Qing Governors and Their Provinces

Qing Governors and Their Provinces

The Evolution of Territorial Administration in China, 1644–1796

R. KENT GUY

A China Program Book

UNIVERSITY OF WASHINGTON PRESS

Seattle and London

This book was supported in part by the China Studies Program, a division of the
Henry M. Jackson School of International Studies at the University of Washington,
and by the Donald R. Ellegood International Publications Endowment.

University of Washington Press
PO Box 50096, Seattle, WA 98145, USA
www.washington.edu/uwpress

Library of Congress Cataloging-in-Publication Data
Guy, R. Kent, 1948–
Qing governors and their provinces : the evolution of territorial
   administration in China, 1644–1796 / R. Kent Guy.
p. cm. — (A China Program book)
ISBN 978–0–295–99295–2 (pbk. : alk. paper)
1. China—History—Qing dynasty, 1644–1912.
2. China—Politics and government—1644–1912.
3. Governors—China—History—17th century.
4. Governors—China—History—18th century.
5. Chinese provinces—History—17th century.
6. Chinese provinces—History—17th century.
7. China—Territories and possessions—Politics and government—17th century.
8. China—Territories and possessions—Politics and government—18th century.
I. Title. DS754.25.G89 2010   951'.032—dc22   2010001806

To the memories of

Robert S.

and

Ernestine Guy

Contents

Tables

Acknowledgments

The first acknowledgment to be made here is recognition of the almost inconceivable patience with which friends, family, and colleagues have awaited this manuscript. The project began with a research trip in 1984 to the First Historical Archives in Beijing, funded by the Committee on Scholarly Communications with the People's Republic of China. The purpose of the trip was to examine the transition between the Yongzheng and Qianlong reigns in the Qing, in order to determine the most important political and administrative changes that took place during the late 1730s. What changed the most, it developed, were provincial governors: No less than eight provincial governors, leaders of half of China's provinces, were changed in the year 1736. As I contemplated this fact, I realized that I had absolutely no context for evaluating it. How unusual was it for eight governors to be appointed in one year? Were governors changed more frequently in some provinces than in others? Could appointment practice be read as a record of the central government's engagement with regional affairs? These questions led me to assemble a database of governors' appointments during the "high Qing" period (see appendix). A summer stipend from the National Endowment for the Humanities in 1988 permitted preliminary analysis of the data, as did a subsequent sabbatical leave from the University of Washington. Further leaves from the university have allowed me to explore the rules governing appointments of governors, and civil officials more generally, in the Qing; the nature of governors' biographies; and the different appointment patterns in different regions. This project has taken me away from the original archival work I did in Beijing in 1984, but it has served, I hope, to provide some context for the work Qing historians will be doing in archives for years to come.

No book is the product of a single individual, and this one owes much to colleagues and friends. Like many books produced in the University of Washington History Department, this one has benefited significantly from the generosity of Howard and Frances Keller. The Department of History and the Jackson School of International Studies and its China Studies Program have all supported this effort, as have the successive chairs of these groups: Jere Bacharach, David Bachman, John Findlay, Richard Johnson, Robert Stacey, and Anand Yang, with Richard Johnson, in particular, offering very valuable comments on the manuscript. Patricia Ebrey has been a wonderfully stimulating and supportive colleague, as were the late Jack Dull and James Palais. Farther afield, Dai Yi, Guo Chengkang, Tom Gottschang, Philip Kuhn, Susan Naquin, Willard Peterson, Edward Rhoads, William Rowe, Ma Ruheng, Jonathan Spence, Karen Turner, Tsing Yuan, and a particularly vigorous anonymous reader for the Press have all provided help and encouragement as this project developed. I am grateful to several generations of University of Washington graduate students who have read the manuscript and to Andrew Eisenberg, Patrick Walsh, Li Yi, Dai Yingcong, Yi Sumei, Christopher Agnew, Bradley Davis, and Cheng Hsiaowen, who have assisted me in various stages of the work. Lorri Hagman of the University of Washington Press has been the soul of patience and competence throughout the process. My father Robert S. Guy has lent me his fascination with personnel processes and the results of his many years of practice and teaching in this area. My immediate family, Chris Cordell and Alexis Guy, have been patient through my years of an obsessive quest to make a computer do my bidding and have added joy and balance to the years. I can never thank them enough.

Over the years, I have been able to repay only a tiny fraction of the debts incurred on this project. I am grateful for opportunities to present my research at Princeton University, the University of Southern California, the University of British Columbia, Holy Cross College, Renmin Daxue, Sungkyunkwan University, and the University of Oslo as well as at the Association for Asian Studies and its West Coast branch. This book is offered in partial payment for the many kindnesses I have enjoyed over the years, but it can be only partial recompense.

Although no book is the work of a single individual, mistakes are. For those that remain here, I take humble and chagrined responsibility.

R. KENT GUY
Seattle, Washington

Qing Governors and Their Provinces

Introduction

As the historian's eye searches for the stuff of grand strategy, the dynamics of policy formation, or evidence of the unseen movement of social change, it usually passes over the routine records of personnel transition and official careers that mark the daily life of any empire. Yet buried in this documentary detritus are stories as rich as any found in more conventional sources, and often more compelling for being cast in the form of human narratives. This is particularly the case in the history of late imperial China. Given the ideology upon which his rule rested, the nature of Qing law, and the routines of the court, no Chinese emperor could afford to neglect recruiting and evaluating human talent, even if he might slight other aspects of administration. In particular, no Qing emperor could or did ignore the task of appointing governors to each of the provinces of the Qing empire, for governors were the imperial court's eyes and ears in a sea of local and regional interests.

This book uses the records of provincial governors' appointments made under four emperors—the Shunzhi emperor (r. 1644–61), the Kangxi emperor (r. 1661–1723), the Yongzheng emperor (r. 1723–36), and the Qianlong emperor (r. 1736–96)—to examine the evolution of provincial government in late imperial China. Each of these emperors had his own approach to provincial appointments; indeed in the seventeenth and eighteenth centuries, the differences among them were probably more apparent than the similarities. The Shunzhi emperor was concerned with finding people who were at least moderately loyal to the new dynasty to fill positions originally established by the Ming. The Kangxi emperor, the first ruler to confront the diversity of the Qing empire, built a system to contain it. The Yongzheng emperor sought governors with energy and vision equal to his own and endeavored, through their appointment, to infuse provincial bureaucracy with new vigor and probity. The Qianlong emperor built a multiethnic corps of governors who functioned within an increasingly standardized and regulated administrative world. At the beginning of their reigns, the Yongzheng and Qianlong emperors even announced by edict their different preferences for provincial governor. But together, the three monarchs built one of the central pillars of Qing rule, the structure of provincial administration.

Qing provincial rule took about a century to evolve. New provincial institutions occupied by civilian personnel were established in north China in the 1650s; in the late 1660s and early 1670s, provincial government began to assume a recognizable form in the lower Yangzi valley. Civilian provincial order came to the southeastern coast in the 1680s, and it was really not until 1700 that the middle Yangzi and Lingnan were actually governed rather than merely occupied. The southwest became a part of China's provincial order in the 1740s, and not until the 1750s did changes occur in China's northwestern boundaries and jurisdictions. As civilian administration reached all corners of the empire, a corps of officials developed to take responsibility for all aspects of civilian administration. Literate but not selected according to literary criteria, the governors of Qing China were technicians of tranquility, both masters of the routine processes of administration and troubleshooters for the central administration. They proved to be a rather remarkably interconnected group of men prepared by their experience and social station to take up positions of responsibility in the name of the Qing and to execute their responsibilities in accord with the standards of the society in which they lived and the state they served. Some were more capable than others, and, as the politics of incompetence were as fascinating in China as everywhere, these have attracted scholarly attention. Yet most of the 532 individuals who served as governors in the eighteenth and nineteenth centuries performed with competence and even distinction, products of an official order that regularly measured their fitness and ability.

By the end of the eighteenth century, all the Chinese territories of the Qing had been provided with provincial administration—the empire had been administratively mapped. At this point, the pace of innovation in Qing provincial administration slowed significantly. On the one hand, the growing body of administrative law and practice made absolute novelty more difficult. On the other hand, beginning in the early nineteenth century, the compelling political problems of the empire were increasingly regional rather than national; local innovations that evolved to meet local crises were seldom applicable in other parts of the realm. A study of nineteenth- or twentieth-century Chinese history could well take provincial government as its focus. Governors played a prominent and, one might argue, the predominant role in most of the great events of nineteenth-century history, and they continue to play major administrative roles in the Chinese state today. But a study of the nineteenth or twentieth centuries would focus on not the institution of governorship itself but the way in which China changed around it. The elements of provincial government all existed earlier, and it is the work of this volume to show how they were created.

GOVERNORS AND THE STATE IN THE HIGH QING PERIOD

The Qing practice of appointing provincial governors as middlemen in the civilian administration established the foundation for one of the signal accomplishments of the late imperial era in China: the stability of the first half of the Qing dynasty. For a number of years, historians of China have used the term "high Qing" to describe China's long eighteenth century, the period between the suppression of the last resistance to Qing rule in approximately the 1680s and the beginning of rebellion against the dynasty in the last years of the eighteenth century.[1] The coinage describes, with the felicitous adjective "high," a period of relative peace, political stability, and rising commercial prosperity. The Chinese empire recovered more quickly than did any other contemporary empire from the crisis of the seventeenth century—a perilous junction marked by climate change and political and social instability—and enjoyed a long period of relative peace and stability. Demographic evidence alone, namely, the doubling of China's population between 1644 and 1800, suggests that Chinese of the eighteenth century were living better, healthier, and more secure lives than in any earlier period of Chinese history. Chinese society grew in answer to its own dynamics, but the growth would not have been possible without a vigilant and effective administrative presence.[2]

The agents of this new presence were provincial governors, who translated central policy into local programs. In a study of civilian administration, the focus on provincial governors should require little justification, for governors played vital roles in almost every facet of territorial administration. Provincial governors supervised lower-level local officials, appointing some and recommending the dismissal of others as needs and opportunities arose. Assisted by lieutenant governors, also known as provincial finance commissioners, Qing provincial governors were responsible for expenditures from the provincial treasuries, which contained nearly one-quarter of the revenue collected by the dynasty. In times of natural disaster, governors made the preliminary damage assessments on which government grants or relief and tax remissions were based. They oversaw and often personally attended provincial examinations, the most important step in the civil service examination ladder. Governors also provided logistical support for military garrisons located in their provinces and, after the Wu Sangui Rebellion (1673–81), assumed command of garrison forces. They supervised and were responsible for financial accounting on local engineering projects and reviewed all criminal and civil sentences meted out by local officials before the decisions were sent to the capital for approval. Provincial governors not only were important functionaries but were the authors of palace memorials, the documents on which the central government relied in assessing local policy and the state of the empire.

The notion that the Qing dynasty "created" provincial governors belies the image, quite correct in many other respects, of a broad institutional continuity between the Ming and Qing dynasties. However, the appointment of a single governor to each of a series of large territorial divisions in China was neither a proven nor a popular idea at the end of the Ming. Province-size units and their governors were so closely associated with some of the debacles of early Chinese imperial history that the Song dynasty (960–1279) had done away with them altogether. The Mongol Yuan dynasty (1279–1368) offered a more stable model for delegating territorial authority, but it was one that few Chinese regimes could follow. The Ming (1368–1644) did appoint regular provincial officials, but their role was one of military coordination. Their functions were sufficiently different from those of their Qing successors that, long ago, Charles Hucker instituted the practice of translating xunfu, the term used for the chief provincial officer in Ming and Qing times, as "grand coordinator" when it referred to a Ming official and as "governor" when it referred to a Qing official.[3] What the Qing created was not the title or the office of xunfu but a group of regularly appointed provincial officials who had both military and civilian functions to perform. Qing practice improved on the Ming in at least three respects. Ming touring pacifiers had military and civilian responsibilities, but their specific functions in either sphere were ill-defined. This meant that they often did not have access to the civilian resources that were necessary for the military initiatives they were meant to lead. They were irregularly appointed, at least in the early days of Ming rule, and served in a constantly changing administrative environment, sometimes subordinate to supreme commanders, sometimes posted in the same localities as imperial princes, often opposed to eunuch military officials.[4]

Qing innovations to the office of governor, chapter 2 argues, lay in the relations governors were meant to enjoy with the other strata of central and territorial officials. Governors' relations with lower territorial officials were prefigured in the Shunzhi reign, when the seats of provincial administration were located in sites appropriate for supervising civilian administration rather than in the strategic military locations where Ming provincial officials had served. With their location in the principal civilian cities of what were to become provinces, governors unambiguously became the senior civilian officials in dynastic hierarchies of territorial governance. In the Kangxi reign, governors' positions were further solidified when all territorial officials were made subordinate to them and in the procedures established for appointing them. There were two such procedures: one routine and the other special. It was in the routine appointments procedure, which linked governors to the subordinate territorial officials they supervised,

that the Qing most significantly changed the Ming era practice. Under this procedure, qualified lieutenant governors could be promoted to governor, and the
two positions stood near the top of a ladder of posts that stretched from county
magistrate, the lowest centrally appointed territorial official in Qing China, to
governor-general, the superior of governors. In each period of Qing history, at
least a few governors ascended this ladder.

Assessing the skills of officials and the credibility of those who reported them
was a challenge, but the effort to do so was implicit in the Qing territorial order.
More directly than earlier dynasties, the Qing had to confront the question—or
perhaps it was really a conundrum—of competence and to define how, by whom,
and to what ends ability could be measured. As the dynasty progressed, the tasks
of assessing territorial administrators and matching individuals to postings
increasingly fell to governors themselves. The Yongzheng emperor contributed
significantly to the growth of evaluative procedures, creating a culture of achievement and rigorous assessment, which guided officials long after his death. This
structure was quite impressive, and it is tempting to regard it as the beginning
of a modern sensibility in China. However, as Angela Zito has warned, we must
guard against reading the Qing imperial structure as evidence of "transcendent
rationalism" as it was defined in Europe.[5] In fact, the new discourse of assessment that came to prevail during the reign was, at least in part, a product of the
emperor's remarkable personality and the peculiar set of personal and political
circumstances that had brought him to power. Nonetheless, some notion of
reward for competence and sanction for incompetence was implicit in the dynasty's project of linking its senior and junior officials.

Routine procedures only partially served the dynastic purpose in the appointment of provincial officials, for governors were not only supervisors of territorial
subordinates but also special emissaries of the emperor on the local level. Qing
procedures also allowed the emperor to appoint whomever he chose to a provincial post—regardless of the appointee's rank or previous service—simply by designating a vacancy as requiring a special appointee. Although such a decree was
not entered into the official record, it is possible to identify special appointees,
since they held positions at the time of their appointment from which they would
not have otherwise been promoted to governor. Special appointments allowed
the court to respond to real or perceived emergencies and to change provincial
personnel in order to accommodate a new emperor or courtier or the demands of
a new policy. The Qing emperors' capacity to wield the power of the unexpected
in personnel matters was one of the authorities that made it possible for them to
rule as well as reign. Concentrations of special appointments at particular points
in time and space provide a measure of the central court's political and strategic concerns. This was particularly true of the spate of special appointments that

marked the Yongzheng emperor's ascension to the throne, a similar if smaller bulge of appointments when the Qianlong emperor came to the throne, and the new appointments that occurred when new chief grand councilors with new strategic concerns took office during the Qianlong reign.

Special appointments were made not only to meet immediate purposes; they were also intended to serve larger policy ends. New appointments responded to the perceived, and changing, imperatives of continuity in Qing history. In eighteenth-century China, special appointments were often necessary to handle particular problems that arose as the Manchus moved into the realm of civilian government from the seventeenth-century military order. Special appointments were also used to transfer governors to provinces that were perceived as requiring officials with more experience; such appointments were one among a series of administrative actions that expressed de facto recognition of regional diversity in an empire committed to de jure consistency. That these appointments were used cautiously was, however, a mark of the importance the Qing attributed to procedures and the assumptions on which they were based.

Although the creation of provincial governors was fraught with implications for the structure and capacity of rule, the dynasty inserted governors fairly seamlessly into the conceptual framework of imperial government. Traditionally, the work of governing China was divided into six categories, represented by the Boards of Personnel, Finance, Rites, Punishments, War, and Public Works; historically, Chinese writings on government were organized in a like fashion. When officials during the Qing dynasty were assigned to edit *Collected Statutes of the Qing* (Da Qing huidian) or the much larger *Statutes and Precedents of the Qing* (Da Qing huidian shili), they had to deal with a relatively new institution—the provincial government—that did not fit any defined categories. The editors' solution to this problem demonstrates the pervasiveness of provincial institutions and the remarkable capacity of Qing rulers to adapt their innovations to existing Chinese administrative patterns. Instead of creating a new chapter for governors, Qing editors inserted references to governors' tasks throughout existing chapters. Both editorially and institutionally, the Qing achieved the delicate feat of inserting a foundation under a structure of territorial rule that had become rather shaky during the late Ming.

The Qing changes to China's provincial government were not so much the unfolding of a new order of things as a case of inspired tinkering, an institutional bricolage punctuated by missteps but blessed on many occasions with luck. Like the intellectual bricolage Claude Lévi-Strauss describes, the Qing had to make do with the institutional elements at hand, but the result of their work was to "renew and enrich the stock of concepts and tools with the remains of previous constructions."[6] The Qing brought new vigor, urgency, and imagination to tasks left over from the Chinese past, namely the incorporation of senior officials into the hierarchy of territorial administrators and the systematization of local government. Nothing the Qing created was absolutely new, but in capacity and character, Qing territorial rule was qualitatively different from that of any previous dynasty.

THE PROVINCES

It is now generally accepted that although nature creates geographic features, human actions give them meaning. The investing of geographic space with human meanings is a cultural act, a construing of physical locations as far or near, and as destinations, routes, or boundaries according to their locations in a mental rather than a physical universe. Chinese had been mapping and naming, remembering, and redefining their land for millennia. The early Manchu rulers were hardly in a position to wholly reinvent the map of China, but they had to come to some understanding of the territory they ruled in order to create meaningful space out of the conquered landscape. Michel de Certeau has argued that "daily practice" is what articulates the opposition between place and space, between the "being there" of inert objects and the attributions of meaning characteristic of human subjects.[7] It is perhaps only a small distortion of his conception to suggest that the daily political practice of imperial administrators during the Qing created the spatial meanings of the late imperial empire. The record of appointments made by the dynasty provides a key to the new rulers' mental map of the empire. The new political units of the Qing were probably less important in the long run compared to the new relations the dynasty created among geographic areas. In this process, provincial governors were crucial, for they were the officials who most commonly moved from one part of the empire to the other.

Despite the impression of homogeneity fostered by the common titles and tremendous centralization of the Qing official order, China's provinces were quite different realms. The most useful means of conceptualizing regional differences in China is the model set forth by G. William Skinner in his essays on marketing and the structure of regional systems in China. Skinner proposes considering China as consisting of "nine major 'islands' of relatively dense population . . . , each surrounded by concentric gradients of declining population." Most of these "islands" were defined by a major river valley and its tributaries and consisted of a functionally integrated urban system, essentially the hinterland of a major city.[8] These regions were not the political units of Ming or Qing China. While there was some correspondence between provincial boundaries and macro-regional boundaries, it was, as Skinner remarks, "grossly imperfect."[9] In fact, Skinner hypothesizes that certain political boundaries were drawn expressly to divide up concentrations of economic power that could pose a threat to the state.[10] Macroregions were not provinces, but they did define the economic, social, and cultural realities the Qing dynasty confronted as it set out to define its provinces.

A study of Qing provincial government shows the human ties that bound these disparate identities together, how they stretched, and when they broke as the official world encountered each region's different realities and political imperatives. Indeed, the very order in which China's provinces were listed in Qing official sources provides some preliminary insights into the workings of Qing provincial government: Zhili, Shandong, Shanxi, Henan, Jiangsu, Anhui, Jiangxi, Fujian, Zhejiang, Hubei, Hunan, Shaanxi, Gansu, Sichuan, Guangdong, Guangxi, Yunnan, and Guizhou.[11]

At first glance, the provinces appear to be listed in order of their proximity to the capital. Closer examination, however, suggests other principles at work; for instance, despite the fact that Shaanxi was closer than Hunan to Beijing, Hunan is listed before Shaanxi. The order was not accidental, for the break between Hunan and Shaanxi constituted the break between "inner" provinces, as the Chinese sometimes called them, where the dynasty collected the bulk of its revenues, and "outer" provinces, where the majority of the dynasty's military forces were located. Conceptually, the list reflects the fact that the tasks of governing these two types of provinces were different, and this fact is also reflected in institutional arrangements and formal and informal appointment practices.

Within these two categories, the order of provinces broadly accorded with proximity to the capital. Among the outer provinces, Shaanxi and the provinces of the northwest are listed first, followed by the Lingnan provinces, and then the provinces of the southwest. The same is broadly true of the inner provinces, for which the list moves from north China to the lower Yangzi provinces, to the southeastern coast, and finally to the middle Yangzi. Even within these constraints, however, a second sort of spatial anomaly can be observed. Fujian was farther from the capital than Zhejiang, and Yunnan was farther than Guizhou, yet Fujian and Yunnan are listed before Zhejiang and Guizhou. In fact, all the provinces that contained the seat of a governor-general were listed before the provinces that were subordinate to it. Distance from the capital was but one principle governing the enumeration of provinces, and perhaps the least important. More important were the tasks of governance required in each province and the way in which physical space was administratively organized in order to perform them.

The record of appointments and the types of appointees sent to given postings offer a second measure of how space was experienced. Here, the Qing dynasty faced constraints. Qing rule was legitimate in China only to the extent that it was exercised in the name of universal principles. What was good for one region had to be good for another: a distinction between provinces that was too apparent, lasted too long, or was unrelated to current realities would surely have undermined dynastic claims. Yet there were practical limits to evenhandedness and also, from the dynasty's point of view, a limited number of qualified and available personnel. There were, in fact, differences—consistent over decades if not over generations—in the depth and character of experience appointees brought to provinces and in the likelihood of being promoted to or from certain provinces. Also important were the moments when the character of appointments to a province changed abruptly, as when civilian governors replaced military governors in Jiangsu after the Jiangnan tax riots of 1661 or in Hunan after that province began to serve as a breadbasket for the empire.

In view of the growing body of English-language scholarship on single regions of China and the long tradition of such writing in Chinese and Japanese, it may seem an act of hubris, or even of academic imperialism, to propose considering all of China's provinces in a single account.[12] This volume is not a critique or a synthesis of regional studies but an examination through comparison of how and to what degree regional knowledge penetrated and shaped political consciousness. The issue for the Qing central administration was not merely recognition of the differences between regions or the geopolitical imperatives they entailed, for these were as readily apparent to the Qing as they would have been to any ruler of China. Rather, the question was how to incorporate into one coherent polity the several regions of China and the political formations they contained. In some cases, regional differences were accommodated by sending different sorts of men to govern; in other instances, unique institutional arrangements served this purpose. At some points in the dynasty's history, strategies changed, and with them boundaries and jurisdictions.

Collectively, the provinces of the north and northwest, considered in chapter 6, demonstrate just how flexible the provincial order could be as well as how it eventually broke under the strain of strategic need and economic and political change. The different logistical demands of the central government coupled with the varying natural ecologies produced different regimes in north China, which the Qing naturalized as provinces. The governorship of Henan was dominated by the great river that flowed through the province; the Shandong governor was confronted with the flow of goods, ideas, and officials along the Grand Canal; and in Zhili, administrators constantly had to be aware of the relations between civilians and bannermen in the strategically significant coastal plain. In the northwest, Shanxi governors dealt with border issues, and Shaanxi governors could never ignore the garrison directly adjacent to their yamen. The changing role of the provinces further complicated the picture of provincial government in the north. In the seventeenth century, northwestern governors were essentially border guardians, while the governors of the rest of north China presided over military outposts scattered along the north China plain. By the eighteenth century, both sets of governors became economic and political administrators who played crucial roles in the management of a larger and more complex empire than the Chinese had ever known. These dramatic changes were driven in part by Qing conquests in central Asia, in part by the growing economic prosperity Qing rule brought to north China, and in part by changes within the Manchu elite. The provincial regimes the Qing had established in the seventeenth century strained against the new tasks they were called upon to perform, and signs of this tension are visible in a series of spectacular corruption cases that marked the end of the eighteenth century in the region.

Chapter 7 examines the lower Yangzi valley and highlights the process of negotiation involved in the development of all Chinese provinces. In Jiangsu and Anhui, negotiations addressed provincial boundaries and the jurisdictions they imposed, tax obligations, the politics of river control and the allocation of resources it entailed, and the relationship of literati communities to the centers of political power. Negotiations were also required along the southeastern coast, but there the Qing encountered a far more multi-centered world with many more nodules of political power. The early Qing government on the southeastern coast was far more variegated in its human and social constitution than it was elsewhere in the empire, displaying a diversity that was in some respects more characteristic of the preconquest Manchu order. The coastal region shows how the variety of the early, preconquest period was transformed into the more regular social and political patterns of the imperial era. As this happened, the two provinces on the coast, Zhejiang and Fujian, which were perceived in the seventeenth century to have much in common, grew apart and came to follow very different paths.

The provinces of the middle Yangzi and Lingnan regions have been set apart in chapter 8 because their political structures were far more protean in the seventeenth century than were those north of the river. This is not to say that there were not very real and powerful political forces south of the Yangzi. But it was unclear in the mid-seventeenth century how these forces, and the vast economic and social potentialities the region embodied, were to be incorporated into a centralized empire. The Qing transformed regions into provinces through the circulation of qualified personnel and a concomitant transformation of regional into political identities. In particular, the middle Yangzi, located in the center of the empire at the intersection of north-south and east-west trade routes, shows the character and success of the dynasty's policy of transferring officials from one jurisdiction to another. All the southern provinces had an untapped potential for dynamic development, and extraordinary differences in wealth marked the far south in the eighteenth century. Growth in the south throughout the eighteenth century strained even the fairly new administrative structures that had evolved in the seventeenth century. Chapter 9 examines the process by which new means of communication changed the character of political relations between the far southwest and the capital, as the court became more aware and perhaps also more in control of developments in the farthest reaches of the empire.

One reason why the differences in Qing provinces have not been fully explored is that the dynasty was particularly successful at naturalizing them. All governments, particularly imperial systems, are faced with the task of making their structures of rule appear normal and necessary. In spite of the fact that province-size entities had existed in China for centuries, Chinese subjects were far more likely to associate themselves with their native districts or with the empire as a whole than with intervening territorial units.[13] It was beyond the capacity of the considerable image-making apparatus of the Qing dynasty to change such a vision, nor was it entirely desirable to do so, since that could have led the dynasty to produce alternative political centers in competition with the state. But it was important for the dynasty to legitimate the political structures through which most of the state's business was transacted at the local level. It did this through the small action of assigning provincial abbreviations that referred to historical events or geographic features in which local residents could justifiably take pride. Perhaps more important, late imperial central governments borrowed a record-keeping genre from elite culture to describe structures of provincial rule. By late Ming times, the "local gazetteer" (fang zhi) had become the favored way in which the local elites described their accomplishments and the landmarks of their social and communal life. During the eighteenth century, the Qing dynasty ordered provincial governments to prepare provincial gazetteers that incorporated at least some of the same information, organized in the same categories, as was available in privately published county gazetteers. Provincial gazetteers included, in sequence, reprints of the most important imperial edicts concerning the province as well as discussions of physical and administrative geography, provincial political institutions, and local society. The last section usually highlighted local notable individuals, monuments, and literary and artistic achievements. In effect, imperial pronouncements were set out as the precondition for rule, and the institutions of provincial government were inserted, as bridge and facilitator, between the natural environment and the human realm.[14]

THE GOVERNORS

The proposition that a study of provincial governors would illuminate the structure of the Qing state would seem to require little argument. What may need more defense is the use of personnel records and the biographical materials to which they were linked as a way of approaching the subject of provincial government in China. Until recently, studies in Qing history have often proceeded on the assumption that the narrative frame provided by the life of the ordinary official was too narrow to allow exploration of the sort of changes in policy and institutions of interest to later imperial historians. Governor Chen Hongmou has rightly received attention, but this interest has been stimulated more by his writings, preserved in the early nineteenth century, which evoked the commitments and attitudes of early eighteenth-century officials, than by the details of his career.[15] The substance of official résumés has received less interest. Moreover, Chinese biographies were rather specialized works, usually written on the occasion of their subject's death, at the moment when the decedent passed from history into memory.[16] As such, they were hardly appropriate vehicles to reflect the individual's subjectivities. On the other hand, biographical writing such as the Chinese practiced it was a well-established genre in Chinese history, which, taken together with writings in chronological and topical form, constituted one of the three primary forms of historical writing. Biographies preserved documents, memorials and letters, and snippets of gossip that escaped other types of source material. Perhaps as important, biographies preserved snapshots of the aspects of an individual's life that his contemporaries perceived as worth preserving and those sets of connections and personal ties that seemed most salient to those who had survived. Surely no one would set out to write a study of "life and times" in this age when Foucault has redefined the meaning of "life" and Braudel has restructured our notion of "times." But neither should one approach the history of policy making in China without a healthy recognition of the role of human contingency.

Biographies also traced the paths governors followed in their journeys through the empire. In *Imagined Communities*, Benedict Anderson writes of the imperial functionary's experience of geography:

> He sees before him a summit rather than a centre. He travels up its corniches in a series of looping arcs which, he hopes will become smaller and tighter as he nears the top. Sent out to township A at rank V, he may return to the capital at rank W; proceed to province B at rank X; continue to vice-royalty C at rank Y and end his pilgrimage in the capital at rank Z. On this journey there is no resting place; every pause is provisional. The last thing the functionary wants is to return home, for he has no home with any intrinsic value. And this: On his upward spiralling road, he encounters as eager fellow pilgrims his functionary colleagues, from places and families he has scarcely heard of and surely hopes never to have to see. But in experiencing them as travelling companions, a consciousness of connectedness (Why are we . . . here . . . together?) emerges, above all when all share a single language of state.[17]

Here, Anderson means to contrast the experience of the imperial functionary with, on the one hand, the feudal official, who makes one trip to the capital to be invested in office and then returns to his native place, and, on the other hand, with the popular representative, who makes repeated trips to the capital serving the interests of those he represents. Elements of Anderson's picture of course do not apply to Chinese officials of the late imperial era. No Chinese official would ever have publicly admitted that he had no home of any intrinsic value, and not every Chinese official's career ended in the capital. But Anderson's arresting description is nonetheless valuable for the Chinese historian insofar as it turns attention to the lessons Chinese officials learned as they journeyed down the dusty byways of empire.

If the focus on the lives of individual officials is narrow, the focus on the collective life of officials is crucial. A prosopographic approach to Chinese governors affords an opportunity to examine a group of Chinese officials who have hitherto received little study. On close examination, those appointed governor during the Qing do not appear to be the corrupt and effete mandarins of twentieth-century imagination. In fact, many of them were not "mandarins" at all, if that much abused term is meant to describe holders of jinshi degrees. Overall, less than half the Qing provincial governors were jinshi-degree holders, though many held lower-level or purchased degrees. Even under the Qianlong emperor, who prided himself on a reign in which knowledge and power were conjoined, only 26 percent of the governors held the degree. Degrees were very important for governors in some places, such as Jiangsu in the last years of the seventeenth and first years of the eighteenth century, and at certain times, such as in the late Kangxi reign and the years following the crisis of provincial government in the mid-Qianlong period. But except for instances when certain types of appointments were meant to make a political and cultural statement, governors inhabited a stratum of Chinese officialdom in which accomplishment, or, perhaps more precisely, a perceived capacity for accomplishment, was more important than any single objective qualification for office.[18]

Chinese governors were men at the middle of their careers, usually between forty and sixty years of age, and who were ten to thirty years away from their entry into government service.[19] Those governors who were appointed directly by the emperor tended to be somewhat younger, and those who had worked their way up the ladder of promotion somewhat older, at the time of their first appointment.[20] Prior to their first appointments as governor, most appointees had served at the capital and, particularly if they had worked their way up the provincial hierarchy, in at least two regions of China in postings of increasing responsibility. Once appointed in one province, most governors could expect to be transferred to another governorship, often one perceived as more difficult. After their service as governor, some were promoted to the rank of governor-general or to a posting of comparable rank in Beijing. Governors seldom retired unless they were quite ill, and most of those who left office because of illness died shortly thereafter. The successful official spent his entire life in service to the state.

Set apart by their travel and the necessary immersion in the details of territorial administration, governors were often closer to their peers than they were to either those they governed or those they served. Governors seldom had occasion to visit their own homes, except for the required period of mourning for the death of a parent or brief visits as they crossed the empire to accept appointments or fulfill imperial commissions. This meant that few of their neighbors were inspired to write reminiscences. Similarly, in the course of lifetimes filled with administrative obligations, few governors had or took the leisure to cast their reflections in literary form, although there were some who had attained reputations as scholars before their appointments and continued their habits of scholarly reflection in territorial office. In other instances, eager students or protégés collected governors' political papers at the end of their lives. But most governors did not leave significant literary remains.

Instead, territorial officials were usually dependent on organs of the state to preserve their histories for posterity. Most Qing governors were the subjects of "working biographies" (ben zhuan) prepared by the State Historiographical Commission (Guo Shi Guan) shortly after their deaths. The primary purpose of this commission, which was staffed by members of the imperial Hanlin Academy, was to prepare the official version of the orders issued by the emperor, known as Veritable Records (Shilu), for each reign. But in addition, the commission assembled biographical materials for important officials. Typically, this process began a few months after an official's death, when the commission requested a "résumé" (luli) of the recently deceased official from the Board of Personnel or other appropriate agency.[21] This text would be supplemented with passages copied from what were perceived to be the official's most important correspondence. A draft biography was prepared, then edited and re-edited for both accuracy and style. In a memorial submitted to the emperor, the State Historiographical Commission undertook to prepare biographies for governors-general, governors, and military intendants who had "genuine achievements in office worthy of emulating" or who had been dismissed from office in ways that would be instructive to future generations.[22]

In addition to these official sources, there were, for some governors at least, epitaphs and reminiscences prepared by friends, associates, or admirers at the time of their deaths. The quality and availability of these writings varied widely. For instance, no one wished to remember the life of Tian Wenjing, the longest-serving governor of Henan in the Qing; his lower-class origins, innovative approaches, and brusque administrative style earned the admiration of few of the literary men who wrote epitaphs. In contrast, Zhang Boxing, who self-consciously took on the task of serving as cultural bridge between the court and the Jiangnan literati, was celebrated repeatedly in private epitaphs. Existing epitaphs must be read cautiously, for although such writings conventionally open with a statement of the relationship between the author and the subject, many of the episodes they narrate are essentially gossip that cannot be authenticated from other sources.

Often halfway between official biography and private epitaph were the accounts preserved in History of the Qing (Qing shi), first printed in 1927–28. The advantage of these biographies is that the editors of the collection were in a position to compare the individuals they wrote about, drawing on materials from different times and places, in a way that few historians of the twentieth century have been able to do. Occasionally, the results of their comparisons are incorporated in a single biography, as in their account of Bian Sanyuan, one of the first Qing governors of Guizhou, whose biography includes a debate over his significance that went on nearly a century after his death. More often the editors of History of the Qing expressed their judgments rather more obliquely through the order in which individuals were considered. The disadvantage of this work is that it is informed by an early twentieth-century vernacular narrative of Qing dynasty history, a Republican period understanding of the Qing past that must be as often deconstructed as accepted. But even when such a narrative exists, it often constitutes a datum, evidence of how the past was remembered.[23]

It would be a vast exaggeration to claim that governors formed the glue that held the Chinese empire together. Military conquest, economic complementarity, and even the cultural conception of China as a whole were also important forces. But governors certainly did articulate the understandings of regional significance that proved the working basis of a unified administration. When Tian Wenjing wrote about the significance of the Yellow River, or the governors of Yunnan and Guizhou explained that vast distances impeded the capacity of southwestern officials to act in accordance with the will of the central government, they were setting forth data on which understandings and actions were to be based. Conversely, when officials carried administrative paradigms from one province or region to another, they defined the nature of the empire for those they ruled. In both cases, territorial officials were the ones who mapped the empire for subordinates and superiors as they traveled along its highways and byways.

This book uses the records of governors' appointments and the laws and practices that shaped them to reconstruct the development of the office of provincial governor during the first century and a half of Qing rule in China. Part 1 traces the development of the office itself. Part 2 examines the histories of governors' appointments in each of China's provinces. Both are illustrated with history drawn from the governors' biographies. A single volume can hardly do justice to the complex world of those who administered the territorial affairs of one of the largest and longest-lived empires in history. There is room for much more work on the lives of governors, the administration of regions, and the central government's attitude toward territorial administration. The observations in this volume are offered as a resource to fuel a continuing quest for the sources of Qing success and the diagnosis of its failures.

PART I

CHAPTER 1

The Burdens of History:
Pre-Qing Territorial Government

In China, as in most early modern empires, provinces as administrative units were created from the earlier military jurisdictions through which territories had been conquered and controlled. The situation in China was unique in that the military jurisdictions that gave rise to provinces had much longer and more daunting histories than did military jurisdictions elsewhere. This history was both a burden and an opportunity. In the Chinese metaphor, historical records offer opportunities when they serve as mirrors of the past, reflecting the dangers and values of various institutional arrangements, and when they demonstrate the advantages of certain territorial divisions. Consciousness of history could be a burden when certain courses of action were determined to be historical dead ends and history constrained the exploration of roads not taken. Knowing history too well, the Chinese were in a sense condemned to repeat it, or rather to repeat the actions that they believed its lessons taught.

Imperial Chinese governments never had difficulty delegating authority to territorial subordinates. Nearly a century before the first Chinese dynasty, the redoubtable Shang Yang (d. 338 BCE) laid the foundation for subsequent imperial rule by replacing feudal lords with centrally appointed officials.[1] Lord Shang created territorial units known as "commanderies" (jun) and subsequently supplemented them with "counties" (xian). Together, these became the basic building blocks of Chinese empires. Inserting an intermediate layer of officials was more difficult, as it evoked fears of deceit and double-dealing at the central level and specters of harsh oppression at the local level.

There were probably many reasons why stable provincial governments eluded the Chinese, but two phenomena were both recurrent and telling. First, Chinese imperial regimes initially turned to provinces as units of military administration, only to find institutions with weak ties to the center and local leaders who were willing to put regional—even personal—interests ahead of those of the central government. The rebellions that ensued were read all too often as a caution against precisely the sort of institution building that would have made provinces effective supports for the central government. The rebellion of An Lushan during the eighth century is probably the most famous example of this cycle.

The second had less to do with historical contingency than with political vision and philosophy. In classical Chinese visions of the just political order, the middleman was suspect. Early Chinese political thinkers such as Shen Buhai and Han Feizi may have developed, as Herrlee Creel has argued, a theory of bureaucracy.[2] However, early Chinese thinking about bureaucracy was marked by an enormous interest in the problem of the ruler's control of officialdom and concerned itself primarily with "impersonal, objective mechanisms for limiting the power of officials and subordinating them to the ruler."[3] As Jack Dull has pointed out, in earliest times there was an order in China that is conventionally called "feudal," but there was no tradition of feudal subinfeudation. This means there was no way in which an imperial subordinate could legitimately exact from an inferior the same obligations he owed to the emperor.[4] As the imperial system evolved out of the ancient feudal order, much more emphasis was placed on the loyalty that all officials owed to the center than to the more nuanced obligations officials owed to one another. There was simply little speculation about the duties of a subordinate who served by supervising lower-ranking officials or about the lower-ranking appointee who served, not a sagely emperor, but that emperor's all-too-human delegate. The most effective model for delegation came ironically not from China itself, but from empires of the steppe, such as the Mongol Yuan (1279–1368), in which delegation of authority over a wider territorial scope was crucial for maintaining order. But "order" meant something different for the Yuan than it had for traditional Chinese regimes, and the Yuan produced a fairly loosely integrated regime that rested on an unholy combination of trust, distrust, and disorganization.

It fell to the final two imperial governments of China, the Ming and, particularly, the Qing, to integrate the values of sedentary empires into the institutions of nomadic regimes. The first emperor of the Ming, Zhu Yuanzhang (r. 1368–98), borrowed Yuan boundaries and appointed Chinese-style officials to oversee what he envisioned as the rather circumscribed role of the central state within them. Seeking greater security, his successors appointed coordinators of military affairs to serve alongside Zhu Yuanzhang's provincial officials. The resulting provincial order was only a partial success, but it provided the offices that the Qing would use to create its more successful synthesis. In view of the history of false starts and new beginnings, rebellions and restorations, it is no wonder that the foremost institutional historian of the early Qing period, Gu Yanwu, had little faith in the province as a territorial unit, seeing governors as nothing more than the supernumerary servants of overweening autocrats.

PROVINCES IN THE EARLY IMPERIAL PERIOD

The history of Tang provinces in the eighth and ninth centuries, which is reasonably well known both in English- and Chinese-language historical works, is
almost universally considered to have been a disaster. The details of this disaster
—stories of scheming palace women, barbarian perfidy, and court intrigues—
have been most often deployed to examine changing social status during the
mid-Tang.[5] The notion that social change in the Tang was either reflected or produced by the collapsing provincial order has been successfully challenged, but
the details of the Tang story can still tell us much about evolving Chinese views of
territorial governance. What is most interesting about the Tang system of provinces is not so much the system itself but the mistakes the dynasty made in its
implementation. On what models of provinces were Tang rulers drawing? Why
did the court turn to outsiders to govern these provinces, and how has the Tang
history been read in succeeding dynasties, or, to put it another way, what was the
impact of the Tang experience on subsequent institutional development?

The Tang rulers were not the first to confront the ambiguities of provincial
power or the dilemmas of delegation. In the Han dynasty (206 BCE–220 CE),
there were two types of territorial officials established to oversee the eighty or so
commanderies that had existed from its beginning. Each commandery was governed by a *taishou*, a term that is customarily translated as "grand commander"
when it refers to a Han official. A group more comparable to later imperial provincial governors, at least in geographical span of control, theoretically oversaw
the grand commanders. These were the thirteen regional commanders, or *cishi*,
who were charged with supervising and coordinating the efforts of the governors
of commanderies. The establishment of this position by Han Wudi in 106 BCE
marks the apogee of his power, a moment when the empire was at its greatest
physical extent and the Han emperor was experimenting with new ways of governing in many spheres. It also represents one of the rare instances in early imperial history when provincial-level officials were created at a moment of imperial
power rather than one of weakness. In practice, however, the regional inspectors were quite weak; in fact, they ranked below the officials they were meant
to supervise.[6] So long as the central regime remained the dominant power in
the empire, this arrangement was perhaps workable. But low-ranking territorial subordinates could not command the resources necessary to defend a falter-
ing center. Crisis demanded a different kind of official, and, by 1 BCE, the Han
dynasty created the new post of "regional shepherd" (*mu*), which brought with it
high rank and wide authority.[7] The Later Han dynasty shifted between these two
approaches to territorial governance, at times appointing low-ranking officials
and at times dispatching senior officials. In 188 CE, the Han committed itself

to governing via senior officials and appointed regional shepherds throughout the empire.[8] From the dynasty's point of view, these proved to be wolves with shepherd's titles, and the competition between strong regional leaders and the central government eventually brought down the ruling house. Thus, in the Han, provincial officials created in moments of power proved too weak to preserve the dynasty in moments of crisis; those created in moments of weakness were too independent to rally to the emperor's side in times of trouble.

Like the founders of the Han dynasty that preceded them, the early Tang rulers saw little need for provinces. The Tang followed the pattern of the Sui, which had distrusted the political units the commanderies represented and so reduced their size and renamed them; eventually the Tang were to create 350 *zhou*, customarily translated as "prefecture" in early imperial history, which presided over nearly fifteen hundred counties.[9] Tang Taizu dispatched regional inspectors to review local governments in his empire, but his successors saw little need to continue the practice. In a stable order, with the borders guarded by Tang standing armies, the empire policed by garrisons from the divisional militia system, and the tax regime secure and productive, there was little need for the aggregation of resources and men that a regional unit could provide. There was also little desire for the threat such a leader could pose. But by the middle of the eighth century, the situation and needs of the Tang had changed. The dynasty was at the height of its power and geographic extent. As Charles Peterson has argued, provinces were made necessary for the Tang by changes occurring along the borders and within China during the eighth century. Along the overextended boundaries of the eighth-century empire with the Qiang in Tibet and the Khitans in the northeast, military threats necessitated the expansion of standing armies, which in turn required the establishment of stronger and more permanent structures of control. Within China, "population growth, [an] increased incidence of vagrancy, tax registers falling out-of-date, a growing complexity of administrative procedures, occasional lawlessness plus the perennial tendency of bureaucrats to become lax" forced the creation of new regional units.[10] Provinces were thus new institutional structures in eighth-century China, created not because of the logic of bureaucratic order but in order to meet the emergent needs of an enlarged state.

Because the province was a new institution, there were few rules or even useful precedents for incorporating them into the bureaucratic order.[11] In particular, there were no procedures or precedents for appointing individuals to serve as regional coordinators. It would have been possible for Tang aristocrats to take on this responsibility, and some members of old court families were sent to establish order in the empire. But more often political leaders, such as the autocratic prime minister Li Linfu, preferred to appoint to these new and powerful positions men who had no ties to factions in the capital and would therefore pose no threat to established structures of authority. In fact, Li preferred outsiders who would have little expectation of rising within the Tang political hierarchy and whose skills, in his view, better suited them for service on the borders of empire. Combining flattery with practicality, Li Linfu argued that a brave emperor required brave subordinates:

> In view of your majesty's talent and bravery and the power and wealth of the state, if the foreign barbarians are not destroyed it is only because the [Chinese] generals are timid and fearful and incapable of military office. Your majesty surely wants to destroy the barbarians and extend your prestige to the four corners of the world. For this purpose nothing would serve better than military leaders, and among these, nothing would be better than foreigners. From their birth they have a brave temperament, and from their childhood, they ride horses. When they reach adulthood, they are used to fighting enemies. This is their natural disposition.[12]

Li Linfu imagined that he had found such a person in An Lushan (702–757). A soldier who had risen through at least the upper ranks of the Tang army, An Lushan was of mixed Turkish and Sogdian parentage, an illiterate who had no significant period of residence at the Tang court. As a young officer, he had been admired by the emperor for his bravery and had even been granted a special pardon from the court in 736 after a battlefield defeat. In 740, he received his first appointment in the Tang territorial government and, by 742, was established as a regional governor in what is today northeastern Hebei, around modern-day Beijing, which adjoined the territory of the Khitans. Each of these characteristics distinguished him from the oligarchy that dominated Tang politics, composed as it was of hereditary descendants of the Tang founder and literati examination takers from southeast China.

Although the emperor bestowed honor after honor upon An Lushan, many in the capital came to resent his influence. The tenuousness of his connections— even to those with whom he was most closely associated—was legendary. According to one tale, An Lushan broke out in a profuse sweat whenever he met Prime Minister Li Linfu or received a communication from him through an emissary. On one occasion, when he met Li during the winter, it is said that Li requested a blanket for his damp and perhaps clammy protégé, who was no doubt shivering. An Lushan's large physical size and his "gaucherie in matters of court" became the stuff of capital jokes. On his birthday in 751, he was formally adopted as a son by the emperor's favorite concubine, Yang Guifei. Several days later, she and her ladies "wrapped his huge hulk in baby clothes and went through a burlesque of the ceremony of washing a new-born infant."[13] There were reports that An Lushan failed to recognize and appropriately honor the heir apparent. When Li Linfu died in 756, his successor Yang Guoqing (brother of the imperial concubine) engineered several deliberate provocations. An Lushan became convinced that he would fall victim to a purge at court and therefore assembled his troops to march on the capital, which they did in 757. They eventually occupied Chang'an, and a civil war ensued in which the armies of An Lushan and his successors fought the armies of the Tang for eight years, nearly ending China's second great imperial regime. When the Tang finally achieved victory, it did so only at the cost of conceding even more authority to An Lushan's fellow governors.

Perhaps less important than the details of the rebellion and its suppression, for the purposes of this volume, was the way in which the history of the rebellion has been told and read. Given the Confucian penchant for explaining political, or even social and intellectual, change in personal terms, the stories of An Lushan's slights at the hands of the Tang court must be discounted. They may well have been created by An Lushan himself in order to foster his own self-image as the unsophisticated soldier-savior of a corrupt and decadent court. But the stories should not be completely discounted. They dramatized the weak and uncertain ties between center and periphery in the personal and psychological terms of which Confucian historians were so enamored. Twentieth-century scholarship has argued that the rebellion arose primarily from institutional tensions. After examining the argument that An Lushan's rebellion was caused primarily by economic or ethnic issues, Edwin Pulleyblank concludes that the roots of the affair lay in the relations between governor and center. Similarly, Charles Peterson concludes in his essay in *The Cambridge History of China* that the "social and cultural gap between the court and its frontier commanders did not necessarily nurture antagonism. But it did permit a powerful commander, acting purely out of his own personal interest, to collect support from his fellow officers and declare war on a court with whom they felt little in common. In this sense, the rebellion is best explained by the dynamics of the T'ang political military structure as it had evolved by the end of Hsuan-tsung's reign."[14]

The political tensions of the Tang provincial order persisted after the suppression of the rebellion, which confirms Peterson's view. In fact, the Tang court soon found itself embroiled in conflicts with the very provincial leaders on whom it had relied to suppress the rebellion. These conflicts centered around a predictable range of issues. The Tang court found itself unable to transfer governors, who began to style themselves "kings" of their respective provinces, and was forced to consult with local garrisons about the suitability of potential appointees. Local governors remitted to the center only such revenues as they pleased, so the court struggled throughout the first half of the ninth century to force governors to content themselves with the revenues of the prefecture in which the provincial capital was located.[15] By the end of the ninth century, although the Tang court had succeeded to some degree in bureaucratizing the relations between center and province, it did so at the cost of undermining the military power of the dynasty and thus weakening the state as a whole.

One might have drawn from this dismal history the lesson that regional governments needed to be more fully integrated with the center, and that in the absence of such linkages, local commanders could not be called upon to save a declining center. An empire as large as Tang China in the mid-seventh century required some sort of delegation of authority to units larger than its 350 prefectures. The Tang central government was not misguided in the creation of regional authority, but, lacking a model or recent experience with large territorial units, it was careless in the way it delegated power and weak in the institutionalization of regional power. Authority was vested in military commissions explicitly regarded as temporary, subject to the whim of the central court and given to men whose loyalty was not ensured. As David Graff has noted, the term for "regional commander," *jiedushi*, probably derived from the expression *jiedu* (to regulate with the insignia of command), which was used in the early Tang to indicate the authority the commander in chief of an expeditionary army wielded over his subordinate commanders.[16] The civilian functions that might have supported military commissioners were usurped rather than assigned, and their performance was not regulated from the center. The issue in the Tang was not the fact of delegation but the way in which power was delegated and constrained.

But the founder of the Song, successor dynasty to the Tang, drew a rather different lesson: that the province and the regional aggregations of men and money it represented had little place in a Chinese empire. The founder of the Song was himself a former regional commander and, from the earliest days of his rule, concentrated on reducing the power of his fellow military commanders, offering them incentives to settle at the Song court and centralizing military control. Territorial administration was clearly differentiated from military service, and both were made directly responsible to the court. Centrally appointed prefects were in charge of local administration. In order to emphasize that prefects owed their allegiance to the emperor rather than to any superior territorial administrator, they were given the right to memorialize the throne directly. Moreover, the titles of local officials identified them as belonging to central rather than local administration. As Jack Dull has noted, this meant that local officials, at least in the early Song, came to hold "a bewildering array of titles and offices."[17] Interregional coordination was achieved through the appointment of a series of circuit intendants, traveling central officials with ranks lower than those of the officials they were meant to supervise. These officials specialized not in the affairs of a region but in one of the functions of the government, in matters of finance, justice, commerce, or the military.[18] The districts these circuit intendants supervised were originally known as *dao*, one of the terms that had been used to designate Tang provinces. Lest any confusion remain, the name was changed early in the Song to the synonym *lu*, which had none of the historical associations of *dao*.

THE PROVINCE DURING THE YUAN

The vast conquests of Chingis Khan and his successors created a state unlike any other in world history, and certainly unlike anything in East Asian history. The Mongols' Yuan dynasty differed from earlier Chinese dynasties in the physical extent of its territories and the range of ethnic minorities it incorporated. It differed from earlier nomadic regimes in that Chingis's successors actually sought to rule the territories they had conquered rather than raid and plunder them. Control of such vast lands required a stable system for delegating territorial authority. The Mongols set out to create such a system, drawing on their own cultural traditions and those of the people they governed. The resulting Yuan territorial regime, though marked by under-institutionalization and duplication of functions, formed a much more solid foundation for provincial rule than that of earlier Chinese provincial forms.

Initially, the Mongols drew on what they had by way of indigenous political traditions. As Thomas Barfield has argued, "Inner Asian nomadic states were organized as imperial confederacies, autocratic and state-like in foreign affairs, but consultative and federally structured internally. They consisted of an administrative hierarchy with at least three levels: the imperial leader and his court, imperial governors appointed to oversee the component tribes within the empire, and indigenous tribal leaders."[19] A functionary like the provincial governor was crucial for the Mongol confederate order, bridging the gap between the local and the imperial. So long as this official was loyal to the central government, his place of origin, ethnic identity, and even native language didn't matter. In the early 1220s, Chingis's conquests brought him to the sedentary empires of central Asia and East Asia, the Khitan kingdom of northeast China, and the Kwarezm empire in central Asia. Faced with the task of how to establish rule over urban and sedentary societies, he conceived of the idea of using administrators from one state to rule another. As *The Secret History of the Mongols* relates:

> Once he had conquered the Moslem people,
> Chingis Khan appointed agents to govern in each of their cities.
> From the city of Gurganj came two Khwarezm Moslems,
> a father and son named Yalavech and Masgud,
> who explained to Chingis the customs and laws of the cities

and the customs by which they were governed.

Chingis Khan appointed the Khwarezm Masgud

the head of the agents

who governed the cities of Turkestan:

Bukhara, Samarkand, Gurganj, Khotan, Kashgar, Yarkand, and Kusen Tarim.

And made his father Yalavech the governor of the city of Chung-tu in Cathay.

Since among the Moslems Yalavech and Masgud

Were among the most skilled at the customs and laws for governing cities,

He appointed them governors of Cathay

Along with our own agents.[20]

So it was that Yalavech, a Muslim from the central Asian city of Gurganj, where the Oxus River empties into the Aral Sea, came to govern in the area of Dadu near modern-day Beijing.

Little is known of Yalavech's tenure, which must have been concerned primarily with overseeing a military occupation and somehow communicating to Mongol masters the niceties—or even the realities—of urban life. As the Mongols settled in, they built a more enduring office at the territorial level, as the career of Menggu Baer (1204–1274) suggests. Unlike Yalavech, Menggu was a Mongol, as were most of the senior territorial administrators of the middle Yuan period.[21] After his appointment to the Zhangde circuit in 1236, many of the functions Menggu performed were military. He was known for restraining the occupying Mongol troops for the purpose of securing the lives and commerce of Chinese subjects and also for pursuing rebels, resettling refugees, and capturing bandits. But Menggu also went beyond these functions to secure the central court's assistance in providing food to peasants whose crops had been destroyed by locusts, praying in the ritually correct manner for rains in time of drought, and judging and reviewing legal cases.[22] During the course of his career, he served in four different postings, rising each time to a more important position as he proved his competence. The source for this description of Menggu, an epitaph ordered by sons and grandsons who had married into a Chinese family, would certainly have been meant to cast him in the best light and perhaps to put the patina of Confucian benevolence on military occupation. Still, the record cannot have been without foundation. Menggu may not have been the complete Chinese administrator, but the progression from military occupier to supervisor of the economic and social functions of the occupied society was a logical and perhaps even necessary one if the dynasty was to endure.

The term used to describe the jurisdictions of Yuan appointees is *xing zhong shu sheng*, sometimes translated as "branch secretariat" but perhaps more precisely rendered as "the office responsible for carrying out the functions of the

Central Secretariat" within a jurisdiction. It clearly marked its holder as a delegate of the central administration and implied no separate military rank or function. The term was customarily abbreviated as *sheng* in imperial times and has come to refer to the territories under the jurisdiction of a governor. This usage troubled Gu Yanwu and other institutional historians. In modern times, *sheng* has come to mean "province," though this attempt to render Chinese territorial divisions comparable to European territorial divisions conceals the term's original reference to an office rather than to a region.[23]

In the last third of the thirteenth century, having conquered the territories of the Southern Song, the Yuan took the further step of dividing its empire into ten jurisdictions. Seven of these were located south of the Great Wall and, together with a broad swath of territory that was governed from the national capital in Dadu, comprised the territory of later Chinese empires.[24] The central geographic feature in the Yuan political map of China was the Yangzi River, which separated the northern jurisdictions from the southern. Three jurisdictions were north of the river: Shaanxi, which took roughly its modern form; Henan (also known as Henan-Jiangbei), which included the territories between the Yellow River and the Yangzi River from the Shaanxi border to the coastline of the East China Sea; and the Northern Metropolitan Region, which included the eastern coastal plain and the Shandong peninsula. The area south of the Yangzi River was divided into four vertical strips, each of which stretched south from the river to the southern border of the empire. The easternmost was Jiang-zhe, which extended from the seacoast on the east to the Wuyi mountain range in the west, and, from the Yangzi River in the north to what is today the boundary between the provinces of Fujian and Guangdong in the south. Next was the province of Jiangxi, which extended from the Wuyi range in the east to the range of low mountains that today divide Hunan and Jiangxi in the west and from the Yangzi all the way to the South China Sea. West of Jiangxi was Huguang, which included all of what is now Hubei, Hunan, and Jiangxi and extended from the Yangzi to the border of Vietnam. Yunnan, in the far west, included the territories conquered by the Mongols in the early twelfth century before their campaigns against the Song dynasty had begun. The only province that included lands both north and south of the Yangzi was Sichuan, a territory defined by its mountainous borders.[25]

These boundaries suggest some of the purposes for which territorial divisions were created in the Yuan. G. William Skinner has demonstrated that provinces in late imperial China often divided the natural marketing networks of Chinese society.[26] Yuan boundaries may not have been quite so out of synch with economic realities, but only because there were fewer of them: economics were certainly not what the Mongols had in mind in establishing their branch secretariats.

The Mongols' provincial boundaries also ignored long-established Chinese cultural identities. Shandong, recognized as a region with its own identity since the time of Confucius, was incorporated into the territories governed from the Yuan capital. Fujian and Guangdong, which had existed as separate provinces in the Tang, were incorporated into Jiangzhe and Jiangxi, respectively. The most obvious characteristic of Yuan boundaries was that they were militarily defensible.

Jurisdictions were divided by rivers and mountain ranges that could not be easily crossed, constituting territories that could not be easily invaded. This division of territory served a military aim, but it was rather different from the aim of meeting emergency needs that had shaped Tang provinces. Yuan provinces were built not to meet crises but to endure and to provide secure seats for the central Asians who governed them. And endure they did. Although political needs and demographic realities compelled some changes in provincial boundaries over the next seven hundred years, the broad outlines of Yuan jurisdictions formed a template for provincial organization in the later imperial period and are still visible today in the territorial divisions of the People's Republic of China (PRC).

Stable territorial boundaries formed a spatial frame within which administrative routines could emerge and develop. This was no small matter in an agrarian society in which consistency—in the assessment of tax and military service obligations, administration of justice, and provision of relief—was a central desideratum of any territorial regime.[27] Although these boundaries were an enduring contribution to successive Chinese governments, ironically, the Mongols could not readily realize the potential advantages of the Yuan provincial order. For although individual governors such as Menggu Baer were capable of benevolent rule, the Mongols as a whole found it difficult to establish a system of benevolent rule, or any system for that matter. Part of the problem was that in addition to branch secretariats, the Mongols established other offices with separate lines of authority to the capital and overlapping jurisdictions. There were, for instance, six "branch pacification offices" (xuanweisi) in northern and central China, many of which were not located in the same cities as branch secretariats.[28] These were primarily military offices, but they could also exercise civilian functions and in this latter capacity overlapped with branch secretariats. As described in History of the Yuan (Yuan shi), the interaction of branch surveillance offices and branch secretariats was awkward and must have created confusion, in the minds of both the governed and the governors: "Whenever a regional secretariat handles an official order, then the pacification office proclaims it below; whenever localities have a request, then the pacification office transmits it up to the regional secretariat."[29] Two branches of the censorate, located in the northwest and in Jiangnan, further muddied the administrative waters.[30] There were also twenty-four surveillance offices whose officials "periodically inspected the records of all government agencies; they accepted and investigated complaints about injustices; and . . . went out annually or semi-annually to make tours of inspection."[31]

Elizabeth Endicott-West has argued that these multiple parallel offices of Yuan local administration reflect the Mongols' preference for conciliar governance. She traces this pattern back to the *khuriltais*, great gatherings of Mongol clans on the plains of inner Asia held to select khans and to confirm plans for major military campaigns and policy departures. At the local level, she observes, officials representing different branches of government were expected to meet in daily conferences—the first item of business in a Yuan official's day—at which the affairs of the day were discussed and decided.[32] David M. Farquhar is not so sanguine about the relationship between political institutions in the Yuan. Drawing on Japanese scholarship, he sees the branch secretariats as "separate vassal states surrounding a nuclear state, the emperor's domain."[33] In this vision of Yuan government, the parallel structures of rule, particularly the provincial surveillance offices, were meant to keep watch on the branch secretariats and prevent the emergence of regional separatism, to which the large and secure Yuan provinces were especially vulnerable.[34] These explanations seem contradictory on first reading, suggesting as they do that different cultural traditions guided the delegation of authority. It is not impossible, however, to maintain cultural traditions with different implications within a single, transitional political order. The Mongols had always had to delegate authority but never for such a length of time or for an enterprise as complex as ruling the sedentary state of China. It is perhaps only in retrospect that the contradictory implications of Yuan rule become apparent.

Certainly, the combination of trust, distrust, and disorganization prevented the Yuan from further developing their proto-provinces. In the final analysis, what the Yuan contributed to Chinese territorial administration were a set of boundaries and the legacy of a sort of rule radically different from those of the Tang and other middle imperial empires. Indeed, the contrasts between Tang and Yuan provinces could hardly be sharper. Where the Tang sought to rule through regional strongmen with tenuous ties to the center, the Yuan appointed agents with shallow roots, if any, in the locale where they were stationed. Where the Tang sought military commanders, the Yuan aimed for stability and established territorial boundaries with this concern foremost in mind. Where the Tang and other early empires were deeply suspicious of creating a permanent extra layer of authority between the court and the prefecture, the Yuan were equally suspicious of temporarily appointed regional strongmen. Historical events seldom unfold with the clarity that the model builder would like. It does not distort history too much, however, to suggest that the Tang and the Yuan afforded two different models of the province: one created to provide the central government with the capacity to respond to crises, and the other created to provide a foreign dynasty the means of securely administering a conquered territory. It fell to the founders of the Ming and Qing dynasties to incorporate these two structures of provincial rule.

MING PROVINCES

The Ming dynasty did not so much integrate the two styles of territorial rule it had inherited from its predecessors as create parallel establishments in the countryside, each with different goals and personnel. Zhu Yuanzhang, the founding emperor of the Ming, moved quickly to build on the advantages of the Yuan order, its clear boundaries and permanent delegation of authority, by converting the branch secretariats into administrative units and reshaping their boundaries to suit Chinese conceptions of history and geography. This reshaping no doubt reflected Ming nativism—a desire, as Edward Farmer has expressed it, to "recreate China."[35] But it also was a product of the founding emperor's profound desire to impose order on the formless military chaos in which he had come to power. Succeeding emperors, less in control of military matters and more in need of the services of regional leaders who could show the dynasty's flag at the local level, began to appoint central officials to "tour and pacify" the regions of their empire, in effect to coordinate military affairs. These officials' title, *xunfu*, has customarily been translated as "grand coordinator"; they were appointed to serve as and where they were needed. The difficulty with this arrangement was that administrative commissioners reported to the bureaucracy and grand coordinators reported to the emperor; even when the two officials served in the same city, there was no mechanism for them to work together. The Ming employed a parallel system, in which regional military leaders were established alongside provincial administrators. Although Ming territorial arrangements brought stability to the countryside in the early years of the dynasty, they proved inadequate to the rising violence of the dynasty's last century.

Provincial Administration Commissioners: The Routine System

Initially, Ming provincial administration drew on Yuan precedents. The Ming did not, however, aim for direct replication. Rather, the first emperor sorted through the institutional accretions of the Yuan years, discarding some and domesticating others. The process was not so much analytical as intuitive, a matter of assigning officials where they were needed in Chinese perceptions of the empire. While he was still known as the Prince of Wu, before the dynasty was formally founded, Zhu Yuanzhang established branch secretariats in the lower Yangzi valley as military circumstances permitted. In 1376, nine years after declaring himself emperor, Zhu placed his own stamp on these units by converting branch secretariats into the seats of "commissioners for the promulgation and dissemination of government policies" (*cheng xuanbu zheng shi* [later abbreviated *bu zheng shi*]). Commissioners were dispatched to the seven locations where branch secretariats had been located as well as to six additional locations: Beiping, Shandong, Shanxi, Fujian, Guangdong, and Guangxi.[36] Most of the added locations were not new to Chinese administrative geography. Shandong and Shanxi had been the sites of branch pacification offices during the Yuan; in effect, the Ming emperor was appointing civilian officials to replace the organs of military occupation in these areas. Fujian had briefly been a branch secretariat during the Yuan, before it was absorbed first into Jiangxi and then into Jiangzhe. Guangxi and Guangdong had been independent provinces at various points in Chinese history. Moving jurisdictional administration into more traditional locations hardly made Ming provinces "natural" units. Provinces in the Ming were, and remain today, units of control imposed from above, yet the early Ming changes did create territorial divisions that more closely corresponded to the way the Chinese had historically imagined their empire.

Some jurisdictions were new in form, though not necessarily in conception. As had been the case during the Yuan, the first emperor of the Ming decided to administer the area around his capital from within the capital city itself. In the first years of the Ming, however, the capital was located at Nanjing rather than Beijing, and so it became necessary to establish boundaries for what would be called the "southern metropolitan region." Within these boundaries, the founding emperor of the Ming included eight prefectures north of the Yangzi, which had formerly belonged to Henan-Jiangbei, and eight prefectures south of the river, which had formerly belonged to Jiang-zhe.[37] In the first years of the fifteenth century, Zhu Yuanzhang's son, Zhu Di, known as the Yongle emperor, established his capital in Beijing and abolished the Beiping commissionership. Yet again, the capital city—this time Beijing—served as the emperor's administrative seat for the surrounding area, which he called the "northern metropolitan region."[38] There were two further changes to the provincial order during the tumultuous Yongle reign. In 1407, flush with the success of his conquests in the south, the emperor established administrative commissioners for a region known as Jiaozhi, located in the northern part of Vietnam. Similarly, in 1413, he established a commissioner for Guizhou. In 1428, as the court met with military reverses and abandoned its positions in northern Vietnam, the Jiaozhi commissionership was abolished.[39] Guizhou was retained, and the fourteen commissioners' posts established in 1428 remained unchanged until the end of the dynasty.

Like the Yuan branch secretariats, the Ming commissioners were meant to serve as conduits through which central policy would reach local officials. According to the brief account of this office provided in *History of the Ming* (Ming shi), the commissioner's role encompassed publicizing the benevolence and laws of the central government as well as supervising local officials, evaluating them, and reporting about them to the central government as necessary. Every three years, the provincial commissioner was to accompany local officials to an audience with the emperor, and every ten years, the commissioner was to submit tax and population registers to the capital for review. The commissioner was also responsible for distributing stipends and grain rations to members of the royal family, officials, government students, and the ranks of the army. His other duties included entertaining official visitors, submitting local products to the emperor on appropriate ceremonial occasions, caring for orphans and widows, recommending rewards for the filial and virtuous, and reporting drought and flood conditions to the central government. The court provided for each commissioner to have at least nineteen regular staff members who were divided among the five offices of the registrar, record keeper, judicial secretary, jail warden, and keeper of the granary.[40]

The founding emperor of the Ming had a minimalist view of government in which local communities would be left to govern themselves, with limited influence from the central administration. But the tasks of administration grew over time, and the commissioners' relatively small staffs needed to be supplemented. By the Wan-li reign (1573–1619), two vice commissioners were being appointed to every province except Shandong, and additional, more specialized staff members were appointed as necessary.[41]

By the middle of the dynasty, administrative tasks at the local level also transformed the role of the "provincial surveillance offices" (*anchashi*) established in the early Ming. These offices were modeled on the Yuan branch censorates, except that the Ming established thirteen such offices, each in a provincial capital. The original function of these offices was to review the activities of provincial and local governments. This task often required provincial censors to conduct inspection tours around the province and remonstrate with appropriate offices in cases of injustice. Inevitably, judicial matters came to be the purview of the provincial surveillance officials and eventually constituted most of their work.[42] By the end of the dynasty, provincial surveillance officials were so fully engaged in this work that their title is commonly translated as "provincial judge." Even with this addition, of course, provincial-level bureaucracy was hard put to cope with the demands of administering territories as large as some European countries. Nevertheless, the Ming provincial staffs were a far more stable and effective presence at the local level than anything the Yuan had attempted and probably were greater in number than any staff that had existed in earlier Chinese dynasties.

Grand Coordinators

Interactions between the local administrative establishment and the government organs responsible for maintaining Ming military authority presented a problem. In the early years of the dynasty, the founding emperor had appointed thirteen regional military commissions, analogous to the branch pacification offices of the Yuan, which reported to the Ministry of War. Although these offices existed until the end of the dynasty, they were never as important as the grand coordinators appointed directly by the court. The title "grand coordinator" was first used to describe the responsibilities of the founding emperor's son and heir apparent when he was sent to Shanxi in the autumn of 1391, probably to determine the suitability of the province—particularly the city of Xi'an—as a national capital. The title died with him in the spring of 1392.[43] It was revived some thirty-four years later to describe the role of two officials, not members of the royal family, who were sent to coordinate political and military affairs in the northern metropolitan region and in Zhejiang. This mission originated in imperial suspicions of how the military and civilian administrations were getting along and of possible abuses by civilian officials. When these two coordinators returned to Nanjing, they reported to the emperor that important offices were being left vacant and that the people's poverty was unabated. They recommended to the emperor that he appoint his own delegates to tour and pacify the people in all regions of China. Four years later, grand coordinators were appointed for Henan, Shandong, Shanxi, Jiangxi, and Huguang.[44]

These appointments provided the occasion for a rare instance of explicit editorialization on the part of the editors of *History of the Ming*, who commented that "this was the beginning of the institution of *xunfu*."[45] There was some truth to their comment, since, from 1426 onward, the appointment of grand coordinators became a frequent practice. Most secondary scholarship has, however, treated this claim very cautiously. There was really no "system" of grand coordinators in the Ming; in fact, very little about the Ming dynasty's appointment of coordinators was systematic. Throughout the Ming, the role of coordinator was simply an additional charge conferred on certain officials who derived their rank from the appointments they held at court. The practice of appointing grand coordinators was so weakly established that when the Tianshun emperor returned from his captivity in 1457, he recalled all grand coordinators and abolished the post, only to reestablish it two years later.[46] The appointment of provincial governors did become a systematic practice in the Qing dynasty, however, and it seems likely that the Qing dynasty editors of *History of the Ming* were assigning, perhaps at court request, the origins of the powerful institution they saw around them to the Ming period. The account of Ming grand coordinators in *History of the Ming*, *juan 73* in "Treatise on Officials" (Zhi guan zhi) was produced several centuries after the events it described, in a world where political realities and administrative desiderata were much changed. Many of the early appointments it outlines seem to have been temporary affairs, the details and circumstances of which have been obscured by time and editorial practice. Moreover, the very organization of the account, in which "provinces" were set as the basic headings and the inconsistencies of appointments detailed under them, probably reflects a world in which provinces had become the administrative norm. Read with these caveats, the account suggests not an institutional creation but a dynasty slowly and perhaps provisionally evolving a new administrative instrument for coping with its political problems.[47]

Grand coordinators were not consistently appointed after 1426, even to the most important provinces, which is one reason to regard the appointments of 1426 as ad hoc actions rather than as the beginnings of a concerted strategy of institution building. Although an official was sent to Zhejiang in 1426, appointments were made in the province only as required until the middle of the sixteenth century. Zhejiang acquired a regular grand coordinator at that time when growing piracy along the coast forced the appointment of new officials. Even when a coordinator was established in 1547, the post was abolished only two years later. It was reestablished in 1551, this time permanently.[48] Permanent appointments were made sooner to Henan, but still the process was an irregular one. In 1430, a coordinator was made responsible for affairs in Henan and Shanxi, but when the first appointee returned to the capital in 1449, the coordinator's territory was shifted to include Henan and Huguang.[49] Finally, in 1450, a permanent coordinator was appointed for Henan, and, in 1579, the Henan coordinator was made responsible for the maintenance of the Yellow River dikes.

Other grand coordinators were not so much administrators as special imperial representatives empowered to address specific problems in the empire. The contingent needs appointees were meant to address become especially clear if Ming provinces are grouped according to the dates when grand coordinators were first appointed. Grand coordinators were appointed in twenty-nine locations during the Ming. Thirteen were in cities where there was already a commissioner for the promulgation of government policies, and sixteen were located in other cities. Table 1.1 lists the locations where grand coordinators served and the dates when coordinators were first appointed.[50] The coordinators who were appointed to locations not included in the original north China appointments may be divided into three groups. In the latter half of the fifteenth century, new coordinators were appointed in the north and northwest; during the middle years of the six-

TABLE I.I. First Appointments of Ming Grand Coordinators

Year	Location	Year	Location
1426	Shuntian	1551	Yunnan
1426	Zhejiang	1556	Fujian
1430	Shandong	1566	Guangdong
1430	Shanxi	1566	Nangan
1430	Henan	1568	Guizhou
1430	Jiangxi	1569	Guangxi
1430	Huguang	1583	Yunyang
1436	Liaodong	1597	Tianjin
1436	Xuanfu	1621	Denglai
1436	Ningxia	1623	Pianyuan
1450	Yansui	1637	Anqing
1450	Xi'an	1638	Miyun
1450	Ganzhou	1638	Huaiyang
1472	Baoding	1643	Chengtian
1474	Datong		

Source: *Ming shi*, 73:1776–79.

teenth century, they were appointed to south-central and southern China; and in the seventeenth century, new appointees served around the capital. Each of these sets of appointments reflects a preoccupation of the Ming court.

Coordinators were dispatched along the northern and northwestern borders in the mid-fifteenth century, when the dynasty, in retreat from its earlier aggressive policy toward the Mongols, sought to secure its flanks. The transition from offensive to defensive postures in inner Asia produced a series of institutional rearrangements along the border. The founding emperor had established his sons in princely fiefs along the northern border and given them military responsibilities. When the Yongle emperor, himself a formerly enfeoffed prince, usurped the throne, these fiefs were supplemented with border garrisons commanded by regular army officers appointed from the capital. During the Zhengtong reign (1436–50), coordinators were appointed to oversee military and civilian governance in the north. The first such appointments were made in 1436 for coordinators in Liaodong, Xuanfu, and Ningxia. Three new coordinators were appointed in 1450 at Yansui, Xi'an, and Ganzhou; *History of the Ming* appears to read these appointments as responses to the capture of the Ming emperor at Dumu in 1449, although Zhang Zhelang has shown that substantial institutional development preceded these appointments.[51] In 1474, after yet another Mongol raid, a seventh border coordinator was appointed to serve at Datong.

These posts were clearly meant to be defensive positions—essentially, border guards—and they came to serve at the same places where Ming princely fiefs had been located.[52] The positions had often evolved out of earlier military positions, and all those who served as governors in the north bore the concurrent title "associate military commissioner" (*canzan junwu*). This title was more often held by eunuchs than by civil officials, and, in one telling case, the appointment of a grand coordinator followed an urgent request from the field that a literate civil official be sent to manage military matters.[53] Circumstances often left these coordinators vulnerable to attack from the princes, from eunuchs who held military posts, and from within their own garrisons. In 1510, a grand coordinator in the northwest was killed when one prince revolted against his sovereign.[54] In the 1520s, when eunuchs in the central court tried to raise tax revenues in the north the northern garrisons mutinied, two grand coordinators were killed.[55] One northwestern coordinator took a more activist approach to administration. Zeng Xian, who served as the grand coordinator of Datong in the 1540s, advocated, unsuccessfully as it turned out, a major military campaign on the steppes of central Asia.[56] After his proposal was defeated, the northwestern coordinators returned to their rather supine position on the borders of the Ming.

In the late fifteenth century, the Ming created two unusual postings, essentially adapting the form of the border guardian to suit the needs of domestic control. In 1475, a military commander was assigned to Yunyang, a prefecture in northeastern Huguang, which sat on the edge of trade routes connecting north and south. This official's mission was to deal with the disruptions caused by travelers, particularly immigrants, as they moved from Shanxi to south China and from Sichuan into the middle and lower Yangzi region. The disruptions must have been severe, for the commander was provided with a garrison, whose rebellion in 1574 led to the creation of a permanent coordinator's position.[57] Later, when rebellion consumed southern Jiangxi, the court granted Wang Yangming's request to create a coordinator's post in southern Jiangxi at Nangan.[58] Like several of the border posts, these positions were created in locations where there was no civilian administrator, but unlike border postings, the geographic scope of these new positions included the territories of more than one province. The Yunyang coordinator was responsible for activities in Huguang, Henan, and Shaanxi, while the Nangan coordinator oversaw military activities in Jiangxi, Huguang, Fujian, and Guangdong. Both postings were less prestigious than coordinatorships in other parts of the empire, and neither official had civilian responsibilities.[59]

In the sixteenth century, the focus of Ming attention shifted from the north to the south and the southeast. A grand coordinator was appointed to Guangxi in 1569; coordinators were appointed to Fujian and Zhejiang in 1556; and a coordinator was first appointed for Guangdong in 1566. This rash of appointments coincided with, and responded in rather particular ways to, two major developments that were transforming south China in the sixteenth century: economic growth and interethnic violence. The growth of a vigorous commercial order brought prosperity and social change to the cities of the southeast. As Timothy Brook has characterized the economic situation of the south, "merchants were drawing producers and consumers into regional and national commercial networks that neither could do without, and exports were luring Japanese and Spanish silver into the Chinese market and helping to lubricate the economy."[60] Economic development afforded new opportunities for individuals and, theoretically at least, for the state. In other early modern empires, commercial opportunities structured the provincial governments. But in China, the coordinators' appointments were a response not to the opportunities but to the dangers brought about by economic development. In Fujian and Zhejiang, coordinators were appointed to contain the piracy spawned by lucrative coastal and international trade. The coordinator for Guangdong was appointed after a major raid against south Chinese pirates liberated more than ten thousand Chinese in south China from involuntary servitude.

In these southern appointments, the court was often aiming more for the image than for the reality of administrative consistency. As James Tong's research has demonstrated, throughout the sixteenth century, south China was being torn apart by collective violence of largely rural origins. In particular, two waves of rebellion swept through the south in the late sixteenth century, one culminating between 1506 and 1515 and the other between 1566 and 1575.[61] Much of this brigandry was probably related to tensions between indigenous peoples and Han inmigrants to the area. During the fifteenth century, the Miao, a mountain-dwelling minority people who lived scattered through the southeast, rebelled three times, and the Yao peoples engaged in two rebellions. In response, during the early sixteenth century, the Ming dispatched military personnel to the south in a variety of capacities. The shift to grand coordinators in the later sixteenth century had more to do with the court than with south China. By the mid-sixteenth century, there were in the capital a series of strong grand secretaries who wanted or needed to represent victories in the south as their own accomplishments. The victories were often rough-and-ready affairs rather than the result of administrative innovations. Gao Gong, a powerful grand secretary during the Wan-li reign, was said to have remarked of the Guangdong appointment: "I gave Yin Zhengmao one million *taels* of silver; he may have pocketed half of that, but he got the job done."[62] A similar attitude may have prevailed in the case of the appointment, in the last years of the seventeenth century, of new officials in the southern and northern areas of one of the largest jurisdictions in China, Huguang. During the Yuan, there were two branch military commissioners in Huguang, one in the north and one in the south. The Ming had seen no need to reproduce these structures until disorder in the region led to the first appointment of an official in southern Huguang, at Pianyuan, in 1623. Initially, the appointment was not meant to be permanent, though a coordinator served in the area more often than not between 1600 and 1644, and the post was made a regular one in 1629. In the very last years of the dynasty, a parallel coordinator was established at Chengtian for the northern part of Huguang.

In the seventeenth century, trouble moved from the frontiers to the dynasty's doorstep. Between the late 1590s and the fall of the dynasty in 1644, five new grand coordinators were appointed to secure Ming defenses. Seaborne threats were addressed first. A grand coordinator was established at Tianjin in 1597, and in 1620, a coordinator was posted at Denglai, the port on the northern coast of the Shandong peninsula nearest to Manchuria. These new posts appear to have been produced as a response to Toyotomi Hideyoshi's invasion of Korea, though they later became outposts for defense against the Manchus. A seventeenth-century Qing governor attributed the origin of this post to long-term changes in trade patterns along the coast. He noted that, in earlier times, the eastern end of the Shandong peninsula had been a poor area surrounded on three sides by ocean from which peasants could barely make a living fishing and processing salt. But in the thirteenth century, this pattern changed. During the Yuan, the practice of shipping grain by sea (from the lower Yangzi to north China) began, and hundreds of thousands of *shi* of grain flowed through Denglai on its way to Tianjin. The Ming stopped this practice, but merchants from south China continued to ship goods through Denglai; northern merchants shipped goods from Tianjin to Denglai and thence to Liaodong.[63]

The land routes to the capital were perhaps even more important than the coasts. In 1638, a coordinator was established at Miyun to guard the Great Wall gateway at Gubeikou, the closest gateway to Beijing. As the Manchu menace mounted, and the wealthy and titled fled south from the capital in increasing numbers, the dynasty established grand coordinators in the lower Yangzi valley, where they were to protect lives and property. In 1637, a coordinator was posted at Anqing, and in 1639, a coordinator was established at Huaiyang. The first and only occupant of the Anqing post was the tragic hero Shi Kefa, whose death in 1645 marked the end of Ming rule in north China.

The habit of responding to crises through ad hoc appointments was so deeply woven into the pattern of Ming government that emperors of the late Ming, faced with the dynasty's most serious challenges, elaborated the system rather than questioned it. Between 1610 and 1620, the government instituted a new stratum of military appointees who were directly responsible to the court, known as "supreme commanders," or *zong-du*.[64] Like grand coordinators, supreme commanders derived their authority directly from the emperor, and their rank came from the separate appointments they held at court. Commanders differed from coordinators in the geographic scope of their authority, and for this reason, they were called upon to address problems perceived to be of a regional nature. Early in the Ming, the title was used for officials responsible for overseeing the transport of grain to the capital. In the fifteenth century, when the grand coordinators appointed to Guangdong and Guangxi proved incapable of dealing with the ethnic rebellion of the southeast, a supreme commander was appointed with the responsibility of overseeing the two southern provinces. Later supreme commanders were sent to the coast to coordinate active measures against pirates and to deal with border threats in the northwest. But at no time in the middle years of the Ming were commanders as important, or as numerous, as they were in the last years of the dynasty. Commanders were established in the provinces of the north China plain, the northwest, and the middle and lower Yangzi regions.

Military administration, born in crisis, readily becomes routine. During the Ming, the posts of grand coordinator and supreme commander originated during times of emergency, but as the initial coordinators were replaced by their successors, procedures were established and prerogatives elaborated. In some instances, this process of elaboration significantly expanded the local scope of the coordinator's authority. In 1454, many governors received the concurrent title "censor in chief," which allowed them to indict officials in their jurisdictions. Some governors were given additional charges of managing taxation, granaries, or river works; a Sichuan coordinator even had the special responsibility of providing timber for building projects. All of these prerogatives, however, derived from the coordinators' roles as special imperial representatives; where powers were needed to accomplish the court's ends, they were granted, but few if any rights were permanently delegated. As Zhang Zhelang concluded: "The limits of Ming grand coordinators' powers—whether in the area of finance, administration, military affairs or the law—were never clearly delineated. Coordinators' powers depended on the seriousness of the circumstances of their appointments, and were in some cases even contradictory."[65] Conceptually and organizationally, governors were never fully incorporated into the regular Ming civil service hierarchy and so remained exceptions, stationed rather awkwardly around an empire administered theoretically by provincial administration commissioners and their staffs. The problems related to this situation were apparent to those who served in the office but were particularly clear to the late Ming institutional historian Gu Yanwu.

The appointment of supreme coordinators gave the Ming a larger territorial administration than that of any previous Chinese dynasty. Supreme coordinators, who held their commissions directly from the emperor, oversaw grand coordinators, who also held their appointments from the emperor; supreme commanders and grand coordinators served together with administrative commissioners who, through their staffs, supervised all local officials. Provincial censors supervised all territorial officials, and regional military commissions routinely monitored local military forces. The system had been several centuries in the making and reflected a variety of social and political concerns. But in the seventeenth century, this proliferation of provincial officials was seen, at least in some circles, as the product of an inept and overreaching monarchy. In an essay probably written shortly before the fall of the Ming dynasty, Gu Yanwu argued that China would be better served by territorial officials who had roots and property in the communities they ruled and some hereditary rights to office.[66] Much of Gu's essay, "On Prefectures and Commanderies" (Junxian lun), is dominated by a rather utopian description of the details of how a system of hereditary magistracies would operate. But in one striking section, he deals with the strata of officials between the district level and the central court. Gu likened the Ming emperor to the owner of herds of horses and oxen:

> Now, caring for the people resembles the work of a family in raising domestic animals. One person is assigned the task of raising the horses and the oxen, and someone else tends the grasses and beans. If, however, the master's majordomo is sent to oversee them, he will not even be able to estimate the harvest without consulting the master, and the horses and oxen will waste away. . . .
>
> The reason the empire's troubles have become numerous is that the masters, not trusting the grooms, have sent servants to oversee them. Not trusting even these, the master's eyes and ears become confused. Thus, if one loves his horses and oxen, he will not calculate the cost of their fodder. If the horse is tended by a single groom, he will grow fat. If the people are governed by a single official, they will be content.[67]

This passage does not mention the provincial officers by name, but the analogy is unmistakable. In his major work *Record of Knowledge Diligently Accumulated* (Ri zhi lu), Gu devotes a *juan* to the origins and nature of the traditional territorial posts in Chinese empires, the *zhou*, the *xian*, and the *fu*, reflecting on the important role they played in local administration. His only reference to "province" in that volume is a short paragraph on the term *sheng*, in a *juan* devoted to military affairs, in which he objects to the use of the term as an abbreviation of *xing zhong shu sheng*.[68] Possibly for this reason, when de Bary translates a portion of this essay in *Sources of Chinese Tradition*, he translates Gu's reference to the offending supernumerary officials as a direct reference to "provincial governors and governors general."[69]

As animals would grow fat when the intermediate level of servants, grooms, and majordomos was pared back, so, too, would the Chinese people grow prosperous when the number of levels of government officials was reduced. Gu's metaphor was, in certain respects, an odd one, for although natural metaphors were quite common in Chinese political philosophy texts, the metaphors were more often of an agrarian than of a pastoral nature. In addition to being a Ming dynasty degree holder and landholder, Gu was perhaps one of the most knowledgeable institutional historians of his generation. Although Gu's pastoral metaphor would not have called to mind the Chinese past, it could easily have reminded his readers of the Mongols, pastoral peoples who had, after all, originated the practice of appointing permanent officials at the provincial level. Gu was offering a double critique of emperors who established levels of provincial officers: they were in effect clumsy imitators of an alien tradition of rule. This may be stretching Gu's pastoral metaphor a bit far, but he was not the only late imperial political critic who attributed the office of provincial governor to the baneful influence of foreign conquerors.

Gu also had a point, or perhaps several points, in suggesting that it was imperial distrust that spurred the development of provincial offices. At one level, this may simply have been a matter of attributing blame for an unbearable political and social situation. Faced with what must have seemed an incomprehensible loss of property, status and even life as Manchu armies occupied the lower Yangzi valley, Gu blamed the disaster on that distant and unknown entity in the late Ming, the emperor. But his critique was more than a cry of personal anguish. The appointment of special imperial envoys had been, since at least Tang times, a mark of the central government's lack of confidence in the ability of local officials to restore order and meet their fiscal and political obligations. This lack of confidence had often been transferred to the envoys themselves. While no Ming governor was subjected to the scorn that An Lushan had suffered, the Ming record is full of accounts of governors being recalled, humiliated and even executed. There was surely no more conclusive demonstration of imperial distrust than the appointment of supreme commanders to supervise grand coordinators, who, in turn, supervised local military affairs.

In "On Prefectures and Commanderies," Gu's proposed solution to this problem was to abolish intermediate layers of officials. Elsewhere in his corpus, however, Gu acknowledged that abolishing established official posts was difficult. With documents growing more complex and lawsuits becoming more numerous every day, the need for officials constantly increased, and the effort to abolish offices only led to frustration and pressure to restore them. Quoting the Jin dynasty (265–317) intellectual Xun Xu, Gu argued that abolishing posts was not as good as abolishing work, and that abolishing work was not as good as relying on the good intentions of those who govern. Gu was arguing, not so much for a change in organization, but for a reduction in the scope of government itself and urging the central state to rely on local people to govern themselves.[70] Taken together, Gu's arguments represent a strong assertion of the traditional Chinese preference for light government, with local people bound to the state by ideological fealty rather than by ties of bureaucratic authority.

Another argument could have been made that seemed more compelling as the Chinese empire expanded and encompassed a wider range of peoples and social and economic environments. In this view, the weakness of the Ming system of provincial government was not in the number of officials who were appointed, or even in the scope of the duties they were expected to undertake, but in the lack of arrangements made for coordinating their efforts. Despite their impressive titles and personal mandates, individual grand coordinators and even supreme commanders in the Ming were simply imperial envoys, strung out along the vulnerable borders of empire or scattered through the vast chaotic south, with few resources and no institutional connections with other dynastic representatives. While administrative commissioners and grand coordinators often served in the same cities, there was no mechanism that enabled them to work together. Military coordinators sent from the court could not depend on the resources and personnel of the civilian administration, and local civilian administrators had little influence over the way in which grand coordinators disposed of military affairs.

Some extraordinary officials were able to rise above these institutional barriers and fulfill their appointed roles, but when they did so, it was more a mark of their own energy and charisma than a sign of a strong political system. Providing a case in point are the efforts of Hu Zongxian, the Ming official who was appointed supreme commander of the dynasty's resistance to pirates in the mid-sixteenth century.[71] Arriving on the coast in 1556, Hu defeated the pirate Xu Hai and his lieutenant Wang Zhi. But, as Charles Hucker points out in his description of Hu's career, Hu succeeded only through his extraordinary ingenuity. Hu's was hardly a routine arrangement, but one in which he used borrowed troops, "offers of pardon, patronizing friendship, subornation of colleagues, poisoned wine, moral principles, false intelligence, procrastination, beautiful women, solemn and fair promises, bribery, banquets, threats, intelligence, lies, cajolery, assassination, and [the] deployment of troops to accomplish his ends."[72] What Hu did not rely on was the support or advice of subordinates. As Hucker notes, while Hu did consult his subordinates, he often made decisions they opposed, and he did so on "his own authority with full and heavy responsibility for them."[73] Hu's tenure in office, while successful, served to highlight what James Tong has called the "horizontal fragmentation in most administrative levels and functional areas" of Ming government, which left territorial officials isolated from the very sources of support that they needed to confront local problems and so fundamentally undermined the regime's capacity to respond to challenges.[74]

Under these circumstances, Gu Yanwu may perhaps be forgiven for not regarding the provincial governorship as a particularly promising institution. In a world in which history mattered, the provincial governorship had no historical record of success. On the contrary, governors were associated with some of the greatest debacles in Chinese history. Many viewed the fall of the Han dynasty, the implosion of social and political order in the mid-eighth century, and the inability of the Ming to resist foreign invasion during Gu's lifetime as results of ill-conceived territorial administration. In a world in which ethnicity increasingly mattered and Manchu armies marched on the Ming capital, the institution of provincial governor was tainted by its association with a foreign dynasty. Not only were the branch secretariats, which formed the basis of Ming territorial administration, of Yuan origin but the whole notion of a ruler delegating authority to individuals rather than among a morally united elite was, at least in Gu's view, foreign to China. Finally, in a world in which titles mattered, grand coordinators had no formal place in the hierarchy of officials and were left isolated, with no support against the many who opposed them. The remarkable achievement of the Qing dynasty was to convert this fairly unpromising institution into one of the pillars of the Chinese empire. The Qing rulers overcame the burdens of history.

CHAPTER 2

The Qing Creation of the Province

Early Qing rulers were uniquely able to tinker with Chinese institutions and, in doing so, fashioned a viable instrument of civilian governance out of an institution that had been more of a problem than a solution in the Ming and earlier dynasties. The creation of this form of administration represented a milestone in Chinese imperial rule, and much of the work for which the Qing dynasty was known—its ability to secure borders, collect and transfer revenues, supervise local governments, manage grain stocks to provide relief in times of dearth, repair roads, dikes, and irrigation works, and maintain local elite hegemony—was accomplished through provincial governors. How were the Manchus able to build such an institution? The answer lies not in any specific Manchu vision of territorial administration but in the details of their postconquest confrontation with the realities of rule in China. Qing leaders were not revolutionaries; they were practical and concrete men whose actions were determined more by perceived needs than by ideological or political visions. Perceptions of need were, of course, a product of the cultural and political milieu, and so in certain respects, the Qing provincial governor was a product of a particular moment in the early years of the dynasty. Nonetheless, the creation stood the test of time, for the Qing dynasty governed more territory for a longer period of time than did any comparable empire in the world.

From the Yuan and Ming dynasties, the Qing inherited a geographic template for provincial administration, but it had been stretched out of shape by the military contingencies of the fifteenth and sixteenth centuries. Once in China, Qing leaders established stable boundaries for existing provinces and created new ones where political and economic realities called for them. By 1664, eighteen provinces had been established; thirteen had capitals in locations where the Ming had posted grand coordinators, while the other five had newly founded capitals. In each of these provinces, a *xunfu*, the Qing term for "governor," served along with a "lieutenant governor" and a "provincial judge," the usual Qing translations for *buzhengshi* and *anchashi*.[1] Groups of two or, in some cases, three provinces formed the jurisdiction of a "governor-general," the usual translation of *zongdu*. In this new order, governors became the middlemen that the Ming had so conspicuously lacked between local and central government, and between military and civilian authority.

Next, the Qing had to sort out the relationships between governors and other territorial officials. The dynasty accomplished this by assigning ranks to offices that had not had rank in the Ming dynasty and by developing a procedure for appointing officials to these offices. Together, these provisions provided a blueprint for provincial administration. But at least as important as the procedures were their application and the human pathways created among the provinces by central court personnel decisions. Qing official positions were endowed with human meanings that were as much a part of the dynasty's design for empire as the provincial boundaries were. These meanings derived from the government's appointment of prominent officials to some posts and less well-known but experienced officials to others and of experienced border officials to new frontier areas and regional specialists to their areas of expertise.

SHUNZHI DEPLOYMENTS

Historians have differed in their representations of the Qing conquest. Those viewing the event from a historical distance have tended to emphasize broad social and institutional continuities between the Ming and the Qing. For many, as Lynn Struve has observed critically, the Qing conquest seemed nothing more than a "minor blip on the very long electrocardiogram of Chinese history."[2] In contrast, for those who experienced the conquest, it seemed nothing less than a meltdown of the late Ming social, institutional, and intellectual order, a vast conflagration that destroyed much that was familiar and memorable about the late Ming. In the realm of territorial administration, a metaphorical compromise position is possible. Fires certainly burned throughout China between 1644 and the late 1670s, but their effect could be compared to a smelting process that produced a harder and more durable metal from the ore of late Ming institutions. In the first decades of Qing rule, the dynasty adopted and then adapted Ming territorial institutions. Initially, the Ming territorial order was re-created, staffed, in part at least, by Ming holdovers who were appointed by traditional methods. Later, new posts were created and others eliminated as the Qing moved in its own directions.

During the most intensive phase of province building, the twenty-seven years between 1644 and 1671, the foundations of provincial rule were laid down as leaders sorted out the roles that the various types of troops of the Manchu conquest armies would play in the occupation. Manchu troops, known as bannermen, were organized into garrison forces and stationed around major cities as the Qing occupied and pacified them. Manchu "commanders" (*jiangjun*) or "brigade generals" (*fu dutong*) stationed within the garrisons commanded these forces. In the north, Manchu banner troops were garrisoned by 1647 around Beijing and, outside the capital, in Xian, Nanjing, and Hangzhou.[3] As Mark Elliott has argued, these northern garrisons preserved the purest form of the "Manchu Way," the mix of martial skills and cultural characteristics that marked preconquest Manchu life.[4] Perhaps in part because of the presence of these garrisons, the legacy of military occupation lasted longer in the north than in other regions of the empire, and military needs and personnel dominated the politics of north China throughout the seventeenth and well into the eighteenth century. Farther south in the Yangzi valley, Chinese bannermen constituted a larger portion of the occupying force. There were garrisons at Jiangning (the Qing name for Nanjing) under the joint command of one Manchu and one Chinese bannerman.[5] The Hanzhong, Guangzhou, Guangxi, and Guizhou garrisons were manned by Chinese martial banner troops, in part because there were not enough Manchu troops to populate all garrisons and in part because the southern terrain of mountains and seas was not suitable for Manchu styles of warfare.

This preponderance of military force was the foundation on which the Qing built its territorial administration. During the initial years of the dynasty, many of the Chinese martial bannerman who had participated in the conquest were installed as governors-general of the newly conquered territories.[6] This move made good sense, as many Chinese bannermen had performed very well during the conquest, and the regent Dorgon held high expectations for them as civil officials. Moreover, as Robert Oxnam has noted, "being Chinese, they would be more adept at dealing with provincial China than their Manchu counterparts, whose knowledge of Chinese people and government was often superficial."[7] Initially, Qing governor-generalships were ad hoc appointments, "created according to the exigencies of military conquest" and "attached to the person not to an area."[8] Later, however, as borders became fixed, these officials were embedded within the developing hierarchy of local officials. Governors-general were a half step below garrison commanders in rank and had a rather different function. Their role was not to command but to oversee the projection of Qing power into the countryside. In 1645, five territorial and two functional appointments were made. Governors-general were posted in Shanxi, Shaanxi, the Huaiyang area, the southeastern coast, and Huguang and assigned to manage grain transport and river conservancy. Subsequently, governors-general were established for Jiangnan in 1646, Liangguang in 1647, north China in 1649, and Yungui in 1653. In 1661, regents for the young Kangxi emperor experimented with a denser network of military control by creating eight new governors-general, a move that allowed them to install protégés in territorial posts around the empire.[9] This experiment was soon abandoned, however, in an action that anticipated future development of the territorial regime. On 4 July 1665, the Qing decreed that henceforth there would be eleven governors-general.[10] Despite the seeming finality of this pronouncement, the north China governor-general's post was eliminated the next year, leaving ten positions, a number that would remain fairly stable until the end of the dynasty.[11]

With military power secured in the hands of Manchu and Chinese banner commanders and governors-general, there was less need for governors to play the role of military commanders at the local level, although it took some years for the Qing to establish these conditions.[12] Initially, the effort seems to have been aimed at filling Ming posts with competent, trusted men. In 1644, the new rulers appointed governors to eight locations on the north China plain where the Ming had posted grand coordinators. By the end of 1645, the Qing had placed their own appointees in eleven more Ming locations in the north, the northwest, and the Yangzi valley. The Qing also placed three governors near the capital. A governor was appointed to Baoding, presumably to protect the approaches to Beijing; to Nanjing, to replace the administrators of the Ming southern capital; and to the lower Yangzi valley, to manage transport and commerce along the river. By late 1645, the Qing had thus largely replicated the Ming system and, in order to do so, had largely used Ming personnel.[13] Of the twenty-two Qing governors serving in early 1645, fifteen were former Ming officials. Eleven of these were senior Ming officials who had declared themselves loyal to the Qing and been reassigned or promoted to new responsibilities, while four had been promoted from the lower ranks of Ming territorial administration. Of the surrendered Ming officials, three had served as grand coordinators, five had served in senior posts in the capital, and three had held local office during the Ming.[14] As Qing armies moved into the south, six new governors were added in Fuzhou, Sichuan, Guangdong, Guangxi, and, later, Guizhou and Yunnan. In many of the southern postings, Qing armies were still in active pursuit of Ming loyalist forces. Most often in the south, the leaders of conquering armies worked together with the members of southern society who could be persuaded to collaborate with them to establish civilian government.[15] By 1659, Qing governors served in twenty-six locations where Ming coordinators had been appointed. The only Ming posts to which the Qing did not make appointments were Liaodong, Chengtian, Miyun, and Datong, posts that had been created to secure defenses against the Manchus.

Having fully staffed the Ming order, the Qing then began to adapt the system to suit its own needs. The most important development of the 1650s was a reduction in the total number of positions as the dynasty came to reassess its own needs. Table 2.1 summarizes the changes in governor posts between the mid-1640s and the early 1670s. Financial considerations dictated the first cut, at Tianjin, a location that the Qing came to regard as unnecessary in a north China that was securely under central control by the late 1640s. Several months later, Baoding was eliminated, as were several posts in the lower Yangzi valley when Manchu and Chinese troops originally stationed there were transferred to the south.[16] The

TABLE 2.1. Changes in Governors' Postings in the Early Qing

Year	Govs. (G)	Lt. Govs. (LG)	Posts Added	Posts Eliminated
1645	22	8		
1646	22	8		
1647	23	10	G: Fujian LG: Fujian, Guangdong	
1648	24	10	G: Sichuan	
1649	22	12	G: Guangdong, Guangxi LG: Sichuan, Guangxi	G: Baoding, Tianjin Anhui, Fengyang
1650	22	12		
1651	22	12		
1652	20	12		G: Xuanfu, Denglai
1653	20	12		
1654	20	12		
1655	20	12		
1656	20	12		
1657	20	12		
1658	21	13	G, LG: Guizhou	
1659	22	14	G, LG: Yunnan	
1660	24	14	G: Baoding, Anhui	
1661	23	14		G: Shuntian
1662	22	14		G: Yansui
1663	22	14		
1664	21	14		G: Yunyang
1665	18	14		G: Fengyang, Ningxia Nangan
1666	18	14		
1667	18	17	LG: Anhui, Gansu, Hunan	

Source: Adapted from *Qing dai zhi guan nian biao*, 3:1516–17.

position at Fengyang was briefly re-created in 1657, when the troops returned from the south, but it was abolished permanently in 1665. Beginning in 1652, the Qing eliminated posts that were primarily of military significance along the northern borders, at Xuanfu and Denglai.[17] Later, Yansui, Yunyang, Ningxia, and Nangan were eliminated, as it became apparent that Manchu garrison commanders in the north and governors-general in the south could control the situation without the assistance of other officials. In 1666, eighteen governor positions remained.[18]

There appears to have been a specifically Manchu component to the policy of eliminating governorships. With the exception of the 1649 reorganization, all the eliminated governorships were cut at moments when the relatively pro-Chinese policies of the imperial regent Dorgon and the Shunzhi emperor were under attack by elements of the Manchu aristocracy. Dorgon's death in December 1651 was followed by a series of impeachments of key Chinese officials whom he had appointed. Among the first of those impeached was Song Quan, the first provincial governor Dorgon had appointed.[19] The governorships that were cut in 1665 were eliminated by the same edict that expanded the number of governors-general, a policy fairly clearly associated with the Oboi regents for the Kangxi emperor. The elimination of these posts presented the paradox of a conquering dynasty abolishing fairly early in its rule the very posts from which it had accomplished its conquest. Moreover, it did this not during a time of civilian rule but at a moment when former military commanders were serving as regents for the young Kangxi emperor. The regents themselves were fundamentally conservative men, and as peace was restored in much of China, they found the overlapping civilian and military Ming system to be frightfully expensive and unnecessary for controlling their vast new empire.

The provincial map of China took its final form in the 1660s when the Qing created four new provinces. Two of these were created by a traditional method: as the armies of Wu Sangui battled their way down the long and winding road to the southwest, the Qing reestablished the two Ming provinces of Guizhou and Yunnan. The two other new provinces were created in a novel way, by accretion rather than by decree. Beginning in 1661, in the lower Yangzi, and in 1667, in the Xiang River valley, the court began to move elements of provincial administration from military outposts at Jiangning and Pianyuan into the river valley cities of Suzhou and Changsha. In neither case was there an expressed desire to create new provinces. In fact, Hunan and Jiangsu were not designated as provinces until 1676 and 1723, respectively. These two innovations are reflected in the establishment of lieutenant governors in Hunan and in Anhui in 1667. The lieutenant governorships eventually grew into full-blown provincial administrations and represented two of the Qing's most enduring contributions to territorial administration.

At the same time that the locations of governors were being established, the number of areas served by lieutenant governors was increased, so that there was a lieutenant governor wherever a governor served. Initially, the Qing appointed such commissioners to twelve of the thirteen sites to which the Ming had assigned them—Beijing being the exception. The number was increased to fourteen in 1659 and to eighteen in 1667.[20] The eighteen locations established in the mid-1660s were stable throughout the remainder of the seventeenth century.[21] Table 2.2 compares the locations of Ming grand coordinators and Qing provinces. In its

TABLE 2.2. Locations of Ming Grand Coordinators and Qing Governors

Ming and Qing	Ming Only	Qing Only
Zhejiang	Shuntian*	Zhili
Shandong	Liaodong*	Anhui
Shanxi	Xuanfu*	Jiangsu
Henan	Ningxia*	Hunan
Jiangxi	Yensui*	Sichuan
Shaanxi	Datong*	
Gansu	Nangan*	
Yunnan	Yunyang*	
Fujian	Tianjin*	
Guizhou	Denglai*	
Guangdong	Baoding	
Guangxi	Anqing	
Huguang	Pianyuan*	
	Miyun*	
	Huaiyang	
	Chengtian	

*Existed briefly during the Qing; abolished by 1675.
Source: Adapted from *Qing dai zhi guan nian biao*, vol. 3: 1516–17

final form, the Qing re-created less than half, that is, thirteen out of twenty-nine, of the Ming postings.

By itself, the decline in the number of provincial administrators from the Ming dynasty to the Qing does not indicate a change in approach to territorial governance. The locations of the postings that were retained, abolished, and created, however, do suggest new priorities. The provinces that the Ming and Qing dynasties shared most closely resemble the territories of provincial administrative commissioners established by the first emperor of the Ming in his nativist reorganization of Yuan territorial jurisdictions. This reestablishment of the Chinese geographic order may have resulted from the advice of the Qing government's Chinese collaborators. But it also represented a return to the civilian arrangements that had existed before Ming emperors began the practice of appointing grand coordinators to deal with military crises.

The locations involved were, for the most part, river valley cities of trade and commerce where civilian populations paid taxes and did business, centers the Qing had to control if it was to govern, rather than merely campaign in, China. It may even have been more important for the Qing to show its colors in these cities, as a native Chinese dynasty could more readily establish its legitimacy. The posts eliminated by the Qing (listed in the middle column of table 2.2) were precisely the ones the Ming had created for emergencies. These included the outposts along the northern border—Xuanfu, Ningxia, Yensui, and Datong—that the Ming had established in order to shield their retreat from the steppe as well as the internal southern control posts of Nangan, Yunyang, and Pianyuan. The disappearance of these posts pointed to one of the fundamental characteristics of early Qing rule, that the Manchus, in effect a nation-at-arms, were simply better prepared to maintain the preponderance of military force through their own organizational resources rather than add these tasks to the portfolio of civilian administrators.

The "new" provinces in the Qing were hardly new Manchu conquests; all existed in territories that had been firmly a part of the Ming empire. None of the jurisdictions the Qing created was a post of military significance. Sichuan was the only province situated on the empire's border, and that border was not particularly contested during the middle of the seventeenth century. (Sichuan also had a grand coordinator, but the appointment was quite brief, existing sporadically in the fifteenth century, from 1449–50, 1452–62, 1469–73, and 1507–9.) By the later seventeenth century, when Sichuan was contested territory, the Qing turned over control in the region to a governor-general and abolished the governorship. The other new provinces were reorganizations of territories, and, in the geographic sense, there was nothing new under the sun in Qing China. Yet provinces, as the Qing reorganized them, have survived into the twentieth century, in large part because they corresponded to changes going on within China. The creation of Hunan arguably represented a response to the new economic realities of the middle Yangzi region; as commerce and people began increasingly to flow to the south and southwest through the Xiang River valley, the dynasty required an administrative as opposed to a strictly military presence there. Jiangsu and Anhui came into being because Nanjing was no longer the southern capital as it had been in the Ming. But the two new posts also provided a foundation for more specialized administration of a region of increasing social and economic complexity. The same may be said of Zhili, although in this instance, the presence of Manchu troops in large numbers and a fairly fragile ecology led to a number of different administrative arrangements. The longer-range significance of the Qing provincial creations was not always apparent in the seventeenth century; what was apparent was the new dynasty's commitment to putting provincial administration to work on the central administration's domestic tasks and to developing the institutional structure for doing so.

KANGXI CONSOLIDATIONS

In the eyes of historians, the fact that governorships in the Qing became permanent is at least as important as the locations of Qing provincial governors. Ming appointments of grand coordinators were ad hoc affairs. Although individual postings were announced by imperial edict, the assembled regulations of the dynasty did not treat the positions to which appointments were made. In the Qing, both governors and governors-general came to be regarded as part of the standing political apparatus of the dynasty.[22] Permanence brought a series of changes to provincial administration. Relative ranks and responsibilities, which could remain protean when arrangements were temporary, were more firmly established. Hierarchies and reporting relationships were decreed among positions that were continually being filled. The Qing developed appointments procedures that allowed subordinate officials to move up to more senior positions. Much of the work of building local administration was accomplished during the later years of the Kangxi reign. Administrative reform was not a sort of activity often associated with the remarkable second Qing emperor; he was far better known as a conqueror who consolidated Qing territories in the southwest and added new lands in central Asia and as the patron of newly rejuvenated Song Neo-Confucianism. But it was Kangxi conquests, of land and, metaphorically, of the lower Yangzi elite, that made some sort of systematization of territorial administration necessary. The ideas for change did not necessarily come from the monarch himself: throughout his reign, the emperor found many Chinese willing to apply their knowledge of traditional Manchu and Chinese institutions to the problems of geographic diversity.[23]

RANKS AND RELATIONSHIPS

As might be expected of conquerors, action—in this instance, dispatching officials to deal with the problems of postconquest reconstruction—was easier than formalization for the early Manchus. The task of incorporating Qing territorial appointments into the bureaucratic order was not accomplished nearly so quickly or cleanly as were the appointments themselves. One issue was the relationship of governors and provincial administration commissioners. As a result of early Qing changes in the locations of governors, for the first time in late imperial history, the functions of coordination and security associated with Ming grand coordinators were being performed in the same locations with the civilian administration functions carried out by provincial administration commissioners. This transition had an impact on both offices. By at least the Wanli period, it was the Ming practice to appoint two administrative commissioners in each provincial capital. The senior of these was known as the "administration commissioner of the left" and the junior was the "administration commissioner of the right"; it was the practice to promote accomplished junior commissioners to the senior post.[24] From very early on, the new Qing rulers were skeptical of the need for two commissioners. In 1646, an edict observed tartly: "the administration commissioner of the left is a very busy office. But what does the commissioner of the right do? If this is not an empty post [rong yuan], then it must have some function. The officials of the six boards are unwilling to provide details."[25] In 1667, the Qing court ordered that henceforth there would be only one administration commissioner in each province. De facto, Qing governors replaced administration commissioners of the left in provincial capitals and were thus positioned to take on, over the next decades, many of the civilian functions the commissioners had performed. Provincial administration commissioners became, in effect, administrative subordinates of the governors; in recognition of this fact, it has become the practice to translate their title as "lieutenant governor" when referring to the Qing dynasty.

In the early Kangxi reign, two further changes in the organization of territorial administration produced administrative consolidation. During the Ming, the central Censorate regularly assigned "regional inspectors" (xun-an) to local jurisdictions. These officials, who served one-year terms, were responsible for "checking files, auditing accounts, interrogating officials, accepting complaints from the people, especially inspecting all prison and trials records [and] participating in policy deliberations of provincial level officials."[26] In early 1660, this office was abolished, and its functions were reassigned to the regular provincial administrators. Following a proposal by the president of the Censorate, Wei Yijie, the court assigned to lieutenant governors the task of auditing civilian and military fiscal accounts; to prefects and circuit intendants, the evaluation of magistrates; and to the provincial judge, the review of judicial decisions and inspection of prisons.[27] In 1671, the dynasty pruned another layer of provincial administrators when it eliminated the position of assistant to the lieutenant governor. The Ming had assigned an "assistant" (can zheng) to every provincial administration commissioner. In 1666, the Qing decreed that such assistants would be provided only where they were necessary. There would be two assistants to the lieutenant governor in Zhejiang, Jiangsu, Fujian, and Guangdong; there would be one in Huguang, Shanxi, Henan, Shaanxi, Guangxi, and Guizhou; and in the other provinces, there would be none.[28] In 1735, the post of assistant provincial administration commissioner was abolished, and its occupants were renamed "circuit intendants" (dao tai).[29] Both reforms had the effect of putting all those who served in local administration into a clear hierarchy under the direct control of governors. Table 2.3 provides a comparison of the two systems of territorial administration.

This hierarchy was reinforced by early Qing rules for the promotion of territorial officials from subordinate to supervisory posts. In 1655, the dynasty ordered that provincial judges could be promoted to administration commissioner and that circuit intendants could be promoted to provincial judge. Through the 1670s,

TABLE 2.3. Ming and Qing Territorial Administration

Ming Territorial Administration

		Emperor		
Supreme Commanders	Grand Coordinators	Censorate	Board of Personnel	Board of War
		Provincial Censors	Provincial Admin. Comm.	Regional Military Comm.
			Asst. Admin. Comm.	
		Prefect		
		Department Magistrate	District Magistrate	

Qing Territorial Administration

	Emperor	
Banner Administration		Board of War
Garrison Commander (2A)	Governor-General (2A) (Formerly Supreme Cmdr.)	Military Intendant (2A)
	Governor (2B) (Formerly Grand Coordinator)	
	Lt. Governor (2B) (Formerly Admin. Comm.)	
	Provincial Judge (3A) (Formerly Prov. Censor)	
	Circuit Intendant (4A) (Formerly Asst. Admin. Comm.)	
	Prefect (4B)	
	Department Magistrate (5A)	District Magistrate (7A)

Sources: Adapted from Hucker, A Dictionary of Official Titles, 70, 83; for Qing ranks, Brunnert and Hagelstrom, Present Day Political Organization.

senior officials at court were allowed to recommend individuals who had not served in territorial office for the positions of provincial judge and lieutenant governor, but such recommendations were no longer allowed after 1679.[30] Governors' appointments were a little more complicated, in part because governors represented the hinge between central and territorial administrations in the evolving Qing system; thus, they needed to be anchored in both. The basic Qing rule on the promotion of governors—first articulated in the Yongzheng edition of *Collected Statutes of the Qing*, but likely operative earlier—was that an individual could be promoted to provincial governor from the positions of subchancellor of the Grand Secretariat, senior vice president of the Censorate, prefect of the capital city or prefect of the District of Feng-tian, and lieutenant governor.[31] The capital posts from which governors could be appointed suggest the importance of governorships in the official hierarchy. During the Kangxi years, the Censorate and the Grand Secretariat were two of the most prestigious organs of central government, likely seats of some of the most influential advisers of the Manchu emperors. Mayors of the capital cities had the opportunity to demonstrate their administrative and political skills directly under the imperial court's eye. The stipulation that lieutenant governors could be promoted to governor separated both offices from the military hierarchy and reinforced the emerging role of the governor as leader of the local civilian administration.

As the civilian authority of governors increased, the military responsibilities that had been the raison d'être of Ming grand coordinators declined. In 1661, the phrase "overseer and adviser on military affairs" was formally eliminated from the official letter of appointment for governors.[32] In 1671, a censor for the Shandong circuit memorialized the Kangxi emperor, asking him to remind governors of their military responsibilities so that banditry could be held in check and the people's security assured. The emperor responded that governors need not be responsible for all the particulars of military activity. "Hadn't the dynasty," asked the emperor, "established governors-general and provincial military intendants for this purpose?"[33] Governors should share command with the appropriate local officials. Clearly, the dynasty felt it could maintain the preponderance of force at the local level through its own military hierarchy; it no longer had to rely solely on its provincial governors.

The functional hierarchy established with the reorganization of the provincial bureaucracy was further solidified as ranks were assigned to the various offices. In the official ranking system the Qing inherited, there were eight grades, each subdivided into an upper and a lower division. Rank inhered in the office rather than in its occupant: an official technically held no rank until he was assigned to a post, and a post always had the same rank regardless of the age, qualifications, or experience of the individual who held it. In assigning ranks, the Chinese political system was rating the importance of the functions officials performed, not commenting on the qualifications of officials themselves.[34] In the Qing territorial bureaucracy, the positions of lieutenant governor and below were ranked in a graduated hierarchy. Provincial censors held the rank 3A, circuit intendants held 4A, prefects held 4B, department magistrates held 5B, and ordinary magistrates held 7A. The ranks of governors were a bit more complicated. In the Ming, governors and governors-general had derived their rank from the positions they occupied, usually at court, at the time of their appointments; there was no rank specifically assigned to the territorial posts. As the Qing regularized provincial posts, they assigned ranks to them, thereby attaching priority to the duties associated with each. The early Qing, accustomed to hierarchy, decreed that a governor's rank was to be one grade above the rank he held at the time of his appointment.[35]

This system created anomalies, however. Officials might hold the same office but different rank, so rank came to bear no particular relationship to the importance of the office. The Yongzheng emperor tried to correct these anomalies in the first year of his reign by decreeing that a person who had been appointed provincial governor after senior service in the capital should hold the concurrent ranks of senior vice president of the Censorate and junior vice president of the Board of War. A provincial governor who had been appointed from a more junior position in the capital should hold only the concurrent rank of senior vice president of the Censorate. If the new governor's principal experience had been in the provinces, he should be given a special concurrent rank, roughly translatable as "assistant vice president of the Censorate." This practice meant, however, that the titles of some governors would be different from those of others, based on the offices they held at the time of their appointments. In 1748, the Qianlong emperor ordered that all governors should have the same concurrent title "senior vice president of the Censorate." Receiving this edict, the Board of Civil Appointments memorialized the emperor, asking whether all governors should also receive the title "member of the Board of War."[36] The emperor failed to respond, but, in fact, all governors appointed subsequently were given this title.

Over time, the logic of the new bureaucratic order required more clarification. Throughout the early Qing dynasty, governors were regarded as having the same rank as lieutenant governors. This anomaly was a product not of dynastic intent but of the history of rank assignment. No officials in China were ranked 1A, and rank 1B was reserved for the most senior officials at court. Governors-general held rank 2A, and when governors were assigned ranks, these clearly had to be below that of governors-general. There was only a half step between the rank of governors-general and the rank historically assigned to the position of lieutenant governor. Governors had to hold the same rank as either governors-general or lieutenant governors, and the Qing chose the latter. In 1748, however, the emerging hierarchical logic of the territorial order finally forced the Manchu court to define relations between the two offices. Even at this point, the concession was a somewhat grudging one. "In the past," wrote the Qianlong emperor, "we established the provincial administration commissioners as the leaders of local government. However, governors and governors-general preside over the hundred offices, and in fact administration commissioners . . . are subordinate to them. The governors and governors-general ought to be ranked first, followed by administration commissioners."[37] The edict offered no direct antecedent for the policy change, but a case that occurred just two years before the emperor made this pronouncement suggests the dimensions of the problem. In this case, a Guangxi governor and a lieutenant governor disagreed over policies for copper mining. Eventually, the governor came around to the lieutenant governor's position, but as the governor was well connected, the case caused a stir within Qing officialdom.[38] The Qianlong edition of *Collected Statutes of the Qing* compiled in 1763, unambiguously ranks governors 2B, adding in a footnote that a governor might hold a higher rank if he were president of a board.[39]

The changes the Qing made to the individual ranks of governors, and to the overall ranking system itself, were probably fairly minor. Governors had an ambiguous identity in both the Ming and the Qing, as emissaries of the central government and as the heads of local administration. In the Ming and earlier, this ambiguity was necessary to assure a powerful official's loyalty to the center. In the Qing, however, the ambiguity became problematic, and perhaps increasingly anachronistic, as the dynasty imposed a more hierarchical vision of administration. This was, of course, a subtle change carried out by stages over nearly a hundred years rather than a matter of revolutionary pronouncements. But such designations determined the self-image and public persona of governors.

APPOINTMENTS PROCEDURE

Once provincial yamens had been established at appropriate locations throughout the empire, the next step was to populate them with officials who were capable of serving as middlemen between civilians and military officers, between central and local governments, and between Manchus and Chinese. Each of these several elements in the still somewhat protean Qing polity had a claim on provincial governors' offices. Initial territorial administrators during the Qing, and many of the grand coordinators of the Ming, had been military figures; thus, the habits of military occupation could easily have prevailed in governors' offices. At the same time, most governors in the Qing were in locations that called for experience in the patterns and routines of civilian governance. The multiethnic character of the

Qing regime further complicated the task of selecting provincial governors. Most of the initial governors were Chinese, but as Manchus grew accustomed to their new role in the state they had established, they became more prepared to enforce claims on at least some of the Qing empire's territorial posts.[40] Finally, most Ming grand coordinators had wide experience in the capital, and many senior capital officials in the early Qing became involved in the selection of governors. But as the office of governor developed, it made increasing sense to promote individuals from the lower ranks of territorial administration to the governors' yamens. It fell to the Kangxi court to reconcile these several claims on territorial office and, in so doing, to establish the character of the Qing office of governor.

At the heart of the Qing procedure for the appointment of governors was the question of the relationship between bureaucratic and imperial authority—the power to recommend and the power to decide. The most complete description of how governors were appointed is found in the second *juan* of the Jiaqing edition of *Collected Statutes and Precedents of the Qing*. According to this account, both institutions were given a role in the appointment process. When a governor left office, the Office of Civil Selections within the Board of Personnel first declared the post "vacant" (*kai que*) and then memorialized the emperor inquiring whether he wished to make a "special appointment" (*te jian*). If the monarch chose to make a special appointment, any person he selected could receive a posting, regardless of his rank or location in the empire. If the emperor did not choose to make a special appointment, the Board of Personnel compiled a "ranked list" (*kai lie*) of all candidates eligible for appointment, from which the monarch made a selection.[41] The conception behind this procedure was fairly clear. The court reserved for the Qing emperor the Ming emperors' right to appoint governors on a fairly ad hoc basis. But the regulations additionally set forth a systematic procedure by which officials from lower-level territorial offices might be promoted to governorships. Cautiously, and probably wisely, the dynasty set forth no criteria specifying when an appointment of either type would be made, leaving the decision solely to the emperor and his counselors.

It was in the procedure for making ranked lists that the Qing made its greatest innovations. All dynasties in China had mechanisms for promoting officials in rank. In the Ming, most middle- and senior-level positions were filled through personal recommendations, in a process known as "collective recommendation" (*hui tui*). The Ming dynasty procedure for grand coordinator seems to have been that if a grand coordinator was to serve in a location of military significance, the appointee was recommended by the members of the Board of War. If the grand coordinator's main responsibility was to be tax collection, members of the Board of Revenue recommended him.[42] This had the advantage of assuring that an appointee would be well known to his superiors and to the court. But insofar as it tied the new governor to those in the capital who had recommended him, the procedure fostered a ferocious factionalism, which many saw as a root cause of Ming decline. The advice of former Ming officials to new Qing rulers no doubt corresponded to their own belief that the paralysis of late Ming factional politics must be avoided at all costs.

In the absence of recommendations, the ruler's problem was how to gather informed data about officials without creating networks of partisans. The Qing solution was to order the Board of Personnel to list officials eligible for promotion and rank them according to the date and circumstances of their qualification for office.[43] This meant that, at the moment of appointment, rulers would be presented with a fairly complete list of all those eligible for advancement. Additionally, office holders could be assured that their names would reach the court and be presented relatively systematically. In effect, the Qing court used the Board of Personnel as a buffer against the factionalism of Chinese officials. This apparent solution to the perennial problem of recommendation was particularly possible in the Qing, when Manchu rulers were set apart from Chinese officials by both rank and ethnicity and interacted with those they supervised by means of set procedures rather than personal ties. The term kai lie, which is used frequently and prominently in Collected Statutes of the Qing, does not appear at all in Collected Statutes of the Ming (Da Ming huidian). Moreover, the Encyclopedic Dictionary of the Chinese Language (Dai kanwa jiten) bases its definition of the term kai lie on the Qing example.[44]

Although there is evidence that ranked lists were used to select junior territorial positions earlier in the dynasty, it was not until the early 1670s that candidates for provincial governorships were subjected to the routine ranking and evaluation procedure. Before the 1670s, the Qing followed the Ming practice of allowing senior officials at the capital to recommend candidates for office by individually or collectively memorializing the throne. In 1653, it was decreed that any person could be recommended as governor or governor-general, regardless of rank, provided that the man's accomplishments were carefully detailed in the recommending document. Presumably these detailed documents, or the reasoning behind them, would have been prepared in advance by people fairly in the know, for, in 1654, the court ordered that recommendations for a governor's position should be submitted on the day after the position was declared vacant.[45] In 1663, regents for the young Kangxi emperor approved legislation stipulating that if a recommended candidate proved to be "inappropriate" (bu dang), both the candidate and the recommender would be punished. Nearly a decade later, in 1671, the Kangxi court approved the recommendation of the Board of Personnel that a ranked hierarchy be established among candidates for provincial governorships, thereby cutting through the knotty problem of appointing governors.[46]

According to *Veritable Records of the Kangxi Emperor* (Kangxi shilu), Ai Yuancheng, president of the Censorate, proposed that the procedure of making ranking lists be applied to provincial governorships in 1671. As redacted in the emperor's edict, Ai's proposal read:

> Previously, an edict was received ordering that in the cases of Chinese in the banner armies who were eligible for promotion, the precedent of Manchu officials should be followed. [In the case of Manchu officials] a ranked list of candidates eligible for promotion is prepared, then an edict calling for collective recommendations is issued. Now the promotion of officials to governor-general, governor, and commandant of the Green Standard Army should be made consistent with this procedure. At present, there are inconsistencies [in the procedures for appointment to senior posts]. Hereafter, when there is a vacancy for governor-general, governor, or garrison commander, let the Board of Personnel first prepare a ranked list of all candidates eligible for promotion, then request that the emperor decide whether to entertain collective recommendations.

> The proposal was referred to the Board of Personnel for deliberation, and then was implemented.[47]

Ai Yuancheng was one of those unsung (or perhaps undersung) heroes of the early Qing who advised the new emperors on the organization of empire. He received his *jinshi* degree in 1646, the third year of the Qing dynasty, and, during the late 1640s and early 1650s, rose through what was later to become the Qing Grand Secretariat. In 1662, he was appointed senior vice president of the Board of Revenue and, in 1670, achieved the same position at the Board of Personnel. One year later, in 1671, he was appointed president of the Censorate, where he served until his death in 1675. All of his proposals bespeak a man intent on facilitating Manchu governance of the new and diverse empire. During the course of his career, he warned the Qing emperors against too readily believing allegations of factionalism lodged against Chinese officials.

In another memorial that was likely related to the later proposal on ranked lists, Ai warned about the dangers of allowing members of the central administration to send their clerks out to inspect territorial administration. The problem was that the supposed "inspectors" demanded bribes from those they were sent to inspect, which disrupted local finance.[48] The practice of territorial officials giving gifts to central government officials or their delegates was a serious and fairly widespread problem in the early Qing. Gifts were given for birthdays, "for coal" in the winter, and "for ice" in the summer; many other sorts of irregular payments existed as well. Some of this gift giving was meant to ensure that reports were properly processed when they were received at the capital and that financial accountings were certified. But much of it was related to the competition for positions. In a world in which a word from a board president would secure a lucrative post for a potential governor, few board presidents could be left unrewarded.[49] Ai's proposal did not, of course, completely eliminate the involvement of central officials in territorial promotions, as members of the Board of Personnel were still responsible for preparing the lists. Nevertheless, the preparation was subject to regulations that became increasingly detailed the longer the dynasty existed.

By his own account, Ai's proposed innovation in civil appointments was borrowed from the military. A method first used to promote Manchu banner commanders, and extended to Chinese bannermen, was to be applied to provincial governors. In the 1670s, this may not have seemed like much of an innovation, for during these years, Chinese bannermen still had important claims on territorial office. In fact, Manchu and Chinese military officers were the primary beneficiaries of the new procedure: three-quarters of those promoted between 1671 and 1691 were bannermen serving in provinces with extensive Qing garrisons.[50] In the same entry in the Kangxi edition of *Collected Statutes of the Qing* that ordered the establishment of ranked lists, the Kangxi emperor decreed that when a governor's post became vacant, the Board of Personnel had to first memorialize, inquiring whether the emperor wished to appoint a Manchu, a Chinese bannerman, or a non-banner Chinese official, and then submit an appropriate ranking.[51] The fact that the selection of an ethnic status group was decided on *before* candidates were actually considered serves to highlight the importance of such groups. On the whole, the choices of status groups to serve in specific provinces were relatively consistent from the time this rule was initiated until it was repealed in 1691. In all provinces south of the Yangzi, except Fujian and Zhejiang, only Chinese bannermen were appointed governor before 1691. In Fujian and Zhejiang, the appointees between 1671 and 1691 were always non-banner Chinese. In the northwest, governors were always Manchus. The lower Yangzi provinces of Anhui and Jiangsu had Chinese bannerman governors until 1676 and degree-holding Chinese officials thereafter. Zhili usually had a bannerman as governor, but the other north China provinces—Henan, Shandong, and Sichuan—had mixed records, with degree-holding Chinese favored in Henan and bannermen favored in Shandong.

Ai's argument for making ranked lists rested on an assertion that consistency was needed in military and civilian territorial appointments. In context, however, Ai's proposal was not so much the defense of an abstract principle as an attack on the policies of the men who had served as regents for the young Kangxi emperor in the early 1660s. Men personally connected to the regents were increasingly chosen to govern China's territories. By 1671, all but one of the four regents were dead, and power had shifted from the hands of the conservative

Oboi regents to representatives of the Plain and Bordered Yellow Banners who served an emperor now ruling in his own name. Throughout the Qing administration, officials and positions were reshuffled. In the central administration, the Inner Three Courts that had served as advisory bodies to early Manchu monarchs were reorganized into the Grand Secretariat, and a new group of Chinese and Manchus was appointed to serve as grand secretaries.[52] In the territorial service as well, there were new faces in the ranks. The number of bannermen appointed to governorships was not new in itself, since most of those who were appointed as governors during the Oboi regency were bannermen. The difference was that the Oboi governors were usually senior officials serving in the capital at the time of their appointments, whereas, after 1671, most of the bannermen were men who had come up through the ranks. There were new men to serve a new emperor, and the mechanism of ranked lists was designed to bring them to the monarch's attention.[53]

One of the first civilians promoted by the Kangxi emperor in the 1670s proved to be one of the most beloved and honored governors of the Qing dynasty, Yu Chenglong.[54] Yu had worked his way up the ranks of the Kangxi service. His first posting was as magistrate of Luocheng county in Guangxi, a district so depopulated by the war between the Qing and the southern Ming that its capital boasted only seven families when Yu arrived. Four of his nine servants died shortly after arriving, and another four fled, but Yu persevered. In his seven years at the post, Yu oversaw the repopulation of the county and restored relations between Han in-migrants and the indigenous populations. He was promoted to the post of department magistrate in Sichuan. There he encountered the devastation that several decades of rebellion and war had wrought on China's westernmost province and consequently pursued policies that represented the core of Qing postwar reconstruction: refugee resettlement, demilitarization, and land reclamation.[55] He was then transferred to a prefecture in Hubei, where he served during the first years of the Wu Sangui Rebellion (1673–81), when most of the fighting was taking place in the middle Yangzi valley. Under his leadership, districts were taken back from Wu's forces. Some years and promotions later, while Yu was serving as lieutenant governor of Fujian, Governor Wu Xiangzuo recommended him for the highest grade in honesty and capacity. By the time Yu attained the governorship of Zhili, to which he was appointed in 1698, his reputation was such that the Kangxi emperor styled him the most upright official in the empire. When he was promoted to Jiangnan, he was called "Clear-Skies Yu," in recognition of his honesty and incorruptibility.

Yu's ability and his rapid rise from the lowest to the highest levels of Kangxi territorial administration inspired many admiring accounts of his life during the Qing. His first biographers were Jiangnan literati serving in the late seventeenth-century Kangxi court. They admired Yu's dedication to state service and his personal and administrative frugality.[56] In the eighteenth century, Yu was transformed from a living exemplar to a legend. He was posthumously admitted to the dynasty's Temple of Eminent Statesmen in 1732; biographies dwelled, not on his ethics or political attitudes, but on his association with the great events of state building in the seventeenth century.[57] His story became the stuff of legend in the later eighteenth century, when a popular novel appeared celebrating the accomplishments of his protégé, who took the rather bizarre step of assuming his mentor's name, exactly the same in both sound and characters. By the early twentieth century, Yu seemed to the editors of History of the Qing to be the rarest of Qing dynasty officials, one who could rise through the official hierarchy without being tempted or tainted by corruption. He has been celebrated in all of these accounts, not only as an extraordinarily effective official, but also as an official who served an effective dynasty. His life was a testimony to the capacity of the Qing dynasty, and of the personnel procedures established in the Kangxi reign, to attract officials of talent and promote the worthy.

THE EXPERIENCE OF EMPIRE

In 1691, when the Kangxi emperor suspended the requirement that the Board of Personnel had to ascertain the appropriate ethnic group for a provincial post before recommending candidates, he took what in retrospect was a crucial step toward expanding promotion possibilities for junior Chinese officials. Henceforth, candidates would compete for office everywhere in the empire on the basis of their ability rather than their ethnicity.[58] In the short run, the Kangxi emperor's goal may have been to increase the number of bannermen in office. The early 1690s were years of preparation for the war against Galdan in central Asia, an undertaking in which the emperor took an extraordinarily personal interest and which colored many aspects of government and politics. In fact, after returning from one trip to central Asia, the emperor called upon military commanders to recommend bannermen who would be qualified to hold territorial office, asserting they were every bit as capable as Chinese civilian officials were.[59]

In the long run, however, the 1691 order opened the floodgates for the routine appointment of junior Chinese officials to senior territorial office. As officials moved routinely through the ranks of territorial offices, self-images changed. Occupants of all territorial posts came to see themselves not only as imperial representatives but also as members of a corps of territorial officials charged with the responsibility of carrying out the empire's civilian administration. Such a shift in the conception of the offices of governor and governor-general was as much subjective as objective and emerged slowly in the late seventeenth and early eighteenth centuries. Although more bannermen than civilians were promoted to governorships in the Kangxi reign, by the Qianlong reign, Chinese civilians serving as governors were more likely than their bannerman counterparts to have reached their position by means of promotion. By the nineteenth century, the vast majority of those promoted were Chinese civilians. As the numbers of promoted Chinese civilians grew, so did the importance of promotions in Qing territorial administration as a whole. In last twenty years of the Kangxi reign, promotions of lieutenant governors accounted for 39 percent of all governor appointments and for 45 percent of the appointments of new governors. In the Guangxu reign, 46.5 percent of all appointments were promotions, and 66 percent of new governors reached office through promotion. As the number of men promoted to governor grew, so did the salience of those promoted in political affairs and in history. Fu Zongmou has examined the careers of the provincial governors significant enough to be included in *History of the Qing*. According to his statistics, 20 percent of the Kangxi governors who have biographies in *History of the Qing* began their terms as governor by means of promotion. In the Tongzhi reign, the figure was 80 percent.[60]

Most of the routine promotions of the eighteenth century were of lieutenant governors, although the rule permitting promotion to governor from the positions of grand secretary, censor, and mayor of the capital cities remained a part of the Qing administrative code until the end of the dynasty. The twenty-five individuals appointed from capital agencies during the first quarter of the eighteenth century constitute about a sixth of the governors appointed. The seventeen individuals appointed after 1725 represent a negligible percentage of the nearly fourteen hundred people appointed in these years. For much of the eighteenth and nineteenth centuries, the vast majority of those promoted to governor were lieutenant governors. This shift occurred, in part, because the Yongzheng emperor grew to distrust those who served around him in the capital, trusting instead those who came up from the ranks whose careers he had monitored through personnel reviews and secret memorials. Perhaps as important, governors acquired more management tasks, which required them to have more practical experience.

From the end of the seventeenth century, the advancement of junior territorial officials into governorships became a central and stable element of Qing imperial administration. One reason for the system's longevity was the ability of dynastic leaders, within the confines of the promotion system, to address at least three continuing challenges to the Chinese administration. The first of these was the fact that certain areas required more specialized expertise to govern, and as the dynasty progressed and economies and ecologies became more diverse, the need for specialization in administration grew more urgent. A second issue was the need for more experienced governors in certain provinces, either because of the size of the governing apparatus they sustained or because of their military and fiscal significance to the dynasty. A third conundrum was the question of how to involve central leadership in a process of appointment that came increasingly to rely on the assessments of peers and supervising officials. None of these issues were—or perhaps could have been—resolved by decree; all three were addressed in practice through rules on intra-province promotions, differential provincial promotion rates, and the role of the emperor.

INTRA-PROVINCE PROMOTIONS

In principle, Chinese territorial administration, with its provision for regular evaluations of subordinate personnel and their promotion by routine means, was well structured for developing officials with regional specialties. In fact, at the lower levels of the territorial order, the rule put in place after 1729 allowed governors to select and promote the most able of their subordinates within their own provinces. At the provincial level, however, the court's intent was different. In 1677, it decreed that finance commissioners could not be promoted to governor in the same province in which they had served as lieutenant governor.[61] This rule may have had its origins in fears that a senior official left too long in one province could amass a local following and thereby challenge central authority, or that officials who had interacted with one another for a long time could more readily collude to deceive central authority. Regardless of its origins, such a rule ensured that qualified administrators—and thereby their knowledge of procedures and statutes—would circulate from one province to another. In this respect, the rule expressed one of the central principles of Qing administration.

The fate of this rule provides a remarkably clear example of how contingencies strained against rules in the Qing personnel order. As Qing provincial administration matured, regional specialization became more common, and the prominence of the rule against intra-province promotions for finance commissioners declined. There were 172 cases of intra-province promotions during the eighteenth and nineteenth centuries. Table 2.4 displays the numbers of these promotions by reign and by province.

In the last twenty-three years of the reign of the Kangxi emperor, who had issued the decree prohibiting intra-province promotions, 14 percent of lieutenant governors were promoted to serve within the same province that they had been appointed to govern. Intra-province promotions nearly doubled from 14.2 percent during the last twenty years of the Kangxi reign to 27 percent during the Yongzheng reign. They remained at roughly 30 percent until the first quarter of the nineteenth century. Military needs were almost certainly behind the growing number of intra-province promotions in the nineteenth century; for example,

TABLE 2.4. Intra-Province Promotions, 1700–1900, by Reign and by Province

A. By Reign

	Intra-Province Promotions	Total Promotions	Percentage of Promotees
Kangxi (1700–1723)	6	42	14%
Yongzheng	12	44	27%
Qianlong	45	146	30.8%
Jiaqing	22	77	30.5%
Daoguang	26	86	30.2%
Xianfeng	18	36	50%
Tongzhi	16	33	48%
Guangxu	27	80	35%
Totals	172	541	31%

B. By Province

	Intra-Province Promotions	Total Promotions	Percentage of Promotees
Jiangsu	16	24	67%
Shaanxi	17	32	56%
Shandong	12	27	44%
Yunnan	16	37	43%
Henan	13	33	39%
Guangxi	19	52	36%
Fujian	10	36	38%
Zhejiang	8	29	28%
Shanxi	9	33	27%
Guizhou	13	49	27%
Anhui	12	42	26%
Jiangxi	9	36	25%
Hunan	8	32	25%
Guangdong	5	19	16%
Hubei	5	45	11%
Total	172	526*	31%

*The total number of promotions in Table A includes 15 promotions in Gansu, Sichuan, Taiwan, and Xinjiang that are not listed in Table B.
Source: Qingdai zhi guan nian biao (QDZGNB).

eleven of the nineteen promotions in Guangxi occurred during and in the immediate aftermath of the Taiping Rebellion (1850–64). As the rule ceased to guide
bureaucratic practice, its salience in the Qing regulations declined. Decreed by the
Kangxi emperor, the rule appeared in the Yongzheng edition of *Collected Statutes
of the Qing* but shrank to a footnote in the Qianlong edition.[62] The Jiaqing period
manual of the Board of Personnel, *Regulations of the Board of Personnel, Authorized by
the Emperor* (Qin ding Li bu ze li), contains reference to the practice, but there is no
mention of the rule in the Guangxu edition of the *Collected Statutes*.[63] The rule was
never formally repealed, but it was ignored in practice and eventually was erased
by editors.

All provinces had intra-province promotions, and in half of the provinces, the
rate of such promotions was usually within 5 percentage points of the 31 percent
national average. There were, however, several outliers. Two-thirds of the governors promoted in Jiangsu, and more than half of those promoted in Shaanxi,
held office within those two provinces at the time they became governors. In the
case of Jiangsu, a structural anomaly accounted for the high promotion rate of
local lieutenant governors. Tax collection in the lower Yangzi delta was always
a vexing matter; in fact, it was in the wake of a tax resistance movement that the
Qing divided the region it had governed from Nanjing into two provinces, Anhui
and Jiangsu. Even with this change, most Jiangsu governors reported tax arrears
through the seventeenth century, and it appears that the Yongzheng emperor
nearly despaired of collecting all the revenue the province owed.[64] In the delta's
memory, the first Qing official to master local tax affairs fully was the jinshi-
degree-holding Manchu aristocrat, Governor-general Yinjishan. In 1760, Yinjishan proposed to the court that a second lieutenant governor be appointed to
Jiangsu—one to serve in the provincial capital of Suzhou, and one to serve upriver
in Jiangning, the Qing dynasty name for Nanjing.[65] This meant there were two
lieutenant governorships from which one could be promoted to the governorship of Jiangsu. More generally, the situation spoke to the specialized character
of revenue collection in one of the empire's wealthiest provinces.

The other provinces with high rates of intra-province promotions also had
specialized needs, although they were not reflected in so obvious a structural
anomaly. Shaanxi, Shandong, and Yunnan all had a rather heavy and active military presence. The troops themselves were not the responsibility of the governors,
but the logistics of their support was. In these provinces, lieutenant governors
would have had to work closely with the governors and with military authorities
to ensure the provisioning of troops without unduly burdening local populations.
In Shandong, governors were often so closely connected to the court that their
strong recommendation for a subordinate would be heard in Beijing. In these
instances, differences in promotion records reflect real and rather specific differ-

ences among provinces.[66] But these are only examples of a much broader issue, the fact that some provinces of the empire required different sorts—or even different levels—of skill compared to other provinces. In these provinces, the question was not how ranked lists were to work but how regional diversity was to be contained within a single, centralized administrative structure.

THE EMPIRE OF EXPERIENCE:
DIFFERENCES IN PROMOTION RATES AMONG PROVINCES

As the appointment of lieutenant governors to the post of governor became a routine practice, the interesting question became not so much *who* was promoted but *where* promotions occurred. In principle, any lieutenant governor could be promoted to fill any vacant governorship. In fact, however, not all posts saw the same number of promotions. Unlike the junior positions in Qing local administration, which were rated according to degree of difficulty, there was no formal acknowledgment of the greater responsibilities some posts entailed. Yet, different posts posed different challenges, requiring different sorts of skills as well as different levels of experience. These challenges were reflected in differential promotion rates.

In table 2.5, the fifteen provinces that retained a consistent form between 1700 and 1900 are listed in the left column.[67] The next three columns show the numbers of lieutenant governors promoted in each province, the numbers of governors appointed to each province, and the percentage of appointees who were promotees. Promotions occurred with some frequency in all provinces; in no province did promotees constitute less than 21 percent of the appointees. But there were also significant variations in provincial promotion rates. For example, a governor of Guangxi or Guizhou was twice as likely to have just been promoted as was a governor of Shandong. A comparison of the Guangxi and Zhejiang provincial governments during the Jiaqing and Daoguang reigns offers a clear illustration of the impact of differential promotion rates. Between 1796 and 1836, fourteen lieutenant governors were promoted in Guangxi, serving for a total of 321 out of 480 months, or 66.8 percent of the time. By contrast, only four promotees served in Zhejiang, for a total of 48 months, or 10 percent of the time.[68] The Guangxi governors were not inexperienced; collectively, they brought many years of experience to their posts. But they were not well enough connected to the capital or conversant enough with the province they governed to convey fully to Beijing the dangerous ethnic and economic conflict developing in Guangxi that would break forth in the 1840s in the Taiping Rebellion. Zhejiang, in a era of influence and prosperity, was governed for many of these years by the distinguished scholar Juan Yuan and several senior Manchu appointees from Beijing and Shenyang.

TABLE 2.5. Promotions to Governor, by Province, 1700–1900

Province	Number of Promotions	Total Appointments	Percentage of Promotees
Anhui	42	98	44%
Fujian	36	89	40%
Guangdong	19	89	21%
Guangxi	52	99	53%
Guizhou	49	92	53%
Henan	33	95	35%
Hubei	45	115	39%
Hunan	32	103	31%
Jiangxi	36	94	38%
Jiangsu	24	94	26%
Shandong	27	99	27%
Shanxi	33	98	34%
Shaanxi	32	105	31%
Yunnan	37	83	45%
Zhejiang	29	102	28.9%
Total	528	1455	37.8%

Source: *Qingdai zhi guan nian biao* data. These figures are revisions of numbers originally published in Guy, "Imperial Powers," 255, table 1.

Provincial promotion rates reflect a series of discrete decisions made over the course of two hundred years rather than an outcome of any single deliberation or judgment. Inevitably, the differences in promotion rates among the provinces could be explained in a variety of ways. One of the most consistent and telling comparisons, however, is between a rank ordering of the provinces based on the amount of land tax revenue each was required to remit yearly to the central government treasury and a rank ordering in terms of promotion rates.[69] These two rankings are compared in table 2.6A. The comparison suggests, on the one hand, the dynasty's realistic recognition of provincial differences. Not surprisingly, revenue contributions mattered. Broadly speaking, the greater the contribution of a province to the center, the less likely it was to have a governor who had been recently promoted from the ranks of lieutenant governors.

More specific comparisons are also suggestive. Table 2.6B compares the order of the provinces when ranked by remittance rates with their order when ranked by percentage of promotions. Eight of the provinces occupy the same or adjacent (plus or minus one or two positions) rankings in the two series. Three provinces in north China—Shanxi, Henan, and Anhui—had more promotions than

TABLE 2.6. Land Tax Remittances and Promotions, by Province, 1700–1900

A. Tax Remittances and Promotion Rates

Province	Land Tax Remittance (liang)	Percentage of Promotions
Jiangsu	2,836,302	26%
Shanxi	2,678,779	34%
Shandong	2,504,209	28%
Henan	2,268,602	35%
Zhejiang	2,188,575	29%
Jiangxi	1,525,637	38%
Shaanxii	1,277,096	31%
Anhui	1,153,291	43%
Guangdong	1,006,377	21%
Fujian	866,448	40%
Hubei	821,754	39%
Hunan	487,419	31%
Guangxi	243,969	53%
Guizhou	61,692	53%
Yunnan	0	45%

B. Comparison of Rank Orderings

Province	Rank Order in Land Tax Remittance	Rank Order in Percentage of Promotions	
Jiangsu	1	2	
Shanxi	2	7	+
Shandong	3	3	
Henan	4	8	+
Zhejiang	5	4	
Jiangxi	6	9	
Shaanxii	7	6	
Anhui	8	12	++
Guangdong	9	1	– –
Fujian	10	11	
Hubei	11	10	
Hunan	12	5	– –
Guangxi	13	14	
Guizhou	14	15	
Yunnan	15	13	

Sources: For revenue quotas, Zelin, *The Magistrate's Tael*, 28. For rank orderings, *Qingdai zhi guan nian biao*, table 2.5; these figures are revisions of numbers originally published in Guy, "Imperial Powers," 255, table 1.

might be expected based on their revenue contributions. In the cases of Shanxi and Henan, revenue submitted to the capital may not be the best indicator of perceived importance, since both provinces were close to Beijing and remitting revenue was inexpensive. Both provinces were nonetheless in the top half of the ranking. Anhui appears to have functioned rather like a training ground where newly promoted governors could develop their skills before moving on to more complex positions. Yunnan, Zhejiang, Hunan, and, most spectacularly, Guangdong had unexpectedly fewer promotions, meaning that they were more often in relatively experienced hands. Zhejiang and Guangdong were coastal provinces, where governors had garrisons to feed and supervise as well as responsibilities for collection of customs and salt tax revenues. Yunnan and Hunan had diverse populations, which frequently required military action, and dynamic regional economies central to Qing growth.

The relative magnitude of the differences between revenue collections and promotion rates is as interesting as the rank orderings. If the size of revenue contributions had been the sole determinant of where promotions occurred, one would expect rates of promotion to differ far more than they did. For instance, Jiangsu remitted ten times the amount of revenue Guangxi did but had only twice the number of promotions. No amount of wealth precluded promotions; similarly, no level of poverty condemned a province to being governed by neophytes. Even with these qualifications, the practice of promoting lieutenant governors did seem to serve as a guarantee that there would be a certain level of administrative consistency throughout China's provinces and was in this regard a crucial element in the dynasty's territorial design.

THE BELEAGUERED EMPEROR

It has been argued that the routine appointments system contained implicit mechanisms for assessing the abilities and experience of candidates. The system as a whole functioned reasonably well enough to establish official hierarchies and career ladders and assured that men of competence and experience were available for appointment when needed. There were, however, some practical difficulties. While the Chinese civil service was not large in comparative terms, there were enough positions to be filled that the process of reviewing ranked lists could take a fair amount of the emperor's official day. On one day in 1736, for instance, the Qianlong emperor was presented with lists of candidates for seven positions that needed to be filled for the metropolitan examinations of that year. When the representatives from the Board of Rites had finished, officials from the Board of Personnel arrived with more lists of candidates. The emperor was presented with one list each for the posts of commissioner and secretary of the Office of

Transmission (Tongzheng Shisi), one each for the censor of circuit positions in Guangdong and Guizhou, and one for a circuit intendancy in Shandong. The emperor then met five persons recommended for the position of prefect by the governor of Henan, followed by three magistrates recommended as outstanding by the governor of Yunnan. His final meeting was with one circuit intendant from Shandong who had recently received administrative discipline.[70] Confronted with such an array of officials from different parts of the empire, each with different concerns, the actual act of imperial selection became rather perfunctory, simply a matter of placing a vermilion circle beside the name of a successful candidate. It became the practice of imperial diarists to note simply that the emperor "circled" appointments on a given day.

The demands that routine personnel transactions placed on the emperor's time were clearly apparent in the regulations governing the circumstances under which lieutenant governors could request an imperial audience. As Philip A. Kuhn has noted, such interviews were one of the monarch's few opportunities to personally take the mettle of his servants, and the comments he made on such occasions could be tart and to the point.[71] Getting such an audience was not easy, however. Once appointed, for instance, lieutenant governors were allowed to request an audience with the emperor only once every three years. If the request was not granted, they were allowed after their third year of service to request an audience once during each subsequent year until they were finally allowed to meet with the emperor. Somewhat ominously, the regulations stated that if the lieutenant governor, having been granted an audience, got to Beijing and found the imperial calendar full, he was to proceed to the Board of Civil Appointments for investigation.[72] Clearly, in the case of provincial officials, one of the problems was the time spent away from one's post that an imperial audience could entail. Probably for this reason, in 1752, it was stipulated that if a finance commissioner had been granted an imperial audience within three years, as a result of having been found to be "outstanding and distinguished" in the triennial evaluations, he was not to come to the capital for an audience before being promoted.[73] The practical significance of this regulation was that the finance commissioners most likely to be promoted to governor, those rated as outstanding in the routine evaluations, were the ones least likely to have received an imperial audience before promotion.

In other contexts, the retreat of a monarch from direct involvement in the selection of office holders signaled a decline in the importance of an office. For instance, when British monarchs ceased to personally select sheriffs and began to signify their assent to appointments by approving a list, a process known as "pricking sheriffs," the role of the sheriff in local law enforcement decreased. In Qing China, however, this was not the case.[74] The eighteenth century saw an increase in the salience and importance of governors in territorial administration even as more appointments were merely "circled" by the emperor. In part, this occurred because territorial administration became the duty of a self-regulating corps. As emperors withdrew from the selection process, the importance of accomplishments and the judgments of peers expressed through the evaluation process became more important in the advancement of administrators. Having imposed their vision of organization and responsibility on Chinese officials in the early years of the dynasty, Manchu emperors did not need to reimpose themselves at every moment of personnel selection.

There was a fair distance, in time and conception, between the first Qing appointments of surrendered Ming officials to territorial office and the mid-eighteenth-century emergence of a corps of administrators who took as their mission not service to an emperor but administration of an empire. What began as a hasty attempt to fill Ming dynasty territorial posts with men of a basic standard of loyalty to the Qing eventually led to the creation of a flexible and fairly sophisticated system that adequately served the dynasty's needs for nearly three hundred years. This system has provided the template for Chinese governance in the twentieth century. What began as a tentative effort to map the empire gradually resulted in a relatively well-evolved vision of the demands of different provincial posts, and consistent patterns in the assignment and circulation of personnel, which imparted stability to the whole provincial order. In fact, such officials are consistently described with the term *wai-guan*—literally, "those who served outside (the capital)"—in *Collected Statutes and Precedents of the Qing*. Regular promotion patterns, based on what must have been commonly held images of the various postings in the empire, created a corps of territorial officials of shared perspective and ability who were capable of evaluating each other.

In the longer context of late imperial history, the creation of an official who served as middleman between central and local administration and between the military and civilian realms was also significant. It was not without reason that early twentieth-century patriots such as Qian Mu accused the Qing of inserting a "tribal authority" into Chinese government and militarizing provincial administration in order to assure its control.[75] But it seems more plausible to argue that the Qing transformed *xunfu* from military functionaries appointed exclusively by the emperor into civilian authorities who were products of the bureaucracy. Whether the glass is half full or half empty surely depends, in part, on whether the observer is thirsty. Anti-Manchu patriotism blinded Qian Mu, and others like him, to the possibility that the Qing had productively innovated in the creation of the provincial governor's post and, in so doing, forged a link between court and locality that had been patently missing in the Ming. If asked whether this was their goal, few in the Qing would have answered in the affirmative. But few would have denied the importance of the tasks provincial governors performed for the new dynasty.

Developments comparable to the Qing creation of a corps of territorial officials had occurred earlier in Chinese history, but in critical aspects, the Qing development brought the potentials of a Chinese bureaucratic order to new fruition. Financial officials in the Song, as Robert Hartwell has described them, established their professional credentials and then moved through a fairly well-established sequence of postings in the course of what might be termed a career.[76] Unlike their predecessors in the Song, Qing territorial officials had to master no body of professional knowledge over and above what was required for the examinations. Officials could consult a growing body of writings in the eighteenth century on the principles and practice of administration, including the collected state papers of famous officials, manuals for junior territorial officials, and, in the nineteenth century, collections such as *Essays on Statecraft in Our Times* (Huangchao jingshi wenbian). Moreover, Qing territorial officials had to be jacks of all trades, who could be asked as easily to supervise engineering projects along rivers and canals as to collect taxes. The Qing territorial hierarchy did not define a corps of specialists. Another difference between the Qing and the Song, however, was that the steps of the Qing professional ladder were more clearly defined, and the sequence by which officials moved up them is easier to examine. At best, Hartwell's argument is based on the coincidence of common appointments. The Qing system was consciously and carefully built over nearly a century to serve the needs of the Manchu state.

John Dardess has argued that Confucian literati could take on the character of a professional class, particularly under autocratic rule such as that of a foreign conquest dynasty.[77] Administrators under the Yuan, he argues, came to see themselves as professionals serving a Mongol "client" with the specialized knowledge they had gained from their study of the Chinese past. As with the Qing, the Yuan situation described by Dardess was the product of an effort by a foreign regime of military occupation to set up a civilian government in China. In both cases, civilian officials organized themselves to serve in essentially military hierarchies. The Qing territorial system, however, informed as it was by much more Chinese experience and expertise, was far better organized than that of the Yuan. Moreover, Qing officials could move further up the official ladder—indeed almost to its top—before they reached what might be called an ethnic glass ceiling. In fact, on an ideological level, the system of promotions was meant to emphasize that all who served the state had an opportunity to advance.

There may never be anything totally new under the Chinese sun. Qing governors bore the same titles as their Ming predecessors, exercised an authority that was shaped by Manchu preferences for clear lines of authority and responsibility, and realized the potentials for bureaucratic organization and professionalism long implicit in the late imperial Chinese political order. But in combining these elements, tinkering with the bits and pieces of older administrative forms, Qing monarchs created something decidedly new, which would form the basis of their rule of China for nearly three centuries.

CHAPTER 3

The Conundrum of Competence

Implicit in the territorial order that Qing rulers built in the seventeenth century was a commitment to assess the qualifications of those who served in lower offices and to determine, on some regular basis, who among them was most suitable for promotion to senior office. As territorial administration became more powerful and salient in the eighteenth century, the Qing was forced to confront more directly than had its predecessors the issue—or was it really a conundrum?—of competence. The Qing had inherited from earlier dynasties several formulations of assessment procedures, which provided vocabularies and conceptual frameworks, but these were hardly up to the challenge the Qing faced in the eighteenth century. Most classical definitions of ability in Qing China focused more on attributes than on accomplishments, and previous dynasties had not evolved mechanisms for assessing practical achievements as fully as those they applied to other aspects of the personnel process. The reasons were not hard to imagine. Measuring and comparing individuals' achievements at mid-career was an extraordinarily difficult task, complicated by the fact that officials achieved their successes in different venues and under different circumstances. There was no simple solution to many questions of assessment; therefore, rules for evaluating and promoting officials were continually elaborated during the dynasty. The growth of procedures was particularly evident during the first third of the eighteenth century and resulted in substantial growth in the authority of provincial governors.

The importance of these evaluations to Qing officialdom is demonstrated by the enormous amount of documentation the subject produced. Even considering their barest forms, *Collected Statutes of the Ming* and *Collected Statutes of the Qing*, the Qing dynasty regulations for promoting officials were nearly 60 percent longer than those of the Ming.[1] As elaborated in *Collected Statutes and Precedents of the Qing*, the extent of the rules is even more daunting. In the modern reprint of *Statutes and Precedents*, the expansion of the rules of promotion managed by the Bureau of Appointments (Wen Xuan Si) takes up 560 pages. The rules are divided into five subsections: rules governing initial qualification for office (*quanxuan*), preparation of ranked lists for promotion to higher office (*kailie*), selection of individuals to be promoted (*linxuan*), procedures to follow when a promotion was ordered (*shengbu*), and extraordinary promotions (*chushou*).[2] The Bureau of Evaluations (Kao Gong Qing Li Si) managed further aspects of the evaluation and review process, and the regulations for this office occupied another 786 pages in the *Statutes and Precedents*. They are divided into seven sections. First are rules about the process of evaluations, and specific rules and precedents for the punishment of officials follow, grouped according to the six traditional functions of central administration: personnel, revenue, rites, punishments, war, and works. Early in the nineteenth century, separate volumes were produced for the regulations surrounding each of these six functions.[3]

There were multiple reasons for this explosion of documentation during the eighteenth century. By 1725, the Qing system for circulating officials through territorial postings had been operative for nearly a generation; both monarchy and officialdom felt the need to modify and define its workings, and the personnel order would probably have required elaboration regardless of the monarch on the throne. However, the Yongzheng emperor, who succeeded his father in 1723, preferred to work from within the palace and so needed written documentation on which he could rely in making appointment decisions. Conversely, Chinese officialdom, ever anxious to define its prerogatives in the face of an all-powerful monarchy, recorded each concession that could be used as precedent for subsequent decisions. The convergence of these trends produced a force of unholy power, and the Qing dynasty was second to no regime in the eighteenth century in the recoding and rationalization of its administrative procedure.

Ample as such documentation is, it is not easy to interpret. Deconstructing personnel manuals is an odd task, yet there are few sorts of documents for which it is more important to separate author's intent from readers' constructions and to establish the changing and often unwritten assumptions that inform readings. To speak of "readings" of a personnel manual is a bit of a stretch, as they tend to be more often perused than used. A personnel manual is usually reviewed once and then set aside, to be consulted only when promotion looms or a procedural dispute arises. Rereadings on such occasions were less concerned with the meaning of the text than with how it authorized or constrained future actions. Accounts of personnel procedures seldom describe reality. Rather, personnel manuals set forth a set of parameters within which, ideally, very human contingencies were measured and the necessary responses formulated. The issue in reading manuals is not fully, or even primarily, one of textual criticism, for the real challenge is to establish how the parameters expressed in manuals impinged on the consciousness of those they regulated. A single understanding of the rules will not suffice, for parameters shifted over time, occasionally in ways that were explicitly acknowledged in successive editions of the manuals and sometimes by means of practices and interpretations that were not formally part of the record.

Printed texts considered together with records of practice, and statements made by officials about practice, may approximate the desired nuance. In the matter of practice, provincial governors were a small enough group that it is often possible to reasonably establish the full range of cases in which a rule or rules were applied. Few governors wrote about their offices, but statements by a wide range of officials about personnel regulations are preserved in such works as *Essays on Statecraft in Our Times*.[4] Together, these sources attest to a dynasty that labored to come to terms with the implications of the personnel system, which its early regulations prescribed, drawing on the resources of its classical heritage and the dictates of practical experience.

LENGTH OF TERM

Term lengths and the evaluation of officials were first discussed, and first linked, in two texts from Chinese antiquity. The first is *The Book of Documents* (Shang shu), a collection of documents from the classical age of Chinese historical imagination. The relevant passage from "The Canons of Yu" tells of the sage-king who, in addition to taming the rivers, instituted a procedure in which: "Every three years there was an examination of merits, and after three examinations the undeserving were degraded, and the deserving promoted."[5] A second, equally influential passage is from *Rites of Zhou* (Zhou li), a work that purports to describe the rituals of the ancient Chinese state of Zhou and outlines in some detail a rather utopian scheme of political organization, including official titles and lists of official functions. In this volume, the vice prime minister is said to have the responsibility of conducting a regular evaluation of personnel on the basis of six criteria: benevolence, capacity, caution, rectitude, observation of the law, and discernment.[6]

Neither of these texts can be taken as a reliable guide to ancient practice. The "Canons of Yu" chapter is not regarded as a particularly reliable chapter in a work that is in significant measure a forgery. *Rites of Zhou* is a work of uncertain provenance, probably compiled some centuries after the fall of the Zhou. Moreover, the two texts present no end of practical difficulties. A nineteenth-century student of *The Book of Documents*, for instance, asked with reason why a ruler would wait until the end of a nine-year term to remove an incompetent official from office if the ruler had determined at the end of three years that the official was not capable.[7] In spite of these problems, the passages were unavoidably linked to personnel administration. The phrase from *The Book of Documents* "to demote the undeserving and promote the worthy" (chu-zhi you-ming) became synonymous with the process of personnel evaluations.[8] The legacy of these texts was not in their specific provisions but in terms of three broad principles they established. These were, first, that officials' tenure of office should be reconsidered at regular intervals, usually some variation of three years. Second, reconsideration of postings should involve some mechanism for evaluating officials. Third, there should be a procedure for removing from office those who did not meet central standards and calling attention to those who exceeded them. It fell to the various rulers of China to develop means of implementing these desiderata.

In theory, all territorial officials in China were eligible for transfer from one post to another at prescribed intervals. During the Qing, these intervals were different for officials located within the boundaries of the empire, posts rather colorfully referred to as "belly positions" (*fu feng*), and at positions located on the "borders of the empire" (*jiang feng*). Within the empire, prefects and those in positions below them were eligible for transfer after the three-year terms specified in *Rites of Zhou*, and circuit intendants were meant to serve for two years. Shorter terms—by as much as half—were prescribed as an incentive for officials who served in posts along the borders. [9] Term limits were as ambiguous in imperial China as they seem to be in the modern-day democratic United States, and these stipulations were probably far more important for the conception they expressed—that all officials would move on a fairly regular basis—than as guides to the practice of appointments.

There was a continuing debate in imperial China over the benefits of long and short official terms. Many late imperial institutional historians argued that the longer an official was allowed to serve, the better it was for the state and the people. The rationale for this argument was that local officials who served in one place for a long time were less likely to be deceived by and more likely to take seriously the needs and concerns of those they governed. Gu Yanwu even argued that local officials should serve for life and be allowed to pass on their posts to their heirs. Gu's scheme was utopian rather than practical, and as he was a holdout against the Qing conquest, he would not likely have carried much weight in administrative circles. Wang Mingyue, who received a *jinshi* degree from the Qing in 1655 and rose to a position in the Censorate, and Wei Yijie, who received his *jinshi* in 1646 and rose to be a grand secretary, were probably more influential. In two memorials anthologized in *Essays on Statecraft in Our Times*, they proposed that educational and prefectural officials should be left at their posts as long as possible. Wei even suggested that a special title be created for prefects who had served successfully in the position for a long time and argued that long terms were the hallmark of Han dynasty local administration, the closest period in time to the golden age of early China, and that they fostered careful practice by those who governed and respect among those who were governed. [10] On the other side of this debate were activist officials and late imperial monarchs who argued that the ability of the central government to place officials at appropriate locations and times constituted one of the most important political powers of the monarchy. Among Qing rulers, the Yongzheng emperor was the strongest advocate of this point of view, and his exchange with Ortai, anthologized in part in *Essays on Statecraft in Our Times*, is the most famous statement of this argument.[11]

Governors' Terms

Given this debate, it was not surprising that provincial governors, who were associated more with the powers of the central government than with the needs of local society, would serve relatively short terms. The median term for a Qing governor appointed between 1700 and 1900 was seventeen months, and a third of those appointed served less than nine months. Traditionally, the short tenures of Qing provincial governors and governors-general have been attributed to central government insecurity, namely the fear that long-serving officials would develop local followings and would contend with the central government for power and control.[12] There were certainly cases before the Qing of danger arising from extended tenures, and during the Qing, the case of Wu Sangui, who dominated southwest China between the 1650s and 1670s, illustrated the dangers of long provincial tenures. Certainly insecurities or, to put it another way, respect for the historical difficulties of establishing provincial government in China, shaped an environment in which governors were assigned to serve limited terms.

One the most striking features of the data, however, is the variation in governors' terms. Governors could serve terms as short as one month, even, in one instance, one day, or as long as twelve years. Table 3.1 presents a summary of the term lengths of governors appointed in Qing China between 1700 and 1900. The distribution of governors' terms is far from statistically normal. The mean was 24.3 months, but the standard deviation was 22.6 months. The distribution was heavily skewed toward longer terms. While short terms were most common, longer terms were frequent, and more than one-fifth of the terms were between three and five years. In fact, terms of short, medium, and long duration all served the purposes of the Qing, and they should be understood in terms of thick descriptions, considerations of moment and function, rather than thin statistical ones.[13]

Long and Short Terms

Longer terms of service were found in all reigns and all provinces in the empire. The tendency, however, was for the longest terms to be concentrated in provinces located on the borders rather than at the center of the empire. The insecurity hypothesis is problematic in explaining this fact, for it would appear the dynasty was most likely to leave governors in their posts for a long time in precisely those locations where it had the most to fear from independent regimes. The tendency

TABLE 3.1. Term Lengths of Qing Governors, 1700–1900

Number of Months	Percentage of Terms	Cumulative Percentage
0–10	34.4%	34.4%
11–20	21.4%	55.8%
21–30	14.0%	69.8%
31–40	11.0%	80.8%
41–50	6.3%	87.8%
51–60	4.6%	91.7%
61–70	2.9%	94.6%
71–80	1.4%	96.0%
81–90	1.5%	97.5%
91–99	0.9%	98.4%
Over 99	1.6%	100%

Source: *Qingdai zhi guan nian biao* data.

toward long terms on the borders was most pronounced among the governors who served longest in Qing China, the twenty-four governors who served ninety-nine months or longer (see table 3.2). The four provinces of Guizhou, Yunnan, Shaanxi, and Shanxi accounted for nearly half of the long terms. Ironically, governors served their longest terms in precisely those provinces where lower-level officials had to be lured by the incentive of a reduced term.

But the locations where governors served long terms may have been less important than when and upon whom these terms were conferred. Nearly a third of the governors in table 3.2 presided over strategically important territories at moments of crisis or war. For example, Nian Gengyao governed Sichuan from 1709 to 1721, during the brief but important Sino-Tibetan War at the end of the Kangxi reign. Guo Hong (governed Guangxi, 1728–36), Zhang Yunsui (governed Yunnan, 1730–47), and Zhang Guangsi (governed Guizhou, 1735–47) continued and perhaps intensified the military subjugation of indigenous peoples of the southwest, which their mentor Ortai had begun. Qin Cheng'en (governed Shaanxi, 1789–99) and Jiang Sheng (governed Hunan, 1791–1800) held their offices during the great White Lotus Rebellion in central and north China at the end of the Qianlong reign. In Jiangxi, Liu Kunyi (governed 1865–74) and Ding Baozhen (governed 1867–76) presided not over war but over the perilous task of rebuilding the peace in the wake of the Taiping Rebellion. However, not all of the long-serving governors were appointed in times of war; the appointments of the late Kangxi years (1700–1723) and the Daoguang period (1820–40) may simply have reflected the preference of those rulers for more stable territorial administration. Many of the governors allowed long terms in more peaceful times had special relationships with the courts that had appointed them. For example, Zhao

TABLE 3.2. Longest-Serving Governors of Qing China

Governor	Province	Years
Ehai	Shaanxi	1701–10
Zhao Hongxie	Zhili	1705–22
Sukeji	Shanxi	1709–21
Li Chenglung	Anhui	1716–28
Nian Gengyao	Sichuan	1709–21
Liu Yinqu	Guizhou	1709–17
Tian Wenjing	Henan	1724–32
Shilin	Shanxi	1727–40
Guo Hong	Guangxi	1728–36
Zhang Yunsui	Yunnan	1730–47
Zhang Guangsi	Guizhou	1735–47
Min Eyuan	Jiangsu	1780–90
Qin Chengen	Shaanxi	1789–99
Jiang Sheng	Hunan	1791–1800
Zhu Xun	Shaanxi	1813–22
Yinlibu	Yunnan	1825–35
Deng Tingzhen	Anhui	1826–35
He Changling	Guizhou	1836–45
Jiang Weiyuan	Guizhou	1851–60
Liu Kunyi	Jiangxi	1865–74
Ding Baozhen	Shandong	1867–76
Yu Rong	Anhui	1874–85
Tan Jixun	Hubei	1889–98
Dexing	Jiangxi	1884–95

Source: *Qingdai zhi guan nian biao* data.

Hongxie (governed Zhili, 1709–22) was from a family of bannerman administrators whose services the Kangxi emperor especially valued. In the case of the Tian Wenjing (governed Henan, 1724–32), the Yongzheng emperor was willing to expend considerable political and symbolic capital in support of the policy innovations of his favorite governor. He Changling (governed Guizhou, 1836–45) was repeatedly appointed to some of the most important administrative positions in the empire and is known to history as the editor of *Essays on Statecraft in Our Times*. Although it hardly endeared him to the court, it is perhaps worth noting that Tan Jixun (governed Hubei, 1889–98) was the father of the firebrand and revolutionary martyr Tan Sitong.

Clearly, these long-term appointments demonstrate that the Qing court could, when it chose to do so, entrust single individuals with major powers over por-

TABLE 3.3. Effects of Unforeseen Circumstances on Term Lengths, 1700–1900

	Mourning	Death or Illness	Total
Short terms			
(less than 9 months)	4.6%	10.3%	14.9%
All governors	3.7%	13.6%	17.3%

Source: *Qingdai zhi guan nian biao* data.

tions of the empire for a long time. In a remarkable sign of the evolution of the Qing territorial order, 75 percent of the longest-serving governors were Chinese rather than Manchu, and 70 percent of them were promoted from the lower ranks of territorial administrators rather than appointed from the court. Only one of the twenty-four governors in table 3.2, Nian Gengyao, was perceived to have overstepped the authorities granted to him.

The very short terms that many governors served are less comprehensible, and explaining them becomes especially difficult if the insecurity hypothesis is discredited. The circumstances of individual short terms are less revealing of the court's motives than are the historical situations of those who governed for longer periods. Political crises often produced short appointments. But perhaps as influential were events in individual lives. Governors were generally men of middle age; scattered biographical information suggests that they were usually between their late forties and their seventies, and illness or death in office was always a possibility. Moreover, the Qing civil service system required that an official leave office for twenty-seven months when his father died and for a briefer time when a mother died.

Governors serving very short terms were not disproportionately affected by these circumstances. Table 3.3 compares the number of governors who left office after short terms because of mourning, death, and illness with the numbers for all governors. Governors who served short terms were slightly more likely to leave office for mourning and slightly less likely to leave office because of death or illness compared to the total population of governors, but overall, their terms were less likely to be affected by unforeseen circumstances.[14]

The more significant fact may be that one in six terms ended for reasons other than those related to the central government. If subsistence or military crises were added to the list of unexpected events that could end governors' terms, the ratio might well be one in five or even one in four. The very centralized Qing personnel system, which rested on personal ties between governors and the center, was not organized to cope with rapid change. At any given moment, the pool of officials the court was willing to entrust with the office of governor was relatively small, and even minor demographic or historical events could have a fairly large

TABLE 3.4. Term Lengths under Different Qing Monarchs, 1700–1900

Reign	Lower Third (in Months)	Median (in Months)	Upper Third (in Months)
Kangxi			
(1700–1723)	20	31	47
Yongzheng			
(1723–36)	8.5	15	22
Qianlong			
(1736–96)	8	14	23
Jiaqing			
(1796–1820)	8	14	24
Daoguang			
(1821–51)	10	22	31
Xianfeng			
(1851–61)	8	16	22
Tongzhi			
(1861–75)	14	25	35
Guangxu			
(1875–1900)	14	25	31

Source: *Qingdai zhi guan nian biao* data.

impact.[15] When a governor died or was forced to leave office, either for mourning or because of administrative discipline, a string of temporary appointments might precede more permanent arrangements. Or an emergency in one province might be seen as requiring a manager who could serve until the immediate crisis passed and then be diverted to a new appointment. Frequently in the case of emergency appointments, emperors noted that only one trustworthy person was available, which testifies to the small pool of proven candidates for senior office and to the strains that sudden transfers could place on the system as a whole. In some cases, appointments were so short that the appointee could not have taken office, suggesting that changes in appointees merely reflected changes in the court's thinking about who should be assigned.

Different standards of what constituted long and short terms prevailed at different moments during the dynasty's history. Table 3.4 provides a comparison of the lengths of median, short, and long terms during the reign periods of the seven emperors who ruled China between 1700 and 1900. Most striking of all in this data is the precipitous decline in term lengths between the late Kangxi and the Yongzheng reign. In part, this can be attributed to the Kangxi emperor's preference for long terms; a disproportionate number of the very long terms in table 3.4 are from the Kangxi reign, and three such terms were initiated in the year 1709 alone. This may have stemmed from the emperor's quest for stability or perhaps from the gradual disengagement from the political process that occurred at the end of his life. But most of the change must be attributed to the Yongzheng emperor, a restless, dynamic, and perhaps slightly unstable ruler who devoted inordinate amounts of time and energy to managing the bureaucracy. The short terms of governors—on whom the Yongzheng emperor lavished so much of his rather feverish attention—were associated in his reign with central government activism and optimism about what an emperor could accomplish by dedicating himself to the management of the civil service. In the matter of term lengths, the Yongzheng emperor left a permanent mark on the office of provincial governor, for median term lengths remained the same through the century after his death. They grew somewhat in the nineteenth century, increasing by about 50 percent in the Daoguang reign. Confronted with internal rebellion and foreign invasion, the Xianfeng emperor—an activist by necessity if not by choice—reverted to the eighteenth-century pattern of short terms. But after the traumas of the mid-nineteenth century had passed, growth in term lengths continued. Both in the aggregate and in individual cases, marked shifts in term length were the product of imperial action.

Mid-length Terms

Although it is most convenient to approach the subject of governors' terms by averaging their individual terms, we gain a different perspective by considering the actual amount of governing time for governors who served terms of various lengths. For instance, although the Qing made an extraordinarily large number of rather short appointments in pursuit of its various political aims, these appointees did not have a great impact on the provinces they governed. In fact, the 521 governor appointments of fewer than ten months represent only 7.3 percent of the period between 1700 and 1900. This was less time than was served by governors with terms of more than ninety months. Chinese provinces were governed 50 percent of the time by governors who served for forty months or more and 70 percent of the time by governors who served more than twenty-seven months. Table 3.5 summarizes the amount of time governors serving terms of various duration spent actually governing.

For most of the Qing dynasty, men who served relatively long terms governed China. Governors serving such terms had the time to impose their stamp on the provinces in which they served, and it was possible to identify in any single decade the one governor who was most important in the administrative life of the province. In view of this, what was the relationship between longevity of service and promotions? Initially, little thought was given to this issue, but as the Qing

TABLE 3.5. Governors' Term Lengths and Time Spent Governing, 1700–1900

Term Length	Percentage of Time Spent Governing
0–10 months	7.4%
11–20 months	13.3%
21–30 months	16%
31–40 months	14.5%
41–50 months	12%
51–60 months	10.4%
61–70 months	8.8%
71–80 months	4.2%
81–90 months	4.5%
91–100 months	10.1%

Source: *Qingdai zhi guan nian biao* data.

territorial order matured, officials formulated clearer answers to this question. The Manchus fairly consistently rejected the idea that longevity of service per se should constitute a ground for promotion. In 1655, it was decreed that officials whose terms were complete would be promoted only if taxes within their jurisdictions had been fully paid, there were no outstanding legal cases, and they had not received administrative discipline. In 1676, those who had completed terms without any sort of distinction were listed last among the categories of local officials eligible for promotion to lieutenant governor.[16] The only officials for whom length of service was unambiguously a criterion for advancement were those who served in border posts, which were considered "unhealthy." In this instance, the guarantee of promotion after completing a successful term was offered to encourage officials to accept problematic and isolated positions, as discussed below. For other officials during the first century of the dynasty, there was no guarantee that service at one level could lead to an appointment at another. In 1748, however, the Qianlong emperor issued a fairly complex decree addressing the situation. In it, he ordered that those officials who served in the most important prefectures of the empire should be considered for promotion after five years of service and that lower-ranking officials should be given an additional title after three successful years of service.[17] This was a fairly cautious pronouncement with all the hallmarks of a compromise. It afforded all officials the opportunity of promotion, without restricting the length of time that they were eligible to serve in office, and it acknowledged the value of experience at one post without necessarily guaranteeing promotion to the next.

According to statute, Qing governors who served successfully could either be promoted to governor-general or return to the capital. For the purpose of this analysis, an appointment to the capital will be counted as a promotion if the new

TABLE 3.6. Governors' Term Lengths and Likelihood of Promotion, 1700–1900

Term	Percentage of Governors Promoted
0–9 months	9.4%
Greater than 10 months	28.2%
Greater than 20 months	30%
Greater than 40 months	29.4%
Greater than 50 months	33.3%
Greater than 60 months	35.7%
Greater than 70 months	37.7%
Greater than 80 months	40.4%
Greater than 90 months	47.4%

Source: *Qingdai zhi guan nian biao* data.

position was the same rank as governor or higher. Table 3.6 presents the percentage of governors serving terms of various lengths who were promoted. These figures demonstrate that the Qing, as it claimed, promoted officials without regard to longevity of service, for some governors were promoted after very short appointments. It is tempting to imagine that governors promoted after short terms had in fact held other governorships, and in some cases, this was true. Nevertheless, a higher percentage of those promoted before twenty months of service (41 percent) than of those promoted after twenty months of service (31 percent) were appointed directly from the capital. Conversely, even those who served very long terms as governor had no guarantee of promotion; even after ninety months or more in office, such governors had less than a 50 percent chance of being promoted. On the one hand, exactly half of the twenty-four governors with the longest terms in table 3.6 were promoted.[18] On the other hand, although there was no discernible threshold above which promotion became decidedly more likely—neither the three-year nor five-year term envisioned for lower officials made much difference—longevity clearly mattered. Governors could reasonably expect that the longer they served successfully in office, the better their chances of being promoted to higher office.

Tours of different lengths served different purposes for the Qing. Governors sometimes were transferred quickly from one post to another and promoted rapidly to meet emergent needs, and sometimes they stayed in office for long periods in order to accomplish the court's ends. In these instances, Qing governors served much as the *xunfu* had served during the Ming, as imperial emissaries to the regions in which they served. Alongside these appointees, however, were others, men who served terms of middling length and who had reasonable expectations of advancement along the bureaucratic ladder upon completion of their service. Retaining the capacity to tailor term lengths to its political needs, the

Qing territorial order never wholly succumbed to the whims (or lack thereof) of a disinterested monarch as had the Ming, or to the triumph of system over purpose that is often the fate of rigid bureaucratic orders.

EVALUATIONS

In 1653, Manchu rulers were first presented with and accepted a proposal from their Chinese advisers to institute a system of triennial evaluations of serving territorial officials, known as the "grand accounting" (*da ji*).[19] *History of the Qing* records this proposal as the beginning of evaluations in the Qing, asserting that the dynasty followed the precedent of the Han, Tang, and Song in establishing such a system. Rather paradoxically, the account proceeds to describe the very tortuous process through which the final evaluative procedure evolved. During the Oboi regency, the triennial evaluations of sitting officials were abolished and replaced by an evaluation carried out at the "end of an official's term" (*kaoman*).[20] The two types of evaluations produced somewhat different results. The triennial evaluation of sitting officials resulted in a statement of a superior's perceptions of a subordinate official's abilities. The end-of-term evaluation produced a written record of the official's accomplishments, which was checked by his superiors before being submitted to the capital. The Oboi regents may have preferred a straightforward statement of accomplishments; more likely, as Frederic Wakeman has argued, the grand accounting was associated with a sinicization of Qing administrative procedure that the regents wished to avoid. When the Kangxi emperor began to rule in his own name, end-of-term evaluations ceased, and triennial evaluations were reestablished.[21]

The next issue to arise was the relationship between written evaluations produced by the territorial bureaucracy and personal evaluations performed by the emperor. In the Ming, it had been the system for provincial administrative commissioners to personally accompany officials to an imperial audience once every three years, carrying with them the records of the grand accounting in their jurisdictions.[22] Initially, this practice continued in the Qing, but by the end of the Shunzhi reign, orders were issued ending the mass visits to the court. Only lieutenant governors, the successors to the Ming administration commissioners, were then required to attend court. This was followed by protest that the emperor was evaluating only senior officials and junior officials were thereby being ignored. In 1685, all visits to the capital were suspended, and the court relied solely on the written evaluations of governors and governors-general.[23]

These written evaluations were fashioned to embody a common rhetorical metric that would serve as a corrective to the sometimes exaggerated language in which the recommendations of officials were usually cast. As the evaluation system was practiced in the Qing, reports were initially prepared by the local official's superior and then submitted to governors and lieutenant governors for final review. Provincial officials bound the results for the several hundred officials under them into a small volume and were required to submit them in triplicate to the capital within the year the evaluations were conducted. Four characteristics had to be measured in the evaluations: "talent" (*cai*), "stewardship of office" (*shou*), "administrative ability" (*zheng*), and "age and energy" (*nian li*). Evaluators were allowed to choose one of two or three descriptions for each characteristic. Talent could be "exceptional" (*zhang*) or "ordinary" (*ping*); stewardship of office could be "incorrupt" (*qing*), "careful" (*jin*) or "ordinary" (*zhuo*); administrative style could be "vigorous" (*tong*), "diligent" (*jin*), or "lazy" (*dai*); and candidates could be "young" (*qing*), "middle-aged" (*zhuang*), or "mature" (*jian*). Evaluators were discouraged from using language other than the terms prescribed in their reports. As they were making these rankings, governors were to recommend the dismissal of officials who were not up to standard and the retirement of officials who were no longer able to perform their duties effectively.[24]

Governors were further authorized to identify certain officials as "outstanding." Since this was the category that most affected personnel status, it was the most carefully regulated. As the dynasty progressed, the regulations governing "outstanding" recommendations became ever more specific. Initially, outstanding officials were to have the highest possible ratings in the categories of talent and stewardship of office, the two categories most directly related to administrative efficacy. Later, not only were they required to have spotless records in terms of corruption but they must also have collected all provincial taxes, dealt with all legal cases in their jurisdictions, and shown their ability to effectively proclaim the sacred instructions of the Kangxi emperor at the local level. In 1664, governors could be demoted if they recommended as outstanding any officials who were involved in corruption cases during current or subsequent appointments. At the end of the Kangxi reign, governors were urged to stick to the basics in their recommendations and to avoid flowery language.[25] By the early eighteenth century, the process of making "outstanding" recommendations had become so highly regulated that governors were reluctant to do so. The triennial evaluations conducted in seven provinces in 1730 produced only twenty-eight recommendations of outstanding. In 1733, the same evaluations carried out in ten provinces produced only twenty-nine such recommendations.[26] In light of these reports, the Yongzheng emperor "suggested" that each province might designate about ten people as outstanding and recommend the dismissal of approximately the same number.[27] At the end of the Qianlong reign, each province was given a quota of "outstanding" recommendations. Zhili's governor-general was entitled to recommend thirteen officials above the rank of magistrate, while the governor-general of Sichuan could recommend eleven; the governors of Shandong, Henan, and Shanxi were each allotted nine recommendations; the governors of Jiangxi, Fujian, and Guangdong could recommend eight officials; Hubei, Hunan, Shanxi, Yunnan, and Jiangsu were granted seven recommendations; Gansu and Guangxi were entitled to six; and Guizhou could recommend five officials.[28] Those recommended as outstanding were eligible for promotion and ranked ahead of those who had to complete their terms of office without such distinction. During the first one hundred years of the dynasty, those recommended were given an official robe as a mark of favor. Beginning in the late Kangxi reign, recommended officials were given the additional privilege of an audience with the emperor.

Those identified as outstanding were a select group; the designation could positively influence one's career for years and even decades afterward. The term "outstanding" (zhuo-yi) appears sixty-five times in History of the Qing, and fifteen of these occurrences, mostly from "Treatise on Officials," deal with the evolution of "outstanding" recommendations. Fifty references occur in individual biographies; twenty-three of these are for officials who served before 1800, and twenty-seven are for officials who served in the nineteenth century. The twenty-three references occur in nineteen biographies; sixteen of these were eventually promoted to provincial governor (see table 3.7). Quantitative conclusions cannot be drawn here. There is no guarantee that the biographies in History of the Qing always include their subjects' "outstanding" recommendations, or that such recommendations appear in the biographies of all those who received them. Stories in History of the Qing are more likely models for other officials to follow than exact descriptions of personnel procedure.

As carefully regulated as "outstanding" designations were, they were still subject to all the pressures of the Chinese political system. Three of the sixteen officials listed in table 3.7 were the sons of powerful officials who were themselves still serving at the time their sons were honored. Ding Sikong's father, Ding Wensheng, had been active in the establishment of Qing rule in Shandong and served as governor of that province from 1645 until 1647.[29] Yang Wenqian's father, Yang Zongren, who had himself been recommended as outstanding, was serving as governor-general of Huguang at the time his son received such a designation.[30] Yu Chenglong's own grandson, Yu Jun, was designated as outstanding while his grandfather was governor-general of Liangjiang.[31] A fourth official, Fang Gui, was designated as outstanding while his father, Fang Xian, was governor-general, but Gui died shortly after receiving the honor. In each of these instances, reputations were clearly at stake, although it is difficult in retrospect to establish the roles individual accomplishment and family prestige played. Administrative competence may have run in families, particularly when sons accompanied their fathers to official postings, as was the case in the Yang family. It was also possible

TABLE 3.7. Governors Who Received Outstanding Recommendations in Qing China

Name	Dates Recommended	Governorships and Governor-Generalships
Shi Weihan	1652	Shandong, 1679–82 Zhe-min, 1682–83 Fujian, 1683–84
Yu Chenglong	1665, 1672	Zhili, 1686–90 River, 1692–1700
Adusi	ca. 1667	Shanxi, 1672–73 Liangjiang, 1673–81
Yao Diyu	ca. 1670	Sichuan, 1685–88
Wu Dian	1673	Huguang, 1687–92 Huguang, 1694–96
Zhu Hongzuo	1673	Guangdong, 1687–92 Zhe-min, 1692–94
Yang Suyun	1677	Anhui, 1687–88 Huguang, 1688–89
Zhang Pengge	1678	Zhejiang, 1689–94 Liangjiang, 1698–1700 River, 1700–1708
Ding Sikong	1681	Hunan, 1682–84 Huguang, 1688–94
Kong Yuxun	1689	Guangdong, 1722–23 Liangguang, 1723–29 River, 1729–30
Yu Jun	ca. 1690	Guizhou, 1704–5 Jiangsu, 1705–9
Yang Wenqian	ca. 1695	Guangdong, 1718–22
Yang Zongren	unknown	Guangdong, 1718–22 Huguang, 1722–25
Cha Li	1743	Hunan, 1782
Li Shijie	1745	Hubei, 1769–71 Hunan, 1771–73
Liang Guozhi	ca. 1752	Guangxi, 1779 Hunan, 1781 Henan, 1782

Source: *Qing shi*, 240:3744, 269:3920, 271:3935, 274:3951, 275:3954, 289:3968, 278:3969, 280:3986, 293:4061, 293:4062, 321:4249, 325:4278, 333:4331.

that a father's accomplishments were read into a son's behavior, or that a son's superior was expressing respect for a father's accomplishments. Each of these possibilities evokes the rather small world in which senior Qing officials lived and served, particularly after the middle of the seventeenth century.

In the early eighteenth century, an ethos of evaluation was building, a discourse of official life that focused on measurable accomplishments and popular respect. The growth of this ethos was not, however, unchallenged, and the death of the Yongzheng emperor proved to be a moment of protest. The new Qianlong emperor began his reign by inviting officials to submit their own views on all aspects of Qing government, an invitation known in classical Chinese as "opening an avenue for opinions" (kai yan lu). In response to this invitation, a young intellectual from the lower Yangzi valley, Cao Yishi, submitted a memorial on the Qing evaluation procedures.[32] Cao opened his memorial by analogizing the senior officials' treatment of their subordinates to the subordinates' treatment of the people they governed. If the emperor wished his realm to be at peace, Cao argued, he should avoid disturbing the people. In order to prevent his officials from disturbing the citizenry, he must make certain that senior officials did not harass their subordinates: "If the governors and governors-general do not disturb lower territorial officials, the lower territorial officials will not disturb the people, and all the world will be at peace." This analogy was natural in a world in which political and social order was conceived of as a matter of maintaining appropriate symmetries. It implies, however, a rejection of the view of which centralizing leaders were so fond, that the official was a tested instrument hewing to its intended course.

In Cao's view, evaluations had become a tool for harassing officialdom. Even worse, a procedure, based more on cleverness than on virtue, had evolved that had the potential to select the wrong people for government positions. As he reasoned:

From the great officials to the minor functionaries, there are those who are worthy [xian] and those who are capable [neng]. The best are those who are both worthy and capable; next are those who are worthy but not capable. The rest who are capable but not worthy are the least valuable to a ruler. What do I mean by worthy? [I mean] those who are aware of the great principles of government and cause the people to be at rest are worthy. What do we mean by capable? [I mean] those who can handle government affairs with dispatch and assure that names and realities match in administrative matters.[33]

The problem with those who were merely capable, Cao argued, was that they were capable of both good and ill. They could just as easily extort bribes as balance official accounts. Similarly, they could just as easily burden the people through inappropriate exactions as build peace and trust in government. Cao declared that only "those who are truly worthy can rescue the world from those who are merely capable." A government by the clever was not one founded in virtue. A process of evaluation that focused exclusively on relatively few characteristics and accomplishments, namely, the routine evaluation categories—integrity, clear-headedness, physical fitness, amounts of grain collected, numbers of criminal apprehended, and the ability to keep clear accounts—inevitably favored the capable over the worthy.

How had such a system come to exist? "Is it," asked Cao, "that we have emphasized capacity over worthiness? Or is it that we have been ensnared in a bureaucratic pattern which takes capacity to be worthiness?" Too often, he argued, it was the latter. In its concern to implement regular evaluations, the Qing bureaucratic order actually confused capacity with worthiness:

> If we take the ability to handle matters with dispatch as capacity, then those who are honest and steady will seem lazy and obtuse. If we take the ability to formulate clever responses as capacity, then those who are cautious in speech will seem to be inarticulate. If we take those who are fortunate in their management of affairs to be able, then we take those who are careful and quiet to be lazy and dilatory.[34]

Cao's arguments are a remarkable combination of both premodern and modern themes. Like many who have contemplated the increasing bureaucratization of society and politics, he lamented the "iron cage" the routine evaluation process imposed upon officials who served the empire. In the contrast he made between worthiness and capacity, however, he sounded an ages-old theme in Chinese history. Worthiness, as he defined it, was not so much a measurable attribute as an absolute value, a value that could not be judged by fallible fellow officials on the basis of mundane accomplishments.

Cao's memorial found a willing listener in the Qianlong emperor. Early in his reign, the emperor had complained that the territorial evaluations were nothing but an "empty letter" administered "sloppily and perfunctorily," with the result that good officials were not recommended and bad ones were not impeached. As the emperor wrote: "Our governors-general and Our governors are Our arms and legs. If they treat such a crucial government function as mere routine, on whom can We rely?"[35] Some years later, a censor proposed emphasizing "concrete accomplishments" more in the evaluation process, accomplishments such as founding schools and establishing a mutual guarantee group among the population. He was rebuffed by an emperor who questioned whether these evaluations, like the existing verbiage of assessments, would become merely empty words. A true government by men, rather than a government of laws, could not be established by setting up procedures that would simply generate conventional documents.

In his fascinating account of the 1768 sorcery scare in China, Philip Kuhn rightly emphasizes the skepticism with which the Qianlong emperor viewed routine evaluations. The middle of the eighteenth century was a time when complaints like those of Cao Yishi hit their mark, when the procedures of evaluation in the Qing seemed to be producing an administrative consistency that limited, rather than extended, Chinese officialdom's capacity to manage the empire. "Rules," Kuhn writes, yielded "predictability and standardization. They also limit[ed] the freedom of those who applied them."[36] For Kuhn, mechanisms of bureaucratic evaluation were an integral mechanism in a bureaucratic order whose strength lay mainly in its durability rather than in its creativity.

But it may be important to put this picture in historical context and to read the reaction against evaluations in the middle Qianlong years not as an inevitable structural flaw but as a reaction to the very success of the Qing in establishing a territorial order. It is possible to read the Qianlong emperor's response to Cao not as a rejection of the system but as an expression of concern that it was not working well enough. As ineffective as governors may have seemed to the emperor, he accepted it as a given that they were the "arms and legs" of the state and that their evaluations were crucial to its performance. In the first years of his reign, the emperor was more inclined to rely on governors to whose "worthiness" he could personally attest, but routine personnel procedures and the products thereof dominated the decade after 1768. Later in his reign, the emperor chose not to eliminate the system but to reinforce it by setting quotas for "outstanding" recommendations for each governor in the empire. Rules may well have limited the emperor's freedom, but they made possible consistent territorial government in which the central government could move officials from one post to another, with reasonable expectation of uniform performance.

LOCAL NEEDS AND PRIORITIES

Although the central evaluation of officials was ideologically important in China, it could not solve a problem that presented itself with increasing urgency as the geographic shape of the later Chinese empire emerged. This was the need of some regions for specialists, officials with knowledge of the particular social and political geographies associated with certain posts, while others demanded officials with a high level of skill and experience. No solution to this problem was offered by the Confucian vision, which held that a person was qualified for service if he mastered classical texts and passed the state examinations. In this, as in so many other respects, the Qing modified traditional procedures to meet practical needs. In broad terms, the Qing solution to the problem of regional expertise was to acknowledge that provincial-level officials, who were closer to local postings and their problems, were better qualified to judge the fitness for office of specialized local officials than was the central Board of Personnel and to accord these officials special prerogatives in evaluating such postings. At several points in the late seventeenth and eighteenth centuries, special rights of appointment were granted, creating a patchwork of personnel regimes at the local level. As the needs of each province were different, sometimes markedly so, the prerogatives of each provincial governor differed. Governors were both the products and the managers of a complex, differentiated territorial personnel order crafted over decades in order to suit particular local needs.

During its early history, the Qing developed a variety of mechanisms for recognizing postings that required special knowledge or expertise. In the Qing, as in earlier dynasties, a rather small number of local postings that were deemed strategically important were designated as "autonomous departments" (zhili zhou) or "autonomous subprefectures" (zhili ting).[37] Officials in these areas reported directly to the governors of the provinces in which they were located rather than to the prefects and circuit intendants who normally served as middlemen between the governor and local officials. As G. William Skinner has argued, such an arrangement, "entailing as it did close supervision and minimal competition for channels of communication, was highly desirable for centers vulnerable to military invasions, or other violent disruptions."[38] The governors of provinces with such jurisdictions were allowed to select magistrates for the independent departments and subprefectures from among the most competent officials serving elsewhere in the province. This seemed to guarantee not only that the local officials in these districts would be experienced and accomplished but also that they would enjoy the confidence of the provincial governor.[39]

When the Wu Sangui Rebellion was defeated in 1684, the Kangxi court faced a different sort of problem. In the far south, it appeared, the dynasty had to offer special incentives to qualified officials for postings that were perceived as dangerous and unhealthy. In 1684, the Kangxi emperor decreed that those who served in the far southern postings, which he termed "malarial and miasmic" (yan zhang), would automatically be eligible for promotion after they had served successfully for three or five years, depending on the difficulty of the position. Fourteen posts in Guangxi were identified as "malarial and miasmic" in 1684, and five more posts in Guangdong were labeled as such in 1731.[40] When the Kangxi court set out to establish a local administration on Taiwan in 1695, the two existing special-status markers were combined. Taiwan officials were deemed eligible for promotion after three years of successful service and were to be selected by the governor of Fujian from among the most competent magistrates serving in the province's mainland jurisdictions.[41]

During the Yongzheng reign, the number of counties designated for special incentives increased significantly and came to include those in border regions and in areas located well within the frontiers. In 1724, the Yongzheng emperor decreed that the governors of Guangdong and Guangxi should choose the magistrates of "malarial and miasmic" districts from among the most talented magistrates in their provinces, making the terms of service in Guangdong and Guangxi comparable to those in Taiwan.[42] Later that year, the new emperor ordered the same terms of service for magistrates serving in counties located along the seacoasts of Shandong, Jiangsu, Zhejiang, and Guangdong.[43] He further ordered that a number of magistrates in Henan, Shandong, and Jiangsu be selected to serve in counties located along riverbanks in those provinces and that they be eligible for promotion after three years of successful service. In the case of the riverbank posts, "successful service" was further defined to mean that there had been no breaks in the dikes during the magistrate's term of office and that the magistrate had not spent excessive government funds on dike maintenance.[44] It would seem that magistrates were offered incentives not only to serve along the riverbanks but also to avoid the graft that was often associated with dike maintenance projects. In 1727, the Yongzheng emperor ordered that appointments in five border districts in Shaanxi and Gansu be made by the governors of those provinces.[45] Later the same year, magistrates of forty districts and departments in the "Miao frontier areas" of Hunan, Guizhou, and Yunnan were offered promotion after three years of successful service, and provincial governors were correspondingly ordered to appoint them.[46]

Early Qing regulations of borderlands and internal frontiers addressed one side of the problem with differences in postings. Nevertheless, some postings located well within China, away from frontiers, required more experience and skill than did others. The Qing had a system for identifying and characterizing difficult postings. As Skinner has described this system, each territorial post in the empire was characterized according to the presence or absence of four attributes, each of which was identified by a single character. A post could be "troublesome" (*fan*), meaning that there was a great deal of official business; "thoroughfare/frequented" (*chong*), meaning that it was a center of communications or commercial importance; "difficult" (*nan*), meaning that the magistrate had to cope with an "unruly, crime-prone population"; or "tiresome" (*pi*), meaning that it was difficult to collect taxes. A posting could have from one to four of these attributes; altogether, there were sixteen possible designations, and, in general, the more attributes a post had, the more difficult it was considered to be. As Skinner has argued, the more attributes a posting held, the more likely it was to be of some economic centrality. Difficult and tiresome posts were "strongly concentrated in regional cores," and the most common three-character combinations—troublesome, frequented, and difficult and frequented, difficult, and tiresome—were "over-represented among cities that ranked high in the regional hierarchy."[47]

In 1728, the governor of Guangxi, Guo Hong, proposed to the emperor that provincial governors be permitted to select the governors of the districts in their provinces that had four designations (i.e., those districts that were perceived to be the most difficult to administer). He reasoned that centrally appointed officials, who were assigned to districts by lot, might be mismatched with their new appointments. Assigning a talented official to an easy posting or a less gifted official to a very difficult post was a waste of human talent that ill-served the dynasty's interest in good government. He recommended that governors carefully review all the jurisdictions in their provinces and prepare a register of the posts and their degree of difficulty for the Board of Personnel. The board would review the lists, and when they were approved, governors would be entitled to recommend for the posts with four designations an official who had served effectively in the province.[48]

The emperor was clearly impressed with this proposal. He recognized that government had become sufficiently specialized in many quarters of the empire that the traditional "one size fits all" model of personnel assignment, in which new graduates were assigned by lottery to their first postings, would not suffice. In arguing his case, however, the emperor drew on somewhat more traditional grounds. As he noted, governors often recommended officials in times of emergency, which could readily lead to abuses. Specifically, it could result in a situation he had earlier condemned in which governors turned the power of selection over to subordinates who were biased toward sycophants. Worse still, they might extort money from those who desired to be recommended, forcing the newly appointed magistrate to spend the first years in office trying to earn back the money he had spent to acquire his office. Such rapacious underlings were like "rivers that dug their own beds," forces of nature whose effect on their own environment was inevitable and uncontrollable. Setting up standard procedures regulating governors' use of the power of appointment could only serve to eliminate these abuses and provide for smooth government.[49] The emperor recommended that the Board of Personnel deliberate on the matter, and in 1731, the system Governor Guo proposed was implemented. It would appear that the needs of governing a complex and diverse empire overcame the reservations of even this most activist of emperors regarding the local appointment of local officials.[50]

By the end of the Yongzheng reign, Qing governors had acquired control over the appointment of a substantial number of magistrates in a wide variety of venues. The terminology used to designate these positions pointed to their political significance. Posts were labeled as "very important posts" (*zui yao que*) if they had received a four-character designation or "important posts" (*yao que*) if they had either received a three-character designation or been placed under a governor's control on the basis of their location.[51] Governors were said to have control over both important and very important posts. Postings under the control of governors were also known in official records as postings for which the "selection was made outside [the capital]" (*jian xuan zai wai zhi que*). Because of the common terminology used to describe these posts, it is impossible to tell how many of them were set aside for strategic reasons and how many were set aside because of their economic importance. According to the 1899 edition of *Collected Statutes of the Qing*, appointments to 410 magistracies, departments, and subprefectures in the empire had been placed under the control of governors.[52] During the early eighteenth century, a total of 181 districts and departments was set aside on the basis of their location in the far south, along the seacoasts, riverbanks, and "Miao frontier regions."

These postings were distributed unevenly over the provinces. Table 3.8 compares the number of governor-controlled magistracies in each province to the province's total number of magistracies. Overall, the governors of Zhili, Zhejiang, Jiangsu, Shandong, and Hunan had the largest numbers of positions under their control. The governor-general of Zhili controlled the most magistracies; he also had, as noted above, the highest quota of both "outstanding" recommendations and densest populations of local officials—and not to mention military forces—of any province in the region. With "seacoast" and "riverbank" posts within the borders of their two provinces, as well as large commercialized areas, the governors of Jiangsu and Shandong controlled a relatively high numbers of posts. Because of Jiangsu's comparatively small number of counties, its governor had control over a larger proportion of his subordinate officials than did the governor of any other province. Taken together with the fact that more governors of Jiangsu than of any other province were promoted from within, this gave the lower Yangzi administration an insular quality unmatched in any other region. Zhejiang had not only seacoast postings but a relatively large commercial core and relatively few counties, so that its governor also had a large proportion of counties under his control. Sichuan's and Guangxi's governors controlled the fewest counties. Guangxi had its "malarial and miasmic" regions but relatively few commercialized areas; none of the counties in Sichuan was set aside by imperial edict, and relatively few of its postings were characterized as difficult.

Governors not only had different degrees of control over appointments in their provinces but also exercised different kinds of control. In some counties where appointments were under a governor's control, the governor could only

TABLE 3.8. Counties, Departments, and Subprefectures under Control of Governors, 1899

Province	Number of Posts under Governor	Total Number of Posts	Percentage of Posts
Anhui	17	55	31%
Fujian	13	63	21%
Henan	21	102	21%
Hunan	25	71	35%
Hubei	17	69	25%
Jiangsu	30	68	44%
Jiangxi	22	79	27%
Guangxi	20	105	19%
Guangdong	23	85	27%
Guizhou	23	57	40%
Shanxi	18	95	19%
Shandong	32	113	28%
Shaanxi	23	86	27%
Sichuan	24	131	18%
Yunnan	22	86	26%
Zhejiang	27	77	35%
Zhili	53	146	36%
Total	410	1488	27.5%

Source: *Da Qing huidian*, 1899 Guangxu ed. (reprint, Beijing: Zhonghua, 1990), 8:11a–14b (reprint, 74–76).

appoint an official who had served successfully in another, perhaps less challenging posting. Since such appointments constituted transfers of sitting magistrates from one county to another, the counties were known in Qing parlance as "transfer posts" (*diao que*). These were mostly the postings with four designations, the Qing system's "most important."

In other counties, however, governors were allowed to recommend any available person by submitting a petition. Known as "petition posts" (*ti que*), these often required skill and experience but were difficult to fill, owing to their location or special challenges. Many were in border provinces, like Shanxi and Guizhou, while others were located in parts of China's interior that posed special difficulties, such as areas of southwestern Hunan inhabited by Miao peoples, the banks of the Yellow River in Henan, and parts of northern Anhui. Particularly along China's southern and southwestern borders, petition posts replaced many of the jurisdictions of hereditary "native chieftains" (*tu si*) in the Ming and early Qing. Like the chieftains, Qing magistrates in petition posts were selected for their local expertise; unlike chieftains, they held formal titles that placed them in

TABLE 3.9. Transfer and Petition Posts, 1899

Province	Transfer Posts	Petition Posts	Total Posts
Anhui	3	14	17
Fujian	5	8	13
Henan	5	16	21
Hunan	9	16	25
Hubei	14	3	17
Jiangsu	30	0	30
Jiangxi	21	1	22
Guangdong	20	3	23
Guangxi	15	5	20
Shanxi	3	15	18
Shandong	30	2	32
Shaanxi	18	5	23
Yunnan	14	8	22
Zhejiang	18	9	27
Zhili	46	6	52
Guizhou	9	14	23
Total	309 (69%)	101 (31%)	410

Source: *Da Qing huidian*, 1899 Guangxu ed. (reprint, Beijing: Zhonghua, 1990), 8:11a–14b (reprint, 74–76).

the official hierarchy and were subject to the disciplinary and personnel rules of the empire. Table 3.9 shows the proportion of petition posts and transfer posts in each province.

THE DYNAMICS OF GOVERNORS' INCREASING CONTROL

Several edicts ordering specific provincial governors to select appointees for local territorial positions make clear the Qing's reasons for setting certain districts aside. But they do not address the larger question of why a new principle of selection was being introduced into Qing personnel administration. As usual, Qing tinkering emerged more from practice than from principle, but there were several strands of thought that supported the new attitude toward local administration. First, giving governors control of jurisdictions within their provinces in central China replicated the arrangements of military occupation that had been established successfully along the borders, and so represented the transfer of the patterns of military administration to China's heartland. But new appointments procedures also served civilian needs, or at least needs articulated by Chinese civilian institutional historians. Perhaps most important, new appointment procedures served the needs of the increasingly activist governors who were appointed in eighteenth-century China.

The Yongzheng emperor successfully extended to inland Chinese provinces the methods of administration that had evolved on the frontiers. What the monarch sought to achieve through this process needs to be carefully established, since he was hardly a proponent of all things military. To be sure, the military was involved in most of the major events of his reign, such as his ascension to the throne, his wars in central Asia, and the establishment of the Military Affairs Bureau, later to be known as the Grand Council. But the emperor's attitude toward these developments was ambivalent. On the one hand, many of his most famous enemies, whom he hounded out of office and sometimes executed, were military men; he devoted considerable energy during his reign to eliminating what he perceived to be the dangers of the Manchu banner system. On the other hand, it is apparent from his comments on memorials and edicts that the emperor carefully and supportively watched over the careers of young officers; the most favored governors of his reign—Tian Wenjing, Ortai, and Li Wei—were all bannermen. Although Yongzheng was hardly a militarist, he does seem to have admired certain military virtues. Among these was the principle of direct supervision and reporting, which was characteristic of a military chain of command. As many of his edicts and rescripts make clear, he very much distrusted arrangements in which responsibility was indirect and supervision impossible. Moreover, Guo Hong, who proposed the extension of governors' powers of appointment to counties with multiple designations, was himself a bannerman. It probably appealed greatly to the Yongzheng emperor that when governors were allowed to appoint their own subordinates, direct relationships were fostered between governors and the magistrates in charge of most important territories.

Others in Qing China were also concerned about the way the dynasty assigned officials to important postings. As Gu Yanwu pointed out in *Record of Knowledge Diligently Accumulated*, dynasties before the Ming had recognized the differences in local postings. In the Han, Tang, and early Ming dynasties, magistracies were divided into three or sometimes six grades, and the officials assigned to each grade had held different ranks. Therefore, it had been possible to "promote" local officials to more difficult magistracies. Gu regarded it as a loss that postings in his own day were all treated equally.[53]

Gu's contemporary Cai Fangbing also addressed this problem and its implications for the appointments process.[54] Cai noted that the practice of "drawing lots" (*che-qian*), which the Board of Personnel used to make appointments to posts under its control, was not one of great antiquity.[55] In fact, as he pointed out, it dated only to the Wanli period (1573–1619), when the court was concerned about officials manipulating the selection process for local office.[56] Drawing lots,

Cai argued, made it impossible to match talents with the localities in which they might most usefully be employed. It would be more appropriate if governors were to carefully observe the local officials who served under them and memorialize the throne regarding their transfer.[57] In a later essay on the same subject, he pointed out the difficulties that could ensue if inappropriate appointments were made to important magistracies, citing as examples his own home region of central Jiangsu and the areas around Hangzhou in Zhejiang.[58] Cai was motivated as much by practical needs as by institutional history and believed that developing a more effective means of appointing local officials would lead to better government.

Governor-controlled appointments answered some of the requirements of a centralizing monarchy and met needs articulated by civilians like Cai Fangbing. But the greatest supporters of the new system, those responsible for its expansion if not necessarily its inception, were the activist governors who the Qing state appointed in the mid-eighteenth century. The right to make appointments represented a substantial grant of authority to provincial officials, and they moved rapidly to protect and expand their prerogatives. In 1733, Lieutenant Governor Liu of Sichuan memorialized the throne, proposing that the appointment of local officials of thirty-five districts of Sichuan be turned over to the provincial governor. Sichuan was not affected by any of the late Kangxi and early Yongzheng edicts that set aside territories for local control; similarly, few of its regions were noted for their economic centrality. Even in 1899, Sichuan did not have many posts under the control of the provincial government. In 1733, the situation was yet more marked; at the time of Liu's memorial, governors could recommend the appointment of only six local officials in the province. Lieutenant Governor Liu's proposal would have rectified the situation, but it was not accepted. The emperor submitted the memorial for review to Ortai, who was then grand secretary and grand councilor. Ortai consulted with his nephew Echang, the governor of Sichuan, and Huang Tinggui, the governor-general of Sichuan. He also conferred with Xiande, a former governor of the province who was then in Beijing. The result was an acknowledgment that the status of Sichuan's official posts needed some reassessment, but the wholesale reclassification Liu had proposed was rejected. In the end, Ortai and his colleagues recommended reclassifying only four of the thirty-five districts identified by Liu. These were Nanchiong, the capital of Shunqing prefecture and a center of communications and river transport; Guanxian, which was in the northern part of the province and adjoined the territories of minority peoples; Wanxian, a district on the Yangzi that adjoined Hunan; and Yibin, the capital of Xuzhou prefecture and an important city along the route from Sichuan to Yunnan. Ortai further recommended that the designations of nine districts be upgraded to "important" but concluded that in none of these cases was it necessary for appointments to be placed in the hands of governors. The report concluded that no further change was necessary in the remaining twenty-two districts.[59]

There were two apparent repercussions of the Sichuan proposal. Two months after Ortai delivered his assessment of Sichuan post designations, Lieutenant Governor Liu was cashiered. The charges seem to have been initiated by Governor-General Huang Tinggui, but they struck a responsive chord with the emperor, who wrote:

> I did not know Liu very well [when I appointed him]. But in his capacity as intendant of the Jianchang circuit [in Sichuan], he had several praiseworthy accomplishments. So I promoted him to lieutenant governor, thinking by this means to "drive a light cart over a familiar road." In the past few years, as I have read his memorials, I have come to realize that they are neither substantive nor honest, and may even have harmed local interests. Now, according to Governor-General Huang Tinggui's memorial of indictment, there is evidence [that he has engaged in] extortion and the pursuit of private interest.[60]

Much probably remained unsaid here, but several points seem noteworthy. First, Liu had spent a great deal of time in Sichuan, so his appointment as lieutenant governor was an easy choice, like driving a light cart over a familiar road. In the course of this service, he developed a set of relationships with local officials, whose status he sought to advance by having their posts designated "important" or "very important." It would appear that he sought to profit from these relationships, or perhaps Governor-General Huang Tinggui was embarrassed by Liu's advocacy and the rejection it had elicited. Whatever the precise circumstances of Liu's official demise, it was clear that local officials ran risks when they tried to expand their authority too greatly over local offices.

If the court rejected Liu and his proposals, it could not reject the principle behind the proposals, which was that post designations needed to be reviewed periodically, particularly in light of the importance they had assumed in the appointments process. Liu's was not the only proposal to make this point. It was reiterated in a memorial submitted by none other than Li Wei, governor-general of Zhili and one of the Yongzheng emperor's favorite officials.[61] In response to Li's request, the emperor issued an edict in October 1734, ordering governors and governors-general to review the post designations in their provinces and memorialize their findings. This was, however, to be a one-time review. The edict continued that if after a governor had submitted his requests for revision, a successor requested further changes, the original governor was liable for punishment. The emperor was not inviting a rolling reconsideration of post designations. Four responses to this edict are extant. The Fujian governor declined to make any recommendations, noting that many jurisdictions in his province were being changed and that their classifications would be determined after officials had been appointed.[62] The governor of Gansu reported in another response that there should be three "most important" positions, thirty-two "important" positions, forty-two positions of "middle" importance, and ten "easy" positions. The governor of Shaanxi reported that his province should have eight "most important" positions, all under the governor's control. He additionally stated a need for twenty-nine "important" positions, another twenty-nine positions of "middle" importance, and forty-two "easy" positions. In the cases of Shaanxi and Gansu, it is not clear what changes were advocated. The governor of Jiangxi, however, clearly identified ten positions that deserved status upgrades and whose officials needed provincial-level appointments. Presumably, other governors also availed themselves of the opportunity to reorganize local territorial governments in their provinces.

The edict of 1734 demonstrates that the Qing central government of the early eighteenth century envisioned the possibility that post classifications would change, albeit at moments and under circumstances prescribed by the court. The edict also recognized the central importance of governors, who not only exercised the prerogatives of appointment but were in the best position to judge where these prerogatives should be exercised.[63]

But there were limits to the extent of reclassification, and limits to the number of positions the Qing were willing to turn over to provincial governors. John Watt describes the efforts of a Fujian governor, carried out over a period of some years, to effect the reclassification of one of his magistracies in the 1880s.[64] The magistracy was finally reclassified as "important" when the governor offered to downgrade one of the existing "important" posts. It seems likely that changing the appointment process for any local magistrate in Qing China—involving as it did the power to assign status and the control of people and resources—could easily be a matter of dispute. But such disputes were a necessary part of the personnel regime the dynasty had implemented. The tension between governors' prerogatives and central interests was manifested in other ways as well.

It is beyond the scope of this account to explore all of the changes in post designations that occurred during the eighteenth and nineteenth centuries. However, two large, multicolored maps found in the Number One Archives in Beijing in the 1990s make collective assessment possible. The maps show the degree of importance associated with each posting in the empire; they are not dated, but Yasuki Masui has established that they represent the status of posting around the turn of the eighteenth century.[65] Altogether, 270 positions were labeled "important" or "most important" on the map and hence under the control of governors. This represents an increase of 89 positions over the 181 positions placed under governors' control before the edict of 1733, which placed most of these positions under the control of governors. In Sichuan, for instance, governors were authorized to fill 6 positions before Lieutenant Governor Liu's memorial; 4 were added as a result of that memorial. By 1800, 12 positions were added to the list. The governor of Jiangxi, who had been authorized to fill 10 positions in 1734, could fill 20 positions by 1800. The steady increase in the number of positions filled at the provincial level continued through the nineteenth century, as a comparison of post designations in the 1800 maps with those listed in the Guangxu edition of *Collected Statutes and Precedents of the Qing* demonstrates. If Gansu and Sichuan, which did not have provincial governors in 1800, are removed from consideration, the remaining provinces in 1900 account for 410 posts, an increase of 140 posts over the number in 1800, or about 1.4 posts per year. While all provinces saw some increase in the nineteenth century, the largest took place in Guizhou, Guangdong, Hunan, and Shanxi.

As power grew, there were inevitably abuses. Beginning in the Qianlong reign, governors had to follow rules when selecting magistrates for "important" and "most important" posts. They could not nominate for appointment any individual who had a record of disciplinary demotion, with or without retention of duties, or who had been officially warned about the collection of taxes. Nominees were also required to have apprehended all accused at-large criminals in their current or previous postings.[66] By the middle of the eighteenth century, some governors reported in secret memorials to the emperor that they could not find any officials within their provinces who met all the criteria for appointment to an important post and nominated individuals who did not meet one or more of the criteria.[67] Most often the court accepted these nominations, although in 1806, the Jiaqing emperor complained, "Recently, recommendations in violation of the regulations have been particularly numerous." He continued:

> Now, a province is a big area, and the department and county magistrates and their assistants are not few. Have those whose nomination would be in accord with regulations not been considered for vacancies? How is it that if one official is not appointed, none other will do, and the rules must be violated? Governors who bear the public interest at heart act for the good of government and have no other motive. But there are others who pretend to act in the public interest, but have private motives. They don't consider the appropriateness of an appointment, but look to the profit [lit., "fat"] of the position. The effect on the personnel order is significant.[68]

Competence may always be a problematic notion, but it is particularly so when it serves as the basis for complex administrative and political decisions.

Chinese history offered the late imperial state a fairly wide range of thought about talent and competence and a variety of models for institutionalizing different notions of talent within a political and administrative order. None of these various conceptions fully satisfied the Qing, however, as the dynasty struggled with the questions of how to set term lengths for officials, how to recognize merit in central government deliberations and record keeping, and at what level to judge ability and fitness for local office. Over the course of the eighteenth and nineteenth centuries, the Qing drew on its own experience to evolve workable, though not always optimal, solutions to these questions. These solutions not only affected the character of territorial government in China but shaped—probably decisively—the careers of its principal territorial servants, the provincial governors.

Central regulations, actual practice, and thought inside and outside of government affected the evolution of Qing practices in the areas of term lengths, central evaluations, and local decisions on fitness. For each of these issues, Qing solutions involved compromises between principles—often those of long historical standing—and realities of local circumstances. The dynasty implemented a system in which China was governed most of the time by men who served in office long enough to have a real impact on the regions they governed. This was achieved, however, only through a barrage of rapid transfers that must have been confusing to the governed, if not to the officials who were being appointed. In the matter of central evaluations, the Qing implemented a system that, at least in the eighteenth century, served to identify officials whom the people deemed to be among the most distinguished in the empire. But this system was hampered in at least two respects. First, central evaluations could be achieved only through the imposition of categories that some literati, and even the Qianlong emperor, found inappropriate at times. Equally as important, such an evaluation system could not be fully separated from a cultural context in which the family was the basic model for political interactions. The system of designating post and setting aside governor-controlled local offices met the dynasty's need for local expertise and allowed the state some mechanism for keeping up with changing relationships among the empire's territorial components. But as it fully evolved, it produced a remarkable patchwork of personnel regimes that was subject to manipulation and difficult to monitor and to maintain.

This examination of the evolution of regulations in three relatively narrow but significant areas of territorial administration highlights the role governors played in managing the territorial order. It may also suggest something about the nature of bureaucratic development in late imperial China. Bureaucratization has acquired a rather checkered reputation within the field of Qing history. In the 1970s, Thomas Metzger demonstrated that the conceptual system for Weberian rationality existed within Neo-Confucianism and so argued that Chinese governments had already achieved a fairly sophisticated bureaucratic order in the late imperial period.[69] Recent writers have been more skeptical. Examining the behavior of Qing officials, Philip A. Kuhn finds some praiseworthy elements but much room for doubt; he thus offers two rather less-than-hearty cheers for the Qing bureaucracy.[70] Angela Zito finds the assumptions of the late imperial Chinese to be sufficiently different from those of contemporary bureaucratic politicians that she recommends referring to the Chinese government as an "imperium" rather than a bureaucracy.[71] More recently, Evelyn Rawski has argued that Qing bureaucratization, which she sees as a hallmark of the dynasty, proceeded from the specific needs of Qing rulers for order and hierarchy among those with claims to office.[72] Rawski's finding, along with the others offered here, suggests that the Qing bureaucratic order derived neither from the universal quest for modernity nor from a timeless Chinese penchant for such forms. Rather, Qing bureaucratic forms may have originated, at least in part, from the need of a conquest dynasty to sort out and enforce the obligations and prerogatives of its various strata of servitors. This is not to grant Manchus all the credit for China's seventeenth- and eighteenth-century political successes or to blame them entirely for the woes of a system labeled as dysfunctional in the nineteenth century. Instead, it is meant to suggest that the institutional forms of the Qing grew out of a specific historical context and can best be understood as conscious responses to specific historical problems.

CHAPTER 4

The Power of the Unexpected

Like all Chinese dynasties, the Qing maintained an elaborate image-making apparatus that employed the full range of rhetorical resources at its command —allusion, metaphor, and reference to historical precedent—in making its case, and its products have rightly been read as statements of the dynasty's political intentions. Ironically, however, it was probably at the very times when the court set aside precedent and procedure that it made the most historically interesting statements.

This was particularly true of governors' appointments. To some degree at all times and especially in moments of crisis, governors were the executive agents of the Qing monarchy, responsible for the preservation of order, provision of relief, maintenance of defense, and even on occasion diplomatic negotiations. During crises, the Qing court needed more power over appointments, more ability to scrutinize accomplishments, and more authority to change mandates and jurisdictions than were allowed under the established procedures of the Board of Civil Appointments. In the matter of appointments, central prerogatives were clear. Provincial governorships were among a very few positions within the Qing bureaucracy—the others, significantly, included governor-general, president of one of the six boards, and members of the palace guard—to which the court reserved the right to make appointments without following routine procedures. When one of these positions became vacant, the Board of Civil Appointments was required to submit a memorial to the emperor asking whether he wished to appoint someone of his own choosing before it prepared a ranked list. If the emperor chose to select his own man, no list was prepared at all. When this occurred, the emperor was said to have made a special appointment.

Emperors' power to affect unexpected outcomes through special appointments was central to their ability to set the political agenda of their day. A changed vision of how government could or should function was often behind rapid changes of senior territorial officials; the new man and the new mandate often came together. In individual cases, this was often readily apparent. At least as significant and potentially far more revealing were multiple appointments of governors or the simultaneous or serial removal from office of several governors. Such events often reflected a perception of crisis, either one of military origin or one of confidence in provincial officialdom.[1] Particularly interesting in this regard were moments in the early eighteenth century when the Yongzheng and Qianlong emperors used the power of appointments to shape the evolving office of governor to their respective visions of empire. The Yongzheng emperor's personnel policy was the most dramatic. But personnel crises during the Qianlong reign highlight changes in policy during the eighteenth century, providing benchmarks in a reign that is all too often seen as a seamless whole. Governors' appointments also underscore the systemic crisis the Qing faced after the death of the Qianlong emperor in 1799.

HOW SPECIAL WAS "SPECIAL"?

In English, the word "special" has acquired a range of meanings. There are "special friends," persons to whom one feels tied by unusually strong bonds, and "special elections," plebiscites held when a previously elected official proves unable to serve, and presumably there is a wide range of usages in between. The character *te* had a similar range in Chinese, conveying varying measures of personal involvement and institutional irregularity. Most of the documents and actions labeled *te* in Qing administrative discourse, however, refer to instrumentalities or activities performed on an occasional basis in response to unusual needs. There were "special decrees" (*te yu*), edicts that were not meant to be taken as precedents for subsequent actions;[2] "special indictments" (*te can*), accusations of corruption or malfeasance not submitted through regular channels; "special budgetary allocations" (*te zhi*) to meet emergency needs; and "special commissioners" (*te shi*), individuals appointed to undertake particular tasks for the court.[3] These special actions reflect the particular engagement of the court in a region, problem, or issue, but they also represent an overriding of established precedent. Collectively, they define a realm in which emperors could rule as well as reign.

In some instances, it is possible to reconstruct fairly clearly the perceptions that lay behind special actions. In early 1723, the newly enthroned Yongzheng emperor spelled out in some detail the reason why he was making a special appointment to the governorship of Shandong. As the emperor related the matter, Xie Celu, the serving governor of Shandong who had been appointed by the Kangxi emperor less than a month before, was a competent administrator and a man of good character. But the demands of the Shandong government, which were likely to include repairs to both the Grand Canal and the Yellow River dikes, were very great for a man of fairly limited experience. Therefore, Xie, who had in fact only served as an expectant provincial censor in Shandong, was relieved of responsibility and ordered to return to Beijing to wait for another appointment. In his place, Huang Bing, a Chinese bannerman who had served as provincial censor in Shandong since 1716, was appointed Shandong governor. The

TABLE 4.1. Special Appointments, by Reign, 1700–1900

Reign	Number of Special Appointments	Total Number of Appointments	Percentage Special Appointments
Kangxi (1720–23)[a]	27	107	25%
Yongzheng (1723–36)	52	121	43%
Qianlong (1736–96)	153	532	29%
Jiaqing (1796–1820)	52	201	26%
Daoguang (1821–51)	67	220	30%
Xianfeng (1851–61)	26	76	34%
Tongzhi (1861–75)	35	83	42%
Guangxu (1875–1911)	43	172	25%
Total	455	1,512	26.4%

[a]Governors routinely appointed from the capital are excluded.
Source: *Qingdai zhi guan nian biao* data.

same edict set forth a series of orders facilitating the new political arrangements. Qisule, a Manchu student at the Imperial Academy, was ordered to take Huang's place as censor after a brief visit to Henan during which he was to consult with the Yellow River administrator and a former Shandong governor about the engineering work to be accomplished.[4]

Such explanations, perhaps occasioned by the fact that the Yongzheng emperor was making his first provincial appointment, replacing one of his father's appointees scarcely a month after the Kangxi emperor's death, were rare. More often, special appointments were announced, without comment, by the rather terse bureaucratic formula: "X is made governor of Y province" (*Yi X wei Y xunfu*).[5] On an ideological level, since the power to make special appointments derived from the emperor's heavenly mandate to rule, no explanation was necessary. On a practical level, the fact that special appointments were not announced as such was probably advantageous for the Chinese monarch. The monarch was free to comment on the circumstances that had led to a special appointment at a moment of his own choosing, or he could decline to comment altogether. The insertion of an imperial favorite into the ranks disrupted provincial bureaucratic routine to a limited extent. Moreover, expectations of appointees perceived to be the emperor's personal selections were minimized. Table 4.1 summarizes the special appointment records of the eight emperors who governed Qing China between 1700 and 1900.[6]

The consistency of special appointments was perhaps their most visible and surprising characteristic. Special appointments occurred in every reign of the dynasty, and in almost every year between 1700 and 1900. Moreover, their distribution was relatively constant. In no reign were more than 45 percent of appointments made by special means, and in no reign except the last were less than 20 percent of appointments special. During the Kangxi, Qianlong, and Jiaqing reigns, special appointments constituted between 20 percent and 25 percent of special appointments, and this number seems to have met the needs of emperors and central courts at most times. Considered as a whole, Qing emperors were quite cautious in their use of this instrument, one of their most powerful means of control.

Some fairly clear initiatives are apparent in the data, however. The Yongzheng emperor made many more special appointments than his father had. The Qianlong emperor reduced the number of special appointments to a level slightly above that of the Kangxi reign, and it remained at that level for the latter half of the eighteenth century and the first quarter of the nineteenth century. Then the rate of special appointments climbed slowly through the middle of the nineteenth century, interrupted only by a slight decline in the latter years of the Xianfeng reign that seems to have reflected a documented period of imperial despair. After this minor interruption, the number of special appointments continued to grow, reaching in the Tongzhi years a peak slightly below that of the Yongzheng era. In the last reign, the numbers fell to their lowest levels in the dynasty.

In the case of special appointments, however, the specific years in which they were made is as interesting as the reigns in which they were made. If the 435 special appointments made between 1700 and 1900 had been evenly divided among the years, there would have been 2.3 such appointments per year. In fact, the range was from 0 to 9 special appointments in a given year, and there were twenty-five years in which 5 or more special appointments were made. There was a significant correlation between the years in which large numbers of special appointments were made and years when large numbers of governors were dismissed from office. Governors were dismissed in four ways during the Qing: they could be cashiered from the civil service,[7] demoted to a post of lower rank,[8] relieved of responsibility pending further investigation,[9] or summoned to the capital for consultation upon designation of a new appointee.[10] Between 1700 and 1900, there were 343 dismissals of governors.[11] Had the dismissals been evenly spaced, there would have been 1.7 per year, but in fact the range was from 0 to 7 dismissals per year, with twenty-one years in which 4 or more dismissals occurred. In eleven of the twenty-one years in which more than 4 dismissals were made, there were more than 5 special appointments. In two additional cases, 5 dismissals were made in one year, and the subsequent year saw 5 or more special appointments. Circumstances serious enough to require the dismissal of a governor called for a special appointment to remedy the situation. There is a somewhat weaker correlation between years in which unusual numbers of special appointments were made and those in which more than the usual number of appoint-

TABLE 4.2. Years of Unusual Personnel Activity during the Qing

Three High Indicators	Two High Indicators		One High Indicator			
1725	1723	1790	1700	1751	1800	1845
1726	1735	1809	1715	1761	1802	1849
1727	1757	1854	1722	1762	1818	1852
1728	1763	1863	1724	1766	1819	1859
1769	1768	1895	1740	1782	1821	1865
1802	1780		1743	1785	1822	1884
1853	1786		1748	1795	1825	

Source: *Qingdai zhi guan nian biao* data.

ments were made. Here, the range was from 0 to 21, with twenty-eight years in which there were more than 12 appointments. In ten of the twenty-eight years in which unusual numbers of appointments were made, unusual numbers of special appointments were also made.

Using the thresholds of 5 special appointments, 4 dismissals from office, and 12 total appointments, it is possible to define the years in which the Qing court seemed most pressured, from the standpoint of governors' appointments. Obviously, these indicators overlapped. Governors had to be removed from office in order to make way for new appointments, and when needs were sufficiently urgent to require a dismissal, the office was filled by special appointment. In forty-six years between 1700 and 1900, the number of total appointments, special appointments, or dismissals was above the thresholds defined above. In seven of these years, all three were high; in another twelve years, two thresholds were crossed; and in twenty-seven years, one of the indicators was high (see table 4.2).

Nearly half (twenty-two of forty-six) of the years in which unusual numbers of governors were appointed or dismissed were contiguous. The periods of greatest appointment activity were 1722–28, 1768–69, 1800–1802, and 1852–53. Smaller, but still discernible clusters of appointments occurred in 1735, 1819–22, 1862–65, 1883–84, and 1895. Together, the nine periods accounted for all the years in which three indicators were high, six of the eleven years when two indicators were high, and five of the twenty-seven years with one high indicator. A consideration of the appointments and dismissals in each of these eras suggests something of the character of those periods. It is striking that five of the nine periods of most activity were the first years of new reigns; these include 1723–28 (Yongzheng), 1735 (Qianlong), 1800–1802 (Jiaqing), 1819–22 (Daoguang), and 1852–54 (Xianfeng). In these cases, special appointments were often the first practical actions of new monarchs and so expressed fairly clearly attitudes that were brought to the throne. To be sure, in several of these instances, notably the beginning of the

Jiaqing, Xianfeng, and Tongzhi reigns, the change of emperor was not the only event affecting appointment policy. Even in these instances, however, special appointments often provide a good guide to the new emperor's take on existing problems.

REFASHIONING THE TERRITORIAL ORDER, 1723–28

The first and the most protracted period of central interference in territorial government were the years between 1723 and 1728, when the Yongzheng emperor sought to impose his will on a reluctant and defensive bureaucracy. Developing the palace memorial system to serve his needs, this monarch left no province of the empire and few institutions of its government untouched. Governors of the emperor's choosing were sent to every province of the empire, although Jiangsu and the provinces of the northwest were particular targets of imperial concern. When appointees displeased the emperor, they were relieved of responsibility and returned to the capital. What did this churning of the governor corps mean? Unlike his son the Qianlong emperor, the Yongzheng emperor did not comment on specific appointments; his personnel policy must be deduced from his statements on the personnel process and its desiderata. Hostile portrayals of the Yongzheng emperor have represented him as mercurial and insecure, greedy, and liable to change officials on the flimsiest suspicions. But in the emperor's own view, the rapid turnover of governors was a fundamental part of his approach to reform of the territorial service. This reform was necessitated, in part at least, by structural problems that had emerged in the system of territorial government the Qing had implemented.[12]

Some of these problems are apparent in the stern edicts the Yongzheng emperor issued on the first New Year's Day of his reign, reminding territorial officials of their duties. The edict to governors voiced complaints not only about governors' inaccurate or dishonest assessments of their subordinates but also about their management of provincial treasuries, relief grain stocks, acting appointments, military forces, and indictment of subordinate officials. The most pressing issue was the process of evaluating subordinate officials. The emperor complained:

> From the lieutenant governor and provincial judge down to the local magistrate, people's abilities are judged through random gossip, and then we try them in office. We then judge the popular reaction. It then becomes impossible to sort out the confusion over who is good or bad, pure or corrupted. Senior officials are prejudiced in favor of those who flatter them and are especially partial to glad-handers, promoting them as men of ability. Those with integrity

who love the people are never noticed. When it comes time to demote the inefficient and promote the competent, or make a recommendation for a vacant position, [senior officials] either extort bribes or take their revenge, and only then do they make a recommendation. Also, they rely on the eyes and ears of their assistants, who listen to the gossip of private secretaries, to the point that impeachments are unfair. Through secret animosities, haste, and fear, the process of rewarding the competent and demoting the corrupt misses its mark. How can local government office be filled with good men?[13]

The Yongzheng emperor was hardly the first activist leader to complain of the role of gossip in personnel affairs. A rather similar complaint came from Zhang Juzheng (1525–1582), probably the most famous and powerful central administrator of the late Ming period.[14] Both statements express the frustration of Chinese leaders who contemplated making significant appointments on the basis of limited information and proceeding in important matters on the basis of gossip. Both worried, in nearly the same terms, about the honest local official who is ignored in a world of flatterers and sycophants. Both further lamented that there was no adequate means for assessing blame when matters went awry. The Yongzheng emperor seemed to be somewhat angrier than Zhang Juzheng, or at least more inclined to blame the situation on the abuses of senior officials. Zhang tended to emphasize the contributions of those who are talented yet ignored, who are capable of straight speaking but are seldom given the opportunity to do so. These differences in tone may have been related more to role than to choice. As Son of Heaven, the Yongzheng emperor was responsible for upholding the moral order; Zhang probably counted himself among the straight-speaking officials whose views should be consulted. While in their statements both the emperor and Zhang seek to shape talents to their own needs and contain gossip and slander, the emperor is a little more honest in suggesting that there are times when the state's need for competent officials must be put above popular opinion.

The matter of provincial treasuries was also urgent. This was to become one of the central political and administrative issues of the Yongzheng reign.[15] "Recently," wrote the emperor, "the arrears in grain and money in the provincial treasuries have grown to as much as several hundreds of thousands of taels." He continued:

The resources of the provincial governor are collected and disbursed from the lieutenant governor's office. Either the two officials, in their weakness, maintain overly friendly relations and interfere in each other's affairs, or the governor audits the provincial lieutenant governor's accounts and then uses his authority to extort money. As they divide the fat for themselves, the resources of each office are commingled. This renders meaningless the idea that it is the court's money that is stored in provincial treasuries. Once an affair has begun, it is difficult to conceal. Then, there is only thought of how to refill the treasuries with new exactions, rolling over the financial burden onto the people. No abuse is more serious than pursuing private interests in the name of the state.[16]

Although managing provincial treasuries was formally the lieutenant governor's responsibility, the emperor laid the blame for arrears at the feet of the governors. Governors either were lax in the supervision of their subordinates or, worse, used their authority over their subordinates to extort or misappropriate public money. The lieutenant governors had little recourse to such demands. "When a governor wants money, few indeed are the lieutenant governors who would not agree."[17]

Governors' mismanagement and the manipulations they tolerated by subordinates were also responsible, in the emperor's view, for the depletion of grain stored to provide relief in case of emergency. The Yongzheng emperor had some personal experience of this problem, for, as a prince, he had been sent to Tongzhou, a prefecture near the capital, to investigate grain storage facilities. Of 276 grain storage sites, he found 100 compromised in some way: 7 were empty, 45 were less than half full, and another 48 contained spoiled grain.[18] The trip was probably motivated by famine conditions in the capital area, which continued to worry the new emperor throughout the first year of his reign. As a prince, he had recommended a more rigorous system of monitoring the transactions of grain storage managers. As emperor, he would expand on these observations:

> The counties and prefectures store grain for the purpose of providing relief during years of flood, drought, and poor harvest. This has a very important impact on the life of the people. But now this stored grain is simply regarded as an extra exaction from the people. It is withdrawn from the storage granaries in the name of replacing the grain. But in fact, half of it has been squirreled away by unscrupulous underlings, and the other half of it has been used to make up the arrears in local treasuries. As a result, when there is a disaster, there are no reserves for relief. This is all because governors are very inexact in their reports and tolerate the consequences of these manipulations.[19]

Not only were provincial governors derelict in their civilian duties, the emperor complained, but many ignored their military responsibilities altogether. Military duties had traditionally been associated with *xunfu*, but the specific responsibilities to which the Yongzheng emperor referred were relatively new in the eighteenth century. In the early Kangxi reign, the Qing court had seemed to signal that territorial defense was largely the responsibility of governors-general, but after the Wu Sangui Rebellion, each provincial governor had been given a regiment that ranged in strength from one thousand to two thousand troops and charged with local defense.[20] But governors, and particularly the civilians promoted through the territorial service, regarded military matters and the strength or weakness of provincial forces as outside their purview. The Yongzheng emperor may have been particularly conscious of this issue in the early days of his reign, when he was particularly influenced by the military figures Nian Gengyao and Lungkodo. Nian Gengyao alone recommended at least three governors' appointments and two dismissals in the first six months of the reign.[21] Several of the new appointees were drawn from military ranks, but according to the emperor, all governors needed to be more concerned with the troops who were subordinate to them. As the emperor observed, through governors' neglect, provincial regiments often went untrained, their weaponry decayed, vacancies in the ranks were left unfilled, and the provision of food and supplies became an occasion for private profit rather than a matter of public responsibility. As a result, the provincial regiments were unable to fulfill the purpose for which they were created, and the people were left unprotected.[22]

Governors were tied to the court, and the court to governors, by a series of personal undertakings, and the emperor concluded by reviewing the terms under which these undertakings took place: "You gentlemen governors have all received your commissions to preserve order in your separate provinces by the grace of my late father. I have now inherited the central power, and will respect established traditions and honor with ritual the great officials, in all matters great and small." In return for imperial respect for the integrity of governors' offices, the emperor expected loyalty from his governors. But as a part of loyalty, the emperor expected action. "As for the matters I have discussed," wrote the emperor, "if there are those among you who are guilty, recognize and regret your guilt and swiftly correct your practice. If you have no guilt, continue to examine yourselves and redouble your efforts." If governors failed to remember the great benevolence that the Kangxi emperor had exhibited in appointing them to office, leaving local affairs "to the evil ministrations of underlings," they would bring only guilt and tears upon themselves. Should this occur, the emperor asserted ominously, "How could I possibly bend the law to take a benevolent attitude?"[23]

In its tone, this edict certainly was prophetic; no Qing emperor was as genuinely concerned with the details of local affairs, or as withering in his rebukes of local officials, as the Yongzheng emperor. But in certain respects, what the edict did not say was as interesting as what it did say. Many of the problems the emperor pointed out in territorial administration were structural in nature. Conflicts between lieutenant governors and governors had their origins in the fact that both officials had equally important functions and had enjoyed equal rank before the practice of the Qing placed more emphasis on the role of the governors. The relationship of governors to the provincial military order was also a matter of institutions. As the territorial service became routinized, its products became distinctly civilian, unaccustomed to the military functions long associated with *xunfu*. Even the conception of provincial governor revealed challenges within the office. Throughout the edict, the emperor anachronistically referred to governors with metaphors drawn from China's pre-imperial feudal tradition, invoking the loyalty "gentlemen governors" owed to the monarch who had dispatched them. But clearly, governors increasingly lived in a bureaucratized world guided by procedures of regulation, evaluation, and routine procedure. In no case, however, did the emperor propose systematic change. Despite his acute perception of the difficulties of local administration in China, the conclusion the emperor drew from his survey of provincial maladministration was that the governors, not the system, needed to be changed.

But changing governors—chastising sitting governors for their failures and appointing new ones to replace them—did bring about a flow of new ideas, which the emperor was able to transform into structural change. The reform of local finance, which occupied so much of the new emperor's time in the first years of his reign, represented an attempt to provide regular support for the underfunded subordinates whose collusive behavior disrupted the proper functioning of local government. But although the revenue source that provided such support, the silver wastage surcharge, is mentioned three times in the early edicts on government, the Yongzheng emperor (like his father) urged in each of these references that local officials to reduce the surcharge. Not until provincial officials such as No Min of Shanxi, Tian Wenjing of Henan, and Li Wei of Zhili suggested regularizing the surcharge as a means of providing for the support of yamen underlings did the new dimensions of policy reform emerge.[24] Similarly, although the edict expresses concern for the state of people living under native hereditary chieftains, the means the Yongzheng government adopted for changing their situation, the forceful military transformation of hereditary chieftainships into regular administrative posts, reflects the ideas of activist administrators as much as it mirrors the language of the early edicts on government.[25] In each of these instances, the emperor relied on the suggestions of provincial officials while formulating his policies, a pattern that prevailed not only in the great matters of empire but in the small ones as well. In seeking new governors, the emperor was seeking ideas and allies for his quest to reform Qing government.

The key to reform in the Yongzheng era was thus, as Kent Smith has argued, the "new men" whom the Yongzheng emperor dispatched to provincial office.[26] The question of where and how to find competent administrators resonated through Yongzheng edicts. A Chinese emperor was surrounded with potential servitors, and those closest to the throne, other than the bondservants who actually served the royal family's needs, were probably those masters of ritual and text who maintained the records and the legitimacy of the dynasty. In the later years of his reign, the Kangxi emperor had often turned to such people in his search for governors, to establish the Confucian legitimacy of his Manchu dynasty and surely in part because of their convenient proximity to the monarch. In 1700, the Kangxi emperor appointed his *Classic of Changes* (Yijing) tutor Xu Chao governor of Henan, and in 1711, he appointed his poetry tutor Chen Yuanlong governor of Guangxi.[27] When he came to the throne, the Yongzheng emperor, by his own testimony, knew few court ministers. Moreover, by temperament he distrusted the pretension and social manner of classically trained Chinese scholars and suspected many of having sided against him in the conflict over succession to the throne.[28] For the Yongzheng emperor, the Kangxi scholar-administrators were a source of corruption at the local level, not part of its solution. The great conundrum of Yongzheng appointments policy was thus that those officials who were closest and hence best known to him were in his judgment the least effective, while the farther he reached in seeking the men he needed, the more he had to rely on intermediaries and extraordinary bureaucratic expedients.

Several references early in the Yongzheng emperor's reign indicate the seriousness with which he approached the task of finding the right people. On one occasion in the summer of the first year of his reign, a censor urged the emperor to accomplish his aims by clarifying and expanding the framework of law. The emperor responded that while there could be government by men, there could be no government through laws. "If we obtain the right people to govern, then there is no task that cannot be satisfactorily accomplished. Without such people, although we play with documents and manipulate words, nothing can be accomplished."[29] In 1726, he wrote to Ortai: "Since the time when the ancients governed the sub-celestial realm, finance and personnel policies have dominated political discussions. But from my point of view, making good appointments is more important than managing finances. If you find the right people [for office], what need is there to worry about financial mismanagement or affairs not attended to?" To Governor Yinjishan of Jiangsu, he wrote simply, "My duty is nothing more than to appoint competent governors and governors-general."[30]

In 1725, the emperor offered a particularly vivid description of the challenges he faced in finding the right men:

When I was still a prince, I did not have contact with ministers of the Outer Court, and thus I knew very few of them. When I succeeded to the Throne and there were vacancies in metropolitan and provincial posts, how could I not appoint people? I have had to search widely and use people whom I never knew. After I have appointed them and in due course observed them, then if I find them unworthy, I have no choice but to change them. Therefore every time there is an opening—starting from governors-general, governors, provincial commanders in chief . . . on down to local magistrate—if I do not find the right men, I pore through the monthly records of the Board of War or the Board of Civil Office repeatedly. Often I go without sleep all night. I must get the right man before I can relax. This is my predicament as a monarch, which words cannot describe.[31]

By night, the emperor reviewed secret memorials and personnel dossiers in his study, in bursts of insomniac energy; by day, he interviewed candidates who had been recommended for office. In 1983, the First Historical Archives in Beijing published the records of 259 interviews the Yongzheng emperor held with candidates for the post of prefect.[32] Each interview record contains a brief résumé of the candidate followed by an imperial ranking and the emperor's personal comments. Rankings were in two categories: *shang* (superior), the highest category, and *zhong* (average); apparently no candidates were presented to the emperor who could be classified as *xia* (inferior). Each of the two broad categories were further subdivided into *shang*, *zhong*, and *xia*, creating six possible designations, from *shang-shang* to *zhong-xia*.

In making his personal assessments, the emperor drew on a limited vocabulary, but his comments were not formulaic. No two comments were absolutely alike, and when the emperor's comments could be checked against other observations, they prove him to have been a fairly shrewd judge of character.[33] In the hierarchy of capacities the emperor valued, certainly the most important was "talent" (*cai*) and the capacity to be a "great vehicle" (*daqi*) for the state. Of the characteristics that made up talent, "clear-headedness" (*mingbai*) was the most important. Less often, a candidate's "energy" (*jingshen, liliang*) or his "conscience" (*liangxin*) was praised. Sometimes these talents were fortunately combined in a single individual, like Zhuang Gui, a *jinshi* from Changzhou, Jiangsu: "This man is very clear-headed. He seems to have a conscience. There is great hope that he will develop into a mature talent. He can handle an important [*jinyao*] circuit intendancy"[34] Sometimes, however, all elements of talent were not present in a single individual: "This man is a very experienced and trustworthy individual who has an active conscience," wrote the emperor of another candidate. "He can be used in the future. My only fear is that I don't have a sense of how talented he is."[35] In the case of Chen Hongmou, the ubiquitous governor of the Qianlong era, the emperor remarked not that Chen was clear-headed but that he was "clear-hearted" (*xin yi mingbai*), to which comment the emperor added the intriguing if rather enigmatic qualifier "not at all like a native of Guangxi." The emperor went on to praise the fact that Chen took his parents with him to his official postings and turned to them for advice.[36]

Terms the emperor used to damn with faint praise or to condemn are also interesting. He noted "honesty" (*laocheng*), "loyalty" (*zhong*), and "reliability" (*laoshi*), but these did not in themselves qualify an official for office. An official might be "reliable and honest but of mediocre talent"[37] and so rate only as middle grade. The emperor also rejected literary ability and examination success as an indicator of an official's ability. Commenting on one candidate who had achieved the highest rating in the metropolitan examinations, he wrote, "A *zhuangyuan*, who is accomplished in writing. He resembles Wei Tingzhen. The senior officials at the Board of Personnel speak well of him and recommend him for office. But I fear he is too fond of the soft life. He is clear-headed, young, and honest." Wei Tingzhen was one of the few governors the Yongzheng emperor publicly upbraided. A student at the Hanlin Academy in the late Kangxi reign, Wei was appointed to territorial office, being appointed governor twice and removed twice.[38] On both occasions, the emperor complained that Wei was unable to make hard decisions and impose consistent standards; underlying the emperor's complaints seems to have been a view that the scholar's indecisiveness ill-fitted him for administrative responsibility. With vigilance, however an official could overcome the liability of a literary background. The Yongzheng emperor wrote of another candidate, Wang Shu: "If in the future, he does not develop the bad habits of the examination class [*ke jia mao bing*], he will be a great vehicle." Wang rose to the position of governor in the early Qianlong reign.[39] Most troubling to the emperor were officials like the bannerman Chang'an, who was "clear-headed and knows his way around banner officialdom. But I fear he is too clever [*congming*] and not trustworthy." In fact, Chang'an rose to occupy a governor's post during the Yongzheng reign and was reappointed governor in the Qianlong reign, but he proved to be corrupt and was dismissed and ultimately executed by the Qianlong emperor.[40]

In emphasizing talent and clear-headedness over more traditional, moral characteristics, the emperor was building a new paradigm for the selection of officials, one that emphasized administrative capacity over morality or even examination success. In view of the often elusive and always intangible nature of the realities associated with characterizations of personalities, one must be cautious in assessing the importance of the emergence of new semantic clusters in individual assessments. Nonetheless, new forms of discourse often generate new modes of political and social organization. Confronted with officials whose training and backgrounds did not suit the work they were expected to perform, the emperor tried to reform officialdom. In a comment to Wang Guodong on the occasion of his appointment as governor of Hunan, the emperor rejected Sima

Zhao's famous standard that an official must be pure, upright, and diligent: "The governor's office has many important responsibilities. It may not be the case that one [only] who is pure, upright, and diligent can master the job. In personnel matters, one does not demand perfection, but in the case of governors, a wide range of skills [*quan cai*] are needed."[41]

As the Yongzheng emperor searched for a new paradigm of officialdom, there was an experimentalism about the era's appointments . When he found persons he regarded as promising, he would appoint them and then watch carefully to see whether they fulfilled or failed to meet expectations. If they succeeded, they were lavishly praised and rapidly promoted. If they did not, they were removed from office, but usually quietly. Although the Yongzheng emperor did not hesitate to discipline his officials, he very seldom condemned them in public edicts while they were in office. More often, he relieved of responsibility those with whom he was dissatisfied or summoned them to the capital. The result was an appointments record with many hasty, unexplained transfers, shifts of policy, and apparent favorites.

Emperors were not, of course, obliged to defend their practices, but on one occasion the Yongzheng emperor commented to officials at court on the rapid changes of senior personnel in his reign:

Circumstances change, and one can never hold fast to a single approach. Sometimes it seems as if I am fond of overturning past patterns. What people don't know is that in truth I take great pains in such matters, always seeking the right course. For this reason, I may seem repeatedly to change people in a single post, or move a single official from post to post. I change with the times, in order to achieve what is appropriate.[42]

Extraordinary circumstances provoked this explanation. Early in the reign, the emperor relied on Nian Gengyao for recommendations for governors. In the spring of 1726, Nian lost favor with the emperor and was transferred from his post in the northwest to the command of the Hangzhou garrison. Within the same month, three governors who had been appointed on Nian's recommendation were dismissed from office. In private, the emperor seemed at pains to explain what he had done; in public, an edict was issued urging officials not to form factions or inappropriately indict colleagues whom they disliked.[43] Although extraordinary circumstances provoked the emperor's comments, there is little reason to doubt that they reflect his true attitude toward personnel matters. Certainly the record of appointments and dismissals provides ample evidence of the emperor's constant and restless effort to produce a new type of official, and his extraordinarily detailed comments on secret memorials offer additional testimony. Early in the reign, these reports and the emperor's comments on them were meant to be strictly confidential; any official who showed an imperial rescript even to another family member was liable to be prosecuted. In the tenth year of his reign, however, the emperor decided that the record of his comments on territorial officials' memorials would constitute the clearest evidence of his dedication to provincial government, a legacy comparable in scope, for instance, to the Kangxi emperor's sacred edict. He ordered the publication of a collection of memorials that had been submitted and received vermilion inscriptions. The task of editing the memorials was assigned to one of the emperor's favorite officials, Ortai, and was completed in 1738.[44]

Perhaps the most remarkable thing about this first period of crisis was how abruptly the appointment pattern changed at the midpoint of the reign, in 1729. After having made 78 appointments (13 per year) and dismissed 32 governors (5.4 per year) for the first six years of reign, the emperor made 39 appointments (6.5 per year) and dismissed 12 governors (2 per year) in the second six years. It may have been that the emperor was satisfied that he had refashioned the provincial bureaucracy. The emperor commented in a rescript to Tian Wenjing in 1726 that his goal was to shake up the bureaucracy, and eventually the day would come when such churning was no longer necessary.[45] In 1729, his attention was diverted from domestic affairs by a short, ill-starred war in Mongolia, which proved particularly difficult for him to manage in the absence of his brother Prince I (Yin-xiang), who died in 1729. Beatrice Bartlett has emphasized the prince's importance in many of the undertakings of the reign and the Yongzheng emperor's heartfelt grief upon his brother's death.[46] The prince was not likely to have been directly involved in governors' appointments, although he very often served as a messenger from the court to the governors. It would appear that the prince's willingness and ability to handle many of the political matters of the day freed the emperor to address other matters. Whatever the precise mix of causes, the emperor's attention seems to have shifted rather sharply at mid-reign from internal to external matters, and he thus spent less time managing—one might almost say micromanaging—provincial affairs.

But in spite of the much lower number of governors' appointments made after 1729, many innovations in the Yongzheng territorial order became permanent features of the Qing provincial system. The secret palace memorial and the Grand Council, the agency created in the late Yongzheng years to read and process secret memorials, became central parts of the communications structure of the Qing empire. The reduction during the Yongzheng reign in the average length of time governors served became a permanent feature of personnel administration. Perhaps most important, the new imperial scrutiny of governors' records and accomplishments established by the Yongzheng emperor became a part of

Qing political discourse. Taken together, Yongzheng reforms represented an effort to use the power of the monarchy to rationalize territorial administration. The Yongzheng emperor's experiments with new principles of appointment had effects that went far beyond the lives of the men appointed or the provinces they governed, to affect the very yamens in which they served and the system they sustained. As one governor loyal to the Yongzheng emperor expressed it in the early Qianlong reign, when the Yongzheng emperor came to power, he found an administration that had grown lax and ineffective under the Kangxi emperor. By dint of hard work and attention to detail, the Yongzheng emperor was able to lay the foundation for secure and stable administration. There had been excesses in this reform process, the governor acknowledged: supervisors had mistaken severity for clarity, public accounting had become dominated by trifles, and punishments had not matched crimes. But these had been minor faults of a bureaucratic order, not the product of Yongzheng policies. By the end of the reign, the government became more harmonious. Officials respected the emperor and were secure in the knowledge that whatever he did was in the interests of good government.[47]

QIANLONG RECENTRALIZATION: 1735–37

The Yongzheng emperor has been much admired by twentieth-century Western and Japanese scholars for his modernization of Qing administration, but he was hardly a loved monarch in the eighteenth century. Few centralizing rulers of the early modern world were popular, but the Yongzheng emperor's attempt to change the norms of official service in China, and enforce his views with rapid transfers and trenchant reprimands, was particularly unpopular among the traditional Chinese elites on whom Manchu rule relied. The main problem for the Qianlong emperor, the Yongzheng emperor's son, in the early days of his rule was deciding how to signal a retreat from his father's most unpopular policies of provincial government without losing the capacity to monitor and influence local affairs or appearing to repudiate his father, which would have been unacceptable in a state that considered filial piety a cardinal virtue. The period of political change, as measured by changes in the governors' corps, was fairly short, as it had to be. The Yongzheng reform of territorial service resulted in an extended period of turmoil and attendant anxiety, and the Qianlong emperor could not afford to reproduce this aspect of his father's rule. Nonetheless, during a relatively short period, the Qianlong court made new appointments in nearly half the provinces in the empire, announced its policies on some of the major political issues of the day, and reasserted the prerogatives of the central government, particularly its boards and councils, over territorial administration.

A process of personnel change began within days of the Yongzheng emperor's death, on 8 October 1735.[48] On 3 November, an edict was issued inviting senior officials at the court to nominate experienced civil servants for positions in the new government.[49] By the beginning of the Western calendar year 1736, a parade of appointments began that would bring new leadership to seven of the empire's eighteen provinces. In January 1736, the governors of Henan, Jiangxi, and Guizhou were replaced; in February, a new appointee was dispatched to Zhejiang; in April, the governor of Gansu was dismissed; and in September, new governors were appointed for Guangxi and Sichuan. In four cases—Jiangxi, Zhejiang, Guangxi, and Sichuan—the transfer of power to new appointees was accomplished quietly. The Yongzheng appointees were simply summoned to the capital for consultation or relieved of their responsibilities and new appointees dispatched, without fanfare, to take their places.

In three cases, the change of governors occasioned comment. In Guizhou and Gansu, the emperor justified his actions publicly; in Henan, the dismissed governor refused to go quietly and, once safely reappointed, wrote a memorial that cast in relief some of the issues at stake in 1736. The issue in Guizhou was the welfare of refugees from a recent rebellion of non-Han peoples against Qing rule in the southwest. The plight of these refugees was brought to the court's attention by Zhang Guangsi, a former governor of Guizhou, who indicted his successor. Endorsing the indictment, the emperor wrote:

> As I read Zhang Guangsi's current memorial, I realize that all is not well among the refugees of Guizhou. Yuan Zhancheng has obviously been trifling with public affairs, and lightly regarded the people's livelihood, in spite of having enjoyed the grace of an imperial appointment. Let him be cashiered from office and returned to the capital for interrogation.[50]

In Gansu, the ostensible issue was similar, though the basic problem in the northwest was Governor Xu Rong's inability to manage disruption of the local economy caused by the need to provision the armies who fought the Mongols in the last years of Yongzheng's reign.

> Examining Xu Rong's character, I find him not only to lack concern for the pains of the people but to be disobedient to imperial orders as well. How can a provincial official [so conspicuously] fail to calculate whether or not the common people have the means of subsistence that he is in the process of beginning relief measures at the moment when hundreds of thousands of refugees are already on the move to other jurisdictions?[51]

Neither of these cases was quite as it appeared. In Guizhou, the dismissal of Governor Yuan Zhancheng reflected the powerful grand councilor Ortai's reassertion of control over a region that had been his special concern for much of his career. Ortai had served as governor-general of Yunnan and Guizhou for much of the Yongzheng reign and wrote the Qing plans for stabilizing the region.[52] After Ortai left the region to command Qing forces in the northwest in 1732, a rebellion broke out in Guizhou, which local officials were unable to suppress. This rebellion was particularly embarrassing to Ortai, who surrendered the hereditary rank he had been awarded for his work in the southwest.[53] With the death of the Yongzheng emperor, however, Ortai became regent and then the leader of the Grand Council for the Qianlong emperor. Zhang Guangsi, the official who indicted Yuan, was a protégé of Ortai's, while the imperial commissioner who had overseen the unsuccessful Qing response to the rebellion was a protégé of Ortai's rival, Zhang Tingyu. Yuan Zhancheng was dismissed, and Zhang Guangsi was appointed to serve concurrently as Guizhou governor and Yun-gui governor-general, an unusual double charge that signaled Zhang's mandate to oversee all military action in the southwest. Under Zhang Guangsi, the military conquest of the southwest that had begun under Ortai continued. If anything, Miao peoples in the southwest were treated more violently in the first years of the Qianlong reign than during the Yongzheng reign. In the first years of the Qianlong reign, Zhang Guangxi's armies were said to have destroyed 1,324 Miao stockades, sparing 388. He also killed 17,600 people and wounded more than 25,000. Although the document that dismissed Yuan Zhancheng seemed to embody a language of leniency, in fact it announced Ortai's reassertion of control in the area and, if anything, heralded a harsher policy.[54] Neither Yuan Zhancheng, who was almost immediately reappointed governor of Gansu, nor his subordinate, Zhang Tingyu's protégé, whose calligraphy resembled that of Dong Qichang and was much admired by the Qianlong emperor, was particularly hurt by the affair. The dismissals were equal parts political statements and disciplinary actions.

The repudiation of Xu Rong was as much a statement about the war in which he had been involved as it was about the governor himself. Aggressive action in northwest China was a long-standing policy of the dynasty. The conquest of the Eleuths, completed with the death of their leader Galdan in 1697, had constituted one of the Kangxi emperor's proudest achievements and was one that his son—though not a monarch with a military reputation—could not afford to ignore. The death of Galdan's successor in 1728 seemed to provide the opportunity to continue the campaigns in the northwest, and the Yongzheng emperor overcame the reservations of many of his senior Chinese courtiers and undertook the campaign. Two armies were dispatched in the spring of 1729. One, under Yue Zhongqi, was to proceed along the "western route" through Sichuan, to

Lanchow and Hami. A second army, under the Manchu general Furdan, was to proceed along the "northern route" through Gansu to pursue the enemy. While the western armies met with reasonable success, the expeditions of the northern army came to tragedy, from the Chinese point of view, when the main force of the Eleuths decisively defeated Furdan near Khobdo. Despite this defeat, victories by Yue Zhongqi and the Qing Mongol ally Tsereng forced the Eleuths to enter peace negotiations in 1734.[55]

Despite its relatively successful outcome, the war cast a shadow over court politics. Ortai was said to have advised against continuation of the war on his return from the northwest, and there was probably other opposition as well. At some point in the last years of the reign, Fang Bao, a courtier who knew firsthand the conditions of the northwest since he had spent some time in exile there in the early Yongzheng reign, submitted a long and forceful critique of Yongzheng policy in the region, which raised not only the traditional Chinese scholar's opposition to war but specific objections to the strategy adopted in the late 1720s.[56] Opposition to the war was also reflected in a debate over the burden that supporting the northern army had imposed on the people of Gansu and how Governor Xu Rong had managed it. This debate must have been complicated by the fact that the Yongzheng emperor had handpicked Xu Rong to govern a province that had been the scene of frequent dismissals and special appointments.[57]

But in a sense the reasons for the dismissals, both ostensible and real, may not have been as important as the way in which they were made. The Yongzheng emperor often quietly removed from office those with whom he was dissatisfied, relieving them of responsibility, which did not require him to spell out their misdeeds. The Qianlong emperor made firings very public acts. He took the occasion of an indictment to spell out an official's faults, often at length, referring to unimpeachable moral principles. The emperor seized the moral high ground, defending his actions and those of his counselors in ways that were unassailable on merely political grounds. The new Qianlong appointments served to make a political statement rather than build a foundation for future policy. Qianlong's new governors served short terms in provincial capitals, often just long enough to dislodge existing governors and carry the message that a new emperor was on the throne. Their role was much more one of repudiation than construction, more a rejection of what many probably saw as the chaos of the Yongzheng years than the inauguration of a new era.

The dominant figure in the new administration was Ortai, the former governor-general of Yunnan and Guizhou and confidante of the Yongzheng emperor, who served as regent for the young Qianlong emperor and as senior grand councilor for the first nine years of the reign. Ortai had grown to political maturity at a time when opportunities for Manchus without hereditary rank were decreasing, and with the Yongzheng emperor's support, he made his mark in territorial administration before moving to the highest levels of central policy making.[58] Having risen to power through the territorial hierarchy, he retained a firm control over it once he was in central office. Unlike his mentor the Yongzheng emperor, Ortai was not experimental in his personnel policies; he appointed known entities to office and guided them in the pursuit of established policies. Although the language of the court was new, the faces associated with it were not. An edict of 1739 identified as protégés of Ortai several governors appointed in the first years of the Qianlong reign: Fude (governed Henan, 1735–37), Chang'an (governed Zhejiang, 1741–47), and Fa Min (governed Shandong, 1736–38).[59] This list could also include Chen Hongmou (multiple appointments, 1739–65), Huang Tinggui (governed Gansu, 1741–48), and Yin Huiyi (governed Henan, 1737–39), among others.[60]

In the years immediately following his death, three of Ortai's sons were appointed provincial governors. His eldest son, Erong'an, served three years as governor of Henan (1748–51), one year as governor of Shandong (1751–52), and briefly as governor of Jiangxi.[61] A second son, Ening, governed Hubei and Hunan (1766–67), Guangdong (1767–68), and Fujian (1768–69), and a third son, Ebi, was governor of Shanxi (1759–61) and Shaanxi (1762–63).[62] Two of Ortai's nephews also served as provincial governors: Echang governed Guangxi (1746–48), Gansu (1748–51, 1754–55), and Jiangxi (1751–52); and Eleshun governed Gansu (1752–53) and Anhui (1754–55).[63]

Whereas the Yongzheng emperor had sought allies among provincial governors in a quest to reform the Qing bureaucracy, the Qianlong emperor selected his assistants from among officials of the central government and proved, on the whole, rather uninterested in administrative reform. The implications of the new imperial rhetoric were not lost on provincial officials, particularly those who perceived themselves as having a stake in the Yongzheng order. One of the governors the Qianlong emperor dismissed refused to go gently into the bureaucratic night. Wang Shijun was in some respects the quintessential Yongzheng official. He had been appointed a local official in Tian Wenjing's province of Henan in the first year of the Yongzheng reign. His skills so impressed the lieutenant governor of Henan, Yang Wenqian, that Yang arranged for Wang to follow him to Guangdong. After several promotions in Guangdong, and a brief stint as governor of Hubei, Wang found himself appointed Tian Wenjing's successor. Early in 1736, Wang was indicted for careless administration of the Yongzheng policy of forgiving taxes on land reclaimed for agricultural use after warfare or disruption.[64] Wang's accusers claimed that far too much land was being held off the tax rolls, raising the tax burden for those who were not exempt. The object of this indictment may have been not Wang but the policy, which was subsequently abandoned. Nonetheless, Wang was dismissed and later appointed to Sichuan.[65]

Once in the southwest, Wang memorialized, protesting that a few senior officials at the capital controlled all the affairs of the dynasty, making it impossible for the voices of territorial officials to be heard. Such officials, he alleged, were more concerned with central policies than with local realities and devoted most of their attention to faction building. Here, he may have been referring obliquely to Ortai, who had been a rival of Tian Wenjing during the Yongzheng administration. Wang also complained that all at court were bent on destroying the Yongzheng legacy. His complaints, though cast as a warning for the new emperor, elicited an edict in which the Qianlong emperor firmly rejected these complaints and asserted that administrative change was necessary if the dynasty were to achieve the ideal central point between leniency and severity. Wang himself was dismissed permanently from official service.[66] The angry reaction to Wang's charges lent them credibility; he must have been speaking some truth, or there would have been little point in issuing a public edict to refute a secret memorial. But the reaction also demonstrated that from the beginning of the Qianlong reign, the center of gravity in provincial affairs was located firmly in Beijing.

Centralization of authority continued under Ortai's successor Fuheng, although it was turned to different ends. Fuheng's ties to the emperor were those of family and common Manchu military heritage.[67] In 1727, Fuheng's older sister was married to the young prince who would become the Qianlong emperor. The prince became especially devoted to her, designating her the Xiaoxian empress when he ascended the throne, and she bore two of his seventeen sons and two of his ten daughters before she died in the spring of 1748.[68] Fuheng was the emperor's brother-in-law, if it is appropriate to apply such a term to the complex connubial relationships surrounding a Chinese emperor, when he became a member of the Grand Council in 1745. He rose to the post of chief grand councilor in 1746 and held it until his death in 1770. Fuheng's appointment and continuing tenure were all the more remarkable in view of his youth. Not yet fifty when he died in 1770, he could not have been older than twenty-six at the time he became chief grand councilor. Youth may have been precisely what the Qianlong emperor sought in the mid-1740s.[69] Having reigned for a decade under the watchful eyes of his father's aging counselors, and suffered through their factional and personal conflicts, the Qianlong emperor was anxious to shape the direction of the empire he had inherited, assisted by a man of his own generation.

The young Manchu's ascent reflected the reemphasis on Manchu military heritage that was a tenet of the Qianlong emperor's definition of empire. Fuheng's background was principally in military matters, and during his tenure as chief grand councilor, the Qianlong court embarked on the great military campaigns that so clearly define the Qianlong reign in history. One of Fuheng's first services for the Qianlong emperor was to rescue the failing campaign against the Jinquan rebels in the southwest, replacing Noqin in command of the armies. Fuheng went on to organize and lead the Qianlong campaigns of the 1750s in northwest China and central Asia. The Qianlong emperor remarked in one edict that Fuheng should be counted one of the principal architects of strategy in the northwest, and in another edict he compared Fuheng to Mingju, the sole courtier who had advised the Kangxi emperor to go to war against Wu Sangui.[70]

All of Fuheng's children did very well in Qing administration, although none held the post of provincial governor. Rather, like their father, they specialized in military affairs and central administration. Fuheng's eldest son, Fuling'an, inherited his father's hereditary rank and fought in the Burma campaign of 1767. Fuheng's other sons were Fuchang'an, who was president of the Boards of Revenue and Works and commander of the Bordered White Banner; Fulong'an, who served as president of the Boards of War and Works, held the post of grand councilor and married the Qianlong emperor's fourth daughter; and Fukang'an, who was repeatedly appointed governor-general and commanded Qing forces in the campaign against the Gurkhas in the 1790s.[71]

One of Fuheng's contributions to provincial administration in the Qianlong reign was his practice of appointing Grand Council clerks directly to office as provincial governors. Grand Council clerks were not mere calligraphers, although good calligraphy was probably a factor in their selection. The more appropriate comparison, Beatrice Bartlett has argued, is to law clerks for U.S. Supreme Court justices. Grand Council clerks were young or in early middle age and had been selected for their intelligence and ability to handle "high-level discretionary tasks."[72] During the Qianlong reign, twenty-nine individuals who had served as Grand Council clerks were appointed governors of China's provinces, which represents about 15 percent of those who served as governor (see table 4.3). Of the individuals, twenty were Manchus and ten were Chinese. There was a small but steady increase in the number of clerks who served as governors during the reign: four were appointed in the late 1740s, four in the 1750s, six in the 1760s, six in the 1770s, seven in the 1780s, and four between 1790 and 1796.[73] The first clerks were appointed as governors in 1748; among them was Erong'an, Ortai's oldest son, who became governor of Henan, three years after Ortai's death. Thus, Ortai was not involved in the appointment and in fact had objected to Erong'an's appointment as Grand Council clerk, but the Yongzheng emperor overruled his objections.[74] In 1755, Erong'an's younger brother Ebao, also a former clerk, was appointed governor of Guangxi. Several years later, a father-and-son team, Mingshan and Haining, moved through the Grand Council to the provinces. Mingshan began as a clerk in 1754 and was appointed governor of Jiangxi in 1762; while he

TABLE 4.3. Grand Council Clerks Who Became Governors, Qianlong Reign

Name	First Service in Grand Council	First Appointment as Governor
Jiang Bing	1731	Henan, 1752
Changjun	1731	Henan, 1761
Yaerhashan	1732	Jiangsu, 1748
Asiha	1731	Jiangsi, 1749
Erong'an	1733	Henan, 1748
Fang Guancheng	1737	Zhejiang, 1748
Hu Baoquan	1737	Shanxi, 1753
Liang Guozhi	1742	Hubei, 1769
San Bao	1744	Shanxi, 1771
Wen Fu	1743	Fujian, 1769
Ebao	1748	Guangxi, 1755
Bayansan	1748	Shaanxi, 1772
Haoshuo	1747	Shandong, 1777
Chang Tao	1748	Hubei, 1768
Fude	1754	Jiangxi, 1761
Mingde	1754	Shanzi, 1756
Mingshan	1754	Jiangxi, 1762
Feng Guangxiong	1753	Hunan, 1790
Chen Huizu	1755	Guangxi, 1769
Yingshan	1763	Guizhou, 1793
Laibao	1762	Shanxi, 1768
Yongbao	1768	Guangxi, 1784
Huiling	1768	Hubei, 1788
Haining	1769	Shanxi, 1788
Fusong	1770	Zhejiang, 1782
Sun Shiyi	1775	Yunnan, 1779
Sun Yongqing	1785	Guangxi, 1785
Chenglin	1780	Guangxi, 1795
Haicheng	1784	Jiangxi, 1772

Sources: Liang, Shu yuan ji lue, 4:1a–8b, 18:1a–4a; Qingdai zhi guan nian biao.

was governor, his son Haining became a clerk and then was appointed governor of Shanxi in 1788.[75] During the chaos of 1768–69, four former Grand Council clerks were appointed governors—Liang Guozhi, Cheng Tao, Chen Huizu, and Wen Fu.

Grand Council clerks who were appointed governors were bearers of the centralizing impulse of the Qianlong court, but they were also representatives of the new military emphasis of Fuheng and his generation. Jiang Bing accompanied

Ortai on his inspection tour of the northwest campaign in the late Yongzheng years and received an outer court appointment to the Board of War before being appointed governor of Henan (1752–55) and Hunan (1756–57).[76] Hu Baoquan accompanied Fuheng on his journey to investigate the campaign against the Jinquan that resulted in Fuheng's elevation to chief grand councilor and was then appointed governor of Hunan (1753–55), Jiangxi (1755–57), and Henan (1757–63).[77] Changjun accompanied Fuheng on the campaign against the Dzungars before his appointments as governor of Henan, Jiangxi, Gansu, Hubei, and Yunnan (1761–67). The Qianlong emperor wrote a short poem during one of his southern tours expressing his pleasure at finding Changjun, an old military colleague, ensconced in civilian administration.[78] Ortai and those he supported often had a hand in both civilian and military administration, but Ortai probably saw his main contribution as bringing order and competence to territorial administration. With Fuheng, the Qianlong government went on a war footing, and officials shuffled back and forth between military postings and service in territorial administration.[79]

DEFEAT AND GENERATIONAL CHANGE: 1768–69

The concerted effort of the court to justify policy in terms of unchanging virtue rather than expedience has always made it difficult to establish political benchmarks in the reign. But a transition of some sort occurred in 1768–69, years in which more governors were appointed and dismissed than in any other year of the Qing dynasty. The Qianlong emperor's attention was drawn to the corruption and failings of an aging corps of provincial governors by the strange appearance of a group of bandits who were reputed to clip the queues of unsuspecting individuals and then conjure with the queues, causing victims to do their bidding. In *Soulstealers: The Chinese Sorcery Scare of 1768*, Philip Kuhn has provided a thoroughly engrossing narrative of this episode. Kuhn is inclined to attribute the court's awkward handling of this odd case to the inherent limits of the traditional Qing bureaucratic order, and certainly much other scholarship on the Qing confirms these limits. However, other changes taking place in the Qianlong court in the late 1760s also affected its capacity to respond to challenges in the provinces.[80] Not only were central authorities maladroit in handling the soulstealers, but the court, overconfident after its victories in central Asia, embarked on an ill-conceived war in Burma that ended with Manchu troops bogged down in the muddy headwaters of the Irrawaddy River.[81] This defeat suggested the limits of Manchu arms; it also proved especially costly to the Qianlong emperor personally, as Fuheng, his trusted councilor for twenty years, died of malaria contracted on the campaign. The period 1768–69 was hardly typical for the Qianlong monarchy. It was a critical moment of transition between the military endeavors associated with Fuheng and the much more civilian concerns of Fuheng's successor Liu Tongxun.

The bases of Liu Tongxun's power could not have been more different from those of his predecessor. Liu Tongxun came from a scholarly Shandong family.[82] His father had received a *jinshi* degree and risen through the provincial administration to become lieutenant governor in Sichuan. Tongxun began his career as a student at the Hanlin Academy in 1724 and advanced through the central administration. In 1741, he caught the court's attention with a memorial complaining of the nepotism and factionalism associated with Grand Councilor Zhang Tingyu and Grand Secretary Noqin.

In succeeding years, he became famous as an incorruptible troubleshooter for the central government. He investigated a number of cases in which Manchu appointees or relatives of senior officials were charged with malfeasance in the provinces. In 1753, one month after joining the Grand Council, Liu was sent to investigate river conservancy in the lower Yangzi valley; this may have been a difficult commission since the two officials responsible for Yangzi River conservation were famous and well-connected river-work specialists. Gao Bin, the director general of the Southern River Conservancy, had served most of his career in the management of Chinese rivers and had the additional advantage of being the father of one of Qianlong's concubines. He was assisted by Zhang Shizai, who had also spent most of his career in river work, as had Zhang's father, the much beloved governor of Jiangsu, Zhang Boxing. Despite their illustrious pedigrees, Liu found that Gao and Zhang had inadequately supervised their underlings, with the result that river conservancy work had been mismanaged and financial accounts had become confused. Both Gao and Zhang lost their positions in the autumn of 1753; neither was further punished, though Gao Pin was ordered to watch the execution of the subordinates whom he had failed to supervise.[83] Two years later, in 1757, Liu Tongxun was sent to investigate charges made by a Chinese governor, Guo Yiyu, that Hengwen, the Manchu governor-general of Yunnan and Guizhou, had ordered Guo to purchase gold from him at inflated prices. Eventually, both officials were found guilty of extortion, and Hengwen was ordered to commit suicide.[84] In 1759, Liu was called on to investigate charges by the new Manchu governor of Shanxi, Ta-yong-ning, that the former lieutenant governor of the province, Jiang Zhou, had not accounted for deficits in the Shanxi provincial treasury before his promotion to the governorship of Shandong. This task was potentially difficult because Jiang Zhou was the son of the former grand councilor Jiang Tingxi and nephew of the regent Jiang Tingyu. Jiang Zhou was found guilty and ordered to serve without pay in the Qing armies in Gansu, and a number of the Manchu officials under whom he had served were also reprimanded.[85] In 1760, Liu was sent to investigate charges by the Chinese education commissioner of Jiangxi that Governor Asiha had received gifts from a subordinate in return for recommending him for a post and had extorted loans from local gentry members. Asiha, a former Grand Council clerk, was found guilty and cashiered, but in two years he was reappointed governor of Henan, a post he held for four and a half years.[86]

Remarkably, in view of his long experience in investigating the corruption of Manchu territorial officials, Liu Tongxun reduced only slightly the number of Manchus appointed as governors. However, the era must have been a very confusing time for both those at court and those in territorial offices, when signals from court to provincial capital could easily appear mixed and intentions might be misunderstood. This confusion would have been especially pronounced when the issue turned on the prerogatives of Manchu officials for symbols of Manchu rule, like the queue. In the sorcery case, Kuhn has argued, it was not until Liu Tongxun was established as chief of the Grand Council and was able to persuade the Qianlong emperor to abandon the hunt for the elusive soul stealers that the case began to wind down.

Similarly, in the matter of governors' appointments, once Liu's influence was established at court, the pattern of rapid appointments and dismissals that marked the 1760s came to an abrupt end.[87] Between 1766 and 1771, the Qianlong court appointed an average of 13 provincial governors a year; from 1771 to 1778, the average was 5.4 appointments per year. Also, the character of appointees changed. As befitted one who had announced his presence at the Qianlong court with a memorial complaining that Grand Councilor Noqin had taken too many duties upon himself, Liu was more inclined to let the routine procedures of promotion and evaluation produce officials of experience and competence. Under Fuheng, most new appointees had some experience in the capital; in fact, capital experience was probably more important than civil service degrees. During the Liu Tongxun years, men raised to governorships were more often Chinese official degree holders and were somewhat more likely than earlier governors to have had experience in the territorial service. Liang Guozhi (governed Hubei, 1769–71, and Hunan, 1771–73) and Bi Yuan (governed Shanxi, 1773–79, 1780–85) were both *zhuangyuan*, the highest-ranked members of the *jinshi* classes; Liang Guozhi went on to be a grand councilor himself in the 1770s.[88] Yu Wenyi, promoted to governor of Fujian in 1771, and Li Hu, promoted to governor of Guizhou in 1770, both took their *jinshi* degrees in the first years of the Qianlong reign. At the time of his appointment, Li Hu had twenty-eight years of experience in Qing territorial administration, during which he had risen from magistrate to governor.[89] Neither He Wei, promoted to governor of Henan in 1771, nor Chen Huizu, appointed governor of Guangxi in 1769, had *jinshi* degrees, but both had ample experience in the territorial service. He Wei had worked in river conservancy since the late Yongzheng reign, and Chen Huizu had grown up in the yamen of his father, Governor Chen Dashou (governed Anhui, 1739–41; Jiangsu, 1741–46; and Fujian, 1746–47).[90]

Scholarship on the eighteenth century has emphasized the growth of central and monarchical powers during the Qianlong reign, and at an initial level of generalization, this characterization is correct. Closer examination via consideration of governors' appointments, however, reveals multiple dynamics. Ortai continued the Yongzheng policy of using the monarchy's power to rationalize territorial administration, although he did so from a firmly established position of central authority, rejecting the Yongzheng emperor's experimentalism. Fuheng reorganized the state for war, drawing on his close and friendly relations with the Grand Council staff to project central power into the provinces. Liu Tongxun reacted against the central appointment of governors but asserted the importance of central regulation of official behavior. Each of these policies had the effect of advancing the power of the central government over that of the provinces, and each arguably represented one dimension of the Qianlong emperor's design for the empire. Centralization in eighteenth-century China was not the product of a single autocratic will to power but the result of several thrusts, guided by men of different generations.

REEMERGENCE OF THE BUREAUCRACY: 1799–1802

The crisis that occurred in Qing territorial administration between 1799 and 1802 was the result of a change in emperor and, more importantly, of another change in grand councilors. In February 1796, the Qianlong emperor, not wishing to appear unfilial by ruling longer than his grandfather, abdicated in favor of his fifth son, who was enthroned as the Jiaqing emperor (r. 1796–1820). Despite this formal abdication, control over political matters and probably territorial administration remained in the hands of the Qianlong emperor's chief grand councilor, Heshen, while the retired emperor was alive. Much has been written about Heshen. But on the whole, studies have focused on his relationship with the old emperor and the enormous fortune he accumulated during his lifetime.[91] Seeking a scapegoat for the corruption of Qing government in the eighteenth century, scholars have failed to set the career of this notorious court favorite in context by comparing his position and accomplishments with those of his predecessors. While the precise sources of Heshen's influence over the emperor may never be known, it was an influence that did not differ, at least in kind, from that enjoyed by previous chief grand councilors. Like Ortai, one of the Yongzheng emperor's favorites and the first chief of the Grand Council, Heshen was rescued from an obscure position in the ranks of the Beijing Manchu military establishment by imperial notice. Like Fuheng, Heshen was related by marriage to the emperor: Heshen's son was married to the emperor's youngest and favorite daughter. Like Liu Tongxun, Heshen secured his place in the capital by investigating charges brought in the provinces. In Heshen's case, the accusation was that Li Shiyao, the governor-general of Yunnan and Guizhou, had accepted gifts from his subordinates and sold them pearls at inflated prices. These charges very much resembled the accusation that Governor Hengwen had forced his subordinate Guo Yiyu to buy gold at inflated prices, which Liu Tongxun had investigated for the Qianlong court in 1757.[92]

Corruption spread significantly during the few years between Liu Tongxun's death and Heshen's rise to power. Seventy-three years old, Liu Tongxun served as chief grand councilor for only three years. His successor Yu Minzhong also came out of the examination system, having become a *zhuangyuan* in 1737. Like Liu, Yu performed most of his official service in the capital, but unlike Liu, Yu had earned the emperor's attention with his literary abilities, serving as the monarch's chief editor and literary amanuensis. Despite their common backgrounds, Liu Tongxun had a firmer hand in personnel matters compared to Yu Minzhong, who was involved in several corruption cases. It was Yu who approved the scheme of contributions and honors that lay behind the great corruption case in Gansu under Governor Wang Danwang. Yu probably was also on the take in Shandong, where his younger brother served as Guotai's lieutenant governor. Prince Zhaolian notes that, although earlier grand councilors received modest gifts, the practice of making large cash payments to members of the council really began during Yu Minzhong's term.[93]

Heshen differed most conspicuously from his predecessors in the degree to which he profited from office. Like earlier chief grand councilors, he appointed relatives to provincial office. Jiqing, who governed in Shandong from 1791 to 1793 and in Zhejiang from 1793 to 1796, was Heshen's cousin. In fact, the unusual number of appointments made in 1780, 1785, and 1790 probably reflect the grand councilor's actions. During Heshen's tenure, the ratio of Manchu to Chinese appointees in provincial governorships, which had fallen to 0.36 to 1 during Yu Minzhong's term, rose to 1.1 to 1. But Heshen was most famous for appointing Manchu associates to provincial office and then extorting money, gold, precious stones, and works of art from them. At his death, he had amassed one of the largest personal fortunes of his day and secured the permanent enmity of most of Chinese officialdom.[94] His years as chief grand councilor produced some of the most spectacular corruption prosecutions of the eighteenth century. In 1782, Guotai, himself the son of a famous Manchu general of mid-century, was charged with embezzling during his five-year rule in Shandong, from 1777 to 1782.[95] Four years later, Fusong was cashiered from the governorship of Shanxi when he was found to have accumulated arrears of 3.3 million ounces of silver and manipulated salt tax revenues during his previous posting as governor of Zhejiang.[96]

Although these cases took place on Heshen's watch, he may not have been responsible for them. Traditionally, Guotai has been regarded as Heshen's protégé, but a careful consideration of the archival record casts doubt on this association. Fusong was quite clearly opposed to Heshen, and, if anything, Heshen was responsible for his prosecution rather than his transgression.[97] Heshen may have been not as much the author of corruption in the late eighteenth century as its fortunate beneficiary, for it seems that corrupt practices were beyond the control of any individual. As Guo Chengkang has noted, the Qing system did a better job of providing for the livelihood of territorial officials than of capital officials. Given that territorial officials owed their appointments to capital officials, it was perhaps inevitable that mentor-protégé relations would be reified with flows of cash, as officials appointed to wealthy postings rewarded those in the capital who had been responsible for their advancement. As Guo further notes, the extremely hierarchical character that territorial administration had acquired in the Qing further fostered corruption. Unlike the Ming, in which the various officials who held territorial appointments reported to different superiors, Qing territorial officers were obligated to only one person, which made it easy for senior officials, often under pressure from the center, to extort money from their subordinates.[98] Several courageous Chinese officials tried to bring Heshen's corruption to the attention of the Qianlong court, but the Qianlong emperor rejected their pleas.[99]

The situation changed, however, with the Qianlong emperor's death on 7 February 1799. Five days later, on 12 February, the Jiaqing emperor accepted senior statesmen's recommendation that Heshen be put to death. Not quite a fortnight later, on 24 February, the Jiaqing emperor began to dismantle the provincial power structure Heshen had built. The first governor to be dismissed was Governor Yinjianga of Shandong, who had inserted into a palace memorial—in principle, written for the emperor's eyes only—a letter to Heshen in which he consoled the Manchu councilor on the Qianlong emperor's death. The memorial offered no sympathies to the new emperor, and although friends of Yinjianga suggested that the letter was merely a routine, general expression of grief, the new emperor took it as a sign of factional allegiance. Removed from provincial service, Yinjianga returned to his post in the Manchu banner order.[100] Some months later, the emperor dismissed Governor Yixing of Jiangsu, whom he described as an arrogant alcoholic who extorted special gifts from his subordinates. This dismissal must have been particularly embarrassing for the Jiaqing emperor, who had made Yixing governor by special appointment just two years before. As the imperial edict of dismissal made clear, the Jiaqing emperor did not approve of Yixing's haughty attitude and flaunting of his special status as a member of the imperial clan. Someone obviously had recommended Yixing to the Jiaqing emperor; the evidence pointed in this instance to Heshen.¹⁰¹

Most of the Jiaqing emperor's dismissals were not cast in such ad hominem terms, however. The problem with Heshen, the emperor asserted in his edict ordering the councilor's execution, was that he had not attended to the military affairs of the dynasty, with the result that the large White Lotus Rebellion in central China had been allowed to continue for far too long. Justifying Heshen's execution, the Jiaqing emperor compared Heshen to Nian Gengyao, whose execution the Yongzheng emperor had ordered for monopolizing military affairs in west and southwest China, and Noqin, whom the Qianlong emperor had ordered beheaded for cowardice in front of his armies during the first Jinchuan campaign in 1749.¹⁰² After dismissing Yijianga and Yixing, the Jiaqing emperor turned to Shaanxi, the scene of the rebellion, and cashiered two governors in sequence in order to turn around the dynasty's war efforts there.¹⁰³ In 1801, the emperor turned his attention to the fighting in the far southwest, dismissing two Yunnan governors out of dissatisfaction with the performance of imperial armies there.¹⁰⁴ Only in 1802, when the emperor was satisfied with the performance of his armies, did he consider central China, replacing the governors of Jiangxi and Guangdong and appointing second governors to Guizhou and Yunnan.

As governors were being appointed and dismissed, a new and rather curious phenomenon emerged. Illness was always an acceptable reason for leaving office in the Chinese civil service. Confronted with two provincial governors who had become incapacitated in the course of their duties, the Yongzheng emperor ordered that when a governor became ill, he should submit a memorial describing his condition and turn over his seals of office to a subordinate who could act until a replacement arrived.¹⁰⁵ The emperor's order left open the question of what might happen if an official recovered, but this did not happen often in the Yongzheng or Qianlong reigns. A total of seventy governors left office for reasons of illness in the eighteenth century, and none were reappointed; in every case for which sources are available, governors who left office because of illness died within six months of their departure. The first governor to be reappointed after recovering from an illness was Governor Jiang Zhaogui of Shanxi, who became ill in 1797, recovered, and was reappointed governor of Shandong in 1800. The circumstances of his illness were somewhat suspicious. After having spent most of his career in Shanxi, he became ill just at the moment when the White Lotus Rebellion reached his province. Once Heshen was dead, Jiang presented himself at the capital, declared himself recovered, and was appointed governor of Shandong. After five months in office, however, old age and the accumulated weight of corruption in Shandong caught up with him, and he was removed from office again, this time permanently.[106] Many governors in the nineteenth century pronounced themselves afflicted, only to recover and be reappointed or enjoy healthy and extended retirements. The circumstances of each case no doubt differed, but it is hard to avoid the conclusion that a "bureaucratic flu" affected at least some governors in China's troubled nineteenth century and that the imperial power of special appointment was used to smooth their departures and reentries into the official order.

The Jiaqing emperor found replacements for those he dismissed among the followers of his close advisers, often officials who had themselves been victims of Heshen. James Polachek has pointed out that many of those who were appointed to senior territorial positions in the early Jiaqing years owed their appointments to their connections with Zhu Gui. The Zhu family had resided in Beijing for at least two generations and had served as the center of a circle of Beijing intellectuals and officials. Zhu Yun organized this group to propose and guide the *Complete Library of the Four Treasuries* (Si ku quan shu) project in the 1770s.[107] Zhu held a jinshi degree and was a former Hanlin academician; he was originally recommended to the court by Liu Tongxun, who had served as the Jiaqing emperor's tutor.[108] In the 1780s, Heshen blocked Zhu's advancement in the central government and that of a number of his Chinese associates, but Zhu embarked on a territorial career, which culminated with his service as governor of Anhui (1790–94) and Guangdong (1794–97). On Heshen's downfall, Zhu was recalled to the capital to serve as president of the Boards of Personnel and Revenue. His return marked the return of degree-holding Chinese to posts of influence in the capital. Among those he recommended as governors were Jing Daoqian (governed Anhui, 1799–1802) and Sun Erjun (governed Anhui, 1821–23, and Fujian, 1833–36).[109] Other governors recommended by Zhu Gui's circle included Sun Yuting (governed Guangdong and Guangxi), 1802–7; Guizhou, 1808–10; Yunnan, 1810–15; and Zhejiang, 1805–6); Fei Chun (governed Jiangsu, 1795–97), and Jiang Youxian (governed Jiangsu, 1809–11).[110]

In view of the continuing importance of individual grand councilors like Zhu Gui in the appointment process, twentieth-century historians have suggested that the Jiaqing emperor did not so much reform as reshuffle the bureaucracy. But for those in the early nineteenth century, such as Prince Zhaolian (1780–1833), the Jiaqing emperor's actions seemed nothing less than a "restoration" (*wei-xin*) of Qing government.[111] Zhaolian was a Manchu aristocrat whose father had served at the Qianlong court, but as a poet, not as a warrior.[112] Coming of age just when the Jiaqing emperor ascended the throne, Zhaolian shared the passions of the Chinese officials who were promoted. In fact, one theme of his rich and gossip-filled *Miscellaneous Notes of the Xiao Pavilion* (Xiao ting Za Lu), a history of mid-Qing politics, is the contrast between the corruption and incompetence of the previous generation and the promise of the new one.

Personnel change was not the only mark of the new reign. Conditioned by Chinese tradition and the assumptions of seasoned Chinese officials who surrounded him, the Jiaqing emperor responded to crisis by reasserting the importance of the rules, standards, and norms of procedure that were the Chinese officials' traditional response to discrepancy and corruption. All the state collections of regulations on governing were reissued during the reign in new and considerably expanded editions. The Yongzheng edition of *Collected Statutes of the Qing*, the Qing operations manual, had grown to nearly 250 juan, and the Qianlong emperor, wanting to separate the dynasty's enduring statutes from their changing interpretations, shrank the collection to 100 juan but published 180 juan of supplementary material in another volume, *Collected Statutes and Precedents of the Qing*. In the Jiaqing era, *Collected Statutes of the Qing* itself was further edited to 80 juan but was accompanied by 920 juan of precedents.[113] A separate book of 52 juan, *Regulations on Punishments of the Six Boards Newly Authorized by the Emperor* (Qin ding xin xuan liu bu chufen zeli), issued shortly after the emperor died but prepared during his reign, dealt exclusively with regulations for the administrative punishment of officials.[114] Unlike *Collected Statues of the Qing*, the Board of Personnel regulations identify every potential infraction as either a public offense, an administrative error made in the course of official duties, or a private offense, an intentional violation of public order that served the offender's private interests. It also specifies punishments for each infraction.

In these new publications, procedures that were probably known, if at all, only by word of mouth or were available only in private publications were made transparent. For instance, the Jiaqing edition of *Collected Statutes and Precedents of the Qing* includes the first clear description of the prerogatives the Grand Council had assumed during the Qianlong reign, including the right to determine whether the emperor wished to make a special appointment in the event of a vacancy among the governors corps. This seemed a minor modification in procedure, and yet it represented a formal acknowledgment of the involvement of councilors in selecting governors. In context, this announcement served to emphasize that the Chinese councilors who served the Jiaqing emperor made decisions about appointments in accord with the dynasty's standing rules and statutes. This new emphasis on procedure and order affected not only the dynasty's rule books but the emperor's own pronouncements. Where the Yongzheng emperor had merely announced that an official was dismissed because he had been "implicated in a certain matter," the Qianlong emperor offered extensive moralistic commentary on official offenses, and the Jiaqing emperor specified in detail the statutes officials were accused of violating.[115]

THE NINETEENTH-CENTURY REPRISE

Bureaucratic influence in the Qing served, as it had since time immemorial in Chinese history, to modulate the force and unpredictability of imperial actions. As crises went, the Jiaqing one was a relatively small episode. In only two of the four years of reshaping the bureaucracy, 1799 and 1802, did the Jiaqing emperor dismiss four governors. Moreover, in four years, the Jiaqing emperor made only forty-three appointments, nearly the same number as his father had made in the two years of 1768 and 1769. Of the Jiaqing emperor's forty-three appointments, only sixteen were special appointments. This was not an insignificant number, but it meant that well over half of those appointed by the Jiaqing emperor between 1799 and 1802 were promoted from within the territorial service or transferred from one governor's post to another.

Throughout the early nineteenth century, the territorial service itself was becoming more important as a source for new governors. Strikingly, this trend continued with the Daoguang emperor's ascension to the throne in 1820. Although there was a shake-up of territorial administration between 1818 and 1820—with five governors dismissed in 1818 and twelve appointed in 1819, 1821 and 1822—very few of the appointments were special appointments. Instead, some lieutenant governors were promoted and others reassigned in a process of reorganization that had all the hallmarks of being managed by a group of central officials who were well informed about the capacities and experience of territorial officials.[116] Chastened by the experience of the late eighteenth century, and constrained by those whose role it was to preserve the memory of such experience, Qing emperors ceased in the early nineteenth century to use the power of special appointment to shape the character of the state. This perhaps limited the capacity of the early nineteenth-century state to respond to crises as they arose, but it provided for greater stability in a large and increasingly complex empire.

Significantly, however, the powers of special appointment, though unused, were not forgotten. When crises did confront the Qing order in the later nineteenth century, emperors made good use of their power of special appointment. When Izhu, the fourth son of the Daoguang emperor, ascended the throne as the Xianfeng emperor on 9 March 1850, he began to remake the corps of provincial governors; as this process was under way, the emperor confronted the Taiping Rebellion, which brought chaos to territorial administration in much of central China. The result was a long period of provincial change. In 1851, he dismissed four governors; in 1852, three more governors were dismissed and twelve provincial appointments were made; in 1853, twelve governors were appointed, eight by special appointment, and six governors were dismissed; and in 1854, there were ten appointments, five special appointments, and four dismissals.[117] After 1854, the Xianfeng emperor's interventions in routine personnel processes declined abruptly, nearly as suddenly as had the personnel-related activities of his great-great-grandfather, the Yongzheng emperor. Unlike the workaholic Yongzheng emperor, who then turned to the management of warfare in central Asia, the Xianfeng emperor (at twenty-three, a much younger and less seasoned monarch) was said to have turned to entertainment and dissipation. In the language of a later account that probably reflects early twentieth-century Manchu chauvinism, the Xianfeng period was one in which "whatever was left of virility and patriotism in Beijing gnashed its teeth in impotent rage."[118]

There was a comparable period of reorganization of territorial administration during the Tongzhi period. Following the end of the Taiping Rebellion, Tongzhi statesmen used the power of special appointment to field a largely new territorial administration tasked with reconstruction and rebuilding. In 1862, there were eight special appointments and two dismissals, and in 1863, there were five special appointments and four dismissals.[119] The goal of the central government in the early 1860s was to reshape the provincial bureaucracy. As Mary C. Wright has written, "The able senior officials of the Restoration realized than their policies would be ineffective unless the quality of junior officials was improved, and moreover, unless the rot were checked at once, tomorrow's senior officials would be drawn from today's unimpressive junior officials."[120] The special appointments of the Tongzhi period had two significant characteristics: 1862—63 was the first period of personnel change when all the appointees were Chinese, and most held lower-level positions in the provinces, rather than at the capital, at the time of their appointments.

The nineteenth-century concentrations of special appointments differ from those of the previous century in three respects. First, under the Yongzheng and Qianlong emperors, bursts of special appointments were provoked by crises of confidence at the center, whereas nineteenth-century appointments were spurred by military crises. A second difference was that as a result, while eighteenth-century appointments affected all regions of the empire, nineteenth-century appointments were concentrated in regions affected by war or rebellion. The Xianfeng emperor made special appointments to the middle and lower Yangzi regions in response to the Taiping Rebellion, and the appointments of 1883–84, responses to the Sino-French War, occurred in Fujian and the southwest. Third, nineteenth-century special appointees had more direct military responsibilities than did their predecessors. This development has been the subject of much commentary by historians of late Qing and twentieth-century China, who have argued that the transformation of territorial administrators into proto-warlords, or the general militarization of late Qing society, led to the downfall of dynastic rule in China.[121] As the late Qing is not the primary focus of this volume, no attempt will be made here to engage this debate in detail. But the history of the office of governor described in these chapters suggests that the developments of the mid-nineteenth century represent not so much a novelty as the reemergence of an element long dormant in provincial affairs. The Qing provincial governor had evolved from the Ming grand coordinator, whose role was primarily military. While the nineteenth century may have seen a shift in the governors' military role from logistical to tactical responsibilities, the governors' involvement in the dynasty's military undertakings was hardly new in the nineteenth century.

The more important fact may well have been that when the dynasty was confronted with mortal peril, its leaders relied on the well-established tools of imperial rule, the emperor's capacity to make special appointments to shape the political agenda. Qing imperial powers of discipline and special appointment existed in part to deal with precisely the sort of emergency presented by the military challenges of the nineteenth century. The frenzied appointments of the Xianfeng years, and the more systemic remaking of the bureaucratic order in the Tongzhi period, were certainly dramatic but hardly represented a violation of the principles underlying the Qing provincial government. Even more striking, such measures were at least temporarily successful, giving the dynasty an additional generation of rule after the century's civil war and foreign invasions. Until the dynasty's last days, the power to interrupt routine and produce unexpected results remained a central element of Qing power.

CHAPTER 5

The Imperatives of Continuity

Special appointments made at moments of crisis offer a vivid picture of the politics of discontinuity in Qing China, the moments when specific imperatives forced changes in the direction of policy and the character of leadership. But in the case of a long-lived institution like the Qing dynasty, continuity as well as discontinuity must be explained. Continuity posed its own imperatives, broader perhaps than those that brought about change at specific moments, but equally compelling. Special appointments were used to achieve these purposes, and the use of the prerogative in this way was a particular feature of eighteenth-century politics. Early rulers of dynasties had the liberty to impose their stamp on dynastic institutions by fiat; the Kangxi and Shunzhi emperors could simply decree new procedures. Succeeding emperors did not have such freedom; the canons of filial piety dictated that emperors not overturn the precedents of their ancestors, and change, if it was to come, had to happen incrementally and was often effected through new types of appointees and new interpretations of existing policy. In the Qianlong reign, groups of appointees and the directions they represented were as revealing of the political agenda as were individual postings.

At least three initiatives were apparent in the eighteenth century. The first was the effort, which began in the mid-1740s, to appoint more Manchus to civilian office in China. New Manchu appointments were a result of the Qianlong emperor's changing vision of the role of Manchus in the Qing empire, a vision expressed and reinforced in many of the court publications of the eighteenth century. The vision was informed by the changing demographic situation of the Manchus and the physical growth of the empire. Manchus were sent to every province in the empire and were the beneficiaries, not only of special appointments, but of a variety of other personnel practices the Qing evolved in response to the demands of empire. A second initiative is seen in the dynasty's attempt to forge closer relations between provincial officials and the agencies of central government to which they reported, and so alleviate the hostility and often corruption that attended this nexus. The early Kangxi regulations for appointments established fairly specific tracks leading to territorial office; with the passage of time and the succession of emperors, new offices became important. The special appointment mechanism was used to place in governorships individuals from offices other than those from which routine appointments could be made. The geography of the Chinese empire posed a third imperative for the Qing state. At junior levels in the territorial service, the dynasty formally recognized the different degrees of difficulty of postings, using the system of post designations and placing appointments in certain districts under the control of governors. No such designations were applied to whole provinces, but the issues must have been similar. There were some provinces on the empire's borders in which governors were concerned primarily with matters of military control, and other inland provinces where the somewhat more routine tasks of collecting revenue and adjudicating disputes occupied most of a governor's time. For much of the eighteenth and nineteenth centuries, men who were transferred from one governorship to another administered China's more difficult provinces. In principle, the transfer of governors among provinces could have been accomplished by routine means; governors, like all officials, were eligible for transfer after three years of service. But the pattern of transfers was hardly random. Rather, inter-provincial transfers were guided by a system of priorities comprehensible in terms of the broad geopolitical goals of the state. In brief, the dynasty developed a ladder of appointments, by which officials regularly moved into and through the provinces of south China on their journeys to the prestigious and prosperous provinces of the north.

THE MANCHU IMPERATIVE: HISTORY AND FAMILY

Qianlong appointments of significant numbers of Manchus to provincial office in the middle decades of the eighteenth century represent one of the clearest examples of the use of the special appointment prerogative to change the composition of Chinese officialdom. The practice was not particularly unusual in the eighteenth century; by the early eighteenth century, Manchus already occupied most of the senior offices in Qing bureaucracy and had even moved into the imperial academy and scholarly bureaucracy. What attracted the attention of eighteenth-century literati and, following them, twentieth-century historians were the Manchus appointed to territorial office in the early Qianlong reign.[1] According to the calculations of Narakino Shimesu, Manchus governed China's provinces 13.1 percent of the time in 1738. By 1750, the high point of Manchu influence in the provinces, Manchus governed 71.1 percent of the time, and they occupied provincial governorships at least 50 percent of the time until the early 1770s.[2] The average ratio of Manchu to Chinese appointees for the first thirty-three years of the reign was 1.25 to 1, meaning that five Manchus were appointed governor for every four Chinese during this period. After a brief interlude in the early 1770s, when the numbers of Manchu governors were reduced significantly, Manchus and Chinese were appointed in roughly equal numbers until the end of the Qianlong

reign. Although scholarship has charted the change in numbers of Manchu officials, no reason has as yet been offered for this growth. This was perhaps because
the appointments were the products not of a single initiative but of a variety of
imperatives derived from the changing circumstances of Manchu rule in China.
Specifically, in the early eighteenth century, a group of energetic Manchus accustomed to the ways of Chinese administration found in the Qianlong emperor a
patron willing to use the power of the monarchy in order to achieve his ethnic and
political ends. The result was a flow of appointments that brought Manchus to all
provinces of the empire and had an impact on the office of provincial governor.

Fathers and Sons

One factor in the increased numbers of Manchu appointment was the steady
growth in the Manchu population after the conquest. Population growth was
partly a matter of government policy: as an ethnic minority, Manchus were
encouraged by the state to reproduce, and since Manchus could be legitimately
employed only by the state, positions had to be found for them. There was a
rapid increase in the number of posts in the Manchu officer corps after the Wu
Sangui Rebellion, motivated to some extent by the Qing's perceived vulnerability
in China and also by the growing numbers of those qualified for military office. In
the early Qianlong reign, Manchu population growth may have been particularly
pronounced. In their study of the imperial lineage, James Lee, Cameron Campbell, and Wang Feng note that until the early eighteenth century, birth rates and
death rates were quite high among males in the lineage. In the first decades of
the century, however, death rates fell considerably more rapidly than birth rates,
resulting in an especially large cohort of Manchus who were contemporaries of
the Qianlong emperor.[3] This is not to say that the emperor appointed Manchus
to governorships for the purpose of relieving an overpopulation or underemploy-
ment problem. But it does suggest that a large and active generation of Manchu
officials came of age in the 1740s and 1750s, many of whom could trace their
ancestry to noble families and who sought opportunities to serve their state.

   The publication of *The General History of the Eight Banners* (Ba qi tong zhi) in 1739
served to confirm the entitlement of many young Manchus to Qing office. As the
emperor proclaimed in the edict ordering the volume, the work was meant to
parallel the provincial gazetteers that the governor of each province had been
ordered to compile. But it also had a more specialized purpose—to celebrate
the generation of heroes who founded the dynasty, particularly those who manifested good Confucian virtues in doing so. The book was meant to provide an
account of the "loyal officials and filial sons, virtuous women and martyred wives,
those of hidden virtue and occluded glory."[4] More than half the volume deals

with histories of Manchu heroes, lists of their descendants, and records of heirs to the hereditary captaincies of the banner system. For many Manchu families, this volume represented the first account of their heritage to appear in print and served as written confirmation of their place in the Qing order.

Two eighteenth-century governors, Korjishan (ca. 1670–1750) and his son Dingchang (ca. 1700–1768), could look with pride on their family's records in *The General History of the Eight Banners*. The two men are particularly interesting examples of those who served in Qing territorial service in the eighteenth century, not only because, cumulatively, they served as governors in six Chinese provinces over a period of twenty-six years, but also because they were the fourth and fifth of six generations of their family to serve the state. For more than two hundred years, from the last years of the sixteenth century to the middle years of the nineteenth, ancestors and descendants of Korjishan were appointed to office by Qing emperors, rewarded with hereditary ranks and honors, and celebrated in dynastic historical accounts. It was Hecen (d. ca. 1615) who offered the first service and made the first sacrifice for the new dynasty. In an age when the Manchus were a growing but as yet unnamed confederation of tribes and clans on the edge of the Ming order, Hecen led his clan to swear allegiance to the dynamic leader of the new confederation, Nurhaci. Nurhaci employed Hecen, and presumably his family members, in wars against the rival Ula tribe and then sent Hecen as emissary to urge yet another set of rivals, the Yehe, to join him. The Yehe heard him out on his first visit, but on his second visit they executed him, and Nurhaci responded by launching a military expedition against them. This expedition was successful in 1619, and when the defeated leader of the Yehe was brought to Nurhaci for execution, Hecen's son Keifu (ca. 1600–1650) was allowed to plunge in the dagger in revenge for his father's murder.[5]

After this experience of diplomacy mano a mano, Keifu entered the Manchu armies and participated in a number of Hong Taiji's preconquest battles against the Chinese. While Keifu was serving in the vanguard of the forces accompanying Hong Taiji, who had recently returned to Manchuria after a raid inside the Great Wall, Keifu detected and thwarted a Ming ambush, saving Hong Taiji's life. The grateful ruler bestowed on Keifu a hereditary captaincy in the Plain Yellow Banner, which his family members would inherit into the eighteenth century.[6]

Keifu's descendants extended the dynasty's sphere of control throughout China. One died while holding the family captaincy; another was killed in action in Yunnan in pursuit of the Ming pretender known as the Yongli emperor.[7] But it was Keifu's nephew Kacilan (ca. 1630–1698) who contributed most to the family fortunes. Kacilan inherited hereditary rank in 1649 and commanded troops in armies that attacked Chusan Island in 1654 in pursuit of followers of the Ming pretender Prince Lu. Twenty-four years later, Kacilan led the first wave of troops across the Yangzi River to put down the rebellion of Wu Sangui. As a reward for his services, Kacilan was given command of the Mongol Plain Yellow Banner and, in 1680, given the rank of vice-commander of his own Manchu Plain Yellow Banner. In 1683, the company Kacilan commanded was divided into two; Kacilan continued to command one and passed it on to his son Kaimbu (ca. 1652–1720), while three of Kacilan's other sons commanded the second.[8]

The contributions of Hecen's descendants to the nascent Qing order were those that were required in their times. The names Keifu and Kacilan in fact both mean "arrow" in Manchu, *keifu* being the arrow used for shooting tigers, bears, and deer, and *kacilan* being the sort of arrow used in target practice.[9] By the late Kangxi reign, however, the family began to reorient itself toward civilian service. This process occurred in slow stages, beginning with Korjishan's father Kaimbu, who, after inheriting the family captaincy and demonstrating his administrative talents, was sent as a censor to investigate the condition of the Manchu arsenal in Shanxi. Upon his return, he began his ascent through the ranks of the civil bureaucracy, rising to the post of Manchu member of the Board of Finance. He was then transferred to the military service and was appointed vice-commander of the Chinese Plain Yellow Banner, then of the Manchu Plain Yellow Banner, before he was dispatched to Guangdong to put down a rebellion of the Miao. After the rebellion, he returned to the capital and was appointed Manchu president of the Board of Finance in 1701.[10]

When Kaimbu died at the beginning of the Yongzheng reign, he had every reason to expect that his family's place in the Qing order was secure. Both he and his father had enjoyed personal relations with Qing monarchs, and the main and collateral branches of the family were spread throughout the Qing civil and military orders. In the Yongzheng reign, however, the social and political worlds of the Manchus were changing, and the security the banner elite had enjoyed in the late seventeenth century was eroding. During the course of his reign, the Yongzheng emperor dismissed twelve commanders and seventeen vice-commanders of banner armies for various sorts of incompetence and ordered that banner captains would be appointed on the basis of heredity only when more competent persons were not available.[11] The new regimen touched Korjishan directly. When Kaimbu died, Korjishan's older brother Siming initially inherited one of the two family captaincies. By the middle of the reign, Siming had also become an assistant department director at one of the six boards in the capital. In 1727, he was cashiered for unspecified offenses and passed on the family captaincy to Korjishan.[12]

Korjishan met the Qianlong emperor for the first time in the summer of 1736, beginning an official relationship that would continue uninterrupted until Korjishan's death in 1757. But the circumstances under which Korjishan met the new monarch were quite different from the occasions on which his ancestors had met early Qing rulers. In the spring of 1735, Korjishan had submitted, in his capacity as a member of the Imperial Stud, a report on horse husbandry that was found to be inaccurate. The Yongzheng emperor, still smarting from the failure of his campaigns in the northwest, was angered by the report and dismissed Korjishan from his civil and military offices. The Manchu officer was ordered to return to the Plain Yellow Banner lands in Manchuria. Shortly after the Qianlong emperor came to the throne, he was apprised by the Board of War that there were a number of senior Manchu officials in Korjishan's position, "officials whose talents were being wasted" (*fei yuan*) because of administrative discipline undertaken in the Yongzheng reign. Acknowledging that the transgressions of such senior officials were probably not minor matters, the emperor nonetheless interviewed the most promising of these officials and arranged for them to work without salaries until they had sufficiently compensated the government for their errors. Five days later, on 24 June 1736, Korjishan was one of eleven high-ranking Manchus who were ushered into the emperor's presence. Two were appointed to positions as vice-commanders of banner armies, and a third had his name entered on the lists of those waiting appointment as vice-commander; six were appointed colonels in banner armies; and one (Echang, Ortai's nephew) was ordered to serve as a clerk in the Grand Council. Korjishan was one of two selected for service in the elite companies that guarded the imperial summer palace.[13]

After rescuing Korjishan from the ignominy of life on the farm, the Qianlong emperor proceeded to employ the Manchu as a troubleshooter, circulating him throughout the empire as necessary. In 1740, Korjishan received his first appointment as governor, in Shanxi, where he was charged with untangling the corruption associated with his predecessor in the province, Shilin, a Manchu of the Aisin Gioro clan and the Plain Red Banner. After thirteen years in office, during which he was reputed to have lined his own pockets, Shilin left the province's hydraulic works in disrepair and the provincial treasuries empty when he departed office to mourn his mother.[14] After Korjishan reorganized finances and hydraulic works in Shanxi, in 1743 he was transferred to Shandong, where he arrived in the second year of a three-year drought. His memorials from Shandong dealt with refugees from the famine, the delicate task of balancing grain reserves in order to meet subsistence needs and feed the armies garrisoned in the province. In 1746, Korjishan was promoted to governor-general of Min-zhe, a post he held until his death in 1757. In this post he was concerned primarily with border defense and disorder in Taiwan, although three Manchu governors of Zhejiang also were indicted and dismissed for corruption during his term.

Dingchang, Korjishan's son, had a somewhat smoother ride to high office but ultimately enjoyed a career parallel to his father's. Dingchang was the first in his family to possess a civil service degree, although his status, that of *jiansheng* (licentiate), was the lowest within the Chinese system. He was nonetheless appointed as prefect in 1744 and within six years rose through the hierarchy of territorial positions to the post of governor of Guizhou, where he served a largely routine term, from 1752 to 1757. In 1757, Dingchang, along with many Manchus of his generation, was sent to the northwest with the Qianlong campaign. Dingchang's role was to manage military garrison lands. When the wars were over, a remarkable sequence of events unfolded, which spoke volumes about the late eighteenth-century Manchu world. The Qianlong emperor had noted with pleasure that both Korjishan and his son were serving successfully in territorial service at the same time. After the war, the monarch went a step further and appointed Dingchang to the governorship of Fujian, where he served from 1761 to 1766. The governorship of Fujian was located in the same city as the governor-generalship, which meant that father and son presided over the coastal political order for nearly twenty years. After his successful service in Fujian, Dingchang was promoted to governor-general of Huguang, a post he held until his death in 1768.[15] A governor-generalship was the highest position the descendants of Hecen attained, but the family continued to play an administrative role after Dingchang's death. During the Jiaqing reign, Eyunbu, Korjishan's grandson and Dingchang's nephew, served as governor of Guizhou (1809–10). The family seemed an almost paradigmatic case of a Manchu family that extended its range of competence as it grew, responding to the new opportunities and demands of the Qing state. They achieved as much as could be accomplished in Qing China by Manchus who were not members of the imperial lineage, and they did it with grace and dignity

MANCHU IDENTITIES: FOUR CAREERS

Numbers alone—of young Manchus either available for or appointed to office—did not tell the full story of Manchu careers in the eighteenth century; politics and policy played their parts. As the Qianlong emperor favored Manchus in senior appointments, he also sought to articulate a new role for them in the Qing state. Both the Kangxi and Yongzheng emperors had seen the problem of relations between the Manchus and Chinese in terms of the paradigm of assimilation. They were inclined to argue that the "Aisin Gioro lineage . . . had been culturally and morally transformed and for this reason were fit to rule China." Perhaps the strongest statement of this position was the Yongzheng emperor's assertion in *A Record of Great Righteousness Resolving Confusion* (Da yi jue mi lu) that the transforming effect of the Chinese culture was sufficiently great that even the beasts, if they embodied the way of the ancient sages, were fit to rule.[16] The Qianlong emperor, however, in Crossley's argument, rejected the prospect of cultural and moral transformation. "The Qing were fit to rule China because heaven had backed the struggles of Nurhaci and Hong Taiji against the Ming, and because the emperor's consciousness was an extension of the mind of heaven." In short, Manchus of Qianlong's generation were no longer to be subjected to the pressures of conforming to Chinese ways of life and government. They were to be not the assimilated managers of a Chinese state but the proud administrators of a universal empire.[17]

Such a view of the Qing polity opened the way for the appointment of many more Manchus to office in the eighteenth-century Qing state. It also meant that such appointments could not be made through mechanisms of premodern affirmative action, special rules that permitted Manchus to occupy particular positions. Rather, all positions had to be opened to Manchus who were assumed to prevail, to the extent that they did, on the basis of talent, not origins. This represented a new position and raised concern among Chinese scholars who observed it. In 1742, a Chinese censor memorialized the throne on the subject of Manchus holding territorial appointments, expressing fear that since "Manchu officials were not learned or practiced in the way of caring for the people, if they were suddenly assigned as territorial officials, they might well fail in their duties, and be indicted," which, as he remarked, would be "much to be regretted." The Qianlong emperor responded:

> In heaven's creation of human talent, there is no difference between physical places of origin. In the past Manchus haven't been used as prefects or magistrates because the Manchu population was not large. However, now the number of talented Manchus has grown by several fold. There are more than enough of them to fill capital positions, and the queues for certain offices have become clogged. Positions in the capital or in the territories are all in service to the throne. How could it be that Manchu officials can occupy all the capital posts managing punishments and the collection of revenue, and not serve as magistrates? Or that Manchus could be qualified to serve as governor, or censors of circuit, and not be able to hold lower posts?[18]

Five months later, the classicist Hang Shijun wrote in answer to a policy question posed on the civil examinations that "court opinions should neither be preformed nor biased" when it came to making appointments. "Although there are many talented Manchus, Chinese occupy only about 30–40 percent of the governorships, and Manchus occupy the majority of posts. There is not a single Chinese among the governors-general." Hang further complained about the locations of Manchu and Chinese officials: "Why is it that Manchus are posted in the interior provinces of China, whereas Chinese are posted in the border provinces?"[19] The

Qianlong emperor responded: "There has never been any single technique for finding and appointing talented people. There is simply the way of ancient kings and emperors. Even though Manchus and Chinese are different, they are both united in one body. I have never had any prejudice for one over the other."[20]

The rhetoric of both emperor and censor implies that Chinese and Manchus were two consistent orders. But since the time of the conquest, social differences had emerged among the Manchus and were only accentuated by the eighteenth-century competition for office. Korjishan and Dingchang had many advantages as they contemplated official careers with the Qing. They held hereditary office in one of the prestigious upper three banners, directly under control of the emperor, and their family had proved its competence in both peace and war. They had personal relationships with the Qianlong emperor, and, in Korjishan's case, the tie was secure enough to allow him to attack other Manchus for corruption without fear of being disciplined himself. Not all eighteenth-century Manchus had such advantages. Most deployed such cultural and social capital as they could in the competition for office. Some turned to the civil service examinations, earning degrees beyond that of *jiansheng* Dingchang held; others became master of complex administrative procedures; while still others committed themselves to military service or to Manchu traditions like the hunt, what Mark Elliott has called the "invented tradition" of Manchu identity in the eighteenth century.[21] The process undermined the coherence of the Manchu order, but it also produced Manchu officials with very different specialties and personalities.

Different Manchu attributes were prized by the Qing court at different times during the dynasty. In the early eighteenth century, most Manchus who sought to advance their careers within the Qing bureaucracy did so by conforming to the model for Chinese officials, learning classical Chinese and bureaucratic terminology and earning official degrees. Ortai, for instance, held the *juren* degree, and the *nianpu* (chronological biography) written by his son emphasized the early age at which he had learned to read Chinese and his literary abilities. Ortai's protégés were both Chinese and Manchu. His political career had begun in the Yongzheng court, where administrative ability was prized above all else, including ethnic identity and linguistic skills.[22] The poet Yuan Mei, who was briefly a protégé of Ortai's, experienced this firsthand when the grand councilor evaluated his examination in Manchu. After determining that Yuan Mei had failed, Ortai invited him to dinner and assured him that the failure would not unduly affect his career. "When the emperor sees you," he said, "I am sure your appearance alone will make him anxious to use you. I do not doubt that as a provincial official you would show yourself perfectly competent."[23] In fact, Yuan was appointed prefect in two districts in Jiangsu, posts in which he served from 1742 to 1753.

After the middle of the eighteenth century, however, imperial attitudes toward

Manchus changed. Events in the late 1740s seemed to conspire to undermine the emperor's faith in the Manchus who served closest to him. The deaths of his father's close friend Ortai and his beloved Xiaoxian empress provoked a rethinking of mission, perhaps even a midlife crisis for the forty-eight-year-old monarch. At the same time, the failure of Qing armies to suppress a rebellion of Tibetan-speaking peoples in western Sichuan tested the emperor's patience. The most spectacular instance of Qianlong reaction against sinicized Manchus was the execution of Nuoqin in 1749. Nuoqin was a hereditary Manchu noble whose first appointment was to the Grand Council in the late Yongzheng reign. During the early Qianlong reign, as the council became more important, so did Nuoqin, who served as president of the Boards of Revenue and Personnel. Nuoqin proved to be a capable although rigid and arrogant administrator; his career before 1748 had unfolded entirely in Beijing and rested on his mastery of Chinese administrative procedures. In 1748, Nuoqin was dispatched to the southwest to supervise the response to the Jinchuan Rebellion. Having no military experience, he was at first too bold, then too cautious, and ultimately ineffective. After an investigation marked by numerous factional charges and countercharges, Nuoqin was found guilty of cowardice and ordered to commit suicide using his grandfather's sword.[24] Also in 1748, the Qianlong emperor engaged in sharp and extended criticism of his fellow Manchus for not observing ancient mourning rituals for the empress by letting their hair grow and not shaving the front of their heads. Certainly the emperor's grief, and a concern for ritual propriety, led him to react with such passion to the evidence that Manchu governors were not mourning in the proper way. But the emperor's accusation took the form of an angry cry that Manchu governors had forgotten their heritage. Governor Saileng'e who seemed to the emperor a particularly egregious offender, was cashiered and eventually executed. Saileng'e was the first provincial governor executed in the Qianlong reign.[25]

If a Manchu was qualified to serve in office by virtue of being Manchu, then there was little need for ambitious young men to earn Chinese-style credentials. In fact, as the emperor made clear, an effort to earn Chinese credentials could lead Manchus to develop bad habits. Some years earlier in 1758, he had written to Kaitai, another Manchu *jinshi*-degree holder, "I had never expected that among Manchu officials there would be a thing [*wu*] quite as useless as you."[26] The emperor wrote to the *jinshi*-holding Zhongyin in 1777: "There is probably not a single good man among Manchu degree holders."[27]

Neither reprimand was entirely fair. Kaitai had governed Hubei (1745–46), Jiangxi (1746–48), Hunan (1748–50), and Guangxi (1750–53) and coordinated the logistics of the first Jinchuan campaign. Zhongyin had governed Shaanxi (1753–54, 1758–62), Guangdong (1767–68), and Gujian (1770–71). In these instances, the emperor was expressing his displeasure, but he did not mean to suggest that either official should be removed. Nonetheless, his rebukes reflected a genuine suspicion of Manchus who had abandoned their (imagined) heritage for Chinese ways. Abandoning Manchus who affected Chinese administrative styles, the emperor turned after 1748 to Manchus whose expertise was primarily in military matters. In some instances, civilian postings as governor were rewards for military officers who had distinguished themselves on the field of battle, while in other instances, managers of military logistics, once promoted to governor in provinces that provided supplies to the army, went on to govern in other provinces of the empire.[28]

Until the end of his reign, the emperor held to his vision of appropriate Manchu conduct, which he endorsed at mid-century. There was, however, some reduction in Manchu appointments in the 1770s. Liu Tongxun did not significantly reduce the number of Manchu governors, but Yu Minzhong did. After Yu's death, approximately equal numbers of Manchus and Chinese were appointed until the end of the reign. Heshen himself proved to be a somewhat ambiguous model for his fellow Manchus. He was a poor manager of military affairs, although he was extremely defensive about his performance. In fact, Heshen seems to have gained the emperor's attention by his ability with classical texts and his talent for writing poetry.[29] In the last decades of the reign, Manchu careers may have depended less on how officials acted and more on whom they knew or could come to know by the presentation of appropriate gifts.

There was no model Manchu career in eighteenth-century China, just as there was no typical Manchu. Rather, there were multiple career paths created as individuals and families dealt with the challenge of living in an empire much changed from the one their fathers and grandfathers had conquered. The record of careers begun and ended changed conceptions of the elements that constituted true Manchu-ness, and the often serious consequences of violating the standard speak vividly of the challenges of the eighteenth century. In the case of governors, there were some whose careers were founded on association with the emperor, military prowess, and ascent of routine career ladders. Each sort of governor made a different contribution to the eighteenth-century state, and the effect of "the Manchu imperative" must ultimately be measured in individual lives. The careers of four—Henian and Guilin, Mingde and Tuerbing'a—suggest some of the range of possibilities.

Henian and Guilin

In the Qing as in any political system, being a favorite, or more charitably, a trusted friend of the court, could lead to special appointments and perquisites. Qing emperors were not capricious in their personal selections, however, and most special appointees from the court possessed fairly predictable categories of social elements necessary for the preservation of the dynasty. Only thirty-one of the special appointees held positions close enough to the throne to have had significant regular contact with the emperor prior to their appointments as governors.[30] The most common position was superintendent of the capital granaries (sixteen appointees). This was essentially a military institution, concerned with the logistics of feeding the capital military establishment.[31] In the eighteenth century, the position was held mostly by Manchus, and for Manchu officers, it served as a stepping-stone from the banner administration into civilian administration. Henian, a Manchu who held a *jinshi* degree, followed this route in the 1750s. Henian came from the same banner as Ortai, the Bordered Blue, which was traditionally ranked last among the banners, and like the family of Ortai, Henian's family tried to raise its prestige with classical studies. Both Henian and his father Chunshan earned the *jinshi* degree, Chunshan in 1708 and Henian in 1736. No source attests to an association between Henian and Ortai, but they certainly would have known each other; Henian could well have been a protégé.[32]

Throughout his career, Henian was a man marked for senior service. After receiving his *jinshi* degree, Henian spent the first five years of the Qianlong reign at the Hanlin Academy and the next five years with the title Diarist of Action and Repose, responsible for recording the actions and words of the emperor. After spending the first fifteen years of his career at the Qianlong court, he was appointed superintendent of capital granaries in 1750 and served in this post for three years. Henian may have had much to learn in the world of line administration. In 1751, he was formally cashiered for shortages in the granaries but remained at his post; the next year, he indicted one of his Manchu subordinates for incompetence and indolence. Having served his apprenticeship in the capital, Henian was appointed governor of Guangdong (1753–56) and then Shandong (1756–57). Much of his early work in both provinces was in the area of grain management and military garrisons. During his term as governor of Shandong, Henian developed an interest in the maintenance of the Grand Canal and expressly requested that he be left at his post to devote himself to this work rather than accept the promotion to governor-general he had been offered. The emperor initially ordered Henian to go to Guangdong because, as Qianlong remarked, Henian was the only man he knew (or could trust?) for the position. Two months later, the emperor relented and left Henian in Shandong, where he died in 1757.[33] Throughout his life, the emperor took an interest in Henian's career, even writing a poem in 1757 to celebrate Henian's talents. Henian's career was marked by pragmatism above all; although he had a *jinshi* degree, he applied himself to the tasks he saw before him, earning imperial praise and canonization.

Guilin, Henian's son, was equally pragmatic, but when he came of age, the

Qing state's needs were different. Despite his father's academic credentials, Guilin did not pursue an academic career but used the *yin* privilege his father had earned and claimed a place on the staff of the Board of Works and then the Board of Revenue. He also apparently served briefly as a Grand Council clerk, and in this capacity, he was sent to oversee the military response to the second Jinchuan Rebellion. His activist response initially earned the emperor's praise, and Guilin was appointed governor-general of Sichuan. Then, when his armies failed, he was condemned and exiled to Ili for six years. Eventually, his name was cleared, and he was reappointed governor-general of Sichuan and then transferred to Guangdong, the post his father had turned down in order to remain in Shandong and work on the Grand Canal.[34] Henian's career in itself, and particularly its early years, suggests a pattern of assimilation to Chinese ways and administrative style. But the lives of father and son together were more complex and highlight changing assumptions about Manchu success through the Qianlong reign.

Mingde

The combination of roles that Henian and Guilin undertook in civil and military administration was fairly common in the middle of the eighteenth century, and it created its own potentials and problems. Specifically, it placed Manchus, whose primary experience was in military matters, over civilians; unless care was exercised, the flows of money necessary to support both roles could easily become commingled. This peril is reflected in the career of Mingde, a Manchu of the Plain Red Banner who held ten governorships, more than any other Manchu, in the middle of the eighteenth century.[35] Mingde had some provincial experience early in his career, and was even governor of Shanxi for a year. But his career took off after he served as Huang Tinggui's lieutenant governor in Sichuan. In the early years of his career, Huang Tinggui had been a leader of troops in the campaigns against the Miao in the southwest, but by the late 1740s, he was specializing in military logistics.[36] Together, Huang and Mingde managed the logistics of the wars against the Mongols in 1754–56 as well as of famine relief in Shanxi. During the war years, Mingde held brief appointments as governor of Shanxi and Gansu.[37] After the war, he returned to both provinces for longer terms but remained concerned with issues related to military logistics. From 1765 to 1768, he served as governor of Jiangsu and earned the emperor's praise with his vigorous investigations of provincial affairs. In 1768, he was moved to Yunnan, where he was meant to oversee logistics for the Burma campaign, but as that effort bogged down, he was blamed for its failure. Having been promoted to governor-general of Yun-gui in the winter of 1769, he was demoted to Yunnan governor, a post he held until his death in the autumn of 1771.[38]

During the course of this remarkable career, Mingde had several brushes with administrative discipline. In 1757, during his second term as governor of Shanxi, he served alongside lieutenant governor Jiang Zhou, the son of the Kangxi era courtier Jiang Tingxi. Shortly after he was promoted to governor of Shandong, Jiang Zhou was found guilty of having extorted money from local officials in Shanxi. No proof was found that Mingde had profited personally from this extortion, but as the emperor noted, how could Mingde, whose yamen adjoined that of Jiang Zhou, not have been aware of such extortion?[39] Mingde was reprimanded but not removed from his post. Sometime later, he was involved in the case of Duan Chenggong, prefect of Suzhou, who seemed unable to prevent his domestic staff from extorting money from those they encountered in their official capacities.[40] Before Mingde's appointment, officials in Jiangsu suspected Duan's underlings of extorting funds, but his predecessor Zhuang Yougong reported that Duan was unaware of his underlings' activities. Once in office, Mingde reported that Duan was well aware of what his staff was up to.[41] As it developed, Duan had a long history of extortion, much of which he had practiced while he was a subordinate of Mingde's brother, Governor Heqizhong of Shanxi. In fact, Duan had illicitly raised the money to support Heqizhong's visit to the imperial summer palace at Rehe, which, what with clothes and gifts and transport, was an expensive proposition. During interrogation, local officials in Jiangsu confessed that Zhuang Yougong had advised them to protect Duan, because of his connection with the incoming governor Mingde and his brother.[42] Infuriated, the emperor ordered Zhuang Yougong dismissed, Heqizhong executed, and a host of other officials sentenced to execution following the autumn assizes (this postponement usually resulted in a commuted sentence).

In this case, Mingde emerged as something of a hero, reporting the crucial information that led to his corrupt brother's execution. But the association between Manchu governors and corruption was obviously complex. Manchu governors seem not, of themselves, to have created a culture of corruption in provincial office. Edicts on corruption cases focused more often on the Chinese officials who facilitated Manchu corruption than on the Manchus themselves. This may have been a way of protecting Manchus from accusation, but clearly the governors themselves did not create new sorts of financial manipulation. The problem was that Manchu governors were members of a very small and intertwined elite that had extraordinary access to the emperor. Chinese officials who wanted to profit professionally from this access served Manchu officials in many ways, licit and illicit, and Manchus could often profit personally from their services. Mingde escaped accusation, perhaps because he was more honest, more useful, or better connected than most, but his career illustrates some of the weaknesses of Qianlong's Manchu appointments practice.

Tuerbing'a

The Qianlong emperor's vision of Manchus serving as the equals of Chinese precluded the development of special procedures for the appointment of Manchus. But in many respects, Manchus were different from their Chinese counterparts: their experiences had been different, they enjoyed different relations with their colleagues and the court, and their educations often were different from those of their Chinese counterparts. For these reasons, special procedures were often called for, but they more often represented new emphases in existing procedures, not new procedures. This was the case with the eighteenth-century practice of reappointing to office those who had been indicted, cashiered, and dismissed from office as a result of administrative discipline.[43] Such a reappointment was a mark of imperial favor, although in this instance, imperial benevolence for governors paralleled that offered to other officials. The threat or reality of administrative discipline was probably more of a presence in the lives of all Qing officials than it had been for their counterparts in previous dynasties. As the Qing administrative order developed, not only were most official actions subject to regulation, but penalties were established for nonperformance or malfeasance. This danger was compounded for senior officials by the growth of the secret palace memorial system, which allowed officials to report on one another confidentially without the strictures on evidence provided in routine memorials of indictment.[44] Faced with the growth of accusations and administrative punishments, the Yongzheng emperor reflected in 1729 that, "in instances in which territorial officials have been cashiered, I fear that there are often talents that could still be employed. The reasons for their dismissals may only be technical, and I cannot bear the thought of rendering officials useless for the rest of their lives."[45] Yongzheng's concerns were probably directed at junior officials, but as the eighteenth century progressed, the principle behind them was applied to senior officials. In the Qianlong reign, a dismissed governor could seek reinstatement by greeting the imperial carriage as it passed through his home district or volunteering his service as a manager of logistics for a military campaign or engineering project.[46] Governors could also be reinstated after a time in exile, and Joanna Waley-Cohen has argued that in mid-eighteenth-century China, exile often meant serving as an administrator in the territories of central Asia that the Qing had conquered in the 1750s and 1760s.[47]

There thus existed procedures through which a governor might be reinstated, but not all governors used them. Reappointments after dismissal were most common during the Qianlong reign, when at least sixteen of the eighty-one governors who were removed from office by means of administrative discipline—cashiering, demotion, relief, and summons—earned reinstatement in one way or another (see table 5.1).[48]

TABLE 5.1. Governors Dismissed and Reappointed, Qianlong Reign

Name of Governor	Dismissed	Reappointed
Xu Rong	Gansu 1736–44	Jiangsu 1738–45
Yuan Zhancheng	Guizhou 1735–43	Shanxi 1737–39
Tuoyong	Guangxi 1746–54	Anhui 1761–62
Tuerbing'a	Yunnan 1750–57	Honan 1761–62
Yonggui	Zhejiang 1751–1812	Shaanxi 1757–1810
Zhou Renji	Zhejiang 1756–62	Guangdong 1756–1810
Mingde	Shaanxi 1757–1810	Gansu 1759–1801
Asha	Jiangxi 1760–1810	Henan 1763–66
Song Bangsui	Hubei 1763–65	Guangxi 1765–73
Tang Bin	Jiangxi 1763–65	Hubei 1765–1811
Li Hu	Yunnan 1775–82	Hunan 1778–83
Sun Shiyi	Yunnan 1780–83	Guangxi 1783–85
Fusong	Shanxi 1786–89	Jiangsu 1790–92
Changlin	Shandong 1790–99	Jiangsu 1790–1810
Qin Cheng'en	Shaanxi 1790–1810	Jiangxi 1802–11
Chen Yongfu	Guizhou 1795–1802	Anhui 1799–1801

Sources: *Qingdai zhi guan nian biao* (QDZGNB) data; QDZGNB.

About half of the reinstated governors were Manchus, particularly those appointed during the era of Fuheng, but clearly the procedure was open to Chinese governors as well. One Manchu who benefited from the Qing reappointment policy was Tuerbing'a, a member of the Plain White Banner, who was twice dismissed and twice reappointed during seventeen years as provincial governor.[49] He was dismissed from his first appointment, as governor of Yunnan, when he was accused by his superior, the Yun-gui governor-general, of colluding with his subordinates to cover the arrears of one magistrate by reporting that the money had been used for military provisions. When an imperial commissioner ascertained the truth of the charge, Tuerbing'a was recalled to Beijing and turned over to the Board of Punishments for discipline.[50] The emperor intervened and appointed Tuerbing'a to the Board of Personnel. Two months later, he was appointed lieutenant governor of Henan, where he served for four years before being promoted to governor in 1754. A year later, as the emperor passed through Zhili on a southern tour, a former Jiangsu lieutenant governor from eastern Henan, Peng Jiaping, greeted the imperial carriage and informed the emperor of a flood in his native district. When the emperor asked Tuerbing'a about the flood, the governor reported that the region had mostly recovered, and there was no need to distribute relief. Upon investigation, his account was found to be inaccurate, and he was dismissed from office.[51] But in the meantime, Tuerbing'a found a favorable biography of Wu Sangui hidden in one of the counties affected by the flood, and the emperor judged that Tuerbing'a's accomplishment in finding the treasonous book outweighed his failure to report the flood. The matter became even more complicated when Peng Jiaping admitted during interrogation that his family also possessed writings from the late Ming dynasty that were critical of the Qing.[52] However, Tuerbing'a was later found to have been niggardly in the distribution of flood relief, supposedly because of a grudge against the flooded area, and he was formally cashiered and ordered to Uliasutai to manage military logistics.[53] Five years later, in 1765, Tuerbing'a was recalled and appointed governor of Guizhou, where he served without incident until his death in 1765.

In both these cases, there were reasons the emperor chose to become involved. Tuerbing'a was clearly at fault in the Yunnan case, but the amount of tax revenue involved was not great, and the emperor seemed more impressed that Governor-general Shuose had discovered and reported the irregularities than that Tuerbing'a had erred. In the Henan case, levels of guilt and responsibility were quite intricate and probably could not be left to routine procedures of assessment. In fact, the case developed into an ideological grudge match. Chinese accused Manchus of failing to provide for the welfare of the Chinese population, and Manchus accused Chinese of treason. Removing the Manchu governor from the scene was probably the most effective way of defusing a complicated situation without spelling out responsibilities. Tuerbing'a was fortunate that he was called upon to expiate his guilt at a moment when Manchu armies were on the march in central Asia and there were opportunities for well-placed Manchus to demonstrate their capacities. He served until the end of the campaign and then returned to a posting in China proper.

Assessing the impact of the series of appointments, which is here termed the "Manchu imperative," is a complex task. One reason is the sheer number of Manchu governors, who brought very different backgrounds to their roles and had rather different accomplishments. Moreover, there is little in the primary source record with which to assess the special contributions of Manchus, since it was an assumption of state policy that they were equal to their Chinese peers. Certainly, the appointment of significant numbers of Manchus did have the effect of demonstrating that Manchus could govern the empire they had conquered, as the Qianlong emperor intended. There were many competent, though often unsung, governors among the Manchus. Korjishan dealt effectively with corruption in Shanxi and famine in Shandong; Henian reorganized military supply procedures in Guangdong and worked on refurbishing the Grand Canal. The most effective Manchu governors had to concede nothing to their Chinese counterparts in terms of ability or achievement. There may have been some tendency among Manchu governors to specialize in certain spheres of territorial administration rather than to affect the role of the Confucian gentleman-generalist, but given the growing complexity of eighteenth-century administration, this was perhaps a necessary trend, which all governors should have observed. The main characteristic of Manchus in office in the eighteenth century may have been their interrelatedness: they had a denser, and, for Chinese, impenetrable, web of ties among themselves and to the inner court than did Chinese officials. This surely complicated their lives, as the curious episode of Mingde and Heqizhong suggests, introducing new variables of connection into an already corrupt world. Finally, as the cases of Tuerbing'a and the protest of Hang Shijun suggest, even if the emperor believed that Manchus could serve in the same capacities as Chinese, not all Chinese saw the matter in these same terms. To many, the appointment of Manchus to provincial office represented a regrettable militarization of civilian administration. The currency of this perception, together with the corruption cases of the last years of the eighteenth century, may well have been the reason for the rapid decline in Manchu appointments after the turn of the nineteenth century. If the Qianlong emperor was convinced that Manchus could govern the empire they had conquered, his descendants and the Chinese who advised them were not, and they ceased to use the special appointments procedure as a means toward securing this end.

APPOINTMENTS FROM THE SIX BOARDS

Some degree of functional specialization is implicit in all bureaucratic orders: if officials are to be rewarded for the effective performance of duties, then those who have repeatedly performed the same function are at an advantage. In China, there were limits to this phenomenon established by the Confucian concept of the generalist, the view that a gentleman was never to be merely a tool of the state. Nonetheless, much of Qing administrative reform centered on the creation of hierarchies, through which officials might rise as they gained skill and the good opinion of senior colleagues. *Collected Statutes of the Qing* set out in some detail the separate functional hierarchies within the Qing civil service and even provided for a special form of appointment, known as "transfer" (*gai*), for officials who were moved from one hierarchy to another.[54] These regulations did not discuss provincial governors, whose appointments were decided by the emperor, but they did highlight systematic differences in career patterns that often produced varied outlooks on the problems of government. Both text and appointment records demonstrate that special appointments were used throughout the Qing to move officials from one career ladder to another. This was done both to assure that the perspective of one branch of government was represented among the other branches and to accommodate inevitable changes in the power of government branches as personnel and policy evolved.

Table 5.2 groups the 399 special appointees to governorships between 1700 and 1900 according to the positions they held at the time of their appointments. These appointments can be broadly divided into three groups. Special appointees from the court and the senior military service as well as those reappointed after discipline were the first group, likely to have been known by the emperor prior to their appointments. In fact, most of the Manchus appointed to governors' posts came from these categories. Appointees raised to governorships from posts in the territorial service and the grain, salt, and river administrations, a second group, were likely recommended by territorial officials, and their increasing numbers in the latter part of the eighteenth century suggest the growing importance and independence of the provincial service. Although these appointments violated hierarchical principles, they did so in service of perceived needs, which had to be addressed in order for the Qing to continue its rule in China. Perhaps most striking, more than one-third, 155 out of 473, of the men appointed by special order to provincial governorships between 1700 and 1900 came from a third group, men who were serving at one of the six boards in the capital at the time of their appointments.

Early Qing regulations on the appointment of provincial governors provided for the routine appointment to governorships of individuals from the Grand Sec-

TABLE 5.2. Positions Held by Special Appointees at Time of Appointment, 1700–1900

Agency	Number of Appointees	Percentage of Appointees
Capital		
Six boards	155	33%
Other agencies	104	22%
Reappointment after mourning and discipline	66	14%
Military	25	5%
Provincial office	52	11%
Grain, river, and salt administrations	44	11%
Miscellaneous	27	5%
Totals	473	100%

Sources: *Qingdai zhi guan nian biao* (QDZGNB) data; QDZGNB.

TABLE 5.3. Governors from the Six Boards

Board	Number of Employees	Percentage of Total Boards	Governors	Percentage of Governors
Personnel	157	12.5%	14	8.4%
Revenue	313	24.9%	28	18%
Rites	87	6.9%	14	8.4%
War	151	12%	25	16%
Punishments	301	24.4%	56	35%
Works	242	19.2%	18	11.3%
Total	1,249	100%	155	100%

Sources: For governors' appointments, *Qingdai zhi guan nian biao* (QDZGNB) data; QDZGNB. For numbers of officials in Boards of Revenue, Personnel, Rites, and War, *Da Qing huidian shili*, Guanxu ed. (DQHDSL), juan 20. For numbers of officials in Boards of Punishments and Works, DQHDSL, juan 21.

retariat, which created a conduit from the court to territorial administration. This practice declined precipitously in the Yongzheng reign, in part probably because the emperor was suspicious of those around him in the capital. But in the long run, the six boards, agencies of the specialized functions of Qing government, eclipsed the Grand Secretariat, formerly the office in the capital with the most control over territorial administration, and as this happened, board personnel replaced grand secretaries as provincial governors (see table 5.3).

The largest group of appointees from a board, fifty-five (35 percent), served in the Board of Punishments; the next largest groups were from the Boards of War and Revenue, with Revenue contributing more in numbers, but War contributing more as a proportion of its size. In fact, judicial, military, and financial affairs were the areas of most conspicuous interaction between provincial governors and the central government. In the Ming, the members of the Boards of War and Revenue had the prerogative of nominating provincial *xunfu* for provinces in which military or financial affairs were particularly salient. Judicial affairs perhaps became more important in the Qing, as the provincial judge became a direct subordinate of the governor.

The regular exchange of personnel between the boards and governors' yamens highlights an increasingly important and somewhat vexed relationship in the eighteenth-century Qing state. The six boards were fairly small organizations of midlevel officials at the capital who exercised control over affairs of state in the six traditional divisions of Chinese government—personnel, finance, ritual, public works, justice, and military administration. One of their responsibilities was to review and record governors' reports within their spheres of competence; when governors' submissions did not accord with regulation and precedent, the boards had the right to refuse their reports, in effect refusing to legitimize their actions. The Boards of War, Revenue, and Punishments were organized explicitly for the purpose of reviewing provincial affairs and were divided into offices corresponding to the provinces. Most often, these offices combined a territorial purview with a more specialized function. Thus, for instance, the Jiangsu provincial office of the Board of Punishments dealt with documentation from Jiangsu and imperial pardons. The Shaanxi office reviewed that province's affairs along with cases from Gansu and Xinjiang and also managed the prison system. The boards thus served as a check on the authority of territorial officials, giving rise to opposition between the governors and the boards.[55]

This opposition had to be contained if government was to function at all. Informally, cash helped ease this particular administrative problem. Governors provided the boards with certain amounts of cash, known as "board fees" (*bu fei*), in order to assure that their reports and accounting would be approved. In the early days of the Qing, board fees seemed to many to be excessive and a major source of central government corruption. During the later Kangxi reign, the amounts of fees may have been restrained; at least, complaints of excessive fees declined, although "food money to the Board when reporting annual accounts" and "food money to the Board of Punishments at the time of the autumn assizes" were still in the listing of Guizhou public expenses presented to the emperor in 1725.[56] All early Qing emperors urged that a middle ground be found between the interests of the board and the governors. Governors were not to arrogate to themselves the functions of the boards, and boards were not to harass governors with petty or vexatious complaints.[57]

In the course of one such pronouncement, the Qianlong emperor, inadvertently perhaps, articulated the rationale for the regular exchange of personnel between the boards and governors' offices. Refereeing a conflict between the Jiangsu lieutenant governor, the commissioner of grain tribute, and the Boards of Revenue and Personnel over the handling of forgiven taxes in the lower Yangzi delta, the emperor wrote:

> Senior officials are all appointees of the state; they cannot be prejudiced. Many of those who are now board presidents or secretaries have at one time been governors, or will be sent out as governors at some time in the future. In the provinces, they are inclined in their requests to err on the side of leniency, saying "I empathize with the people's miseries." At court they are inclined to err on the side of severity, saying, "I protect the state treasury." The positions their offices occupy are different, and so their opinions are different. If officials change opinions as often as they change offices, how can we ever expect to achieve harmony in the government?[58]

The predominant tone of this edict was certainly frustration that board members and governors continued to cling to their points of view in spite of imperial exhortations to cooperate. But the cause of the emperor's frustration was the underlying assumption that the practice of transferring officials regularly from the boards to the territorial hierarchy would resolve the problem. The emperor sought to achieve cooperation within the government by creating an informal link between the central and territorial administrations.

In some instances, this link proved to be quite productive. The careers of Wu Shaoshi and his son Wu Tan showed that the alternation of board and provincial appointments could work. Both combined legal specializations developed at the Board of Punishments with territorial service. Wu Shaoshi's first appointment in Qing civil service was as an apprentice at the board, where he served from 1724 to 1736. During the early Qianlong reign, he held a number of junior positions and then was reappointed to the Board of Punishments following a term of mourning. He was governor of Jiangxi from 1766 to 1769 and then returned to the capital to serve at the Board of Punishments. His sons, Wu Yuan and Wu Tan, both had their first appointments serving with their father at the Board of Punishments. Wu Tan was there from 1761 until 1768, and again from 1772 until 1779. He alternated service at the board with service in Jiangsu, first as lieutenant governor and then as governor. Wu Yuan also spent the first fifteen years of his career at the Boards of Personnel and Punishments, before he was appointed governor of

Guangxi and Hubei. Commenting on these remarkable careers, *History of the Qing* explains that "Shaoshi and his sons clearly comprehended the legal system and were valued by the Qianlong emperor for their knowledge. Yuan and Tan both served at the board and were especially exempted by the emperor from the rule of avoidance," which would have prohibited father and son from serving in the same agency at the same time. In the early Qianlong years, Shaoshi was responsible for editing *The Great Qing Code* (Da Qing lüli), and Wu Tan wrote *General Commentary on the Qing Code* (Qing lüli tongkao), the most important late eighteenth-century commentary.[59]

The case of the Wu family, though interesting, is perhaps atypical. Few of those appointed governor while serving at the Board of Punishments had been there long enough to develop a substantive specialty; the average term of service at the board prior to an appointment as governor was fifteen months, and very few stayed more than two years. For many who became governors, time at the boards represented a sort of apprenticeship at the central government agencies responsible for recording and reviewing provincial affairs, or an interlude in the capital when contacts could be made, connections cultivated, and the central administration's new concerns could be absorbed and processed.

Xiong Xuepeng, whose previous experience of government service was at the Censorate, served for fifteen months at the Board of Works and six months at the Board of Punishments before being appointed governor of Guangxi (1761–62) and Zhejiang. There was a certain irony in Xiong's service at the Board of Punishments since one of his most famous writings as a censor was his accusation that capital punishment was dispensed too freely, a charge that the emperor, who approved all capital sentences, rejected forcefully.[60] Yeh Cunren seems to have been summoned to the capital to learn something of administrative procedure before being promoted in the territorial service; after nearly twenty years in subordinate territorial positions, he was summoned to the Board of Punishments for a year before being appointed governor of Henan.[61]

For Manchus who were appointed governors after serving at one of the boards, another sort of apprenticeship may have been involved. Manchus who had not passed the examination often began their civilian service as clerks, posted to an agency of the capital government. At the boards, positions were reserved for Manchus, so a promising clerk could attain a ranked position, from which he could be appointed to others of comparable rank in the territorial service. At the Board of Punishments, for example, 255 of the 342 ranked positions were reserved for Manchus, 59 for ordinary Chinese officials, 18 for members of the Chinese banners, and 9 for Mongols.[62] The majority of the slots reserved for Manchus, 179 of the 255, were for clerks, making it possible for many young Manchus to learn the ropes of Qing administration within the Board of Punishments. The boards not only were convenient places to start but proved to be useful places to park Manchu officials whose careers had, for whatever reason, been interrupted. Yude was a Manchu official who began his career by working his way up from a clerkship to a ranked position in the Grand Secretariat. He occupied a number of junior territorial posts from 1774 to 1776, and then returned to the capital to observe the mourning period for his mother. During this time, and for some time after, he served what seems to have been an apprenticeship at the Board of Punishments. When his next territorial appointment ended in demotion in 1783, he was again assigned to serve as an apprentice at the board, worked his way up from apprentice to senior vice president with responsibility for investigating accusations, and was appointed governor in 1796.[63]

The practice of selecting governors from among individuals serving at one of the six boards fulfilled several purposes for Qing rulers. It facilitated the exchange of perspectives, which the Qianlong emperor, among other Qing rulers, saw as essential to the smooth functioning of government. The boards provided training for the young Manchus whom the Qianlong emperor wished to appoint to office. The practice may also have reflected the changing character of the Qing government itself. Guo Chengkang, who has examined the competition for power between governors and the boards, argues that the relation between the boards and territorial government changed over the course of the eighteenth century. In the Kangxi era, boards and governors were fairly evenly matched. Governors acquired an advantage when they received the right to secretly memorialize the throne; then the boards fought back with new regulations in the eighteenth century.[64] The argument is plausible, though as stated, it rests on anecdotal evidence. Nonetheless, Guo suggests the interesting possibility that the growth in the numbers of board appointees in the Qianlong reign, which continued into the nineteenth century, represented a small triumph of the boards' routine procedures over the special powers of governors and the emperors who appointed them. If this was indeed the case, it confirms that the powers of special appointment, though vested in the emperor, represented one of the means by which the Qing administration could change its form without changing its constitution.

LATERAL TRANSFERS

The circulation of experienced administrative personnel lay at the core of the Chinese design for empire. Perhaps no other early modern empire more clearly expressed or adhered to the principle that officials should regularly change posts and locations. In China, the movement was meant to combat administrative provincialism or, worse, the formation of regional cliques. It also facilitated the circulation of ideas and talents that had been proved in one context to other parts of the empire. So common in fact were the movements of senior officials over thousands of miles, through regions of vastly different natural and political ecology, that they seldom elicited comment in eighteenth-century biographical materials. Nearly a third of Qing governor appointments were transfers of sitting governors from one province to another, and the average governor could expect to serve in two or three provinces during his career. Individually, these lateral transfers seemed random, but collectively they followed broadly predictable patterns that served the needs of a centralized empire.

As in the cases of special appointments and promotions, the locations of lateral transfers are suggestive. Lateral transfers of governors occurred in all provinces, but, as with promotions and special appointments, they were more common in some provinces than in others. The spatial distribution of lateral transfers follows a somewhat different pattern from that of the other two types of appointments.

Revenue contributions, which seem to have been such an important factor in determining which provinces would be governed by special appointees and promotees, were apparently much less of an influence on lateral transfers. More important, it would appear, was location. Only one of the provinces to which governors were transferred most frequently was on a border (Guangdong); the others (Jiangxi, Henan, Shandong, and Hubei) were at a safe distance from the special complexities of trade and defense imposed on provincial government by border locations. Most of the transfers occurred among a core of provinces situated along China's water transport network—the Grand Canal and the Yellow River in the north, and the Yangzi, Xiang, Gan, and Pearl Rivers in the south. These riverine highways bore the bulk of China's domestic commerce and, apparently, also the bulk of China's official travelers. The provinces with the fewest transfers were located on the edges of the empire, including Shanxi in the north, Jiangsu in the east, and Guizhou and Guangxi in the far south. In the southern border provinces, governors were more likely to be brought in through promotion rather than transfer, and in the northern border provinces, governors were more likely to be special appointees. Like a vast living organism, the Qing circulated its personnel and the capacities they represented, primarily along its main arteries rather than through its peripheries.

In principle, these appointments could have been effected in two ways. All governors were regarded as eligible for transfer after a term of three years in office. At this stage, the Board of Personnel was authorized to enter their names on ranked lists for appointment to another governorship, and as they reached the top of the list, their transfers would have been a routine matter. It is equally possible, however, that as the emperor contemplated possibilities for appointments, he might well have turned to sitting governors and ordered one of them moved to another post; in such an instance, the lateral transfer would have been in effect a special appointment. Both the anecdotal evidence of the careers of governors with multiple terms and the record of appointments considered as a whole suggests that the court played a significant role in lateral transfers.

The most spectacular example of a repeatedly transferred governor in the Qing is Chen Hongmou, who held twenty-one positions, sixteen of them governorships, in the course of a thirty-year career in the Qing territorial service. Several of Chen's terms as governor were of substantial length. He served three years and five years as governor of Shaanxi, three years in Jiangxi, and four and a half years in Jiangsu. But he also served shorter terms, appointments of five months in Henan and six months in Hunan, and some even shorter, during which he could scarcely have reached and occupied the office to which he was assigned. As William Rowe writes: "Fairly shortly after Qianlong's succession, he came to utilize the multitalented Chen as provincial troubleshooter. Chen's gubernatorial transfers usually came quite suddenly as he was needed to deal with food supply emergencies, revive collapsing hydraulic structures, or handle urgent minority relations problems, or clear up critical litigation gluts, or simply rescue a province mired in maladministration." As Rowe argues, Chen's role as troubleshooter did not mean he was intimate with the Qianlong emperor; in fact he very seldom met the monarch during his journeys between Qing provincial capitals. But his transfers were clearly not accidental; rather, they were the work of a court well aware of his capacities and provincial needs.[65] No other governor came close to serving this many terms as governor. Mingde, whose career was shaped by the state's military concerns, served the second-highest number of terms in the eighteenth century.

Although not as mobile as Chen or Mingde, most governors were appointed to two or three terms before being promoted to governor-general or before death or illness removed them from the corps of provincial governors. Two sorts of evidence suggest that more of these transfers were products of imperial action than of routine personnel actions. First, the terms that ended in lateral transfers were relatively short and did not approximate the standard of three years envisioned by the Qing. In fact, terms ending in a lateral transfers were even shorter than average. The median term of a Qing governor was twenty-five months, but the median term of a governor who was transferred to another governorship was eleven and a half months.

A second sort of evidence about the nature of lateral transfers concerns the provinces in which they occurred. As has been argued above, behind the spatial distribution of special appointments and promotions was an implicit geographical hierarchy, in which provinces that contributed more money to the central

TABLE 5.4. Lateral Appointments, by Province, 1700–1900

Province	Number of Lateral Appointments	Total Appointments	Percentage Lateral Appointments
Guangdong	41	89	46%
Jiangxi	34	94	36%
Henan	34	95	36%
Shandong	34	99	34%
Hubei	40	115	35%
Hunan	40	103	39%
Zhejiang	34	102	33%
Shaanxi	34	105	32%
Fujian	30	89	34%
Yunnan	29	83	35%
Shanxi	29	98	30%
Jiangsu	40	94	40%
Guangxi	24	99	24%
Anhui	23	98	24%
Guizhou	17	92	18%
Total	483	1,455	33%

Source: Qingdai zhi guan nian biao data.

government treasury received more special appointments and fewer recent pro-motees. The mechanism of lateral transfer served as a means of moving governors who had experience in one province to another province. One would expect that those provinces perceived as requiring more experience would be net recipients of transferred governors. In provinces deemed more appropriate for beginners, the pattern would more likely have been reversed. An official would be promoted in and then, if he had been successful, transferred out to other more difficult posts. Such "beginner" provinces would be net givers of transferred governors. The measure of whether lateral transfers achieved this end lies in the relationship between the number of transfers into a province and the number of transfers out of that province. These data are presented in table 5.4.

The rank orderings of provinces in this table rather closely resembles the rank orderings in table 2.4, in which provinces are grouped according to their percent-ages of newly promoted governors. Provinces with significantly more transfers in than transfers out, where in effect the mechanism of lateral transfer resulted in the inflow of experienced governors, are listed first. These include the revenue-rich provinces of Jiangsu and Zhejiang as well as Shandong and Henan, which adjoined the capital, and Guangdong. In the middle group are provinces where the numbers of transfers in and transfers out are fairly equivalent, composed of much of the central part of the empire—Fujian, Yunnan, Shanxi, Hubei, Hunan, Shaanxi, and Jiangxi. At the bottom of the chart are provinces that functioned as training grounds, places where governors were frequently promoted and served first terms before being transferred elsewhere. These provinces are Guangxi and Guizhou, along the southern borders, and Anhui.

This ordering resembles earlier orderings too closely to have been coincidental. It suggests that lateral transfers were driven not by accidents of local emergency or the expiration of terms but by design based on a mental map of the empire. The court would have had ample reason to promote experienced governors up the provincial hierarchy. This would have ensured that those confronted with the challenges of more important provinces would have faced broadly similar tasks before and shown their ability to master them. But there was probably another motive involved. The corps of provincial governors was relatively small; at any given moment, only fifteen individuals held governorships, and another fifteen or so lieutenant governors were in training for higher posts. It was quite possible for the emperor, or those who served him at court, to keep fairly close track of who was where, who had proved himself, and who might require only a bit more experience before shouldering a larger task. Comments recorded in edicts of appointment or edicts issued shortly after an appointment suggest that, in addition to attending to the needs of provinces, the court often referred specifically to an official's personal character. These comments were seldom detailed or consistent enough to form a picture of the Qing concept of human potential. But they do indicate, as perhaps they were meant to, that the court paid close attention to the personalities of those who served as governors. The Chinese court was consciously alert to human potential, seeking to develop officials who could respond to ever increasing challenges.

It was therefore not surprising that officials, particularly in the eighteenth century, rose up the hierarchy of provinces in the same way they rose through the ranks. Table 5.5 presents schematic outlines of the careers of four governors, excluding brief appointments. Lateral transfers took each of these governors through a sequence of more prestigious provinces; insofar as these provinces often had higher revenue obligations, appointments also took these four governors to positions of greater financial responsibility. Since two of the provinces in which governors were most frequently promoted, Guizhou and Guangxi, were located in the far south and, generally speaking, the provinces in which transfers were likely to occur formed a corridor leading from south to north, the career paths of these governors often paralleled those of Chen Huizu and Li Hu (see table 5.6).

Careers like these, which approximated statistical expectations fairly closely,

TABLE 5.5. Lateral Transfer Ratios, by Province, 1700–1900

Province	In-Transfers	Out-Transfers	Ratio of In-Transfers to Out-Transfers
Zhejiang	34	21	1.619
Jiangsu	40	26	1.538
Shandong	34	23	1.478
Guangdong	41	31	1.322
Henan	34	27	1.259
Hunan	40	35	1.114
Yunnan	29	27	1.07
Shaanxi	34	35	.971
Fujian	30	29	.966
Hubei	40	45	.888
Jiangxi	34	40	.85
Shanxi	29	36	.806
Guangxi	24	36	.667
Anhui	23	42	.547
Guizhou	17	35	.485

Source: *Qingdai zhi guan nian biao* data.

were relatively rare, as several factors could interfere with a governor's rise. The Qing dynasty's rules of avoidance represented the most formal of these barriers. Qing territorial officials were not permitted to serve within 500 li of their native places, or, in some instances, of their ancestors' native places or the places where their natal families had temporarily resided. Also, they could not serve as subordinates of relatives or of the officials who had been their civil service examiners.[66] Few governors were actually obliged to move because of these regulations. Special appointees were exempted from the rules of avoidance by a precedent established in 1724, when the Yongzheng emperor appointed a native of Jiangsu governor-general of Liangjiang.[67] Although governors frequently were connected to local officials, either by blood or because the officials had served as their examiners, governors were more often the senior parties in these relationships, and the rules of avoidance obliged the junior party to move.

One case in 1757, when Chen Hongmou was appointed to serve briefly as governor-general of Liangguang, illustrates the effect these rules could have. The appointment in itself was in conflict with the rules of avoidance since Chen was from Guangxi, which was part of the Liangguang jurisdiction. However, the Qianlong emperor, asserting that Chen was an experienced and trusted official, and would at any rate be spending most of his time in Canton rather than upriver in Guangxi, exempted him from the rules.[68] When Chen arrived in Canton,

TABLE 5.6. Sample Careers, 1700s

Name: Chen Hongmou	Province	Transfer Ratio
Native place	Guangxi	
Lieutenant governor	—	
Governor	Jiangxi, 1741–43	.850
	Shaanxi, 1743–46	.862
	Shaanxi, 1747–51	.862
	Fujian, 1752–54	.966
	Jiangsu, 1758–62	1.619

Name: Li Hu	Province	Transfer Ratio
Native place	Jiangxi	
Lieutenant governor	Jiangsu	
Governor	Guizhou, 1770–72	.485
	Yunnan, 1772–75	1.017
	Hunan, 1778–80	.875
	Guangdong, 1782–85	1.322

Name: Bi Yuan	Province	Transfer Ratio
Native place	Jiangsu	
Lieutenant governor	Shaanxi	
Governor	Shaanxi, 1773–1785	.862
	Henan, 1785–1788	1.259

Name: Chen Huizu	Province	Transfer Ratio
Native place	Hunan	
Lieutenant governor	—	
Governor	Guangxi, 1769–71	.667
	Hubei, 1771–79	.888
	Zhejiang, 1781–83	1.619

Sources: Governors' careers, *Qingdai zhi guan nian biao*; transfer ratios, table 5.5.

however, he found that his former examinee Zhou Renji was governor of Guangdong, which necessitated a series of changes. Zhou was transferred to Guizhou, the Guizhou governor was transferred to Fujian, and the Fujian governor was transferred to Guangdong.[69] When Zhou reached Guiyang, he found that one of the magistrates was a former student of his, and the magistrate was transferred to Yunnan.[70] As it happened, Chen Hongmou served as governor-general at Canton for only five months before he was appointed to the governorship of Jiangsu.[71]

Clearly, the dynasty was prepared to risk considerable upheaval to preserve the proprieties. In fact, at the beginning of the nineteenth century, the price of certain kinds of avoidance proved too high. In 1803, the rule against students serving under their former examiners was abandoned.[72]

Another reality of Qing administration was the requirement that when an official's parents died, he had to resign formally and return home on leave to observe a specified period of mourning, twenty-seven months for the death of a father and three months for a mother. These leaves could occur relatively frequently, particularly for officials of middle age, such as provincial governors. As Norman Kutcher has argued, the Qing modified rules on mourning in several important respects, in order to limit the impact of the mourning requirement on government service.[73] The most important modification had to do with the procedures to be observed before an official left office to mourn. In the Ming, officials were encouraged to leave office immediately upon the death of a parent, in testimony to the sincerity of emotion the properly moral individual would feel on such an occasion. The Qing modified this rule, requiring that an official formally notify the central government of his bereavement and request leave; only after the central government had approved leave could the official depart from office.[74] These modifications made clear that Qing officials should put loyalty to their state above loyalty to their parents; the changes also reduced the havoc wrought on administrative continuity by unpredictable leaves.

The dynasty's reaction when Zhang Shicheng, an early nineteenth-century governor of Jiangsu, left his post to the lieutenant governor in order to be at the bedside of his dying father without first receiving official permission illustrates Qing sensitivity on this latter point. "This has never happened before," wrote the Jiaqing emperor, "and is extremely irregular. Zhang Shicheng is a governor with heavy responsibilities for territorial administration. As his father's illness worsened, he should have petitioned the throne requesting that he be allowed to vacate his post in order to return home. I would certainly have granted his request." Declaring a post vacant was the formal prelude to making a new appointment. Given the Qing penchant for promoting lieutenant governors of Jiangsu to govern the province, it was likely that the outcome in Zhang's case might not have been any different had Beijing made the appointment. The emperor was objecting to the procedural irregularity, in fact, the expression for "irregular," *dan wang*, had connotations of extravagance and disorder. The Qing fear of such disorder, and the need to respond to irregular circumstances in a way that expressed dynastic control, were surely reasons why its appointments seemed so irregular in length and character. Governors simply could not take to the road when private matters required it. In Zhang's case, the emperor continued, the danger was not too great:

His home is on Huzhou [Zhejiang], which is quite close to Suzhou [the Jiangsu provincial capital]. But if governor and high officials who serve far from home were to do the same, wouldn't this be a matter of wasting the public in service of the private? As for the official postal system, it is meant for matters touching official policy. Zhang's memorial about his father's illness was a family matter. Why was it sent through the official post?[75]

For inviting disorder, Zhang Shicheng was cashiered and, despite a distinguished record of territorial administration since the beginning of the Jiaqing reign, had to wait four years until the ascension of the Daoguang emperor before he could return to the territorial service.[76]

In practice as well as in principle, the Qing administered the mourning system in such a way as to reduce its impact on administrative continuity. Between 1700 and 1900, fifty-five governors left office to mourn. Of these, eighteen were not reappointed to the territorial service; they either changed the branch of government in which they served or, in many cases, simply retired from the civil service, perhaps to attend to new family responsibilities. Of the thirty-seven who were reappointed as governor, twelve found themselves appointed to the same province in which they had served before mourning, and another six were appointed to neighboring provinces. Although those at the junior levels of civil service who had completed mourning obligations were supposed to register with the Board of Personnel and wait for the first available position, there were few random reassignments at the senior level. In some cases, governors who were reassigned to the same provinces after mourning were men identified with the provinces, like Yang Xifu, who was twice reassigned to Hunan after fulfilling obligations, and Ruan Yuan, who was returned to Zhejiang after mourning. Lateral transfers of substitutes for governors in mourning were used to implement such arrangements.

Viewed as a whole, the pattern of lateral transfers appears to have a rather random quality, in which the central government's role was like that of an untutored hand carelessly removing and inserting pegs in a cribbage board. However, when the transfers are disaggregated and considered in terms of the life histories and career trajectories of those transferred as well as the specific needs of the state, a more rational picture emerges. The price the Qing paid for transferring talented people from post to post and maintaining the rules of avoidance was striking discontinuity at the provincial level. The language of costs and benefits here can only be a metaphor, since the notion that the dynasty rationally calculated the costs of its policies is problematic, as is the notion that such calculations can be reconstructed at all, absent the cultural context in which they were made. Nonetheless, there must have been recognition that the benefits of a mobile officialdom outweighed the costs of discontinuities in provincial governors' yamens. Insofar as lateral transfers were perceived as a valuable element of the Qing personnel system, it was not surprising that the Qing court became involved in orchestrating them.

The dynamics of special appointments made for the purpose of achieving continuity were complex. It seems clear that the emperor was behind the appointment of Manchus to court. Those appointed in the early years of his reign were men of the his own generation, and he seems to have known many of them personally. Certainly he offered ample personal testimony to the importance of appointing Manchu officials. In the other two initiatives traced here, the appointments of men from the six boards to governorships and lateral transfers, the Qianlong emperor's personal role is not so clear. The emperor certainly supported the regular exchange of personnel between the Beijing boards and the provinces, and he may have been involved in decisions to return certain governors to the boards, as in the case of Tuerbing'a. But there is little evidence of a personal association between the emperor and those selected from the boards for service in the provinces. Lateral transfers lie in a gray area in this regard. When, as was most often the case, they resulted in the movement of experienced people from less difficult to more difficult posts, some human judgment must have been applied in evaluating capacities and challenges. The monarch may have supplied this judgment himself, or it may have come from those closest to him, but clearly the decision to move an experienced person from one post to another relied on the powers of the emperorship. To the extent that decisions to move such officials realized elements of the Qing concept of empire, they represented a vital element of Qing rule. Without some power vested in the emperorship to realize such a design, it could hardly have been accomplished, and the critical element of circulation of personnel might well have been neglected. Emperors cannot be ignored in Qing history, but neither should contributions made in the name of the emperor, uses of the great reservoir of executive authority vested in the Qing emperorship, be dismissed.

It was probably in the latter half of the eighteenth century, when nearly three hundred officials were promoted and transferred among the empire's provinces, that the circulation patterns of officials highlighted above were likely established. As these developed, officials with more experience and education were brought to China's southernmost provinces and even the provinces of the middle Yangzi region. There, a new generation of officials came to implement a scheme of territorial governance more like the classical Chinese administration of the north than the haphazard arrangements that had often prevailed south of the Yangzi. The argument may be stretched a bit further. Arguably, the innovations of the first half of the eighteenth century, which have recently been described in the literature—the creation of relief granaries, famine relief procedures, construction of dikes along China's rivers and lakes—should be counted as a creation of eighteenth-century officialdom rather than of the eighteenth-century monarchy. At least, these innovations came to depend more on the administrative achievements of officials than on the efforts of a monarch reading documents in the wee hours of the morning. It is tempting to imagine that, had the court retained its political initiative, it might have been better able to cope with the serious challenges of the eighteenth century. But, in fact, the empire, and particularly its most dynamic quarters, might not have been able to reach the nineteenth century without the administrative developments of the eighteenth century. Using monarchical authority during the Qing to build a stronger territorial bureaucracy was probably a good thing for the Qing state. A view of the Qing monarchy that emphasizes its capacity to build a territorial order may not fully accord with traditional conceptions of the nature of Qing emperors. But it may capture, in part at least, the executive ability that allowed the dynasty to adapt for most of its history to the changing realities of early modern East Asia.

PART II

CHAPTER 6

The Legacy of Military Occupation:
The North and the Northwest

O ne of the principal innovations of the Qing territorial order was the provision it made for shared responsibility—governors and lieutenant governors shared responsibility for the tasks of civil administration, and both shared
military responsibilities with governors-general. This arrangement was not
administratively tidy, but it was durable. Perhaps more important, it was flexible. Where civilian needs were important, the role of governors could be emphasized over that of governors-general, and where military needs were the primary
concern, governors-general could bear the larger share of responsibility for governing. This flexibility was vital to the dynasty in establishing a territorial order
in the north and northwest. The provinces considered in this chapter—Henan,
Shandong, Zhili, Shanxi, Shaanxi, Gansu, and Sichuan—had different, in some
instances radically different, natural and human ecologies. Yet at some point in
the seventeenth or eighteenth centuries, they were all sufficiently important to
the Qing dynasty to be the scene of heavy concentrations of military force. Provincial government evolved around and on top of these military concentrations,
with different institutional arrangements made in order to accommodate strategic needs and local ecology.

As a consequence, the relationship of military conquest and civilian governance in Qing China was highlighted more clearly in the northern and northwestern provinces than in the provinces of other regions. The issue is one of
general interest, since provincial forms in many parts of the world grew out of
earlier military jurisdictions. But it is also of specific interest for Chinese historians, as there is a growing consensus within the field of late imperial Chinese
history that the Manchus retained the form, language, and institutions of a conquest regime far longer than had earlier been imagined, indeed perhaps throughout the dynasty. Most of the studies illustrating this proposition have, however,
focused on the Manchus and their military establishment rather than the territorial organs they developed. This chapter argues that the most important legacy
of the conquest period in the north is the creation of a series of governors who
had unique relations with their superiors and with the Qing court. In Henan and
Shandong, powerful governors reported directly to the central government; in

Shaanxi and Gansu, governors-general predominated over weaker, and, in some instances, dispensable, governors. In Shanxi and Zhili, the Qing made a remarkable series of compromises with its principles of territorial order for the purpose of assuring the safety of the capital and the loyalty of its defenders.

As interesting as the synchronic question of how northern and northwestern provinces differed from those of other regions is the diachronic question of how the governors of these provinces addressed the changing circumstances of the regions they governed in the seventeenth and eighteenth centuries. Manchus conquered north China in an era when a declining central government, the scourge of banditry, and a series of colder than usual winters conspired to weaken the region, rendering it nearly prostrate before the invaders. But over the course of the seventeenth and eighteenth centuries, partly through the actions of the Qing conquerors themselves, prosperity, or at least such prosperity as was possible in a region that rested on a fragile economic base, returned. Grain and goods began to move along the restored Grand Canal from the lower Yangzi region, and a secure government was able to direct resources to the northwestern borders. As the northern economy revived, the role of territorial administration changed, though many of the institutional forms and patterns of the early conquest days remained, at least through the eighteenth century. Not all of the rather uniquely privileged governors of the north and northwest dealt with economic and political evolution effectively. Indeed, a series of celebrated prosecutions of officials at the end of the eighteenth century reflects the strain of new economic prosperity built on an old set of institutions.

HENAN AND SHANDONG: FIRST AMONG EQUALS

It was hardly a foregone conclusion in the early Qing that north China would be the seat of strong civilian governors, for the military significance of the region in Chinese history was enormous. However, in the Qing, the problem in north China was not the need to hold the plain militarily but the requirement to extract from and transport through it the disproportionate share of resources the region was obliged by tradition and statute to provide to the central court. This was complicated by the fact that the physical geography of the region could barely support the apparatus needed to govern and defend it, let alone the apparatus necessary to accomplish the dynasty's logistical goals in the region. The situation was broadly similar in the two provinces of north China, but the dynasty provided different sources of support. In Shandong, the dynasty provided help in the form of support for the Grand Canal, which made the burden bearable, at least for most of the eighteenth century, but in Henan, governors relied largely on their own resources in coping with the logistical and political challenges of the north.

Geographically, north China consists of the lower basin (essentially the delta) of the Yellow River plus the drainage areas of several smaller rivers, including the Huai and the Wei, which flow across the plain.[1] The dominant political feature of the region was the national capital, Beijing, which was located at the far northern extremity of the productive lands that constituted the economic core of the region. Beijing was the region's metropolitan city, but beyond this, its political influence affected the region's administrative structure in a variety of ways. The city obviously had to be defended, and the troops garrisoned within it and along its approaches had to be fed and supplied. Moreover, since the agrarian surpluses of the region could not support the regime, arteries of communication had to be maintained linking the north with other regions. The most important of these arteries, the Grand Canal, which linked the capital with the productive lower Yangzi valley, was the effective responsibility of a governor-general for river transport, who was provided with a contingent of troops and based in Shandong along the canal. For all of these reasons, government was more present in north China than in other regions. Comparing the urbanization of north China with that of the lower Yangzi, Skinner finds that there was administrative presence in much smaller cities in the north compared to the Yangzi valley, and a higher proportion of the existing urban centers in the north were political capitals than in the south.[2]

This fairly large political establishment had to be maintained in a region where nature was notoriously inconstant. As Philip Huang has observed, the rain-bearing monsoon winds imposed a particularly harsh agrarian regimen on north China. Wet years could have seven or eight times as much rain as dry years, and drought during the spring growing season could be especially devastating. In the two thousand years of Chinese imperial history, drought struck the north 1,078 times, according to one Chinese scholar. In years of flooding, waterlogging was an equally serious problem, especially along the flood plains of Shandong and Zhili.[3] Nature's inconstancy in the north had its social effect as well. Because there was little profit to be made from the land, the institution of landlordism was never strongly developed in north China, except in its most commercialized regions.[4] In the absence of a strong elite, the state, particularly in its local manifestations, had to be strong if order was to be maintained. The region posed the following problem for central governments: how to maintain the security essential to dynastic survival without overtaxing agrarian surplus or diverting resources from other essential tasks.

The Ming resolved the dilemmas of governing the north by dotting the north Chinese landscape with grand coordinators. Eleven of the thirty coordinators the dynasty appointed were posted within 200 miles of the capital; six were located in north China, and there were also two governors-general in the area. This was partly an artifact of the Ming dynasty's fears in its beleaguered final days, but there may have been a certain logic to it. Studies of the nineteenth-century collapse of the Qing order in north China have emphasized the extent to which Shandong in particular consisted of a series of microregions, small worlds with significantly different political economies, social structures, and military traditions. Joseph Esherick divides Shandong into six subregions: the Peninsula, the North Slope, the South Hills, Jining, the Southwest and the Northwest. Kenneth Pomeranz adds another subregion, Huan-Yun, which incorporates portions of Henan.[5] Esherick writes of the nineteenth century, and it is possible that some of the subregional differences he observes were the product of nineteenth-century economic changes. But many of these differences were enduring. Assuming that a similar situation prevailed in the sixteenth century, the assignment of numerous separate military commands may have made sense. The Qing initially followed the Ming pattern, appointing its own personnel to replace grand coordinators in Shuntian, Tianjin, Baoding, Denglai, Henan, and Shandong between June and November 1644.

Within a few years, however, the Qing began to find fault with the Ming pattern. First, the creation of small, separate jurisdictions was expensive. In 1649, the Board of Revenue memorialized the throne, proposing a number of steps to deal with what must have been a serious shortfall:

In our dynasty's establishment of government, the most important thing has been sympathy for the people. Since the conquest, we have abolished illegal taxes in order to succor the people. Now, however, armies are on the march, and the border areas have not yet been settled. Yearly income does not match yearly expenditures. [Yi sui suo ru bu zu heng yi sui suo chu.] This office therefore proposes that *jiansheng* and lower-ranking officials be allowed to purchase office, that Daoist and Buddhist ordination certificates be sold, that criminals be allowed to pay fines rather than suffer corporal punishments, and that the governorships of Tianjin, Fengyang, and Anhui be abolished.[6]

Three years later, when revenues still did not cover expenditures, eliminating the provincial governorship at Denglai was the first of fourteen measures the board proposed in order to balance the dynastic books.[7]

A further problem with the Ming order was that the assortment of small divided governorships made it difficult to respond to challenges to the state's monopoly of force. Because the initial Qing conquest of the north had proceeded smoothly and rapidly, aided, as Frederic Wakeman has argued, by the collaboration of north China elites,[8] the Qing in its early years did not feel the need to establish a governor-general in the north. But with no single individual in command, it was difficult to combat the banditry endemic in postconquest north China. "In areas where many provincial boundaries adjoin," wrote one official in 1649, "troops and horses are kept on either side of the border. Governors do not have the authority to give orders to garrisons in another province, and troops are not authorized to cross boundaries." For this reason, "crafty bandits" found ways to evade capture. The memorialist's solution to this problem was to convert the governorship at Baoding into a governor-general's post and to charge the governor-general with responsibility for order throughout the north China plain. In making this proposal, the memorialist was careful to stress that the position would not entail additional expense: "No additional provision need be made for troops, equipment, orderlies or lodgings," since the establishment of the Baoding governor would be used for the new governor-general.[9] The court accepted the recommendation, and the post existed for the remainder of the Shunzhi reign. In 1658, the governor-general committed suicide when deficits were discovered in his treasury, and the Qing court, reasoning that banditry on the north China plain had subsided, chose to convert the position into a governorship responsible for Zhili alone.[10] The north China governor-generalship was briefly reestablished between 1665 and 1669, in the panic that followed the Wu Sangui Rebellion, and was recreated for Tian Wenjing from 1728 to 1732. But for most of the dynasty, there was no governor-general with responsibility for north China. This left the region in the hands of three governors, one each in Henan, Shandong, and Zhili, half the number of territorial officials as had served in Ming times.

As a practical consequence, these governors were stronger than their counterparts, both in relation to the court, with which they dealt directly, and in relation to the territories they governed. The uniqueness of the Henan and Shandong governorships was recognized officially in several ways. The governors of these provinces were among a few in the empire who were given command of the Green Standard Army detachments in their provinces. In addition to the governor's brigade, which contained about three thousand troops, as well as two naval units, the Shandong governor commanded three brigades, each headed by a brigade general, stationed at Dengzhou and Yanzhou.[11] The Henan governor also commanded three brigades, one at Kaifeng, another centered in the north of the province, and a third in southern Henan. But as important as the number of troops under the command of northern governors was the prestige involved. Since Green Standard Army provincial commanders in chief technically ranked with governors-general, and so outranked governors, their absence made governors the highest-ranking officials in their respective capitals.[12] In recognition of this special responsibility, the governors of Henan and Shandong were allowed to wear an additional peacock plume as part of their official regalia. The plume probably recognized more than the simple fact of an administrative arrangement, since the governors of the three other provinces without provincial commandants—Shanxi, Anhui, and Jiangxi—were not allowed to wear it. In the early nineteenth century, in an effort to systematize the personnel system, the governors of these three provinces were allowed to wear the plume; however, in 1847, the plume was eliminated from all five uniforms.[13]

The governors of Henan and Shandong were also the only two in the empire whose responsibilities for maintaining the imperial infrastructure were formally acknowledged in *Collected Statutes and Precedents of the Qing*. The Grand Canal and the Yellow River were primarily the responsibilities of the director-general of river conservancy, but this official had such vast obligations that, particularly in times of emergency, he required assistance from the governors. De facto, the Henan and Shandong governors shared responsibility for the hydraulic works of the north, much as governors in other provinces shared military responsibilities with governors-general. The burden of river work probably fell most heavily on the governor of Henan, who had to manage the perils of the Yellow River with less help from the downstream governor-general than his colleague in Shandong had. Certainly the great river dominated his province.[14] As it flowed out of the Zhongshan mountains onto the plain, it slowed, and as it slowed, its capacity to carry silt diminished. Throughout much of the province, the river deposited silt in its own bed and so came to flow at a level higher than the surrounding farmlands. To prevent disaster, either the speed of the river's flow had to be increased or dikes had to be built and maintained along the edges of the river. Tian Wenjing, who served from 1725 to 1735, the longest-serving governor of the province during the Qing dynasty, pointed out that everyone in the government recognized that failure to control the river in Henan brought disastrous consequences, not only for the province itself, but also for downstream regions in Anhui and southern Shandong. The Henan governor had a responsibility to both his province and the larger empire.[15]

Maintaining and repairing the dikes involved not only supervising engineering works but raising and accounting for revenues, hiring workers, and providing relief for farmers whose lands were damaged by flood. River repairs often had to be carried out at the same time that relief was distributed to those whose crops and homes had been destroyed by flooding. Distribution of relief was especially urgent in Henan, since the population of that province could rely on little except agriculture. As Governor Yin Huiyi wrote in 1737, "the customs of Henan are rustic and simple, not at all comparable to the luxury of Jiangsu and Zhejiang. If they mismanage their lands, the people of Henan have no other way of making a living. Their public and private lives depend exclusively on what heaven produces."[16] It may have been the case, as Kenneth Pomeranz has argued, that the Qing state at its height accepted financial responsibility for river work in Shandong. But in Henan, governors were usually forced to cobble together packages of central government relief along with provincial and local monies in order to accomplish necessary work along the rivers.[17]

The Henan governor also bore special responsibilities that derived from his province's status as the main grain-producing region of north China. In the late Kangxi reign, discussions were initiated about creating special stores of Henan grain for relief of famine in Shanxi and Shaanxi.[18] State demands for Henan grain were exacerbated during the wars of the mid-eighteenth century, when the western-route armies marched through Henan on their way to Shaanxi, Gansu, and Xinjiang. All of the governors of Henan in mid-century came with backgrounds in military strategy and policy. Jiang Bing (1752–55), Hu Baoquan (1757–63), and Asha (1763–68) had all served as Grand Council clerks; Jiang Bing had accompanied Ortai on his tours of the northwest military front in the late Yongzheng reign;[19] and Hu Baoquan had traveled with Fuheng to Sichuan to oversee the Jinquan wars. Despite the Jiangsu native Hu Baoquan's protest that he was only a clerk, he was in fact sent to Henan to inspect the military in 1745.[20] Tuerbing'a's service in Henan came at the height of the war in Xinjiang, and he was nearly destroyed by his need to balance famine relief with supplying the army, as described in chapter 5.[21]

The Shandong governor could expect help with maintaining the Grand Canal from the director-general of river conservancy, since the canal was more of a lifeline for the dynasty than was the Yellow River, but in many respects, canal maintenance was more daunting. The Grand Canal was one of the first pieces of Chinese infrastructure in which the Qing made significant investment. Maintenance of the canal and its embankments was probably the responsibility of a director of river conservancy. But perhaps as important, at least in Shandong, was the flooding caused by the canal's diversion of southern waters into the Shandong watersheds. Gu Yanwu had noted the flooding this frequently caused,[22] and his concerns were echoed by an early Qing director of grain transport who pointed out in 1666 that if the dynasty expected the regular supply of nearly 4 million shi of grain that moved annually to the capital, the court had to keep the embankments along the canal and its subsidiaries in good repair. The subsidiaries included six lakes and, as the director estimated, 250 rivers and streams that joined the canal along its course in Shandong.[23] Work in Shandong likely fell to the Shandong governor, along with the task of maintaining order among the peasantry pressed into corvée service in the southwestern part of the province. When the Grand Canal was in good repair, wrote the seventeenth-century geographer Gu Zuyu, Shandong and the capital were as close as lips and teeth; when the canal failed, the relationship between the two was like that of the elbow and the armpit, close but never touching.[24]

Compounding the importance of the Yellow River and the Grand Canal was the fact that they were such visible symbols of the success or failure of dynastic rule. Official and private travelers to the capital had to pass along the canal or cross the river on their way to Beijing, and Shandong received special allocations for the support of horses and post stations. Moreover, the two northern provinces were among the few that Manchu emperors actually passed through, bound either for destinations in the north or for the cities of the lower Yangzi valley. In 1705, the Kangxi emperor wrote on the occasion of a visit to the province:

> The Grand Canal in Shandong transports grain to the capital; it is vitally important and cannot be overlooked. When I traveled along the canal several months ago, there were embankments that did not hold. Now on my return, in the space of two or three months, they have been repaired. In the future, I hope repairs can be accomplished with such alacrity, and it is not the case that once I have passed, they can be forgotten.[25]

The Shandong governor was surely the only governor who had to face the problem of Potemkin embankments.

The nearness of the northern provinces to the capital was important in another respect as well. The Qing empire assessed its land tax through a series of quotas; each province had a quota of tax to collect as well as quotas of revenue to be retained in the provincial capital and remitted to the center. The percentages of remitted revenue ranged from 97.6 percent to nothing. The remittance rates in the north were all high: Zhili remitted 83.7 percent, Henan remitted 83.6 percent, Shanxi remitted 88 percent, and Shandong remitted 78.5 percent. Together, the four provinces of the north accounted for 37 percent of the total revenue Beijing received each year.[26] This is not to argue that the northern provinces were overtaxed, for the effective rate of taxation was greater elsewhere in the empire. But it did mean that provincial officials in the north, governors and the lieutenant governors who oversaw the tax collection process, bore an unusual responsibility for the support of the capital establishment.

Perhaps not surprisingly, governors of the north China provinces were more often appointed directly by the emperor than were the governors of any other province. Between 1700 and 1900, 36 percent of the governors of Shandong and 29 percent of the governors of Henan were selected by the emperor. If lateral transfers are included in the numbers of those personally selected by the emperor, as chapter 4 has argued that they should be, then nearly 75 percent of the governors of Shandong and 66 percent of those in Henan were imperial delegates.[27] Proximity to power had both a premium and a price in Qing government. The governors of Henan and Shandong were more likely than their colleagues in other provinces to be promoted to governor-general, but they were also more likely to leave office through disciplinary proceedings. Statistical evidence suggests the likelihoods involved. Between 1700 and 1900, 24.7 percent of Chinese provincial governors were promoted either to governor-general or to a post in the capital of rank equal to or higher than governor. The province with the fewest promotions was Jiangxi, from which only 12.8 percent of governors were promoted; Henan, at 31 percent, and Shandong, at 35.4 percent, had among the highest rates of promotion.[28] Conversely, 11.7 percent of Chinese governors in the eighteenth and nineteenth centuries were either cashiered or demoted. Guangdong had the fewest cashierings and demotions, 5.6 percent; Henan, at 15.8 percent, and Shandong, at 14.2 percent, had the highest rates. For the governors of Henan, the risks of service close to the capital marginally outweighed the benefits. Henan governors were 28 percent more likely than their colleagues to be promoted and 35 percent more likely to be disciplined. For the governors of Shandong, who were 43 percent more likely than their colleagues to be promoted and 24 percent more likely to be demoted, benefits outweighed the risks. In Henan, most of the dismissals came in the nineteenth century, when the north China economy was weakening and the dynasty's attention was focused elsewhere. In Shandong, firings were sprinkled throughout the two and a half centuries of Qing rule.

In Shandong, the strengths and limitations of governors closely connected to the capital were particularly evident. One of the most striking aspects of the list of Shandong governors is that they were twice as likely as governors of other provinces to be the brothers, nephews, or children of governors. In the Yongzheng reign, Chen Shiguan, the son of the Kangxi governor Chen Shen, and Yue Zhun, the son of Yue Zhongqi, governed Shandong from 1724 to 1726 and 1728 to 1730, respectively. In the Qianlong reign, Shandong governors Aligun (1746–48), Erong'an (1751–52), Yang Yingju (1753–54), Jiang Zhou (1755), Eleshun (1755–56), and Guotai (1777–82) were all related to other governors. Consistently, it appears, the eighteenth-century Qing court turned to men it knew, or whose families it knew, to govern this strategically crucial province.

The Shandong dismissals provide a vivid picture of the perils and prerogatives of life at the top. Table 6.1 lists the Shandong governors who were cashiered in the seventeenth and eighteenth centuries.

Establishing the causes for a governor's dismissal is a tricky proposition, since a variety of circumstances usually conspired to end a senior official's term; nonetheless, the proximate reasons for proceedings usually may be established from the edicts ordering the dismissals. Shandong governors were dismissed for the usual range of reasons; they presided over large staffs who prepared rivers of routine paperwork, and all governors were vulnerable to charges that reports had been carelessly written or intentionally falsified, leaving famine conditions unreported or local disturbances inaccurately described. As was the case with

TABLE 6.1. Shandong Governors Dismissed, 1600s and 1700s

Name	Term	Cause of Dismissal
Zhao Xiangxing[a]	1673–79	Bribery, collusion
Qian Yu[b]	1687–89	Personnel
Yang Tinghui[c]	1695–96	Inappropriate behavior
Li Wei[d]	1696–98	Failure to report famine conditions
Zhuntai[e]	1748–51	Censorship
Eleshun[f]	1755–56	Extortion in previous post
Jiang Zhou[g]	1757	Racketeering in previous post
Guotai[h]	1777–1782	Extortion
Changlin[i]	1787–1790	Inaccurate report of local disturbance
Yinjianga[j]	1796–99	Inappropriate correspondence with Heshen

Sources: Da Qing shilu; Gaozongshun (Qianlong) Huangdi shilu (QLSL); Qingdai zhi guan nian biao (QDZGNB); Renzong Rong (Jiaqing) Huangdi shilu (JQSL); and Shengzong Ren (Kangxi) Huangdi shilu (KXSL).

[a]KXSL, 85:2 (4:1076).
[b]KXSL, 142:17–19 (5:565–56).
[c]KXSL, 175:3a (5:890).
[d]KXSL, 187:11b–12a (5:995).
[e]QLSL, 397:17–18 (14:220).
[f]QLSL, 506:31b–34a (15:392–94).
[g]QLSL, 541:11b–17b (15:977–78).
[h]QLSL, 1160:17a–19b (23:537).
[i]QLSL, 1360:19–21 (26:274–75).
[j]QLSL, 38:13b–14a (28:437).

all governors, manipulation of personnel matters was the most frequent cause for dismissal of Shandong governors. What was unique about Shandong governors, however, was the extent to which their histories and connections got them in trouble. Two governors were dismissed for actions that had occurred in previous appointments. Eleshun extorted money from salt merchants during his term as governor of Zhejiang, and Jiang Zhou was dismissed for running an extortion scheme while he was lieutenant governor of Shanxi.[29] It was not that the Qing deliberately appointed corrupt officials to Shandong. Rather, in order to be appointed in Shandong, one had to be both powerful and accomplished, and such governors had already run afoul of the administrative code. Even when Shandong governors were punished for events in Shandong, they often acted in collusion with officials in the national capital. When Zhao Xiangxing and Qian Yu fell, they took numerous capital officials down with them.[30]

The Guotai Case

Probably the most celebrated dismissal of a Shandong governor was that of Guotai, governor from 1777 to 1782, for implementing a systematic scheme for extorting money from local officials. This episode has been treated previously as a case study in court factionalism, a prosecution initiated by enemies of the imperial councilor Heshen against one of his protégés, and certainly it had some of this character.[31] But in fact, the case highlighted not only national but local circumstances.

Guotai governed Shandong for five years at what was nearly the height of north China's late imperial economic cycle, a time when the region was as prosperous as it was ever to be during the Qing. He was the son of an important political family and was surrounded by others with close ties to the capital. The extortion scheme he implemented in Shandong rested on one of the peculiar prerogatives of the Shandong governor, the power to effect promotions to nearly a quarter of the county offices in the province. Guotai's inability to resist the temptations of the revenue flowing through Shandong brought his family to ruin, but it also cast into vivid relief the network of ties that bound Jinan and Beijing and how these strained to contain the new realities of the later eighteenth century.

The prosperity that made possible Guotai's excesses was both a cause and a consequence of the dynasty's interest in Shandong. Much of the literature on Shandong has described the province in decline. Frederic Wakeman and Jonathan Spence have each portrayed a poor province where officials and elites could not control the paramilitary organizations of the mid-seventeenth century.[32] Joseph Esherick and Kenneth Pomerantz paint a similar picture of the late nineteenth century, when the arrival of Western powers further undermined the province's economic stability.[33] Each picture is a correct rendering of a moment, but none captures the middle of the eighteenth century, when realities, at least in parts of Shandong, appear to have been very different.

The Grand Canal and the flow of goods and revenues it brought through the province had much to do with the transformed economy of this period. The waterway did not have a consistent effect throughout the province, however. As Esherick has argued, for the peasants and landholders who lived along the canal, the effects of flooding and salinization and the need for corvée labor likely made the waterway a liability. For political and social elites who lived in the cities, the picture likely was very different. Susan Mann documents the transformation of elites in Grand Canal port cities such as Jining from an austere group "ashamed to place elegant trappings on the chariots and horses" in the early seventeenth century into a world of nouveaux riches by the last years of the century. By the dawn of the eighteenth century, the rich of Jining were "throwing elegant banquets where, it was said, each guest consumed enough food in one evening to nourish the average person for several months. Funerals had become great extravaganzas with parades and great lines of mourners."[34] For officials, who dwelled primarily in cites, Shandong by the eighteenth century had become a province of comfort and reward.[35]

Through much of the middle of the eighteenth century, the reward of postings in Shandong went to representatives of the Manchu military elite. Manchus governed Shandong for twenty-five of the forty years between 1736 and 1776. Each of these Manchu governors had his own ties to the capital, but Governor Guotai's can be spelled out in some detail. Guotai was born into the Fuca clan, which had given the Qing most of its military leaders and senior counselors in the mid-eighteenth century and had also provided the Qianlong emperor with his cherished first empress and Chief Grand Councilor Fuheng.[36] Guotai was not a member of Fuheng's immediate family, but his own immediate family had its share of distinctions. His father Wenshou had served as governor of Shaanxi in 1768–71 and governor-general of Shaanxi in 1771–72, Huguang in 1773–76, and Sichuan in 1776–81. The Qianlong court not only assumed but celebrated family connections of this sort. When Wenshou returned to the capital for an audience, the emperor ordered Guotai to leave Shandong and make his way to the capital so father and son could be reunited in the imperial presence.[37] Guotai's family connections were not the only ties between Jinan and Beijing. In 1778, the brother of Chief Grand Councilor Yu Minzhong, Yu Yijian, who neither held a civil service degree nor had any previous official experience, was appointed lieutenant governor of Shandong and served alongside Guotai during the remainder of Yu Minzhong's life.[38] Yu Minzhong's successor as chief grand councilor was Heshen, who served together with Liu Yong as investigator in the case. The Shandong corruption case, perhaps like Shandong government itself, was a family affair, or the affair of several of the few families who constituted the ruling elite of late eighteenth-century Manchu China.

Guotai was a presence in Shandong administration for more than a decade. He was first assigned to the province in 1771 by a special appointment that elevated him from the post of department director in the Board of Punishments to provincial judge for Shandong. A year later, he was promoted to lieutenant governor of the province, and five years later, he was appointed governor. This appointment was in contravention of the seventeenth-century rule against promoting lieutenant governors to the governorship of the province in which they were serving. Indeed, the circumstances of Guotai's term, in which a single official made use of a long period in one location for his own gain, may have illustrated a reason for the rule. But Shandong was one province in which this rule was violated relatively often, as the province's special needs were perceived to be more important than the operating procedures of Chinese administration.

Rumors about Guotai began to circulate soon after his promotion to governor. Yu Yijian arrived in Jinan as a provincial judge shortly after Guotai's promotion to governor, and after two lieutenant governors proved unable to serve because of mourning obligations, Yu was promoted to lieutenant governor. In 1781, the Qianlong emperor became aware that local officials in Shandong didn't like Guotai and summoned Yu Yijian to report on his superior. After consulting with Yu, the emperor was inclined to attribute the trouble in Shandong to the Manchu's brusque and severe manner and left him at his post after reprimanding him for being overly severe.[39]At this stage, Guotai was protected by his status as a Manchu, by the fact that both he and Yu Yijian were known personally to the emperor, and by the emperor's assumption that his own people, though unpolished, were surely devoted to Qing interests.

In the summer of 1782, however, the Chinese censor Qian Feng openly accused Guotai and Yu Yijian of engaging in massive extortion at a moment when the province was falling ever deeper into arrears in its tax obligations.[40] This indictment was no doubt a courageous act on the part of a fairly low-ranking Chinese civil servant, though Qian may well have been emboldened by Wenshou's fall from imperial favor and subsequent exile to Ili in the late fall of 1781.[41] Whatever the political circumstances of the accusation, the facts from Shandong proved to be striking. Careful investigation of the tax registers carried out by Guotai's successor showed that the province was almost a year behind in its tax obligations, despite the era of relative prosperity. Guotai and local officials in Shandong claimed that the arrears had been incurred during the military action undertaken against White Lotus rebels in the province in 1779. But the emperor observed that the military phase of the rebellion had required only a few weeks, and that if Shandong officials had been truly pressed to meet military needs in this period, they could have requested special allotments.[42] The matter of tax arrears also produced a rather telling episode. Although in principle the Grand Council deliberations were secret, word of the brewing political controversy leaked out to the Manchu community in Beijing. Guotai's younger brother Guolin heard of the matter and dispatched a bondservant to Shandong post haste with word of the investigation. The news reached the governor, and Guotai set about moving money around in the provincial treasuries and leaning on local merchants to provide short-terms loans so that tax obligations would appear to have been met. The episode raised the question of how the family had learned about the case. Under interrogation, Guolin testified that he had merely meant to warn his mother, who was traveling along the road to Shandong, to watch out for the imperial investigators, who would be traveling fast. When asked how he knew about the appointment of investigators, Guolin, who was serving at the time as a Grand Council clerk, responded merely that he had heard some gossip while loitering around the Grand Council offices. Subsequent histories have assumed that Heshen revealed the proceedings to Guotai's family, although in view of the interlocking family ties that bound Shandong to Beijing, the warning to Guotai could easily have come from many other quarters.[43]

The tip-off, and the actions that followed, also suggest that the court was dealing in Shandong with a collusive network of senior officials, junior territorial officials, and merchant elites. The primary focus of the case was Guotai himself and what he collected, rather than the junior officials who presented items to the governor. Nonetheless, the list of junior officials named in the case is revealing. Eleven officials were specifically identified as having presented items to the governor: four were named by Qian Feng himself, and imperial investigators uncovered another seven.[44] Five of these eleven officials were prefects, nearly a quarter of the twenty-three prefects in the province. Fewer district magistrates, only 7 of 113, were named. These were the magistrates of Licheng, Zhangqiu, Dongping, Yidu, Linqing, Liaocheng, and Pu counties. Most of the magistracies named contained cities. Licheng was the county in which the provincial capital was located, Yidu was the seat of the Taian prefect, Linqing and Liaocheng were prosperous cities situated along the Grand Canal, and Dongping was also located on the canal. Pu and Zhangqiu were somewhat unusual, though Zhangqiu was quite close to Jinan, and Pu seems to have been part of the trading network around Daming in southern Zhili. This list associates Guotai's extortion fairly clearly with the successful cities of central Shandong whose economies were most influenced by the prosperity of the mid-eighteenth century.

Perhaps as important, each post was in effect controlled by the provincial governor of Shandong. As discussed in chapter 4, all Qing governors had the prerogative of selecting certain of the officials who would serve as their subordinates in the province. The Shandong governor's prerogatives involved primarily the ability to move officials from less to more difficult postings; he was authorized to fill 25 of 113 posts by transferring officials. This prerogative was significant in a province with economic disparities, insofar as it allowed the governor to move officials from one economic zone to another. Not all of the transfer posts in Shandong were in wealthy areas, but all of the "urban" magistrates identified in the Guotai case were in transfer posts over which the governor had control. In view of Guotai's long service in Shandong, it was likely that the governor had selected all the appointees named in the prosecution. It is possible to read the Shandong case, therefore, as one in which Governor Guotai was systematically using the powers of office to place pliant officials in urban posts and thus skim the cream off the north China economy that Qing policies had created.

The one subordinate official on whom the case focused was Lu Erchang, the prefect of Jinan, the Shandong capital district, who served as Guotai's henchman. The role of bagman is always a complicated one in illicit transactions with figures of authority, and the Shandong case provides a nice example of how such a position was described.[45] Lu's relationship with Guotai was one of the issues that had been brought to the court's attention in 1781, though at that time, the emperor had been convinced that there was nothing untoward about it. According to Lu's 1782 confession, he had become friendly with Guotai when the two were serving together in the Board of Punishments. In 1777, Lu received an appointment as prefect of Denglai in northern Shandong, but in 1778, newly appointed Governor Guotai transferred him to Jinan. Once in the provincial capital, according to his testimony, Lu was ordered to buy objects of jade and precious metal for Guotai and to transmit gifts from various subordinate territorial officials to Guotai. Lu professed uncertainty as to the source of the funds for these purchases, but investigation suggested that Lu received money from provincial officials who meant to bribe the governor and then used these funds to buy objects. Lu clearly proved himself diligent in his duties, for he was promoted first to the post of circuit intendant in Shandong and then to the position of provincial judge in Anhui. Lu's successor as Jinan prefect was exhorted to follow Lu's example.

Families who lived by the sword, or at least the powers that Qing swords had earned in north China, could also die by it. The consequences of this case were grave for both Wenshou's descendants and Yu Minzhong's family. Guotai and Yu Yijian were sentenced to death, but in view of their families' eminence, they were allowed to commit suicide in prison. The emperor, however, sent a member of the Grand Council to observe the suicides and announced them in public edicts. The honors that had been granted to Yu Minzhong during his lifetime and posthumously were revoked, and the emperor wrote a poem comparing Yu to the corrupt ministers of the Ming dynasty.[46] The Imperial Household Department seized the assets of Guotai's family. These included a house of 135 rooms in Beijing, nineteen male and female slaves, two commercial rental properties with a combined total of forty-one rooms, more than fifty jade objects, and more than a hundred other items, including pearls, furs, and household furnishings.[47] The list of objects seized was detailed in part because Guotai, like other governors, seems to have preferred his bribes in the form of art objects. This is not to suggest that Guotai or other governors were connoisseurs, except perhaps in the very status-conscious sense of connoisseurship articulated by Craig Clunus in *Superfluous Things*, his study of late Ming material culture. Rather, these governors may have appreciated that the art objects, after being sold and resold (perhaps in the very commercial properties Guotai's family owned in the capital), could effectively conceal the source of the money that had been used to purchase them. Regardless of how it had been collected, all the family's wealth was gone, and when Wenshou returned from exile in 1784, his son was dead. Wenshou himself died two years later.[48]

Perhaps Guotai's case was extreme, but behind it were the basic realities of north China government. The governors of Henan and Shandong were powerful and visible representatives of the Qing order, and they ruled populations whose loyalty was important to the dynasty. In both the military and the civilian sphere, they exercised formally (and likely informally as well) powers that far exceeded those of other governors. Henan and Shandong governors directly commanded the Green Standard Army detachments located in their provinces, and their power to recommend officials for promotion exceeded that of other governors. They presided over flows of grain and revenue that were essential to the support of the Qing administrative apparatus. They were first among equals in the elite corps of Chinese governors. For all these reasons, the governors of Shandong and Henan were very closely tied to the capital and much more sensitive than their colleagues to the winds of political change.

For the seventeenth and much of the eighteenth century, the regime the Qing implemented in north China was arguably successful, if not in alleviating poverty among north China peasantry then at least in creating a stable basis for dynastic rule and secure urban seats for its officialdom. In fact, one could argue that the Manchus were in some sense the victims of their own success, much of which was based on the principle of vesting unusual powers in a few individuals who were closely tied and well known to the ruler and those around him. This was a very effective strategy in the early years of the dynasty, when circumstances and resources offered the Qing few choices in north China. However, by the middle of the eighteenth century, when resources permitted the pursuit of multiple goals in the region, the close ties between Jinan and Beijing made it far more difficult to exercise the kind of supervision in north China that was routine elsewhere. In this environment, central control of the northern provinces became less stable, and the region that had been a great success story during the first half of the Qing dynasty became an Achilles heel.

ZHILI AND SHANXI: KEYS TO THE CAPITAL

Nowhere in the empire was the Qing penchant for consistency tested more sorely than in the provinces adjacent to the capital. Like all the governors of north China, the governors of Zhili and Shanxi had the general responsibility of supplying the capital; unlike their north China colleagues, however, officials in Zhili and Shanxi had a specific responsibility for access routes to the capital and the military officials and men who guarded these routes. In both provinces, special arrangements were made to accommodate the unique relations between the governors and the central government and the special responsibilities the governors bore. Most of these arrangements stood somewhere between statute and practice, in a legislatively liminal world where the dynasty preserved the freedom to act as it chose. How the Manchus operated in that world as well as how they represented and justified their decisions are especially revealing of changing identities and political realities. In both Shanxi and Zhili, the issue was the dynasty's representation to the outside world, but the specific problems were different. In Zhili, the dynasty was confronted with a world of bannermen and bandits, and it navigated its way among them as its perceptions of danger permitted. In Shanxi, the issues were how to control access to the Qing capital from central Asia and what role ethnically Manchu officials were to play in the Chinese state.

Zhili, the third province wholly within the north China plain, was a Qing dynasty creation. Both the Yuan and the Ming had set aside the area around Beijing as a special administrative region, but both dynasties governed the region from the capital. The Qing established the area around the capital as a separate jurisdiction with a full quota of provincial administrators. But the name given the area—Zhili, which means "directly under the control (of the capital)"—emphasized the area's current and historical relationship with Beijing. The Qing also set aside much of the province's land, some 29 percent by one estimate, as land grants to support its own Manchu banner troops.[49] From the time of its creation, the Zhili provincial administration was meant to have obligations both to the territories it governed and to the capital, and Qing emperors seem to have been ambivalent about how these obligations should be marked.

The province also had an odd shape. Zhili's boundaries encompassed the coastal plain, which extended from the suburbs of the capital to the south and the east, but they also included a rather long "tail," which extended south from the coastal plain along the eastern and western borders of Henan and Shandong, respectively. Skinner has suggested that this tail was a product of high-level gerrymandering. "One effect of extending a leg of Chihli deep into the southern portion of the regional core," he argues, "was to split the metropolitan and regional-city trading systems of both Kaifeng and Tung Ch'ang-fu, and to tie the interests of the powerful gentry of Ta-ming Fu (the prefecture forming the southern leg of Chihli) to the metropolitan province rather than to Honan or Shantong, the provinces on which the interest of the Ta-ming merchants were focused."[50] Provincial boundaries seemed to Skinner to have been designed with the intent of breaking up natural concentrations of economic power. It should be noted, however, that the Daming merchants gained as well as lost in this administrative arrangement. The boundaries of Zhili derived from the three-province governor-generalship created during the Shunzhi reign. The shape was proposed by Yao Wenran, a Ming era *jinshi*-degree holder who chose to serve the Qing. Yao is included in *History of the Qing* in a chapter devoted to Chinese officials of the early Qing who, through their advice to the Manchus, gave the dynasty its political and fiscal form. Yao was certainly well aware of the several types of economic activity in southern Zhili, for he warned of the danger that arises when banditry prevails: "Trade cannot flourish and agricultural tasks cannot be accomplished in season." Yao proposed incorporating parts of eastern Henan and western Shandong into the new jurisdiction. His proposal did tie the merchants of southern Zhili to the metropolitan province, but it also placed a governor-general and his order-preserving troops in the merchants' native city of Daming.[51] Through the 1650s and 1660s, the "tail" was allowed to wag the dog in Zhili, that is, Qing administrative presence was concentrated in the portion of the province that was sandwiched between Henan and Shandong. By 1665, however, the northern three-province governor-generalship was judged to be unnecessary, and the senior official in Zhili was designated a governor. When this occurred, the capital of the province was moved north and east. In 1660, the capital moved to Zhengding on the coastal plain, and in 1664, it was moved to Baoding Fu.[52] For much of the eighteenth century, the senior official of the province was designated a governor-general rather than a governor. But such a distinction was never formally proclaimed; it was granted, and then withdrawn, according to the will of the monarch. Indeed, Zhili was one of the few provinces of the empire to take different forms depending on who governed.

The province was not designated a governor-generalship until the term of the longest-serving governor of Zhili during the Kangxi reign, Zhao Hongxie, who was appointed in 1704. Zhao was, in some respects, the perfect governor for Zhili. His father Zhao Liangdong had surrendered to the Qing armies when they invaded Shaanxi and had risen through the ranks to become a general. He fought beside Manchu generals in the conquest of the southwest, commanded the Ningxia garrison, and again fought beside (and was punished with) Manchu generals in the Wu Sangui Rebellion. Zhao Hongxie started his career as a magistrate in Zhili, was promoted to circuit intendant, and finally, after he had inherited the hereditary rank given his father, became governor.[53] In 1715, the Kangxi emperor observed that since Zhao had acquitted himself with distinction for ten years and maintained harmonious relations with the bannermen stationed around the capital, it was appropriate that his rank be raised to governor-general. While the edict certainly represented an acknowledgment of the region's strategic importance, the promotion seems to have been meant mainly to reward a senior official who had mastered the demanding job of presiding over both bannermen and civilians in China's metropolitan province.[54] In fact, when Zhao Hongxie died in office, leaving tax arrears in the province, the matter was resolved by the stratagem, curious in a bureaucratic order, of appointing his son to serve in the province until the family name was cleared.[55]

The title "governor-general" was allowed to die with Zhao in 1722, but two years later, when the new Yongzheng emperor appointed an official of his own choosing to the post in Zhili, he designated the official a governor-general. "Since Li Weijun [the new governor] is so able, and can preside over the gentry of the province and organize its military forces, let him serve as governor-general. Let

the provincial commandant and the brigade commanders take orders from him."
Even on this occasion, the emperor was not willing to make the post of governor-
general permanent. "This is a special order [te zhi]," wrote the editors of *Collected
Statutes and Precedents of the Qing*, "and should Li Weijun be promoted or move elsewhere, appointees in Zhili should once again be governors."[56] However, all subsequent appointees to the post were designated governors-general, and the title
became permanent. The title distinguished the senior official in Zhili from all the
other governors in the empire, although the emperor was at some pains to deem-
phasize Zhili exceptionalism. In the same edict in which he appointed Li Weijun,
the emperor moved to rectify an irregularity in the province. When lieutenant governors were appointed to China's provinces in the 1660s, none was established
for Zhili, and the functions of the lieutenant governor were assigned to special
censors serving in the province. Asserting that Zhili was a "province just like any
other," the Yongzheng emperor ordered that it be provided with a lieutenant governor, creating the only province in which a lieutenant governor served without a
governor. In fact, in the case of north China governors, the distinction may have
been a matter more of degree than of kind. Although the Zhili governor-general
could issue orders directly to the provincial military commander, the north China
governors could command their troops directly.

The political arrangements made for Zhili in the Yongzheng and Qianlong
reigns reflect very clearly its obligations to the capital and the constraints they
imposed on its officials.[57] The task of defending the approaches to the capital
from the south entailed a regime of extraordinary vigilance: more troops were
garrisoned in Zhili than in nearly any other province, and the arrangements
made for their subsistence and security were elaborate. Zhili contained seven brigades of Green Standard Army troops, more than in any other province except
Guangdong, which also had seven.[58] In addition, Manchu troops were garrisoned
throughout the province, and by an order of 1732, they were also placed under
seven tactical commanders.[59] Troops guarding the capital were garrisoned on a
rather narrow, low-lying coastal plain that was extremely susceptible to flooding. The area of Zhili constituted the northeastern extremity of the Yellow River
delta, and, as such, it was crossed by numerous rivers and streams that rose in
the Daxing Mountains along the western border of the province and flowed east.
The watercourses of the province were customarily divided into five river systems,
which converged like spokes of a wheel in Tianjin city. There, they merged to
form the Haihe, which flowed to the ocean. The Grand Canal, the main commercial waterway linking the capital with Jiangnan, flowed almost due north and
south; from the southeast came the Ziya River; flowing almost directly west to
east was the Qing River; and the Bei River flowed in from the north. From the

northwest came the Yongding River, the longest of the Zhili river systems, which rose in central Shanxi and flowed past Beijing, feeding the reservoirs that supplied the city's water.[60]

When excessive rain beginning in the spring of 1725 flooded the areas south of Beijing, the Yongzheng emperor ordered his younger brother Prince I to investigate Zhili's water conservancy projects. The outgrowth of this investigation was the creation of a new circuit intendant in central Zhili, who was responsible for overseeing local administration in the eight magistracies nearest Baodingfu and supervising the river works in the area.[61] As if to assure itself that the disaster of 1725 would not be repeated, the Qing court renamed the Hunhe, the "River of Chaos," the Yongding, or "Permanently Secured River." Considering the number of troops garrisoned in the province, threats to subsistence could have been disastrous, and it was perhaps not surprising that the longest-serving governor-general of Zhili, Fang Guancheng, was also the author, according to Pierre-Etienne Will, of the model regulations for relief of famine in cases of drought or natural disaster.[62]

Just as the Zhili governor-general who controlled the approaches to the capital from the south and the east was differentiated from other governors, so the provincial administrator who controlled the approaches to the capital from the north and the west, the governor of Shanxi, was marked off from his colleagues. The geopolitical imperatives of Shanxi, however, were very different from those of its eastern neighbor, and so the provincial markers employed were different. The province was created to serve defensive purposes; in the seventeenth century, Gu Zuyu, who had characterized Shandong as the empire's elbow and armpit, likened Shanxi to the empire's backbone.[63] As befit a province that was likened to a spine, Shanxi sat athwart a macro-regional boundary. Water and trade routes linked the eastern part of the province to the coastal plain, while the Fen River, which drained into the upper Yellow River basin, the defining feature of the northwest, dominated its western part. The merging of these two subregions dated from the Yuan dynasty, when the Mongols established a defense bureau in Taiyuan in order to protect their capital near Beijing. The Ming appointed a provincial administration commissioner to Shanxi as well as two grand coordinators, one in Taiyuan and the other in Datong. The Qing established a banner garrison at Guihuacheng even before Beijing fell.[64] In 1644, the Qing replaced the two Ming coordinators with Green Standard Army regional commanders,[65] appointed a governor in Taiyuan, and posted a governor-general to oversee the province and the border regions to the north. The governor-generalship was abolished in 1658 but reestablished sporadically in the early Kangxi reign. During the Kangxi era war against Galdan, a Manchu garrison was established in the province, but when the wars were over, it was allowed to shrink and was placed under the control of the Shanxi governor.[66] As peace prevailed in inner Mongolia, the northern areas of Shanxi, which had been governed as garrisons, became counties and prefectures and were subject to the rules and procedures of civilian administration.[67] Like the governors of north China, the Shanxi governor after 1731 was commander of his own provincial garrison.

The province that resulted had, to be sure, some agriculturally productive valley land, but much of it was a mountainous border region.[68] Its wealthiest subjects were merchants who underwrote long-distance trade throughout the empire. The main study of this group, *The Shanxi Merchants* (Sansei shonin no kenkyu), by Terada Takenobu, focuses on the Ming dynasty, but Wei Qingyuan has used Imperial Household Department documents to trace this family's fortunes during the Qing. As Wei demonstrates, descendants of the Ming Shanxi Fan family became licensed monopolists in service of the Qing, supervising trade with the Mongols at Guihuacheng and other northern cities. From this role, they seem to have moved into the business of purchasing copper in Japan and transporting it to mints in north China, supervising the official trade with the Koreans and selling salt on behalf of the Qing state throughout north China. The Fans also served as purchasing agents for the grain supplies needed in the Kangxi and Yongzheng emperors' military campaigns in Mongolia. When the family fell on hard times in the late eighteenth century, the state seized property including twenty salt shops in Henan, a salt warehouse in Tianjin, a copper warehouse in Suzhou, three shops in Beijing, six shops in Zhangjiakou, four shops in Guihuacheng, and 100 *mu* of land near Zhangjiakou.[69]

But what really set the Shanxi governor and his northwestern colleagues apart from his fellow governors was the decree, said in *Collected Statutes of the Qing* to have been issued by the Kangxi emperor in 1668, that only Manchus would be allowed to serve as governors of Shanxi, Shaanxi, and Gansu.[70] There was, however, some mystery about this decree. Issued only four months after the court had consolidated its provincial bureaucracy by limiting the number of provincial administration commissioners, the rule seems to have been a fundamental part of the new provincial order being created. However, although the decree was referred to in the Kangxi, Yongzheng, and Guangxu editions of *Collected Statutes*, there is no mention of the edict in *Veritable Records of the Qing* (Qing shilu). There was no question about the dynasty's intent, since new Manchu governors, lieutenant governors, and provincial judges were appointed to Shanxi and Shaanxi within a two-week period in 1668. Similar appointments were made in Gansu in the summer of 1670, and for the remainder of the seventeenth century, all the province-level appointments in Shanxi, Shaanxi, and Gansu went to Manchus. There could have been many reasons for the policy: the strategic importance of the approaches to the capital and the defense tasks that devolved upon local governors, or indeed the delicate business of dealing with the Shanxi merchants. But either the dynasty never set out to explain its reason for appointing only Manchus to the northwest or the edict has been lost or suppressed. Since references to the rule were preserved, it seems unlikely that the document was actually suppressed. More likely, Chinese editors simply made a rule out of a practice. In itself, this instance of editorial reification was of relatively little interest, except insofar as it suppressed an element of contingency in the governance of the region. Up until the middle of the eighteenth century, as it appears, Qing rulers were consciously choosing to send Manchus to the northwest.[71]

But the reasons for their choices likely varied over the seventeenth and eighteenth centuries.[72] In the beginning, the issue may well have been military. In the 1670s, it was quite likely that the Kangxi emperor wanted military forces along the northern borders under firm control as he prepared to go to war in the south and contemplated the threat of Galdan in Mongolia. However, the role of the Qing provincial governor was usually more logistical than tactical. In Shanxi, military logistics probably meant dealing with the Shanxi merchant bankers, or supervising the cross-border trade between Manchus and Mongols at Guihuacheng. Later seventeenth-century governors of Shanxi were better known for their entrepreneurial rather than military skills. Maci, who served as lieutenant governor and governor from 1685 to 1688, was best known before his appointment to Shanxi for having increased the revenue from the Wuhu customs station along the Yangzi River in the mid-1680s.[73] Gali, who served as governor from 1703 to 1709, is described in *Eminent Chinese of the Ch'ing Period* as a clever if covetous executive.[74] Gali never quite shook his reputation for corruption, and Zhang Boxing used this fact quite skillfully, as explained in chapter 7, in his campaign to have Gali dismissed in Jiangnan. Managing flows of revenue was part of the Manchu heritage, for Manchus had been traders—of ginseng and furs along the borders of the Ming empire—before they were conquerors.

The Case of Shilin

As provincial offices were regularized in the eighteenth century, the anomaly of the Shanxi situation became more apparent. Manchus serving in Shanxi reported to no senior territorial official; they were overseen only by the central court and in fact had little to do with provincial administrations outside the northwest. Before 1740, twenty-one of thirty governors who served in Shanxi were either promoted from the lieutenant governorship of the province, appointed from other provinces in the northwest, or appointed directly from the capital. Few of those who served in the northwest had ever served south of the Yangzi, and some had never served south of the Yellow River. While some of the northwestern governors had been promoted from below, those who were promoted had usually served shorter terms in fewer subordinate positions than had their Chinese counterparts. Combining modest experience in Chinese administrative practice with close ties to the court and banner elite, the Manchu governors of Shanxi were fairly unique figures in Qing administration.

Some of the characteristics of this Manchu *imperium in imperio* are suggested by the career of the longest-serving governor of Shanxi, Shilin, a Manchu of the imperial Aisin Gioro clan. Like most Manchus of the eighteenth century, Shilin qualified for office by first serving in an agency of the central government in Beijing as a "clerk" (Chinese, *bitieshi*; Manchu, *bithe*); in Shilin's case, it was the Board of Works. He then moved to the Office of Transmission, the agency responsible for transmitting routine memorials from provincial governors to their appropriate locations in the capital, usually the Grand Secretariat. This appointment brought Shilin one step closer to the provinces, not only because correspondence from all the provinces passed through the agency but because the Office of Transmission was the capital agency to which lieutenant governors were appointed if they were not promoted to governor. When Manchus actually moved into the territorial service in eighteenth-century China, they started fairly near the top, usually in the positions of provincial judge, lieutenant governor, or sometimes governor. This was true of Shilin, but, either because of his demonstrated competence or because of his clan connection with the imperial family, he started even higher than most and was appointed lieutenant governor of Jiangsu in the spring of 1726. The Yongzheng emperor repeatedly assigned well-connected Manchus to this position in the hope of introducing an element of central control into lower Yangzi valley finances. After a year and a half of service in this position, Shilin was promoted to the governorship of Shanxi, a post he held for thirteen years.[75]

As governor of Shanxi, Shilin's main achievement, according to the draft biography prepared by the State Historiographical Commission, was regulating Shanxi's provincial grain storage. During the first half of the eighteenth century, as Bin Wong, Pierre-Etienne Will, and their colleagues have shown, the amount of grain stored against subsistence crises in provincial granaries was as great as it would ever be in China.[76] In Shanxi, the concern was how to maintain the reserves necessary to prevent civilian disasters while still providing enough food for the troops stationed in the province. Shilin undertook this task, using as his purchasing agent the Shanxi merchant Fan Yuqi. Other elements of Shilin's experience in Shanxi, perhaps not so praiseworthy, were not recorded in the commission's draft. During the course of his service, he was technically demoted thirteen times and restored to office only because of the administrative commendations he had received by imperial favor. When he left office, his successor Korjishan found a province rife with corruption. His first tasks were to shore up the dike works along the Fen River and monitor more carefully relations between miners, bannermen, and traders in the area of Guihuacheng, along the Mongolian border. Six months after taking office, Korjishan memorialized, accusing the Manchu lieutenant governor of failing to maintain proper accounts of monies handled in the province. Two months later, he accused the Manchu education commissioner of Shanxi of demanding sexual favors from the wives and concubines of examination candidates in return for positive evaluations.[77]

Juicy as these charges were, the bill of particulars may not have been as important as the impact of the indictments and what they said about the price the Qing court was willing to pay for the specialized administration of Shanxi. Under the control of an official whose special access to the court precluded effective supervision, a provincial regime had developed that undermined the dynasty's claim to rule by universal standards. Korjishan's indictments certainly had ethnic overtones, but the Qianlong emperor seemingly could comment on ethnic implications only obliquely. This was probably because Korjishan's indictments pointed not to tensions between Chinese and Manchu officials but to Manchu officials' inability to police one another. To suggest that Manchu officials had a particular problem in this regard would have seriously undermined their claims for Chinese civil office. Rather than speak of such a matter, the Qianlong emperor chose to emphasize the structure of incentives for proper behavior and disincentives for malfeasance that had been built under his father and to reflect on the question of the ways in which corrupt (and coincidentally Manchu) officials came to be appointed. In so doing, the emperor provided a fascinating glimpse of how senior provincial appointments were made in the 1740s and revealed at least one of the reasons for the predominance of Manchus among appointees.

The emperor's edicts on the Shanxi cases emphasized first the responsibilities all officials shared in the evolving Qing bureaucratic order. As he had in the early days of his reign, he emphasized that his own contributions to official life were meant to be positive ones, from the official's point of view. "Since the beginning of my reign," he wrote, "I have tried to sympathize with officials, provided them with increased salaries and new nourishment of virtue payments," in the expectation that officials would exert themselves to the fullest. "Not in his wildest dreams" (*zhen meng-xiang zhi wai*) had the emperor imagined that officials would be as corrupt as the Shanxi officials appeared to be. Officials, wrote the emperor, seem to have ignored both his own good efforts and those of his father, who had labored for more than ten years to clean up the Qing bureaucracy. Even though he had earlier rejected the severity of his father's rule, the model for punishment of officials was to come from the Yongzheng reign.[78] In fact, in investigating the indictment against Karchin, the imperial investigators were to take as precedent the case of a Chinese education commissioner, Yu Hongtu, who had been found guilty of corruption and executed in 1731.[79]

Perhaps Shanxi officials could be corrupt because they were being protected. The emperor continued: "As for Karchin and Sahaliang, I long ago heard of their evil nature. But among the nine ministers, there were none who spoke of them. As for Shilin, the Shanxi governor, even though there were Shanxi natives at court, I have heard nothing at all about his misdeeds." Even the censors had reported only insignificant matters when they wrote of Shanxi. Could it be, the emperor seemed to ask, that the whole court was in league with the Shanxi bureaucracy and its senior Manchu appointees to prevent the emperor from learning what was going on? Imperial frustration appears to have been high. Subsequent events suggest that the issue may have been not selective testimony from senior officials as much as selective imperial hearing. The emperor certainly heard the accusation against the two junior officials and punished them severely. But no action was taken against Shilin, a member of the Aisin Gioro clan, who had been governor of the province for thirteen years; he was allowed to return to his banner office after completing the mourning period for his mother.[80]

The thrust of the emperor's edict—perhaps illogical but not entirely surprising—was that Manchus, subjected to the rules of the Qing personnel system, could be as capable as their Chinese counterparts. In effect, the Qianlong emperor achieved something of a compromise between the notion that Manchus should serve in only those postings to which their historical role as border guardians would have consigned them and the view that Manchu and Chinese officials should have exactly the same qualifications. In the northwest, however, the new attitude toward appointing Manchus meant that the governors of Shanxi after 1740 were much more likely to have had experience outside the northwest than those who had served in the province before. Twenty-six out of thirty-four of the governors who followed Shilin in Shanxi during the Qianlong reign held positions in other provinces at the time they were appointed to Shanxi. Manchus continued to govern Shanxi through the Qianlong reign, but increasingly they were officials in the generalist tradition of the Qing civil service rather than specialists in the military arts.

Ironically, when the moment came for a military specialist in the province, during the White Lotus Rebellion, the court turned to a Chinese candidate, Jiang Zhaokui, who was appointed in 1792. Jiang was a straight-speaking military man who had earned his stripes as a governor under Fuheng's nephew Fulaihun in Sichuan during the Jinchuan Rebellion.[81] His appointment signaled the beginning of an era in the northwest when Chinese could be as knowledgeable as Manchus about military matters. More important, perhaps, the appointment suggested that the Jiaqing emperor and possibly the Qianlong emperor himself did not find Manchu officials as inherently trustworthy as the Qing once had, a conclusion that could easily have been drawn from accusations against Qianlong's chief grand councilor Heshen, which dominated the first few years of the Jiaqing emperor's reign.

The Qing dynasty did not set out to create anomalies in the provinces of Shanxi and Zhili. At the time the first arrangements for the regions nearest the capital were made, there was no standard against which the situation in Shanxi and Zhili could be compared. Later, when there was a standard form for Chinese provinces, arrangements in Shanxi and Zhili were adjusted without fanfare. Crucial decisions about the two provinces often bore the hallmarks of personal imperial involvement and were quietly, if unimpeachably, proclaimed. In fact, all Qing imperial pronouncements on Shanxi and Zhili governors had a truncated feel, as if the emperors had more to say but were unwilling to reveal themselves in public. Unlike the other provinces of north China, where the capacities of the Qing state were on public display, matters in Shanxi and Zhili were held close to the imperial vests and suggest something of the hearts that beat beneath them.

NORTHWEST CHINA: CIVILIAN GOVERNORS IN MILITARY CONTEXT

Like his colleagues in north China, the Shanxi governor controlled routes to the capital and was marked off from other governors. Like the governors of the northwest, he presided over a fairly poor province that bordered on non-Chinese territories. As the official traveler moved farther west from Taiyuan, the differences between north and northwest China became even more pronounced. The northwest, which Skinner has defined as including the upper Yangzi basin and the drainage systems that supported the oases of the Gansu corridor, was an empty and rugged land that posed different strategic dilemmas from those of north China. The physical area of the northwest was only slightly larger than that of north China. But the northwest had in the nineteenth century less than one-fifth of the population of the north, which gave the region the second-lowest population density of the eight regions in China proper. Somewhat more of the northwest's population was concentrated in cities than was the case in other regions, but the cities were often of administrative origin, military or political outposts linked by official communications system.[82]

The region was bordered on the northeast by inner Mongolia, whose peoples had pledged allegiance to the Qing before the conquest. But to the north and the west were the outer Mongols, against whom the Qing warred in the 1680s, the 1730s, and the 1750s. To the west was Xinjiang, with its complex religious, linguistic, and ethnic divisions, and to the south lay Tibet, the key—or so the Qing came to understand—to the religious life of Mongolia and the steppes. Northwest China was the Qing bridge to each of these areas, but its people were few and its resources sparse. This set limits on the type of government that could be effected in the region. R. Bin Wong has expressed the situation of the northwest quite cogently:

> In the northwest, the government faced fundamental strategic concerns, a threat of a Mongol federation preying on Chinese settlers and a fear of Mongol alliance with the Tibetans against the Chinese. Moreover, Islamic religious movements held the potential for serious social disruption as Russian advances threatened Qing territories all along China's northern frontiers. The Manchus who ruled China's last dynasty therefore acted out of concerns over political security. The absence of cultural homogeneity reflected the importance of social and material strategies of control.[83]

Normative control, Wong argues, was less of an option in the northwest than in the provinces of central China. Normative controls were also ineffective in Sichuan, but for slightly different reasons. As in the northwest, peoples who were intermittently hostile to the Qing, including those in Tibet, the regime of Wu Sangui, and the Jinchuan rebels in the eighteenth century, inhabited territories around Sichuan. But as important, for most of the first century of Qing rule, Sichuan itself was a land of armies on the march, where early Qing government more closely resembled martial law than the civil administration of other provinces.

Government in Sichuan, Shaanxi, and Gansu was unstable, not in fact but in form; provincial boundaries and the administrative arrangement within them shifted frequently as the dynasty changed its strategies in the far west. As a consequence, the region's history nicely highlights some of the central questions of territorial government in China: At what point in time or in space were military controls judged to be necessary? At what level, how, and by whom was such a decision made? The military regimes established in the three provinces in the early years of Qing rule evolved on somewhat different trajectories. Shaanxi moved toward the model of a civilian province, particularly during the long term of Governor Bi Yuan, who served in the province from 1773 to 1785. Sichuan and Gansu moved in the opposite direction, losing their civilian governors in the middle of the eighteenth century. The contrasting trajectories of these provinces highlights Qing strategic dilemmas in the seventeenth and eighteenth centuries.

Shaanxi

Like the Ming, the Qing addressed the problems of governing the northwest by garrisoning troops throughout the region. The largest Qing garrison in China was at Xi'an, but other garrisons were added later at Ningxia (1696), Suiyuan (1744), and Qinghai (1729). Unlike the Ming, however, the Qing built a civil administrative structure around its northwest garrisons. The dominant figure in this structure was a governor-general, who was usually based in Shaanxi. The office was one of the oldest and most enduring in the Qing territorial order; created in 1645, it existed continuously until the fall of the dynasty in 1911. Perhaps the secret of the office's longevity was that the Qing reshaped it periodically to meet evolving needs. Table 6.2 lists the several titles enjoyed by Shaanxi governors-general and the years during which the titles were used. The element designating Shaanxi province, *shaan*, appears in all the titles. Sometimes, the title indicates that the governor-general's authority was limited to Shaanxi or to Shaanxi and its neighbor Shanxi. These were mostly periods, as in the early years of the dynasty (1645–52) and during the early Kangxi reign (1661–65), when the dynasty perceived a direct threat from Mongolia. During the years 1673–80, the situation was particularly critical, as the threat of a Mongol invasion at a time when the dynasty was involved in the Wu Sangui Rebellion in the southeast could well have brought the new regime to its knees.[84]

At other times, however, the dynasty could redirect the Shaanxi governor-general's attentions toward other regional dangers. At other points in history (1653–61, 1681–1717, 1721–30, and 1735–48) the dynasty gave the Shaanxi governor-general authority over Sichuan because, in the early days of the dynasty, warfare in the south and southwest was supported and supplied from the dynasty's bases in the northwest. In the wake of the conquest of the middle Yangzi region in 1650 and the Rebellion of the Three Feudatories in the 1670s, the court turned to the Shaanxi governor-general to regulate the flow of supplies and restock the garrisons of both the northwest and the southwest. The third permutation of the Shaanxi governor-general's title, *shaan-gan*, occurred twice in the eighteenth century (1731–35 and 1749) when the dynasty turned its attention to the conquest of Mongolia and added Gansu to this adaptable governor's territorial portfolio. The governor-general even resided at Lanzhou, the capital of Gansu, briefly during the 1750s. The *shaan-gan* version of the title ultimately became permanent as large territories in the northwest were incorporated into the empire.

It was perhaps not surprising, given the nature of the region, that its provincial governors fell under the shadow of this powerful and pivotal governor-general. The governor of Shaanxi was outranked in his own capital, not only by the com-

TABLE 6.2. Governors-General in the Northwest

Title	Years in Office
Shaan-shan	1645–52[a]
Chuan-shaan	1653–61[b]
Shaan-xi	1661–65[c]
Shaan-shan	1665–72[d]
Shaan-xi	1673–80[e]
Chuan-shaan	1681–1717[f]
Shaan-xi	1718–20[g]
Chuan-shaan	1721–30[h]
Shaan-gan	1731–35[i]
Chuan-shaan	1735–48[j]
Shaan-gan	1749–1911[k]

Sources: Da Qing huidian shili (DQHDSL); Dai Yincong, "The Rise of the Southwestern Frontier"; Gaozongshun (Qianlong) Huangdi shilu (reprinted in Da Qing shilu, 1937; reprint, Beijing: Zhonghua, 1985), vols. 9–27 (QLSL); Shengzong Ren (Kangxi) Huangdi shilu (reprinted in Da Qing shilu, 1937; reprint, Beijing: Zhonghua, 1985), vols. 3–6 (KXSL); Shizong Zhang (Shinzhi) Huangdi shilu (reprint, Beijing: Zhonghua, 1985), vol. 2 (SZSL); Wakeman, The Great Enterprise; Shizongxian Huangdi shilu (reprinted in Da Qing shilu, 1937; reprint, Beijing: Zhonghua, 1985), vols. 8–9 (YZSL). Citations include juan and page numbers for the original; volume or juan and/or page numbers for the reprint are in parentheses.

[a] SZSL, 15:18b (2:138); see also Wakeman, The Great Enterprise, 683–98.
[b] SZSL 76:3a (3:598); DQHDSL, 23:5B (290).
[c] KXSL, 4:15a (4:87).
[d] KXSL, 15:15a (4:224). DQHDSL, 23:9b (292); see also Dai Yincong, "The Rise of the Southwestern Frontier," 104.
[e] KXSL, 389:25a (4:515).
[f] KXSL, 93:2b–4a (4:1174).
[g] KXSL, 28:13b–14a (6:750–51); see also Dai Yincong, "The Rise of the Southwestern Frontier," 328–29.
[h] KXSL, 292:12a–b (6:842).
[i] YZSL, 103:31b–32a (8:374).
[j] QLSL, 8:7b (9:300); DQHDSL, 23:13a (294).
[k] QLSL, 329:21a–b (12:451–52); DQHDSL, 29:14a–b (294).

mander of the local banner garrison, who was always a Manchu, but also by the governor-general when he was in residence.[85] In fact, the governor's yamen in Xi'an was located midway between the governor-general's yamen and the garrison commander's yamen, just inside the "Manchu city."[86] In the seventeenth century, much of the Shaanxi governor's time must have been spent supplying armies that were marching elsewhere. "All of the grain and money for the troops in Sichuan comes from Shaanxi," the Shunzhi court declared in 1655, as it justified placing Sichuan under the Shaanxi governor-general's control. Similarly, at the end of the Wu Sangui Rebellion, three separate officials complained to the Kangxi emperor of the famine that had been created in Shaanxi as a result of efforts in the south. Unfortunately, just a few months after these complaints, the Kangxi emperor ordered the governor of Shaanxi to transfer another 60,000 liang to the Xi'an garrison treasury in order to deal with a military emergency to the south.[87]

Most officials in Shaanxi had served much of their careers in the northwest, as was true of most northwestern provinces; in fact, Shaanxi had the second-highest rate of same-province promotions in the empire, 56 percent. But there was a glass ceiling of sorts in Xi'an. Although it was possible for a governor to be promoted to governor-general, this seldom happened in Shaanxi: only five of the seventy-three officials who served as Shaanxi governors during the eighteenth century were promoted to the governor-general's position. This is to suggest not that the Shaanxi governor's post was unimportant but merely that the governor was an official responsible for civilian matters in a region that was primarily of military importance.

As in the other northwestern provinces, the Shaanxi governorship was de facto reserved for Manchus in the Kangxi reign. Possibly because of the civilian tasks associated with the province, the Qing assigned Chinese to govern it as early as 1737. The first Chinese governor of the province was Cui Ji, who served from 1737 to 1738, a *jinshi*-degree holder who was originally from Shanxi. Cui was followed over the next five years by two Chinese and one Manchu bannerman and then by Chen Hongmou, who served in the province, with some interruptions, from 1743 to 1757. From 1757 until 1789, during the central Asian wars of mid-century and for some time thereafter, the province was governed by Manchus, but from 1789 to 1799, Bi Yuan, a *jinshi*-degree holder and patron of Chinese literature, served as governor.

Despite the appointments of Chinese in the province, differences between the military and civilian worlds remained, as illustrated by an episode from the biography of Chen Hongmou. At the end of his first term, Chen was charged by his superior Qingfu with various crimes, including being slack in handling public affairs, being lenient in prosecuting criminality, showing favoritism to subordinates, and being "excessively fond of his own cleverness in getting things done."[88] His accuser, Governor-general Qingfu, was a descendant of the banner elite that had conquered China and the son of Longkodo, the head of the Beijing garrison during the early Yongzheng reign. Once Qingfu had been transferred to another posting, Chen Hongmou was reappointed governor, with an imperial instruction: "This is territory you know well. If you are fair, and don't insist on your own opinions or pursue a name, then you can still achieve much in this post."[89] Acknowledging that Qingfu's charges may well have been made in order to deflect attention from his own military failure, William Rowe is nonetheless inclined to accord them a certain plausibility. Chen Hongmou did, Rowe asserts, seek popular approval for his projects in a way that Manchu military administrators did not, and this habit could well have earned him the resentment of an official who held his position as a result of entitlement rather than popular approval.[90]

More may have been involved here than a simple clash of personalities, however. Qingfu's charges echoed the charges that Manchu governor-general Gali made against Zhang Boxing in Jiangsu in the early 1700s (reviewed in chapter 7) and reflected the Manchu establishment's concern with public order and the dangers that could result from lax, faction-ridden Chinese administration. One of Chen Hongmou's successors lost his office in nearly the same way. Zhongyin had the advantage in northwest politics of being a Manchu, but he also held a *jinshi* degree and had served in the Hanlin Academy before embarking on a territorial career that took him to Fujian and, in 1757, to Shaanxi. His nemesis was Songchun, a member of the imperial clan, who was appointed garrison commander at Xi'an in 1762. When Songchun arrived in Shaanxi, local officials did not receive him with the deference he felt was due his person and his rank. The emperor ordered Governor Zhongyin to investigate, and Zhongyin had the, from the imperial point of view, audacity to suggest that some of the rituals for receiving senior officials were out of date. The emperor was horrified, commenting that such matters were not even to be discussed, and ordered Zhongyin recalled to the Board of War.[91]

During the Mongolian wars of mid-century, the governors of Shaanxi were Manchus, but after the wars, Chinese governors returned to the province. The career of Bi Yuan, the longest-serving governor of the province in the seventeenth and eighteenth centuries, offers an example of how northwestern realities were assimilated into Chinese administrative patterns.[92] There was little in the young life of Bi Yuan to suggest his remarkable career. He was raised by his widowed mother, and his youth was a model both in Jiangnan and in the capital of what could be accomplished by maternal care and scholarly diligence. Availing himself of the best education Jiangnan could offer, Bi went to the capital in 1755 and served as a clerk in the Grand Secretariat. Shortly thereafter, he was seconded to the Grand Council as a clerk and is said to have attracted the attention of Fuheng, the imperial confidante, brother-in-law, and likely architect of Qing military victories in the northwest. After five years of service, Bi took his *jinshi* degree, placing second in the palace examinations. The emperor, however, raised him to first place on the strength of a policy essay he wrote about the newly conquered Qing territories in Xinjiang. The most likely possibility here would seem to be that Bi was aware, through his connection with Fuheng, of the nature of imperial thinking on Xinjiang and so was able to write an essay that would be well received. It is also possible that Fuheng influenced the emperor on Bi's behalf.[93] Probably on the strength of this essay, Bi was sent to Xinjiang, where he rose rapidly through the territorial administration. The province was a long way from Jiangnan, but his mother was hopeful. In an ode marking his departure, she wrote:

The people of the west are pure by nature;
Their character is simple, and few are given to extravagance.
The sounds of the ancient Zhou capitals still echo;
Arts and learning flourish there and thrive.[94]

Bi Yuan was eventually to be one of the instruments by which the rosy vision of Qing Shaanxi was realized.

But first he had to pay his dues. All Shaanxi officials had to provide for the supply of the armies fighting around the province, and Bi Yuan did this diligently and effectively.[95] As a lieutenant governor, he earned a commendation for supplying the armies that were fighting in the Jinchuan Rebellion in Sichuan. Promoted to governor, he provided supplies for the armies battling Muslim rebellions in Gansu. In fact, so successful was Bi at performing the supply role of the Shaanxi governor that when his mother died, the emperor ruled that Bi's services were necessary in the northwest and ordered that the period of official mourning, already shorter than that required for a father, be further shortened so that Bi could return to his duties. "The Shaanxi governor's post is vacant and is very important," wrote the emperor. "Bi Yuan has been in Shaanxi the longest, and is familiar with the situation there. However, if he observes the required mourning period, he would not be available for a year. Let him proceed [to Xi'an]."[96]

But Bi Yuan went further than a military role. When he was appointed governor in 1773, the provincial capital of Xi'an was flooded, and one of his first tasks was to coordinate relief efforts. He is credited in his *History of the Qing* biography with shoring up the banks and dikes of fourteen Shaanxi rivers and also with successfully encouraging agriculture in the province. This claim may represent a bit of hyperbole.

One theme in the writings of all the Chinese officials who governed Shaanxi is the need to maintain the province's irrigation works in order to foster agriculture. Cui Ji, the first Chinese governor of the province, a *jinshi* degree holder from Shanxi, submitted an extensive series of memorials on hydraulic work in the province but was dismissed from office when the emperor found that little action had been taken on any of the proposals.[97] Chen Hongmou completed some of Cui Ji's projects, but the issue remained on the governor's table, and the editors of *Essays on Statecraft in Our Times* devote nearly a *juan* to proposals regarding Shaanxi's waterways.[98] Recent research, cited by R. Bin Wong, suggests that during the late eighteenth and nineteenth centuries, a new agrarian economy based on New World crops that could be grown on marginal lands was evolving in Shaanxi.[99] In highlighting Bi Yuan's commitment to fostering agriculture in Shaanxi, the biographies may simply be taking note, in one of the few ways Chinese historiography could, of a new regional development. Whether Bi was responsible for it or not, the increasingly agrarian economy of the province was certainly making it more suitable for Chinese-style government and Chinese-trained administrators. Bi Yuan's association with this policy was made clear in what appears to have been his valedictory memorial as governor, in which he asserted the fundamentally agrarian basis of the Chinese lifestyle and set forth a number of proposals for irrigation work that would have been necessary to facilitate this lifestyle in Shaanxi. The memorial appears to have been widely admired, though it had little effect. Reprinted in *Essays on Statecraft in Our Times* and excerpted at some length in Bi's biography in *History of the Qing*, it did not appear in his State Historiographical Commission biography because it did not lead to significant consequences.[100]

But Bi was most famous for using the resources of the Shaanxi governor's yamen to support scholars in their specialized research projects. Initially, these research projects celebrated the northwest and included gazetteers and collections of stone inscriptions from the region as well as works on northwestern geography. Most celebrated was the edition of the *Mozi* published under his patronage. This was a text that had been ignored for centuries, but the editors of the *Complete Library of the Four Treasuries* judged it worthy of notice, and thereafter it became a subject of scholarly study. Ironically, it dealt, at least in part, with the subject of military defense, although it did so in a style and with language that engaged the attention of eighteenth-century philologists. With these publication projects, Bi Yuan seemed to fulfill the prophecy his mother had made when he had departed Jiangnan for the northwest.

Gansu

During the eighteenth century, Shaanxi moved from being a province concerned with border defense to one increasingly within the Chinese cultural orbit. Gansu moved in the other direction, eventually so far that the dynasty had to make institutional changes in order to accommodate it. The history of Gansu is an interesting case study of the cultural construction of borders and the changing goals of late imperial Chinese governments. The province consisted of a wide swath of territory extending to the northwest from the mountainous western border of Shaanxi and included a string of oases leading across central Asia to Xinjiang. When the Mongols first set it aside as a province, it was not a border region but the gateway to their larger domains in central Asia. The Ming, reluctant after the Dumu incident to advance too far into Mongolia, saw the region as land to be garrisoned, not governed. Although Ming troops were sent to outposts in Gansu, no provincial administration commissioner was appointed for the province. The Manchus reverted to the Yuan pattern, appointing a governor to the area in 1645. In 1671, when the Qing reduced the number of administration commissioners from two per province to one, they ordered the second administration commissioner in Shaanxi to relocate to Gansu and thus laid the foundation for full civilian administration of the area.[101] In the early eighteenth century, Gansu was regarded as sufficiently comparable to the Chinese provinces that it required its own gazetteer, separate from Shaanxi, and Governor Xu Rong produced the first Gansu provincial gazetteer in Chinese history.[102]

Gansu administration, however, proved to be the preserve of officials with previous experience in the northwest: nearly three-quarters of the governors and virtually all the Gansu finance commissioners were appointed to their posts from other positions in the region.[103] As was the case in Shaanxi, Manchus exclusively occupied Gansu positions until the middle of the Yongzheng reign, after which time Chinese held the posts intermittently until the 1750s.

Unlike Shaanxi, however, where provincial government acquired a somewhat more civilian character following the wars of mid-century, warfare in Gansu highlighted the military element of Qing territorial administration. This occurred as part of a general shift in administrative boundaries beginning in the late 1740s. During the middle decades of the eighteenth century, the Qing went to war in both the southern and the northern sections of the northwest. To the south, the dynasty found itself battling the Jinchuan rebels, a Tibetan-speaking group in western Sichuan. To the north, the dynasty embarked in 1755 on a series of three ambitious campaigns that led to the Qing conquest of Xinjiang. In 1749, in order to facilitate the campaign in the southwest, the dynasty separated the Shaan-gan and Sichuan governor-generalships; the separation eventually became permanent.[104] Six years later, when the Qing armies were about to move in the northwest, the Shaan-gan governor-general was ordered to move from Xi'an to Lanzhou, the capital of Gansu. During the war, the Shaan-gan governor-general's territorial portfolio was limited to Gansu alone, and Shaanxi was subordinated to Sichuan, although the dynasty recognized fairly soon that with supply lines for the northwestern armies reaching into Shaanxi, it made the most sense to place both provinces under one governor-general.[105]

When the war against the Zunghars concluded in 1764, Gansu had changed to such an extent that the emperor judged that the province no longer required a governor. He wrote:

> Formerly, because of the necessity of supplying the western-route armies, I ordered the governor-general of Gansu to move from Lanzhou [in the eastern part of the province] to Suzhou [in the west] to facilitate the dispatch of supplies. Now the great military enterprise is complete, the regulations for the military agricultural colonies of Xinjiang are established, but the governor-general still resides at Suzhou. This is very far from Xi'an, and the territories, archives, and personnel who are subordinate to the governor-general [in Shaanxi]. Therefore, it occurred to me that it would be appropriate to move the governor-general from Suzhou to the governor's yamen in Lanzhou, so that he would be

equidistant from the eastern and western extents of his jurisdiction. It would be less difficult for him to exercise control from a central location, and the governorship of Gansu could be eliminated.[106]

There was a certain irony to the fact that as soon as Gansu ceased to be on a border, it ceased to have a governor. During the Ming, the area had no civilian administration precisely because it was on a border—remote, inhospitable, and not susceptible to the normative controls of traditional Chinese administration. A distant and forbidding frontier during the Ming, Gansu became a fairly natural part of the nascent and rather protean multinational seventeenth-century Qing empire. As this empire expanded in the eighteenth century, Gansu became a corridor linking the Manchus' Chinese domains with their conquests in central Asia. Hundreds of thousands of taels worth of supplies passed through the magazines that the Qing built along this corridor. As Peter Perdue has argued, this logistical achievement, which gave the Qing the capacity to field armies farther from its agrarian base than could any contemporaneous state, represented one of the crowning achievements of mid-eighteenth-century society.[107]

As Gansu became merely corridor, its already specialized civilian administration focused increasingly on the task of supporting armies and military colonies, and the government structure was altered to facilitate this change. The force of precedent probably prevented the emperor from directly acknowledging this change. In fact, the elimination of the Gansu governorship seemed almost an afterthought in an edict that was concerned primarily with the location of the governor-general; it appeared that once the governor-general moved into the Lanzhou yamen, there would be no space for the governor. But physical "space" could not have been the real issue. Governors-general resided in the same cities as governors in the capitals of several Qing provinces. Moreover, while the expense of building a new yamen to accommodate a governor-general might have been a concern in north China in the middle of the seventeenth century, this could hardly have worried a court that had just spent millions of *liang* conquering Xinjiang. At stake was a new conception of Gansu, and as the emperor continued to describe the process of change in Gansu, he demonstrated the formation of political imagination in mid-Qing China. Noting that the idea of making a change in Gansu had occurred to him earlier, the emperor continued: "Then, in an imperial audience with Changjun, I inquired of the situation, and he responded that my original intention, to order the governor-general to move, accorded with realities. I then issued an edict to Yang Yingju, ordering him to draw up the necessary plans. Yang memorialized in return, confirming my views." It would seem that imperial prescience was confirmed by official perspicacity. Yet in this instance, the acknowledgment of official perspicacity suggests that it may have been the driving force.

The officials the emperor consulted were those who were likely to know what was going on in Gansu. Changjun, the last governor of Gansu, had served as a junior official in the province, accompanied the Qing armies on campaign in the 1750s, and commanded one of the banner armies. He served in Gansu from the late summer of 1761 through the late autumn of 1763 and, according to his State Historiographical Commission biography, proposed the new administrative arrangements in Gansu during an audience with the emperor as he moved to his next posting.[108] Yang Yingju was governor-general of Shaan-gan from the end of the war in 1759 until 1766, and in this capacity, he would have responded to the emperor's edict sometime in the early winter of 1764.[109] Most likely, then, administrative change in the province reflected changes in actual practice, and the officials who were engaged in that practice were the very ones who made the proposal. Although it was convenient for the emperor to claim the change as his idea, Gansu's administration was reshaped in order to reflect better what the province had become.[110]

On the ground in Gansu, changes in the titles of those occupying the yamens in Lanzhou may not have made much difference. However, changes in the character of the province—from outpost to conduit—did affect the province's place in the political economy of the empire as a whole. When Gansu was merely Qing China's most northwesterly province, governors constantly struggled against the poverty of the land in order to meet the food supply needs of residents and troops. Despite being the Yongzheng emperor's personal choice to govern Gansu, Xu Rong was reprimanded twice during his eight-year governorship (1728–36) for squeezing grain out of an overburdened peasantry. As soon as Gansu became the gateway to Xinjiang, merchants lined up to travel through the province to the markets of central Asia. As James Millward notes, by 1776, "the flow of people was so great that there were long delays in getting through the Jiayu Guan."[111]

In Gansu, new streams of revenue came to flow to and through the province after the 1750s, some to secure the conquered territory in Xinjiang and some to secure the route through the Gansu corridor. One of these revenue streams generated considerable controversy in the mid-eighteenth century, producing one of the most notorious official investigations of the Qianlong reign. The revenue in question was the result of a scheme for providing relief grain to this chronically drought-prone province. In most provinces of China, stores of relief grain could be set aside from the surplus in good years and sold at reduced prices in times of dearth. But in Gansu, grain had to be imported, as there was seldom surplus, and silver drawn from other parts of the empire paid for these imports. Rather than pay for relief grain out of the central treasury, the dynasty implemented a scheme whereby private contributions toward relief grain supplies in Gansu would be rewarded with state recognition in the form of low-level official degrees. If aspirants contributed to Gansu relief funds, they would be rewarded with the status of "tribute student" at the imperial academy. Although hardly an instrument of choice for Chinese governments, the scheme was in fairly common use, particularly when military circumstances strained official resources.

Administrative units in Gansu thus received significant payments, usually in cash, from aspirants to official rank and were expected to disburse this money in times of emergency. Cash in Gansu, like flows of money anywhere in the Qing administration, had the habit of finding its way into the pockets of those who administered it. In the mid-1770s, Gansu officials appear to have engaged in a conspiracy of silence about the amount of money they were pocketing out of the relief payments. The emperor became suspicious when a Muslim rebel known as Su Forty Three laid siege to Lanzhou in 1781, and the lieutenant governor of the province was able to contribute the entire cost of defending the city out of his own pocket.[112] The emperor then observed that the lieutenant governor's predecessor, Wang Danwang, had personally contributed half a million *liang* for the construction of seawalls in the province to which he had been transferred after serving in Gansu. Where, the emperor asked, was all this money coming from?

It was, of course, coming from relief funds that had made their way into the pockets of the two officials. It is noteworthy that these officials, though certainly corrupt, were not entirely self-interested. They had enough public spirit to direct their ill-gotten gains toward fulfilling the ends of the state. In Gansu, public and private were readily confused: private funds, contributed to secure private ends, were being recycled through public officials to individuals in need. Even in a world where the legal boundaries between official and private resources were clearly established, such redistribution would have been complicated. But in Gansu, it proved impossible. The Qianlong court was impressed, however, not by the uses to which revenues were put, but by the number of officials involved in the conspiracy. No less than 140 officials were caught in the conspiracy; in fact, the numbers were so great that the Qianlong emperor had to establish an ad hoc standard for punishment. Officials who were guilty of pocketing more than 20,000 *liang* were to be executed, and those who took less than this amount were to be cashiered. By this standard, some 56 officials were executed and 84 cashiered.

In the course of the investigation, the property of each accused official had to be inventoried and the inventory reported to the court.[113] Since officials came from all over China, every provincial governor in the empire had to investigate the property of at least one of the accused, and this was surely part of the reason the case became such a cause célèbre, generating more than six hundred documents. One governor was caught up in the case even as he investigated it. Governor Chen Huizu of Zhejiang had to investigate the circumstances of Wang Danwang, who was serving in Zhejiang as lieutenant governor at the time the case broke; his own younger brother, who was a Gansu official; and the son of Governor Min Eyuan of Jiangsu. While faced with this triply delicate task, Chen Huizu was himself charged with corruption. The Chen family property was seized, and Chen was cashiered, ending the official service of a family that had provided governors to the court throughout the entire Qianlong reign.[114]

If the presence of so many Chinese officials among those charged in Gansu tells us anything, apart from the possibility that Heshen was using the case to carry out a vendetta against Chinese territorial officials, it was that corruption in late eighteenth-century Gansu cannot be blamed on the province's military administration. A civilian governor might have restrained his subordinates, but more likely he would merely have taken his cut. The problem in Gansu was not military administration per se but military needs and the flows of money necessary to meet them. In his study of the Qing occupation of Xinjiang, James Millward has richly demonstrated the capacity of Qing military administrators to respond creatively to the challenge of securing financial support. Concerns about the cost of military occupation probably lay behind many decisions about the governance of north and northwest China. Such concerns, detailed above, probably determined the locations of government on the north China plain, for instance. The case of Wang Danwang in Gansu provides a relatively late, and hence fairly well documented, example of the woes of maintaining an administration in a land that could not support it. Unique perhaps in the scope of profiteering it generated, the case was not unusual in its underlying cause, the tension between Qing military ambitions and resources.

Sichuan

In the mid-eighteenth century, provincial structure also changed in China's great southwestern province of Sichuan, although from the nineteenth- or twentieth-century point of view, comparing the two provinces seems incongruous. The clear blue skies of the northwest could hardly have been more different from the leaden, rain-bearing skies that created in the upper Yangzi basin one of the great agrarian engines of the late Qing empire. Nineteenth-century Sichuan was, in contrast with Gansu, a relatively densely populated area with a regional trading system, well developed and efficient, that formed the inspiration for G. William Skinner's model of peasant marketing in China. The grain of Sichuan's "Red Basin," shipped down the Yangzi River, made possible the more specialized economic production of the middle and lower Yangzi regions, and the revenues that moved back upriver formed the basis for a strong landed elite. The capacities of Sichuan agriculture were amply recognized in the nickname "heaven's storehouse," which is traditionally attached to the province.

As Dai Yingcong has argued conclusively in "The Rise of the Southwestern Frontier under the Qing," however, Sichuan has not always been so central to the Qing economy or polity. In the early years after the Qing conquest, Manchu rulers had little idea of what to do with the vast, depopulated basin that Sichuan had become after the wars of the late Ming. Dai writes that Sichuan, like the other provinces of southwest China, "was viewed as the least important from the center—it was remote, bleak and even 'uncivilized.'" Far from solving Sichuan's problems, Qing policies may have exacerbated them as armies marched through the province on their way north, west, and south. It was not until the end of the seventeenth century that the Qing "came to realize that the key to resolving a cluster of frontier problems in the vast north, northwest and west border areas lay in controlling the Tibetan Lamaist establishment," and the court in Beijing became aware of the region's importance.[115] Before the middle of the eighteenth century, provincial administration had a rather protean quality, with boundaries and roles changing constantly as the central government conceived and then reconceived the nature of the territory. In this uncertain world, governors could become immensely powerful and, depending on how they used their power, become either allies or enemies of central rulers.

Certainly, early Qing rulers had no clear view of Sichuan's place within the Chinese territorial order, as demonstrated in the assignment of the province to the jurisdictions of different governors-general. The dynasty's first inclination was to attach Sichuan to Huguang, forming one gigantic jurisdiction held together by the Yangzi River, which existed in 1647–52 and 1668–74. When wars in the northwest made the connection between Shaanxi and Sichuan salient, the two provinces were united into one jurisdiction, held together by trade routes through the mountain passes of southwestern Shaanxi. Indeed the combination of Sichuan and Shaanxi was the most common arrangement in the early Qing, existing in 1653–60, 1681–1718, and 1721–31. When the dynasty faced enemies to the west and southwest—during the Wu Sangui Rebellion, the war against Tibet, and the Yongzheng emperor's war with the Oirats—Sichuan had its own governor-general, most often a military figure who was given wide authority over the province's civilian apparatus. This proved to be the most durable organization of the western territories, in effect during the years 1660–68, 1674–81, 1718–20, 1721–35, and 1748–1911. The edicts changing Sichuan's status most often were simply terse military orders conferring authority on an individual, which the editors of *Collected Statutes of the Qing*, hard put to make such governance appear routine, simply repeated.[116] The central government also constantly changed its view of relationships among various jurisdictions in the province. The Kangxi emperor reorganized the territories in Sichuan in order to better prepare the province for war. Most of the jurisdictions Kangxi created were modified by the

Yongzheng emperor as he pursued his policy of converting areas governed by hereditary native chieftains into regular administrative territories of the Qing empire. This process continued well into the eighteenth century, as the Qing tried to digest the enormous territories in the west of the province, which it had acquired in the wars in Tibet in 1720.[117] As late as 1733, the lieutenant governor of Sichuan complained that the dynasty had not established its priorities in the province and called for reclassification of many of the districts and prefectures.[118]

In such an uncertain political world, the role of provincial leaders was not always clear, as illustrated by the career of Nian Gengyao, the longest-serving governor of the province (1710–21) and one of the most powerful men in early eighteenth-century China.[119] Nian was the only one of the twenty-four longest-serving Qing governors (those with terms of more than ninety-nine months) to be dismissed from office; not only was he dismissed, but he was executed, as were a number of his supporters. Nian's term has often been approached as a case study of regional strongmen, highlighting the nature of the challenge powerful governors posed to the central administration. In fact, his power rested on many bases. His father Nian Xialing had a successful career in territorial administration, including twelve years as governor of Huguang (later renamed Hubei) in the years after the Wu Sangui Rebellion. Nian Gengyao himself, though a bannerman, earned a *jinshi* degree and served in the late Kangxi Hanlin Academy. But most significant, he came to Sichuan at a moment when the strategic importance of the distant province was becoming painfully apparent to the court. This awareness was spurred by the looming possibility of a Mongol-Tibetan alliance in opposition to the Qing along the empire's northwestern frontier; Mongol armies did occupy Lhasa in 1720. The Kangxi emperor dispatched his fourteenth son Yinti to lead an expedition against the Mongols. Yinti approached Lhasa from the north, and Nian Gengyao approached from the east. In October 1720, the Tibetan capital was occupied, and a new Dalai Lama was placed on the throne. As a result of these victories, the Qing annexed large territories in the east of Tibet and added them to the province. The Kangxi emperor praised Nian and appointed him to serve concurrently as governor-general of Shaanxi and Sichuan and governor of Sichuan. Combining in his person the distinction of a famous family, personal heroism, and vast territorial authority, Nian was not only unique in his own day but remarkable in the history of Qing governors.[120]

One of the great ironies of Nian's career was that although he was born into a Chinese banner unit that belonged to Yinzhen, the Kangxi emperor's fourth son, he fought by the side of Yinti, the emperor's fourteenth son and Yinzhen's rival for the throne. The dance of loyalties that ensued when Yinzhen became emperor is one of the most famous in Chinese history. The details may never be fully established, but it seems fairly certain that the head of the Beijing gendarmerie,

Longkodo, was at the Kangxi emperor's side when he died, and his troops were assembled around the monarch's villa. Longkodo is also reputed to have been the man who heard the Kangxi emperor's deathbed command that the throne be transmitted to his fourth son, the future Yongzheng emperor. Once the new emperor was enthroned, relations with the military forces in the northwest, commanded by Yongzheng's brother and rival for the throne Yinti, were particularly delicate. The burden of smoothing these relations fell on Nian Gengyao. Nian was likely allied, at least on some level, with the new emperor, as his daughter was Yongzheng's concubine. In 1723, Nian requested an audience with the new emperor, who awarded him hereditary rank and promoted his younger brother from the post of Anhui finance commissioner to the Guangdong governorship.[121]

As a series of edicts issued on the first day of the first new year of the new reign suggest, the Yongzheng emperor was aware of the force of the military for both good and evil. In these edicts, the emperor addressed the various officials in strict accordance with their rank rather than dividing them into civil and military hierarchies. Because of this, the edict addressed to governors-general came first in the sequence, and those addressed to the provincial commanders in chief and garrison commanders preceded those addressed to all subordinate provincial officials and local officials. The sequence certainly had the effect of emphasizing the role of the military in the maintenance of domestic order. But each edict addressed to military officials also stressed that civil and military officials were engaged in the same enterprise and emphasized the need for cooperation between the two orders. In the edict to provincial intendants, the emperor observed that when civil and military officials cling to their separate points of view and refuse to cooperate, both military and civilian suffer, and grudges acquire a long history, leading only to arrogance and evil. He quoted a passage from *The Book of Documents* asserting that the social arrangements and duties of the Chinese empire are given by heaven, and "when sovereign and ministers show a common respect for these," they "harmonize the moral nature of the people." Although the emperor did not quote the entire passage, all would have known that it ends with the exhortation: "The business of government!—ought we not be earnest in it? ought we not be earnest in it?"[122]

The emperor's relationship with Nian Gengyao began to sour in the spring of 1725. As the emperor tells it, Nian's arrogant demeanor during a visit to the capital in December 1724 aroused the emperor's suspicions about the bannerman. It appears that Nian, accustomed to having Mongol and Tibetan princes as well as Chinese subordinates kneel to him, expected Manchu princes to do the same. When Nian Gengyao returned to Xi'an, he found that his subordinate Governor Fan Shijie had been relieved of office and returned to his banner post. Shortly thereafter, he received a very cold reply to a memorial thanking the emperor for receiving him in Beijing. Several months later, when Governor He Tianpei of Jiangsu, whom Nian Gengyao had recommended to the emperor, submitted a fairly routine memorial reporting rice prices in Jiangsu, the emperor warned: "I am suspicious of Nian Gengyao's [air of] arrogance and prosperity. He has often been the recipient of my grace. You should terminate your relations with him and put distance between yourself and him . . . if you don't want to be implicated in his misdeeds. Keep this secret!" A few days later, Governor He received an edict ordering him to return to his post as commander of the Nanjing garrison. The emperor issued a secret edict to other governors ordering them to report anything they knew about Nian Gengyao and methodically began collecting evidence against him.[123] The culmination of this effort was a ninety-two-count indictment issued against Nian Gengyao in 1725, accusing him of arrogating powers to himself that appropriately belonged to the state and of extensive bribery and corruption.[124] Senior officials at the Yongzheng court approved the indictment, and Nian and many of his protégés were executed.[125]

Qing historians since Meng Sen, who wrote in the early twentieth century, have generally argued that it was not Nian Gengyao's demeanor alone that worried him. More pressing was the possibility that Nian might ally with the emperor's rivals to challenge his right to the throne.[126] Of critical importance has been the argument that at the time of the succession, "Nian's position as governor-general and his great influence made it expedient that the Emperor should, for a time, treat him with deference, but when he was no longer useful, his knowledge was embarrassing."[127] Meng Sen lived in an age when intellectuals sought to establish the illegitimacy of Qing rule, and Meng in particular sought to establish the illegitimacy of the Yongzheng emperor's rule. For him, Nian Gengyao was a Chinese hero protesting the enthronement of a Manchu usurper, a bannerman swept up in the maelstrom of a contested Manchu succession. In recent years, however, historians have been concerned more with the efficacy than with the legitimacy of Yongzheng's rule. In a recent study of the Yongzheng emperor, Feng Ergang takes at face value the edicts and memorials concerning Nian Gengyao and his faction that were published in *Veritable Records* and *Vermillion Endorsed Edicts* (Zhupi yuzhi) of the Yongzheng emperor. Feng emphasizes evidence such as the report that after indicting Governor-general Zhao Zhihuan, Nian Gengyao extorted a payment of 100,000 *liang* in order to recommend Zhao's reinstatement. Feng also emphasizes the reach of Nian's faction through the Yongzheng bureaucracy, and the fact that so many followers of Nian were appointed that the Board of Personnel came to term certain appointees *Nian xuan* appointees, men selected by Nian.[128] Since Nian corresponded with the Qing court in Manchu as well as in Chinese, Chinese historians have been slow to assess this pivotal figure or to pinpoint the nature of his influence.[129] The job of governor-general of Sichuan did not readily fit into the institutional model of Qing territorial governance, as it involved a degree of control over resources, personnel, and active armed forces that far exceeded what was offered to almost any official of comparable rank. Despite the great power this official wielded, it seems likely that it was not the power per se that got Nian in trouble but the way he used it and the corruption that surrounded an official who was familiar with the pathways of power in the early Qing.

The dynasty made no effort to restrict the power of the office after Nian left it. Nian Gengyao was followed in the post by Yue Zhongqi, in many respects an equally formidable figure.[130] Yue's father had risen through the Qing military system and served as Sichuan commander in chief from 1695 through 1711.[131] Yue Zhongqi initially was appointed to the Qing civil service but petitioned to be transferred to the military service; after reaching the post of Tianjin brigade general, he was transferred to Sichuan, where he followed in his father's foot-steps as provincial commander in chief. After the fall of Nian Gengyao, Yue was responsible for screening Sichuan civil and military officials and eliminating Nian's protégés. During most of the Yongzheng reign, Yue was one of the most important military administrators in China, though he fell from imperial grace during the war against the Eleuths in the early 1730s.[132] He was imprisoned for four years in Beijing and retired after his release.

Even after he retired, Yue enjoyed unusual relations with the state and the region he had governed. Because Sichuan was so depopulated in the early Qing, emperors had offered incentives to Chinese farmers to reoccupy and cultivate ter-ritories in the province; one of these incentives was an offer of free land to sol-diers who participated in the western campaigns in Sichuan. The Yue family had availed itself of this offer, and by the time of Yue Zhongqi's forced retirement, the family inventories listed "dozens of properties, great mansions with tiled roofs and multiple courtyards in several major cities, fine properties scattered across several regions, and scores of caretakers and bailiffs."[133] In short, Yue was not only a retired official of the province but a major landholder. He was also married to the daughter of Governor Gao Qilong of Guizhou, and had seven sons and sixteen grandsons, many of whom served in Sichuan. From this estate, which he named the Court of Peaceful Simplicity, he was able to observe the career of his son Yue Jun, who served as governor of Shandong (1728–36), Jiangxi (1737–40), Guangdong (1747–50), and Yunnan (1750).[134] Yue also had one further asset: he knew western Sichuan better than any official of his day. When rebellion broke out in 1748, he was briefly called upon to serve his dynasty during the Jinchuan wars, but once again punished and retired when the wars ended.

Serving in the shadow of such powerful governors-general, the civilian gover-nors of Sichuan inevitably became protégés. Often, the governors were promoted from the ranks of military officers, as were Ma Huibo and Xiande.[135] Even when Sichuan governors were not merely protégés, they may not have been effective. In the first years of the Qianlong reign, Wang Shijun seems to have been dispatched to Sichuan on his way into administrative oblivion because he opposed the new emperor's policies.[136] When he dismissed Jishan, who was effectively the last governor of Sichuan in 1748, the Qianlong emperor described him as a "Manchu grandee who had not lost the habits of his homeland," continuing that "I only feared when I appointed him that his subordinates would mock and cheat him."[137] The Qianlong emperor could be remarkably frank about his provincial governors, particularly when he was firing them.

In the middle of the eighteenth century, the Qing dispensed with the Sichuan governorship altogether and made do with a single military official. In Sichuan, as in Gansu, the governorship was abolished at the end of a war, but the campaign against the Jinchuan was considerably less glorious than Qianlong's conquests in the northwest a decade later. The war was fought against people whose land the dynasty had annexed during its 1720 war in Tibet. It broke out in 1747 when one native chieftain, Seleben of the Jinchuan, began by warring with his fellow chieftains and ended by attacking Qing military positions along the principal route to Lhasa. The court at first termed the Jinchuan "little wretches" (*xiao chou*) but found that they were capable of very aggressive attacks. Although the Qing assembled an army of more than sixty thousand troops from seven surrounding provinces, it took nearly two years to force the Jinchuan to surrender. The campaign cost two Chuan-shaan governors-general, as well as Governor Jishan, their careers and provoked much concern in Beijing about the corruption and loss of vigor in the southwestern armies compared to the late Kangxi years.[138] The Qianlong emperor probably sought to address the latter problem when he ordered changes in the administrative structure of the west in 1748:

> The Shaan-gan governor-general governs Sichuan, Xi'an, and Gansu, an area that includes truly vast areas of borderland. In ordinary uneventful times, I worry that such an official will not be able to manage [literally, "his whip will not reach"]. But now, with the Jinchuan matter not yet resolved, local affairs and the management of military affairs cannot be controlled from Xi'an. Even when matters are more settled in the future, we will still require a single individual for Sichuan. In the past, separate governors-general have been established on occasion in Shaan-gan and Sichuan. Let Yinjishan, who is currently in Shaanxi on a special mission, be appointed as Shaanxi governor-general. Let Celeng serve as governor-general of Sichuan, concurrently managing the affairs of the governor's yamen. . . . Let the Board of Personnel examine the precedents for the establishment of a separate governor-general's post and memorialize.[139]

As in the case of Gansu, the abolition of the governor's post was almost an afterthought, but the origin of change in Sichuan was different from what it would be in the northwest ten years later. In Gansu, the impetus for administrative change probably came from officials on the scene; in Sichuan, territorial administration was reshuffled at a moment when all the relevant provincial administrators had been dismissed. The impetus for change came from the capital, where the emperor confessed to having spent sleepless nights worrying about whether he could send trustworthy officials to the south and still staff the Grand Council in Beijing. Other edicts at the time suggest that the emperor's main confidant at this point was his "brother-in-law" Fuheng, who was on his way to Sichuan to mop up operations against the Jinchuan.[140]

In a narrow sense, change came about in Sichuan in 1748 because the dynasty's administrative chickens had come home to roost: The court was finding that the vast territories it had annexed in the west after the war with Tibet required a firm military hand. It wasn't that the Qing changed its mind about Sichuan; rather, the court simply made up its mind about a heretofore puzzling territory. By the middle of the eighteenth century, three images of Sichuan were current in the Qing historical imagination. The province was "heaven's storehouse," the rich inland agrarian basin that could feed the rest of the empire. It was also, as Gu Yanwu had argued, a crucial strategic juncture—the dynasty that held Sichuan controlled the north China plain. Finally, it was a frontier, the point where the Han areas of the Qing empire met the Mongol and Tibetan territories. In coming to its decision about Sichuan, the court relied more on central perceptions of the territory, the sort of local perceptions that lay behind administrative changes in Gansu. Throughout its political history, the administration in Sichuan seems to have been influenced more heavily by central government decisions than by local initiatives. This is not to say that there weren't important changes in local economy and society in Sichuan, but these seem not to have influenced central attitudes toward the province as much as did central conceptions of strategy and image. Sichuan was so distant from the capital, and posed so many baffling problems, that it was easy for the court to think of the province in terms of images rather than realities.

Pamela Kyle Crossley has recently chided Qing specialists for too often forgetting that the Qing was a conquest dynasty.[141] In north and northwest China, the fact was unforgettable and its consequences undeniable, but the military legacy was many faceted. Although it is convenient from a narrative viewpoint to regard military conquest as a single phenomenon, the military enterprise in fact involves a number of different activities, each with its own social and economic concomitant. Feeding and transporting troops required extensive consultation with civilian authority. Although these functions could be militarized in times of emergency, the dynasty more often relied on degree-holding Chinese civilians to perform these tasks in Henan and Shandong. A custodian presiding over those who guarded the approaches to the capital, as in Shanxi and Zhili, had to enjoy credibility with both the guards and the civilians among whom they lived. Policing the relations between military and civilian communities, and monitoring the flow of goods and travelers to the capital, involved a regime of vigilance that was best accomplished by those in whom the court had confidence. Officials who were both governors and tactical commanders played the most problematic role in the occupation. In their role of controlling the troops who defended or expanded the boundaries of empire, they needed more authority than the procedures of civilian government normally allowed, and these exceptions were easily abused by officials like Nian Gengyao. Maintaining the bases from which armies might be dispatched was a third task. Base maintenance, though vital, was never as prestigious as tactical command, and where tactical commanders were present, as in Shaanxi before the 1750s, base commanders inevitably took a backseat.

As interesting as the different roles of northern and northwestern governors during the occupation were the ways in which these roles changed during the seventeenth and eighteenth centuries. The events that brought about change in the Qing territorial order were not of a single kind, for provinces in Qing China were formed at that uncertain boundary where political, military, and economic history met. Military circumstances were always important, but the role of military action in changing provinces evolved. Initially, boundaries were formed as new lands were conquered and incorporated. Later, provincial boundaries changed, as in Gansu and Sichuan, as wartime expedients became peacetime necessities. Even as tasks changed, the continuing military imperative in the region was apparent, not only in the direct familial ties between northern and northwestern governors and elements of the conquering elite, but also in the special grants of power the Qing made to northern governors, the extraordinary arrangements created for governing provinces adjacent to the capital, and the special needs of the northwest. These arrangements, however, acquired a different significance as the region's economy changed and its importance to the dynasty evolved. Appointments of officials of military background to north China posts, which had begun as a necessity, became a prerogative, at least in Shandong and perhaps in Shanxi. The survival of the military element in the north throughout the eighteenth century, and its rather precipitous decline in the beginning of the nineteenth century—reflected in the White Lotus Rebellion and the Manchus' inability to combat it with their own resources—was one of the most important elements of the Qing eighteenth-century history.

Changing economic circumstances were also reflected in changes in the Qing provincial order, although this was a subtle matter. Qing economic policies were not exclusively or even primarily expressed in the establishment of provinces. Moreover, as Skinner has argued, provinces are not the appropriate units for measuring economic history in China. But when the economic circumstances of a region changed sufficiently to alter the nature of the political challenges of governing, the dynasty responded, often with a new sort of appointee but occasionally with a formal change in provincial institutions. The identity and background of appointees were important for the dynasty's economic policies, since the dynasty relied on those it had appointed—men such as Guotai and Shilin, Yang Yingju and Changjun—to apprise it of changing local realities and to implement and even formulate policy. In the early days of Qing rule, the court could rely on officials' advice, and court and governors had the same interest, the resuscitation of the north China economy. But as north China's resources grew, along with the ambitions of its governors, reliable advice about economic conditions of the realm became harder to secure. Wang Danwang's assurances that the contributions of Chinese degree holders were being put to effective use to prevent famine in Gansu highlights the dynasty's difficulties in relying on its subordinates in the latter years of the eighteenth century. Posts crafted for the leaders of Qing occupation forces could only with difficulty be transformed into positions for managers of economic development, particularly when the issue was dealing with economic decline rather than growth. Chen Hongmou or Bi Yuan in Shaanxi was able to fill both roles, but many of their Manchu colleagues could not.

Much of the analysis in this chapter relies on descriptions of three prosecutions of provincial officials in the eighteenth century: Shilin in 1740, Guotai in 1782, and Wang Danwang in 1780. Traditionally, these episodes have been viewed as reflections of declining bureaucratic morale or perhaps more specifically the desire of territorial officials to emulate the practices of a court on the take. There is certainly merit to this view; indeed, as the case against Guotai was winding down, the courageous censor Qian Feng submitted a second memorial pointing out that the emperor was accepting too many gifts from his subordinates. He made no direct connection, but the inference certainly was that had the emperor not accepted so many gifts, his subordinate Governor Guotai would not have felt entitled to such quantities himself. But neither the Qianlong court nor its eighteenth-century governors could have taken so much if there had not been so much to take. Rather than attribute the eighteenth-century governor's penchant for corruption to a collective psychological malady, this chapter has argued that the dynasty's success in governing the north generated a prosperity that made corruption possible. It may be most useful to approach corruption by using (or perhaps slightly abusing) the metaphor of the market. Corruption, in this metaphor, could be seen as the product of a demand for illicit revenues interacting with a supply of extortable revenues. Human nature being what it is, demand was inflexible except in the technical sense; presumably, demand from officials would be relatively constant. This is not to say that they were inflexible in their quest for personal gain. But it may ultimately have been the supply of revenues that determined the level of corruption in provincial administration. Without painting an excessively Panglossian picture, it is possible to argue that the opportunities for corruption north China offered its officials in the eighteenth century were a mark of the dynasty's administrative success in the north.

CHAPTER 7

Negotiated Orders:
The Lower Yangzi Valley and the Southeastern Coast

In recent years, it has become the fashion in works of Western social science to characterize a variety of moments and events as "sites of negotiation." In most instances, this term is used metaphorically to describe events, series of events, or verbal formulations that appear to have resulted from a reconciliation of several sets of interests. In this chapter, the term "negotiation" is used both in the metaphorical sense and literally in order to describe the interactions between Manchu conquerors and Chinese living in the lower Yangzi valley and along the southeastern coast. There was, of course, no negotiating conquest; Qing military presence along the southeastern coast was a given from the very earliest years of the dynasty. But there was room to negotiate the terms of coexistence for Qing and local authority on the coast. This transaction was vital, since in the broad swath of territory from the southern mouth of the Yellow River to the Guangdong border, more than in other quarters of China, the Qing encountered coherent and self-conscious communities with whom it had to negotiate power and obligations. A local elite proud of its literacy and traditions recorded these encounters for posterity. So recorded, stories of the encounters became the stuff of legends that have shaped images of the early Qing for three centuries.

These images are vivid and powerful, but they hardly set the tone for Qing rule in the delta. The Manchu conquest of China did not end with the death of the last Ming loyalist's hopes for restoration or with the death of the last loyalist. It ended with the creation of a structure of rule in which the especial tensions and contributions of China's regions could be incorporated into the structure of empire. This occurred in stages. In the first, conquerors confronted coastal communities directly. In the lower Yangzi, the issue was tax revenues, and farther south along the coast, the question was whether groups would be loyal to the Qing state or to the multiple power centers existing in a complex and conflicted region. A second stage of accommodation consisted of each side's recognition of the other's legitimacy, and the legitimacy of representatives who could speak to and for the various elements of court and community. The work of this stage was the creation of a cadre of specialized governors whose experience and abilities suited the particular needs of the southeastern provinces to which they were assigned.

These governors served, in the third stage of negotiations, as representatives of local groups and court interests under the tense circumstances that marked Qing government in the south.

Negotiations were not uncommon in early modern polities, in both empires and nation-states, and concerned a wide variety of matters, including tax and service obligations, religious obligations, and the like. What made the Chinese case unique was the extent to which negotiations were carried out through appointments. The centralized nature of Chinese administration, and the fact that appointed officials were the primary source of information for central policy makers as they built and rebuilt institutions, meant that those who served fundamentally affected what took place at the local level. In the case of the southeastern coast, appointed officials and the particular information they conveyed produced a rather unique institutional pattern of southeastern government. This pattern included borders that divided up major marketing systems among several political jurisdictions, placed governors-general at odd removes from the governors who were subordinate to them, and added two new provinces, Anhui and Jiangsu, to the map of late imperial China.

THE LOWER YANGZI VALLEY

No region of the Qing empire was typical, so surely no region was atypical. Yet the lower Yangzi valley was of such importance to the Qing dynasty that rulers and historians have given its particularities special attention. The history and economy of the region produced contradictory imperatives for the Qing. On the one hand, the elites of the lower Yangzi valley were the wealthiest and most educated of the Chinese empire; if any regional elite was entitled to regard itself as the custodian of Chinese heritage, it was the wealthy of the lower Yangzi valley. Perhaps not surprisingly, the lower Yangzi was the only region in China where the Manchus encountered significant elite resistance to their establishment of territorial governance. The military phase of this resistance was fairly short-lived, but its heroes and memories lingered in the local imagination for several generations. On the other hand, the lower Yangzi valley was also, by a tradition that long predated the Qing, the most heavily taxed region of China, a rich delta land whose already thoroughly commercialized economy provided the economic underpinning for late imperial Chinese government. The lower Yangzi society posed this challenge for the Qing: how to control the territory without so alienating the local elite as to make tax collection impossible.

Territorial governments in the delta needed not only to collect money but to spend it, often in very significant amounts. In order for delta residents to prosper, and the delta to play its accustomed role in the political economy of the empire, it was necessary that the network of dikes, channels, and hydraulic works be maintained in the southeast. Maintaining this infrastructure was so costly that it required the participation of both central and local governments and so complex that it required the active input of multiple officials and communities of landowners. Local government in the region could be successful only to the extent that it recognized and reconciled the interests of all involved in managing the rivers. The conflicts here could be significant, especially when the officials involved represented different strata of Qing officialdom. The loudest interofficial conflict in delta history, between Governor-general Gali and Governor Zhang Boxing, highlights both the potential for conflict and the administrative interface that constantly sustained central rule in the region.

Confrontation

The short-term cause of the violence attending the arrival of Qing forces in the delta was the confrontation between conquerors and conquered, but long-standing strains in the relationship between delta elites and the central government were also a factor. For this reason, military action did not represent the solution to delta political problems; rather, the armed conflict of the mid-seventeenth century produced a moment's pause in the conquest and an era of rethinking and institutional creativity. From a period of misunderstood violence and misguided leadership emerged the durable recognition of the nature of local interests.

The military phase of resistance was quite brief. After the fall of the Ming dynasty's northern capital and the death of the Chongzhen emperor, elements of the Ming court and members of the royal family retreated to the dynasty's southern capital of Nanjing and there allied with southern elite families against the northern invader. The military leader of the resistance was Shi Kefa, who was appointed supreme commander in the lower Yangzi valley during the late Ming. Through late 1644, Shi attempted to knit together a coalition of forces in the south while at the same time resisting the Manchus' offers of positions in the new Qing order. Perhaps fatefully, perhaps inevitably, Shi took as his strategy the defense of rich lower Yangzi delta cities. This meant that the Manchu advance most often involved laying siege to and then occupying the centers of southern culture and elite life. Yangzhou fell first in May 1645 after a relatively short siege, and its inhabitants were subjected to ten days of looting, massacre, and rape.[1] Probably during the siege or shortly after, Shi Kefa was captured and committed suicide. Shortly afterward, Nanjing fell, and Qing forces captured the Ming prince who had been enthroned there as the Hongguang emperor.[2] Later in the summer, armed resistance developed in other delta cities such as Jiading and Suzhou.[3] The tales of this resistance were heroic, but as Lynn Struve has observed, "these locales had no natural defense advantages, aside from the many waterways which made cavalry and artillery movements inconvenient. District gates and city walls simply became fodder for Qing cannon, and the efforts of resisters to counter sabers with bamboo poles and crossbows with flung pots of excrement" were totally ineffective.[4] By the late fall of 1645, Qing armies had already moved south, leaving an occupying force in the delta.

Vivid and romantic as the stories of delta resistance often were, neither side in this conflict was quite as it seemed. On the one hand, the Qing armies, though led by Manchu officers such as Dodo and Bolo, were composed of northern Chinese troops, many of whom had surrendered to the Qing in 1644 or earlier. The victimizers of cities like Yangzhou may in fact have been not Manchus but poor northern peasants turned loose on the wealthy and vulnerable southern elite. On the other hand, the southern elite was hardly unified behind the southern Ming court at Nanjing, which was riven by the same tensions between military and civilian leaders and among civilian factions as afflicted the Beijing Ming court. In some areas of the south, such as the Anhui district of Tongcheng, where peasant rioting had occurred in the last years of the Ming, local landholders conspicuously preferred the order more or less guaranteed by Qing armies to the anarchy of late Ming rule.[5] Even residents of Nanjing, supposedly loyal to the Ming, were found looting the imperial palace as the Qing armies arrived. Armed resistance to Qing rule was neither universal nor terribly effective, but the memory of heroes, even (and perhaps particularly) flawed ones lived on long after their deaths. This was especially true in a land where the elite, in their capacity as keepers of local traditions, had the power to turn memory into history and legend into ideology. Accounts of southern resistance, like the chilling "Ten Days at Yangzhou," survived in lower Yangzi valley libraries until the nineteenth century. As did the residents of another famously subjugated delta, William Faulkner's fictional Yoknapatawpha County, Mississippi, in the early twentieth century, the Chinese southern elite sentimentalized the heroes of their "lost, irrevocable, unreconcilable debacle."[6]

This atmosphere would have provided ample reason for Qing conquerors to move slowly and carefully in establishing territorial administration in the delta. But there was a further complication in the establishment of provincial structures in the region; namely, that Ming institutions did not provide a usable geographic template for Qing provincial administration in the delta. Under the Ming, the lower Yangzi region was governed from the southern capital of Nanjing and comprised a territory known as Nan Zhili (Southern Territories under Direct Control). The Qing had no need for a second capital in China as they already had one in Manchuria; the central government apparatus was to be housed entirely in Beijing, which was firmly under the control of Manchu banner forces. To highlight their determination in this regard, the Qing renamed Nanjing (Southern Capital) Jiangning (Place of River Repose).[7] But if Nanjing was not to be a capital, it still was a site of enormous strategic significance, not the least because it contained the tomb of the founding emperor of the Ming dynasty. In late summer of 1645, the Qing established in Nanjing their first official presence in central or south China with the appointment of Hong Chengchou, a surrendered former Ming supreme commander, as "grand secretary and pacifier of the south" (*Zhaofu nanfang neiyuan daxueshi*). Hong was given the fairly large mandate of arranging military supplies and logistics for Manchu armies operating in south China and overseeing military-civilian relations in the Yangzi delta, Henan, and Jiangxi. Two days after Hong's appointment, 373 former Ming dynasty officials were restored to local and intermediate offices in the Yangzi delta area. These officials were ordered to serve under four officials of governor's rank. One of these was posted at Fengyang, the ancestral home of the Ming royal house; a second was stationed at Jiangning; a third was posted at Anqing upriver from Jiangning; and a fourth was charged with responsibility for managing the river.[8]

For an area that was smaller than most Chinese provinces, the territorial administration there was fairly dense. It was also an unusual administrative arrangement that probably reflected the court's uncertainty about the centers of power and dynamism in the lower Yangzi valley. Qing administrative density in the south increased with the establishment of a banner army garrison at Nanjing in 1646. The first step toward bringing the lower Yangzi area into line with arrangements being established in other parts of China came when Hong Chengchou retired from office to meet his ritual mourning obligations. His successor Ma Guozhu was appointed as a regular governor-general, with jurisdiction limited to the provinces of Jiangxi and Jiangsu. As Ma's biography makes clear, however, most of his time was spent directing the dynasty's response to rebellions in what was to become the province of Anhui and coordinating the dynasty's campaigns in the far south with the Manchu commanders of banner armies.[9] The governor-level appointees also spent most of their time on military matters. During most of the late 1640s and early 1650s, the governor at Fengyang was apparently away from his post, participating in the campaign to recapture Canton. Even those officials who stayed in the delta were probably mostly engaged in police actions, often of a fairly rough-and-ready sort. The first governor at Jiangning, Tu Guobao—a former Ming "regional commander" (*zongbing*)—was demoted and temporarily transferred to another posting for executing criminals he had captured without formally requesting permission from Beijing.[10]

Such an administration was able to keep the peace in the delta, after a fashion. But it was not able to accomplish the other task required of all lower Yangzi governments, tax collection. Or to put the matter more precisely, the earliest Qing regime in Jiangnan was unable to produce for the central government the amount of revenue to which the institutional records suggested it was entitled. Tax delinquencies were endemic in the Yangzi delta for several reasons. First, the basic tax rate in some of the largest delta counties was higher than in other parts of China. The founding emperor of the Ming set an extraordinarily high tax for these counties in the late fourteenth century, partly to punish the area for supporting a rival and partly to ensure that the large estates of the region would be profitable only to a resident landholder. This high tax burden was somewhat mitigated during the later Ming, but not completely, and it was axiomatic in Qing times that the region had the highest land taxes in the empire.[11] The wealthy delta could probably have borne a somewhat higher tax burden than the rest of the empire if it were not for problems with collection. A survey of tax arrears carried out in the late 1720s, at a moment when the Qing's administrative capacities had significantly increased, found that nearly 50 percent of the delta's arrears were attributable to clerical corruption and fraud.[12] In the seventeenth century, there was an additional political problem. The amount of arrears reported in the 1660s strongly suggests that some families had paid few, if any, taxes since the time of the conquest. Armed resistance, it would appear, changed by degrees into tax resistance.

All this posed an increasingly serious problem for a government that declared in 1649 that its revenues did not cover its expenses. In an effort to address this problem, the Qing had in 1655 decreed that local officials would henceforth be fined or demoted according to the percentage of uncollected taxes in their jurisdiction.[13] Trouble in the lower Yangzi has been seen as having begun with an edict issued shortly after the death of the Shunzhi emperor in January 1661. This edict reiterated the regulations of 1655, adding the additional stipulation that officials whose taxes were unpaid would not be eligible for promotion. What was new about this edict were not so much its terms, which moderately increased pressure on magistrates, but the way in which it was read in Jiangning. Strangely, the edict itself did not mention the south at all but referred only to tax problems in Zhili.[14] However, inspired by the severity that the regents for the new emperor seemed to exhibit toward the habits and foibles of Chinese officials, Jiangning governor Zhu Guozhi—himself a bannerman—moved vigorously to collect outstanding taxes in the delta.[15] In late March 1661, he began to see results, in the form of a demonstration carried out by the Suzhou gentry against the burden of back taxes they were being forced to pay. This demonstration occurred on the occasion of a memorial service for the Shunzhi emperor in the Confucian temple at Suzhou, which the governor was attending. In June 1661, Governor Zhu submitted to the court a list of 13,517 names of tax-delinquent households and 254 delinquent yamen clerks in the delta. In the proceedings that ensued, many local gentry lost their civil service degrees, temporarily or permanently, and some were arrested.

There were even reports of Qing troops surrounding and occupying the homes of delta residents who were on the register.[16]

In the long run, however, the most important aspect of the Jiangnan tax arrears prosecutions of 1661 was the yawning gap they revealed between the Qing military officers who ruled from the garrison town of Jiangning and the local elite. Meng Sen, a Republican era historian of the Qing period who was himself from Suzhou, has speculated that Governor Zhu was motivated in the case not only by a desire to collect taxes but by his general frustration with the delta elite. This frustration was compounded when the elite failed to support government forces in a recent conflict with pirates. The elite were certainly not inspired to write accounts of Zhu's activities. His biography in *History of the Qing* records his charges against the Jiangnan rate payers and then observes with delicious understatement "for this he earned a reputation for cruelty."[17] The psychological distance between the garrison town of Jianging and Suzhou in 1661 was so great that when a party of Manchu officials arrived in the southeast to investigate the demonstration at the Confucian temple, they chose not to go to Suzhou so as not to cause trouble there. Shortly thereafter, Governor Zhu fled his post in Jiangning, for which act he was cashiered and demoted five ranks.[18]

As the regents knew well enough, this gap could not be allowed to continue if the new empire was to endure; they had to develop a new basis for interaction between the landowning elite of the delta and the central government. Frederic Wakeman and others have discussed the new means of tax assessment and collection that grew out of the Jiangnan tax arrears case of 1661.[19] Not so fully remarked upon is the fact that the process set in motion in 1661 would eventually lead to a new administrative arrangement giving the elite of Suzhou and the lower delta their own means of direct access to the central government. Much of this process is not fully accessible to the historian, for as the late Meng Sen observed in his classic study of the Jiangnan arrears case, there are few references to Jiangnan in the *Veritable Records* for late 1661. But there is ample circumstantial evidence to suggest that administrative change was in the works in late 1661 and the years thereafter in Jiangnan.

The process likely began when Governor Zhu Guozhi abruptly left his post at Jiangnan in the autumn of 1661. In December 1661, the Shunzhi court ordered the Chinese bannerman Han Shiqi to take his place. Han had moved from a posting in the Imperial Household Department in the capital to the position of governor of Shuntian, the district around Beijing, in the early summer of 1661. He was to serve as governor of Jiangning until 1669.[20] A series of further changes also began in Jiangnan in 1661. Under the Ming and in the first years of the Qing, two administrative commissioners, a senior commissioner of the left and a junior commissioner of the right, were appointed in each province; in the lower Yangzi valley, both officials served in Jiangning. According to the 1730 *Jiangnan Gazetteer* (Jiangnan tongzhi), beginning in 1661, there was a territorial distinction as well as a distinction in seniority between the two administrative commissioners. The senior of the Jiangning administrative commissioners was given responsibility for the upper delta; the other was made responsible for the counties of the lower delta, where the tax arrears case had occurred. The *Jiangnan Gazetteer*, the *Revised Anhui Gazetteer* (Chongxiu Anhui tongzhi), and, following them, *History of the Qing* date the founding of the province to this reorganization of administrative commissioners' duties.[21] The actual change in responsibilities seems likely to have occurred when a new commissioner of the right for Jiangnan arrived in the delta in early January 1662, one month after the new governor Han Shiqi.[22] Several other pieces of circumstantial evidence suggest that the Qing was moving toward a new administrative presence in the delta in the early 1660s. After Governor Han arrived in Jiangnan in late 1661, he ordered the Suzhou city walls strengthened and expanded, with structures incorporated for guardhouses and granaries. This was the first work done on the Suzhou city walls since the late 1360s and the last major rebuilding in the later imperial period.[23] Two years later, in the summer of 1663, the Qing central government further increased its presence in the lower Yangzi delta by appointing two provincial judges for Jiangnan. Both judges had the same title, but the *Anhui Gazetteer* and, following it, *A Chronological Table of Qing Officials* (Qingdai zhi guan nian biao) identify one of the two Jiangnan provincial judges as the Anhui judge and the other as the Jiangsu judge.

None of these steps committed the dynasty absolutely to the establishment of a province of Jiangsu with its capital at Suzhou. Indeed, there is no mention of Jiangsu in appointment edicts in the *Veritable Records of the Qing* (Qing shilu) until the mid-1670s, although both the *Jiangnan Gazetteer* and *History of the Qing* refer to the formal establishment of a Jiangsu lieutenant governor in 1666. Forced to rethink the disposition of Qing administrative forces in the southeast, Qing leaders in the 1660s took tentative steps toward the creation of a new geographical order in the region. This was to be an order in which local elites had access to Qing centrally appointed personnel in locations other than garrisons. Suzhou, although not a new city in the seventeenth century, was known not as a city of administration but as a city of wealth, a city of gardens rather than governments.[24] There, elite families could afford to turn valuable orchards into pleasure gardens and pay enormous sums for fantastically shaped rocks to add interest to their landscapes. It was a city, in short, where the Chinese elite could meet Qing officials on its own terms. In fact, with the assignment of a governor to Suzhou, the Qing created an anomaly: Jiangsu was the only province in the empire where a governor and governor-general were posted in the same province but not in the same city.[25]

A new provincial capital was also being created in the upper Yangzi delta. At the time of the conquest, the Qing seemed not to know which of the challenges in the upper delta would be most serious. Three governors were assigned there; one to manage the river, one to manage the river valley elite, and a third to manage the Ming ancestral home and the rugged counties north of the Huai River. Circumstances took the decision of which governor should be maintained out of the dynasty's hands. The Fengyang governor was needed to lead troops in the south, and mounting expenses forced the dynasty to abolish the governors' posts at Fengyang and Anqing in 1649. In 1659, the functions of the river-managing governor and the governor at Anqing were combined into one position, that of the Anhui governor, who resided at Anqing. The Fengyang post was briefly recreated in 1660, when the Oboi regents were particularly concerned about military security, but was abolished in 1665.

Out of the conflicts of the early 1660s emerged two new provinces, two new centers of civilian authority in the Yangzi delta, Anhui in the upper delta and Jiangsu in the lower delta. This innovation seemed to offer advantages for the delta elite, since it afforded them access in more neutral locations to Qing officials. The Suzhou governorship in particular proved to be a location where scholar-gentry and scholar-officials could meet on fairly equal terms. But the arrangement also had advantages for the Qing, both in the seventeenth century and later. For, as G. William Skinner has pointed out, an alliance between the local elites of the delta, as the tax case of 1661 suggests was possible, could have posed a real threat to imperial power. "By drawing provincial boundaries so that the core of the region was divided among" several provinces, and the "metropolitan trading systems were split between administrative units," the Qing forestalled the possibility of such a debilitating alliance.[26] In some sense, the fact that both local elites and the Qing gained something from the territorial innovations may account for their durability, for the lower Yangzi provincial boundaries formed in the 1660s still exist today.

Accommodation: The Civilian Governors of Jiangsu

Having created two provinces in the Yangzi delta, the Qing set about to create two different administrative orders, and in this endeavor, Qing accommodation to the enduring realities of the delta was most apparent. Much of this accommodation was accomplished with different sorts of appointments. Anhui became a stopping place on official journeys through China's heartland. Governors of Anhui were often recently promoted and came to Anqing from all the provincial capitals in China except Guizhou. At the conclusion of terms that ranged from several months to nearly five years, they were generally transferred laterally to other governorships, often in other regions. As relative newcomers to the corps of governors, Anhui governors were probably somewhat weaker than their colleagues and were certainly weaker than their neighbors in Suzhou. Southern Anhui, where the provincial capital was located, was one of the most heavily commercialized regions of China and home to a very powerful merchant elite. In other parts of China where mercantile elites effectively organized economic and social life, for instance, Hankow, the Qing contented itself with a relatively weak political presence. This may have been the case in Anqing as well. The dynasty's relations with the southern Anhui merchants were more likely to have been managed by the Lianghuai salt commissioner than by the provincial governor.

Jiangsu, in contrast, became one of the most specialized provincial postings, with frequent internal promotions and many intraregional transfers. Of those promoted to governor in Jiangsu, 66 percent were lieutenant governors there at the time of their promotions, and 46.9 percent of those promoted and transferred to the governorship of Jiangsu held posts in the lower Yangzi region at the time of their promotion. Only Yunnan and Shaanxi were comparably specialized. But in those places, it was quite clearly military need that dictated patterns of appointment. Jiangsu was the preeminent site of civilian rule in the delta. In a world where military and civilian portfolios so often overlapped, it may be problematic to insist on a distinction between the two realms. Yet if such a distinction existed anywhere in seventeenth-century China, it was in Jiangsu, where governors and governors-general occupied two different cities, located a hundred miles apart.

After the disasters of the early 1660s, it took the Qing the better part of a generation to build a stable civilian administration at Suzhou. But when the task was accomplished, by the last years of the seventeenth century, most of the lower Yangzi elite had at least accepted Qing rule and routine, and the dynasty, for its part, had rebuilt much of the hydraulic infrastructure on which the economy of the region depended. Much of this was accomplished by a remarkable series of governors in whose lives the themes of intellectual accomplishment, public service, and the creative reframing of loyalties were intertwined.

It took nearly fifteen years for the dynasty to make a decisive commitment to civilian rule in the lower Yangzi valley. When the Kangxi emperor established procedures for promoting finance commissioners to provincial governorships in 1671, the Board of Personnel was ordered to memorialize first on whether the appointee should be a Manchu, a Chinese bannerman, or a Chinese civilian. This meant that, until the regulation was rescinded in the 1690s, the category of officials was chosen before the individual appointee. In Jiangsu, all governors appointed before 1676 were either bannermen or surrendered Ming military officials, and all those appointed from 1676 to 1719 were civilians, that is, offi-

TABLE 7.1. Governors of Jiangsu

Governor	Date of Service in Jiangsu	Date of Jinshi Degree	Native Place
Mu Tianyan	1676–81	1655	Gansu
Yu Guozhu	1681–84	1652	Huguang
Tang Bin	1684–86	1652*	Henan
Zhao Shilin	1686–87	1664*	Yunnan
Tian Wen	1687–88	1664*	Shandong
Hong Zhihao	1688–90	1659	Huguang
Zheng Rui	1690–92	1659*	Zhili
Song Luo	1692–1705	*	Henan
Yu Zhun	1705–9	*	Shanxi
Zhang Boxing	1709–15	1685*	Henan

Sources: *Qingdai zhi guan nian biao; Qin ding "Si ku quan shu" zong mu ti yao;* and *Zeng jiao Qing chao jinshi timing peilu fu yinde.*

*Works included in *Complete Library of the Four Treasuries* (Si ku quan shu).

cials who held no military rank or appointments. Table 7.1 lists the governors of Jiangsu and their dates of service during this time period.

The governors who served in Jiangsu between 1676 and 1719 were more than mere civilians, however; most held that special mark of accomplishment in the Chinese intellectual world, the highest civil service degree, the *jinshi*. Conventionally, it is assumed that the *jinshi* degree was a required credential for holding office in later imperial China, but in fact only about half the provincial governors during the Qing held the degree. During the reign of the Qianlong emperor, who prided himself on establishing a regime in which knowledge and power were joined, only 60 of 232 governors (26 percent) held the degree.[27] For most of the dynasty, and particularly during its early years, competence proved by deeds or recommendations was more important than an academic credential for the post of provincial governor. Mu Tianyan and Yu Guozhu seem to have been transitional figures. Mu Tianyan held the highest degree, but he came from Gansu, a region better known for its military than for its scholarly life. During his terms as lieutenant governor and governor at Jiangsu, he was known for distributing relief grain in times of famine and memorializing on the work needed along the rivers.[28] Although Yu Guozhu held a degree, he was better known for being the protégé of Mingzhu, one of the few Manchu counselors of the young Kangxi emperor who supported the decision to go to war against Wu Sangui.[29] Both governors were surely competent, but neither was the representative of the lower Yangzi elite that their successors would be.

During the governorship of Mu Tianyan, the Qing took several steps to cultivate delta elites. In Beijing, the dynasty took the important step of inviting recommended scholars to participate in a special examination, known as the Boxue Hongru. Those who passed were appointed to participate in scholarly projects in the capital, such as the compilation of the dynastic history of the Ming. Certainly it did not erase the memories of conquest, but the Boxue Hongru examination did have the effect of separating the minority of intellectuals who refused to serve the Qing under any circumstances from the majority who were willing to serve under what they regarded as appropriate circumstances. The first true scholar-governor in Jiangsu was Tang Bin, appointed in 1684. Tang had earned his *jinshi* degree and begun an official career early in the dynasty, then responded to the invitation to participate in the Boxue Hongru examination, passed it, and was appointed general editor of *History of the Ming* before being appointed to Suzhou. In 1687, Tian Wen was appointed governor. He had a history in the delta. Shortly after the Boxue Hongru examination, the dynasty responded to court pressures to appoint a *jinshi* holder as education commissioner of Jiangsu and chose Tian Wen. Tian was so successful in his work with the local elite that Mu Tianyan, his colleague in Anhui and the governor-general of Liangjiang, joined in recommending his promotion.[30] Tian Wen's *Chronological Biography of Meng Zhai* (Meng Zhai nianpu) presents a transcript of Tian Wen's interview with the emperor on the occasion of his appointment as well as the full text of the appointment letter. In the imperial interview, the emperor remarks that Jiangsu is indeed a hard province to govern and Tian Wen should make it his goal to assure that the scholars and the military lived in peace.[31]

Tang Bin and the governors who followed him in Jiangsu were not only consumers of contemporary intellectual discourse and effective test takers; they were also writers and editors of scholarly works. Tang Bin and six of his successors had works listed in the *Annotated Catalog of the "Complete Library of the Four Treasuries," Authorized by the Emperor* (Qin ding Si ku quan shu zong mu ti yao), which was published in the 1780s. Tian Wen, Zhao Shilin, and Yu Zhun each had one entry in the catalog; Tang Bin had three entries; Zheng Rui had four; and Zhang Boxing and Song Luo had eight entries apiece. Even for officials as distinguished as provincial governors, this was an unusual degree of recognition. The collected writings of Song Luo, Tian Wen, and Tang Bin are among the few works of their genre by Qing dynasty authors to be copied into the imperial library and are described in a chapter of the catalog that opens with descriptions of the poetic works of the Kangxi, Yongzheng, and Qianlong emperors.[32] Of course, more than purely literary judgments may have been involved here. Although literary criticism is perhaps always implicitly political, in the case of the *Complete Library of the Four Treasuries*, it was explicitly so, as the collection was commissioned by the Qing dynasty in order to celebrate its own contributions to the Chinese literary world. In featuring the work of Jiangsu governors so prominently, the editors of the collection were asserting, perhaps at the behest of their Manchu superiors, that Chinese who collaborated with the dynasty could be every bit as productive as those who refused to serve. The same political motive may have been behind another signal honor bestowed on Jiangsu governors Tang Bin and Zhang Boxing, who were two of only three officials recommended by the dynasty for elevation to the Confucian temple.[33]

The Qing accomplished several things with their appointments of scholar-governors to Jiangsu. First, they achieved a certain kind of social acceptability. Although he did not hold the *jinshi* degree, Song Luo was known as one of the two or three best poets of his day, and during his term as governor at Suzhou, he interacted with local literati on fairly equal terms. Specifically, he bought and renovated an estate that had belonged to a Song dynasty poet and held gatherings there for local literati; he wrote a small volume commemorating the site and the gatherings, which was listed in the imperial catalog. Also during his term as governor, he edited an anthology of poetry by Suzhou authors that was also noted in the catalog.[34]

Beyond sociability, the appointment of scholar-governors allowed the elite and the emperor to explore the terms and possibilities of cooperation. The appointment of Tang Bin provides an apt illustration. When the post of Jiangsu governor became vacant in the spring of 1684, two candidates were recommended to the Kangxi emperor. One, Chinese bannerman Shi Lin, had been a hero of the Wu Sangui Rebellion and had served for several years as finance commissioner of Zhejiang. The other was Sun Zaifeng, a *jinshi*-degree holder then serving in the Hanlin Academy.[35] Both would have been good appointments: Shi Lin was shortly appointed as governor of Hunan, and Sun Zaifeng was active in river conservancy work in Jiangsu through the 1680s. But in 1684, the Kangxi emperor set aside both recommendations and chose Tang Bin instead. He explained his choice in an edict on the role of scholars in government. In it, he asserted that "What is to be valued about those learned in the Way is their personal vigor and their capacity to achieve concrete results." This formulation already put a Qing spin on the matter. What the emperor meant by "learned in the Way" was mastery of what twentieth-century scholars have called Neo-Confucian philosophy, the body of ideas associated with the Song dynasty scholar Zhu Xi that had become the basis for the imperial civil service examinations. In broadest terms, these ideas focused on how the individual moral and political actor might best understand his obligations and his relation to the moral forces underlying the universe. "Concrete results" were only one of the standards by which those "learned in the Way" measured themselves in the seventeenth century, but this was clearly the standard by which the dynasty proposed to measure them. In effect, the Kangxi emperor was saying that he was prepared to support the learned so long as they focused on concrete results and did not lose themselves in debates of "empty words."

The emperor was articulating a middle ground between the dynasty's concern with effective administration and the scholar's concern with moral obligations, and inviting intellectuals to occupy that ground. On these terms, the emperor could profess admiration for the profundity and difficulty of Chinese learning, which there was every indication he actually felt. "Since ancient times," wrote the emperor, "penetrating to the essence of the Way has been difficult. I have heard that the academician Tang Bin, who formerly studied with Sun Qifeng, has achieved significant results. Moreover, he has conducted the Zhejiang provincial examinations, and proved himself to be a man of integrity. Let him be appointed governor of Jiangning."[36] The emperor's reference to Sun Qifeng was especially telling. Sun had been active, as a scholar, rather than an official, in the literati politics of the late Ming and had organized the resistance of his Zhili community to the Manchu invasion. When that resistance proved futile, and his properties were expropriated to serve as banner lands, he retired to Henan to a life of teaching and writing.[37] Tang Bin was his most famous student but had also passed both the *jinshi* and the special Boxue Hongru examination and served the new dynasty. In his edict, the emperor was asserting that as long as Tang and those in a similar position in the delta focused on the future instead of on the past, on results instead of on resentments, there could be a place for them in the new Qing order.

Negotiation: River Politics

The test of the new regime in the delta was not how much poetry it produced, although for the elite the production of poetry certainly marked the return of civility to political life. The real test was how effectively the new constellation of forces could negotiate the conflicts and commitments of delta life. The most important of these, and probably the most costly, was the maintenance of river-control structures and canals in the low-lying delta. River work in the delta served two purposes, flood control and transportation. Flood control was the more urgent to delta residents, particularly after the neglect flood-prevention structures had endured in the late Ming; transportation of food grain and tax revenue from the wealthy delta to the capital was more important to the central government. These two purposes were, of course, congruent; delta residents had an interest in shipping their grain, and the state had a concern with local welfare, and to some extent the same physical structures could serve both purposes. But there was room for different emphases, especially in projects that involved spending vast amounts of revenue and employing thousands. In discussions of how to proceed along the rivers, lower Yangzi officials spoke for the constituencies their posts had been created to represent; negotiations in the delta came to be exchanges not between residents and the state but between different officials reflecting different interests. A full description of the technical problems and practical tasks entailed in this massive undertaking awaits a longer study. But it is possible here to sketch some of the remarkable political disputes and what they reveal about the changing nature of government in the southeast.

In the seventeenth century, Jiangsu province contained the mouths of two transcontinental rivers. In the south, the wide mouth of the Yangzi River was broad enough to contain Chongming Island, itself a county of the province; in the north was the relatively narrow, shallow southern mouth of the Yellow River. The counties around both mouths suffered from neglect during the chaotic last years of the Ming. Restoring flood-protection structures in the southeast was one of the highest priorities of the Qing in the last quarter of the seventeenth century, and the effort provided the first tangible benefits of Qing government to the regional elite. Problems around the mouth of the Yangzi were addressed first. In 1678, Governor Mu Tianyan proposed dredging the Bai Mao River from Changshu to the Yangzi, a distance of forty-three li, and dredging the Mengdu River from Wujin to the Yangzi, a distance of forty-eight li, so as to provide drainage for floodwaters. The project was approved and accomplished at a cost of 90,000 *liang*, much to the approbation of the residents of the province's southern Susongtai circuit.[38]

The problems in the north, at the mouth of the Yellow River, were much more serious, and the fix was vastly more expensive and controversial. Unlike the relatively fast-flowing Yangzi, the Yellow River was slow and silt-ridden throughout its lower course and flowed through lands in northern Jiangsu that were barely above sea level. This was a particularly crucial span, because for a distance of about sixty miles in northern Jiangsu, the Yellow River served as the channel for the Grand Canal, the critical man-made artery that linked the rice-producing areas of south China with the capital. To complicate matters further, Qinghe in northern Jiangsu was the site of the confluence of the Yellow River and the Huai River, which drained northern and central Anhui. Late Ming practice, associated with Pan Jixun, who was in charge of Yellow River conservancy off and on between 1561 and 1595, had been to allow the three streams to flow together. The idea behind this approach was that the combined currents of the Huai River and the Grand Canal could be used to move the silt down the Yellow River, or as it was described in late imperial times, to "use the water to attack the silt" (*shu shui gong sha*).[39] The problem with this strategy, according to Qing commentators, was that the combined currents of the three rivers was not strong enough to prevent the

Yellow River from building up silt, overflowing its banks, and blocking transport along the Grand Canal. Using local and national gazetteers, Hou Renzhi has shown that there was flooding in northern Jiangsu in all but two of the first thirty-three years of the Qing dynasty. Moreover, floods became more serious and affected a longer span of the river as time went on.[40]

In the 1670s, the Qing dynasty's point man on the Yellow River was Jin Fu, a Chinese bannerman who received a special appointment to serve as governor of Anhui from 1671 to 1677 and was then promoted to director-general of river conservancy in May 1677, in which position he served until 1688.[41] Rather like his contemporary Cao Yurong in the southwest, with whom he appeared to share a factional allegiance, Jin Fu had a broad regional vision and sought to use the new dynasty's financial resources to transform the physical environment. Three months after becoming director-general of river conservancy, he submitted five major proposals for work along the lower course of the Yellow River and Grand Canal. In a sixth memorial, he estimated the cost of the proposed work to be 2,158,000 *liang*, the equivalent of one year's tax revenue from Jiangsu. As a means of financing this work, he proposed selling military *shengyuan* degrees, charging for private commerce along the Grand Canal, and levying a special tax on reclaimed land in Anhui. He also proposed collecting 10 percent of the Zhili, Jiangsu, Zhejiang, Jiangxi, Hupei, Shandong, and Shanxi tax revenues one year early in order to provide working capital for the project. This cost was too high for the Kangxi court, which was already heavily committed financially to suppressing the Wu Sangui Rebellion, and so Jin pared back his proposal to only the most urgent tasks and resubmitted it. He chose as the most pressing eight projects for repairing levees, water gates, and canals in the vicinity of Lake Hongze, which he estimated would cost 350,000 *liang*, and restoring the Grand Canal and received approval to undertake them.[42] In 1678, after the rebellion ended, Jin embarked on an even larger project, construction of a canal that came to be known as the Zhong He, parallel to the Yellow River. This canal, which was eventually used for Grand Canal transport, was one of the major engineering accomplishments of the Qing dynasty.[43] A second permanent contribution Jin Fu made to Qing institutions in the delta was the establishment of a contingent of "river troops" (*he bing*), which he created with a view toward subjecting the management of rivers to the fiscal and organizational disciplines of the military order.[44]

Unfortunately, although Jin Fu was effective in securing water transport along the Grand Canal and repairing waterworks in northwestern Jiangsu, flooding did not abate along the lower course of the Yellow River, between the Grand Canal and the Pacific Ocean. There were major floods in 1681, and between 1684 and 1686, Tang Bin reported further flooding in northern Jiangsu. This devastation, the governor argued, coming as it did on top of ongoing major engineering and construction work, was driving the peasantry to the brink of starvation, forcing families to sell daughters in order to survive.[45] In response to this disaster, Jin Fu proposed several projects. The most prominent of these was to build new water gates and reinforce existing dikes along the western edge of Lake Hongze. This lake, along Jiangsu's western borders, formed a natural catchment basin for both the Yellow and Huai Rivers. Governor Tang Bin, his successor Tian Wen, and Mu Tianyan, who had returned to the delta as director-general of grain transport with control over the Grand Canal,[46] all opposed this plan. This conflict pitted Jiangsu's "civilian" governors against the delta's Chinese banner administrators. It was a battle the governors were especially qualified to fight, for they knew their rivers. Tang Bin's native district was in the Yellow River valley in Henan, near Zhengzhou, and Tian Wen came from Dezhou, a city along the Grand Canal in Shandong, where the older, northern mouth of the Yellow River crossed the canal.[47] In addition to their personal expertise, the Jiangsu governors could cite the rising opposition of a waterlogged peasantry as well as the cost, some 600,000 to 700,000 *liang* by Mu Tianyan's estimate.

Opposed to Jin Fu's proposals, the governors of Jiangsu rallied around a proposal made by an official with a name familiar to all in the delta, Yu Chenglong. This name was familiar because, in a rather bizarre expression of political allegiance, Yu had taken the exactly same name—both sound and characters—as Yu Chenglong, the governor-general of Liangjiang. The elder Yu was the younger Yu's political mentor, having requested his appointment as prefect of Jiangning prefecture and then recommended him as provincial judge for Anhui. The elder Yu was a Chinese bannerman (though the younger Yu was not), but his reputation was radically different from Jin Fu's. Whereas Jin Fu had proposed gigantic and expensive engineering projects, the elder Yu Chenglong was known for his extraordinary honesty and frugality. During his terms as governor-general, he acquired the nickname "Yu of the Clear Skies," and his lifestyle was so austere that it was said that on his appointment, Jiangnan people abandoned their frivolity and markets.[48] The younger Yu's river proposal was similarly restrained. Instead of building expensive dikes along Lake Hongze, he proposed the relatively less costly and more direct expedient of widening and deepening the mouth of the Yellow River so that water could more readily flow to the sea. This proposal had the additional merit of attacking the problem closer to its source and using the existing riverbed as a conduit for floodwaters. Jin Fu, however, opposed it, arguing that since the lands between Qinghe and the Pacific Ocean were below sea level, no amount of dredging in the riverbed would produce an acceptable channel.[49]

In this controversy, as often happened in Chinese history, policy differences eventually turned into accusations of factionalism and corruption as courtiers took sides in the dispute. As H. Lyman Miller has argued, the case became the focus of a dispute between the "Northern Faction," a group of officials centered around Mingzhu, and a "Southern Faction" made up of Jiangsu scholars at court.[50] Finally, neither plan was fully carried out: the dikes along the lake were not reinforced, and although some dredging was completed along the lower course of the Yellow River, Jin Fu blocked full execution of Yu's plan. With such dredging as was accomplished and the opening of the Zhong He canal, the problem in northern Jiangsu seemed to subside.[51]

The details of charge and countercharge in these cases, though amply documented in the historical record, were probably less important than what the case as a whole said about the evolving government of the delta lands. The effort to restore flood-protection structures in northern Jiangsu clearly demonstrates that the dynasty was willing to commit very scarce resources to protect Jiangsu's livelihood and maintain communications with the southeast. But in China, as perhaps in most empires, large flows of resources to or from one region produced controversy. The problem in the late 1670s and 1680s was local use of expenditures authorized by the capital. A similar issue had arisen in Jiangnan in the late 1650s. To be sure, in the earlier period, the flow of money was to rather than from Jiangsu, and the issue was by what means to extract revenue, not how to spend it. Still, in both periods, provincial officials were the crucial cadres in determining the effect of financial decisions at the local level. One difference between the 1650s and 1680s, however, was that in the 1680s, Jiangsu governors were more attuned to local needs and in a better position to communicate local desires to the capital.

Zhang Boxing versus Gali

Negotiations between state and society in the delta were effective, in a rough-and-ready sort of way, but they were also noisy. This was in part because the issues and the amounts of money involved were serious. But it was also because the role of provincial middleman in Jiangsu was a contested and somewhat congested space. Regional decision making involved not only Jiangsu governors but also three directors-general —of river conservancy, grain transport, and Liangjiang—all of whom had interests in the security of the delta. Each official often felt himself especially empowered to communicate his will and his challenges to the capital.

Before the beginning of the eighteenth century, conflicts were often suppressed, as all delta officials labored under the requirement of silent loyalty to their Qing masters. The first to break the silence were Zhang Boxing and Gali. Within months of Zhang's arrival in Suzhou in 1709, he found himself locked in hand-to-hand bureaucratic combat with his superior, Liangjiang governor-general Gali. Both officials broke the code of silence, indicting each other in one of the loudest and most colorful exchanges of official broadsides in the early eighteenth century. The charges and countercharges are worth examining, both for what they say about political life in the delta and for what they tell of the conflicts between Manchus and Chinese officials and the structures the dynasty had evolved, three-quarters of a century after the conquest, for containing them.

Zhang Boxing was the last of Kangxi's scholar-governors in Jiangsu, and he was also the most prolific writer. In addition to the eight works listed in the imperial catalog, Zhang edited two large collections of major works of Song dynasty philosophy and works by his contemporaries. Because Zhang Boxing's philosophical position, which involved vigorous promotion of the work of Zhu Xi, had fallen out of favor by the late eighteenth century, only one of his works was actually copied into the imperial manuscript library. This was a work on river conservancy, written when he was director-general of river conservancy late in his career, which the editors of the Complete Library of the Four Treasuries described as the most useful book Zhang had ever written.[52] This was a harsher judgment on the remainder of Zhang's scholarship than most in the seventeenth century would have hazarded, since the sort of work on Song philosophy that constituted the remainder of his corpus was much favored and patronized by the Kangxi emperor. But it may have been true that Zhang's work on river conservancy was valuable, since his career effectively began and ended with efforts to tame China's rivers. After receiving his jinshi degree in 1685, he was appointed to a series of positions in the capital, reaching the Grand Secretariat in 1692. The death of his father in 1695 necessitated a return home to Henan, where he worked on coordinating flood defenses. He probably owed his next promotions to his success in these endeavors, for which he was singled out for especial praise. From Henan, he was promoted to provincial judge in Jiangsu and in that capacity entertained the Kangxi emperor on the emperor's tour of the south in 1707. When the emperor inquired who was the most upright and able official in Jiangsu, Zhang's superiors put him forward. The favorable impression Zhang made on the emperor during this tour led to his special appointment to governor of Fujian. In 1709, there was famine in Jiangsu, and the emperor, seeking a trustworthy governor, identified Zhang. According to a story written down in the early eighteenth century, two grand secretaries disagreed over this appointment, with one pleading that Zhang should be retained in Fujian and the other begging for his transfer to Jiangsu. The emperor supposedly laughed and responded "Don't you southerners fight. I have a plan for the empire."[53] Because of his scholarship and his previous administrative accomplishments, Zhang had every reason to assume that he enjoyed the full respect and support of the emperor during his term as Jiangsu governor.[54]

In terms of connections and imperial confidence, however, Zhang met his match in Gali. Gali was of a distinguished Manchu family—his great-grandfather was one of the five most trusted counselors of the Qing founding emperor. Gali had a special connection with the Kangxi emperor: his mother had served as the emperor's wet-nurse. The two men were "brothers at the breast," in Chinese parlance.[55] Gali began his official career managing logistics for the Kangxi emperor's campaign against Galdan in Mongolia. After Gali served for three years in the Board of Revenue at Shengjing, the emperor chose him to be governor of Shanxi. Despite several attacks on his administration of Shanxi, Gali was promoted to the Liangjiang governor-generalship in the summer of 1708 and had been in office about four months at the time of Zhang Boxing's appointment.[56]

The source of the two officials' disagreements cannot be pinpointed. Personal enmity or ethnic resentment could have been factors, although it was hardly new to find Chinese officials serving with or under Manchu banner officers in the delta in the early eighteenth century. Ever since the disastrous term of Governor Zhu Guozhi, Manchus had roughly alternated with Chinese in the Jiangnan governor-generalship. If there was resentment, it could have as easily come from Gali's side as from Zhang's. Both extant biographies of Gali comment on his fondness for indicting Chinese subordinates. The Manchu governor-general announced his arrival in the delta with a joint indictment of the governor of Jiangsu, Yu Zhun, and the lieutenant governor Yi Sigong over tax arrears in the lower delta. Zhang and Gali first disagreed over how the arrears were to be made up. Gali proposed that officials in the delta should make up the tax arrears from their own salaries; Zhang felt that Jiangsu officials could not bear such a burden. The Kangxi emperor, who finally forgave the arrears, reprimanded the two officials for their disagreement. In the face of this reprimand, Zhang resigned on account of illness, but the emperor refused to accept his resignation.[57]

The feud between the two officials climaxed with the charge, made by Zhang Boxing in the autumn of 1711, that Gali had accepted bribes from candidates for the *juren* degree in the Jiangsu provincial examinations of 1711. These charges proved to be so incendiary that the facts of the case became almost impossible to establish. A Chinese official charging a Manchu with undermining one of the central institutions of the Chinese government made for a difficult enough case. But there was the additional problem that the degree candidates and the residents of the delta chose sides, with military personnel generally supporting the governor-general and civilians and degree holders generally supporting the governor. Pressures became so intense that one Jiangsu official who was scheduled to give crucial testimony committed suicide before the investigation took place. Two teams of investigators, each consisting of one Manchu and one Chinese, came to the unsatisfying conclusion that although there had been cheating in the examinations, the blame could not be assigned to any particular official. Both sets of investigators recommended that Gali be demoted but left at his post and that Zhang Boxing be dismissed.[58]

Before a decision could be made to carry out either recommendation, Gali counterattacked with a memorial charging Zhang Boxing with seven instances of dereliction of duty during Zhang's two years as governor. Gali's original memorial is not extant, but most of its text is preserved in his biography and in Zhang Boxing's extraordinary written response to the charges. This response appears as a memorial in Zhang's collected works, although there is no reference to such a document in the official record. If it was submitted as a memorial, it was an extraordinarily long one of thirty-seven hundred characters. There was, to be sure, a self-righteous tone to the document, as might be expected of a piece of writing titled, in effect, "Why I Was Indicted." But the document provides much lively detail of the interactions between Gali and Zhang Boxing and suggests many of the tensions of early eighteenth-century government in the delta. Gali's memorial and Zhang's response center around four issues: the suppression of piracy along the Jiangsu coast, the tasks of capturing and punishing lawless elements, shipment of tribute grain to the capital, and relations between the governor and the Suzhou literati.[59]

Piracy, though frequently ignored in accounts of delta politics, was quite a serious problem for early Qing regimes in the lower Yangzi. All along China's southeastern coast in the late seventeenth and eighteenth centuries, the lines between legitimate commerce, unauthorized but informally permitted trade, and piracy were rather fuzzy ones that merchants and officials alike could both step and trip over. The failure of the Jiangsu elite to respond to Zheng Chenggong's incursions had, at least in some accounts, provoked the anger of Zhu Guozhi in the 1650s. The pirate who figured in Gali's attack on Zhang appears first in the historical record in the autumn of 1709, when the Manchu brigade general of Fengtian reported to the emperor that a band of some three hundred pirates had landed in Jinzhou and looted the official granary. Thirty-six of the pirates were captured, and according to the general, one of them revealed under interrogation that their leader was named Zheng Jinxin. The edict acknowledging receipt of this report was placed next to an edict acknowledging the report from the Shandong governor of similar activity along the Shandong coast.[60] In the early fall of 1709, the court's approach to this situation was to warn coastal governors to guard their granaries in the hope that the pirates could be starved. But later that autumn, the Board of War sent out a circular ordering governors to go out to sea in pursuit. Gali, leaving from Shanghai, apprehended the pirates, but in 1711, he charged Zhang Boxing, in much the same way his predecessor Zhu Guozhi had charged the people of Jiangnan, with failing to follow an imperial order to pursue the pirates.[61] The Kangxi emperor was inclined to believe this charge had some merit: "When I ordered the governors and governors-general to set forth against the pirates, many held back out of fear or assigned the task to subordinates. Only Gali proceeded to Shan-hua Island to capture the pirates."[62] Gali implied in his memorial, and the emperor appeared to agree, that Zhang and perhaps other Chinese governors were jealous of the governor-general's success in apprehending the pirates.[63]

Zhang Boxing took a different view. Noting that he had no naval forces assigned to his command, he asserted that he had tried to communicate with the governor-general about the proposed expedition, but by the time Zhang Boxing's deputy reached Jiangning, Gali had already set off downriver to go to sea. Moreover, Zhang remarked, there were a number of mysteries about Gali's pursuit of the pirates. Instead of going directly to sea from the mouth of the Yangzi, Gali had sailed up the Huangpu River and paused at Shanghai for two weeks. Then when he finally did put out to sea, he did so in an unarmed cargo ship rather than in one of the dynasty's naval vessels. Building up a case from the confessions of the sailors Gali had captured and other circumstantial evidence, Zhang argued that although Gali caught Zheng Jinxin, he had done so only because he was in league with a Jiangsu pirate/official named Zhang Yuanlong. Zhang Boxing then described his own efforts to arrest Zhang Yuanlong, which he said were frustrated because his junior officials were intimidated by the close relationship between the governor-general and the pirate. In his memorial, Zhang painted a vivid picture of Governor-general Gali loading up his flotilla of unarmed cargo ships with pirate loot that he had accepted from Zhang Yuanlong before the two set off in pursuit of Zheng Jinxin.[64]

There were probably two sides to the story. Obviously the court was satisfied that pirates had been apprehended and Gali had done his job; the central government may not have felt particularly inclined to inquire how the task was accomplished. In the watery world of the Chinese coast, some sorts of liaison were necessary if effective action was to be taken. Many Manchu military victories rested on strategic alliances, some of which were no doubt undergirded by payments. Zhang Boxing could not deny that in a world concerned with concrete results, Gali had achieved them. But he could discredit these results by suggesting that the governor-general was on the take. The charge was plausible, apart from the circumstantial and other evidence Zhang Boxing provided, since Gali had a reputation for greed. While governor of Shanxi, he had been charged three times with the personal use of public funds, including accusations that he had pocketed relief funds and levied a 20 percent surcharge on land taxes. Indeed, it might have been Gali's reputation for greed that led Zhang Boxing to accuse Gali of taking bribes from examination candidates. Moreover, Gali would not have been the first high-level Manchu to attempt to line his pockets with the rich revenues of the delta. During the term of Tang Bin, Mingzhu—a Manchu councilor who was then president of the Board of Revenue—had attempted to extort a bribe for approving Tang's plan to restructure the Susongtai district's tax obligations. Jin Fu was also known to be Mingzhu's protégé, so it may be speculated that some of the vast sums appropriated for river work made their way into his pockets.[65] Tang resisted the demand for a bribe, and any payments Jin Fu received are lost to the historian. Zhang Boxing was the first Jiangsu governor to protest the informal demands for revenue that often seem to have been associated with Manchu supervision of Chinese officials in the delta.

Gali's second, third, and fourth charges revolved around the preservation of order in the delta. Ostensibly, each charge concerned Zhang Boxing's failure to arrest lawbreakers; in fact, in each case, the real issue was how Zhang had protected his subordinates from the consequences of their failures in this regard. The second charge accused Zhang of colluding with the Shanghai magistrate Xu Shizhen to change the official record of the dates on which certain criminals were apprehended. The third charge accused Zhang of conspiring with Suzhou prefect Chen Pengnian to prevent Gali's imposition of the bao-jia mutual security system in the delta. In the fourth charge, Zhang is accused of inappropriately seeking a reduction of the penalty imposed on the Susongtai circuit intendant who failed to investigate robbery cases. As with the piracy charges, these accusations rang true for the emperor, who remarked that although Zhang was an official of great integrity, he seemed to be unable to protect the Susongtai area from banditry. But as Cao Yin, an imperial bondservant stationed in the delta, remarked, each of these cases was old by the time Gali brought it to the emperor's attention. In many of the instances Gali cited, the miscreants had died by the time the governor-general prepared his memorial, which made the facts of criminal actions and official inactions difficult to establish.[66]

Formally, Zhang Boxing had a response to each of these charges. He assured the emperor that he believed in the bao-jia system and had ordered his subordinates to implement it. He also carefully described the official actions he had taken on behalf of the Shanghai magistrate and the Susongtai circuit intendant, and, in the case of the Suzhou prefect, he demonstrated that these actions were in accord with dynastic procedures. Throughout his response, he argued that it was the many canals and byways of the delta region rather than any collusion among officials that made it difficult to apprehend criminals in the delta. In the case of the Shanghai magistrate, Gali had accused Zhang of "looking out from the same window" (tong chuang) with magistrate Xu Shizhen, that is, building a faction based on common native place. Zhang responded that although he and Xu were fellow provincials, they were from different prefectures.[67]

Informally, the situation was more complex and ambiguous than Zhang's memorial allowed, as the case of Suzhou prefect Chen Pengnian suggests. Chen was a *jinshi*-degree holder who had a reputation for integrity, reflected in the nickname "Clear Skies," which he shared with Yu Chenglong; however, Chen had a history of shaky relations with Manchu supervisors. When Gali's predecessor as governor-general, Asan, assembled the local officials in Jiangsu and ordered them to levy an additional tax in order to underwrite the cost of the Kangxi emperor's southern tour, Chen Pengnian alone refused. After this, Asan accused Chen Pengnian of bribery and of impropriety in converting houses of prostitution into Confucian lecture halls, and Gali himself was to accuse Chen (falsely, as the court judged) of writing seditious poetry. Chinese officials such as Zhang Boxing admired and respected Chen, however. Zhang was said to have especially relied on Chen's judgment when Chen was prefect of Suzhou and to have treated him with "great honor" (*zhong ya*). Chen was one of only a very few Qing writers whom Zhang Boxing included in his collectanea, and Zhang's was the only published edition of Chen's collected writings until the Chen family brought out an edition in 1762.[68]

Zhang had a similar relationship with Lü Lungqi, another delta official who seemed to be a thorn in the side of his lower Yangzi superiors. Lü Lungqi had also been accused by Mu Tianyan of failure to apprehend criminals, but Zhang's spirited defense of Lü made its way into Mu's own biography. Lü Lungqi's collected writings were also reprinted in Zhang's collectanea. The two officials' biographies appear in the same *juan* of *History of the Qing*, and they were admitted together into the Temple of Eminent Statesmen.[69] Zhang Boxing may have been justified in arguing that informal ties among Chinese officials had not interfered with the prosecution of criminal activity in Jiangsu, but he could not deny that such informal ties existed, or that they often formed a basis for common action, from which senior officials might well be excluded.

There was an internal logic to Gali's indictment, which probably replicated the priorities of many senior Manchu officials as they faced the prospect of governing their empire in the seventeenth century. Having accused Zhang Boxing of exposing the empire to danger from the outside (pirates), Gali then condemned the governor for failing to preserve order within. In the fifth count of the indictment, Gali charged that Zhang Boxing had been unable to fulfill the basic obligations of a Jiangsu governor for the maintenance of the regime, guaranteeing the timely delivery of tribute grain to the capital. Specifically, he charged that under Zhang Boxing's direction, the tribute grain shipment from the Susongtai circuit for 1710 had left the delta for the capital nearly two months after the established deadline for such shipments. The shipment in question was a rather complicated one. Transport of grain to the capital had been delayed by the need to divert some of the grain to relieve a famine in the province of Fujian, where, probably coincidentally,

Zhang Boxing had just served as governor. After this, there was a further delay while grain that represented repayment of a loan made earlier to relieve distressed areas of Jiangsu was delivered and the Grain Transport Administration prepared boats for the shipment north. Then, the boat containing Susongtai grain had to wait in the queue of grain boats before it could start north. As a result, the last boatload of Susongtai grain had left the delta on the twenty-seventh day of the fourth lunar month, some fifty-seven days after the deadline, the last day of the second lunar month.

In his response to this charge, Zhang acknowledged that the shipment was late but asked with some justification who was really at fault. The lines of official communications around this multisourced grain shipment of 1710 must surely have been as congested as the Grand Canal shipping lanes themselves. Despite this, Zhang Boxing had memorialized the throne after the shipment was dispatched, accepting personal responsibility for the delay (and listing the names of other officials who bore some responsibility) and requesting administrative punishment. For Zhang, as for anyone who accepted the logic of the Chinese personnel system, the matter should have ended with whatever penalty the Board of Punishments saw fit to assess. For Gali, however, Zhang's memorial was a case of embellished words fashioned to cover up administrative incompetence. What seems to have been at stake in this charge of Gali's was nothing less than the standard of accountability to which Qing officials were to be held. Gali and Zhang Boxing seemed to speak in their respective memorials as representatives of two quite different political traditions.[70]

Of all of Gali's charges, the seventh and eighth accusations revealed most vividly the gaps among officials in the delta. Both dealt with the role of Chinese intellectuals in Chinese government. In his seventh charge, Gali accused Zhang of having had as a houseguest Fang Bao, who had been found guilty of writing a preface to a work judged seditious by the Kangxi court. Worse, the work in question, *Southern Mountain Collection* (Nanshanji), had been printed in Suzhou, right under Zhang Boxing's official nose. Gali's eighth charge was one that surely resonated with the experience of anyone who has observed a scholar at work. Gali charged that Zhang spent all his time buying and reading old books instead of attending to the responsibilities of his office, particularly the timely review of judicial cases. With these charges, Gali moved from accusations of dereliction of duty to make explicit the broader indictment of Chinese scholar-officials, which was probably behind all of his accusations. Not surprisingly, these charges evoked some of Zhang Boxing's most spirited responses.

On the matter of Fang Bao, however, Zhang Boxing had to be careful. The two men were probably friends, although Gali's charges made it unlikely that either man would formally acknowledge or describe their friendship in writing. They could easily have met when both were serving in Beijing from 1692 to 1695, Zhang as a junior official in the Grand Secretariat and Fang as a senior licentiate. They also shared an allegiance to the philosophy of Zhu Xi and a commitment to a strict construction of his writings. The prosecution of Fang Bao must have been especially troubling to Zhang, not only because it struck within his circle of friends, but also because it seemed to signal the end of an era at the Kangxi court. For the middle years of his reign, the Kangxi emperor had actively encouraged scholarly officials like the governors of Jiangsu, and indeed *History of the Qing* made the claim that such officials could not have survived in the Qing territorial order without the emperor's express personal patronage. By the end of the first decade of the eighteenth century, however, the emperor was aware that Chinese officials were forming factions for the purpose of influencing the choice of a successor. Increasingly frustrated, the Kangxi emperor took decisive action when it was reported to him that an aging Hanlin academician, Dai Mingshi, had published a book that included the reminiscences of one of his kinsmen who had fought with Wu Sangui against the dynasty. Dai was executed, and all of his family members were banished. Fang Bao was particularly singled out because he had written a preface for the volume and was related by marriage to its publisher.[71] In view of all of this, Zhang was probably wise to sidestep Gali's real accusation, that he and Fang Bao were friends, and instead present a detailed description of how he had arrested Fang Bao in Suzhou. He further pointed out that the *Southern Mountain Collection* had likely been published in Suzhou, not because of any relationship between himself and Fang Bao, but because Suzhou was home to the elite publishing industry in the late seventeenth century. He was further unable to resist observing that although Gali had temporary duties as acting governor of Anhui, Fang Bao's native province, at the time Fang was condemned, it was Zhang, not Gali, who had arrested him.

On the matter of buying and reading books, Zhang Boxing could afford to be more vocal. As usual, there was probably something to Gali's charges. There was at least enough substance to them for Zhang Boxing to take especial care to tell the emperor that making just and appropriate decisions in judicial cases took time, especially in Jiangsu, where the organs of territorial government were split between Jiangning and Suzhou. But, at least in Zhang's view, book buying and rendering judicial decisions were separate issues. Elite life in Suzhou had always been a life of letters, and one of the pleasures of a sojourn there was surely the opportunity to buy volumes, both old and new. Zhang's predecessor Song Luo was said to have accumulated a library of more than one hundred thousand volumes during his term as governor, part of which he purchased from the collection of the late Ming printer and bibliophile Mao Jin.[72] Zhang's own book purchases were meant to support the library of the Ao-feng Academy in Fuzhou, which he had founded during his term as governor of Fujian. Zhang had no need to apologize for these purchases. Nor, as he made clear to the emperor, did he need to apologize for the time he had spent reading and annotating during his term as governor of Jiangsu:

> My writing and reading books has its reason. At the end of the metropolitan examinations of 1685, the assembled new *jinshi* [of whom Zhang was one] received an edict from the Kangxi emperor. "When you return home, you should continue to read as you always have. Don't waste your scholarly abilities." In accord with the imperial instructions, from the day I returned home, I closed my door and set about reading. I also worried about not transmitting what was inappropriate. Now the examination curriculum is based on the commentaries of Zhu Xi and the Cheng brothers. But the thought of Zhu Xi accords with that of Confucius, Zissu, Zengzi, and Mencius. Therefore, morning and night, I reviewed these texts until I seemed to make progress. I wrote—but only in moments of leisure. I have recently received an order that the examination questions [for the provincial exam] be drawn from Zhou Dunyi's *Taiji tu shuo*, therefore I have ordered the works of Zhu, Cheng, Zhang, and Zhu printed in order that they could be circulated widely. This has only been in accord with imperial teachings. This has been so that all would know that one cannot fail to read the books of the sages. If one reads these books and embodies their teachings, then one will be a filial son at home and a loyal official at court, and this will further the imperial goal of honoring the Confucian tradition and respecting our traditional Way.[73]

Taken together with the passage that immediately follows it, a reassertion of Zhang's charge of a collusive relationship between Gali and Zhang Yuanlong, this passage put in stark terms the contrast between the political idealism of Chinese tradition and the realpolitik of the Manchus. The court was practically forced to make a choice. The decision was difficult, partly because the conflict was so public and partly because there was substance on both sides. The emperor hesitated for months, pondering the reports of two inconclusive commissions of investigation. Finally, in a rather terse edict, the decision was announced: Both Gali and Zhang Boxing were dismissed from office, but Zhang was allowed to remain at his post. Zhang took this as a victory and returned in triumph to his Suzhou yamen from Beijing, where he had resided during the investigations.[74] Jonathan Spence has emphasized that the Kangxi emperor was acting as a mediator in making this decision, defusing the tensions that were an inevitable element of the multiethnic order over which he presided. The editors of *History of the Qing* emphasized that the emperor's decision was basically pro-Chinese and concluded that governors like Zhang Boxing and his colleagues could not have survived without the active support of the throne.[75]

But the case may be as interesting for what it says about Jiangsu as for what it says about the court. Coming almost exactly half a century after Zhu Guozhi had fled his post, the exchange between Gali and Zhang Boxing illustrates what had been achieved in the delta and the tensions that remained. The exchange highlights, in language that was perhaps larger than life, some of the particular difficulties of Jiangsu government. Officials at all ranks were constantly vulnerable as they balanced the interests of the large landowning families who dominated delta social life against the state's need for revenues. In this province, bayous and byways offered hiding places for pirates and bandits, and in the cities, the whitewashed houses that lined them served as hiding places for dissident intellectuals. It was a province in which trade, particularly waterborne trade, provided many opportunities for fuzzy transactions, some of which posed a threat to the state. In carrying out their duties, governors and governors-general in Jiangsu had to rely on subordinates and colleagues who had their own connections to the capital and sources of legitimacy. Elite libraries and publishing institutions were potentially threats to the state but could also be a source of support for officials, and the elite had a powerful capacity to rally support. Manchu officials had to rely on Chinese officials who preferred to read rather than rule, and Chinese officials had to deal with Manchu colleagues who preferred the company of pirates to that of pedagogues. If there was any substance to these rather heavy-handed characterizations, then the very fact of stability in the delta less than a century after the Qing conquest is indeed remarkable.

In fact, perhaps the most interesting thing about Gali's charges and Zhang's retorts is that they could be made at all. In an earlier, more tentative era of Qing government in the southeast, conflicts of the sort that occurred between the governor and the governor-general in 1711 would surely have been kept quiet in the interests of social and political order. No accounts of the conflicts between Zhu Guozhi and the people of the delta have survived, and the only account of Mingzhu's attempted extortion of Tang Bin appear in posthumous biographies of Tang. The disagreements over Jin Fu's plans for river engineering may have been the first time political conflict in the delta became public. It must have been a mark of Zhang's and Gali's security in their relations with the court and with the delta that they were willing to charge each other so publicly and viciously. The delta had become sufficiently a part of the family of Qing provinces that its officials' dirty official linen could be aired in public. That tensions could be expressed did not mean that they were easily overcome, however. Well into the eighteenth century, the court and the Qing imperium regularly remarked on the unique difficulties of the delta and the tensions there between Manchu and Chinese officials. But at some point, the uniqueness of the delta became a trope of Qing political discourse rather than a new observation; the shocked recognition of discovery became the stuff of cliché.[76]

This could happen because the Qing had succeeded in building a political structure around the needs and tensions of delta life. The outlines of this structure reflected the province's history. Most Qing emperors followed the lead of the Kangxi emperor, who had forgiven the tax protesters in 1661 by acknowledging that delta taxes would often be in arrears. The one exception seems to have been the Yongzheng emperor, who tried to reform the tax system in the delta but gave up in sheer frustration. Most Qing emperors, again with the possible exception of the Yongzheng emperor, also followed the practice of dispatching to Jiangsu governors who were masters of the elite literary traditions of which the local elite fancied itself the custodian. For more than half the Qianlong reign, for instance, Jiangsu was governed by five men who served average terms of six and a half years. Four of them held the *jinshi* degree, and the fifth, a Manchu member of the Imperial Household Department, spent virtually his entire official career in Suzhou. Two of Qianlong's Jiangsu governors, Chen Dashou, who served in 1741–46, and Chen Hongmou, who served in 1758–62, were well known for their published works, and a third, Zhuang Yougong, who served in 1751–56, was adopted into one of the most prominent and intellectually distinguished lineages of the delta.[77]

Even though tax collections in the delta were not always what they were supposed to be, enough revenue flowed to the capital in land taxes and grain tribute to make the region one of the fiscal pillars of the dynasty. Indeed, one might argue that it was as much the rivers of revenue flowing to and from the capital as the flows of water that created the peculiar "river politics" of the delta. Conflicts over the collection and use of state money would remain a relatively constant feature of delta life until the end of the dynasty. They would never again acquire the sharpness or explosive potential they had exhibited in the seventeenth century, however, partly because such conflicts came to be expected. No Jiangsu governor would ever be as vocal about the anomalies of his situation as Zhang Boxing had been, probably in part because none would find it necessary: no later eighteenth-century governor would be accused of reading on the job rather than attending to the duties of empire. Delta politics would be subsumed in the larger politics of empire.

THE SOUTHEASTERN COAST

When the leaders of Qing forces reached the southeastern coast in 1645, they confronted a land that bore a strange resemblance to the place they had left. The dominant characteristic of the southeastern coast was its variegated human landscape. Not only was the Chinese population divided into separate communities by geography, dialect, and social forms; there were also trading communities with ties, sometimes even blood ties, to lands beyond the waters. Catholic communities had links to Macao, the Philippines, and beyond; Dutch Protestant traders called, as they sailed north from their base at Batavia; and well-entrenched pirate groups often had bases in Japan. The southeastern coast was a land with many political and ethnic centers, somewhat like the northeast, where the Manchus had risen to power, and in many respects the strategic pragmatism that marked their rise to power served them well along the coast. But if the Qing were used to transfrontiers, they were totally unaccustomed to the sea frontiers they encountered in the southeast. Lacking naval expertise and naval forces, they were unable to pursue coastal challengers back into their own strongholds. For this reason, the peoples along the coasts often presented themselves as strangers, as John Wills has argued, "non-mediated aliens," unlike people the Qing encountered over a land frontier, where foreigners "formed part of a complex, mediated interaction of cultures and migrating peoples."[78]

During the first decades of the Qing dynasty, government on the southeastern coast passed through the same stages of confrontation, negotiation, and accommodation that it had undergone in Jiangnan, but because of the greater military challenge on the coast, the stages had different markers. The period of confrontation lasted far longer on the coast than it had in the lower Yangzi, both because coastal forces of resistance were stronger and because the Manchus were less sure of their footing. In the early years, regimes along the coast were remarkable hybrids of coastal and central personnel, driven by complex and sometimes crosscutting imperatives. Accommodation with local interests on the coast resulted in the establishment of two very different regimes, as it did in the delta. Fashioning governments along the coast did not require a new province, as it had in Jiangnan, but it did result in the creation of two very different regimes with very little in the way of structure, personnel, or purpose in common. Negotiating with the paramilitary forces along the coast and dealing with an unreconciled elite in Zhejiang were somewhat more complicated than negotiating with Jiangnan elites, who depended on state investments for their hydraulic infrastructure. Although the two political orders along the coast proved to be serviceable, in the long run they seemed less successful at accommodating local interests than were parallel provincial orders in Jiangnan, with the result that social conflicts in the two provinces were more evident throughout the eighteenth and nineteenth centuries.

Confrontation

In the early years, the Manchus had to rely on local, coastal intermediaries, giving rise to a regime that was fascinating in its possibilities but open to conflicts over loyalties and legitimacy.[79] There were several reasons for the different reaction to resistance in the southeast. Whereas military resistance to the Qing in Jiangnan was poignant but ineffectual, on the southeastern coast, it was real and initially insurmountable. Moreover, in the southeast, unlike in the delta, the north Chinese who largely collaborated with the Qing in the early days were often as ill-equipped to deal with local Chinese as were the Manchus themselves. For both of these reasons, it took the Qing nearly a generation longer to reach peace with local interests on the southeastern coast than it had in the lower Yangzi; local conflict dominated the lower Yangzi region only until the late 1660s, but the coast did not see a return to order until the late 1680s.

Early Qing coastal policy was at times hesitant and impossibly heavy-handed, and in its very vacillations, it alienated those who were most necessary for its success. Before civilian government could be established, three sets of enemies had to be defeated, and Qing policies themselves arguably created a fourth. The first enemy was composed of two members of the Ming royal family, Zhu Yihai, known as the Longwu emperor, and Zhu Youjian, known as the regent Lu. The Longwu emperor was captured and executed by Qing forces in 1646, but the regent Lu survived, protected by coastal communities and mercenary military forces, until 1662.[80] A second source of opposition came from within the Qing ranks, from the descendants of Geng Jimao, a Chinese bannerman who was instrumental in the conquest of south China and, as a reward, was granted hereditary titles and broad authority along the coast. Jimao was loyal to the Manchus for all his life, but the Qing's reluctance to extend his privileges to his son Geng Jingzhong was one of the precipitating factors in Wu Sangui's rebellion. Geng Jingzhong participated in that rebellion, massing forces to fight the Qing in northern Zhejiang from 1672 to 1674.[81] The Zheng family, a network of traders-cum-pirates with ties to Japan, Taiwan, and the Philippines who were accustomed to having fairly free rein along the coast, made up the third set of opponents. A fourth source of resistance developed in response to a policy proposed by one of the Zheng's naval commanders who surrendered to the Qing, which required removing the coastal population at least five li away from the sea and interdicting coastal trading. The beginning of this policy is customarily dated to 1655, but as Xie Guozhen has pointed out, it was enforced inconsistently, as need and conviction arose.[82] Although these threats had different origins, they were related. The Zhengs supported, significantly if fitfully, the Longwu emperor and the regent Lu and joined forces briefly with Geng Jingzhong. All the military forces in the region drew on the same pool of resources and alienated the southern people.

The network of posts in Zhejiang and Fujian took some years to evolve to meet these needs. The first Qing official posted on the coast was a governor-general put in place in late 1645. This official was meant to have control over the entire coast and reside at Fuzhou, and his first task was to dislodge the Longwu emperor from that city. Once this task was accomplished, the seat of the governor-general was moved to Quzhou in southern Zhejiang, a more central location. As the perils of the region became more apparent, a second governor-general was appointed in 1658 to serve in Zhejiang. A governor of Zhejiang was appointed to serve under the coastal viceroys in late 1646, and a governor for Fujian was appointed in late 1647.[83] As in the early years of Qing government throughout south China, bannermen often served as governor and governor-general, and appointees commonly moved from one post to the other.[84] The backgrounds of early officials on the southeastern coast were remarkable in at least three respects. First, most seventeenth-century governors in the southeast had close ties, in many cases, family ties, with those responsible for the pragmatic and flexible statesmanship that had marked the Manchus' rise to power. Second, they were willing to make strategic alliances as necessary in order to preserve dynastic interests. Finally, although coastal officials often came as strangers, they usually remained on the coast long enough to acquire some genuine familiarity with the problems of coastal management. The cases of Tong Guoqi (governor of Fujian, 1653–55, and of Zhejiang, 1658–60), Fan Chengmo (governor of Zhejiang, 1668–71, and governor-general of Fujian, 1671–72), and Wu Xingzuo (governor of Fujian, 1678–81) illustrate these contentions.

Residents of the coast could hardly have known what to expect as forces from the north arrived. But perhaps no amount of experience with the Qing propensity for timely strategic alliance could have prepared coastal residents for the governor they welcomed in the late 1650s, Tong Guoqi, a Zhejiang native with the highest connections with the dynasty. Guoqi was a member of the Tong clan, a large, powerful family whose ancestral seat was in Manchuria. Many of the Tongs had come over to the Qing side at an early moment of Manchu victory, when Nurhaci conquered their native town of Fushun in 1621. In the middle of the seventeenth century, Tongs enrolled in the Chinese Plain Blue Banner and fought for the Qing in north China, the lower Yangzi valley, and Hunan. But their connection went beyond military service. A daughter of General Tong Tulai (d. 1658), the most prominent member of the family in the seventeenth century, was given as a concubine to the Shunzhi emperor and became the mother of the Kangxi emperor. Another Tong daughter became a concubine of the Kangxi emperor. The importance of the family was captured, as Pamela Crossley has written, by the expression "Tong ban chiao." This meant both "the Tong who fill up half the court," referring to the number of offices the family held, and "the Tong who are half the court," referring to the blood connections between the family and the Qing monarchy.[85] One could as easily have asserted that the court held up half the Tongs, in a very literal sense, for the politically active members of the Tong family in the seventeenth century all took the character *guo*, meaning "state," as the first element of their given names.[86]

Despite the consistency of their given names, the Tongs were capable of a variety of commitments. Tong Guoqi was from a branch of the family that had settled in Zhejiang and played little role in the Manchus' preconquest history. He was enrolled in the Chinese Plain Blue Banner when the armies of his kinsman, Tong Tulai, passed through Zhejiang in 1645. Once enrolled, he found himself appointed first circuit intendant and then provincial judge in Zhejiang; in 1651, he was transferred to Fujian, where he served as finance commissioner and then governor (1653–55). He next served two years in the Nan-gan governorship in southern Jiangxi (1655–57), where several of his relatives served before and after him, and then was transferred back to Zhejiang, where he was governor from 1658 to 1660. Many of these appointments violated the rules of avoidance, which forbade an official to serve in his home jurisdiction, but there were more important priorities in Zhejiang in the mid-seventeenth century. For the Qing, Tong must have seemed a useful bridge to the coastal elite, a man well connected locally whose loyalties could be readily guaranteed by family members. He was well remembered by the Zhejiang elite, who, it was said, conducted observances in his memory at the official temple for sixty years after his death.[87] Tong also had ties to the Catholic community on the coast. While this group was certainly not the predominant element in coastal society, Catholics were one of several groups— among them foreign merchants, Muslim traders, and others—that made up the human mosaic along the coast. Tong wrote three prefaces to works of Catholic theology, and his wife is known to mission history as Madame Agathe through the writings of Philippe Couplet. During his terms as governor of Fujian and Zhejiang, he supervised the building of cathedrals in Fuzhou and Hangzhou.[88] He was perhaps the only cathedral-building governor in Chinese history. But Tong Guoqi lived during a protean period along the coast, when there were many political possibilities. One possibility, however, Tong Guoqi actively sought to foreclose, and that was the power of the Zheng regime; in his communications with the court, he offered strategies to defeat the Zhengs and descriptions of the problems they posed.[89]

The longer Qing government lasted in Beijing, the more the political situation hardened, and although the character and preoccupation of coastal governors remained the same, their relation to other forces along the coast changed. In the late 1660s and early 1670s, the issue along the coast was loyalties. This was already beginning to be apparent at the end of Tong Guoqi's term, when he was cashiered for having protected from exile the aged mother of a Zhejiang rebel. He was shortly thereafter replaced with a protégé of one of the Oboi regents, who were determined to reassert Manchu control over the Qing government.[90]

Conflicts over loyalties became much more serious during the term of Fan Chengmo, who was subsequently celebrated as a paragon of loyalty to the Qing. All Chinese bannermen were collaborators, but few had the unmistakably collaborationist credentials of the descendants of Fan Wencheng. Although the Fan family was descended from the Song statesman Fan Zhongyan, a branch of the clan had migrated to Manchuria by the early seventeenth century. Fan Wencheng surrendered early to the Manchus and became one of their most important early advisers on things Chinese. He even drafted the document in which the regent Dorgon announced the new regime's intent to assume the throne in Beijing.[91] Wencheng's second son Fan Chengmo took his *jinshi* degree in 1652, served for sixteen years at the Qing court, and was appointed to govern Zhejiang in 1667. When he arrived in Hangzhou, he found a province so devastated by warfare and drought that it was necessary to forgive the land taxes on some 315,000 *mou* of land in the six richest districts.[92] Also pressing was the issue of refugees and the dispossessed, whom Fan likened to the fearsome turtles of Chinese fable that hid in the murky depths and spat poisonous sand at passing travelers. Many of these refugees survived only by forming illicit and temporary relationships with Qing military forces; they "sold themselves in the morning, and fled in the evening." The only solution Fan could propose was to require those who sought to join banner forces to secure the written guarantee of the official of their district before enlisting.[93]

In 1667, he expressed a desire to resign the governorship for reasons of health but was prevailed upon by the local elite and the emperor to remain in office one more year. After this year, he was promoted to the governor-generalship of Fujian and tried four times to be relieved of this new obligation.[94] When he arrived in Fujian, he found conditions there no better than in Zhejiang and memorialized the emperor about the consequences of the policy of removing people from the coast:

> The livelihood of the people of Fukian depends on either farming or fishing. After the prohibition on travel near the coast, more than 2 million *mou* of land have been left uncultivated, causing a loss of revenue of more than 200,000 *liang*. The tax arrears grow every day, and the revenues of coastal provinces are

inadequate for the government's needs. Cottages and cultivated farms have become salt lands unfit for crops. The old and the weak struggle in ditches and in holes, and those who have wandered in all directions are innumerable. The few old and weak remaining are without work or means of subsistence, and the suffering is extreme. Recently the people's minds are especially troubled. The price of rice is rising daily. Unless they are taken care of, they will be oppressed by hunger and cold and forced into banditry.[95]

The consequences of Qing policies on the coast were rendering the region ungovernable, even for an official as committed as Fan.

As Fujian governor-general, Fan Chengmo also confronted the rebellion of Geng Jingzhong. From one point of view, Geng Jingzhong and Fan Chengmo had similar backgrounds. Their fathers had both surrendered to the Qing; Fan Wencheng had told the new rulers which battles to fight, and Geng Jimao had fought them in north, central, and south China before being handed his coastal sinecure. Similarities in their background probably led Geng Jingzhong to hope that Fan Chengmo could be persuaded to join his rebellion against the Qing. Fan Chengmo consistently refused, at one point remarking that he would rather "die with loyalists than live with rebels." Such language of Confucian loyalism was odd indeed in a squabble between collaborators.[96] But on the surface at least, the conflict between these two officials appeared to be one of loyalty to a new, sinicizing Qing dynasty, which the Fans had helped shape, and loyalty to an older regime of military occupation and collaboration. Tellingly, the conflict between these two dimensions of the Manchus' preconquest heritage was played out in the rather protean political arena of the southeastern coast, where the early Qing atmosphere of strategic calculation and opportunism prevailed longer than it did elsewhere.

Fan Chengmo did not survive the rebellion. Early on, Geng Jingzhong captured and imprisoned Fan Chengmo. Then, in a scramble to find a niche in a world of congealing loyalties, Geng first tried to convince Fan to surrender and next tried to cut a deal with the Qing. Failing in both endeavors, Geng ordered Fan to commit suicide, which he did. Only a few months later, Qing forces led by Giyesu, a grandson of the dynastic founder Nurhaci, arrived and defeated Geng Jingzhong and took him prisoner. Once again, a dance of loyalties ensued in which Geng was first offered clemency, while the dynasty tried to ascertain how deeply his rebellion had influenced local loyalties, and then sentenced to death by slicing. When this last grisly task was accomplished, a small piece of his flesh was given to Fan Chengmo's son. In a macabre marriage of ritual filiality and political vengeance, Fan's son used the piece of flesh to conduct ancestral sacrifices at his father's grave.

This was, however, only the first of the long series of political and editorial interventions designed to secure Fan Chengmo a place in the Qing pantheon. Shortly after his death, Fan was canonized as "loyal and conscientious," and early eulogies focused on the circumstances of his martyrdom. Peng Peng, a young Fujian native who hid out for two years in order to avoid responding to a summons from Geng Jingzhong, wrote a long biography of Fan, detailing the circumstances of his resistance to Geng and martyrdom. Peng wrote that he first read the poems written from the "dark valley," the name Fan and his followers gave to his prison cell, with tears in his eyes.[97] Shortly thereafter, Fan Shizong, the son who conducted the filial sacrifices described above, presented all of Fan's poems to the emperor, who favored them with two prefaces.

Both Peng Peng and Fan Shizong rose to be coastal officials themselves; Peng Peng governed Guangdong from 1699 to 1704, and Fan Shizong governed the same provinces from 1706 to 1709. This fact, together with the annual sacrifices instituted by Fujian governor Bian Yongyu, assured that Fan's name would be remembered along the coast. Nearly a century after Fan's death, a second group of writings on Fan appeared, beginning with the review of his collected works published in the *Annotated Catalog of the "Complete Library of the Four Treasuries,"* which was followed by biographies by Dai Zhen and Qian Iji. These works, appearing at a time when the Kangxi emperor had become the sagely ancestor, and his reign became better known for establishing the foundations of Qing peace than for pursuing Manchu wars, emphasized Fan Chengmo's concern for popular welfare and tax reduction.[98] In the late nineteenth century, at a time when the Qing had few admirers and fewer heroes, a Hunan intellectual, Long Xiqing, sponsored the commercial publication of the collected works as a model for his times.[99]

It fell to Fan's successors, particularly Wu Xingzuo, to develop the military forces and political institutions that would make such firm control possible. Like Tong Guoqi, Wu Xingzuo counted Zhejiang as his native place, but his father had contributed to the Manchu cause by serving as the Chinese secretary to Prince Daisan, the eldest son of the dynastic founder Nurhaci. On the strength of his father's service, Xiangzuo entered the Qing regime as a local magistrate in 1650. His early service to the Qing was fairly rocky. He was faulted for failing to anticipate an uprising in Jiangxi and then for failing to put down a White Lotus uprising in Shandong. He distinguished himself, however, as magistrate of Wuxi, where he served from 1662 to 1673, and on the recommendation of the governor-general for grain transport, he was promoted to the post of provincial judge in Fujian. In this capacity, he saw service in the last months of Geng Jingzhong's rebellion and was promoted in 1678 to the governorship of Fujian.[100]

After Geng's forces were dispatched, the main threat to Fujian came from the naval forces of the Zheng family, who held Amoy and Xiamen at the time Wu became governor. Influenced perhaps by the memory of his own unsuccessful experience with anti-Qing uprisings in Jiangxi and Shandong, Wu was determined to have the military forces necessary to resist the Zhengs. After a particularly bloody series of battles along the coast, Wu memorialized the throne in 1677 requesting that a contingent of twelve hundred sailors be assigned to the coast and announcing that he had begun to build a fleet of sixty-seven warships. Perhaps more important, during Wu's term as governor of Fujian, the Qing made the post of naval commander at Fuzhou a permanent one. In Fujian, there had been a commandant of land forces since 1647, and when Shi Lang commanded his first naval attack on Taiwan from 1662 to 1668, he had been given the title "naval commandant" (*shui-shi ti-du*). The position was allowed to lapse with the end of his appointment but was revived in 1677. In 1678, Wan Zhengse, a Fujian native who had risen through the Qing military ranks during service in the northwest and southwest, was appointed to the post.[101] As Wan and Wu Xingzuo noted in a joint memorial, the position and the forces attached to it freed the Qing from dependence on the warships and whims of the Dutch in attacking Taiwan and the Zheng forces there.[102] Wu Xingzuo was also instrumental in introducing the military entrepreneur Yao Qisheng to the Qing; in 1687, Yao was appointed governor-general of Fujian, a position he held until the end of the war.[103] Arguably, it was the institution building accomplished by Wan and Wu that enabled Shi Lang to accomplish his final victory over the Zheng forces in 1683.

Probably Wu's most famous contribution to the coastal order came after he had been promoted from the governorship of Fujian to the governor-generalship of Guangdong and involved the policy of coastal depopulation. Many officials along the coast, especially those who remained in their posts for any length of time, opposed this policy. Fan Chengmo's sad description of the plight of Fujian peasants, quoted above, was the prelude to a plea for more military forces and the flexibility to use them.

> If soldiers are stationed at the strategic points, then the rebels will find no crevice to creep through. The purpose of a navy is to protect the maritime frontier: nobody leaves his door open and guards only the inner chambers. In these days of trouble, the sea rebels are looking for opportunities. I pray Your Majesty to permit me to take measures appropriate for the circumstances. Those prohibitions that are appropriate will be maintained, and those that should be changed will be changed.[104]

The governors of Guangdong and Shandong evidently protested the policy as well, although the texts of their protests have been lost. But policy change had to wait, as Fan Chengmo's memorial implied, until a preponderance of military force had been established on the coast. Once this happened, in part because of Wu Xingzuo's actions, it fell to Wu to submit the memorial that finally provoked a change in the disastrous coastal policy. The court received Wu's memorial in late autumn of 1683, and the emperor dispatched a commission to investigate the situation along the coast. When this commission returned, the emperor swiftly ordered a change in policy, anxious that southern peasants could return to their lands before the 1684 growing season began. Coastal governors were ordered to devise a resettlement scheme. In Guangdong, more than thirty-one thousand people were resettled, and in Fujian, forty thousand were repatriated; in Zhejiang, 9,000 *mou* of farmland and 74,000 *mou* of salt land were returned to those who had occupied them.[105]

Despite the Kangxi emperor's concern about the growing season, the real advantage of repopulating the coast was that trading could resume, and the natural economy of the region reasserted itself. Even the Kangxi emperor recognized this and expressed the hope that revenues from commercial taxes would eventually support the political and military establishment along the coast. This may not have happened immediately for, at least in Guangdong, Wu Xingzuo memorialized requesting a remission of commercial and salt taxes so as to foster economic recovery. But in the long run, commercial revenues transformed the region and its politics. Wu Xingzuo and probably other coastal governors were behind this recovery in both a personal and an institutional sense. In his official capacity, Wu encouraged merchants and sponsored the compilation of a collection of coastal maps that facilitated navigation. Dutch sources from the 1680s show Wu acting in a private capacity, "overseeing an abortive attempt to form a general association of merchants and high officials, a sort of anticipation of the co-hong; standing behind the activities of client merchants; and even sending merchant-envoys to Batavia to discuss a contract for Dutch delivery at a fixed price of Japanese copper for the Canton mint."[106] In fact, it was an attraction to peacetime profits that ended Wu's career as a coastal warrior. In 1689, he was accused of personally profiting from the minting of copper coinage (perhaps the very copper he had bought from the Dutch), reduced in rank from governor-general to assistant brigade commander, and assigned to a posting on the Mongolian border.[107]

The end of Wu Xingzuo's term in Canton marked the beginning of a new era in the southeast, a time when rising commercial prosperity did much to salve the wounds of remaining Ming loyalists. But the early years of Qing rule left their legacy in the region. Even as the coastal provinces were incorporated into the empire, they remained a world of many centers, and tales of violence and legends of heroism lingered. The Tongs continued to thrive until at least the middle of the eighteenth century and were even allowed to change their registration from the Chinese to the Manchu banner system. One of their number, using the Manchu name Longkodo, held the post of commander of the Beijing garrison at the time of the Kangxi emperor's death and may well have played a crucial role in the disputed succession. Peng Peng, Fan Chengmo's biographer, led a rather charmed bureaucratic life following the Geng Jingzhong rebellion, protected by the Kangxi court from attacks on his idiosyncratic administrative style. Fan Chengmo's legend may have been the most useful for the Qing, since his martyrdom in the Qing cause provided such a nice counterpoint to the many stories of martyrdom for the Ming cause.

Beyond legend, however, the main legacy of the early Qing years in the southeast was the heavy concentration of military forces stationed there permanently. Like generals everywhere who prepare to fight the previous war rather than the next, the Qing remained on guard throughout its history against the dangers of seaborne treachery and Ming revivalism. Zhejiang had one of the largest contingent of regular, or Green Standard Army, forces in the empire as well as the Manchu garrison at Hangzhou. Fujian remained until the end of the dynasty the only province in China with two military intendants, one for naval and one for land forces, both of whom outranked the provincial governor. Fujian and Zhejiang dealt with this continuing military legacy in different ways.

Accommodation

In the lower Yangzi valley, the Qing had found it necessary to establish two provincial regimes in order to accommodate the various regional interests that sought a voice in administration. There were already two provinces along the southeastern coast, where the process of accommodation involved a differentiation of the two regimes. The provinces of Zhejiang and Fujian had been pulled in many directions in Chinese history. At times, China's long, exposed coastline and the maritime world beyond formed a realm unto itself, shaped by its own waterborne dynamics and governed by the same means and often the same men. At other moments, when opportunities and dangers from the sea were not so pressing, Fujian and Zhejiang were drawn in different directions. Zhejiang was pulled toward the lower Yangzi delta with which it had natural economic and social ties, and Fujian came to have more in common with other border provinces of the empire in which military administration played a comparably important role. Dynasties before the Qing had devised various ways of coping with the complex conundrum of the coast. Faced with a vigorous littoral, the Yuan created a single, gigantic province stretching from the southern bank of the Yangzi to the borders of Fujian and Guangdong. Time ate away at this province: later in the Yuan, Fujian was set aside as a separate province, and during the Ming, the northernmost prefectures of Zhejiang became part of the province of Nan Zhili.[108]

The Qing similarly wavered over whether there should be one governor-general or two along the coast, and where the seat of military power should reside. Once the decision was made in 1684 to seat the coastal governor-general at Fuzhou, separate institutions were created in Fujian and Zhejiang, separate and ultimately very different officials were sent to govern, and the two provinces acquired rather different personalities within the empire. In Fujian, the end of the seventeenth-century wars led to the creation of a military establishment meant to prevent future wars. In Zhejiang, peace meant the revival of a powerful and wealthy local elite that had ties to both the lower Yangzi valley and Beijing, and the province became a crucial test case of the dynasty's ability to govern. As the political culture of the two provinces grew apart, so did their governors. Where a common cadre of officials had held provincial posts along the coast in the seventeenth century, in the eighteenth century, the governors of the two provinces came from different strata of Qing officialdom. Between 1710 and 1820, no governor was transferred from Zhejiang to Fujian, and no one moved from Fujian to Zhejiang between 1724 and 1834.

In the first years of the antebellum period, there may not have been much difference between the two provinces. Peace has its own imperatives, and in China, these included the reassertion of paradigms of government described in classical texts and derived from Chinese history. Two early "civilian" governors of Zhejiang and Fujian—Zhao Shilin, who governed Zhejiang from 1684 to 1686, and Zhang Boxing, who governed Fujian from 1707 to 1709—highlight some common elements of late seventeenth-century coastal politics. Both were Chinese *jinshi*-degree holders appointed directly from the capital, both moved from their coastal posts to Jiangsu, both had their works reprinted in *Complete Library of the Four Treasuries*, and both were remembered fondly on the coast. Each addressed the tasks of reconstruction, as circumstances and vision permitted. Zhao Shilin was best known in Zhejiang history for clearing the debts local Chinese owed to the banner troops by refunding loaned sums out of his own purse.[109] The beneficiaries of this action were perhaps the very Zhejiang residents whom Fan Chengmo described as "selling themselves in the morning and fleeing in the evening." For his part, Zhang Boxing emphasized the strand of local history in Fujian that most clearly tied the province to the territorial empire in the north, the legacy of Zhu Xi. As governor of Fujian, he devoted time and resources to building an academy at Fuzhou in order to honor the Song sage; apparently, he also devoted himself to this project when he was governor of Jiangsu, where he spent time buying books for the academy library. This emphasis on orthodoxy had its price, at least for some communities in Fujian, for Zhang also converted the cathedral there, probably the one Tong Guoqi had patronized, into a home for widows and orphans.[110] Although it may have been significant that Zhang served in Fujian nearly two decades after Zhao did, it would be hard to differentiate too clearly between their governorships; both were servants of a maturing peacetime state.

A series of changes in formal institutions and informal practices in the early eighteenth century focused Fujian governors' attention more exclusively on the coast. Shortly after the defeat of the Zheng family in 1684, the Qing court consolidated the two coastal governor-generalships at Fuzhou and Hangzhou into one and decided that, since the resulting governor-general would be primarily responsible for coastal defense, he should be located at Fuzhou.[111] In the 1720s, regulations were issued that gave the Fujian governor new authority as well as new responsibility for local government in seaside jurisdictions. An edict issued in 1724 provided that governors should select the magistrates of coastal counties in their provinces. Governors were to select from among the magistrates of their provinces' inland counties who had compiled records of exemplary service for three years or more.[112] This meant that coastal magistrates would always be very experienced, but it also meant, given the principle that recommenders were responsible for the official conduct of those they recommended, that governors of coastal provinces had a double responsibility for what occurred in counties adjoining the ocean.

These regulations affected all the easternmost provinces of China, but in the case of Fujian, there was the additional matter of Taiwan. Local officials in Taiwan were to be selected by the Fujian governor using the same criteria as those for coastal magistrates, but they were also subject to rules governing officials who served on distant and dangerous borders. This meant that they were not to serve longer than three years, and they were automatically eligible for promotion upon their return. Originally, the three-year terms of officials in Taiwan seem to have expired simultaneously. The Yongzheng emperor had ordered that replacement officials should depart from Fuzhou every three years at the beginning of the northwestern monsoon, in late autumn, and serve as understudies to Taiwan officials until the beginning of the southeastern monsoon in spring, when the returning officials would leave. The simultaneous departure of all experienced Taiwan officials seemed to the Qianlong emperor to create too much possibility for local disturbance, and he ordered that appointments to Taiwan be staggered so that not all positions would turn over at once.[113] Many of these special regulations for Fujian local government dated from the Yongzheng reign and perhaps reflected that emperor's particular fears and cautions. But the special rules for local government of the Fujian coast, unlike a number of the Yongzheng administrative innovations, were not rescinded by the Yongzheng emperor's successors. They remained on the books through the eighteenth century and gave Fujian government a somewhat insular quality. Not only was the attention of Fuzhou concentrated disproportionately on the sea and Taiwan, but the province of Fujian itself became an island in the mainland Chinese south, whose officials were absorbed in their particular tasks.

Zhejiang followed an entirely different trajectory. As Fujian officials became more insular, Zhejiang governors became more and more a part of the national discourse, in both military and civilian matters. Both provinces were heavily garrisoned as a consequence of their early history and strategic importance, but the military apparatus of the two provinces faced in different directions. In 1659, the Shunzhi emperor ordered a detachment of Manchu troops stationed near Baodingfu to move permanently to Hangzhou. During the coastal wars, some of these troops were temporarily moved to the Fuzhou area, but in 1683, they were ordered back to Hangzhou, where they formed the southernmost garrison of the Qing empire that was entirely populated by troops who were ethnically Manchu. The official quota of about four thousand Manchu soldiers in Hangzhou represented about 40 percent of the Qing banner forces stationed in the lower Yangzi valley. Another sixteen hundred Manchu troops were stationed in a naval garrison at Zhapu.[114] The Manchu troops in Hangzhou were backed by a force of about forty-three thousand Green Standard Army troops, which, in the eighteenth century, was the third-largest provincial force in the empire, behind Fujian, with sixty-three thousand, and Guangdong, with sixty-eight thousand.[115] This garrison was different from the one in Fuzhou, however, in that it was stationed, not to guard a coast, but to represent the Qing in a province that had significant ties and obligations to the central court. As Pamela Crossley notes, in the eighteenth century, the Hangzhou garrison took on a genteel quality, with its commanders often men being rewarded for their distinguished careers with postings at a "center of literary accomplishments in a scenic and wealthy region."[116]

Zhejiang's wealth distinguished it from other provinces in which the military played a comparable role. Zhejiang's land tax quota of 2,920,629 *liang* per year, with 2,100,000 to be remitted to the capital, was the third-largest in the empire. To this were added the yearly grain tribute shipments and the revenues of the Zhejiang salt monopoly, making the province's contributions to the state's coffers very considerable. Other provinces perhaps contributed as much, but no other province combined such heavy revenue contributions with such a large military garrison. Like most empires, the Qing state survived by collecting revenues from agrarian core areas and expending them, in part at least, on frontier defense, and therefore the responsibilities of defense and revenue collection fell on different officials, perhaps even on different sorts of officials. But in Zhejiang, they fell on a single governor, whose superior was down the coast at Fuzhou. Largely by himself, the Zhejiang governor had to balance the demands of garrison commanders and military intendants, civil officials and tax collectors.

In order to deal with this group and the many issues of Zhejiang, the court appointed some of its most trusted and experienced officials. Between 1700 and 1900, Zhejiang ranked just behind Shandong in the number of governors who were appointed directly by the emperor. Most of those chosen were men of experience, often in military matters, who could manage the multiple tasks assigned the Zhejiang executive. While cashiering was not as common among governors in Zhejiang as it was in Shandong, the province was nonetheless the scene of some spectacular prosecutions, particularly in the eighteenth century. Two of the six officials discussed in *History of the Qing*, in the chapter on Qianlong governors who were executed, were Zhejiang governors, and at least two other Zhejiang governors left office under corruption-related clouds. Among governors who were executed are the longest-serving governor of Zhejiang, Chang'an, who was appointed in 1741 and relieved of responsibility in 1747, and Fusong, who was appointed in 1782 in order to restore probity to the Zhejiang governor's office and executed in 1786.[117] Lu Zhuo, dismissed in 1741, and Wang Danwang, dismissed and executed in 1780, were also cashiered for corruption. Except for Wang Danwang, who was executed for his role in the Gansu grain contribution scandal, the problem in Zhejiang most often was that accused officials used their access to the enormous revenues that passed through Hangzhou, including salt revenues, grain tribute, and funds for rebuilding sea walls, to enrich themselves.

One official who managed the many tasks of the Zhejiang governorship without being accused of corruption was Li Wei, one of the Yongzheng emperor's most trusted governors. At the time of the Yongzheng emperor's ascension to the throne, Li held an appointment as circuit intendant for salt and post in Zhili; the Yongzheng emperor transferred him to Yunnan and then promoted him rapidly from circuit intendant to finance commissioner and finally made him governor of Zhejiang. During the latter years of Li's appointment in Zhejiang, his rank was raised to governor-general; this was a new position in the Qing territorial service, which existed during Li Wei's tenure and shortly after but was abolished by the Qianlong emperor. Like many of the Yongzheng emperor's favored officials, Li Wei was quite young, only thirty-eight *sui* at the time the emperor ascended the throne and forty-one *sui* when he was appointed governor. During the course of his rise through the territorial service, the Yongzheng emperor several times bailed Li Wei out of scrapes Li had gotten into because of his youth and activism. Clearly, the emperor admired Li's capacity for hard work and trusted him to reform administration of the salt monopoly and keep the military in order.[118]

During his stay in Hangzhou, which proved to be one of the longest governorships in the province's history, Li Wei addressed many of its characteristic issues.[119] Five months after his appointment, he submitted his first memorial on what would prove to be an enduring concern, the seawalls that protected the low-lying coastal communities around Hangzhou bay from flooding. As in

Jiangsu, central government investment in local infrastructure paved the way for the recovery of trade and elite loyalties. As was the case in Jiangsu, infrastructure protected the interests of state and elite, ensuring the value of elite landholdings and making possible the reclamation of land and the production of salt. Salt production proved to be another of Li's concerns. Unlike the Liang-huai salt district in Anhui, which was managed by an imperial commissioner, the Liangzhe salt district fell within the purview of the Zhejiang governor. Zhejiang salt was distributed throughout the province and in the lower Yangzi delta as far as Suzhou, and, unfortunately, Zhejiang salt cost significantly more than illegal, privately distributed salt. The Zhejiang governor could prevent the circulation of illegal salt in his own province but had few resources to patrol in Jiangsu, and Jiangsu authorities, like the Nanjing garrison commandant, had little incentive to support their neighbor. Eventually, Li Wei proposed creating a detachment of salt troops in Jiangsu who could secure the salt monopoly. The Yongzheng emperor recognized Li Wei's authority over part of Jiangsu, and the perceived inability of Jiangsu officials, by asking Li to rule on Jiangsu law cases in order to clear the legal backlog in that province.[120]

As Fujian governors focused more exclusively on the sea, the Zhejiang governor's authority grew, and the post became one of major importance on the land of the southeast. In part, this reflected the dynasty's attempt to fashion a political order in the southeast that would suit the needs of local elites. As important was the maturing system of empire that assigned different roles to different regions, and different tasks to their leaders.

Negotiation in Zhejiang

The test of structures of accommodation in the Qing order was the extent to which they preserved order and allowed local interests to flourish. The spectacular prosperity and political influence of the lower Yangzi provinces of Jiangsu and Anhui were testimony to the success of Qing policies of incorporation in the delta. In the southeastern coastal provinces, the evidence was not nearly as clear. Political life in mid-Qing Fujian was punctuated by episodes of low-level violence; the Qing seemed unable to build a framework to contain them, and in many respects, Qing power in the region took on an almost colonial form. In Zhejiang, elite grumbles about the character of Qing rule went on far longer than in Jiangnan.

In the Ming dynasty, the Zhejiang elite constituted a powerful, well-established group whose association with Hangzhou intellectual life gave its members a sense of identity. They suffered in the early Qing, not only from wounds of resistance, but also from weather and thirty years of warfare, from 1645 to 1675. The Zhejiang gentry's slow recovery from this period was reflected in rates of success on state examinations. Overall, Ho Ping-ti's figures on the native provinces of jinshi-degree holders show that Zhejiang produced the second-largest number of degree holders in the empire, behind Jiangsu.[121] This figure conceals a significant temporal variation, however. In the first decades of the dynasty, Zhejiang lagged considerably behind Jiangsu, but by the eighteenth century, Zhejiang was producing more degree holders than its northern neighbor. As the Zhejiang elite recovered from the wars, it became a force to be reckoned with. The wealth of the region gave the elite a unique status with regard to the state. As Timothy Brook has argued, the Zhejiang elite was aristogenic, that is, although its members did not have the guaranteed status of true aristocrats, they had the wealth and symbolic capital to maintain their social status for generations without the marks of prestige the central state could confer.[122] In a sense, the Qing state needed the elite for legitimacy as much as the elite needed the Qing. But members of the Zhejiang elite proved much harder to cultivate than their Jiangsu contemporaries. There was in Zhejiang no single moment of submission and renegotiation, as there had been in Jiangsu at the end of the tax resistance case in 1661. Rather, by the time peace was restored and elite fortunes in Zhejiang had recovered, the empire was a done deal, and the Zhejiang elite became part of it, ambivalence and all.

The ambivalence of the Zhejiang elite lay behind one of the Yongzheng emperor's boldest experiments in provincial administration, the creation of the post of commissioner for the observation and rectification of local customs. This was the only new post created in the Qing territorial service after the middle of the seventeenth century. Like the institutional innovations of the seventeenth century, the creation of this post was initially an ad hoc response to particular local conditions. Unlike the seventeenth century innovations, however, the new post did not become permanent. The creation of the post thus reveals something of the early eighteenth-century attitude toward the territorial service, but it perhaps says more about the nature of Zhejiang in the first half of the eighteenth century and the talents that those who governed it were perceived to require. In Zhejiang in the eighteenth century, much rested on the experience and capacities of Wang Guodong.

Wang was a figure of rather unusual accomplishment in the early eighteenth century. A bannerman by birth, he had taken the jinshi examinations and passed high enough to be admitted to the Hanlin Academy, where he rose through the bureaucracy and was appointed several times to be a provincial examiner. Wang Guodong's first assignment in the Qing territorial service was in Henan, where he served alongside the Yongzheng emperor's favorite activist governor, Tian Wenjing.[123] In fact, Tian Wenjing requested Wang's appointment in order to deal with members of the Henan elite who were boycotting provincial examinations in protest against Tian's river-control policies.[124] There were hints in Tian Wenjing's memorials that the governor wanted Wang Guodong to stay on in Henan and serve as a buffer between governor and elite. But the emperor had another task in mind for Wang. Broadly, this post originated in the emperor's evolving attitude toward China's elite, but a more specific catalyst was the prosecution, undertaken in the autumn of 1725, of the provincial examiner for Jiangxi, the Zhejiang literatus Cha Siting. The prosecution has been the source of one the most curious popular legends about the Yongzheng emperor, that he misinterpreted in rather paranoid fashion an examination question as advocating that the emperor be beheaded. In this question, candidates were asked to interpret a passage from *The Great Learning* (Da xue), "Where the people rest." The last two characters of this passage, *wei zhi*, resemble the characters in the name Yongzheng, except that in the characters *wei* and *zhi*, the top stroke of each character in the name Yongzheng is missing. Such a misinterpretation would indeed have been a serious error, for the passage in question was used very frequently in civil service examinations.[125]

Colorful as this legend is, the edicts in the case do not mention the episode; they do make clear, however, that Cha Siting was guilty of what may have been a far more serious challenge to Qing authority. After reviewing Cha's examination questions, the emperor ordered Cha's house searched and his luggage seized and inspected. Among Cha's possessions was a body of writings about Qing policies toward scholars and intellectuals. Cha Siting's crime was not that he proposed through orthographic legerdemain the emperor's execution but that he indicted, in his writings and examination questions, the dynasty's entire system of incorporating men of talent into its scholarly administration. The emperor described Cha's writing as indicting the Kangxi emperor's "utilization of personnel" (*yong ren*) and his abolition of offices. Cha also offered a series of criticisms of the examination process, particularly the continued testing of Hanlin academicians after they had been admitted to the academy; Cha found the use of Manchu in testing Hanlin academicians a particular case of academic bullying. Once one finished a term in the Hanlin Academy, in Cha's view, matters got worse; he claimed that to move from the scholarly atmosphere of the Hanlin Academy into line administration could only be a cause for shame among officials, that the awarding of *jinshi* degrees by a Manchu emperor was nothing less than extravagant excess. He also condemned the prosecutions of Dai Mingshi and Zhao Qin as oppression and pointed to the waste and dangers of constructing Bishu Shanzhuang, the emperor's mountain retreat. Ordinary administrative punishment would not suffice, in the view of the emperor, for one who had accepted the responsibility of conducting examinations on behalf of the dynasty and then propagated such ideas. He ordered Cha arrested and interrogated and turned over to the Three High Courts of Judicature for criminal punishment. Fearful that such ideas were common in Cha's native Zhejiang, the emperor also suspended the provincial examination in that province and appointed Wang Guodong to be commissioner to observe and rectify customs for Zhejiang.[126]

Wang Guodong thus found himself once again charged with the task of mollifying the local elite after examinations had been canceled, although in the case of Zhejiang, the cancellation came about by imperial order rather than through boycott. Wang Guodong's mandate was actually somewhat broader than this. The edict condemning Cha Siting proved to be the first of a series of four edicts, issued in rapid succession, which together constitute an imperial essay on the role of the literate elite, particularly the Zhejiang elite, in the Qing state. Those who were "leaders of the four sorts of people," the emperor wrote in an edict issued just two days after his edict condemning Cha Siting, had the duty to be a model for the common people and extend the way of the sages down to the ordinary farmer. While the empire did not lack for scholars who cultivated their good names and carefully read the classics by candlelight, there were others who had a negative impact on government, interfering with the operation of the official yamen. It was the duty of local instructional officials to make sure these corrupt practices were rooted out so that the elite could be a model for the common people. But since local educational officials were often men of mediocre talent, it was the duty of education commissioners like Cha Siting and Wang Guodong to model proper behavior. Thus, educational officials should not concern themselves solely with literary style or examination essay form but should be actively engaged in the social and political leadership of local elites.[127]

Several days later, the emperor observed that customs were particularly debased among the elite of Zhejiang. Indeed, the emperor feared that the breakdown of social order was so significant that it might be reversed only by application of the law, a prospect the monarch "could not bear." Therefore, the emperor undertook to appoint a special representative who could observe the "strengths and foibles of local custom" (feng su zhi de shi) and rectify them where necessary. This formulation represents the creation of a new official as the benevolent act of a monarch concerned with properly conveying his intentions rather than as an additional level of supervisory personnel. State leadership of the elite was to be liturgical rather than legal. The edict then decreed that the title of the new official should be "commissioner to observe and rectify customs" (guan feng zheng su shi) and ordered an official seal produced and arrangements made for a yamen for the new commissioner. In a separate edict issued the same day, Wang Guodong was appointed to the post.[128] Wang's appointment supplemented that of his colleague Li Wei who, though respectful of literate elites, did not have an advanced degree.

In a final edict on Zhejiang and the Cha Siting case, the emperor addressed the errors of those who violated the social order he had laid out. Since ancient times, the emperor noted, empires had rested on the common recognition of a common code of conduct that regulated high and low. There was simply no place under heaven to which those who did not acknowledge such a standard could flee. By the early eighteenth century, scholars and their wives, ancestors, and children had enjoyed the dynasty's prosperity for eighty years. How could they not recognize their good fortune and acknowledge its authors? This was a bit of hyperbole, at least for the Zhejiang elite, since economic recovery along the coast had not really begun until the later Kangxi reign; nonetheless, the emperor's point was certainly that all were bound by the social compact and the dynasty had delivered on its portion of the deal. The edict then condemned those literati members of the official order who allied with other officials, or requested favors of them, rather than devoting themselves to the responsibilities the state had assigned. These last remarks were apparently addressed to Cha Siting's complaints, no longer extant, about the nature of the personnel process in the Kangxi and perhaps also the Yongzheng reign and led to a spirited defense of the experimentalism the new emperor had brought to Qing personnel administration.[129]

In fact, Wang Guodong's task as commissioner for the rectification of customs in Zhejiang was to raise the imperial flag over the southeastern elite, so that Li Wei could go about the task of administering one of China's most complex and strategically significant provinces.[130] He seems to have traveled from county to county, observing local officials' conduct and reputations and lecturing local landholders on their obligations to the state. A portion of the text of one of Wang's lectures to the local elite is preserved in one of his memorials and closely parallels the imperial edicts. Much of the language was hyperbolic; one cannot take at face value a memorialist's report of his own comments about the emperor. Nonetheless, even the stereotyped language of the reported talk does not conceal the two themes Wang addressed. The first was that the emperor and the local gentry were bound by the same code of moral conduct, and it was the emperor's role to assist his subjects in following that code. It simply was not the case that the Manchus lived by one political code and Chinese officials lived by another. Since the beginning of his reign, the emperor had respected heaven and modeled himself on his ancestors. Indeed, the emperor's works of benevolence could not be counted. Moreover, since customs in Zhejiang had become depraved and confused, the emperor had issued repeated edicts and established a special official to devote himself exclusively to transforming local customs. All of this was undertaken because the emperor wanted the gentry to understand the workings of heaven and respect for the proper relations of superior and inferior. The second theme was that Zhejiang's local elite needed to remember their parents' or ancestors' commitment to the Qing. As Wang put it: "One's parents' nation must be their children's concern." It would not do for the elite in a time of peace to forget the sacrifices made by their predecessors and, indeed, by the Manchus in times of war. All forms of tax protest, litigiousness, and other obstructionism had to cease. None of this was new to Wang Guodong's audience, but reinforced by the presence of a specially commissioned imperial emissary and the suspension of examinations, it must have made a powerful statement. Wang himself said that all who heard him wept in alarm and fright and pledged with one voice to reform themselves. Wang also reported to the emperor one quantitative mark of his success, although it reads rather incongruously to the modern ear. He reported that the number of new lawsuits declined by about half following his presentations.[131]

Wang Guodong's appointment had its origins in the narrow circumstances of the Cha Siting case, but the appointment and the creation of the commissioner's office in other provinces can be seen more broadly as an attempt to create a stratum of officials on whom the emperor could rely to represent the Qing positively and serve as a model for the local elite. In his first report to the emperor, Wang dealt with the condition of the shed people, a hereditarily disadvantaged minority group; the practice of proxy remittance by the provincial elite and its effect on finances; the competence and appearance of several subordinate officials; and the dangers of the practice of selling hand-copied versions of official documents, produced by yamen underlings, in the markets.[132] In addition to conveying the court's intent to the local elite, Wang took on administrative duties in the province. When eastern Zhejiang was flooded in 1727, the emperor ordered Wang, together with Li Wei, to oversee the reconstruction of dikes and seawalls breached in the flood. It would appear that in Zhejiang, as in Jiangsu, the imperative of ideological conformity was made more palatable to the local elite by investment in infrastructure.

Wang's practice of rating the customs of the counties whose elite he addressed provides additional insight into the nature of his task. Certainly in Wang's mind, as well as in the emperor's, the problem of elite customs was most serious in the prefectures of Jiaxing, Huzhou, and Hangzhou and nearly as serious in Shaoxing and Ningbo. Together, these regions constituted the most commercialized areas of the province, what G. William Skinner and others have called the economic core of the southeast China macroregion. Of the regions Wang visited, the situation was better only in Taizhou, which was fairly far from the commercial center of the province and, at least in the eighteenth century, belonged to a different and relatively less developed marketing area.[133] The correlation between the wealth of the core and the need to reform customs was probably not coincidental. Gentry in the regions Wang identified as most troublesome was precisely that element whose resources and symbolic capital gave its members the prestige and standing to resist the Qing's ideology. Although organized around somewhat different principles, the Yongzheng emperor's attempt to find a bridge to the southeastern elite was comparable to the Kangxi emperor's Boxue Hongru examinations of 1669 and his subsequent appointment of *jinshi*-degree holders to the governor's post at Suzhou.

While the Yongzheng emperor was clearly reaching out to the Zhejiang elite, there were many reasons why his approach was not as successful as had been that of his father, the Kangxi emperor, to the lower Yangzi elite. Unlike in Suzhou, the commissioner's post did not become permanent or evolve into an enduring buffer between state and elite. When Wang Guodong left the post in 1727, he was replaced by Xu Rong, who served as commissioner for seventeen months. Xu was replaced by a third commissioner, who eventually served concurrently as provincial governor; when this commissioner left office, the emperor judged that the position was no longer necessary and abolished the post. Efforts to establish Qing legitimacy among the elite also had a different tone than in Jiangsu. Unlike the elite of Jiangnan, who were invited to participate in the activities of the state, the elite of Zhejiang were being lectured, reminded of the obligations to the central government that their parents, in some cases unwillingly, had assumed. The Yongzheng era was considerably further into the Qing dynasty than the Kangxi reign; social positions had hardened since the 1660s, and the Zhejiang elite had been allowed more time to reflect on its position in the state. The Zhejiang elite had famously long memories; in the eighteenth century, historians of the province, known as the Eastern Zhejiang School, were reputed to have preserved the details of the conquest period far longer than had other historians in China.[134] Zhejiang dissidence in fact followed Wang Guodong from Hangzhou to his new post. Shortly after being appointed governor of Hunan, Wang was ordered to investigate the case of Zeng Jing, who had attempted to use the writings of a disaffected Zhejiang literatus, Lü Liuliang, to lure Governor-general Yue Zhongqi into rebellion against the Qing. Ironically, after a lifetime of dealing with literati dissidents, Wang lost his touch in his attempt to capture and interrogate Zeng Jing and was angrily reprimanded and then dismissed by the emperor.[135] Whereas literati resistance became a trope in Jiangsu, it remained a reality in Zhejiang well into the eighteenth century.

Negotiation: Fujian

Negotiations with the Fujian elite took a different form, in part because the concerns of the Fujian gentry were different from those of their colleagues in other southeastern provinces and in part because, by the time the concerns of the Fujian elite became most pressing, in the early eighteenth century, the central government's capacity to negotiate was more limited. Eighteenth-century administrative history in Fujian took place against the background of the maritime world's declining importance to central politicians. The interaction of governors with the Fujian elite turned not so much on the ocean as on a range of issues, including land tenure, paramilitary organizations, and the resolution of legal disputes that inflamed the province. Although few came to Fujian with experience in these issues, all who governed there encountered them, and some developed special competencies, but the central government proved unable or unwilling to fashion unique institutions.

One might be inclined to attribute the eighteenth-century decline in interest in the maritime world to Chinese attitudes toward the outside world in general, but as John Wills has argued, the reality was more complex. There were, as he notes, many areas of the early modern world where international commerce transformed political economies and remade states. But these areas—the Baltic, the Mediterranean, and the Malay Peninsula—tended to be regions where coastal powers faced "narrow and relatively safe seas" that offered the ready promise of wealth. This was not the case along the southeastern coast of China, with the South China Sea being too dangerous and potential trading partners too far away and too weak to serve as economic magnets.[136] Instead of being seen officially as a source of opportunity, in mid-Qing China, the sea was seen simply as a potential source of danger. As the danger of the sea receded, so did the importance of guarding against it. During the latter half of the seventeenth century, this task was increasingly assigned to Chinese Green Standard Army troops and the Qing military apparatus at Fuzhou. Perhaps in response to both these trends, fewer officials with careers made on the coast were appointed to Fujian. Rather, Fujian in the later eighteenth century became one of a number of stops officials made on their journeys around the borders of the Qing empire. Only three of the eighty-eight governors appointed to Fujian between 1700 and 1900 were transferred from Zhejiang. Seven more came from Guangdong, but the majority were from borderlands. Of those promoted to Fujian, 50 percent came from within Fujian or from Yunnan, Guizhou, Shanxi, Shaanxi, and Guangxi, and 40 percent of those transferred laterally to Fujian came from the same provinces.

In Fujian, difficulties with the Qing order were not so neatly framed by a single event like the tax protest of 1661 or the Cha Siting case. Rather, they turned on the dynasty's inability to come to terms with the system through which local interests were expressed on the coast, an extraordinarily complex system of property rights. This system predated the Qing and probably reflected coastal prosperity during the trading era of the late Ming.[137] The main characteristic of landowner-ship under this order was the presence of two or even three owners to a field, one owning topsoil rights, the other owning subsoil rights, and so forth. This made land leases complicated, and the total alienation of property nearly impossible. It also produced an extraordinary number of legal disputes in Fujian. In the clichéd language of Chinese administrators, every province was "litigious," but there was good reason to apply this characterization to Fujian. Strong lineage organizations, which competed for land, control of water, and market rights, exacerbated the difficulties of the system. They "suppressed class conflict but magnified rivalries based on kinship territories and ethnicity."[138] When the inevitable conflicts over land arose, family-based groups were prepared to back up their claims with paramilitary forces, leading to lineage wars along the coast. In the minds of officials, lineage wars and legal backlogs were intimately related. One governor wrote in a memorial of 1759: "The reason for lineage disputes is that local officials allow legal disputes to go unresolved. If such disputes are not promptly solved, they grow into major warfare."[139]

The problems became particularly salient in the eighteenth century, as the coast's economy declined, and existing organizations were forced to compete for increasingly scarce resources.[140] In her monograph on litigation masters, those who assisted ordinary Chinese in preparing official legal complaints, Melissa Macauley devotes an entire chapter to the study of Fujian legal culture. Some particularly telling examples date from the governorship of Wu Shigong, who served from 1758 to 1761. As Macauley argues, despite an acute perception that legal cases and lineage feuds were related, Wu Shigong could resolve property rights cases only by issuing proclamations urging people to simplify their land deeds. But, as she writes, "his solutions reflected the enormous distance that separated him from such transactions. The litigation and struggling over contract disputes were not primarily due to lack of clarity in the written contracts themselves, as to the complex local practices that law had to attempt to regulate in the southeast."[141] Wu Shigong's solution to the backlogged legal disputes was to provide local officials with small notebooks in which they could record the dates that cases were filed, investigated, and resolved.

The same ineffectual quality that characterized Qing efforts to standardize law in the coastal province also marked its efforts to deal with the conflicts between lineage groups. In 1741, a substatute was introduced into the Qing code to punish those involved in lineage wars: "When those who inhabit riverine or coastal areas attack each other with spears and clubs, let the ringleaders and those who sounded the gong to call the people together be sentenced to 100 strokes of the heavy bamboo and an exile of 300 li."[142] Once again, Wu Shigong made some contribution to the legal order by pointing out to the central government that these were not acts of random violence but conflicts that often pitted large, wealthy lineages against smaller, poorer ones. At his request, the statute was modified to incorporate the different reasons for lineage groups going to war. Even armed with such statutes, however, governors were reluctant to involve themselves in lineage disputes. Feuds, as David Ownby notes, "were messy affairs, embedded in the local social landscape, frequently connected with local elites—in sum, unlikely to be resolved quickly or permanently by the decisive action of 'alien' officials whose tenure in the region was likely to be short."[143] Moreover, "local militarization for purposes of self defense received limited sanction in the Chinese statecraft tradition," and at least some of the actions of Fujian paramilitary groups had the effect of preserving order in a violent and chaotic region.

Macauley's and Ownby's examples notwithstanding, Wu was not incompetent. He had very good traditional credentials; he had passed high on the civil service examinations, served in the Hanlin Academy, and occupied a series of increasingly responsible positions in the Qing administration.[144] Wu's problem, which was probably shared by many of his fellow Fujian governors, was that he had little knowledge of the complex and volatile social environment in which he found himself when he arrived in Fuzhou. He came to the province with experience primarily in the grain transport administration. This was no doubt useful, as the supply of grain for the military garrisons in the province was always an issue, as was regulating grain shipments from Taiwan to the mainland, but it hardly provided him with insight into local conditions.[145] In the early seventeenth century, the Qing had often posted to the coast officials from the southeast who were familiar with its society. One of the consequences of Qing success in Fujian, however, was to bring Fujian fully into the empire, a province to be governed by the same routines as in all the others, and the special arrangements that had prevailed in the seventeenth century could not be continued. Eighteenth-century governors of Fujian could not speak for those they governed as readily as the governors of Jiangnan and Zhejiang did.

The eighteenth-century Qianlong central government was also less adaptable than earlier Qing orders, less willing to engage in negotiations with local elites. The apparatus of the territorial service was more established in the eighteenth century than in the seventeenth, and the emperor himself was less open to experimentation and had less interest in reform than his father or grandfather. The eighteenth-century Qing personnel bureaucracy made some effort to cultivate Fujian expertise, however, by leaving in or returning to the province officials with Fujian experience. The rate of inter-province promotions was 38 percent, below provinces with obviously specialized needs, such as Yunnan and Shaanxi, but above most others in the empire. Closer examination of individual careers reveals the effort to cultivate local expertise. In 1747, the hearty troubleshooter Korjishan, who had successfully dealt with corruption in Shanxi and famine in Shandong, was appointed governor-general of Minzhe and remained there for eleven years, until his death in 1757. Four years later, his son Dingchang returned from mourning obligations and service in the armies of conquest in central Asia to serve for five years (1761–66) as governor of Fujian.[146] Yu Wenyi, who governed in Fujian from 1771 to 1776, had served in subordinate positions in the province for sixteen years and for eighteen years as an official at the Board of Punishments before his appointment as governor.[147] But if this was the dynasty's conscious policy, it was not always successful, for two of those promoted from lieutenant governor to governor in Fujian were cashiered within a year of their appointments.[148] Many governors arrived in Fujian with little local experience. The hapless Xu Sizeng, who presided over the rebellion of Lin Shuangwen, the suppression of which became one of the Qianlong emperor's "ten great campaigns," had acquired experience only in Yunnan before becoming governor in Fujian.[149] While a few governors arrived in Fujian prepared to take on the challenges of this independent, litigious, and complex province, many were not ready for the challenges of governing the province in the eighteenth century, the mire of litigation and low-level violence it presented. The result was that the Qing regime, though serviceable, had to content itself with a less than complete monopoly on the means of military force and limited communications with the elites of the province.[150]

It may seem a considerable semantic stretch to term the lectures of Wang Guodong and the shamed tearfulness with which they were supposedly met as a "negotiation." Yet Wang's activities were fairly typical of the process by which the Qing established what it would provide to and could expect from the elites of southeast China. The appointment of a special imperial envoy to deal with the concerns of elites in the commercialized core of the lower Yangzi valley was hardly a new phenomenon in the 1720s. There were, in fact, striking consistencies in the Qing treatment of the lower Yangzi and the southeastern coast. The continuities grew out of two rather fundamental lessons the Qing learned in its first century in the region. The first was that neither the lower Yangzi nor the southeastern coast could be ruled as a single political unit; both had to be divided into small units where local needs could be addressed more directly. The second lesson was that the constituents of these smaller units had to be given a voice in their government if the region was to produce the grain and revenues required by the central government. Both of these lessons became apparent by stages as the Qing first conquered and then set out to govern the region.

The provincial boundaries the Qing fashioned in the lower Yangzi and along the southeastern coast were a significant innovation and a legacy of the Qing conquest that still shapes Chinese political realities today. As G. William Skinner has argued, these boundaries were not of economic inspiration. The borders between Anhui, Jiangsu, and Zhejiang broke up the natural lower Yangzi macroregional marketing area, and the boundary between Zhejiang and Fujian broke up the southeastern coastal marketing area. Rather, these boundaries were of political inspiration; they represented efforts to divide the various political communities of the coast from one another so that each could be dealt with separately. In the 1660s, the dynasty found it prudent to divide the lower Yangzi delta elite, who looked toward Suzhou as a capital, from the center of military power and regional administration located upriver in Nanjing and to assign a different sort of official to each post. Later and somewhat less formally, the dynasty created a division between a north-facing regime in Hangzhou and a Fujian government that was clearly oriented toward the sea. These decisions were the product of decades of interaction with communities along the coast, rather than sudden impositions from Beijing.

The decisions were made in part so that the dynasty could assure local stability and the regular flows of grain and revenue from the southeast on which the central administration came to depend. The close connection between political form, local stability, and revenue flows first became clear in the tax protests of 1661 in Suzhou. The concern was also implicit in the connection Wang Guodong drew between loyalty to the regime and the abolition of such practices as proxy remittance and interference in the work of the yamen. In the long run, the dynasty's program for governing the coastal region came to rest on the principle of allowing local elites a voice in their own government.

In broad outlines, the development of provincial government in southeast China went through three stages of comparable activity. The confrontation between military forces and local communities, which dominated the first years of Qing presence in the southeast, was painful but not unproductive. The late Ming had seen dramatic changes in the society and economy of the southeast—the commercialization of the lower Yangzi delta and the growth of overseas trade along the coast—and the forceful reimposition of Ming structures of rule might not have been effective. The pause in institution building, which occurred in the early stage of confrontation, allowed new forms of rule to emerge. The stage of confrontation lasted longer along the coast than it had in the delta, partly because there were more forces arrayed against the Qing, and partly because the Qing deferred the process of conquest along the coast until matters in other parts of the empire were more settled. It was the second phase, of accommodation, that produced the political personality of the southeastern provinces during the Qing. In the delta, this was accomplished by the appointment of scholar-governors in Suzhou and promising young administrators in Anqing; farther south, military specialists emerged in Fujian, and Zhejiang was defined as a province requiring men of multiple competences. Individual governors in the delta, and centrally initiated institutional change along the coast, acted to accomplish accommodation. It was a product of needs and also of the different eras when accommodation occurred. In the delta, government took form at a moment when the Kangxi emperor patronized and empowered individuals to act as agents of the state. Government on the coast was formalized during the Yongzheng reign, when political initiatives were developed at the center and were labeled administrative reforms. In the last decades of the seventeenth century, these patterns of control, which had initially been somewhat fluid, began to harden. As this occurred, a third stage began in which governors spoke for the communities they governed, and negotiations occurred not between court and community but between different elements of the political apparatus. Jiangsu governors represented the needs of their communities for flood protection, against the desires of activist central administrators to re-create transportation routes. In Jiangsu, Zhang Boxing's noisy responses to Gali's charges showed that the new order was sufficiently established that its tensions and problems could be argued in public. Farther down the coast, Wu Xingzuo prevailed upon the central government to lift the prohibition on sea travel that so burdened local communities. His successors as governor of Fujian were not as successful at expressing the needs of their constituents or resolving the legal and social problems that animated the community, but a provisional order was at least maintained for the remainder of the Qing.

CHAPTER 8

Regions into Provinces:
The Middle Yangzi and Lingnan

In the classic conception of Qing provincial government, first articulated in an
edict of 1665 and repeated, consciously or not, in textbook accounts and class-
rooms ever since, Chinese provinces were divided into contiguous pairs, and each
pair was put under the control of a governor-general. Although in theory this was
the model for all China, it existed only in four regions south of the Yangzi. Here,
the provinces of Hunan and Hubei formed the jurisdiction of the Huguang
governor-general, Guangdong and Guangxi formed Liangguang, Fujian and Zhejiang formed Min-zhe, and Yunnan and Guizhou formed Yun-gui. There was
little in the geography of the region to dictate this two-in-one structure. Macro-
regional boundaries roughly enclosed the territories of southern governors-
general, but they were no more decisive than they were in the north, and nowhere
were they sacrosanct. Political action rather than geography formed the distinc-
tive two-in-one pattern and many other features of Qing government in the south.
Throughout the middle Yangzi and Lingnan regions in late imperial China, the
interesting question is how the politcal power of the Qing central government
interacted with changing local societies and economies to create new territorial
identities.

The Qing could reorganize political arrangements in the region in this fashion
because relations of control were not so long established there as in the north.
South China under the Ming was certainly not a tabula rasa; the Ming court
assigned six administrative commissioners to the region and posted grand coordinators as necessary throughout the area. But the Ming had built a regime of
control, not of integration, and had established a structure that was ill equipped
to incorporate the vast economic and social changes that transformed the area
from the mid-sixteenth century onward. During the Qing, developments in the
south—population movements and new patterns of domestic and international
trade—were drawing the region inexorably closer to the northern centers of
political power. The changes necessitated a rethinking of political forms in the
region, a process that was nearly continuous from the earliest days through the
middle reaches of the Qing.

Initially, the Qing was inclined to follow Ming patterns of governance, without giving much thought to the region. When regents for the Kangxi emperor issued their edict dividing the territories of the south, they still largely lacked experience of the region. Tellingly, after decreeing the area's political order, they left to Chinese officials at the Board of Personnel the task of deciding where the governors-general would actually reside.[1] Government in the region drifted into a pattern of rule by Chinese military collaborators with the Qing. The most famous of these was Wu Sangui, whose timely shift of allegiances made possible the relatively peaceful occupation of Beijing in the spring of 1644. Wu was given rewards for his service far beyond what was possible within the Chinese bureaucratic order. In 1645, he was made a prince of the blood of the Qing ruling house, though he subsequently declined this honor. In the late 1640s and early 1650s, Wu and the other three generals who had surrendered to the Qing were sent by the dynasty into south China in pursuit of the last of the Ming resistance, and to reestablish order in a region beset by banditry. The assignment of these generals to the south had the effect of reproducing Ming structures of control, in which a central court relied on specially designated military subordinates. In a sense, the Qing had no choice but to turn to Chinese generals and troops to govern the south, since Manchu forces were spread so thinly in the north and northwest.

The Qing's reliance on Chinese generals in the south paved the way for these powerful collaborators to set up relatively independent regimes for themselves in the postconquest period. Wu Sangui not only monopolized revenues from the regions he commanded but demanded ever-increasing subsidies from the Qing court in Beijing. He also exercised veto power over military and civilian appointments in the region; his own appointees were referred to as those who had been "selected from the west" and took precedence over appointments made by the central court. As Wu's influence grew in the southwest, ominous warnings about his ambitions and loyalties reached Beijing. In 1673, in response to these warnings, the twenty-one-year-old Kangxi emperor made one of the most fateful decisions of his reign, siding with the relatively few in his court who favored an attempt to dislodge Wu and the others from the south. The emperor's decision provoked a rebellion that began in the winter of 1674. Wu Sangui himself died in 1678, but his grandson continued the fight for four more years.[2]

It was not until the last Qing armies cleared the region in 1682 and the Kangxi emperor announced victory to his ancestors that the Qing could begin to contemplate how it fit into the empire as a whole. Occupation was in a sense the enemy of integration in the south. So long as it was seen as a region amenable to control only through military means, the central government had no reason to explore the regional difference, recognition of which was central to incorporating the south into the empire. But once the military lid was off, the central government could go about fashioning a government that suited the character of the area and its subregions. This the Qing did, not so much with formal changes in the status of the area, as with informal changes in the character of the men who administered it. The Qing appointments procedure, which allowed the central government considerable flexibility in its choice of personnel, also facilitated the establishment of regional identities. Appointees chosen for one set of skills reinforced the association between their particular skills and the offices they held, until the various postings in central and south China came to acquire their own character. In this way, the regions of military occupation in south China became provinces of the modern Chinese state.

THE MIDDLE YANGZI

The incipient nature of the middle Yangzi region in the seventeenth century is probably better suggested by what it was to become in the nineteenth century than by what it had been in the fifteenth and sixteenth centuries. In the middle of the nineteenth century, the middle Yangzi was moderately urbanized, not yet as thoroughly commercialized as the lower Yangzi valley but considerably more developed than the northwest. More important, the cities of the nineteenth-century middle Yangzi manifested what G. William Skinner has called a "layered effect." That is, when the cities were ranked in order of population, they appeared to be grouped in layers rather than ordered in a smooth line in which size is proportional to rank in the commercial hierarchy. Skinner explains this phenomenon by citing Chauncy Harris: "The existence of two or several large cities of more nearly the same size than might be expected by the rank-size rule . . . is suggestive of residual regionalism." Indeed, a pattern of residual regionalism was embedded in the middle Yangzi region: "The lowland Yangtze corridor is flanked by four regions, each dominated by a major river system and rimmed by mountains except where the tributaries flow into the corridor. Thus, though Wuhan, which dominates the corridor, is unique in having ready access to all the region's other major cities, and though the corridor cannot be considered a region in its own right, rather sharp regionalization characterized each of the four tributary basins."[3]

If the "residues" of regionalism remained in the nineteenth century after nearly two centuries of integration, they must have been powerful forces to begin with. In the late seventeenth century, the river valleys of Hunan—the Xiang, the Zi, the Yuan, and the Li—and the valley of the Gan River in Jiangxi were self-contained regions.[4] Located within these several valleys were a variety of urban centers with claims to economic and administrative centrality. The Ming deployment of its administrative apparatus only partially recognized this reality. The Ming administrative presence was concentrated in two cities, located about 200 miles apart, in the northern quarter of the region: an administrative commissioner and a grand coordinator were located in Wuhan and Nanchang. In addition, the Ming had military outposts in three corners of the area: the southeastern corner of the region at Nangan, in the northwestern corner at Yunyang, and in the mountains, which formed the southwestern border of the region at Pianyuan. Yin Huiyi, a Chinese official who served briefly as governor of Henan in the eighteenth century, contrasted Yunyang and Nangan, articulating the early Qing perceptions of these posts and their significance: "Nangan adjoins Huguang, Fujian, and Guangdong. Yunyang adjoins Shaanxi, Shanxi, and Henan. Nangan is mountainous and its people are crafty. Yunyang is on the plain and its people are schemers. Schemers can easily be assembled into crowds. Therefore if Huguang and Jiangxi were to enjoy order, it was necessary to establish additional civil and military personnel."[5] The words Yin used for "schemers" and "crafty" were essentially synonymous, but the distinction he was trying to make was clear enough. At Nangan, the problem was mountain-dwelling people who secured their access to the scarce resources of the area by preying on others; at Yunyang, the concern was streams of travelers and immigrants moving from north China to the middle Yangzi region and westward into Sichuan. In one case, the problem was mountain men on the take; in the other, it was travelers on the make. But in both situations, the Ming purpose was political control.

As the seventeenth century progressed, the Qing moved away from the principle of government by means of strategic outposts in the middle Yangzi. Initially, the Qing followed the Ming in setting up its main military and administrative establishment at Wuhan, where both a governor and a governor-general were located. Perhaps because of the presence of Wu Sangui's forces in the area, the Qing felt freer in the first decades of its rule to experiment with this position than had the Ming and combined it twice with the upriver jurisdiction of Sichuan. During the Wu Sangui Rebellion, a single governor-generalship for Huguang was reestablished, independent of Sichuan. Several years after the war, the Kangxi emperor again sought to eliminate the governor-general at Wuhan but eventually re-created the post at the urging of his senior officials.[6] In fact, however, in the largely peaceful century and a half following the end of the Wu Sangui Rebellion, the Huguang governor-general appears to have been much less actively involved in the direction of military affairs than were his counterparts elsewhere. In similar fashion, the Qing abandoned the military postings at the corners of the region. Both posts were filled in 1645, but both were eliminated in the early Kangxi reign. The Yunyang post was reestablished briefly during the Wu Sangui Rebellion but was eliminated again in 1679.[7] This left the Qing with three governors in the area, at Nanchang, Wuhan, and Pianyuan.

The Wuhan and Nanchang governors became permanent fixtures of Qing administration, but the Pianyuan governorship saw significant change in both location and function.[8] Yuanzhou, the seat of the Pianyuan governor in the early Qing, was located in the Yuan River valley, the longest but also the narrowest and least densely populated of Hunan's four river valleys. Yuanzhou made sense as a capital only because of the threat to order posed by the non-Chinese Miao and Tujia peoples. Far more densely populated was the valley of the Xiang River to the east. This was a broad flow, navigable for much of its length, that formed a highway linking the far south of the empire with the lower Yangzi valley. The Xiang River valley was the most economically advanced subregion in the middle Yangzi, and was the first of the four southern river valleys where double-cropping was practiced in the eighteenth century.[9] In 1665, when the Qing moved the seat of the Pianyuan governor from Yuanzhou to Changsha, the principal city of the Xiang River valley, the dynasty was opting to base its government in the area on agricultural productivity and commercial importance rather than on strategic necessity.[10] This is not to credit the early Qing with economic foresight. Its attention was probably first drawn to the Xiang River valley by resistance to the Qing conquest, largely from bandit groups rather than Ming loyalists, which Wu Sangui suppressed in the 1650s.[11] Nonetheless, events made clear that the Qing were not merely setting up a regime of military occupation at Changsha. In 1671, when the allotment of lieutenant governors to each province was reduced from two to one, the emperor ordered one of the lieutenant governors in Huguang to move from Wuhan to Changsha and proceeded to build civilian administration there.

A Hunan political identity took a while to emerge, however. The governor at Changsha was known as the Pianyuan governor until 1723, when the Yongzheng emperor engaged in a rectification of regional names, redesignating Pianyuan as Hunan and Huguang as Hubei.[12] By this renaming, the emperor decreed that, semantically at least, Hunan was to be regarded as equal to Hubei rather than as the remnant of a military posting. In the same year, the emperor ordered the Hunan governor to begin building an examination hall in Changsha so that Hunan candidates could take their provincial examinations closer to home, and he also ordered the Huguang governor-general and the governors of Hunan and Hubei to deliberate on how to divide the Huguang examination quota between the two provinces.[13] Even with these administrative changes, in the later Yongzheng reign, when territorial officials were ordered to compile provincial gazetteers, officials in central China chose to compile a single *Huguang Gazetteer* (Huguang tongzhi) rather than separate volumes for Hunan and Hubei. It was not until 1820 that a provincial gazetteer was compiled for Hunan.[14]

Once the locations and titles of middle Yangzi posts had been established, the next task was to fill them, and as appointments were made to the three provinces of the middle Yangzi region, each acquired its own character. Hunan became the seat of experienced governors, men whose trustworthiness and competence came to be admired not only by officials at court but also by contemporaries, who preserved the administrative writings of Hunan officials in various forms long after these officials had left Changsha. Hubei also had its competent managers, but as the remarkable commercial potential of the region developed, its governors came to be sojourners, officials whose peripatetic lives paralleled those of the merchants they governed. Jiangxi saw an extraordinary number of Manchu governors and seemed to develop into a posting in which young Manchu officials from north China found their feet in Chinese civil administration. These appointment patterns were never proclaimed as policy; rather, they emerged over a period of years and sometimes decades.

Hunan Statecraft

The new province the Qing created, Hunan, became one of the most dynamic in the empire, a land that would repeatedly put the flexibility of the Qing territorial order to the test through the eighteenth and nineteenth centuries. From the time of the Wu Sangui Rebellion until the end of the seventeenth century, Hunan was governed primarily by Chinese bannermen. The first post-rebellion governor in the province was Ding Sikong (governed 1683–88), the son of the Qing's first governor of Shandong, Ding Wensheng. Ding Sikong had earned the dynasty's designation of "outstanding official" for his work as lieutenant governor of Jiangsu in the 1670s and devoted himself to postwar relief and reconstruction work in Hunan.[15]

The first non-banner administrator of the province was Zhao Shenqiao, who arrived in Hunan as part of a team of Manchu and Chinese officials sent to deal with a Miao rebellion. He stayed on as governor from 1703 to 1709. As Peter Perdue has written: "Hunan must have been a wild place when Zhao arrived. Throughout his tenure, he had to settle an extraordinary number of murder cases, fight bandits who infested mountainous areas and protect merchant boats from attack on Dongting Lake. Frequent floods and draughts made life insecure, and families were selling themselves into servitude."[16] Zhao laid the foundation for a more orderly society in the province by correcting inequalities in land tax assessments, increasing grain supplies, and encouraging the cultivation of new lands. The Kangxi emperor also especially instructed Zhao to reform what the emperor perceived as the corrupt officialdom of Hunan. Zhao, who had about him a rather stiff incorruptibility that intimidated his fellow officials and inspired several indictments, may have been what was necessary in a frontier province.[17] Hunan administration remained in civilian hands until the Kangxi reign ended in 1723.

Hunan government became more chaotic during the Yongzheng reign. The

TABLE 8.1. Hunan Governors with Experience in Other Provinces, Mid-1700s

Governor	Dates in Hunan	Previous Service
Yang Xifu	1745–48, 1750–51, 1753, 1755	Guangdong, Guangxi
Kaitai	1748–50	Hubei, Jiangxi
Chen Hongmou	1755–56, 1765	Multiple
Feng Qian	1758–62	Hubei
Qiao Guanglie	1763–64	Guizhou
Fang Shijun	1767–69	Guizhou
Liang Guozhi	1771–73	Hubei
Bayansan	1773–76	Shanxi, Shaanxi
Li Hu	1778–80	Guizhou, Yunnan

Source: *Qingdai zhi guan nian biao* data.

first governor the emperor appointed in Hunan was one of the few Yongzheng governors to be cashiered publicly, Wei Tingzhen (governed 1723–25), a hapless Hanlin academician who could never quite grasp the new emperor's expectations for provincial government.[18] After Wei came several Chinese bannermen, but by 1727, the emperor was forced to admit that those he had appointed to the province were not of the highest caliber. He wrote privately to the new governor he appointed in that year: "The situation in Hunan is very pressing. Administrative collapse has proceeded there for a long while, and the need to bring it under control is urgent." The bannerman then serving as governor, the emperor continued, "is competent and his heart is in the right place, but he is a narrow and shallow vessel and cannot lead and transform the province. I have long been unable to find a person for the post, and I am dissatisfied."[19]

As the province's economy developed in the middle decades of the eighteenth century, more civilian governors with experience elsewhere were sent to Hunan, and by the middle of the eighteenth century, the governors appointed to Hunan were the most senior and experienced in central China. Most of the governors appointed in Qing China had some sort of experience, but Qing practice assured that some would reach provincial posts with more experience in the sort of management tasks associated with the office. In the course of the eighteenth century, Hunan emerged as one of the provinces to which governors were transferred after having been promoted elsewhere. Overall, nearly 40 percent of Hunan's governors had served elsewhere, and during the mid-eighteenth century, nearly 70 percent of those appointed in Hunan had served elsewhere These Hunan governors and the provinces in which they served before their Hunan postings are listed in table 8.1.

These governors assembled a striking record of administrative achievement. Four of them—Yang Xifu, Kaitai, Chen Hongmou, and Bayansan—reached the rank of governor-general, and a fifth, Liang Guozhi, rose to the post of grand councilor after his service in Hunan. Yang Xifu's career demonstrates the process by which officials rose to postings in the middle Yangzi. Perhaps most striking, his official life was spent almost entirely in the south: only six of his forty-one years in government service were spent in the capital, and he held no territorial appointments in north China.

But although his experience was almost entirely in the south, it involved rather varied tasks. His first appointment was as circuit intendant in the Guangzhaoluo circuit in central Guangdong. The main feature of this district, a very wealthy one in the core of the Lingnan region, was a large, privately built dike system, known as the Mulberry Enclosure, that surrounded the most productive farmland in the region. Three years before Yang's appointment, these dikes had been the scene of a furious conflict between those who wanted to reinforce the Guangdong dikes with stone and others who thought this would be too expensive.[20] All was quiet during Yang Xifu's term, but the experience may have been his first introduction to the politics of dike building and river control.

From Guangdong, Yang moved on to deal with very different problems as lieutenant governor of Guangxi, the post to which he was promoted in 1736. In Guangxi as throughout the southwest in the first quarter of the eighteenth century, the dominant issue was relations between the indigenous Miao peoples and the Qing government and the Han settlers it represented. During the Yongzheng reign, the court and local officials envisioned military conquest as the solution to this problem. Yang arrived in Guangxi in the first year of the Qianlong reign, the moment in which a new emperor was emphasizing the possibilities of peaceful coexistence. Yang's background as a trained Chinese civil servant well suited him to the new communitarian directions of Qing policy, and when he wrote about establishing *bao-jia* units and mechanisms for interregional cooperation among provincial officials, he received praise and support from Beijing. The combination of experience in the wealthy core of Guangdong and in the borderlands of Guangxi and the southwest would appear to have qualified Yang Xifu superbly for service in Hunan, but one detail may have stood in the way. This was the fact that Yang was from Jiangxi, the province that bordered Hunan. In fact, he was from Jiang Qing district, a community situated about a third of the way along the major thoroughfare from Nanchang to Changsha. Depending on how one read the rules, service in Hunan could have been counted a violation of the Qing rules of avoidance, which held that an official could not serve within 200 li of his native district. However, the Qing had decided early on that the rules of avoidance did not apply to special appointments made by the emperor. That Yang's appointment possibly was in violation of the rules strongly suggests that his appointment was decided upon at the highest levels of the Qing court.

Yang Xifu was best known during his Hunan years for an essay in which he reflected on the relationship between population pressure and grain prices and the importance of maintaining hydraulic infrastructure if a growing population were to be fed. Yang was as good as his word in this instance and devoted much of his time as provincial governor to repairing dikes and irrigation works.[21] The Qing court went out of its way on several occasions to make sure that Yang remained in Hunan. All officials during the Qing were required to observe a period of ritual mourning when a parent died, roughly twenty-seven months when a father died and a shorter period when a mother died. Officials who observed this mourning formally vacated their offices, and upon completion of the prescribed term of retirement, an official was expected to report to Beijing, present his credentials to the Board of Personnel, and wait for the next available vacancy at the appropriate rank.[22] Yang Xifu was unique among eighteenth-century governors in having to go into mourning twice while he was governor of Hunan, once in 1748 for his father and again in 1751 for his mother. After both of these periods of mourning, Yang was returned to Hunan. As officials returning from mourning were officially constrained to wait for the first available vacancy at the rank to which they were entitled, Yang's two appointments to Hunan were very likely to have been the product of official action. After his service in Hunan, Yang was promoted first to the capital and then to the post of governor-general for Grain Transport, which he held longer than any other official in the eighteenth century.[23]

Other Hunan governors listed in table 8.1 had more conventional careers but were equally vigorous in their terms in Hunan. Kaitai and Feng Qian are both remembered in the historical record for articulating and addressing the difficulties of meeting the emergency grain needs of surrounding provinces while maintaining necessary grain stocks in Hunan.[24] This was an increasingly thorny problem as Hunan became more prosperous. In the 1750s, there was a major scandal when one Hunan finance commissioner implemented a scheme by which he would profit personally from purchases of grain made to support relief efforts after a famine in the lower Yangzi valley.[25] Famine was not the only circumstance that required the shipment of Hunan grain. Liang Guozhi was known during his term in Hunan for his ability to meet the grain needs of the armies fighting the Jinchuan rebels to the west in Sichuan, and for his service he was promoted to serve on the Grand Council in Beijing.[26] Li Hu came to Hunan after a career that spanned nearly fifty years and five provinces. Little is known of his accomplishments in Hunan, but according to Li Yuandu, a nineteenth-century Hunan historian, his term was remembered in the province as one of the three most successful in Hunan history.[27] As Li Yuandu and his contemporaries were unlikely to have remembered Li Hu personally, this assessment may have reflected the admiration felt by those living in a troubled period for the political heroes of a more prosperous age. Still, there is every reason to believe that Li Hu, like his earlier colleagues, was a remarkable governor.

Writings by and about Hunan governors, and the ways in which they were preserved, suggest the importance that the court and the eighteenth-century political community attached to the sort of experience governors acquired in the province. Yang Xifu's collected works, *Collected Writings from Sizhi Hall* (Si zhi tang wenji), is a case in point. This collection differed from most other collected writings in several respects. First, the "memorials" section was considerably longer than it would have been in the typical literary collection, occupying nearly half the volume, sixteen out of thirty-four *juan*. The next section, for prefaces and biographies, was markedly shorter than it would have been in most literary collections. The selection of letters was quite long but was composed almost entirely of letters Yang wrote in his official capacity as governor-general for grain transport, discussing shipments and responsibilities with various grain intendants of the lower Yangzi valley. Most of the poetry in the collection celebrated moments in official life, waiting for grain boats along the Grand Canal and admiring its scenic and historic locations. The work celebrated not so much a literary life as an official life, picturing as it did a Neo-Confucian workaholic, mastering the demands of his successively more responsible positions. The work was not compiled by Yang himself, but by his fellow officials. When he died in office in January 1768, his papers were moved to the capital, where his colleagues and contemporaries admired them. These officials carried out the publication of Yang's papers, and two fellow governors, Tan Shangzhong and Fei Chun, provided prefaces for the volume.[28]

Collected Writings from Sizhi Hall celebrated the accomplishments of one man, but later publications highlighted collective accomplishments. It was long-standing Chinese practice to anthologize writings about administration. One group of such anthologies centered on the "ordering of the state" (jing-shi), a phrase more commonly translated into English as "statecraft." As the idea that the world needs ordering implies that things were out of order, these collections usually came in the middle of a dynasty; they were not calls for dynastic overthrow but programs for reform. In 1826, Wei Yuan and He Changling compiled the collection *Essays on Statecraft in Our Times*, an anthology of writings by seventeenth- and eighteenth-century figures. This collection included 113 essays by eighteenth-century governors, and 70 were written by men who had governed in the middle Yangzi region, most of them in Hunan.

The editors of *Essays on Statecraft in Our Times* clearly favored Chen Hongmou, but other governors made significant contributions. No governor who had not served in the middle Yangzi had more than four essays included in the collection, and most of the others governors were represented by only one essay. This apparent favoring of middle Yangzi officials could have been simply a matter of

TABLE 8.2. Hunan Governors Included in *Essays on Statecraft in Our Times* (Huangchao jingshi wenbian)

Governor	Service in Middle Yangzi	Number of Essays
Chen Hongmou	Hunan, 1755–56, 1762–63	49
Yang Xifu	Hunan, 1745–52	10
Qiao Guanglie	Hunan, 1763–64	10
Yan Xishen	Hubei, 1777–78	12

Sources: *Qingdai zhi guan nian biao; Kocho Keisei Bunken So Mokuroku.*

local pride. Both the compilers were from Hunan, and they could simply have selected governors whose accomplishments they knew and admired. But there was probably more to it than this. The governors whose work was reprinted in the anthology had long careers in the territorial service, which culminated in Hunan. In some cases, the essays by Hunan governors that the editors chose to include were not about Hunan at all but detailed problems they had encountered in other postings in the empire. What the editors admired was a certain style of reform, in which officials relatively far removed from the imperial capital identified problems and implemented solutions on their own initiative. Hunan was the sort of province in which this sort of experienced, activist, and relatively independent official would thrive, and so it surely was not accidental that it became known as a center of statecraft, a showplace for what mid-eighteenth-century officials could achieve given opportunity and position.

Hubei Sojourners

Up to a point, the experience of Hubei paralleled that of Hunan, for the two provinces were similar in many respects. Both provinces had fairly large agrarian cores, but both also had their hinterland hot spots—Yunyang in the northeastern corner of Hubei and the Yuan valley along the western border of Hunan. Both provinces were well endowed with river transport, although the dominant rivers of Hunan were regional thoroughfares, whereas the Yangzi River, which bisected Hubei, was a national thoroughfare that joined three large regions. Politically, arrangements for the provinces were similar after they were separated in the late seventeenth century: both provinces had governors and provincial military commandants, and the two provinces had substantially the same tax quotas and similar revenue obligations to the center. Hunan and Hubei both experienced a similar cycle of economic development, in which growth began with recovery from the wars of the mid-seventeenth century and continued until population began to strain natural resources in the later eighteenth and nineteenth centuries. In Hubei in particular, this pattern of growth and decline was apparent in the Qing management of the region's hydraulic infrastructure, as Pierre-Etienne Will has argued.[29]

If anything, the early modern cycle of commercial expansion should have benefited Hubei more than Hunan, since the province had at its center a world-class entrepôt, the city of Hankow. In the markets so vividly described by William T. Rowe, rice merchants from the Xiang River valley met rice buyers from the lower Yangzi provinces, salt producers from the Yangzhou yards sold to middle Yangzi distributors, and tea producers from Hunan and the southeastern coast sold their wares to buyers from north China, indeed from as far away as central Asia and Siberia.[30] The growth of this commercial order produced a core of largely self-governing merchants in the province. This together with the continued residence in Wuhan of the last remnant of Manchu military occupation in the middle Yangzi, the Huguang governor-general, had the effect of circumscribing the provincial governor's role.

Through the last years of the seventeenth century, Hubei, like Hunan, was governed primarily by Chinese bannermen. From 1692 to 1699, the Hubei governor was Nian Jialing, whose son Nian Gengyao was soon to become governor-general of the northwest and leader of the Qing armies in the war against Tibet. Nian was succeeded by another Chinese bannerman, Liu Dianheng, who governed from 1699 to 1717. Liu Dianheng was remembered in Hubei for much the same sort of work for which Zhao Shenqiao was celebrated in Hunan: encouraging land resettlement and reclamation and restoring dikes along the Yangzi River.[31] The Yongzheng years were not quite as turbulent in Hubei as in Hunan, and the early Qianlong reign saw the arrival in Hubei of Chinese governors reputed for their intellectual accomplishments and abilities in statecraft. Chen Hongmou served one term in Hubei in 1743, and Yen Sisheng, an eighteenth-century governor whose writings on statecraft were anthologized as were those of Yang Xifu, governed from 1743 to 1745.[32]

The parallels between the careers of Yan Sisheng and Yang Xifu were strong and demonstrate the parallels between Hunan and Hubei until the middle of the eighteenth century. The most striking fact about the two officials is that they came from the same river valley in north-central Jiangxi. Yan Sisheng's native community of Xin Yu was a mere thirty-seven miles farther down the road to Hunan than Yang Xifu's. Both received their *jinshi* degrees at about the same time, Yan Sisheng in 1722 and Yang Xifu in 1723, the first year of the Yongzheng reign. Both spent the early Yongzheng years as junior officials in the capital, and it is almost inconceivable that two successful Jiangxi natives would not have been aware of each other, perhaps even known each other well, before they found themselves governing neighboring provinces in the 1740s.

Although Yan Sisheng and Yang Xifu were both products of the routine promotion system that was bringing young Chinese officials up through the territorial ranks in the eighteenth century, Yan's experience was somewhat different from Yang's. Yan held his first territorial appointment as lieutenant governor of Anhui in the first year of the Qianlong reign. Flood conditions in Anhui in 1737 required Yan to become expert in the management of relief efforts and the mechanisms for storing grain against subsistence crises. Yan particularly emphasized the creation of charitable granaries but also contributed to the elaboration of rules for famine relief that Pierre-Etienne Will describes in *Bureaucracy and Famine in Eighteenth-Century China*.[33] Perhaps more interesting, Yan experimented in Anhui, as he would in Hubei, with using the governor's financial resources to buy grain from other provinces in times of dearth and selling grain to other provinces in times of surplus. His experience in Anhui prepared him well for the tasks of managing territorial government in Hubei, much as Yang's service in Guangdong and Guangxi prepared him for Changsha. Both were examples, perhaps the best examples that could be cited, of what the routine provincial promotion system could accomplish in the eighteenth century.

Beginning in the middle of the eighteenth century, the political histories of the two provinces diverged. As Hunan became a province to which a governor was transferred after being promoted elsewhere, Hubei became a province where a governor received his first promotion. The dimensions of this phenomenon are outlined in table 8.3. Table 8.3A compares the promotion records of governors of the two provinces between 1700 and 1900. In the left column, the percentage of governors of Hunan and Hubei who were newly promoted from lieutenant governor are compared with each other and with the national averages: the figure for Hunan was 13.7 percent below the national average, that for Hubei was 9 percent above the national average. As would be expected, recently promoted governors were less likely to be promoted to governor-general. The Hunan promotion rate was 14 percent above the national average, and the Hubei rate was 20 percent below the average. Although the discrepancy between the two records was wider at the level of promotion to governor-general than at the lower level, both figures suggest that Hunan governors were the senior officials, more experienced as governors and more likely to move into the higher levels of Qing territorial administration. Just over one-third of the governors promoted in Hubei, fourteen out of forty-one, were promoted between 1740 and the end of the Qianlong reign, 1796. Table 8.3B lists the governors promoted in Hubei, their dates of service in Hubei, and their previous and subsequent appointments. Collectively, these newly promoted governors governed Hubei for almost exactly the same length of time that the officials listed in table 8.1 governed Hunan. However, the average term of the Hubei promotees was less than half the average term of the transfers to Hunan,

TABLE 8.3. Comparison of Hunan and Hubei Promotion Rates

A. *Promotions to Governor and Governor-General, 1700–1900*

	Percentage Promoted to Governor	Percentage Promoted to Governor-General
Hubei	39%	20%
Hunan	31%	28%
National Average	35.4%	24.7%

B. *Promotions in Hubei*

Governor	Length of Service	Previous Appointment	Subsequent Appointment
Fan Can	1740–44	Zhili	Anhui
Hengwen	1751–53	Zhili	Shanxi
Zhang Rozhen	1753–56	Shaanxi	Died
Feng Qian	1758	Shandong	Hunan
Tang Bin	1761–62	Jiangxi	Jiangxi
Song Bangssui	1762–63	Shanxi	Cashiered
Fu De	1763	Henan	Gansu
Wang Jian	1764	Gansu	Guangdong
Tang Bin	1765	Shaanxi	Jiangxi
Cheng Shou	1768	Jiangxi	Cashiered
Kui Yi	1768	Jiangxi	Cashiered
Tusabu	1786	Shaanxi	Guangdong
Li Feng	1786–87	Shandong	Capital
Fu Ning	1790–93	Shaanxi	Shandong

Sources: *Qingdai zhi guan nian biao* (QDZGNB) data; QDZGNB.

fourteen months as opposed to twenty-nine months. The "Previous Appointment" column of table 8.3B indicates that most of those promoted to Hubei came from north China, with five from Shaanxi, two from Zhili, and one each from Henan, Gansu, Shanxi, and Shandong. After their service in Hubei, these officials spread out across the empire. Three went to Jiangxi, two to Guangdong, and one each to Henan, Shandong, Shanxi, and Anhui. As they moved from north China, served brief terms in Wuchang, and then dispersed to various corners of the land, Hubei governors of the late eighteenth century seem to have become sojourners, like the merchants whom they governed.[34]

How did this pattern, so different from the one in Hunan, come to exist in Hubei?[35] The answer lies in part in the Qing state's attitude toward the activity that most distinguished Hubei from its southern neighbor, vigorous interregional commerce. As Susan Mann, William Rowe, and many others have pointed out, the Qing state was hardly hostile to commerce; in fact, local and provincial administrations derived much of their operating revenue from locally levied taxes on commerce. But the Qing state never regarded the encouragement of commerce as its highest priority. In the early eighteenth century, the development of commerce in the middle Yangzi was an important part of economic recovery in the region as a whole. But once this recovery had been established, the long-term trend Rowe sees in the Qing dynasty toward "privatization of many sectors of the Chinese economy" asserted itself, with the result that Hubei governors and their subordinates became less involved in the regulation and encouragement of commercial activity.[36]

As trade became less central to Hubei government, the other reality of Hubei political life, the presence of the Huguang governor-general, seems to have become more important. For seventy years in the eighteenth century, the Huguang governor-general was a Manchu, and frequently a fairly senior and distinguished one. Often these governors-general had relatively little experience in civilian administration, having been promoted to the governor-generalship from garrison commands. Already in the Yongzheng reign, the pattern of Manchu appointments in the Wuchang governorship had become sufficiently well established that the emperor became concerned about posting two non-Chinese officials in the same capital.[37] Over time, Wuchang became one of the places in the empire where the notion of shared responsibilities ran up hard against the reality of different Manchu and Chinese political cultures. In this respect, the experience of the governors promoted in Hubei may tell us more about the eighteenth-century Qing political system than about Hubei specifically. In fact, many of those promoted in Hubei were better known for their run-ins with Manchu authority than for anything they did or wrote about in Hubei.

The career of Tang Bin was probably fairly representative of the later sojourning governors of Hubei.[38] His terms in Hubei were not of great local significance; however, the same could be said of most short-termed governors of Hubei during the later eighteenth century. But Tang Bin's passages to and fro in the middle Yangzi vividly highlight some of the forces behind the short terms. He did have the distinction of having been promoted twice, in 1761 and 1765, to the governorship of Hubei. He was also demoted twice, first from the governorship of Jiangxi, to which he was transferred after his Hubei service, and again from the governorship of Guizhou in 1768.

Tang Bin's two demotions did not make him unique in the Qianlong years, but the phenomenon of double demotions was sufficiently rare to have occasioned imperial comment. At least the emperor had to explain why he had appointed a failed official for a second time and why, after a second appointment, the official had not been reformed. In Tang's case, the explanations invoked the language in which conflict between the new civilian administration of the middle Yangzi and the older structures of Manchu authority might be expressed.

In view of Tang's subsequent experience with the process, it was perhaps ironic that his first appointment after receiving his *jinshi* degree in 1736 was as an apprentice in the office that supervised administrative discipline, the Office of Evaluation and Scrutiny in the Board of Personnel. After ten years with this board, he followed a time-worn path for civilian officials in Qing administration, moving first from the Board of Personnel to a post in the Censorate, and thence to a series of positions in which he administered provincial examinations and guided the studies of provincial examination graduates. In 1754, he received his first appointment in the territorial service, a posting as circuit intendant for southwestern Hunan. He was promoted from this position to the lieutenant governorship of Jiangxi in 1757, and it was in this post that he dodged his first disciplinary bullet. In 1761, he was charged with having given in too readily to Manchu governor Asha's demand for a bribe. The Chinese provincial education commissioner brought the charges, which were investigated by Grand Councilor Liu Tongxun, who specialized in investigations of conflicts between Manchu and Chinese officials. As a result of the charges, Tang was demoted but left at his post.[39]

A year and a half later, Tang found himself rather hastily promoted to the Hubei governorship, which had become vacant because Chinese governor Zhou Wan did not get along with his Manchu superior, Suchang. According to the investigation of the case, Zhou had disagreed with his superior on a wide range of matters, from local policy to personnel decisions, and sought to undercut his authority. Matters had proceeded to the point that local officials in the province were afraid to report to either official.[40] The court clearly sided with Governor-general Suchang, characterized Governor Zhou as perverse and biased in his decisions, and ordered Tang to fill his post. Tang served in Hubei without incident for a year and was transferred back to Jiangxi as governor. But shortly after his transfer, both Tang and his successor Song Bangshou were accused of failing to investigate a robbery case in the provincial capital. The case was complicated by the fact that the robber's name had the same sound (though it did not involve the same characters) as that of an earlier robber in the province. Moreover, the prefect whom provincial administrators tried to blame in the case was the cousin of Qin Huitien, then serving as president of the Board of Punishments. Both Song and Tang were found guilty, and Tang was demoted and ordered to volunteer his service supervising dike repairs in Hunan as punishment.[41]

Five years later, Tang had once again worked his way up through the ranks of provincial bureaucracy and was promoted to the governorship of Hubei.[42] After he served there for a year, Tang was transferred to Yunnan and then Guizhou,

where he was again cashiered for not standing up to the powerful Chinese bannerman Yang Yingju.[43] Tang was retired after this case, having been characterized
by the emperor as a "weak and compliant 'scholar-type,' incapable of occupying high provincial office." The language, particularly the term "bookish one"
(*shu-sheng*), was that of stereotype, used as shorthand for the difficulties a civil
service examination graduate might face in trying to fit into the world of men of
action. Not enough is known of Tang Bin personally to determine whether he had
a character flaw or whether—as was perhaps more likely—he simply was unlucky
enough to have repeatedly been in the wrong place at the wrong time. Whether
or not the language was appropriate to Tang personally, it certainly did capture
the situation of relatively junior Chinese officials serving under senior Manchu
governors-general in many of south China's provincial capitals. The politics of
the Hubei governorship were rooted in the geographic and economic circumstances of the province. Because of its central location in south China, Wuchang
was a logical place to station a governor-general, and it was also a convenient way
station on Chinese governors' long and (if Tang Bin's case is any indication) not
always pleasant journeys across China. But Wuchang's location did not neces-
sitate the form of government that prevailed there, particularly at the end of the
eighteenth century. Rather, the pattern of Hubei government was a product of
the Qing court's reading of local circumstances, which, though never proclaimed
publicly, repeatedly produced common practice. The same must be said of Qing
government of neighboring Jiangxi province.

Jiangxi Manchus

Historically, Jiangxi was one of the most important provinces of south China,
and the Gan River—the dominant geographic feature of the province—was the
main corridor linking the lower Yangzi River valley with the provinces of the far
south. In the Yuan, the province was enormous, a broad swath of territory extending from the southern bank of the Yangzi to the border of Vietnam. Zhu Yuanzhang consolidated his conquest of central China with a battle at Nanchang and
enfeoffed one of his sons there. The Ming later reduced the physical size of the
province, as the lower Yangzi was consolidated and grand coordinators established in Guangxi. Nonetheless, the Gan River remained such an important thoroughfare that an obstruction along its course, caused by banditry in the southern
prefecture of Ganzhou, required the appointment of a grand coordinator in 1450.

Beginning in the latter half of the Ming dynasty, however, the political and
economic centrality of Jiangxi and its capital Nanchang declined almost in proportion to the rise of Wuchang. Wuchang proved to be a superior commercial
center, since it sat across an east-west thoroughfare, the Yangzi, as well as a

north-south highway, the Xiang. As Chinese settlers moved into the lower Xiang River valley and a civilian order was established there, the route to the south through Hunan became as well established as the route through Jiangxi. As Peter Perdue has argued, even Jiangxi merchants moved to Hunan, where they established new markets and trading patterns. As all this was going on, Jiangxi steadily lost its prestige and status, and even its mark of cultural eminence. Jiangxi produced the fourth-largest crop of civil-service-degree holders in the Ming, but its ranking sank to eighth in the Qing.[44] Through the late seventeenth century, the Qing adjusted the shape of its political apparatus in Jiangxi to reflect the province's declining importance. In 1646, the new dynasty appointed a governor and a governor-general to serve at Nanchang. For a brief period, the Nanchang governor-general was made responsible not only for all land between his capital city and the southern bank of the Yangzi but for lands north of the river as far as Henan. Henan was removed from the Nanchang governor-general's portfolio in 1647, but the southern part of the lower Yangzi valley was governed from Nanchang until 1660. When the Oboi regents remapped the south in 1664, however, the Nanchang governor-general was removed to Nanjing, where he remained until the outbreak of the Wu Sangui Rebellion in 1673. The post was reestablished that same year at Nanchang, but in 1681, the governor-general was moved back to Nanjing permanently. The office of Jiangxi provincial commandant underwent a similar evolution: created in 1648, it was abolished in 1668, re-created in 1674, and abolished again in 1683. All this left the Jiangxi governor in a rather anomalous position: politically, his province was a part of the Liang-jiang governor-general's jurisdiction, but economically and socially, his province was independent of the Yangzi.

The Qing court read this situation in different ways in the first and the second half of the eighteenth century. Like the middle Yangzi provinces, Jiangxi was governed by Chinese bannermen from the 1640s through the 1680s and then by a mixture of civilian administrators and Chinese bannermen until the 1740s. The name of the first bannerman governor was well known to many in the region—Tong Guozhen, who governed from 1675 to 1679. Guozhen was a kinsman, likely of the same generation, of Tong Guoqi, who held the Nangan governorship from 1655 to 1658 and governed Zhejiang from 1658 to 1670. Their large clan provided many officials to the young dynasty and a concubine for the Shunzhi emperor. A third and fourth Tong also governed Jiangxi, from 1683 to 1685 and from 1715 to 1717. The first Chinese civilian governor was Song Lao, who governed in Jiangxi between stints as lieutenant governor and governor of Jiangsu. The civilian governor who did the most to establish the routines of civilian administration in Jiangxi was Ma Rulong (governed 1692–1701), who is credited with establishing and filling civilian granaries in the province.[45]

After the 1740s, however, the Jiangxi governorship came to be dominated by Manchus. Manchus served as governor of the province 42 percent of the time during the Qianlong reign, and if the two relatively long terms of Chinese bannerman governors of Jiangxi are added to the total, Jiangxi was governed by bannermen for 56 percent of the Qianlong reign. These numbers clearly distinguished Jiangxi from its two neighbors—Hubei, where Manchus governed for 18.5 percent of the Qianlong reign, and Hunan, where they governed 16 percent of the time. Only in the provinces of the northwest between the early Kangxi and early Qianlong reigns, and in Shandong and Guangdong during the Qianlong reign, did Manchus govern as much of the time as they did in Jiangxi. However, unlike the provinces of the northwest, Jiangxi was never formally "set aside" for Manchus, even by the stroke of an editor's pen, and the subordinate positions of finance commissioner and provincial judge in Jiangxi were occupied mostly by Chinese. Manchus who governed Guangdong during the seventeenth and eighteenth centuries usually served only in Guangdong, whereas those who served in Jiangxi often had experience in two or more provinces in different regions of China before they came to Nanchang and went on to serve in other provinces after they completed their terms in Jiangxi. Shandong's administrative establishment resembled Jiangxi's in that governors there commanded the local Green Standard Army garrisons. Yet, clearly, Shandong, with its Grand Canal and control over routes to the national capital, had greater strategic importance for the dynasty than did Jiangxi.

The Manchus' prominence in Jiangxi was never officially remarked upon, perhaps because of the garrisons in the province. There was significant warfare in Jiangxi during the Ming dynasty, and when the seventeenth-century geographer Gu Zuyu summed up the nature of the province, he did so in terms of its strategic importance.[46] Manchu appointments may, however, had more to do with developments in Beijing than in the Gan River valley. Many of those who governed Jiangxi were part of a cohort of elite Manchus who, probably with court encouragement, began careers in the early Qianlong reign that would be based on positions in civilian territorial government rather than in the banner administration. Some, like Kaitai, who governed Jiangxi from 1746 to 1748 before moving to Hunan, earned Chinese civil service degrees and so competed with Chinese officials on an equal footing. Others, like Asha, followed what was for Manchus a more traditional route to office in the Qing dynasty, first obtaining positions as clerks in Beijing offices and moving from there into upper-middle positions in territorial administration. In many cases, the clerkship in Beijing was in the Grand Council during the years when Ortai was dominant. Table 8.4 compares dates of service in the Grand Council with dates of service in Jiangxi. In view of the time that elapsed between Manchus' appointments as Grand Council clerks and

Table 8.4. Jiangxi Governors Who Served as Clerks in the Grand Council

Governor	Term in Grand Council	Term in Jiangxi
Asha	1731–35	1749–50
Erong'an	1733	1752–53
Changjun	1731	1761–62
Fude	1754	1763–65
Haoshuo	1747	1777–84
Haicheng	1778	1772–77
Mingshan	1762–65	1754

Source: *Qingdai zhi guan nian biao*, table 4.3.

their service in Jiangxi, it seems unlikely that a term as a council clerk per se qualified an official for service in Jiangxi. More likely, the young Manchus appointed as Grand Council clerks were those who had attracted the attention of senior officials, and this attention followed them throughout their careers.

The career of Changjun exemplifies this process. A young clerk in the late Yongzheng Grand Council, Changjun was posted to a number of subordinate territorial posts in the early Qianlong reign and then went to war in the northwest in the late 1750s. Upon his return, he was appointed governor of Jiangxi. When the emperor met Changjun on a southern tour, the monarch marked the occasion with a poem in his honor:

> Returning safe from one hundred battles,
> You set off to hymns of victory, Our shepherd official.
> Setting off to cross the river without knowledge of the south,
> You have the skills to avoid the deep eddies.
> Appointing you is easy, like driving a light cart over a familiar road;
> You bring glory to our house.
> West of the river is a land of fish and rice;
> Resting, you take the people's concern as your own.

The emperor clearly respected Changjun, but not necessarily for his administrative achievements. A respected warrior, of assumed honest intent, Changjun was an easy choice for the post.

But why Jiangxi, when there were many postings in south China to which a trusted Manchu officer might be appointed? The demands of Jiangxi government likely required a certain measure of experience but did not demand the highest caliber of officials. In the absence of great change or challenge, the governor's work in Jiangxi consisted principally of preparing reports in the form prescribed by an increasingly powerful Grand Council. There were routine evaluations of provincial personnel, reports of revenues collected and expended, reports of grain prices and weather, assessments of garrisons' readiness, reports of infrastructural repairs accomplished and proposed, and the like. Much of this was probably done by staff, even under the most experienced of governors. In a quiet province like Jiangxi, Manchus familiar with the Grand Council and its demands could probably be expected to "rest" after their "hundred battles," without much harm being done to a "land of fish and rice."

If this was the calculation, it was partly correct. However, Manchu administration in Jiangxi had a rather rough-and-ready feel that distinguished Jiangxi from other provinces in the middle Yangzi. Three out of seventeen bannerman governors, or 17.6 percent, were cashiered, a rate that was 27 percent above the national average for the Qianlong reign. Governor Asha, whose case is discussed above in connection with Tang Bin, was dismissed for extortion; Haicheng was dismissed in 1777 when a dictionary containing anti-Manchu references was found to have originated in Jiangxi; and Haoshuo was dismissed in 1784 for corruption.[47] A fourth governor was disciplined some years after leaving Jiangxi for having extorted rather than donated funds for the rebuilding of schools and yamens in the province.[48] A fifth governor, Echang, was relieved of responsibility in Jiangxi in connection with the posthumous unauthorized publication of the public papers of Sun Jiagan, a governor-general and board president. It was remarkable that two of the actions against Jiangxi governors, those against Echang and Haicheng, concerned censorship of the written word, which was a particularly difficult issue for the Qianlong government in the eighteenth century. It was perhaps not surprising that the suggestion that gave life to the series of prosecutions known as the "literary inquisition" of the Qianlong court, a campaign directed largely at anti-Manchu writings, came from Jiangxi. It was Hao Shuo, later charged with corruption himself, who suggested that local educational personnel be rewarded with greater opportunity for appointment if they confiscated greater quantities of objectionable books.[49]

The administration of Jiangxi, as portrayed in writings by and about Jiangxi governors in the standard historical sources, looked quite different from those of neighboring Hunan and Hubei. Once across the low mountains separating Hunan from Jiangxi, concerns abruptly shifted from the operation of grain markets and the pressure of population on resources to official corruption and censorship. Valid as this impression would be, it is also deceptive in a certain sense. For, taking a slightly longer view, the important thing about Jiangxi, Hunan, and Hubei was that they all were fairly integrated into the Qing empire by the middle of the eighteenth century. They were ruled by a common corps of personnel who were loyal to a single ruler and responsive to the same set of political signals. Moreover, comparative examination of the corpus of extant memorials submitted by governors of the three provinces would reveal that the vast majority were documents in which governors relayed very similar information to the emperor in forms prescribed by imperial decree or established by long-standing administrative practice. Indeed, it may have been precisely because provincial government had become so standardized by the middle of the century that the Qing court could contemplate assigning a cohort of Manchus with limited classical training and experience in territorial government to provinces distant from the capital. The differences that remained between Jiangxi, Hunan, and Hubei in the mid-eighteenth century were differences between provinces, which were administrative units subordinated to an imperial structure, rather than between contiguous regions with different local traditions.

Politically, the valleys of the middle Yangzi were transformed into provinces of the Qing empire through the circulation of personnel between provinces in the two or three generations following the suppression of the Wu Sangui Rebellion. This is not to argue that political integration did not derive from a more fundamental process of economic and social integration over which the Qing had little control. In fact, considering the histories of other areas in the south, one might argue that the Qing was able to circulate personnel regularly to and from the provinces of the middle Yangzi because the region was steadily becoming more a part of the Chinese empire and society. The differences that emerged among the governors of the three provinces in the mid-eighteenth century were not the residues of persistent localism but the consequences of differences in the process of political integration. Some of the empire's most qualified and admired governors were assigned to Hunan until nearly the end of the century. In Hubei, partly because it was located at the center of so many types of crossroads within the Qing empire, the tensions between "men of action" and "bookish ones," implicit in all Qing government, was particularly vivid. In Jiangxi, the concerns of Manchus at the court were re-created, in a fascinating reprise of national dramas. Each of these provincial histories was inconceivable without reference to the national history; conversely, the national history could not be told without reference to the middle Yangzi story.

TO LIVE AND DIE IN LINGNAN

The process of political integration in the lands "south of the mountains," or Lingnan, the Chinese name for the provinces of the far southeast, involved more direct Qing court involvement than in the provinces of the middle Yangzi and in some respects was less complete. Distance from the capital, in terms of both literal and cultural space, accounted for some of the difference between the political histories of Lingnan and the middle Yangzi. Unlike the capitals of the middle Yangzi region, Canton would always be a destination, never a way station, at enough of a distance from the capital that the central government could hope only to approve rather than to make local policy. But if the central government could not shape Lingnan, neither could Lingnan shape the center. The seventeenth-century geographer Gu Zuyu described Guangdong as a region with more than enough wealth to be independent of the center but without the resources to attack other political centers.[50]

In central China, economic development produced relationships between metropolis and hinterland, as well as among the hinterlands, that were different from those in the far south. In the middle Yangzi, the great tide of economic change lifted the boats of all regions, perhaps not equally but nonetheless significantly. The same tide washed away subregional differences, so that by the mid-nineteenth century, only "residues" of regionalism remained. In Lingnan, the early modern era saw the emergence of the city of Canton, a single center of extraordinary wealth and power, home to an elaborate and often fractious political apparatus, located as far from the national capital as any major city in China. As Canton became more powerful, the region as a whole became less homogeneous. The second province in the region, Guangxi, became clearly subordinate to Guangdong, in both a political and an economic sense. Governing Canton and through it the Lingnan region, proved a continuing challenge for Qing emperors. Most rulers addressed this challenge by sending to Canton men who were, in varying degrees, their personal emissaries. This in turn produced a complex and often combustible mixture of imperial authority, local intractability, and peculiar personality in the southern city.

Conquest of Canton

Readers of Robert Marks's superb economic history *Tigers, Rice, Silk, and Silt: Environment and Economy in Late Imperial South China* will hardly be surprised by the claim that Lingnan in general and Canton in particular experienced sustained and at times explosive growth in the early modern period. As Marks argues, from 1400 to 1550, growth in the south was driven by an increase in population, but "from 1550 on, the process was commercialization driven, with foreign trade stimulating the economy generally and the commercialization of the Pearl River Delta in particular."[51] Canton was the port through which the products of the Pearl River delta passed on their way to south Asia, Southeast Asia, and Europe, and the point at which the inflow of foreign silver entered the Chinese economy. As trade increased and the delta prospered, Canton grew. A series of crises in the mid-seventeenth century, many related to the Qing conquest itself, interrupted this trend.

But it was a mark of the soundness and boisterousness of the south China coastal economy that when these crises had passed, Guangdong and Canton were able to take up where they had left off. By the early nineteenth century, Canton had achieved a level of political and economic primacy in the Qing empire unequaled by other late imperial cities, as it "performed functions for the entire empire not just for Lingnan."[52]

The Qing had little to do with this rising prosperity; in fact, the first forty years of Qing government of Lingnan were a disaster. This was due in part to the difficulty of meeting military challenges from a distance and in part to the court's limited understanding of the needs of the far south. A lightning campaign led by Chinese bannerman Tong Yangjia culminated in the first Manchu conquest of Canton in 1647. Tong was appointed the first Qing governor of Guangdong and concurrently the first governor-general of Liang-guang. In a great burst of optimism, the Qing court appointed an entire provincial administration, a finance commissioner, and twelve circuit intendants to support him.[53] Tong's quick success in the south left the banner armies overextended, however, and the city of Canton weakly defended. When Tong's colleague Li Chengdong switched sides and declared his allegiance to one of the last surviving Ming princes, Tong was left in an untenable position and acquired the distinction of being the first Qing governor to be assassinated in office. Canton fell into the hands of the Prince of Yongli, whose regime, as Lynn Struve has vividly described it, consisted of a motley assortment of Ming aristocrats and all manner of "betel-nut chewers, brine well workers and aborigine whorehouse owners" whose allegiance the court thought it prudent to cultivate.[54] This regime survived in the city until 1650, when the Qing court appointed the former Ming general Shang Kexi to retake the city and the region. After a siege of eight and a half months, the Qing took Canton for a second time in 1651, although fighting continued between Yongli forces and Shang's armies until the late 1650s.[55]

Shang Kexi was one of three former Ming generals—the other two being Wu Sangui in the southwest and Geng Jimao on the coast—who, after playing major roles in the conquest of the south, were given broad powers of governance in the region. But of the three, Shang was probably the most loyal to the Qing, and this loyalty permitted a certain amount of collaboration between Canton and Beijing. In 1660, the Qing garrisoned troops in Guangdong for the first time, although the garrison commander was ordered to consult with Shang on all matters of importance.[56] The garrison, which included both land and naval forces, was probably supposed to assist in the implementation of another Qing policy, the relocation of the coastal population inland to deprive the Fujian rebel Zheng Chenggong of supplies and trading opportunities. The garrison was downgraded to regional command in 1665, and the policy on coastal removal was ended on the pleas of

Guangdong officials in 1668.[57] But scarcely were these debacles over when Wu Sangui's rebellion began, and more Qing troops were dispatched from the south. Fortunately, this war was not as serious in Lingnan as it proved to be in other southern regions, and there was only limited fighting in Lingnan.

Once the Wu Sangui Rebellion was over, the Qing set about fashioning a lasting regime in Lingnan. This process involved a buildup of civilian and military personnel that began in the late seventeenth century and continued into the nineteenth. In 1680, a detachment of banner troops was assigned to Lingnan to facilitate mopping-up operations against the last resistance forces. After the war, this assignment was made permanent, and the troops, who were always Chinese bannermen and were commanded by a Chinese bannerman until 1735, were garrisoned in Canton city.[58] The provincial military commandant who was established in Guangdong in 1661 remained there permanently. This meant that for most of the dynasty, the Liangguang governor-general, the provincial military commandant, and the banner garrison commander all outranked the governor at Canton. There were also a Liangguang salt commissioner and representatives of the Imperial Household Department, known to the foreigners as "co-hong merchants," present in the southern city. Altogether, the 1733 *Guangdong Gazetteer* (Guangdong tongzhi) lists twenty-five government offices in the prefecture of Guangzhou.[59] Only in one other city outside the capital, the Shaanxi capital of Xi'an was such an array of civil and military personnel deployed.

Remarkably, however, the Guangdong governors thrived in this atmosphere. Between 1700 and 1900, fewer governors were cashiered or demoted in Guangdong than in any other Chinese province; the rate of dismissal in Guangdong, 5.6 percent, was nearly a third that in northern provinces. Conversely, Guangdong governors were promoted to governor-general at a rate that was among the highest in the empire, and unlike the governors of Shaanxi, many of those promoted from Guangdong were promoted to the local Liangguang governor-generalship. There were probably several reasons why Canton governors, in a city thick with official positions, seemed to do so much better than their Xi'an colleagues. First, the need to manage wartime logistics, which for so many years dominated the Shaanxi governor's role, was seldom an issue in Canton, where the end of the Wu Sangui Rebellion ushered in nearly 125 years of relative peace. Second, the Guangdong governor controlled more resources than many other governors. The Canton governor, of course, controlled that portion of the land tax revenue that was retained in the province, which was relatively small in the case of Guangdong, but many Guangdong governors held concurrent appointments as salt commissioners.[60] Although it was not the Guangdong governors' primary responsibility, there is much anecdotal evidence that they could profit personally and officially from the customs revenues collected at Canton. Finally, Guangdong governors seem to have been able to hold their own because, more often than the governors of any other southern province, they had been personally chosen by the emperor. Nearly half the governors of Guangdong between 1700 and 1775, and more than half the governors of the province in the 1800s could have achieved their offices only through direct imperial intervention in the personnel process.

The Qing court sent Manchus directly from the court to govern Guangdong before adopting the practice in any other southern province. The first Manchu to serve for any length of time as provincial governor south of the Yangzi was Manpei, a Manchu grand secretary who served in Canton from 1710 to 1714. Manchus governed Guangdong 27 percent of the time during the Kangxi reign, 21 percent of the time during the Yongzheng reign, and 41.3 percent of the time during the Qianlong reign.[61] By the 1740s, Manchus were beginning to make their way into provincial governors' yamens all over China, and so the Guangdong appointments were not unique. Nonetheless, the Manchus appointed in Guangdong were different from those appointed in the other stronghold of Manchu governors in south China, Jiangxi. Unlike their colleagues in Jiangxi, who had often been through a sequence of appointments in other provinces and moved on to other governorships, the Manchu governors of Guangdong tended to serve only in Canton. As much as anything else, it was probably the prestige associated with direct imperial contact that enabled Guangdong governors to contend with the many officials surrounding them in Canton.[62]

Imperial mandates not only may have produced strong governors in Canton but also produced powerful political egos and complicated local politics. One of the best examples of official feuding occurred during the Yongzheng reign, when Yang Wenqian and Akedun came to bureaucratic blows over the range of issues confronting a Guangdong governor.[63] These two officials represented two of the most powerful political families in eighteenth-century China. Yang Wenqian was the son of Yang Zongren, who had served as Guangdong governor from 1719 to 1723 and risen from there to the Huguang governor-generalship. Wenqian's son Yang Yingju, who served as Liangguang governor-general from 1754 to 1757, went from the south to the northwest, where he presided over the Qing conquest of Xinjiang and then returned to the southwest to clean up the mess the Qianlong court had made of the Burma campaign in 1768. Although father-and-son combinations occurred occasionally in the Qing bureaucracy, the three generations of Yangs that served in Canton was remarkable enough to occasion biographers' comments.[64] The family of Akedun was equally illustrious. Akedun was the first of his family to serve in high office and was the father of Agui, grand councilor in the later Qianlong reign, and the great-grandfather of Nayencheng. The careers of father, son, grandson, and great-grandson spanned the era of the Qing's greatest power, and their positions as imperial counselors saw them involved in virtually all the warfare and political change of the period.[65]

Yang Wenqian's career was filled with marks of imperial favor. Reaching office initially through the *yin* privilege, the right the Chinese state granted to senior officials of placing one son in office without passing the examinations, he was appointed first to a prefecture in Shandong and then allowed to serve an apprenticeship in his father's yamen in Wuchang. The Yongzheng emperor subsequently selected him to serve as finance commissioner under Tian Wenjing in Henan. After two years, Yang Wenqian was again picked by the emperor to govern in Canton; in fact, so urgently did the emperor desire Wenqian in Canton that he ordered Yang to observe mourning rituals for his father while in office.[66] Yang arrived in Canton just a month after a flood in the Pearl River delta, and his first act was to send officials to Guangxi to buy grain to support Canton city and the local garrison. He was soon confronted, however, with what he perceived to be a rice riot, led by the banner garrison troops. In April 1726, Chinese bannermen attacked the provincial granaries and began selling grain in the streets; they went on to create disturbances in front of the yamens of the garrison commander and Yang Wenqian. In view of the flooding the previous fall, the troops may have been hungry, but later investigations suggest that tensions within the garrison were more important than hunger.[67] As it developed, the trouble in the garrison had its origins in conflicts between the "old bannermen," descendants of troops who had originally served Wu Sangui and then surrendered, and the "new bannermen," who had marched south after the rebellion. Yang was able to arrest the ringleaders, but the garrison commander ordered their release. Yang refused and called upon the emperor to send a high-level emissary to mediate between himself and the commander.[68]

So it was that Akedun, a former chancellor of the Hanlin Academy fresh from diplomatic duty representing the Qing court at the coronation of King Yongjo of Korea, was sent to Canton.[69] Akedun and the new garrison commander Shi Liha, who was himself the son of a provincial governor, were able to quiet the disturbances among the troops. Matters became dicier when Akedun and Yang Wenqian disagreed over the question of how to repair dikes damaged by the flooding of 1725 and a typhoon that struck south China in the autumn of 1726. Yang Wenqian, remembering service in Henan, where he had participated in Tian Wenjing's struggle to rebuild dikes along the Yellow River, proposed a large engineering project in which existing earth and straw dikes would be replaced by stone dikes, built and maintained by the province. Akedun opposed the plan, arguing that Yang had underestimated the cost of the initial work and would commit the dynasty to much future expense and difficulty in maintaining the dikes.[70] From this initial disagreement, others arose. Akedun indicted two of Yang Wenqian's protégés, and Yang in turn accused Akedun of extorting money from foreign ships visiting Canton and tolerating the corruption of the Manchu finance commissioner Guangda. In best Chinese bureaucratic fashion, the subordinates (and subordinates of subordinates) of Yang Wenqian and Akedun began to attack one another, creating one of the worst cases of open bureaucratic in-fighting during the Yongzheng reign.[71]

Despite such episodes, Qing emperors continued to send their personal delegates to Canton. This was hardly surprising, in view of the city's importance, and yet these appointments should not be read simplistically. There were in fact a variety of reasons why Qing emperors would prefer personal representatives in the southeast. First was the issue of loyalties. Guangdong had both the resources and an appropriate geographical situation to serve as a basis for a separatist regime. Present were not only the Yongli court of the last Ming pretender but also the government of Shang Kexi; echoes of the Wu Sangui Rebellion, reverberating through the Canton garrison, proved to be one of the sources of the riots there in 1725. In the early eighteenth century, these concerns were probably quite important in determining who went to govern Canton. In 1744, Celeng, a grandson of the Oboi regent Ebilun and brother of the then president of the Board of Revenue, Noqin, was promoted from commander of the Guangzhou garrison to the governorship of the province. As most of Celeng's previous and subsequent career was spent supervising military activities, this was more than likely his expected role in Canton.[72] In 1750, Suchang, who had investigated corruption among bannermen in Manchuria and served as mayor of Fengtian, was appointed governor of the province, where he served for three years before returning to the Beijing.[73] But as the century proceeded and Canton grew wealthier, imperial representatives came to provide their rulers with access to and control over flows of money from the province. As this happened, the histories of Guangxi and Guangdong diverged, and the differences between these two provinces became as pronounced as any in the empire.

On the Border: Guangxi in the Eighteenth Century

Physically, Guangxi had as much potential as Guangdong to provide the basis for a separate regime, and historically this potential was more often realized in Guangxi than in Guangdong. Physiographically, Guangxi consisted of the basins of the West and Li Rivers, which were enclosed by the Nanling Mountains on the north, the Yungui Plateau on the west, and the Yunkai Mountains on the south. Within this well-protected basin, strongmen could easily arise to challenge centrally appointed officials. During the Qing conquest, two such strongmen, Chen

Bangfu and Qu Shici, protected and dominated the Yongli court while the Qing held Canton. Thirty years later, regional pressures in Guangxi were so strong that one Qing governor was imprisoned by and another joined the Wu Sangui Rebellion.[74] After order had been established in the east of the province, Guangxi went through a fairly quiet phase. But during the Yongzheng reign, trouble developed in the mountainous west, as the violence associated with Qing efforts to pacify the southwestern provinces of Yunnan and Guizhou spilled over into Guangxi. Guangxi was placed under the control of the Yungui governor-general on two occasions in the early eighteenth century, first in 1722–24 and again in 1728. This sequence of peace and war produced a checkered pattern in late seventeenth-century governors' appointments. When the province was peaceful, it seemed of little importance to the central government, and appointees like Chen Yuanlong, the Kangxi emperor's poetry tutor, found themselves in the province. It is possible that Chen was being punished with exile in the south, for the emperor sent him off with the rather ominous remark that Chen might actually have to learn to command an army.[75] When Guangxi was more troubled, it was governed by the likes of Li Fu, an activist by nature and one of the few followers of Wang Yangming in early eighteenth-century China.[76]

Once peace was restored to the valleys of Guangxi, the political character of the province came to be determined less by central government priorities and more by local realities. As noted above, when Yang Wenqian found that floods in Guangdong had endangered food supplies there, his first reaction was to send officials to Guangxi to buy grain. This was surely not the first nor the last time such purchases were made, for through the sixteenth and seventeenth centuries, Guangxi was becoming the supplier of grain to the commercialized Pearl River delta. A Braudelian relationship of core and periphery developed by the late Ming between Canton and the rich delta lands surrounding it, which were increasingly devoted to commercial agriculture, and the grain-producing areas of the North and West River basins. As Robert Marks argues, "Where the Pearl River delta and the West River basin in Guangxi had previously been separate ecological systems, they became increasingly linked by commercial forces and market transactions."[77] As Guangxi became economically linked to and ecologically leached by Guangdong, government in the upriver province and in the downriver economic center began take very different forms.

After 1730, Guangxi became almost a case study in Qing territorial administration on the peripheries. In this respect, the political pattern in Guangxi more resembled that of its western neighbors Guizhou and Yunnan than of its macroregional partner Guangdong. These three provinces differed most obviously from other Qing provinces in the relatively high proportion of governors who were newly promoted from lieutenant governor. In Guangxi, 54 percent of the

TABLE 8.5. Promotions in Guangdong and Guangxi, 1700–1900

	Percentage Promotions to Governor	Percentage Promotions to Governor-General
Guangdong	21%	32.6%
Guangxi	54%	24.2%
National Average	35.4%	24.7%

Source: *Qingdai zhi guan nian biao* data.

governors were newly promoted, in Guizhou 51 percent were newly promoted, and in Yunnan, 46 percent were newly promoted. In contrast, as shown in table 8.5, the rate of promotion to governor in Guangxi was more than double that of Guangdong. Moreover, the Guangxi rate was 18.6 percent above the national average; the Guangdong rate was 14.4 percent below the national average. The newly promoted governors of Guangxi also did not fare as well in promotions to governor-general, although the difference here was not quite as pronounced. Guangdong governors were promoted to governor-general at a rate that was 7.9 percent above the national average, whereas Guangxi governors were promoted at roughly average rates. The rate of promotion from governor to governor-general was a little higher than might have been expected in Guangxi and throughout the southwest, probably because the personnel process in the region selected for men with some military experience, and the office of governor-general had a more military portfolio than other governors.

It was the large number of promotions to governor that most characterized Guangxi. There were, of course, a variety of reasons why the court might opt to promote lieutenant governors in a given province. In Hubei, for instance, the court could accept relatively weak governors because it had a strong governor-general. However, there were significant differences between Wuchang, which could in no sense be termed peripheral, and Guangxi. Not only was the rate of promotion higher in Guangxi (9 percent above the national average in Hubei versus 52 percent above the national average in Guangxi), but the political power of core and hinterland were reversed in the middle Yangzi and in Lingnan.[78] In the middle Yangzi, weaker governors prevailed in the regional city and stronger governors prevailed in downriver Hunan, whereas in Lingnan, strong governors coexisted with governors-general in Canton and weaker governors were posted in the hinterland. This comparison may say more about the court's attitude toward Guangdong and Hunan than it does about Guangxi and Hubei. But it highlights the isolation of Guangxi governors, who had access to neither the resources of a regional core nor the connections afforded, for better or worse, by access to senior officials. Even governors who arrived in the south with fairly good connections found that their networks failed them when they reached Guangxi. If Yuan

Mei's account may be credited, Tuoyong was much admired by his colleagues and superiors when he served as finance commissioner of Guangdong from 1742 to 1744. But these officials were hardly around to protect him when he was accused and cashiered for mismanaging the copper mines in Guangxi in 1746.[79]

Promotions also came about in Guangxi when the central court judged that a local official could handle a local situation better than could an official brought in from another region. Guangxi was not unique in this. Gansu in the northwest and Jiangsu in the middle Yangzi both saw relatively high rates of intra-provincial promotion. But the pattern further served to isolate Guangxi officials from the centers of power in Qing China. Inter-provincial promotions in Guangxi mostly occurred in the post-Taiping years, when Guangxi had very special problems, but also occurred under special circumstances in earlier periods. Li Xiqin, a *juren*-degree holder from Jiangsu, spent almost his entire career in Guangxi. Appointed magistrate of Luocheng county in the north-central part of the province in 1728, during the next eleven years, he was promoted to prefect and circuit intendant in Guangxi. In 1740, he was placed in command of a detachment of three thousand troops to put down a small rebellion in west-central Guangxi, for which he received imperial commendation. He served as provincial judge for Guangxi from 1741 to 1746 and as lieutenant governor from 1746 to 1753.[80] His one recorded audience with the emperor during these years was a bit of a disaster. He took the opportunity to criticize his former superior Tuoyong and praise his current superior Echang. Since Echang had just given Li an outstanding rating in the triennial evaluations, the emperor suspected some sort of collusion: "How can this not be a case of the evils of factionalism?"[81] Nonetheless, factionalism among officials in far-off Guangxi was not the concern for the emperor that it was elsewhere, and Li was appointed governor of the province in 1752, twenty-four years after his first appointment there. Two years later, Li Xiqin died in office.

Appointed through routine procedures or from the local pool of officials, the governors of Guangxi after about 1730 faced uncertain futures. Statistically, a governor promoted in Guangxi had a less than even chance of moving on to a post of comparable or higher rank after his service in Guilin was completed. Four of the fifty-two promoted to governor in Guangxi were subsequently elevated to governor-general's rank, and another twenty-one were transferred to other provinces. But even those who were transferred did not travel far. An official who was made governor in Guangxi was more likely to be transferred to a nearby province than to one at greater distance. Five Guangxi promotees were subsequently transferred to Guangdong: three each to Hunan and Hubei; two each to Jiangxi, Jiangsu, and Henan; and one each to Anhui, Fujian, Shaanxi, and Yunnan. Just over half (twenty-seven out of fifty-two) of the newly promoted Guangxi governors ended their careers in the territorial service in Guilin. Eleven were transferred to midlevel positions in Beijing, usually at the Board of War; nine died in office; five were disciplined in some fashion; and two left to observe ritual mourning obligations and did not return. The number of promoted governors who died in office in Guangxi is perhaps the most striking. The nine deaths represent about 17.3 percent of those promoted, significantly higher than the average mortality rate of 13.9 percent for all Qing provincial governors. The death rate for promoted governors in Guizhou is even higher, at 20.3 percent. A few of those who died in office in Guangxi and Guizhou died in battle, and perhaps a few more died from the effects of an insalubrious subtropical climate. But the majority of those who died seem simply to have succumbed to old age, for it took a long time for the promotion process to bring an official to governor's rank, and as the dynasty progressed, the process became even lengthier. Yao Chenglie, who was promoted to Guangxi in 1779, received his *jinshi* degree thirty-four years before his first appointment as governor, and Wu Yuan, who was promoted to Guangxi in 1784, had held his civil service degree for nearly twenty years at the time of his appointment. For a lieutenant governor, an appointment to the governorship of Guangxi, though certainly a promotion, seems to have often represented the twilight hour of a long day's journey into bureaucratic night.

Canton Heyday

Those who were fortunate enough to govern in Guangdong in the latter half of the eighteenth century could anticipate a different future. The province became, by the late eighteenth century, one of the prizes of the late Qianlong bureaucratic order, a province so extraordinarily wealthy that it required special means and special personnel, an official such as Li Zhiying. Li governed Guangdong from 1776 to 1780, at a time when commerce in the southern port was thriving. Although the full effects of trade with Britain would not be felt in Canton until the mid-1780s, silk exports and customs revenue in the late 1770s were as high as they had ever been, and the gap between the richer provinces, like Guangdong, and the poorer provinces was growing wider.[82] A relatively rare archival source provides a fascinating glimpse of how the Qing was managing, or at least responding to, this gap and a tantalizing hint of what it must have been like to govern such a wealthy province as Guangdong. The source derives from the practice of allowing officials to atone for their political crimes by making cash payments directly to the Imperial Household Department, the emperor's privy purse. By the end of the eighteenth century, this practice affected many of the governors of China's wealthier provinces, but perhaps none more than Li Zhiying.

Like many of his predecessors, Li Zhiying was probably an imperial emissary to the south, but his particular expertise in the management of flows of resources to the capital suggests the court's conception of the southern province in the last quarter of the eighteenth century. Li was affiliated with the Manchu Plain White Banner but was most likely a Chinese bondservant, as he was hereditarily affiliated with the Imperial Household Department. He passed the *jinshi* examinations in 1737, won a place in the Hanlin Academy, and rose there to the post of compiler. In 1743, however, for reasons not stated in his biography, he was given the lowest possible rating in the metropolitan evaluation of officials and returned to the Imperial Household Department. This may have been a blessing in disguise, for there, Li Zhiying was able to rise through the ranks and was appointed salt commissioner for the Liang Huai District in 1771. This was an extremely important position with major fiscal responsibilities. Since the proceeds of the land tax were budgeted to cover various state functions, revenues from the monopoly on salt constituted a large part of the Qing monarchy's discretionary revenue. As Yang Jeou-yi has shown in great detail, the possibilities for financial manipulation of this vast and nearly constant stream of revenues were nearly endless.[83] After five years as salt commissioner, Li Zhiying served for eight months as Anhui lieutenant governor before being appointed to govern Anhui, which he did for five months. In the spring of 1776, he was transferred to Canton.[84] If a brief term of four months as circuit intendant, which he served before being appointed salt commissioner, is included in his résumé, Li Zhiying had a total of fourteen months' experience in territorial administration prior to his appointment in Canton. This contrasts markedly with the thirty-four years in subordinate posts that Li's contemporary in Guangxi, Yao Chenglie, served before reaching governor's rank in Guangxi. But if Li Zhiying had little experience in territorial posts, he may have had the sort of experience that mattered in Guangdong, making sure that streams of revenue reached the court's desired targets.

From his years in the Imperial Household Department, Li Zhiying probably knew of the Secret Accounts Bureau, the office within the department that kept track of payments officials made in lieu of accepting administrative discipline. The Qing dynasty had an elaborate system of sanctions for officials accused of personal and political crimes, and in a post like Canton, where money flowed like water and officials could find a ready imperial ear for their mutual recriminations, charges were frequent. Traditionally, sanctions had been expressed in terms of the number of strokes an official was to receive if found guilty of a given offense, but during the Qing, these were converted into a series of administrative punishments, dismissals and demotions, and, after the Yongzheng period, salary fines. In the mid-eighteenth century, officials began, at imperial bidding, to offer to make large payments to the state in atonement for their mistakes; such payments caused disciplinary proceedings to be suspended, and there was no adverse impact on an official's career. In the beginning, the emperor suggested an appropriate amount to be paid, but later, officials who had been found guilty or expected to be found guilty began to volunteer payments, although the emperor occasionally encouraged an official to increase the amount of his payment. Most of the crimes for which officials made atonement were perceived derelictions of duty, failing the emperor in some respect, rather than administrative errors.[85] Making payments to the Imperial Household Department was not a new practice, but the sums involved in the late eighteenth century were far more substantial, from ten to a hundred times greater, than any previous salary fines, and payments were made not only to avoid punishments when governors had been found guilty but also to avoid disciplinary proceedings altogether. In this sense, the Imperial Household Department fine system should perhaps be viewed not as an extension of the system of administrative discipline but as a new cash nexus created to link the eighteenth-century court to provincial governors.

By the 1780s, a fairly elaborate bureaucratic apparatus had developed, with the Secret Accounts Bureau keeping track of the amounts of money pledged by officials and the rates of their repayments and making what appear to have been semiannual reports to the emperor on the state of the accounts. In 1935 and 1936, archivists in the Palace Museum published four such reports, dated January 1787, October 1787, March 1795, and October 1795, in their series *Historical Collectanea* (Wen xian cong bian).[86] The number of officials listed as making salary contributions was relatively small, but their collective contribution of Imperial Household Department coffers proved to be fairly significant. The January and October 1787 reports list twenty-seven cases and twenty-five cases, respectively; the March and October 1795 reports list twenty-one cases and twenty-two cases, respectively. The fines levied ranged from 5,000 to 200,000 ounces of silver, but most were between 30,000 and 80,000 ounces. The total of the fines recorded in the January 1787 report is 1,761,586 ounces of silver, which was more than the yearly quota of land tax revenues of all but the seven wealthiest provinces in the empire. Of the total amount, 14 percent, or 250,000 *liang*, was earmarked for public works projects and was paid directly to the governors of Shandong, Henan, and Zhejiang. The remainder of the money was to be paid into Imperial Household Department treasuries in Beijing.

Provincial governors were the culprits in six cases in the 1786 and 1787 reports, and five cases in each of the two 1795 reports; in both instances, they accounted for about one-quarter of the officials charged. Officials' names appear more than once in the reports, as they incurred the fines and then partially paid and finally paid off the amounts they owed, so there was considerable repetition of names in the lists. A total of eight entries in the 1787 and 1795 reports record fines incurred while the officials were serving as governors (see table 8.6). It was probably not a coincidence that most of the governors recorded as paying fines had served in

TABLE 8.6. Provincial Governors Paying Fines to the Imperial Household Department, 1787 and 1795

Governor	Posting	Term	Fine (liang)	Year Repaid
Li Zhiying	Guangdong	1776–80	256,000	1787
Fu Song	Zhejiang	1782–86	200,000	1787
Wu Yuan	Hubei	1785–86	40,000	1787
Yang Gui	Fujian	1781–82	50,000	1787
Shang An	Guangdong	1783–84	40,000	1787
Ming Xing	Shandong	1782–87	30,000	1787
Qifeng'e	Jiangsu	1792–95	30,000	1795
Guo Shixun	Guangdong	1791–94	20,000	1795

Source: "Mi ji dang."

China's wealthier coastal provinces, where both opportunities for corruption and the resources with which to pay fines were greatest. Three of the eight governors fined were from Guangdong.

Li Zhiying owed the largest of these fines, a hefty 256,000 liang, the total of four different contributions pledged in the course of his governorships in Guangdong (1776–80) and Zhejiang (1780–81) as well as two terms as commissioner of customs in Guangdong (1778–80 and 1781–83). His obligations included 100,000 liang for mishandling Guangdong's salt revenues, 20,000 liang for mistakes made as customs commissioner, 36,000 liang for customs tax shortages, and another 100,000 liang for failing to indict a subordinate in Zhejiang.[87] Li was formally reprimanded in only one of these cases. In 1786, a Zhejiang circuit intendant was found to be selling the daughters of his yamen underlings to fellow officials as concubines. As the case unfolded, Li was recalled to the capital and ordered to consider the degree of his own fault in not reporting the case.[88] At the conclusion of this period of court-ordered self-examination, Li promised to pay the court 100,000 taels. In the other cases, Li Zhiying was not subjected to administrative discipline; rather, he proceeded from post to post, acknowledging his mistakes and undertaking financial obligations, and for the most part paying them off.

Perhaps the most remarkable thing about these fines was not that they were levied but that there was a reasonable expectation that Li Zhiying could pay them off. The 256,000 liang he owed was the equivalent of twenty years' "nourishment of virtue" (yang lian) salary, the administrative stipend for the Guangdong governor. Moreover, Li Zhiying owed a personal debt to the Imperial Household Department that was larger than the amount of land tax revenue the governor of Guangxi was required to remit to the capital in the course of a year. The amount of the fines made sense only in terms of the amount of revenue that Li Zhiying was likely handling. The salt tax quota for Guangdong and Guangxi was 503,000 liang per year and, as early as 1721, produced a surplus of 100,000 that provincial officials were willing to admit.[89] It was unlikely that the quota of salt revenues had increased by the 1770s, but the surplus was certainly swelled by inflation. The 36,000 Li Zhiying owed in customs tax shortage was less than 10 percent of the Guangdong maritime customs revenue of approximately 400,000 liang per year, and the fine he paid for "mistakes" was 5 percent of the revenue collected.[90]

Despite these fairly staggering sums, Li Zhiying was able to make good on his debts. By 1785, he had paid 110,000 taels on his accumulated debt and, according to the record books, made an additional payment of 30,000 taels in April 1785. He thereupon entered into an agreement with the Imperial Household Department that he would pay off the balance at the rate of 20,000 taels per year, half in the winter and half in the spring. He was able to make one such payment, but by the end of 1786, he found it impossible to continue repaying the money at the promised rate. In a memorial of the autumn of 1787, Li Zhiying pronounced himself at his wit's end, literally burning the midnight oil to come up with a way of paying off his debt.[91] Li's financial difficulties were probably due to his retirement, in 1783, from active service in China's provinces. From 1784 until 1789, he served in what surely must have been less lucrative posts as manager of the imperial estates at Qing I Yuan and minister of the Palace Stud.

Whatever the reasons for Li Zhiying's financial predicament, it was sufficiently serious that he alluded to the possibility of selling his family property in order to liquidate his official debts: "At present," he wrote, "my property cannot be sold fast enough in order to pay off my debts." The prospect of selling personal property to pay off salary fines must have been a bitter one; however, one should note that for all Chinese officials, and particularly for hereditary bondservants like Li Zhiying, the boundary between private and public resources may have been rather vague. These officials owed their entire lives and rather considerable fortunes to the Qing state, and for them, selling family property may have meant returning to the state resources on which the dynasty had a valid claim.[92] In the end, Li Zhiying was allowed to reduce his yearly payment from 20,000 to 15,000 taels, and between the summer of 1787 and the autumn of 1792, he made nine payments totaling 67,500 taels.[93] In the autumn of 1794, he made a last payment of 10,000 taels, which meant that by the time of the last notation in the Secret Accounts Bureau record books, he owed the state only 2,500 taels. Li Zhiying died in late 1794, surrounded by five generations of his family living together under one, presumably financially unencumbered, roof.

The picture of a Canton governor paying 250,000 liang in personal fines, more than the 243,000 liang the Guangxi governor was required to remit in land taxes on behalf of the province, vividly highlights the difference between the two provinces. The growth of revenue from the tea-for-silver trade in the last decades of the eighteenth century and the beginning of the nineteenth century only exacerbated these differences. Already in the 1780s, however, Guangdong and Guangxi stood at the extremes of what was possible within the Qing territorial order. For a governor, living in Canton was an experience that would be remembered for generations; dying in Guangxi would soon be forgotten. Inarguably, the two provinces were fully integrated into the Qing dynasty by the end of the eighteenth century, but perhaps they could both be a part of one empire only because special arrangements were made for each. In simplest terms, only one province, Guangxi, could have the largest number of newly promoted governors in the empire, and only one province, Guangdong, could have the lowest rate of administrative discipline. To be sure, these concessions to Lingnan exceptionalism were not as great, or perhaps as obvious, as were the policies of the Ming and early Qing that turned over the southern provinces to Lingnan natives or to degree holders who were willing to go. But in some respects, the arrangements the Qing made for the Lingnan provinces may have been costlier in the long run. The Secret Accounts Bureau was certainly not created for Guangdong; fines were assessed and paid by officials of many, if not most Chinese provinces. The system was, however, suited to an environment in which some officials had more resources than others and was crafted so that the punishment fit the criminal rather than the crime.

In the last decades of the Qianlong reign, more Guangdong governors than governors of any other province were paying into the dynasty's coffers. Loss of symbolic capital was the price the Qing paid for the Secret Accounts Bureau. For at its heart was the image of the Chinese emperor methodically taking his cut of the supposedly ill-gotten gains of his ever resourceful minions rather than holding them to a moral standard, as would be required of the ideological image of an emperor who was a center of moral and political authority. Much has been written in Chinese and in English about the corruption of provincial government in the late eighteenth century, particularly that associated with the imperial favorite, Heshen. In part at least, this corruption rested on differences in provincial wealth, like those between Guangxi and Guangdong, and the different circumstances of territorial officials.

The political and economic order that prevailed in Guangxi may have been equally costly. Robert Marks offers a fascinating reflection on the economic relationship between the two provinces, suggesting that Guangxi is paying a price even today for its past role as food supplier to Guangdong. In considering whether the economic relationship between the two provinces, which evolved in the early modern period, was stable, he writes:

> The question of whether or not this was an ecologically sustainable agricultural economy turns in part on the extent to which nutrients and energy from

Guangxi could be replaced. I don't have a firm answer at this time, but I think that in the long run they probably weren't. Guangxi today is one of the poorest provinces in China, experiencing low (or even declining) per capita agricultural yields. . . . The current ecological and economic poverty of Guangxi is a consequence of the centuries of exports of rice sent downriver to Guangzhou.[94]

The newly promoted governors of Guangxi were not inexperienced. Indeed, most had served for many years in the lower ranks of Qing territorial administration before taking up residence in Guilin. But they were nonetheless weak, unable to call on high-level connections or forcefully draw the court's attention to the needs of local society. This sort of government may have sufficed for Guangxi in the eighteenth century, and perhaps for some years in the nineteenth century, when there was little to be done and few resources with which to do anything. But border society had its revenge on the Qing in the nineteenth century, mounting the most serious challenge to Manchu rule during its three centuries in China. This was the Taiping Heavenly Kingdom, which was born in Guangxi and existed largely unnoticed by provincial administration and unreported to Beijing until it was almost too late. As the geographer Gu Zuyu noted presciently in the seventeenth century, unattended, Guangxi could export its troubles down the rivers that linked it to other provinces.[95]

The provincial governments the Qing built in the south were similar in form to those of the north and the southeast but different in social and political role. Unlike the provinces of the north and the northwest, the provincial governments of the middle Yangzi and Lingnan bore only a limited military burden, and, except for Guangdong, provincial governors had no special relationship to maintain with the court. Unlike the elites of the lower Yangzi, those of south China did not have the strength, for the most part, to negotiate the terms of their own provincial administration. Developing largely independent of other forces, a generation after provincial governments were established in the lower Yangzi and two generations after governments were put in place in the north, the south Chinese provincial order demonstrated the Qing's capacity to read regional realities and transform them into effective structures of government.

A second characteristic of middle Yangzi and Lingnan government was that the Qing saw the region through Chinese eyes. There were never many Manchu troops in the area, and with the exception of the governorships of Jiangxi and at times Guangdong, there were relatively few Manchu officials in the region. To nineteenth-century Chinese, the middle Yangzi and the south were where "statecraft thought" was most advanced, the land where the technical tasks of managing the state and the economy had been developed to their fullest potential. In

Western scholarship, the middle Yangzi had become the province, literally and figuratively, of a generation of scholars who have sought to demonstrate and affirm the Qing state's capacities for leadership and flexibility. The Qing's great achievement in the south was to transform what were relatively protean regions in the late Ming into provinces that played crucial and distinguishable roles in the Qing state.

It may be worth reflecting, therefore, on what the Qing state actually did when it converted regions into provinces. Regionalism was a very old and powerful force in China. Transportation routes shaped trading patterns that influenced patterns of human settlement; these in turn were reinforced by differences in local language dialects as well as the force of local and regional religious movements. Little political action was necessary to secure these traditions of association. In establishing provinces, the Qing set up sharp political boundaries between communities and charged a single official, or group of officials, with responsibility for preserving social order within these boundaries. Regions needed no governors, but provinces did. Perhaps more important, the establishment of a province meant that a single official was authorized to speak for a region in central political discourse. This official could articulate the successes and, at least as important, the needs of a region. In the early imperial era, when the central government could do little to meet regional needs, particularly in those regions farthest from the capital, province-size units may not have been that important. But once attention was directed to the capital, either because of the resources it controlled or because it was seen as a symbol of the polity, the ways in which regional needs were articulated became much more important, as did the structures for articulating them. Provincial boundaries hardly changed traditional patterns of association, but they did set the terms in which a region would be integrated into an early modern state.

This chapter has examined the formation of provincial units in central and south China, and the appointment of officials to serve as spokesmen for these units. The process is vitally important, because the provinces under consideration—especially Hunan, Hubei, Guangdong, and Guangxi—have played such an important role in China's modern political transformation. They did so in part because they have been among the most dynamic regions of China, and the Qing process of province building created and shaped the units in which this dynamism was expressed.

CHAPTER 9

Communications and Provincial Government
in Southwest China

Yunnan and Guizhou were the last provinces to be established in the Qing dynasty, nearly half a generation after the first provincial government was ordered in north China. When Qing armies reached the southwest in the mid-1650s, they found a land of cloudy skies, steep mountains, and rapidly flowing but largely unnavigable rivers. Even at the height of the Qing, the most important administrative posts in the two southwestern provinces lay along the main transport route that linked the provincial capitals of Guiyang and Yunnanfu (later renamed Kunming) to the rest of the provinces. This route was of such importance that the perhaps slightly cynical French traveler Bernard-Philippe Groslier would observe in the nineteenth century that the main function of the Guizhou government was to keep open the road to Yunnan.[1] In eastern Guizhou, this route followed the Yuan River southwest from the Hunan border as far as Huangping, then proceeded directly west through Ping Yue to Guiyang. There, it met the other principal route into the province, a north-south artery that led from Chongqing in southern Sichuan to Yunnan. West of Guiyang, the east-west artery proceeded through interlocking river valleys to the Yunnan border, and thence to Yunnanfu.[2] To the west of the Yunnan capital, a series of mountain ranges crossed the province from north to south up to the borders of eastern Tibet. The rivers of western Yunnan flowed north and south, linking the southwest to Thailand, Burma, Laos, and Vietnam. The Red River, which rose in Yunnan and flowed to Hanoi, was probably navigable, but the Mekong, which flowed to Cambodia and Saigon, was not.[3] Linked administrative centers formed the lifeline of the southwest during the early and middle Qing dynasties. In the nineteenth century, the southwest was the least densely populated region of China, "whose centers were very widely dispersed in terms of travel time and only very tenuously interrelated, forming an urban system which was at best only emergent in 1843."[4]

The southwest posed challenges that were substantially different from those of other southern regions. In the middle Yangzi and Lingnan, economic integration preceded political integration: in both regions, the Qing built its political structures on a fairly stable local Chinese society. In the southwest, however, the Qing had first to establish its monopoly of military force and find ways of governing the non-Han indigenous peoples of the region. Only then could territorial administration be established and sufficient resources extracted from the region that government in the southwest could pay for itself. Until this point was reached, the history of government in the southwest is a history of political and military action, grudgingly underwritten by the central government, in which governors and governors-general took the lead and central government mechanisms for controlling distant and powerful political leaders were put to the test.

The Qing dynasty was incapable of achieving social and economic integration of the southwest; only successive waves of migration and patterns of economic development could make the region wholly Chinese. In the seventeenth and eighteenth centuries, the Qing sought a sustainable civilian administration in the region, one that did not depend on the whims and loyalties of military satraps. Between 1660 and 1680, limitations on communication between the court and the southwest seriously hampered the region's political development. Only after 1725, when the dynasty had developed a capacity for nuanced and elaborate political communications, was it able to achieve political incorporation of the region.

TWO CONQUESTS, TWO CONQUERORS

The Qing were first drawn into this rather forbidding corner of the empire by the presence there of the last remnant of the Ming royal family, the putative Yongli emperor, who took his final refuge in the mountains of western Yunnan. The Ming controlled the southwest only tenuously, but when the armies of Shang Kexi forced Yongli out of Canton in 1651, the court fled to the west. Against this pathetic and peripatetic would-be monarch the court sent two Manchu generals and its most trusted collaborator, Wu Sangui, in 1657. The Qing armies did not face a strong opponent. The forces of the Ming pretender in the southwest consisted of a rather fragile coalition of late Ming officials, local warlords, and the forces that could be mustered by the Mu family, descendants of a comrade in arms of the first Ming emperor, who had been hereditarily ensconced in Yunnan.[5] Despite the weakness of this coalition, it took the Qing forces nearly five years, from December 1657 to August 1662, to battle their way across the southwest and find and execute the last Ming pretender.[6] As Qing armies secured the provincial capitals, the first governors were appointed in Guizhou in July 1658 and February 1659.[7] Hong Chengchou, whom the Qing had given control over military affairs throughout the southwest, recommended both of the appointees, which was appropriate, since the Qing presence in the southwest was basically a military occupation. Hong also recommended that overall authority in Yunnan and Guizhou be given to a Manchu prince, and the court chose Wu Sangui, to whom it gave the title "The Prince Who Pacifies the West."[8] In Guizhou and Yunnan, the court did not take the optimistic step of appointing subordinate territorial officials to assist the new governors, as it had in Guangdong, probably in part because it couldn't find civil officials willing to go. In 1659, the Beijing court offered expectant magistrates and former submagisterial officials the opportunity to receive substantive appointments regardless of their qualifications if they were willing to serve in Guizhou and Yunnan.[9]

Those who accepted this opportunity, which was available for only three years, found themselves in positions that were both isolated and, as the experience of the first Guizhou governor Bian Sanyuan illustrates, uncomfortably turbulent. Bian was no stranger to situations involving multiple and complex loyalties. He had received a Ming *juren* degree, but both he and his father chose to serve in the secretariat of the early Manchu court. After the conquest, Bian was appointed a prefect, first in Dengzhou on the northern Shandong coast and then at Yangzhou. The Yangzhou appointment could not have been easy in view of the massacre of Chinese civilians by Qing troops that had taken place there the year before Bian arrived. After Yangzhou, Bian held positions of increasing responsibility in northwest China before arriving in Guizhou in the spring of 1659. His first memorials as governor show his ingenuity in confronting the problems that nearly all his successors in the southwest would have to address. When he arrived, he faced a famine caused by drought and the grain demands of Qing armies; he decided to open the military granaries in the province and provide relief to those who needed it. Normally, this would have required imperial permission, but Bian reasoned that waiting four or five months for communications to travel the nearly 17,000 li to and from the capital would be like waiting for permission to fight a fire, and he therefore acted on his own authority. He also ordered the dredging of the Yuan River, the main waterway to Hunan, in order to improve river transport. He dispatched Guizhou troops to find and execute the Yongli emperor. The court approved of all these actions, and in 1663, Bian was appointed the first governor-general of Yunnan and Guizhou.[10]

The post proved to be his downfall, for it placed him squarely in the middle of the conflict developing between Wu Sangui and the Qing court. All though the south, this conflict tore governors' careers apart, but the pressures were greater and fell sooner on Bian Sanyuan, who resided in the same city with Wu and was under orders from the central government to follow Wu's directives. In the summer of 1677, Wu tested the new emperor's mettle by submitting the first of several resignations, complaining that he was tired and suffered from an eye injury. Injuries to eyes and feet, which could prevent one from doing one's duty but were not usually life-threatening, were often given as reasons for resignation by officials with more complex motives. In 1677, all probably recognized the process of testing that was going on, but none could acknowledge it directly. Initially, the court seemed to call Wu's bluff by issuing an edict accepting the resignation. At this point, Bian Sanyuan memorialized asking the court to reverse its decision and urge Wu to take up his position again. Bian wrote:

> The Prince Who Pacifies the West has labored hard in the affairs of our two provinces, exerting himself to the fullest to pursue bandits and open up new territories with notable success. Now he wishes to resign in order to rest. Our Monarch, cherishing old officials and concerned for the Prince's health, has accepted the Prince's resignation.
>
> Your servant remembers that Yunnan and Guizhou were occupied by the perfidious bandit Li Dingguo for twenty years.[11] Then the heavenly dignity of our founding emperor was made known, and Manchu princes were sent together with the Prince Who Pacifies the West to advance along three routes and conquer the southwest. The exertions of the army over several years and countless amounts of money were expended, and finally the great blessing of a unified empire was achieved. Our founding emperor thereupon appointed the Prince Who Pacifies the West to oversee all the affairs of Yunnan. Later, he received another charge from your majesty to oversee the affairs of Guizhou. In these last years, the Prince has given your court little cause for concern as it faced the west.
>
> Yunnan and Guizhou are lands of myriad mountains. The Chinese are few and the Miao are many. Although rivers flow west and east, there are several spots where we can change their banks and guide their flow. The various indigenous peoples of the area are still uncivilized, and their strange natures have not yet warmed to our presence. They have just begun to turn their backs on the mountain retreats and mitigate their former wildness. If we relax our vigilance over the people on the border, the effect on the troops [guarding the border] cannot be predicted.
>
> Now I have received the rescript announcing that the emperor has accepted the generalissimo's resignation, and I fear that those inside will scheme craftily and those outside will spy stealthily. I have been given the heavy responsibility of governing the two southwestern provinces. I fear that if in the future there is a misstep, I will be reprimanded for not having spoken earlier. I beg your majesty to have a care for the unpredictability of the borderlands. Request that the Prince resume his former position as generalissimo, so that he may coordinate defense in the future and we may hold the borders secure. If in a few more years, the Prince once again submits his resignation, it will not be too late to accept it.[12]

The language of this letter was certainly oblique, as neither Bian nor the emperor could admit that Wu was testing the dynasty, but it was probably not purely partisan in intent. Weaving his themes together elegantly, Bian first appealed to the respect the emperor and his courtiers had for the institutional arrangements that had made the conquest of the southwest possible, reminding them of Wu's successes and his repeated appointments. Bian also calls the court's attention to the precariousness of Qing rule in the southwest, the work that remained to be done if the Qing were truly to be able to govern there, and subtly alludes to the possibility of an uprising among the Qing armies. Whatever the state of Bian's relationship with Wu Sangui, his descriptions of the reality of government in the southwest have the ring of sincerity. The letter at least proved persuasive enough that the Kangxi emperor, rather grudgingly, announced that Wu should continue to coordinate border defenses in Yunnan and Guizhou. As the emperor wrote, "because his health and strength were failing, [Wu Sangui] requested relief. I granted this request. Now affairs in the southwest are fairly peaceful. If I order Wu to resume his duties, I fear he will overexert himself and his strength will fail him completely. Nonetheless, if there are military matters in the region, let Wu Sangui manage them."[13]

In the next year, however, pressures mounted on Bian. In addition to the difficulties of governing the southwest and appeasing Wu Sangui, there were also familial demands. According to a memorial Bian submitted to the emperor in the fall of 1668, his mother had written him complaining of illness and declaring that her eyes could not close peacefully until he returned to her side. It is possible that Bian's mother was truly in decline. But it was also possible that a politically astute mother, sensing danger to her son, took advantage of her motherly prerogatives to summon her son out of harm's way. Or, conversely, a politically astute son saw in his mother's pleas an opportunity to make a sanctioned exit from what was becoming an impossible situation. Either way, filial obligations were trumps in Chinese politics, and the Kangxi emperor granted Bian's request. Bian retired from active service to the dynasty and lived the remaining twenty-eight years of his life at home. During this period, he saw his son rise through the ranks of the territorial service to an appointment as governor of Fujian from 1690 to 1696. When Bian Sanyuan died in 1696, he was canonized and eulogized by the emperor.[14]

All seemed to have worked out well for the Bians, until the Qianlong emperor lowered the boom. In 1781, while perusing the records of the Wu Sangui Rebellion, the emperor came across the story of Bian Sanyuan. Noting that Bian's was the most forceful of the memorials supporting Wu Sangui, the emperor concluded that Bian had been Wu's "servant" (*yong ren*). Then, according to the emperor, once Wu Sangui's rebellion began to reveal itself, Bian took the pretext of his mother's illness to retire and protect himself. Fortunately, the emperor asserted, the cowardly and perfidious Bian was long dead. But to set the historical record straight, he ordered the Kangxi emperor's eulogy of Bian destroyed and the canonization rescinded. The emperor offered no evidence for his reading of the record, and his edict seems to have been a totally gratuitous act, not directed at any official or group of officials. But it may have been precisely because no one was hurt by the edict that the emperor issued it, for it provided him a relatively cost-free way of asserting "in assessing the accomplishments and guilt of all officials, I am fair and consistent."[15] This remark would have been appropriately directed at his own faction-ridden court, and it would appear that the eighteenth-century emperor was using an example from an era when loyalties were larger than life in order to address his own era of epigones.

Bian was probably very glad he had gotten out of the southwest when he did. In the first half of 1671, the governors of Yunnan and Guizhou resigned; two years later, two governors surrendered, one was killed, one fled from his post, and one was taken prisoner. Between 1674 and 1678, no governors were appointed to the southwestern provinces.[16] New governors were appointed in 1679 when Qing armies reached the borders of Yunnan and Guizhou, but the postings proved to be rather optimistic, for it took Qing forces two years to battle their way into the province, following the route Wu Sangui had traveled twenty years earlier. When the armies finally did reach Yunnanfu and Wu Sangui's son committed suicide in December 1681, the two provinces were put under the control of Cai Yurong, the bannerman commander of Qing forces in the southwest.[17]

In the autumn of 1681, Cai submitted ten memorials to the court in his new capacity as governor-general of Yungui, offering an elaborate plan for restoring order in the southwest.[18] Some of his proposals were directed at immediate problems, while others looked further ahead, but all of the proposals suggested how much had to be done in the region before it could be fully incorporated in the Qing empire. In his first memorial, Cai warned the court not to expect much revenue from the new provinces, declaring that until lands were reclaimed and the damages of eight years of warfare repaired, taxes would have to be forgiven. Actually, even more than eight years of damage needed to be undone, since the southwest likely had not fully recovered from Wu Sangui's campaigns by the time of his rebellion.

Cai's next proposals dealt with defeated forces still on the loose. In his second memorial, he recommended that the titles Wu Sangui had given to native chieftains in order to secure their allegiance should be rescinded when they pledged allegiance to the new government. Cai was not advocating changes in the system, which he found to be a satisfactory way of dealing with a knotty problem, nor was he suggesting that individuals be removed, although he did believe that those who were found guilty of disloyalty should be judged by Qing authority.[19] His third memorial argued that the bannermen who had served Wu Sangui had to be found; those who willingly surrendered were to be rewarded, and those who continued to hide were to be punished. As late as the 1720s, some of the Chinese bannermen who were garrisoned in Canton identified themselves as "old banner-men," that is, descendants of those who had served Wu Sangui.

Cai's next proposal was among his most interesting, for it embodied his under-standing of the region's economic future. He contended that agrarian produce and taxation in the southwest could never support the number of troops neces-sary to hold the region. The wealth of the southwestern provinces lay in their mountains and the metals contained therein. The people should be encouraged to mine these metals under official supervision, and the state should establish mints at selected sites in Yunnan where raw ores could be made into currency. Cai also proposed that the estates of the Mu family, collaborators of the first Ming emperor who had been given large territories and hereditary political rights in Yunnan, be seized and operated by the Qing state. In much the same way, the hereditary estates of Ming princes in north China had been converted into lands supporting Manchu banner units there.[20]

Before the economic potential of the region could be realized, it was neces-sary to deal with the large groups among the southwestern population who were caught between banditry and order. Cai's fifth memorial described the people on the borders who had nominally followed Wu Sangui but had fled before the rebel-lion was under way and proposed that they be forgiven. The bands of brigands who were holed up in the mountains presented a somewhat more complex situa-tion. Originally, the native chieftains had controlled these bands, but Wu Sangui had given them titles and incorporated them into his forces. These groups had to be found and instructed on the new political order. In his seventh memorial, Cai proposed confiscating the stores of weapons held in private hands and forbid-ding Chinese to sell saltpeter, niter, and gunpowder in the region, both necessary if the policies proposed in his fifth and sixth memorials were to work.

Finally, since the southwestern provinces had very few grain reserves, Cai rec-ommended in the eighth memorial that wealthy individuals who contributed grain to provincial treasuries be rewarded with official titles and minor offices, a fairly common practice in the far south in the middle and late Kangxi periods. Only when all this was accomplished could the Qing return to what Cai saw as the proper tasks of government, which he described in his ninth memorial as reclaiming lands, encouraging agriculture, establishing bao-jia units, facilitating trade, encourag-ing thrift, carrying out moral instruction, and establishing local institutions that did not make undue demands on local populations.[21] Even here, however, much work remained to be done repairing local yamens and academies—and presumably bridges, roads, and embankments as well. His tenth memorial asserted the necessity of rebuilding local schools destroyed in the rebellion.

This was a fairly tall order. But just as the court was considering Cai's proposals, more requests arrived, for an increase in the number of troops under his command and for permission to use these forces against the people of the southwest, whom the Chinese called "Miao." This term had been used in a variety of different ways in Chinese history, originally as a general appellation for foreigners and later as a term for a specific ethnic group. Its members were non-Chinese people, or at least they spoke non-Chinese languages, a variety of different local patois. Modern linguistic analysts have divided the dialects into three broad families with twelve subdialects and much regional variation. Although Chinese officials conventionally referred to the Miao as one people, recent scholarship has complicated the picture.[22] Groups that became the Miao probably lived originally in central China but moved to south China under the pressure of Chinese population growth; other such groups moved to Southeast Asia, where they became known by the name they call themselves, the Hmong or Hmu. The Miao were mountain dwellers, but not necessarily by choice. As Jenks has observed, they easily lived in river valleys and practiced settled agriculture when political and landholding arrangements permitted. They were, however, fairly insular, residing in stockades behind wooden fences (known as *zhai*), separated from an outside world they regarded as hostile. The Miao would have had several grievances against the Qing and the Chinese in general in the late seventeenth century. There was, first, the matter of the titles that had been proffered by Wu Sangui and then rescinded by the Qing conquerors. But these were only a symptom of the larger problem of unscrupulous Chinese merchants and officials exploiting the Miao. At this level, of course, the Miao had every right to blame Chinese in-migrants, and the military force and political establishment that supported Chinese settlers, for their own precarious situation on the cliffs and mountainsides of the southwest. All Chinese officials who served in the southwest knew of the dangers of the Miao. Bian Sanyuan had written of native peoples, noting that "their strange natures have not yet warmed to our presence." Cai Yurong spoke somewhat more threateningly of bands of brigands assembled in the mountains who needed instruction.

It was perhaps not surprising under these circumstances that Cai wanted to use military force against the Miao, but the prospect set off alarm bells in Beijing. The Qing had not spent eight years and nearly lost their empire fighting one military satrap in the southwest only to turn around and authorize another to build up forces. The Kangxi emperor consistently favored a strategy of appeasement, even objecting to Cai Yurong's proposal that weapons held in private hands should be seized, because it seemed to the emperor that this would interfere with the local peoples' need to hunt in order to support themselves.[23] In 1685, the emperor rejected one of Cai's requests for military support, arguing: "The Miao and the Man[24] have a simple nature. They would not dare to provoke an incident. It is only because local officials treat them unfairly, demanding horses and money without limit that [the Miao], having no way to meet these extortionate demands, rebel. In the past the rebel Wu Sangui also made such demands. . . . I fear that the present case is like this."[25] What the emperor said had the ring of truth to it, but the imperial stance put local officials in an impossible position. Confronted with an incident with the Miao, an official could report it and risk being accused of having provoked it. Or, if the official ignored the incident or attempted to respond with inadequate resources, he would be blamed for the breakdown of local order. This was, to be sure, the classic dilemma of local officials confronted with violence throughout the Qing. But it was particularly acute in the southwest, where distance made consultation with the capital almost impossible, local disorder arose from causes little understood in the capital, and an inflexible communications system left scant room for nuance.

Because of the history of the region, miscommunications could be dangerous, evoking memories of past missteps. Cai Yurong perhaps found it ominous when he was compared implicitly to Wu Sangui in the edict of 1685 quoted above. The comparison was made more painfully explicit when he returned to Beijing in 1686 and found himself charged with arrogating authority to himself as governor-general. The final blow came when Cai was charged with taking Wu Sangui's granddaughter as his concubine, found guilty, and sentenced to execution. The emperor commuted the sentence to exile in Heilongjiang, where Cai remained until he died in 1698.

Ortai and the Palace Memorial System

The non-Chinese peoples of the southwest certainly posed a problem for the Qing; however, had the dynasty's systems for delegating authority and communicating among bureaucracies worked properly, China's conquerors would have been more capable of addressing it. During the Kangxi reign history, distance and memory interfered with these vital functions in the southwest. In the succeeding Yongzheng reign, however, radical changes were made in southwest administration: the dynasty set out to dismantle the system of native chieftains through which non-Chinese peoples of the southwest had been governed since the Chinese had developed a significant presence in the region. The goal of this reform was to put non-Chinese peoples directly under the control of dynastic officials, thereby eliminating a layer of authority and possible confusion in local administration.

Several factors were behind this change. As the dynasty developed its governing structure in the southwest, it relied, as Cai Yurong had predicted, on mining revenues, and the mountain-dwelling Miao often stood in the way of the exploitation of mineral resources. Throughout his reign, the Yongzheng emperor distrusted the special status various ethnic groups, including, incidentally, the Manchus, held in the Qing empire and the opportunities for corruption and maladministration that came with the arrangement. He was also an emperor of extraordinarily activist inclinations, who found in Ortai, the future governor-general of the southwest, a commander he could trust. But perhaps as important was the development of a new medium of communication, the palace memorial system, through which the emperor exchanged private communications with governors and governors-general throughout the empire. These memorials have been widely used and studied in Chinese-, English-, and Japanese-language scholarship. The studies have emphasized quite correctly the power these new sources of information and control afforded the emperor. But the new vehicles also added to the powers of governors and governors-general, at least in the Yongzheng reign, insofar as the memorials afforded them a direct line to the ultimate center of all authority in the Chinese political order, the emperor. In no region of the empire was this change more apparent, nor did it produce more tangible results, than in the southwest under the governor-generalship of Ortai.

Palace memorials were most effective as a means of communication when the emperor and his official correspondent had established some sort of personal relationship. In the case of Ortai, governor and future emperor probably met when the Yongzheng emperor was still a prince and Ortai was a relatively humble bodyguard. As the eighteenth-century poet Yuan Mei subsequently told the story, the prince summoned Ortai and asked him to perform some unspecified service. Ortai refused on the grounds that bodyguards owe their allegiance to the emperor, not to a prince. Later, when the former prince became the emperor, he remembered Ortai's integrity and loyalty to the emperor and specially requested his service. This story has the character of a legend; if Yuan Mei heard it from Ortai while studying the Manchu language at the Hanlin Academy, the event would have taken place eighteen years earlier.[26] However the two met, they would have had much reason to cultivate each other. They were exactly the same age. Ortai was from a relatively poor family, and his father had been in retirement for fifteen years at the time Ortai entered Qing service; for him, the only way out of a lifetime of obscurity in the imperial bodyguard was some form of imperial patronage. As the ruling monarch and presumably as a prince, the Yongzheng emperor was constantly on the lookout for relatively junior officials on whom he could rely to tell him about those senior court officials he distrusted.

The bond the emperor formed with Ortai in the early 1720s was the basis for the monarch's decision in late 1724 to appoint the young bodyguard to one of the most delicate positions in the empire, the post of lieutenant governor for Jiangsu. Ortai so impressed the emperor in this post that the ruler described him as the most capable lieutenant governor in the empire. This characterization was communicated to Ortai in a particularly flattering way. The emperor used the language in an audience with a newly appointed lieutenant governor of Zhejiang and ordered the new appointee to stop off in Suzhou on his way to Zhejiang and publicly repeat the laudatory words.[27] In the autumn of 1726, the emperor selected Ortai for promotion and appointed him governor of Guangxi. By the time Ortai reached Beijing for his predeparture audience, the emperor had become so dissatisfied with the Yun-gui governor-general that he changed Ortai's appointment and made him governor of Yunnan with concurrent responsibilities as governor-general of Yun-gui. Ortai left the capital for the southwest on 4 January 1727. He must have gotten sick shortly after his departure, and some medicine the emperor sent for him caught up with his party in Hupei. Ortai dispatched a brief memorial on 21 January thanking the emperor both for the medicine and for the favor of an imperial audience and reporting that his health had improved. He presumably spent the Chinese New Year in Xiangyang, arrived at the border of Yunnan in late February, and took up his seal of office on 4 March 1726.[28]

Although a bodyguard by birth, Ortai had never commanded troops or formulated military strategy before his arrival in Yunnan, and he had served but two years in the territorial service, in a post very different from the one he now occupied. What Ortai had going for him when he arrived in Yunnan was that rarest of commodities in the early eighteenth century, the trust of the Yongzheng emperor.[29] The problem for Ortai was how to sustain that trust through war and peace from a distance of 17,000 li. In this, the palace memorial system served Ortai extraordinarily well. The record of his memorials preserved in *Memorials Endorsed in Vermilion from the Yongzheng Reign* (Yongzheng zhupi yuzhi), which Ortai himself edited, was meant as a model for the use of memorials. Unlike the governors and governors-general of north China, who had the luxury (or perhaps the burden, depending on the circumstances) of being able to memorialize the throne whenever the need arose, once every fortnight or even weekly, governors south of the Yangzi usually memorialized once a month.[30] Each month, between four and eight memorials dealing with different topics were enclosed in a sealed box and entrusted to a memorial servant who made the journey to the capital. On the return trip, the servant would carry back to the governor rescripted memorials, that is, memorials with the emperor's personal comments written on them in vermilion ink. Usually, however, the servant brought back not the same memorials he had carried to the capital but the previous month's submissions. This meant that Ortai and other southwestern governors could not expect a response

TABLE 9.1. Communications between Ortai and the Emperor

Period	Average Number of Memorials	Ortai to Emperor, Average Length	Emperor to Ortai, Average Length
1726:			
1 June–30 December	4.5	3,000	450
1728:			
1 June–30 December	6.3	9,000	670
1731:			
1 January–30 June 1731	5.1	5,700	240

Source: *Yongzheng zhupi yuzhi*, 2583–2622, 2736–2866, 2972–3003.

Note: Character counts are estimates, rounded to the nearest hundred. Because the conventions of memorial writing resulted in large amounts of blank space, the number of characters was estimated for each page and the sums for all pages were totaled.

from the emperor for three and a half months. These delays allowed ample time for the careful consideration of messages. On 21 April 1726, Ortai was ordered to communicate with Yue Zhongqi about a military operation that was being prepared along the Yunnan-Sichuan border. In a memorial of 14 October, Ortai informed the emperor that he had written the letter; the emperor commented that Yue had moved to the northern part of the province to deal with another matter. On 23 January 1728, Ortai acknowledged receipt, as it were, of Yue's new address and told the emperor that he was awaiting Yue's reply.[31]

Of the four to eight memorials dispatched in an average month, one was usually a memorial expressing Ortai's thanks for the comments written on previous memorials. Two or three more were usually descriptions of the military situation in the southwest, and there might be one or two memorials each on financial or personnel matters. The memorials in a single submission usually did not refer to one another, suggesting that the submissions were not prepared as a single monthly report, although a group of memorials certainly could have been tailored to reinforce one another.[32] Nonetheless, a month's memorials represented a considerable literary effort. Table 9.1 compares Ortai's and the emperor's memorials for three six-month periods during Ortai's term in the southwest. The three periods detailed in the table are the last six lunar months of the first and third years of Ortai's service and the first six lunar months of his last full year of service, which should allow comparison of Ortai's communications early and late in his term as well as during peace and war.

The volume of writing here is daunting. By contrast, Bian Sanyuan's letter to the Kangxi emperor urging Wu Sangui's reappointment, translated in full above, is 287 characters long. The Kangxi emperor's response, 88 characters long, is the only imperial pronouncement regarding the southwest written during that month. To translate the length into slightly different terms, if one were to take, as a conservative estimate, the conversion factor of one character equaling two English-language words, Ortai's monthly memorials to the emperor would constitute a fifty-page report.

Much was surely said in this river of verbiage, but what was actually communicated, and what did emperor and governor take from the communications? In some respects, the most revealing memorials were the thank-you notes, which were always printed first among the monthly batch of memorials in *Memorials Endorsed in Vermilion*. In addition to acknowledging the receipt of rescripts, these memorials also contain personal messages from the emperor and Ortai, descriptions of the ceremony with which memorials were received in Yunnanfu, and lists of gifts the emperor sent to Ortai with each group of returned memorials. The personal greetings are of the sort two old friends might exchange after an absence of moderate duration, questions about health, family matters, and recent life events. In July 1726, for instance, Ortai thanked the emperor for permitting the betrothal of his cousin to Prince Yi, the emperor's brother, an event he had heard of from his family in Beijing. The emperor responded that he was delighted their two families would be joined and regretted that Ortai had not had a chance to meet the prince before starting off for the southwest.[33] Three months later, Ortai acknowledged receipt of a rescript in which the emperor told him that the imperial health was much improved and expressed some satisfaction that whereas those in the capital could see the emperor's good health for themselves, Ortai was among the few to learn about it directly from the emperor.[34] This might have been hyperbole, but the implication certainly was that written communications with the emperor were more reliable and intimate than oral ones. As Ortai was away from the capital longer and was drawn more into the affairs of the southwest, the greetings became slightly less intimate, but the friendly tone remained. In the summer of 1728, Ortai reported with regret the loss of Qing officers in a battle that had gone badly for the dynasty's forces. In 1730, Ortai reported to the emperor that he had returned safely from a journey and thanked the emperor for his support.

Ortai's memorials to the emperor thus preserve some of the character of personal letters, but the very fact that they could be exchanged is of considerable significance. It would, of course, have been a serious breach of confidence for Ortai to reveal to other officials the contents of any of the memorials he received. But he could and did, rather theatrically as it appears, reveal to other officials that he was in contact with the emperor. According to language that is repeated in each of the thank-you memorials, when the bearer of imperial rescripts arrived in the southwest and presented his precious cargo, Ortai would set up an altar in his yamen and burn incense to commemorate the event. Then, he, the governor-general of the southwest, one of the most senior and favored officials in the empire, would kowtow to the altar in gratitude for the communications. This kowtow was most assuredly not the mark of slavish subservience European observers took it to be when they saw it performed in the later eighteenth century. In the first place, Ortai was kowtowing not to a person but to an inanimate object, an altar. To be sure, this altar represented the emperor, but it also represented the power of the Chinese emperorship to unite officials and subjects across the vast distances the Qing controlled. The location of the ceremony was never specified, beyond the report that these acts had taken place in the governor-general's yamen in Yunnanfu or in the quarters he occupied while traveling, but this ceremony likely occurred in at least a semipublic setting, where other officials could observe it. For them, the fact that Ortai had received communications from the emperor surely marked him as a figure of both power and legitimate authority. Moreover, Ortai's act of physical obeisance, three bowings and nine prostrations, surely also identified him as an official committed body and soul to the imperial service.

The corporeal tie between Ortai and the emperor was reinforced by the gifts the emperor sent to the governor-general. Some of these were precious objects that might be collected by a prominent official family—precious stones, sable furs, porcelain from the imperial kilns, and bolts of silk from the imperial manufactories. But in almost every batch, at least one of the gifts was edible and usually reflected the season. In the summer, there were pills and elixirs concocted in the imperial pharmacy, sent perhaps to ward off the fevers of a rainy, subtropical climate. In the late summer, there were fruits—lychees, Hami melons, or tangerines—which were presumably dried or otherwise preserved for their long journey and also several kinds of tea. For New Year's, Ortai received what seems to have been the standard imperial New Year's gift, a piece of deer meat, and one year, he also received the deer's tail. In the spring, there were various kinds of pastries. The memorials did not record how, or indeed whether, these items were consumed, although they almost certainly were used in some way.

More interesting is the very fact that they were sent, not once but repeatedly. In a broad sense, these gifts surely expressed metaphorically the notion that it was the monarch's duty to nourish his officials and that all officials partook in some sense of the emperor's bounty. But clearly, food also had a ritual meaning in China, as it was incorporated in the official sacrifices that marked the monarch's official year. Angela Zito has argued persuasively that in these ceremonies, the emperor and his officials were analogized to the ritual vessels, both consecrated to service of the dynasty and the ancestors. Indeed, the metaphor of the official as a vessel was very common in the Qing order, with weak or incapable officials described as "narrow and shallow" vessels and more capable officials represented as more capacious vessels. In this sense, the emperor had an appropriate concern not only with the body of officials but with the officials' bodies, for these were the instruments he used to offer sacrifice to his ancestors and the gods. Therefore, the gifts of food had a personal as well as a ritual significance, as perhaps did the thank-you notes in general.

Much of Ortai's writing as governor concerned military matters, and changes in the amount of information passing between Beijing and Yunnanfu reflected changes in the military situation.[35] During the first period shown in table 9.1, Ortai was dealing with the aftermath of a relatively limited engagement with the Zhongjia Miao in central Guizhou, his first such experience in his service in the region. In the second period, he was directing open fighting in the two greatest expeditions in the southwest, the conquest of the Bawan-Guzhou area in southeastern Guizhou and a war against the Yi people of northeastern Yunnan. There was no actual fighting in the third period, 1 January to 30 June 1731, when Ortai was concerned with building new structures of civilian government in the conquered areas.[36]

Battlefield Reports

The longest of Ortai's memorials in the first and second periods were descriptions of military engagements. These documents were not dispatched from the front, for Ortai often was nowhere near the front. He did, of course, make trips to disputed areas. During one tour in the autumn of 1728, he quite fortuitously received the surrender of one of the principal native chieftains of northeastern Yunnan.[37] In the autumn of 1730, Ortai made another trip of at least two month's duration from Yunnanfu through Guizhou and into Guangxi and submitted a long memorial to the emperor, describing his trip and the officials he visited on the way.[38] But most often, Ortai and other governors wrote their battle reports from provincial capitals, creating narratives out of their subordinates' reports. They did this knowing full well that other provincial officials in other capitals were crafting their own narratives, often with different underlying messages. All of these accounts were submitted to that ultimate and fabulously fickle critic the Yongzheng emperor.

The main issue in Ortai's early years was the question of how to deal with the non-Han peoples of the region. This was not new; it underlay most of the communications from Yunnanfu to Beijing in the early Qing. Chinese empires traditionally had controlled native peoples of the southwest by appointing native chieftains to govern and collect tax obligations from their own people; such positions were held for life and were often hereditary.[39] This system had suited the Chinese well through much of the late imperial period; so long as the central government's goal was a secure military flank in the region, rule through hereditary chieftains, controlled loosely by a long-term military representative of the center, such as Wu Sangui or members of the Mu family, proved both effective and inexpensive. As soon as the central government proposed to rule as well as reign in the southwest, however, native chieftains began to get in the way. Chieftains' militias could challenge the dynasty's monopoly of military force in the region and could also physically obstruct the infrastructural projects—roads, river works, mines, and garrisons—undertaken to make the area governable. Chieftains' disputes with one another and their conflicts and collusions with Chinese merchants and officials could require military interventions to protect the very people the chieftains were governing. As early as the first days of his reign, the Yongzheng emperor meditated on his obligations to the native peoples of the southeast, and called for officials to provide advice on how these obligations could be fulfilled.

Broadly, there were two strategies for dealing with the native chieftains. On the one hand, the dynasty could employ its military force to suppress non-Han challenges to its rule, eliminating native chieftains and occupying their territories, as Cai Yurong and Ortai's predecessor Gao Qizhuo had proposed. On the other hand, the Qing state could attempt to exercise moral suasion, endeavoring to reach natives through education and indoctrination, as the Kangxi emperor had attempted to do in the last years of his reign.

In the 1720s, each strategy was associated with a particular official. The project of military activism was represented by a young Chinese bannerman named Shi Liha, acting governor of Guizhou at the time of Ortai's arrival in the southwest, whose father Shi Wenzhuo was then governor of Gansu. Shi was likely also related to Shi Wensheng, who had served as governor of Yunnan from 1694 to 1704, and through him to a number of distinguished bannermen active in the Qing conquest.[40] Shi Liha had previously served as the Guizhou provincial military commandant, in which capacity he had developed plans for extending the dynasty's military control in the region. Shi's views were seconded by the military intendant for Guizhou, Ma Huibo, a commander who had passed first in the nation on the military *jinshi* examinations of 1699 and served creditably in the late Kangxi campaigns in Tibet.[41]

The educational strategy was represented by He Shiqi, who was appointed Guizhou governor in late 1725. He had been a local educational official in his native province of Shandong for a number of years before earning his *jinshi* degree in 1708. He then served for eleven years at the Hanlin Academy before receiving appointments to provincial examiner in Shaanxi and Zhejiang and salt commissioner of Liang-huai.[42] It may seem incongruous that the Yongzheng emperor would appoint such a specialist in the examination system and Confucian ideology to a post where minority peoples outnumbered Chinese and military action loomed. But as one aspect of its policy in the southwest, the Qing claimed it was bringing the benefits of Confucian governance to the uneducated minorities of the region. The building of schools and the appointment of a full contingent of civil officials accompanied military expansion in Yunnan and particularly Guizhou.[43] He Shiqi embodied this commitment and was well prepared to preside over the educational efforts the dynasty was undertaking in the southwest. Perhaps imperialism always has a dual face, but in China, the two sides of imperialist conquest were reflected in two different personalities.

Conflict between the Qing's educational and military missions in the southwest was not long in coming. Sometime in late 1725, the Miao of central Guizhou began to obstruct the process of empire building by burning military garrisons, blockading passes, and flogging and then releasing naked an official who had come to parley with them. Considering that naked force could accomplish more than naked Confucians in the valleys of Guizhou, Shi Liha and Ma Huibo advocated using the military to reopen the passes and punish the Miao. He Shiqi opposed this course, making time-honored Confucian arguments against the use of military force. Specifically, he argued that there were both good and bad elements among the Miao, and any broad-scale military expedition would punish both elements equally. Once imperial policies were fully explained and the emperor's benevolent intent proclaimed, He felt that the matter could be resolved without bloodshed. The emperor responded that in all matters He Shiqi should listen to the opinions of Ortai and seek to inspire in the Miao an appropriate mean between benevolence and fear.[44]

Both Shi Liha and He Shiqi wrote letters to the governor-general explaining their positions and requesting a judgment. Ortai effected a compromise. Reasoning that it made no sense to punish the Miao until policies were explained, he ordered military officials to approach the natives and explain what the dynasty was about. Five or six meetings were indeed held at five-li intervals along the main road, and about fifty or sixty people attended each. In the event this effort did not succeed, Ortai also ordered that 2,700 troops from Yunnan and Guizhou be readied should any Miao fail to get the message. Eventually, these troops were ordered to march into the Zhongjia region and "subdued" the Miao in the early summer of 1726. In practice, compromise may not have achieved much. The distinction between a punitive expedition carried out before as opposed to after they had heard an explanation of the Qing mission civilisatrice was probably lost on the Miao themselves. Nonetheless, by the late summer of 1726, quiet reigned among the Zhongjia Miao, and Ortai's policy seemed to have succeeded.[45]

In his support of Ortai, the emperor was sanctioning a course of action that he had been unwilling to endorse when earlier officials had proposed it. In part, the emperor was willing to do this because he had an ongoing relationship with the former bodyguard, nurtured by the monthly exchange of greetings, gifts, and official communications. Both John Herman and Kent Smith have argued that Ortai had the remarkable ability to say exactly what the emperor needed to hear and to justify his actions in precisely the way the emperor was most likely to find acceptable.[46] Such an ability could not have been maintained over time and distance without regular communications. Ortai's presence may also have provided the emperor with a way out of a complex political situation. Shi Liha and Ma Huibo, on the one hand, and He Shiqi, on the other, represented elements of the Qing imperium that the Yongzheng emperor could not afford to alienate. Shi represented the Chinese banner elite, the military force that sustained the Qing conquest of the south and in the 1720s was still largely responsible for its governance. Ma Huibo had likely served under Nian Gengyao, the extremely powerful commander of Qing forces in the northwest. He Shiqi was representative of the examination-taking Chinese elite and stood for a strategy associated with the Kangxi emperor. For the Yongzheng emperor to have sided with either one of these groups would have been a perilous political statement; from the very earliest days of his reign, he had emphasized the need for the military and civilian arms of the Qing to work together. However, the conflict between the banner order and civilian administrators could only be resolved by Manchu central authority. The emperor could endorse the findings of Ortai, a Manchu whose proximity to the monarch was evidenced by monthly boxes of memorials and regular gifts. In fact, relying on Ortai provided the monarch a very convenient solution to a political dilemma that played itself out in regions of the empire that few in Beijing knew well.

The emperor emphasized Ortai's unique ability to reconcile the conflicts in the southwest when he rescripted Ortai's memorial announcing military action:

> Recently, Ma Huibo memorialized about this matter to me, and I feared he was too impetuous. Later, when He Shiqi's memorial arrived, I feared he was too timid. I was just becoming anxious, but when I received this memorial of yours, I began to relax. I knew that you could manage the situation. We must hit the mean.
>
> Once this matter is settled, you should memorialize requesting military honors for Shi Liha. I have already ordered him transferred to be the brigade general at Canton but will order him to delay taking up his post until the matter in Guizhou is concluded.[47]

The formula Ortai and the emperor first devised in 1726 proved to be a template for solutions to other problems in the southwest. In actions in northeastern Yunnan in 1727–30, in the territory known as Sipsongbanna in the summer of

1727, and in the Guwan-Bazhou region of southeastern Guizhou in 1728–29, the emperor endorsed Ortai's activist strategy, and military action followed, so that areas formerly controlled by native chieftains were incorporated into the Qing regular administration. The emperor was not supporting military activism per se. Neither Ortai nor the Yongzheng emperor was a military strategist, and the plans they adopted were often flawed. In 1726, Ortai's delay in sending in troops meant that fighting occurred during the summer rainy season in the southwest, which made the campaign slower and more difficult.[48] Ortai often underestimated resistance to his actions, campaigns wound up taking longer and cost more than he expected and produced results that were less than satisfactory. What the emperor valued in Ortai was his ability to represent the authority of the throne in a complex and troubled corner of the realm. Such a role was inconceivable without the close communication afforded by the palace memorial system.

Personnel and Finance

While Ortai's memorials did not give the emperor the capacity to control Qing forces on the battlefield, they did enable him to exercise with far more sophistication and discernment prerogatives that were obviously within his purview, control of budgets and appointments. In the distant and little-known southwest, where the emperor had to rely on local officials to survey resources and manage budgets, personnel issues were apparently more important that financial matters, although both were clearly a part of the picture. Madeleine Zelin has demonstrated the Yongzheng emperor's interest in budgets and financial matters, which was, in both quality and degree, different from that of his predecessors. Indeed, Ortai was well aware of the financial implications of his actions in the southwest. He knew that northeastern Yunnan, where he sent armies in 1728, contained some of the richest veins of copper in the southwest and proposed reforms of mining and copper transport to the emperor.[49] Moreover, in a memorial in which he proposed transforming areas governed by native chieftains into regions of regular administration, he offered as his principal justification the notion that regular taxation of the formerly native regions would significantly increase the amount of grain they could provide to support provincial military and civilian administration.[50] But such arguments were rare in Ortai's memorials, in part perhaps because the Yongzheng emperor himself was uncomfortable with relying on financial need as a justification for military action. Moreover, the emperor felt that the concentrations of miners necessary to exploit mineral resources held the potential for social disorder, a time bomb set to explode when mines ran dry.[51]

The emperor saw the actions in the southwest principally as political reform carried out in response to social and moral imperatives and was inclined to tell

Ortai to spend whatever he needed in order to accomplish his goals. The relationship between these two issues was the subject of a memorial Ortai submitted in 1726, which was rare in that it dealt exclusively with the philosophy of government rather than with its practice.[52] Ortai opened the memorial by declaring that control of "finance" (*cai*) was the central issue for government, on which all other matters depended. In support of his case, Ortai asserted that Confucius "did not avoid" discussing finances but based his discussions on the notion of a "measuring square." In fact, the term Ortai used for "finances" does not appear in *The Analects* of Confucius. It does appear in the tenth chapter of *The Great Learning*, where the idea of a measuring square is also used, though not in reference to financial dealings. Ortai's reference here was not exact, but it appears to have been close enough for government work.[53]

In his memorial, Ortai argues that finances could not be brought under control without the right people to manage them, and therefore the essence of government lay in the selection of people, and its art lay in matching people's talents to locations, situations, and times. Even men of the most modest talents could be employed if the right positions were found for them. These observations touched a deeply resonant chord in the Yongzheng emperor, and indeed their mutual recognition of the importance of appointments may have been one of the forces that bound the emperor and Ortai. As the emperor read the memorial, he highlighted the phrases translated above, beginning with the expression "finance could not be brought under control unless . . . " At the end of the memorial, the emperor wrote one of his longest rescripts to Ortai, some 400 characters in length. In it, he remarked that Ortai's interest in personnel marked him as a great official. But characteristically, the emperor warned his governor-general that individual characters and loyalties could change and that the official who seemed capable and loyal at one moment might prove to be a disaster at another. Possibly, the emperor was warning Ortai that his own loyalties could change, but more likely he was simply asserting that making good appointments was a process that required constant attention.

In this context, discussion of personnel was more than a consideration of accomplishments and evaluations; it also involved consideration of the special skills a person brought to office and whether these skills suited the individual to a position's particular challenges. This was particularly evident in the exchanges between Ortai and the emperor on He Shiqi's suitability for his post in Guizhou. It was clear from the beginning that the emperor had his doubts about He. Shortly after his appointment, He submitted a memorial regretting that he had not had the opportunity for an audience with the emperor before his departure from north China and asked if the monarch had any advice for the new governor. The emperor responded to this request in an edict of some length:

You should not seek to make your reputation while neglecting the public business; you should not pursue personal probity at the expense of the public business. You should not seek safety in precedent, or mistake stirring up trouble for taking political action, or mistake weakness for benevolence. Don't overindulge your subordinates simply to earn their respect. Don't trust the sentiments of friends or the confidences that are offered only to the powerful. Guizhou is a land of limited resources in cash and grain, and [in managing these affairs,] I know you to be a man of integrity and capacity. But in military matters, it is not appropriate to relax your guard. You must devote yourself fully to it, and be encouraging on occasion. Although the Miao and the Man are simple, they are still people. If local government is in order, and carried out with sympathy, then the people will feel gratitude. If military affairs are in order, then the people will know fear, and I can be assured of their permanent allegiance. By no means can you confuse the words "grace" and "fear." If you confuse them, although there may be short-term gain, there will be tragedy in the long run, and this is not the way to form a policy of long-lasting peace.

Be discerning in your choice of subordinates, and don't rely exclusively on products of the examination process while regarding those who reach office by other routes as lesser men of the market. There has never been any single technique for employing people. How can you distinguish between the wise and the foolish on the basis of examinations alone? Be fair in all things, and don't indulge in prejudice.[54]

Some of this edict addresses the failings to which, in the emperor's view, all products of the examination system were particularly susceptible. But the edict also points to the necessity of dealing with both administrative and military matters, inculcating a spirit of both respect and fear in the southwest. The problem was that He Shiqi did not seem to have gotten the emperor's point. Despite his initial defeat on the use of force against the Zhongjia Miao, He Shiqi persisted in his principled opposition to military force in Guizhou. At one point, he even asserted that the military men around him sought only the victories that would earn them commendations and promotions not those that would ensure peace and the welfare of those they governed.

Both Ortai and the emperor began to tire of these protests, with the emperor at one point labeling He Shiqi a "bookish one." By the autumn of 1726, the emperor began to wonder if he had made a mistake in appointing He Shiqi and asked for Ortai's advice.[55] Ortai's response to this suggestion, in a memorial of early 1727, deserves to be considered at some length, because of what it says about the southwest and about governors' appointments there. Both the emperor's inquiry and Ortai's response turned on the question of the proper relationship between "activism" (zhen-zuo) and "administrative routine" (tiao-li) in the southwest. "Could it be," the emperor asked Ortai, "that the administration of the southwest lies precisely in activism?" Was the military and social situation in the southwest sufficiently chaotic that the traditional administrative concerns He Shiqi represented and articulated were inappropriate? Certainly the emperor was questioning He Shiqi's fitness, but he was also raising the larger question of the sort of governance required in a frontier region. In responding to this query, Ortai admitted that matters were still unsettled in the southwest. Owing to poor administration, provincial personnel had long gone unsupervised, taxable lands were unregistered, bandits went unpunished, and miscreants were undetected. But the chaotic conditions were precisely the reason, Ortai argued, that the emperor should continue to retain He Shiqi. In a passage the emperor highlighted, Ortai wrote:

> Although the burdens of activism and routine administration are different, both begin in caution. The ending of a matter must first be fully envisioned, and only then can it be initiated. If an action is fully planned, then it can be carried out over great spans of time and distance. But if one is impetuous in the slightest, then one will be unprepared when the hoped-for advantage is not obtained and defeat arises. If one is going to root out defects but fails, the harm is worse than if one had left matters alone. It goes without saying that He Shiqi is a man of integrity. He is excessively cautious, but he is not without foresight.[56]

Here, Ortai is clearly reassuring the emperor about He Shiqi's fitness, but he also seems to be commenting on the whole Qing enterprise in the southwest. In urging the emperor to leave He Shiqi in place, Ortai was in effect reassuring the monarch that the effort to install traditional Chinese-style administration in the southwest was on the right track. By implementing activist policies in the region, Ortai anticipated that the standard mechanisms of Confucian administration would be put into place. He Shiqi was eventually dismissed, but not because of his military timidity; rather, it was because a prefect in the province claimed that he was not doing his duty in protecting the people and supervising subordinate officials. Ortai supported He even against this charge, which proved to have originated from the prefect's grudge against He, who had not recommended him for promotion. When He returned to Beijing, he was made a member of the Boards of Revenue and Personnel. Upon his death in 1729, he was given the posthumous title of president of the Board of Rites.[57]

Like Bian Sanyuan sixty years before, Ortai defended a southwestern official against the wrath of a distant monarch, and, as with Wu Sangui, the real issue seems to have been how unique the political arrangements of the southwest had to be so that effective government would prevail. Of course, Wu Sangui posed a far greater danger to the Qing empire than did the innocuous if rather obstinate He Shiqi. But certainly both Wu Sangui and He Shiqi had aroused the suspicions of the monarch, and both Bian Sanyuan and Ortai were arguing that existing arrangements for governing the southwest were adequate and did not need revision. But the respective tones and claims of the two memorials reflect the sixty years of province building that had elapsed between Bian's and Ortai's memorials. In the first place, the closer ties between Ortai and the emperor meant that Ortai was in a much stronger position to defend He Shiqi than Bian had been in defending Wu Sangui. Instead of remonstrating with a distant monarch about a decision that had already been made, always a difficult task in an absolute monarchy, Ortai was offering confidential advice to a monarch before any action had been taken. Moreover, since Ortai and the emperor had exchanged views on He Shiqi before, both were aware of the other's attitudes toward the appointee; as in Bian's memorial, much remains unsaid, but much had been said before. Perhaps most important, Ortai's advice that the emperor stay the course with He Shiqi implies that a course had been set for the southwest. This is not to suggest that either Ortai or the emperor knew exactly what was going to happen, or that any specific plan had been drafted. But it was clear that through Ortai's tenure, the southwest would be fully incorporated into the Qing empire. Ortai was not battling a distant warlord but fighting to keep the southwestern world safe for Confucianism.

TOWARD INTEGRATION

Ortai was a remarkable official, unique in his ability to earn and hold imperial confidence for more than a decade. Empowered by this confidence, he was able to lay down the political foundations for a new order in the southwest. There were, of course, social and demographic forces pushing Chinese into the region, and good economic rationales for Qing expansion into its precious-metal-bearing mountains. Much of Ortai's success in maintaining contact with the emperor and governing in the southwest rested, however, on the new medium of communication, the palace memorial, which the Qing developed in the seventeenth century. It was not that the palace memorial allowed for more imperial involvement in political decisions. Distances and the time it took to cross them meant that neither side could wait for the other's response before making a decision. Rather, the emperor and his officials came to know each other's minds through frequent and frank communications, so that necessary decisions could be made and carried through with force and confidence. Unlike Bian Sanyuan, who could express his views about Wu Sangui only in the most oblique language, Ortai and the emperor exchanged fairly frank views about the quality and capacity of southwestern officials. Unlike Cai Yurong, Ortai could couch his proposals in the careful language needed to assure that they would be read in the capital.

The southwestern provinces were not the only jurisdictions affected by new media of communications in the eighteenth century, and Ortai, power broker and emissary extraordinaire that he was, was hardly the only Qing official whose career was transformed by the ability to maintain personal and confidential contact with the emperor. Throughout the empire, after the first quarter of the eighteenth century, palace memorials were used in many of the functions of Qing government. They conveyed to the emperor appraisals of the capacities and failings of local officials and broached policy proposals before they were formally presented. Palace memorials also kept the court informed about local legal cases or pleaded for more resources for law enforcement or relief efforts. Monarchs were put into closer contact with provincial officials everywhere through palace memorials, but the effect of new media of communications was most evident in the southwest. Many of the developments that transformed the rugged southwest in the eighteenth century were ultimately related to the growth in volume and sophistication of communications.

After Ortai's term, the Qing state set about making conscious efforts to build a more effective postal system in the region. Postal stations replaced the crude forts that had served as relay points during the early Qing, and courier services were professionalized.[58] This made it possible for central communication to reach not only the provincial capitals of Yunnanfu and Guiyang but many of the district and prefectural capitals as well. After the 1740s, a new type of communication found its way along the roads to the southwest. In the early Qianlong reign, Zhang Yunsui, probably with the assistance of Ortai and Zhang Tingyu, succeeded in convincing the court to rescind the Yongzheng emperor's ban on new mining.[59] Copper mined in Yunnan and Guizhou began to flow to many provincial capitals, where it was smelted and minted into the coins that would support an increasingly prosperous empire. In the middle of the eighteenth century, palace memorials were used to announce that copper had been shipped from southwestern mines to the capital and that such shipments had passed through crucial checkpoints along the way. These copper shipment memorials had the effect of keeping the court regularly informed about conditions along the roads to the southwest and became one of the most common sorts of documents moving from Yunnan and Guizhou to Beijing.

With increasingly dense communications, the southwest's place in the empire's political imagination evolved. Laura Hostetler has demonstrated that early writings about southwest China had many of the characteristics of European writings about colonies, dwelling on the exotic characteristics of ethnic "others," the very characteristics of indigenes that made rule by the metropolis seem rational and beneficial. Many early Chinese accounts were travel diaries, subject to all the limitations of perspective and perception that afflict such works in all contexts. As Hostettler notes, with the passing of the seventeenth and eighteenth centuries, these writings became not only more detailed but more realistic.[60] One work situated partly between travel accounts and official reports is *On Guizhou* (Qian shu), by Tian Wen, who was governor of the province from 1688 to 1691, after his service as governor of Jiangsu. Tian presented much in his work that would appear in a standard provincial history. He opened with a history of the province, an account of Miao customs, and a list of the types of Miao in the region.[61] Next came accounts of the province's curious geographic features, followed by a series of biographies of prominent individuals from Guizhou, and a final section of short essays on the province's plants, animals, and insects. Much of this could find its way into an official history, but Tian's was still a private account, valued more for the quality of its writing than for its administrative utility.[62]

Toward the end of his term, Ortai began compiling provincial gazetteers for Yunnan and Guizhou. Both volumes were formally presented to the court by Ortai's two successors in the region, Zhang Yunsui in Yunnan and Zhang Guangsi in Guizhou. These two gazetteers differ from those of other areas in minor, though telling ways. Many Yongzheng period gazetteers begin with official documents concerning the province and proceed to an account of local realities, but the *Yunnan Gazetteer* (Yunnan tongzhi) and the *Guizhou Gazetteer* (Guizhou tongzhi) begin with maps and place official documents at the end, as if recognizing the importance of geography and the limited value of central commands to the region's transformation. The two gazetteers also reprint more memorials by southwestern officials and fewer imperial edicts than did many gazetteers. But more important is the fact that the two southwestern histories present information about the region in straightforward, standard terms, so that it could be readily assimilated by potential officials from other parts of the empire. No longer regions described principally in travel accounts, Yunnan and Guizhou were now standard provinces, interchangeable, at least on paper, with other provinces.

As the place of the southwest in the Qing political imagination changed, so did the region's governors. Early Qing governors in the southwest were rather anomalous figures in Qing territorial administration, long-serving plenipotentiaries who combined civilian and military portfolios. Although they were provided with Qing titles, their situations more closely resembled that of Wu Sangui or the members of the Mu family in the Ming than that of other Qing governors. Ortai, for instance, held the title of governor and governor-general simultaneously, from 1727 to 1731, as did his successors Zhang Guangsi, from 1737 to 1747, and Zhang Yunsui, from 1741 to 1750.[63] But following the two Zhangs, no governor would simultaneously hold the title of governor-general. Moreover, unlike Zhang

Guangsi and Zhang Yunsui, who spent their entire careers in the southwest, their successors began to rotate in and out of the province, serving terms that approximated the empirewide norm. Manchus held the governorship of Yunnan, from 1748 until 1755, and of Guizhou, in 1757. After the late 1750s, Chinese and Manchus served as governors of the provinces with no particular bias for either group, except for a brief period during the Burma campaigns of the late 1760s when the posts were held exclusively by Manchus. After 1770, young Chinese and Manchu officials moved in and out of the two provinces as they would for any other province of the empire. Guizhou in fact became a province where a young territorial administrator could expect to receive his first promotion. Guizhou and Yunnan had been sufficiently integrated into the Qing order that they could be governed by the same men and the same means as the empire's other provinces.

Institutional integration did not produce equality in the southwest; perhaps it does not produce genuine equality anywhere. Postings in Guizhou and Yunnan were never as prestigious as those in other provinces, probably because Guizhou and Yunnan governors never controlled the revenues or faced the stream of official visitors that their colleagues elsewhere did.[64] But perhaps the Qing did not aim for absolute equality in the southwest. Initially, dynastic leaders sought merely a secure flank, protection not so much from attacks by indigenous peoples as from the possibility that the dynasty's Chinese enemies could make common cause with disaffected natives. The Kangxi emperor had sought to educate in the southwest, but his notion of education was founded on the assumption of inequality. The Qing in the late seventeenth century brought the benefits of civilization to the uncivilized. The Yongzheng emperor did feel a duty toward his subjects in the southwest, but he sought fairness, not equity, and ultimately his conception of fairness could be achieved only through imposition by Chinese officials. The Qianlong emperor certainly did not see all regions or ethnic groups as equal, inspired as he was by the prospect of universal Manchu monarchy. What the Qing sought in the southwest was efficacy, the confidence that procedures known to work in one part of the empire were applied in all. By the last third of the eighteenth century, the dynasty had achieved this in the rugged southwest, as the Qing territorial order successfully replicated itself in the last corner of the realm.

Conclusion

The development of the territorial service in the Qing is a critical and largely untold story of the dynasty. What began as a rather hasty attempt to fill Ming dynasty territorial posts with men of at least minimal loyalty to the Qing eventually became a flexible and sophisticated system that served the dynasty's needs for nearly three hundred years. The components included a set of provincial boundaries and capitals still used in contemporary China; a system of appointments that allowed for both routine and emergency actions; a ladder of promotions that offered local officials some hope of upward mobility and guaranteed a certain consistency of administration among those who reached the top ranks; the mechanism of special appointment, which allowed for rapid and minimally intrusive central intervention in provincial affairs; and a means for circulating talented administrative personnel from jurisdiction to jurisdiction. Each component had its origins in Chinese history but was developed further by the Qing, not out of any comprehensive design, but as needs arose. The preceding chapters explore the components of the new order and their methods of deployment throughout the Qing empire. But as important as the individual components was their combination, which gave the dynasty a means of responding to the demands of time and space.

Spatial diversity posed one of the greatest challenges to Chinese imperial administration. Stretching from the deserts of Mongolia to the subtropics, encompassing regions heavily and lightly cultivated, densely and sparsely populated, areas that could be held only with significant military presence and areas that responded best to light and distant government, the Qing empire was hardly a homogeneous land. Neither, of course, were its officials, who were originally men of different regional affiliation, capacity, and political inclination. The task of central territorial administration was to incorporate regional difference into a single administrative structure, to manufacture homogeneity—or at least its image—out of diversity. This it did by dispatching different men to different posts. Much of this book consists of comparisons—among regions and of numbers of promotions, intra-province promotions, special appointments, lateral appointments, and the ratios of transfers in to transfers out. This chapter sums up the account of regional difference by pulling together the various indices of provincial difference.

THE CHINESE PROVINCE IN SPACE AND TIME

North China was a land where the Qing, or any Chinese dynasty, could not afford to fail. The region was the heartland of Chinese civilization, and its governors sat astride essential flows of resources, information, and personnel to and from the capital while maintaining order in an ecologically fragile land. North China governors were very visible symbols of the dynasty they served, and perhaps for this reason, governance in the north was usually in the hands of men who had experience in or strong ties to the capital. Promotions to north China governorships were relatively few, and those who were promoted often came from within Henan and Shandong. More officials were transferred into the region after having acquired experience elsewhere than were transferred out. Because of their relative seniority and frequent close ties with the court, the governors of north China were highly sensitive to changes in the political mood of the capital, securing and losing their positions as policies or favorites changed. The governors of northwest China were also closely tied to the court, and appointment patterns there had much in common with appointment patterns on the north China plain. There were many special appointees and few promotions, and those who were promoted came from within the northwest region. The difference between north and northwest was in the frequency of transfers into the region, fairly common in the north but relatively uncommon in the northwest. In fact, in Shaanxi, more governors were transferred out to other provinces than were transferred in. Government in the northwest was more insular than government in the north, with well over half the governors of both Shanxi and Shaanxi coming either from within the region or from the capital. In Gansu, the situation was even more extreme, until the administration of the province became so exclusively concerned with the transport of supplies and food to Xinjiang that the Qing no longer appointed civilian governors to head it. The reasons for specialization in the northwest are not hard to imagine: the region was among the most sparsely cultivated in China, officials were confronted with a range of tasks not encountered elsewhere, and administrations there were far more concerned with facilitating the defense of the dynasty. This specialization had its echo in the ethnic composition of northwest officials, who were, at least until the late eighteenth century, overwhelmingly Manchu.

The nature of geopolitical imperatives in the north and northwest had a strong influence on government there, and patterns of appointment in the north China provinces of Henan and Shandong were fairly consistent with each other, as were those in the northwest provinces of Shanxi and Shaanxi. In the lower Yangzi valley and along the southeastern coast, appointment patterns varied not only among regions but also among provinces within the same region. In the Yangzi delta and along the southeastern coast, different subregional histories accounted for provincial appointment patterns. Anhui and Jiangsu were both created by the Qing to administer the lands that, during the Ming, had comprised the southern metropolitan region. Jiangsu was created after a series of particularly vocal tax protests by the lower delta elite in the early 1660s necessitated a branch administration in Suzhou. The governor of Jiangsu, located at Suzhou, had the rather specialized tasks of interacting with the wealthy elite of the delta, collecting taxes, and presiding over the Imperial Household Department monopoly enterprises located at Suzhou. As a result, Jiangsu shared with the northwestern provinces the character of a specialized post; there were relatively few promotions, and most of those that did occur were of individuals already in Jiangsu. There were also relatively few transfers, but those who were transferred had often acquired their experience elsewhere. By contrast, Anhui was a crossroads for officials. Half the governors of the upriver province had been promoted from lieutenant governorships, usually in north or central China. Once promoted in Anhui, governors were often transferred to serve elsewhere in north or central China. The one anomalous element in the Anhui record was the high number of special appointments in the immediate post-Taiping period. Zhejiang and Fujian also followed different courses in the eighteenth and nineteenth centuries, although their histories in the early and last years of the dynasty were rather similar. In the middle of the seventeenth century, when Ming pretenders allied with established coastal families posed a threat to the dynasty, the government of Zhejiang and Fujian were somewhat similar. As the menace subsided, however, Zhejiang revived as a commercial and intellectual center and formed close ties with the capital. Special appointees selected by the emperor often formed the bridge between Beijing and Hangzhou. Fujian, in contrast, remained focused on the sea, which for much of the eighteenth and nineteenth centuries was of no compelling interest to the Qing court. As this happened, special appointments to the province declined, and promotions increased.

As the official appointee moved inland from the coast, or south from the northern border, he encountered a central core of provinces that had no special claim on central court attention, unlike the border and seacoast provinces. But for the provinces of the middle Yangzi valley, no niche was itself a niche, for in these provinces, the routine processes of the territorial service operated largely unimpeded by special needs or pleadings. In fact, credit for incorporating the lands of the middle Yangzi into the Qing empire, or, more precisely, presiding over the processes of economic and social change that were tying the area inexorably into the empire, belonged more to Qing officialdom than to the court. In the middle Yangzi, governors moved in and moved on, following routine procedures more than instructions from the court they served. Two of the three middle Yangzi provinces saw frequent transfers of governors and high rates of promotion. Perhaps because of its more complex ecology and diverse human environment, Hunan seemed to receive slightly more experienced governors than did the other two provinces of the region.

In the tier of four provinces along the empire's southern border—Guangdong, Guangxi, Guizhou, and Yunnan—the territorial service played a similar role in incorporating the region into the Qing empire, with two caveats. First, while the territorial servants appointed in the middle Yangzi had governed other provinces relatively often, most appointees in the far south had been recently promoted. Second, the process of incorporation began later; routine circulation of officials through the middle Yangzi region was for the most part established by the end of the seventeenth century, but routine civil appointments did not occur in the far south before the middle of the eighteenth century. Once begun, however, the establishment of routine territorial governance proceeded with a vengeance. Guizhou and Guangxi had the highest promotion rates in the empire and accounted for nearly 10 percent of promoted governors in the Qing. The one exception to this pattern in the south, as it was to many empirewide generalizations, was Guangdong. In fact, no two provinces could have been more different than Guangdong and Guangxi. Guangxi had more promotees than any province in the empire, and Guangdong had some of the most experienced governors in the empire. Service in Guangdong was an extraordinary privilege, at least at the end of the eighteenth century, reserved for the successful and distinguished.

Although these characterizations of provincial difference are schematic, they provide a useful frame within which to display the study of individual governors and their policy emphases. The same is true of the several time sequences that can be constructed with appointments data. Here, of course, qualitative data are somewhat more difficult to come by. Qing officials as well as the emperor wrote about the differences between and opportunities in specific provinces, yet very seldom did anyone, emperor or official, write about how the Qing state used its power of appointment. Regarding human capacities and society's needs as unchanging, rulers strove to be consistent in matching them. Yet, clearly, the court did change its way of making appointments, and not only in response to emergencies. The ebb and flow of central appointments provide a strong indication of the court's ambition and policy. In the seventeenth century, Qing ambitions were best measured by the very project of creating provinces and a means for staffing them. Once a consistent pattern of provincial rule had been established, perhaps the best measure of court intentions is the rise and fall of special appointments. Special appointments rose to a peak in the Yongzheng period, declined through the Qianlong and Jiaqing years, rose again slowly through the Daoguang and Xianfeng periods to a second peak, and then fell through the Guangxu years to the end of the dynasty. Each phase had its own dynamics.

The first period of political activism culminated in the Yongzheng reign. Most of the special appointments of this reign came in its first eight crisis years. But in this instance, crisis at the center had a permanent impact on Chinese government, as the third Qing emperor tried to fashion the territorial service created in his father's reign into an instrument for political reform. The process led to the development of the palace memorial system, "nourishment of virtue" salaries, or administrative stipends, for territorial officials, a decisive and permanent shortening of governors' terms, and a variety of new mechanisms for appointing and evaluating local territorial officials. Effecting these various changes required enormous amount of energy, and the Yongzheng emperor, who seldom left his palace, described nights spent evaluating personnel dossiers and reading governors' memorials in bursts of insomniac activity. The effort also generated much resistance, not only among recalcitrant officials but also among the local elite with whom they formed an alliance.

The Qing dynasty moved away, often with slow and quiet steps, from these policies during the remainder of the eighteenth century and the first reign of the nineteenth. This evolution may have reflected the interests of Chinese and Manchu elites, who must have found the previous ruler's institution building profoundly disturbing. The role of imperial councilors and bureaucrats grew precisely as the number of special appointments declined. The Qianlong emperor rather elegantly expressed himself on the subject of appointments in a corruption case that came to his attention in 1740:

> While I am not prepared to say at this point that the ritual vessels are out of order [that is, to make specific allegations], senior officials have their clients, and all officials have their old friends. There is no way to guarantee that such relations do not exist. Perhaps there are those among officials who have formerly been of great assistance [to those in power], and when I make appointments, former friendships are remembered and supervision is loose. This too cannot be prevented. It's not that I haven't heard of such matters. But to bring up these cases would unavoidably do harm to the body politic.[1]

The statement was as delicate an acknowledgment as one could imagine of a monarch's reliance on his counselors and officials and could not conceivably have been expressed by his father, the Yongzheng emperor. It is tempting to conclude that the decline of central government activism resulted precisely from the influence of Manchu and Chinese who found the previous emperor's institution building very troubling. Although the counselors to whom the emperor refers in this edict passed away, Qianlong became even more dependent on their successors. Indeed, many of the "crisis" years in the Qianlong reign were markers of the change in imperial counselors. Whatever their source, the changes of the Qianlong years represent a critical point in the evolution of the dynasty. Once surrendered, the initiative of political development could be regained by the monarchy only at very significant cost.

But as the court lost the political initiative, governance of the empire as a whole became more systematic. It was probably in the latter half of the eighteenth century, when nearly three hundred officials were promoted and transferred among the empire's provinces, that the patterns of circulation for officials were established. As transfer and promotion routines developed, officials with more experience and education were brought to China's southernmost provinces and even to the provinces of the middle Yangzi region. There, a new generation of officials came to implement a style of territorial governance more like the classical Chinese administration of the north than the haphazard arrangements that had often prevailed south of the Yangzi. This argument may be stretched a bit further. Arguably, the innovations of the first half of the eighteenth century, which have recently been described in the literature—the creation of relief granaries, development of famine-relief procedures, building of dikes along China's rivers and lakes— should be counted as much a creation of eighteenth-century officialdom as of the eighteenth-century monarchy. These innovations came to depend more on the administrative achievements of officials than on the efforts of a monarch reading documents in the wee hours of the morning. It is tempting to imagine that, had the court retained its political initiative, it might have been more able to cope with the serious challenges of the eighteenth century. But the empire, and particularly its most dynamic quarters, might not have continued into the nineteenth century if not for the administrative developments of the eighteenth century.

A third turning point in the life of the dynasty saw a quickening of administrative life in a region that had long been characterized by routine governance. The fact that the rebellions of the nineteenth century arose in regions like Guangxi, long regarded as secure enough to be governed by routine procedures, cannot have been coincidental. Addressing the domestic challenges of the nineteenth century required the dynasty to shift its attention away from the revenue-rich provinces that were its natural strategic bases and turn its attention to the central core of the empire. The direct appointments of the Xianfeng years were among the most irregular of the dynasty. None of the four provinces to which significant numbers of direct appointees were sent during the Xianfeng years had received large numbers of appointees in any other reign. The pattern of appointments in the Xianfeng years suggests a dynasty not so much in decline as shaken to its strategic foundations.

The Tongzhi and Guangxu years saw a restoration of order, but not necessarily a return to the antebellum state. From the standpoint of the center, the period was aptly named "the last stand of Chinese conservatism," for the era saw an almost pugnacious reassertion of authority in the field of central appointments. The Tongzhi rate of direct appointments was matched only by that of the Yongzheng years, the terms of direct appointees were among the longest in the dynasty, and only in this era were direct appointees drawn from the military. However, there were also significant changes. The number of special appointees and the dynasty's traditional concern with north China declined, perhaps paralleling the economic decline of the region as a whole. In its place, the southeastern coast emerged as a focus of government attention. For the first time since the Kangxi years, the coastal provinces of Fujian and Guangdong were governed by special appointees serving fairly long terms. The pattern of direct appointments at the end of the nineteenth century presages China's twentieth-century development into coast and hinterland more than does any earlier pattern of rule.

EIGHTEENTH-CENTURY POLITICAL CHANGE
IN COMPARATIVE PERSPECTIVE

Viewed on its own terms, the eighteenth-century development of provincial government in China represents a remarkable evolution. But the question inevitably arises of how this evolution may be measured. Apparent similarities in the histories of quite different states often turn out to be nothing more than verbal accidents masking quite different realities.[2] Nor is it any longer possible in this postmodern age to base comparative historical discussions on any premise of universal modernity. The constant characteristics that all contemporary states were once presumed to share, and toward which all less developed societies were presumed to be advancing, are no longer clear, and it has become more obvious that the assumptions of modern life need to be deconstructed from a wide variety of sources rather than derived from a simple political or social narrative. Comparisons, if they are to be made, must be less than global, suggestive rather than conclusive, supplementary to the work of establishing narrative rather than constitutive of it. But, insofar as more limited comparisons can draw attention to elements of an historical tradition that may be missed by those immersed in it, or the historians who speak about it, such comparisons are useful; particularly useful in this regard may be the effort to compare elements of the "absolutism" of late imperial China, particularly its territorial component, with institutions of provincial control in early modern Europe.

It must be regarded as a fateful coincidence that the years of early and high Qing rule in China correspond with that period in European history, between the Peace of Westphalia in 1648 and the beginning of the French Revolution in 1789, in which European monarchies were perfecting the structures and attitudes of absolutist rule. The achievements of this era have been variously characterized. Some, who trace the development of the modern state from a sociological point of view, have seen absolutism as "the first mature embodiment of the modern state," providing a ruler with new "flexible and indefinitely extensible and modifiable instruments for articulating and sanctioning his will."[3] Marxian historians, following Engels, have emphasized absolutism's relation to the past rather than to the future. For others, absolutism was essentially just this: "a redeployed and recharged apparatus of feudal domination, designed to clamp the peasant masses back into their traditional social position."[4] Even among Marxians, however, there has been tension between seeing the accomplishments of the era as "counter-poise to the achievements of the nobility" and as "a cornerstone to the new monarchies."[5] In both traditions, European absolutism is seen as a turning point, whether the end of the old era or the beginning of the new, and it is at just such pivotal moments in history that it is useful to compare China with Europe.

The close correspondence between dates associated with European absolutism and the rule of the Qing is somewhat spurious—Spanish absolutism began considerably earlier, and Russian absolutism continued much longer than chronological boundaries would suggest. Dating may be a matter of happenstance, but it was perhaps not so much of a coincidence, given common trends of commercialization, prosperity, and population growth with its concomitant social evolution, that the first 150 years of the Qing also saw the elaboration and perfection of structures of traditional absolutism.[6] In fact, the Qing monarchs seem to have had some advantage over their European counterparts, since they did not need to free themselves from feudal ties and historical obligations. As conquerors different in language and habit from the people over whom they ruled, the Manchus in the seventeenth and eighteenth centuries could focus on the question of how to make the system work for them instead of being bound by the commitments of their predecessors.

One of the areas on which they focused was systematizing territorial administration and rendering it more responsive to central government direction. Every ruler of a state of any significant size requires local subordinates, but these subordinates may be bound to the central ruler by a variety of mechanisms. In a feudal system in which the tie was largely personal, the obligations of ruler and vassal to each other were secured by a personal oath, and different vassals might have different obligations to the same ruler. Even when the tie was not feudal, in the absence of central directives, individual territorial administrators of different premodern empires took very different attitudes toward their roles and responsibilities. The differing powers that the viceroys of fifteenth-century Spain exercised in the territories their empire conquered in the New World, Italy, and the Iberian Peninsula itself constituted a "block to any real unification of the international imperium as a whole, or to the Iberian homelands themselves."[7] Similarly, recent scholarship has argued that the governors of the British empire of the late sixteenth and seventeenth centuries had "commercial as well as bureaucratic and military bases" and has highlighted the vastly differing attitudes of British governors-general to the territories they governed.[8] Even in fourteenth- and fifteenth-century Ming China, grand coordinators, the predecessors of Qing provincial governors, were appointed on an ad hoc basis to deal with military or fiscal crises in the empire, and there was little coordination between the three arms of Ming territorial government.

One element of the growth of centralizing absolutisms everywhere was the effort to organize this territorial chaos into regular administrative practices. The first step in this process was making the local administrative posts permanent fixtures, not subject to purchase, through which qualified officials might be rotated as the center judged necessary. A second step was the perhaps more complex one of regularizing the obligations of provincial administrators appointed in different places and times toward the central government. Possibly the most dramatic case of the regularization of territorial administration occurred in late seventeenth-century France. There, judicial, financial, and police intendants appointed from the center and trained in law and administrative procedure were superimposed on a series of royal governorships held by aristocrats with varying obligations to king and country.[9] This development, and the fiscal and administrative benefits it produced for the state, proved to be the foundation for French political ascendancy in the late seventeenth and early eighteenth centuries.

In China, because the memory of feudalism was so distant by the seventeenth century and the problem of territories acquired under different circumstances was far less apparent, the significance of establishing regularized territorial governorships generated less comment. Nonetheless, it was a signal development and provided the foundation for many of the dynasty's future accomplishments. The universalism implicit in Confucian conceptions of the political order, the idea that governance rests on certain relatively immutable principles as valid in one part of the empire as in another, which was so ringingly asserted by the Kangxi emperor, provided the foundation for the establishment of regular provincial posts in the Qing period. In the Yongzheng reign, this universalism became the basis for a political discourse in which the accomplishments of different officials could be compared, and the innovations of one official were assumed to be transferable to all parts of the empire. The Qianlong emperor carried the process one step further by moving governors among provinces readily and frequently and by this means creating a governorship sufficiently standardized that both Chinese and Manchus were equally qualified to serve.

Consistent in spirit, though on occasion contradictory in practice, the centralizing impulse of absolutist provincial regimes was accompanied by a second tendency common to seventeenth-century regimes, the impulse to rule through personally selected and delegated subordinates. In this era, the monarch ruled "from his court rather than through it. The court made up the expressive aspect of his rule, as it were, but this had to be complemented by an instrumental aspect. Hence, intersecting with the court (rather than nested within it) there was another setting, which placed in a more direct and material relation to the business of rule and which operated as the medium of the ruler's personal power." Monarchs ruled through "small councils of government, each having a small number of members, but each connected with a large number of agents and executors through links all ultimately instituted and activated through the rulers command."[10] This passage was written to describe the government of seventeenth- and eighteenth-century France; it could, however, as easily describe the Yongzheng emperor's formation of the Grand Council, a small informal body of advisers that initially counseled the emperor on military matters but subsequently came to dominate most of Chinese administration and, in the eighteenth century, provided many provincial governors.

The characterization also aptly describes the emperor's appointment of men he knew and trusted to serve as provincial governors, and his creation of a special means of communication by which he could maintain personal and confidential contact with them, the system of palace memorials. Studies of the secret memorial system have focused on the enormous significance of these documents in the political process, and few studies of Qing politics or administration would have been possible without them. But the memorials were also personal communications, not originally meant for public consumption, and could as easily touch upon family matters—the intent behind a gift, the death of a parent, or the promotion of a cousin—as upon matters of policy. Although it is possible to read these documents out of the personal and biographical context in which they were written, to do so is to read anachronistically, inserting the modern concern with policy divorced from personality into a very different eighteenth-century context. As such, they provide a rare example of how an absolutist monarch maintained the personal network of communications on which his reign rested.

Eighteenth-century governors in China, as in some of the most advanced states in Europe, arrived at their posts bearing the special mark of imperial selection. They were also in many cases law bearers, as Chinese emperors (like their European contemporaries) tried to institutionalize their approaches to rule through their chosen provincial subordinates. Indeed, as Poggi writes, "one of the prime concerns of absolutist rule was exactly the authoritative regulation . . . of the private preoccupations of individuals." In the European context, much of this administrative regulation was explicitly economic. In China, though there was no dearth of economic regulation, administrative law was more concerned with regulating the ways in which officials went about the business of governing. Despite the somewhat different explicit concerns of Qing law, the effect was perhaps similar to that of administrative law in European absolutisms, which, as Poggi argues, was promoted not so much to enhance or regulate commerce as to "(1.) Keep the population busy, peaceful and unconcerned with political business, and (2.) to generate the taxable wealth needed to underwrite the expenses of the court," goals with which a Qing emperor could have readily sympathized.[11] Certainly, the growth in volume of such Qing administrative law suggests its importance to the government. This elaboration of the Qing administrative code made it possible for Chinese governors to move from post to post in the eighteenth century without needing to familiarize themselves with local conditions.

The problem with this narrative, one that bedevils almost any discussion of China before the twentieth century, is that although the operation was a success, the patient eventually died. Even in 1768, the limitations of the Qianlong bureaucracy were apparent in its profound commitment to routine procedures, which evoked less than resonant cheers from Philip Kuhn in his study of the 1768 sorcery crisis.[12] Scarcely two decades later, Qianlong's provincial governors were incapable of reporting, much less putting down, a major rebellion in north and central China, and political discourse began a downward spiral dominated by corruption, accusation, and counteraccusation. The full details of this spiral, and how imperial intervention in the early nineteenth century renovated provincial institutions for another century, is a story for another book. But the dimensions of the conflict at the end of the eighteenth century may form an epilogue to this one. This decline came at a moment when differences in provincial needs and resources began to tear at the fabric that held the Qing empire together. Economic change propelled certain provinces far beyond others in levels of wealth and social elaboration. Politically these inter-provincial differences were reflected in the growing factionalism of the government: the wealthiest provinces along the southeastern coast became the preserves of Manchu representatives of the Imperial Household Department and, more specifically, of Chief Grand Councilor Heshen. The style of rule and life in these provinces inevitably attracted the attention and earned the condemnation of Chinese bureaucratic governors of poorer and more troubled provinces. The provisions of the administrative code, however elaborate, proved inadequate to contain both the new social situation along the coast and the increasingly complex situation inland. The Chinese administrators confined to China's inner provinces found themselves bound by codes, without the clout to approach an aging and increasingly insulated Qianlong emperor and without the means or competence to cope with the increasingly violent challenges to Qing rule generated by a new demographic situation. Perhaps more than at any earlier point in Qing history, provinces began to differ. The infamous Imperial Household Department registers of payments collected largely from provincial governors in lieu of salary fines, considered in chapter 8, testify vividly to the disparities in governors' means and circumstances. Put simply, the richest of China's provinces were growing richer, the poorest provinces were growing poorer, and the structure of empire was straining to contain them both.

Such were, at least in part, the domestic origins of China's nineteenth-century crisis. This should not obscure the rather significant achievements of the Qing dynasty in building provincial institutions in the first seventy-five years of the eighteenth century. In few countries of the world did eighteenth-century absolutist institutions survive the challenges of the nineteenth century. But in China they did; moreover, the structures of Qing provincial government and the governors who inhabited them held together a larger physical territory for longer than did any other empire in the world. While they undeniably had their faults, Qing governors must have been doing something right. Their work in provincial capitals and along the dusty byways of empire sustained one of the largest and longest-lived polities of the early modern era.

Appointment Data for Qing Provincial Governors

Historians of monarchical appointments in other empires are somewhat more fortunate than historians of late imperial China. In other realms, the circumstances of individual appointments are revealed in memoirs, correspondence, and, in some cases, even letters of appointment. In China, these materials had much more limited value. While imperial comments on the occasion of a governor's appointment were not uncommon in China, they were often tantalizingly brief. Moreover, the extant records of words spoken at the Qing court were not, in a strict sense, primary sources, being instead edited materials produced significantly after the events they purport to describe. Unable to rely on what emperors said, we must rely on what emperors did. Fortunately, the facts of imperial appointments in China are well documented. Every appointment of an official to the office of provincial governor was announced by an edict, and these edicts, arranged chronologically, were published in the *Veritable Records of the Qing*. Appointments recorded in the records tell us what the court intended and provide a more complete record of appointments than data recorded in provincial gazetteers or the personnel chapter of *History of the Qing*. These edicts have been indexed in a project led by Qian Shifu and his colleagues at Beijing University, completed in 1963 and published in 1980.[1] The record of provincial appointments in volume 3 of this index is nearly complete; in rare instances, the researchers established information using sources other than imperial edicts. As a record of appointments, the entries in the *Veritable Records* are far more complete than the accounts in provincial gazetteers or the "Treatise on Officials" in *History of the Qing*, produced in the early twentieth century.

The material has been used in this volume in two ways. For the seventeenth century, before the provincial order was fully evolved, the entries in *A Chronological Chart of Official Appointments in the Qing Dynasty* establish who governed where and when. Once these basic facts were determined, biographical materials filled in the details of careers, connections, and policy emphases. Since the provinces in these early years were very different from one another, comparisons among them had to proceed in qualitative rather than quantitative terms. Comparable data could be collected for each appointment only after the territorial system had developed fully, and provinces were more consistent units of the imperial order.

For convenience, comparisons begin in the year 1700. Of course, any date is arbitrary, particularly one from the Western calendar. But by this year in China, the great rebellion of Wu Sangui in the south had ended, most provinces had achieved their final form, and changes in personnel procedures in the capital made it more likely that officials could move readily from province to province. I chose 1900 as an end date in order to avoid the changes in personal order that resulted from the political reform the dynasty undertook in its last decade.

A total of 1,512 appointments of 532 officials were recorded. Several of the charts record appointments made in the fifteen provinces that retained a consistent form between 1700 and 1900; in these charts, 57 appointments made in Zhili (3 appointments), Sichuan (17 appointments), Gansu (32 appointments), Taiwan (2 appointments), and Xinjiang (1 appointment) were omitted, resulting in a total of 1,455 appointments.

For each appointment, the institutional, spatial, temporal, and ethnic data were recorded. Institutional data includes mode of appointment and mode of departure. Appointments were divided into promotions from lieutenant governor to governor, lateral transfers from one governorship to another, and special appointments. Since the term "special appointment" is used here to some extent as a proxy for imperial intervention in the appointments process, appointments of individuals serving as board presidents and censors have been classified as special appointments, even though there was a routine procedure for making such appointments. Since appointments of this type were not made for much of the eighteenth century, their inclusion does not affect many of the arguments made here. Modes of departure include unforeseen circumstances (illness, death, or the death of a parent and the required period of mourning this entailed), political circumstances (summons to the capital, being relieved of responsibility, demotion, or cashiering), and routine actions (promotion or lateral transfer). Spatial data includes place of appointment and the applicant's previous and subsequent locations. Temporal data includes year of appointment, year of departure, and length of term. The ethnic identity of the governor, as recorded in the index, is also recorded. Many of the tables on governors' service in this book resulted from computer-assisted tabulations and cross-tabulations of these appointment records, and for these tables, the source is recorded as "*Qingdai zhi guan nian biao* data." In those tables that involve a limited number of appointments, the results of computer tabulations were checked against the original index entries; for these tables, the sources are recorded as "*Qingdai zhi guan nian biao* (QDZGNB) data; QDZGNB."

In this volume, broadly speaking, promotions and lateral appointments were analyzed in terms of space in order to establish the degree to which the Qing central government, when confronted with a vacancy in one part of the empire, turned to officials in another location to fill it. Special appointments were analyzed largely in terms of time, to examine the moments at which the court chose to use its special powers to fill a position. Each sort of analysis has its limits. As I contend in chapter 5, special appointments were sometimes used to achieve policy goals, and lateral transfers were used to move governors to posts where experience was perceived as necessary. Nonetheless, most of the tables in this volume cross-tabulated lateral appointments and promotions by space, and special appointments by time. To complete the circle, cross-tabulations of all appointments, by space and time, are presented in tables A.1 through A.4.

TABLE A.1. All Appointments, by Reign

Reign	Promotions	Lateral Appointments	Special Appointments	Total
Kangxi (1720–23)	42	20	45	107
Yongzheng (1723–36)	41	25	52	121
Qianlong (1736–96)	145	233	153	532
Jiaqing (1796–1820)	77	72	52	201
Daoguang (1821–51)	85	67	67	220
Xianfeng (1851–61)	36	14	26	76
Tongzhi (1861–75)	32	16	35	83
Guangxu (1875–1911)	78	51	43	172
Total	541	498	473	1,512

Source: *Qingdai zhi guan nianbiao* data.

TABLE A.2. All Appointments, by Province, 1700–1900

Province	Promotions	Lateral Appointments	Special Appointments	Total
Anhui	42	23	33	98
Fujian	36	30	23	89
Guangdong	19	41	29	89
Guangxi	52	24	23	99
Guizhou	49	17	26	92
Henan	33	34	28	95
Hubei	45	40	30	115
Hunan	32	40	31	103
Jiangxi	36	34	24	94
Jiangsu	24	40	30	94
Shaanxi	32	34	39	105
Shanxi	33	29	36	98
Shandong	27	34	38	99
Yunnan	37	29	17	83
Zhejiang	29	34	39	102
Zhili		1	2	3
Gansu	8	7	17	32
Sichuan	5	7	6	18
Taiwan			1	1
Xinjiang	2		1	3
Total	541	498	473	1,512

Source: *Qingdai zhi guan nianbiao* data.

TABLE A.3. Modes of Departure, by Reign

Reign	Lateral Transfer	Promotion	Death or Dismissal	Mourning	Total
Kangxi	16	42	27	22	107
Yongzheng	35	35	43	8	121
Qianlong	235	113	110	74	532
Jiaqing	78	50	44	29	201
Daoguang	75	59	42	44	220
Xianfeng	16	22	21	17	76
Tongzhi	15	22	18	28	83
Guangxu	62	30	40	40	172
Totals	532	373	345	262	1,512

Source: *Qing dai zhi guan nian biao.*

TABLE A.4. Modes of Dismissal, by Province

Province	Lateral Transfer	Promotion	Dismissal	Death or Mourning	Total
Anhui	42	20	19	17	98
Fujian	31	18	16	24	89
Guangdong	31	29	14	15	89
Guangxi	39	24	22	14	99
Guizhou	38	15	22	17	92
Henan	35	29	22	14	95
Hubei	48	23	22	22	103
Hunan	35	29	25	14	115
Jiangxi	41	12	28	13	94
Jiangsu	28	27	20	19	94
Shandong	24	35	23	17	99
Shaanxi	39	28	22	16	105
Shanxi	37	23	21	23	98
Yunnan	31	21	21	17	83
Zhejiang	21	28	33	20	102
Zhili		1	1	1	3
Gansu	8	10	12	2	32
Xinjiang	1	2			3
Sichuan	7	4	6	1	18
Taiwan	1			1	2
Total	532	373	345	262	1,512

Source: *Qin dai zhi guan nian biao.*

Abbreviations

The following abbreviations are used in the notes.

DQHD   *Da Qing huidian.* 1899 Guangxu edition. Reprint, Beijing: Zhonghua, 1990.*

DQHDSL   *Da Qing huidian shilu.* Guangxu edition. Shanghai: Commercial Press, 1908. Reprint, Beijing: Zhonghua, 1990.*

ECCP   Library of Congress, Orientalia Division. *Eminent Chinese of the Ch'ing Period.* Edited by Arthur W. Hummel. Taipei: Cheng Wen Publishing House, 1972.

GCQXLZ   *Guo cho qi xian lei zheng.* Edited by Li Huan. Xiangyin, 1884–90.

HCJSWB   *Huangchao jingshi wenbian.* Compiled by He Changling. Reprint, Taipei: Guofeng Chubanshe, 1965.

JQSL   *Renzong Rong (Jiaqing) Huangdi shilu.* 1937. Reprinted in *Da Qing Shilu.* Vols. 28–32.*

KXSL   *Shengzong Ren (Kangxi) Huangdi shilu.* Reprinted in *Da Qing shilu.* Vols. 3–6. Tokyo: Okura Shuppan Kabushike Kaishu, 1937. Reprint, Beijing: Zhonghua, 1986.*

QDZGNB   *Qingdai zhi guan nianbiao.* Beijing: Shifan Daxue Chubanshe, 1997.

QLSL   *Gaozongshun (Qianlong) Huangdi shilu.* Reprinted in *Da Qing shilu.* Vols. 9–27. Tokyo: Okura Shuppan Kabushike Kaishu, 1937. Reprint, Beijing: Zhonghua, 1986.*

QS   *Qing shi.* Edited by Zhao Erxun. 1927. Reprint, Taipei: Guo Fang Yanjiuyuan, 1961.

SZSL   *Shizong Zhang (Shinzhi) Huangdi shilu.* Reprint, Vol. 2. Beijing: Zhonghua, 1985.*

YZSL   *Shizongxian Huangdi shilu.* Reprinted in *Da Qing shilu.* Vols. 7–9. Tokyo: Okura Shuppan Kabushike Kaishu, 1937. Reprint, Beijing: Zhonghua, 1986.*

ZPZZ   *Yongzheng zhupi yuzhi.* Compiled by Ortai. 1738. Reprint, Taipei: Wenhai, 1965.

---

*Citations include *juan* and page numbers for the original; page numbers for the reprint are in parentheses.

Notes

Introduction

1. The term seems to have been first used by Frederic Wakeman, Jr., in "High Ch'ing, 1683–1839." Wakeman, however, draws on the earlier essay by Ho Ping-ti, "The Significance of the Ch'ing Period in Chinese History."

2. For an exchange of the roles of government and society in Qing growth, see Rawski, "Presidential Address"; and Ho, "In Defense of Sinicization," 193–94. This argument builds on a suggestion offered by Wakeman in the concluding pages of his magisterial study of the Qing conquest, *The Great Enterprise*, vol. 2: 1126.

3. Hucker, *A Dictionary of Official Titles*, 255. I will follow Hucker's practice of referring to *xunfu* in the Ming as "grand coordinators" and in the Qing as "governors," although I recognize that the terms "governor" and "province" have rather different associations in European history than they do in Chinese history.

4. On Ming governors, see Zhang Zhelang, *Mingdai xunfu yanjiu*, esp. 233–46.

5. Zito, *Of Body and Brush*.

6. Lévi-Strauss, *The Savage Mind*, 17–18. Here I don't mean to suggest that the Qing were savage or unsophisticated. Rather, I mean to emphasize that provinces evolved not in response to an unfolding metahistorical narrative but through a series of small contingent choices.

7. Certeau, *The Practice of Everyday Life*, 118.

8. G. William Skinner, "Cities and the Hierarchy of Local Systems," in *The City in Late Imperial China*, 281–82.

9. G. William Skinner, "Regional Urbanization in China," in *The City in Late Imperial China*, 218.

10. The "tail" of Zhili and the boundaries of the lower Yangzi valley provinces are discussed in chapters 5 and 6.

11. Zhili was not formally a province after 1723. When Xinjiang was made a province, it was listed after Gansu; Gansu existed as a province only until 1757 (see chapter 3 of this volume). Sichuan existed as a Qing province until 1767. *Da Qing huidian*, 5:4a–5b (29). This is also the order in which prefectural and county officials are listed in DQHD, *juan* 5, and the order in which provincial military establishments are enumerated in DQHD, *juan* 43–45 (387–420) and elaborated in DQHDSL, vol. 7.

12. The regional literature is too extensive to be presented in a single note. For detailed descriptions by region, see the notes for chapters 6–9 of this volume.

13. See the reflections on primordial attachments and provincial narratives in Duara, *Rescuing History*, 177–204, esp. 178–79.

14. Particularly useful for this volume are the imperially ordered gazetteers prepared by provincial governors in the late Yongzheng reign. These were copied into *Complete Library*

of the Four Treasuries *(Si ku quan shu) and reviewed in* Annotated Catalog of the "Complete Library of the Four Treasuries," Compiled by Imperial Command *(Qin ding Si ku quan shu zong mu ti yao),* 68:1481–86. It should be noted that, unlike county gazetteers, provincial gazetteers provided little information that was not available elsewhere, and much of the information in provincial publications suffered from redaction. The volumes have some value as aids for finding information whose accuracy may require confirmation by other sources, but they speak more vividly of the provincial images the dynasty sought to portray.

15. See Rowe, *Saving the World.*

16. Craig Clunas has more appropriately termed these materials "necrologies." *Fruitful Sites,* 104. I continue to call them "biographies" here for expository convenience.

17. Anderson, *Imagined Communities,* 55.

18. In this regard, Qing governors were very different from Ming grand coordinators, the vast majority of whom held the *jinshi* degree. In the Ming, grand coordinators were clearly civilian officials, often poised against the eunuch officials who controlled the military establishment. In the Qing, there were no eunuch appointees in the provinces, and governors had to take on many of the functional tasks of maintaining territorial order.

19. Unfortunately, biographies are not specific enough about age to permit more refined demographic analysis. Age is given in perhaps one-fourth of the cases, but in most instances, one can know only the date on which a governor took civil service exams or entered government service, and in many cases, the date is only an approximation.

20. Insofar as the history of gubernatorial administration displays a range of actions undertaken by a fairly well-documented group, it differs from most existing histories. Both Chinese and Western historians have written about exceptional individuals—men such as Cao Yin, Yuan Mei, Zhang Xuecheng, and Chen Hongmou—whose accomplishments struck their contemporaries and successors as so extraordinary and instructive that they deserved to be retold in detail. At the same time, cultural historians have sought to establish the groundwork of assumptions that underlay official accomplishments. Among these are Thomas Metzger's masterful analysis of the regulations governing administrative discipline in the Qing and the assumptions they reveal about the nature of human fallibility and the human actions needed to overcome it; see Metzger, *Internal Organization of the Ch'ing.* Equally indispensable is Benjamin Elman's *A Cultural History of Civil Examinations in Late Imperial China,* a sweeping and compelling account of the late imperial civil service examination system. But neither the record of the exceptional nor the analysis of norms and their institutional embodiments can adequately convey the world of those who actually governed. For reflections on the relation of narrative and social history, see Paul Ricoeur's chapter "Eclipse of Narrative," in his *Time and Narrative,* vol. 1: 95–120.

21. On résumés, see Feng Ergang, *Qingdai renwu chuanji shiliao yanjiu,* 482–510. In 1997, 55,883 résumés were photographically reproduced in a thirty-volume collection, *Complete Collection of Résumés from the Qing Period* (Qingdai luli dang'an quan bian).

22. These biographies still exist in the Qing archives, but they are most accessible through the work of Li Huan. The son of Li Xingyuan, a Qing governor-general, Li Huan rose to the position of lieutenant governor of Zhejiang before retiring to assemble his massive compilation of biographies, *Classified Collection of Biographies of Worthies of Our Times* (Guo chao ji xian lei zheng). Li Huan had worked at the State Historiographical Commission and, in the course of his employment, copied out many of the working biographies the commission had prepared. Friends and relatives provided him with additional copies while he was preparing his compilation. Li Huan was interested in the lives of territorial

officials. In fact, the category of "provincial officials" (qiang chen) is the third-largest category in the compilation, after those of court officials and princes, accounting for fifty-eight juan in twenty-eight ce. In nearly every case, the entries of provincial officials include the State Historiographical Commission's working biographies. To be sure, these documents are rather dry accounts, really prose versions of official résumés. But they preserved dates and details of an official's service unavailable elsewhere. As important, these working biographies preserve the texts of their subjects' most important official writings. These include policy memorials submitted through the public channel, and hence not readily available elsewhere, as well as secret memorials that may or may not have survived in the dynasty's archives.

DQHDSL 1050:514. The emperor found the standard proposed by the commission to be insufficiently inclusive and ordered it to prepare biographies of women and literary figures as well.

23. Biographical accounts of governors preserved in provincial gazetteers, in which editors produced on imperial command accounts of the most prominent governors in the province, are also useful.

Chapter 1. The Burdens of History: Pre-Qing Territorial Government

1. In "The Beginnings of Bureaucracy in China," Herrlee Creel argues that the Qin borrowed the xian from the state of Chu, where feudal institutions were less well established.

2. See Creel, Shen Buhai, esp. 80–106.

3. Schwartz, World of Thought in Ancient China, 336–37; see also 335–43.

4. Dull, "The Evolution of Government in China," 60.

5. The notion that new provinces reflected a new social order was advanced by Chen Yinko, whose notions influenced Edwin Pulleyblank's Background of the Rebellion of An Lu-Shan. In The Medieval Chinese Oligarchy, David Johnson proposes a much slower model of social change in the Tang. Charles Peterson's "Court and Province in the Mid-Tang" deals with provinces as territorial entities.

6. Loewe, "The Former Han Dynasty."

7. The terms taishou, cishi, and mu became unofficial, literary designations for local officials in the late imperial period. Taishou referred to prefects, cishi to magistrates, and mu to the leaders of independent departments.

8. Beck, "The Fall of the Han," 334. See also the case of a late Han regional inspector demanding higher rank, cited in Gu Yanwu, Ri zhi lu, 271.

9. Gu Yanwu, "Sui yihou zhi cishi," in Ri zhi lu, 13:266–67. The term zhi zhou, used to designate the chief official of the zhou, was coined later in the Song. Gu Yanwu, "Zhi zhou," Ri zhi lu, 13:269. See also Hucker, A Dictionary of Official Titles, 178.

10. Peterson, "Court and Province in the Mid-Tang," 46–47.

11. The great historian of Tang institutions Robert des Rotours despaired of sorting out An Lushan's titles or those of his fellow governors. See his L'Histoire de Ngan Lou-chan, 22 n. 1.

12. Ibid., 39.

13. Pulleyblank, Background of the Rebellion, 95–96; and des Rotours, L'Histoire de Ngan Lou-chan, 97. There is a legend that An Lushan and Yang Guifei had a sexual relationship, but, as Pulleyblank notes, the possibility is "too grotesque."

14. Peterson, "Court and Province in the Mid-Tang," 472.

15. Ibid., 505, 518. See also Twitchett, "Provincial Autonomy and Central Finance."

16. Graff, *Medieval Chinese Warfare, 300–900*, 211.

17. Dull, "The Evolution of Government in China," 74.

18. See Kracke, *Civil Service in Early Song China*, 51–52. See also Hucker, *A Dictionary of Official Titles*, 322.

19. Barfield, *The Perilous Frontier*, 8.

20. *The Secret History of the Mongols*, 176–77.

21. See the statistics for senior appointees collected by Segchin Jagchid, cited in Endicott-west, *Mongolian Rule in China*, 78.

22. Menggu's epitaph, which was drafted by Hu Zhiyu in whose collected works it is found, is translated in ibid., 29–33. It is also in Ebrey, *Chinese Civilization*, 192–94.

23. See Hucker, *A Dictionary of Official Titles*, 244; and Gu Yanwu, *Ri zhi lu*, 29:828. I am grateful to Professor Dai Yingcong for advice on this matter. The term *sheng* has some parallels to the English term "county," which originally referred to the possession of a count but later came to be a geographic unit.

24. *Yuan shi*, 91:2305–7. The dates for the formation of provinces within China proper were Jiangzhe, 1276; Jiangxi, 1277; Henan, 1268; Huguang, 1274; Sichuan, 1291; Shaanxi, 1260; Yunnan, 1274.

25. See the map outlining the borders of these provinces in Rossabi, "The Reign of Khubilai Khan," 440–42.

26. G. William Skinner, "Regional Urbanization in Nineteenth Century China," in *The City in Late Imperial China*, 215.

27. The Yuan retained the traditional counties and prefectures of Chinese imperial administration but changed the term for "prefecture" from *zhou* to *fu*. In earlier dynasties, *fu* referred to military units on the border or to the governing units of major cities. Conversely, *zhou* existed after the Yuan, but as special independent departments, districts that required higher-ranking official than ordinary *xian*.

28. *Yuan shi*, 91:2308–9. These offices moved around as military needs arose, but generally speaking, they were located in modern-day Shandong, Shanxi, Hunan, Hubei, Jiangsu, and Zhejiang. Each office was headed by two commissioners.

29. Ibid., translated in Endicott-West, *Mongolian Rule in China*, 11.

30. *Yuan shi*, 89:2177–78. These were located in Shaanxi and modern-day Jiangsu.

31. Hucker, *The Censorial System of Ming China*, 27.

32. Endicott-West, "Imperial Governance in Yuan Times," ; see also Endicott-West, *Mongolian Rule in China*, 46–53.

33. Farquhar, "Structure and Function," 52.

34. In the middle of the fourteenth century, as various pretenders to the Yuan throne competed for control of the central government, provinces did become, to some degree, bases for the governor's separate political ambitions. But, as John Dardess has argued, this occurred quite late in the dynasty. See Dardess, *Conquerors and Confucians*, 49, 119, and 130–38.

35. Farmer, *Zhu Yuanzhang and Early Ming Legislation*, 1–17.

36. See *Ming shi*, 75:1839–40, for the formation and staffing of these positions.

37. *Zhongguo lishi ditu ji*, vol. 7: 43–44. This produced the boundaries of what would be the provinces of Jiangsu and Anhui during the Qing.

38. On the establishment of the northern metropolitan region, see Farmer, *Early Ming Government*, 98–128 passim, esp. 119.

39. Chan, "Chien-wen, Yung-lo, Hung-hsi and Hsuan-te Reigns," 229–31.

40. *Ming shi*, 51:1835. Translations from Hucker, *A Dictionary of Official Titles*. Hucker finds the translation "registrar" arguable; see 172, entry 1228. The concerns expressed below about the early Qing tendency to systematize Ming institutions, as reflected in *History of the Ming*, may be applicable to this passage as well.

41. *Da Ming huidian*, 4:93.

42. See Hucker, *The Censorial System of Ming China*, 56–57.

43. See *Ming shi*, 3:48. On the substance of this mission, see Langlois, "The Hung-wu Reign," 164; and Farmer, *Early Ming Government*, 93–94.

44. *Ming shi*, 9:116.

45. Hucker, *The Censorial System of Ming China*, 38–39; Chan, "Chien-wen, Yung-lo, Hung-hsi and Hsuan-te Reigns," 292; and Zhang Zhelang, *Mingdai xunfu yanjiu*, 169–77.

46. *Ming shi*, 11:153.

47. Unless otherwise noted, references to the first appointments of grand coordinators are drawn from the *History of the Ming* account. Wherever possible, I have tried to confirm the circumstances of appointments and experiences of Ming grand coordinators from the "Basic Annals" (Benji) section of the history and from other sources.

48. *Ming shi*, 73:1779. On the grand coordinators in Zhejiang in the 1550s, see James Geiss, "The Chia-ching Reign, 1522–1566," in *The Cambridge History of China*, vol. 7, part 1, edited by Frederick W. Mote and Denis Twitchett (Cambridge: Cambridge University Press, 1988), 490–500.

49. *Ming shi*, 73:1779. Yu Qian was the first governor of Henan and Shanxi. See Goodrich and Fang, *Dictionary of Ming Biography*, 1608–10. On the evolution of responsibility for the Henan dikes, see chapter 6 in this volume.

50. In Mingdai Xunfu Zhidu, Zhang Zhe-lang draws on writings other than the *Ming Shi* to identify seven other grand coordinator positions in the Ming. He has also compared *Ming Shi* dates with dates found in other sources. Cases in which Zhang's dates differ from those of *Ming Shi* will be discussed below.

51. Zhang Zhelang, *Mingdai xunfu yanjiu*, 54–56, 58–59, 62–63.

52. For a list of Ming princely fiefs and their locations, see Mote and Twitchett, *The Cambridge History of China*, vol. 7: 171; for a map of the locations, see ibid.: 121.

53. Zhang Zhelang, *Mingdai xunfu yanjiu*, 29–30, 52.

54. Grand coordinators also played a role familiar to students of European history, that is, they acted to defend the monarch against challenges from powerful enfeoffed members of the monarch's own family. But the coordinators' defense of imperial interests was often a matter of duty rather than of conviction.

55. See *Ming shi*, 17:219, 222; and Goodrich and Fang, *Dictionary of Ming Biography*, 524, 892.

56. On Zeng, see Waldron, *The Great Wall of China*, 122–37; and Goodrich and Fang, *Dictionary of Ming Biography*, 1302–5.

57. *Ming shi*, 20:272.

58. Zhang Zhelang, *Mingdai xunfun yanjiu*, 86–87.

59. Ibid., 99. The Nangan coordinator was never called *xunfu*. Until the end of the dynasty, the official was known as *xunzhi*.

60. Brook, *The Confusions of Pleasure*, 19.

61. Tong, *Disorder under Heaven*, 43–56.

62. Ray Huang, "The Wan-li Reign," 521.

63. Memorial of Governor Zhou Yude, quoted in Fu, *Qingdai dufu zhidu*, 13.

64. *Ming shi*, 73:1773–75.

65. Zhang Zhelang, *Mingdai xunfun yanjiu*, 240.

66. Gu Yanwu, "Junxian lun," in *Gu Tinglin wenji*, 12–17. This essay is partially translated in de Bary, Chan, and Tan, *Sources of the Chinese Tradition*, vol. 1: 557.

67. Gu Yanwu "Junxian lun," 5–8.

68. The descriptions of territorial offices are in *juan* 11–13; the reference to *sheng* is at 29.829.

69. De Bary, Chan, and Tan, *Sources of the Chinese Tradition*, vol. 1: 557.

70. Gu Yanwu, Ri zhi lu, 19.241–42.

71. Charles O. Hucker, "Hu Tsung-hsien's Campaign against Hsu Hai," in Fairbank and Kierman, *Chinese Ways in Warfare*, 273–311.

72. Fairbank, "Varieties of the Chinese Military Experience," 23.

73. Hucker, "Hu Tsung-hsien's Campaign against Hsu Hai," in Fairbank and Kierman, *Chinese Ways in Warfare*, 206.

74. Tong, *Disorder under Heaven*, 108.

Chapter 2. The Qing Creation of the Province

1. Since many of the lieutenant governor's duties were financial, the title *buzhengshi* is sometimes rendered as "finance commissioner." However, the Qing clearly regarded this official as an assistant to the governor; therefore, "lieutenant governor" seems the more appropriate rendering. The *anchashi* was number three in the provincial hierarchy, but his duties were primarily judicial, rather than censorial, so it seems most appropriate to refer to him as the provincial judge.

2. Struve, *Voices from the Ming-Qing Cataclysm* 2.

3. This was accomplished after some initial uncertainty about where garrisons were to be located. For an index to the organization and reorganization of garrisons in the first three years of the dynasty, see DQHDSL, 545 (vol. 7: 43–53); QS, 118:1405–7; and QDZGNB, vol. 3: 2218–49, 2428–29 chart.

4. The Qing established a number of temporary garrisons in the seventeenth century and continued to establish garrisons in central Asia well into the eighteenth century. For a fuller history of garrison life, see Elliott, *The Manchu Way*.

5. QDZGNB, vol. 3: 2218–31. On the Hangzhou garrison, see Crossley, *Orphan Warriors*, 63–67; the Hanzhong garrison was initially commanded and subsequently controlled by Wu Sangui.

6. On the establishment of governors-general, see DQHDSL, 23 (vol. 1: 288–97); QS, 116:1385–88; and QDZGNB, vol. 2: 1342–74, 1510–11 chart.

7. Oxnam, *Ruling from Horseback*, 98.

8. Wakeman, *The Great Enterprise*, vol. 2: 1025, 1021–24 passim. In some older works, these officials are known as viceroys, a title that may capture their responsibilities in the early days of the dynasty, though "governor-general" seems a better rendering for most of the Qing period.

9. The posts were created on the thirteenth day of the eighth lunar month, and appointees were designated to fill them on the eleventh day of the ninth lunar month. See KXSL, 4:10b–11a, 15a–b (vol. 4: 84, 86). Fujian is perhaps the clearest example of the consequences of this policy in the provinces; there, a new central official appointed at the begin-

ning of the regency reversed some of the concessions to local practice implemented by his predecessors. See chapter 7.

10. DQHDSL, 23:8b–9a, (vol. 1: 292); KXSL, 15:14a (vol. 4: 229). Robert Oxnam argues that these positions were eliminated because of the corruption of provincial officialdom and because the dynasty seemed to be at peace. *Ruling from Horseback*, 216. Both of these explanations are possible, although none of the regent-installed governors-general were dismissed for corruption and the military situation in 1665 did not seem markedly less threatening than in 1662. I have therefore treated these appointments as a failed experiment, although I acknowledge that the experiment could have been pronounced a failure for a variety of reasons. See also Miller, "Factional Conflict," 23–24.

11. KXSL, 30:13b (vol. 4: 410).

12. For a history of the establishment of governors' posts, see DQHDSL, 12 (vol. 1: 288–97); QS, 116:1388–90; and QDZGNB, vol. 2: 1516–60, 1754–55 chart.

13. See "Shunzhi chunian longluo yu kongzhi Hanzu guanshen shiliao," a collection of 107 memorials written between 1644 and 1646, in which former Ming officials recommend others and offer their own services to the new regime. In a few of these memorials, newly appointed governors in north China describe the conditions they encountered as they took up their posts.

14. QDZGNB, vol. 3: 1516–17. Five of the former Ming officials who served as governors in the first years of the Qing are included in *Biographies of Twice-Serving Officials* (Er chen zhuan).

15. These regimes were somewhat unstable, and it took at least a generation for civilian territorial government to be secured in the far south. See the descriptions in this volume of the governorships of Tong Guoqi in Fujian (chapter 7), Tong Yangjia in Guangdong (chapter 8), and Bian Sanyuan in Guizhou (chapter 9).

16. See SZSL, 45:7a–b (vol. 3: 361), 64:2a–b (vol. 3: 4990). Also see chapter 4 of this volume for discussion of these texts.

17. Ibid., 63:2a (vol. 3: 499).

18. On Yansui, KXSL, 7:7b (vol. 4: 121); on Yunyang, ibid., 11:20b (vol. 4: 178); and on Nangan, ibid., 15:14a (vol. 4: 22).

19. The impeachments of these governors were first published in *Collected Historical Documents* (Zhanggu congbian) in 1928. For a reprint, see "Shunzhi qin zheng hou Han guan bei ke an."

20. QDZGNB, vol. 3: 1758–79; DQHDSL, vol. 1: 24.18b–23a (vol. 1: 306–8).

21. In fact, during the eighteenth century, the dynasty ceased making appointments to Sichuan, Gansu, and Zhili; *Collected Statutes of the Qing* confirms that China had fifteen provinces.

22. Qian Mu, *Guoshi dagang*, vol. 2: 601; Xiao, *Qingdai tongshi*, vol. 1: 537. See also Zhao Xiting, "Qingdai zongdu yu xunfu" ; and Zhao Xiting, "Qingdai ge sheng di zhengzhi zhidu".

23. Accounts of the Kangxi reign have focused more on its conquests than on the institution building that attended them. This was true of the earliest modern accounts of the reign, such as that found in Xiao, *Qingdai tongshi*, vol. 1: 419–99. It has also been true of more recent accounts in Chinese, such as Meng Zhaoxin's *Kangxi pingzhuan* and his earlier *Kangxi dadi quanzhuan* as well as the overall assessment by Shang Hongkui, "Lun Kangxi." The emphasis on accomplishments is also reflected in the basic English-language scholarship on Kangxi, including Spence, *Emperor of China*, and Kessler, *K'ang-hsi*.

Despite the traditional emphasis on the Kangxi reign, several important works have indeed focused on Chinese roles in shaping the political activity of the reign. These include Spence, Ts'ao Yin and the K'ang-hsi Emperor and Miller, "Factional Conflict," an important but unpublished dissertation. For an interesting counterpoint to the dominant Chinese-language emphasis on Kangxi accomplishments, see Liu Danian's 1961 "Lun Kangxi" (to which Shang Hongkui's "Lun Kangxi" may be a response) and, more recently, Huang Chin-Shing's Philosophy, Philology, and Politics, 143–68.

24. Da Ming huidian, 2:1a–b (vol. 1: 93).

25. Qing chao wen xian tong kao, 77:5571. Concerns about superfluous posts were very common in the early Qing.

26. Hucker, A Dictionary of Official Titles, 253.

27. KXSL, 3:1b–2a (vol. 4: 69). On Wei Yijie, see Wakeman, The Great Enterprise, 943–44; and ECCP, 849–50.

28. Da Qing huidian, 1690 Kangxi ed., 5:1b.

29. Hucker, A Dictionary of Official Titles, 517. Liu Ziyang, Qing difang guanzhikao, 89–90.

30. Da Qing huidian, 1690 Kangxi ed., 8:28a–29a.

31. Da Qing huidian, 1733 Yongzheng ed., 8:10b. This language first appears in Yong-zheng edition, but the practice is treated there as the standing procedure of the dynasty and is placed before the Shunzhi edicts on the appointment of governors. Since the Yongzheng edition is 33 percent longer than the 1690 Kangxi edition and had been prepared in an age when bureaucratic prerogatives were being defined, it is likely to have been more inclusive of the dynastic legislation enacted both before and after the compilation of Kangxi edition.

32. KXSL, 4.3b (vol. 4: 91).

33. DQHDSL, 23:7a (vol. 1: 292); KXSL, 35.22a (vol. 4: 480).

34. Xu, Zhongguo fazhi shilunlue, 121.

35. Da Qing huidian, 1733 Yongzheng edition, 8:1b. Like the statute identifying the posts from which an official might be promoted to governor, this statute appears first in the Yongzheng edition but is treated there as the standing procedure of the dynasty.

36. DQHDSL 23:11b–12a (vol. 1: 293).

37. Ibid., 23:15b (vol. 1: 294).

38. The governor was named Tuoyong, and the case is well described in his biography, GCQXLZ. Tuoyong was dismissed in 1746. See QLSL, 263:12a–14b, 264:19a–b (vol. 12: 410, 427).

39. Da Qing huidian, 1760 Qianlong ed., 4:2b.

40. In the Kangxi edition of Da Qing huidian, rules on the appointment of governors are attached to the chapter "Manchu vacancies." Da Qing huidian, 1690 Kangxi ed., 7:1b. A special decree was issued in 1663, providing for the direct transfer of bannermen from their military units to posts such as that of lieutenant governor. Ibid., 8:28a–b.

41. Da Qing huidian, 1822 Jiaqing ed., 2:2a (21). See also Chu and Saywell, Career Pat-terns in the Ch'ing Dynasty, 28–30; and Liu Ziyang, Qingdai difang guanzhikao, 40. The latter two accounts take the Jiaqing wording to represent procedures during the entire dynasty. However, as discussed in this chapter, it was applied to governors' offices in 1671. It was announced for the first time in the Jiaqing reign as part of a spelling out of the prerogatives of the Grand Council.

42. Da Ming huidian, 5:19b–29a (110–15). Xun-fu are discussed on 5:19b (110).

43. Collected Statutes and Precedents of the Qing devotes four juan to ranked-list regulations: two for Manchu and two for Chinese officials. DQHDSL, juan 48–52 (vol. 1: 608–56). Gen-

erally, the chapters move from the rules governing promotions of more senior officials to rules governing more junior promotions. The relatively brief discussion of making ranked lists for governors occurs at 51:1 (vol. 1: 654).

44. Morohashi, *Dai Kanwa jiten*, vol. 11: 721 (entry 41233.406). While it is always danger-ous for a late-imperial Chinese historian to claim to have found the origins of a practice, it seems likely that the idea of preparing ranked lists of officials for promotion was a Qing innovation.

45. *Da Qing huidian*, 1733 Yongzheng ed., 8:10b–11a; DQHDSL, vol. 1: 290.

46. *Da Qing huidian*, 1690 Kangxi ed., 7:3b; *Da Qing huidian*, 1733 Yongzheng ed., 8:11a.

47. KXSL, 35:13b (vol. 4: 476).

48. See "(Ai Yuanzheng) Ben Zhuan," in Li Yuan, *Guochao Qixian leizheng*, 45:14a–15a.

49. Wang and Jin, "Cong qingchu dili zhikan fengjian guanliao zhengzhi," 138–39. See also Lui, *Corruption in China*, 33.

50. QDZGNB, vol. 2: 1540–55.

51. *Da Qing huidian*, 1733 Yongzheng ed., 8:1b.

52. On the reorganization of the Grand Secretariat, see Meng Zhaoxin, *Kangxi ping-zhuan*, 61–60; and Miller, "Factional Conflict," 104. According to *Collected Statutes of the Qing*, the practice of making ranked lists was applied to the appointment of officials in the Grand Secretariat in 1671, but there is no edict establishing this fact in *Veritable Records of the Kangxi Emperor*. In these years, there was also a spate of proposals on reorganizing evaluation and promotion procedures in the lower territorial service. See "Kangxi chunian," 3–19.

53. See Miller, "Factional Conflict," 100–106. There is no suggestion of factional alle-giance in Ai Yuancheng's biography, but his career paralleled that of Mingju, a leader of what Miller calls the Plain Yellow Banner faction at court. It is quite possible that the sug-gestion of making ranked lists was meant to clear the way so the new Manchu faction could place some of its own adherents in provincial office.

54. ECCP, 938–39; QS, 3968–69; and GCQXLZ, zhuan 158. See also Cai, *Yu Qingduan gong (Chenglong) zheng shu*. See also the discussion of Yu's activities in Jiangsu in chapter 9 in this volume.

55. Yu provides a fascinating discussion of Sichuan and its problems in "Qinghua tongliang tiaoyi," in Cai, *Yu Qingduan gong (Chenglong) zheng shu*, vol. 1: 135–42.

56. The earliest biographies of Yu were by Xiong Cili, who wrote his epitaph (reprinted in Cai, *Yu Qingduan gong (Chenglong) zheng shu*, vol. 4: 1329–44); Chen Tingjian, "Yu Chen-glong Gong Zhuan," in Cai, *Yu Qingduan gong (Chenglong) zheng shu*, vol. 4: 1223–90; and Mao Jike, "Yu Chenglong gongzhuan," in Cai, *Yu Qingduan gong (Chenglong) zheng shu*, vol. 4: 1291–1319. Xiong, Chen, and Mao were all members of the Hanlin Academy in the late Kangxi period. Probably the clearest statement of Yu's ethic of public service is in the "Six Admonitions," which he issued to Jiangnan officials during his term as governor-general. See Cai, *Yu Qingduan gong (Chenglong) zheng shu*, vol. 3: 951–60. On frugality as an important theme in Qing political discourse, see Rowe, *Saving the World*, 128–30, 195–97, 327.

57. His eighteenth-century biographies were written by Peng Shaoshu, Yuan Mei, and Dai Zhen. The biography by Dai Zhen was written for the *Fen zhou zhi*. The three eighteenth-century biographies are reprinted in GCQXLZ, 158:37b–49b.

58. *Da Qing huidian*, 1733 Yongzheng ed., 8:1b.

59. KXSL, 152:18b–19a (vol. 4: 696).

60. Fu Zongmou, "Qingdai dufu shixiang zhi fenxi," in *Qing zhi lunwenji*, 256. Fu Zong-mou's is the only prosopographic study of Qing governors. It is, however, a partial one,

based only on the provincial governors whose biographies were included in *History of the Qing*. A list of the governors included in *History of the Qing* and in Fu's study can be found on the large, unnumbered fold-out pages inserted between pages 174 and 175 of Fu's *Qingdai dufu zhidu*. This list includes 571 names for the entire Qing dynasty. My own count of governors, based on appointment edicts indexed in *Qingdai zhi guan nian biao*, produces 792 governors for the years 1700–1900. Fu's work is still useful, however, as it includes all the governors whose careers were judged important enough, by their contemporaries and early twentieth-century historians, to be recorded for posterity.

61. *Da Qing huidian*, 1733 Yongzheng ed., 8:1b.

62. *Da Qing huidian*, 1760 Qianlong ed., 8:3b.

63. *Qin ding Li bu ze li*, 5:55b.

64. On the Yongzheng emperor's attitude toward delta finance, see Zelin, *The Magistrate's Tael*, 253–62.

65. See ECCP, 920–21; and QLSL, 915.41–45a (vol. 16: 918).

66. The case of Guo Tai, discussed in chapter 6 in this volume, illustrates the pressure to appoint lieutenant governors and governors in Shandong and also the dangers of the practice.

67. Sichuan, Zhili, Gansu, Xinjian, and Taiwan all existed for relatively short periods of time, and the governments of these provinces were sufficiently specialized that including them in this comparison would not be meaningful.

68. QDZGNB, vol. 3: 1645–68.

69. Revenue quotas here are taken from Zelin, *The Magistrate's Tael*, 28, which cites the Yongzheng edition of *Collected Statutes of the Qing*. The amount of land tax remitted to the capital by a province is only an approximate measure of provincial importance. The land tax was, of course, only a portion of the revenue a province remitted to the central government; the grain tribute tax, profits from the salt monopoly, and customs and commercial taxes were remitted regularly to the court. Also, strategic military priorities and the cultivation of local elites obviously determined relations between provincial capitals and the center. Nonetheless, land tax remittances provide a first and quantifiable approximation of provincial importance.

70. *Qijuzhu* (Summer 1736): 13–30.

71. Kuhn, *Soulstealers*, 203–7.

72. *Qin ding Li bu ze li*, 5:55a–b.

73. DQHDSL, 50:2a (vol. 1: 635).

74. This English anecdote attributes the origin of the "pricking" of sheriffs to the reign of Elizabeth I. The monarch, as it seems, was doing embroidery in her garden when she was presented with a list of candidates for sheriff. She signified her choice with the only instrument readily available, her embroidery needle. Later, a special silver needle was fashioned especially for the selection of sheriffs. Irene Gladwin has argued that this colorful anecdote should be read as the beginning of a decline in importance of sheriffs. See Gladwin, *The Sheriff*, 196–97.

75. Qian Mu, *Zhongguo lidai zhengzhi deshi*, 116, 128. It is remarkable how much Qian Mu's tone in this passage resembles that of Gu Yanwu.

76. Hartwell, "Financial Expertise."

77. See Dardess, *Confucianism and Autocracy*, 13–84 passim.

Chapter 3. The Conundrum of Competence

1. This figure represents an estimate of the character count in the appointment regulations in *Da Ming huidian*, juan 5: 101–10; and DQHD, juan 9: 76–91.

2. DQHDSL, juan 17–61 (vol. 1: 414–975). This slightly overstates the actual number of regulations, since each subsection of the code is further divided into regulations applicable to Manchu officials and regulations applicable to Chinese officials. Many of the regulations are applicable to both types of officials and so are printed twice. Juan numbers are as follows: qualification for office, 33–42 (Manchu officials), 43–47 (Chinese officials); ranked lists, 48–49 (Manchu officials), 50–51 (Chinese officials); and selections, 52–55 (Manchu officials), 56–67 (Chinese officials). Regulations for extraordinary promotions are not divided and are found in juan 70–77.

3. DQHDSL, juan 78–138 (vol. 2: 1–786). The regulations on administrative discipline associated with functions of the Board of Personnel have been thoroughly studied by Thomas Metzger in *The Internal Organization of Ch'ing Bureaucracy*.

4. On personnel administration, see HCJSWB, juan 15–25. This account is organized on the same principles as *Collected Statutes of the Qing* and *Collected Statutes and Precedents of the Qing*. The following topics are addressed: general comments on personnel practices (*shilun* [juan 15, 16]), "qualification for office" (*quanxuan* [juan 17]), the official hierarchy (*guanzhi* [juan 18]), evaluations (*kaocha* [juan 19]), great officials (*dashi* [juan 20]), local officials (*shouling* [juan 21–23]), clerks (*shili* [juan 24]), and private secretaries (*muyu* [juan 25]).

5. Legge, *The Chinese Classics*, vol. 3: 50.

6. See Lin, *Zhouli jinzhu jinyi*, 19–25; and Biot, *Le Tcheou-li*, 54–55.

7. Zheng, "San dai kaoji," 10–11.

8. The 1761 palace examinations asked candidates to write about Qing evaluation practices. See Man-cheong, *The Class of 1761*, 82–91.

9. On general regulations for calculating the terms of "territorial officials" (*waiguan jifeng*), see *Da Qing huidian*, 1690 Kangxi ed., 8:19a–b; and DQHDSL, 69 (vol. 1: 888–92). One might suggest, pace Lévi-Strauss, that the classificatory terminology was not accidental. In the early years of the Qing, the differences between those who served on the borders and those who served inside the empire were probably so great that the colorful terminology did not seem excessive. For detailed regulations about what constituted a border post, see DQHDSL, 69–70 (838–65); juan 69 concerns the northwest, and juan 70 concerns the southern borders.

10. See Wang Mingyue, "Qiliu jiaozhi shu"; and Wei Yijie, "Zhifu liuren shu." The table of contents of juan 18 of *Essays on Statecraft in Our Times* (Huangchao jingshi wenbian) identifies "Zhifu liuren shu" as written by Wei Yijie. Both Wang and Wei were influential advisers to the Shunzhi court. See ECCP, 848–49; and QS, 245:3780–81. In *Essays on Statecraft*, these proposals are placed next to reprints of passages on the same subject by Gu Yanwu.

11. ZPZZ, vol. 5: 2595–96. Ortai's response to the imperial comments is in HCJSWB, 15:19a–20a (vol. 1: 393).

12. See Chu and Saywell, *Career Patterns in the Ch'ing Dynasty*, 40.

13. John R. Watt examines the term lengths of magistrates in seven lower Yangzi valley districts. He finds it useful to distinguish between the longer and more regular "substantive" appointments and the much more irregular "acting" appointments. Broadly, the distinction made here, between very long and very short terms and those of medium length,

corresponds to Watt's finding that, in effect, two different dynamics shaped term length. See Watt, *District Magistrate in Late Imperial China*, 59–67.

14. The question of why so few governors—both those serving short and long terms—died in office is an interesting one, but the answer can only be a matter of speculation. As members of the elite, governors would have had access to the best nutrition and medical care that Chinese society had to offer. There may also have been a psychological effect; individuals who perceive themselves as successful in worldly terms tend to lead longer and healthier lives than do contemporaries who see their situations differently. Governors were among the most successful people in Chinese society and government.

It is perhaps worth noting that the Qing civil service system did not allow for retirement, but there were ways in which an official could essentially retire. A certain percentage of those who left office to mourn simply did not apply for reappointment after the required mourning period. It was also possible for an official to leave office due to illness, real or imagined, and not return to office. I have found very few such cases in the seventeenth century; most of the officials who left due to illness died within six months of leaving office. This phenomenon was somewhat more common in the nineteenth century.

15. For an example of the ripples a fairly minor event could create in the small pool of territorial officials, see the discussion in chapter 6 of this volume about the series of appointments occasioned by the transfer of Chen Hongmou to the governor-generalship of Liangguang.

16. *Da Qing huidian*, 1690 Kangxi ed., 8:17a–18a.

17. DQHDSL, 60:1a–2b (vol. 1: 762) The Qianlong emperor's system resembles the one proposed by Wang Mingyue except that Wang awarded different titles to junior officials who had served successfully. It is noteworthy that the emperor issued this decree in the same year that he clarified the relationship between the ranks of governors and lieutenant governors.

18. Three governors died in office, two left office to mourn, six left due to some form of administrative discipline, and one was transferred to another governorship.

19. SZSL 71:3b (vol. 3: 560); Wakeman, *The Great Enterprise*, vol. 2: 952. Wei Xiangshu's memorial proposing that the Qing reinstitute the grand accounting, "Qing fu ru jin kao cha shu," is in HCJSWB, 18a–19a (vol. 1: 495–96). On Wei Xiangshu, see ECCP, 848–49.

20. See DQHDSL, 80:4b–6b (vol. 2: 30–31).

21. In the Ming, the end-of-term evaluation was the process for capital officials. Since *xunfu* were regarded as central officials in the Ming, they were subject to these evaluations, which determined their rank at the capital. See *Da Ming huidian*, 12:3b–5a.

22. For regulations of the Ming court visit system, see ibid., 13:1a–9a.

23. *Da Qing huidian*, 1733 Yongzheng ed., 12:9b; QS, 112:1340.

24. *Da Qing huidian*, 1733 Yongzheng ed., 13:2a–b; DQHD, 11:9b–10a (95–96). Translations for the evaluation terminology and characterizations are from Kuhn, *Soulstealers*, 194, with minor modifications. Kuhn's chart shows three evaluations in each of the four categories. The 1899 edition of *Da Qing huidian* defines only two for several categories. See also Metzger, *The Internal Organization of Ch'ing Bureaucracy*, 368.

25. DQHDSL, 80:1a–2b (vol. 2: 28–29).

26. See YZSL, 103.11a–12b, 140.7a–b (vol. 7: 365, 771), for imperial edicts acknowledging receipt of these reports. See also Feng Erkang, *Yongzheng zhuan*, 469.

27. DQHDSL, 80.12b–13a (vol. 2: 34).

28. Ibid., 80:27b–28a (vol. 2: 41). Additional quotas were provided for officials of rank lower than the magistrates as well as for educational officials.

29. QS, 240:3744–45.

30. Ibid., 293:4061–62.

31. Ibid., 278:3968–70.

32. Ibid., 307:4152–53. Cao received his *jinshi* in 1729 and was appointed to the Hanlin Academy, where he served until 1736. After a brief appointment at the Qianlong court, he died abruptly in 1731.

33. Cao Yishi, "Qing fen bie xian neng shu," in HCJSWB, 19:24a–b (vol. 1: 498).

34. Ibid., 19:25a (vol. 1: 499).

35. *Da Qing shichao shengxun*, 92:6, in Kuhn, *Soulstealers*, 196.

36. Kuhn, *Soulstealers*, 190.

37. Hucker, *A Dictionary of Official Titles*, 160.

38. G. William Skinner, "Cities and the Hierarchy of Local Systems," in *The City in Late Imperial China*, 321.

39. DQHDSL, 61:11a–14a (vol. 1: 782–83). In 1899, there were fifty-three autonomous departments and twenty autonomous subprefectures. For a description of their establishment and evolution, see DQHDSL, 28:1a–10b (vol. 1: 352–55). The rule that governors would select the officials of these counties was labeled as *yuanding*, meaning that it was part of the original regulations of the dynasty. This would seem to confirm Skinner's hypothesis that, from the beginning, certain jurisdictions were meant to be special, as opposed to the notion in Brunnert and Hagelstrom that these were areas transitioning to more normal patterns of administration. See Brunnert and Hagelstrom, *Present Day Political Organization of China*, 426.

40. DQHDSL, 67:5a–13a (vol. 1: 848–52).

41. Ibid., 67:18b–28a (vol. 1: 833–36.) For further regulations governing Taiwan officials, see chapter 7 in this volume.

42. Ibid., 69:6a (vol. 1: 849).

43. Ibid., 65:2b–7a (vol. 1: 825–28).

44. Ibid., 63:15a–18a (vol. 1: 811–12).

45. Ibid., 66:1a (vol. 1: 838).

46. Ibid., 67:13a–20b (vol. 1: 853–59). The emperor himself created the term "Miao frontier areas."

47. G. William Skinner, "Cities," 315–16.

48. *Yongzheng zhupi yuzhi*, 5233. A Chinese bannerman, Guo Hong had experience with subordinate offices in the territorial order. He had been promoted from prefect to provincial judge in Guangxi and then became lieutenant governor. In 1728, he was promoted to governor, a position he held until 1736. In view of the region where he served, it is possible that he was one of Ortai's protégés. He also impressed the emperor during the interview before his promotion to provincial judge. See Liu Keyi, "Cong 'shu pi yin jian dan' kan Yongzheng di zhi ren," 28–29. During the course of his service, he changed his surname from Guo to Jin.

49. For the rescript on Guo Hong's proposal, see *Yongzheng zhupi yuzhi*, 5233.

50. DQHDSL, 61:18a (vol. 1: 785); YZSL, 113:11b–12b (vol. 8: 510).

51. Skinner has argued that there was a "secret strategic component" to post designations that raised certain posts to "important" even though they had only two designations.

While I have not examined all the possible cases, in most of the ones I have observed, the posts that counted as "important," even though they had only two designators, were those that had been set aside by the late Kangxi and Yongzheng era edicts. In this case, there was certainly an additional component to these post rankings, but its origin was no particular secret.

52. DQHD, 8:10b–13a (74–76). Governor-controlled postings were also identified in a manual of official postings, *A Complete Guide to Ranks and Postings* (Quezhi quanlan), which was published privately in 1904. The purpose of this volume seems to have been to prepare officials for the postings to which they had been dispatched. The volume not only recorded the fact that a post had been judged "important" or "very important" but also noted the designations assigned to a post and whether the post belonged to one of the categories placed under the control of governors by imperial edict.

53. *Ri zhi lu*, 11:228.

54. Cai and Gu may well have known each other. The Cai family was from Kunshan county in Jiangsu, and Cai's father was killed in the fighting at the time of the Qing conquest. Cai was nominated for the Boxue Hongru examinations but declined to take them. He did not, however, completely spurn the Qing administration. Later in the seventeenth century, he edited the state papers of Jiangsu governor-general Yu Chenglong, *Yu Wenduan gong zheng shu*. Included in these papers was a memorial in which Yu complained that the rigidity of Board of Personnel procedures did not allow him flexibility in choosing the prefect of Nanjing.

55. This system is described in Watt, *District Magistrate in Late Imperial China*, 48–50.

56. On the institution of the lottery, see Pan, *Ming dai wen guan quan xuan zhidu yanjiu*, 189–209.

57. Cai, "Shu dian gu er jishi che qian shu hou" in HCJSWB, 17:29a–b.

58. Cai, "Shu jia Zhongcheng diao que fan jian shu hou," in HCJSWB, 18:31b–32a (vol. 1: 468).

59. "Yongqian shiqi difang guan que shiliao," 3–6.

60. YZSL, 149:2b–3a (vol. 8: 844). The edict also ordered that designations be given to posts that had been set aside, such as the "Miao internal frontiers."

61. I have not seen Li Wei's memorial, but Zhang Tingyu refers to it in a comment on a proposal from Jiangxi to reclassify magistracies in that province. See "Yongqian shiqi difang guan que shiliao," 7.

62. For the reorganization of local government in Fujian, see ibid., 6–7. YZSL, 144:2a–3b (vol. 8: 800).

63. In 1992 and 1993, archivists from Beijing's First Historical Archives published a two-part article containing a series of memorials from the archives of the Grand Council and the Grand Secretariat. In these memorials, governors requested changes in post designations. In addition to the memorials from Sichuan's Lieutenant Governor Liu and the responses to the 1733 edict cited above, the article includes fourteen Qianlong era memorials that request changes in post designations. See "Yongqian shiqi difang guan que shiliao," 17–23. Philip Kuhn has included a memorial on the designation of Chongyang county, Hubei, in his *Reading Documents*, vol. 1: 57–58; vol. 2: 38.

64. Watt, *District Magistrate in Late Imperial China*, 263 n. 8.

65. Masui, "Qianlong chao 'Quan guo sheng fu xian guan que biao' kao."

66. DQHDSL, 59:19a–20b (vol. 1: 756).

67. I have found fourteen such memorials in the volumes of reprinted palace memorials from 1762 that were published by the National Palace Museum in Taipei. It is the first year for which the museum reprinted memorials from all twelve months. See *Gongzhongdang Qianlong chao zouzhe*, vol. 16: 522, 673, 720; vol. 17: 6, 23, 30, 73, 213, 277, 284, 427, 589, 604, 635.

68. DQHDSL, 59:27b (vol. 1: 760).

69. See Metzger, *The Internal Organization of Ch'ing Bureaucracy*, 397–417. The argument is further developed in his later book *Escape from Predicament*; see 167–90.

70. Kuhn, *Soulstealers*, 230–32.

71. Zito, *Of Body and Brush*, 7.

72. Rawski, *The Last Emperors*, and see esp. 286.

Chapter 4. The Power of the Unexpected

1. A full consideration of the circumstances behind every special appointment, fascinating though such a discussion might be, is beyond the scope of this or perhaps any single book. But there may be merit to a broader, composite portrait of special appointments. The field of Qing political history has developed largely through case studies, carefully drawn miniatures of moments and persons. It seems likely, given the nature of training in the field and the character of Qing archival sources, that case studies will predominate in the future. Valuable as such accounts are, they need to be set in context, so that the uniqueness of specific times and places can be more carefully assessed. The discussion that follows describes the points at which appointments of unexpected individuals were made. Against the background of such a quantitative description, it should be possible, both in this volume and in subsequent scholarship, to measure the character and importance of the special events that expressed the will of the Qing monarchy.

2. See Bartlett, *Monarchs and Ministers*, 55–56, 351 n. 40.

3. See Morohashii, *Dai kanwa jiten*, vol. 7: 644–47, provides a broad survey of the uses of *te*.

4. YZSL, 2:15a–b (vol. 7: 52). In 1723–24, the court undertook major repairs on the Grand Canal. See *Qing shilu Shandong shiliao xuanbian*, vol. 1: 116–24.

5. It appears to have been the practice in the nineteenth-century *Diaries of Action and Repose* (*Qiju zhu*) to refer to special appointees and promotees as having rank "bestowed" upon them, whereas transfers of serving governors from one province to another were referred to with the character *gai*. But this is the only consistent linguistic marker of appointment type to be found in the record.

6. In this chapter, I have counted an appointment as special if the appointee held a position from which he would not have been appointed as governor by routine means. These appointments could be effected only by the special intervention of the emperor. This may understate, to some degree, the role of the emperor in the personnel process, since the monarch may possibly have been involved in promotions or transfers that were in accord with personnel routines. But defining special appointments narrowly does identify those appointments that could have been made only by the emperor and points out instances of relatively greater court involvement.

7. Cashiering was the outcome of a legal procedure in which an official was first indicted and then investigated. The court, however, retained the power to characterize the

seriousness of the offense and to decide on the punishment. See DQHD, 11:1a–8a (91–95); DQHDSL, 82.21b–27b (vol. 2: 57–60); Park, "Corruption and Its Recompense," 89–203; and Metzger, *Internal Organization of Ch'ing Bureaucracy*, 235–397.

8. Fewer governors left office through demotion than might be expected, in part because many who were formally demoted remained at their posts, suffering symbolic punishment only.

9. Typically, officials were relieved of responsibility pending investigation. The procedure allowed the court to relieve a governor without having to spell out the nature of his misdeed. When an official was relieved of responsibility, his post was not declared vacant, and therefore no ranked list of possible successors was prepared. See *Qin ding Li bu ze li*, 3:10b–11a.

10. This procedure was often used when military actions were involved, and the court summoned the governor to provide needed information on the local situation. No punishment was implied in such a case.

11. Between 1700 and 1900, there were 126 cashierings. In 94 cases, governors were relieved of responsibility; in 51, they left office as a result of demotion; and in 72, they were summoned to the capital as successors were appointed.

12. For an interesting discussion of treatments of the Yongzheng emperor as reformer, see Gu Zhen, "Dui Yongzheng gaige di pinglun zai pinglun."

13. YZSL, 3:8a (vol. 7: 71).

14. *Zhang Wenzhong gong quan ji*, 4–5. Translated in Crawford, "Chang Chu-cheng," 243.

15. On the roots of financial instability in the Yongzheng period, see Zelin, *The Magistrate's Tael*, 1–23.

16. YZSL, 3:5b (vol. 7: 69).

17. Ibid., 3:14b (vol. 7: 74). This remark actually comes from the emperor's edict to lieutenant governors. The emperor offered no particular solution to this dilemma of rank and responsibility. Sadly, one hundred years later, the Yongzheng emperor's grandson, the Jiaqing emperor, would complain of the same problem. See DQHDSL, 101:4a–b (vol. 2: 296).

18. KXSL, 299:13a–16a (vol. 6: 897–98).

19. YZSL, 3:6a (vol. 7: 69).

20. On the changing military obligations of governors, see Fu, *Qingdai dufu zhidu*, 95–98.

21. The appointments included Li Weijun in Zhili, Fan Shijie in Shaanxi, and He Tianpei in Jiangsu. Nian Gengyao, a distant relative of Li Weijun's, indicted Li's predecessor, Zhao Zhihuan. It was also on the basis of Nian's information that De Yin was dismissed in Shanxi. In the summer of 1723, Nian Gengyao's brother was appointed governor of Guangdong. See Feng, *Yongzheng zhuan*, 99–100.

22. YZSL, 3:6b–7a (vol. 7: 69–70).

23. Ibid., 3:7a (vol. 7: 70).

24. See Zelin, *The Magistrate's Tael*, 96.

25. See Smith, *Ch'ing Policy*, 13.

26. Ibid., p. 16. William Rowe, in his *Saving the World*, sees the southwest as a crucible for "new men," but I am inclined to believe the phenomenon was empire wide. There was a reduction in the numbers of men appointed from the Grand Secretariat and Censorate to governors' positions in the early Yongzheng reign; see Smith, *Ch'ing Policy*, chapter 3, note 43.

27. On Xu, see QS, 277:3962–63; on Chen, see QS, 290:4043–44.

28. On the emperor's relations with two Kangxi holdovers, Fang Bao and his friend Wei Tingzhen, see R. Kent Guy, "Fang Pao and the Ch'in-ting Ssu-shu-wen," in Elman and Woodside, *Education and Society*, 155–57.

29. Feng, *Yongzheng zhuan*, 85.

30. Quoted in ibid., 457.

31. YZSL, 49:19b–20a (vol. 7: 743–4). Quoted in Smith, *Ch'ing Policy*, 14. The emperor was responding in this edict to the cases of Wang Jingqi and Cha Siting. On these cases, see Goodrich, *The Literary Inquisition of Ch'ien-lung*, 80–81, 83.

32. "Yongzheng chao zhupi yin jian dan."

33. See Liu Keyi, "Cong 'Zhu pi yinjian dan'kan Yongzheng di shi ren."

34. "Yongzheng chao zhupi yin jian dan," 143. The term *jinyao* was drawn from the post designation system, reviewed in chapter 3 of this volume. In the case of circuit intendancies, "important" and "very important" positions were filled from the court.

35. Ibid., 99.

36. Ibid., 104.

37. Ibid., 57.

38. Ibid., 91. On Wei Tingzhen, see Guy, "Fang Bao and the Ch'in-ting Ssu-shu-wen," in Elman and Woodside, *Education and Society*, 157.

39. On Wang Shu, see QS, 309:4172–73. Wang Shu's son Wang Rubi served as a governor in the Jiaqing reign.

40. "Yongzheng chao zhupi yin jian dan," 77. On Chang'an's career, see QS, 339:4372–74.

41. Quoted in Feng, *Yongzheng zhuan*, 460. Wang Guodong was a member of the Hanlin Academy and was recommended to the emperor by Tian Wenjing. He rose to be commissioner for the Rectification of Customs in Zhejiang and then governor of Hunan (1727–29).

42. Yongzheng Qiju zhu, entry for Yongzheng 4/3/16, quoted in ibid., 457.

43. YZSL, 31:25b–27a (vol. 6: 478–80).

44. The resulting compilation is *Yongzheng zhupi yuzhi*. On the decision to publish the collection, see Yang Qijiao, *Yongzheng di ji qi mizhe zhidu yenjiu*, 188–214.

45. *Yongzheng zhupi yuzhi*, 5:3217; quoted in Feng, *Yongzheng zhuan*, 458.

46. Bartlett, *Monarch and Ministers*, 68–79. There is a certain irony in the emperor's grief over the loss of his brother when, at least in the view of many twentieth-century scholars, he had spent the early part of his reign killing off or banishing his other brothers. The passions of this remarkable emperor may never be fully understood.

47. This account of Yongzheng reforms is taken from a memorial by Governor Wang Shijun submitted in the first year of the Qianlong reign. The original is held in the Number One Archives in Beijing. For accounts of Wang's memorial, see note 66.

48. The speed of change at the beginning of the Qianlong years suggests that plans may have been in the works before Yongzheng died and raises questions about how, and how rapidly, the emperor died. In a recent biography, Feng Erkang examines the evidence on Yongzheng's death. He finds no proof that the Yongzheng emperor died of foul play or experienced any lingering illness. He also finds no evidence to support the traditional legend that Yongzheng died from overindulging in elixirs of immortality. See Feng, *Yongzheng zhuan*, 540–51.

49. QLSL, 3:7b–8b (vol. 9: 183).

50. Ibid., 7:2ba–29a (vol. 9: 289–97).

51. Ibid., 14:5a–6b (vol. 9: 395–96).

52. For an account of Ortai's role in the southwest, see Herman, "National Integration and Political Hegemony," 181–211; and Smith, *Ch'ing Policy*.

53. For Yuan Zhancheng's role, see GCQXLZ, 171:22a–b.

54. See ECCP, 41, 602; and Tang and Luo, *Qianlong zhuan*, 14–20. On the factional maneuvering about this case, see *Qianlong huangdi quan zhuan*, 96–97.

55. The best discussion in English of this campaign is Dai Yingcong, "The Rise of the Southwestern Frontier," 272–82. See also ECCP, 204–5, 957–59; and Xiao, *Qingdai tongshi*, vol. 1: 835–41.

56. For Ortai's complaint, see ECCP, 602. On Fang Bao, see Fang, "Yu O, Zhang liang xiangguo lun zhiyu xibian shu," in *Fang Bao ji*, vol. 2: 637–46.

57. Xu first attracted the attention of the Yongzheng emperor in the first year of the reign when, as a provincial censor for Shaanxi, he indicted a Manchu salt censor for the Eastern Yellow River District for corruption. When Xu's charges were proved, he was appointed to replace the censor and then rapidly promoted to be lieutenant governor of Zhejiang in the autumn of 1726 and commissioner for morals and ideology in Zhejiang in the summer of 1727. When the emperor was preparing to go to war in the northwest, he appointed Xu governor of Gansu, bringing to an end a particularly turbulent period in the Gansu governorship, during which five persons had served in the office in seventy months. See QS, 292:4058; and *Yongzheng zhupi yuzhi*, 9:5601–55.

58. Erong'an emphasized his father's literary qualifications for office in a *nianpu* (chronological biography) probably written early in the Qianlong reign. His assertion of literary precocity need not be taken at face value. Probably more significant was the fact that Erong'an did not emphasis Ortai's place in Manchu society or the entitlements it might have brought. See Erong'an, "Xiang qin po E wen duan gong nianpu," 56–60.

59. *Qianlong huangdi quan zhuan*, 104. QLSL, 114:5b–8b (vol. 10: 670–71). In this edict, the emperor responds to a proposal that Tian Wenjing be posthumously removed from the Henan temple of eminent statesmen. The emperor read the proposal as an attempt by Henan governor Yaertu to curry favor with Ortai by attacking Tian Wenjing, who had been one of Ortai's main rivals during the Yongzheng reign, and rejected it. On Chang'an, see QS, 339:4372–74. See also the Yongzheng emperor's rather prescient comments on Chang'an cited above. On Famin, see GCQXLZ, 66:16a. There is no biography of Fude.

60. On Chen Hongmou's and Yin Huiyi's relationships with Ortai, see Rowe, *Saving the World*, 127–28. On Huang Tinggui, see *Qianlong huangdi quan zhuan*, 104–5.

61. QS, 313:4207–8.

62. Ortai's second and third sons share a biography with their father in ibid., 289:4033, and are also together in a biography in GCQXLZ, 179:31a–39b.

63. On Echang and Eleshun, see QS, 339:4370–72.

64. QLSL, 17:1a–3b, 15a–b (vol. 9: 439–40, 448). The indictment is quoted at some length in *Qing shi lie zhuan*, 18:13a–b; and QS, 295:4079. It included the lurid detail that poor people in Henan were being forced to sell their daughters in order to meet the heavy tax burden caused by taking reclaimed lands off the tax rolls.

65. QS, 295:4079–80.

66. Wang Shijun's memorial is held in the First Historical Archives, Beijing. For the Qianlong emperor's response to it, see QLSL, 23:16a–21a (vol. 9:522–24); and Guy, "Zhang Tingyu and Reconciliation," 53–57. See also Dai Yi, *Qianlong di ji qi shidai*, 111–12.

67. ECCP, 252–53; GCQXLZ, 29:5a–25b; and QS, 302:4118–20.

68. Sugimura, *Kenryu Kotei*, 21–33; ECCP, 371–72. Fuheng was placed in charge of the empress's funeral. On the complex political and social crisis precipitated by her death, see Kutcher, *Mourning in Late Imperial China*, 153–89.

69. *Qianlong huangdi quan zhuan*, 128–29. The Qianlong emperor was thirty at the time of Fuheng's appointment. Fuheng was thirty-five and the emperor was forty when the Qianlong court went to war in the northwest.

70. QS, 302–4120. The context of this remark is telling. On his return from the failed Burma campaign, the ailing Fuheng memorialized requesting punishment for his failure. The emperor remarked that not all military campaigns start out well and cited the campaign against Wu Sangui. Instead of punishing Fuheng, the emperor rewarded him. Later, the emperor acknowledged that the swamplands of the southwest marked the ecological limits of Qing influence.

71. See ECCP, 249–50 passim. QS, 302:4118–21, treats Fuheng as a fairly cautious and careful administrator. For a spirited defense of the accomplishments of Fukangan, see Dai Yi, "Fu Kang An," in *Qianlong di ji qi shidai*, 499–510.

72. Bartlett, *Monarchs and Ministers*, 201.

73. I obtained these numbers by comparing the list of clerks in Liang, *Shu yuan ji lue*, with the list of provincial governors in *Qingdai zhiguan nianbiao*. As Bartlett has noted, Liang's lists may not be complete; hence, my listing may not include some names, though I have not seen references to the Grand Council in the biographies of other governors.

74. QS, 313:4207.

75. GCQXLZ, 173:34a–41a.

76. Jiang Bing was removed from his governorship in Hunan in part because he used his knowledge of central procedures to save the life of an official the Qianlong emperor had ordered executed. See Guy, "Rule of Man," 98–102; and Guo, *Shiba shiji di Zhongguo zheng zhi*, 404–5.

77. QS, 309:4179; and GCQXLZ, 83:37a–b.

78. GCQXLZ, 172:26a. Neither the earlier experience nor the poem prevented Changjun from being cashiered and exiled to central Asia. He returned from exile, however, and served again at the Qianlong court. See Waley-Cohen, *Exile in Mid-Qing China*, 89, 208.

79. Other Fuheng protégés include Aertai, Sun Shiyi, and Agui. Fuheng was known as a fairly affable man who had good relations with the other members and clerks of the Grand Council. See Zhaolian, *Xiao ting za lu*, 1:11b.

80. It is impossible to measure accurately the extent to which each of the changes in the late 1760s contributed to the court's malaise. It may be worth noting, however, that of the eleven governors who were dismissed from office in 1768–69, three were involved in the soul stealers' case, five held posts along the Burma border, and three were dismissed for miscellaneous matters.

81. On the Burma war, see Woodside, "The Ch'ien-lung Reign," 263–68. See also Zhaolian, *Xiao ting za lu*, 5:1a–21b, which provides an account of all the senior officials who were lost to death or illness in the campaign.

82. ECCP, 533–34; GCQXLZ, 22.221–42a; QS, 303.4126–29. In *The Inner Opium War*, James Polachek describes Liu Tongxun as the patron of a faction of "north Chinese officials" (34). Although Liu certainly had many associates and protégés while in office, I have not seen them described as a faction.

83. ECCP, 51–52, 412–13. Liu Tongxun's role in the event is summarized in GCJXLX, 22:26a–29a. Gao Bin's son Gao Jin was appointed to his first provincial governorship in 1755, and two of his grandsons also served as provincial governors.

84. *Cheng ban tan wu*, vol. 1: 1–208. See also QS, 340:4375–76.

85. QLSL, 548:11b–12a (vol. 15: 977–78); QS, 340:4375. As a result of his lax supervision of Jiang Zhou, Mingde lost his post as governor of Shaanxi in 1757.

86. QLSL, 623:7b–9a (vol. 16: 1002–3); GCQXLZ, 22.35a–b.

87. Liu Tongxun was noted for his ability to tactfully point out to the Qianlong emperor the weaknesses of his policies. Liu did this cautiously, for in 1755, he had been cashiered for pointing out weaknesses in Qing military strategies in the northwest. See GCQXLZ, 29:31a–33a; and Li and Kang, *Qianlong Heshen yu Liu Yong*, 66–68.

88. On Liang Guozhi, see ECCP, 501; QS, 321:4249–50; and GCQXLZ, 29:27a. On Bi Yuan, see ECCP, 622–25; QS, 4337–38; and GCQXLZ, 184:8a–22a. Bi Yuan was one of Fuheng's protégés.

89. On Li Hu, see QS, 325:4278; GCQXLZ, 179:24a–30a; and Guy, "Dusty Byways of Empire." There is no biography of Yu Wenyi. Immediately after his service in Fujian, he was appointed to the Board of Punishments, where he served for one year before he died.

90. Chen Huizu's biography is attached to that of his father in ECCP, 99–100; it is attached to that of Wang Danwang in QS, 340:4377–78. On He Wei, see QS, 4287–89 (326); and GCQXLZ, 176:17a–20a.

91. The sources on Heshen are notoriously limited. There are references to the counselor scattered through *biji* materials and unofficial histories. Probably the most famous treatment of Heshen is an essay by Xue Fuheng, which attempts to estimate the size of Heshen's fortune. In the early twentieth century, William Hong published an article on Heshen's literary works, and Gugong Bowuyuan published central government documents related to the seizure of Heshen's property and his downfall. The subject of Qing official corruption became a particular interest of PRC scholars in the late 1980s and 1990s. In 1989, Feng Zuozhe, of the Chinese Academy of Social Sciences, published *Tanke zhi Wang—Heshen mi shih* [The king of corruption: The secret history of Heshen]. In 1998, Li Jingbing and Kang Guochang of the Qing History Institute published *Qianlong yu Heshen* [Qianlong and Heshen] (Xi'an: Shaanxi Peoples' Educational Press). In 2002, the same authors published an expanded version of their work, *Qianlong, Heshen yu Liu Yong* [Qianlong, Heshen, and Liu Yong] in Taiwan. Citations are to the Taiwan edition.

92. See *Cheng ban tan wu*, vol. 1: 939–1188; the commentaries on the case in Li and Kang, *Qianlong, He Shen yu Liu Yong*, 106–19; and Zhaolian, *Xiao ting za lu*, 4:2b. The apparent similarity between this case and the Hengwen case may simply be that both governors employed the same modus operandi in their corruption. This point has been explored in Park, "Corruption and Its Recompense," 32–38.

93. Zhaolian, *Xiao ting za lu*, 7:13b.

94. See Xue, *Yong'an biji*, 1:61–66.

95. See the discussion of this case in chapter 8 in this volume. Li Jingbing and Kang Guochang raise valuable doubts about Heshen's relations with Guotai in *Qianlong, He Shen yu Liu Yong*, 119–22.

96. QLSL, 1251:18a–19b, 1265:1b–41. See also *Cheng ban tan wu*, 4:3291–3387. Fusong's opposition to Heshen is attested in his biography (QSL, 4374 [339]), and also in draft biographies prepared by the Guoshiguan held in the National Palace Museum, Taipei, Zhuangao #2680–4,5.

97. QS, 339:4374.

98. Guo, *Shiba shiji di Zhongguo zheng zhi*, 440–49, 478–80. These observations come in the midst of a longer, very interesting essay on corruption in the Qianlong reign; see 412–504.

99. David Nivison, "Heshen and His Accusers: Ideology and Political Behavior in the Eighteenth Century," in Nivison and Wright, *Confucianism in Action.*

100. JQSL, 38:13a–14a (vol. 28: 437–38). Yixinga's father, Yonggui, and his grandfather, Bulantai, had also served as provincial governors under the Yongzheng and Qianlong emperors. See GCQXLZ, 91:34a–36a.

101. For the dismissal of Yixing, see JQSL, 48:13a–15a (vol. 28: 595–97). See also GCQXLZ, 100:45a.

102. JQSL, 37:32a–36a (vol. 28: 419–20). See also subsequent edicts in which the Jiaqing emperor ordered word of Heshen's fate circulated to all governors and governors-general and orders suspending provincial presentation of tribute. These edicts are reprinted in Shi liao xun kan, no. 6: 96–100, no. 7: 126–31, no. 8: 149–57, and no. 14: 262–66. See the 1963 Guo Feng Chubanshe reprint, 96–100, 127–31, 149–57, and 262–66.

103. JQSL, 50:28a–b (vol. 28: 634), 74:9b–10b (vol. 28: 988).

104. Ibid., 85:5–8a (vol. 39: 112–14), 102:17b–20a (vol. 29: 265–66). Chu Penglin, a former Hanlin Academy member who had served under Zhu Gui, was responsible for these two dismissals and for the administrative punishment of Jiang Lan, who served as Yunnan governor from 1795 to 1799.

105. Qin ding Li bu ze li, 13:5a–b.

106. QS, 325:4283.

107. See Guy, *The Emperor's Four Treasuries*, 49–56.

108. ECCP, 185–187; QS, 314:4384–85; Zhaolian, *Xiao ting za lu*, 1:14b–15a, 4:11a–b.

109. Zhaolian, *Xiao ting za lu*, 4:10b.

110. Ibid., 10:22a–24a; Polachek, *The Inner Opium War*, 299–301.

111. For Western scholars' comments, see Bartlett, *Monarchs and Ministers*, 242–45; and Philip Kuhn and Susan Jones, "Dynastic Decline and the Roots of Rebellion," in *The Cambridge History of China*, vol. 9, part 1, 116–20. Zhaolian's characterization is in *Xiao ting za lu*, 10.22a.

112. ECCP, 78–80.

113. See the preface to the 1990 edition of *Da Qing huidian shili* for a publication history of the *Da Qing huidian* and *Da Qing huidian shili*. The Jiaqing edition was ordered in 1801, shortly after the emperor came to the throne, but was not completed until 1818.

114. This text is discussed extensively in Metzger, *The Internal Organization of Ch'ing Bureaucracy.*

115. See Guy, "Rule of Man," 91.

116. QDZGNB, vol. 3: 1666–70.

117. Ibid., TK: 1695–98

118. Backhouse and Bland, *Annals and Memoirs*, 406. The language in *Annals and Memoirs* is vivid and probably reflects court perceptions of the period at the end of the dynasty. Given Hugh Trevor-Roper's finding that Backhouse was a notorious forger, this work should not be regarded as a source of factual information.

119. QDZGNB, 1706–8.

120. Wright, *The Last Stand of Chinese Conservatism*, 71.

121. The clearest statement of this hypothesis is Spector, introduction, *Li Hung-chang and the Huai Army*, xxxviii–xliii.

Chapter 5. The Imperatives of Continuity

1. The rise in Manchu appointments to governors' office in the early eighteenth century are noted in Kessler, "Ethnic Composition of Political Leadership,", and Narakino Shimesu, *Shindai jūuyō shokkan no kenkyū*. Neither author attempts an explanation for the growth in numbers of Manchus.

2. Narakino Shimesu, *Shindai jūuyō shokkan no kenkyū*, 250–51; figures reproduced in Wakeman, *The Great Enterprise*, vol. 2: 1023.

3. See Lee, Campbell, and Wang, "The Last Emperors," 361–82.

4. *Ba qi tong zhi*, Fan li, 1.

5. This colorful story became something of an emblem for the family. It was first recorded in *The General History of the Eight Banners* in 1739 (*Ba qi tong zhi*, 150:3832), and the editors of *History of the Qing* prefaced their biographies of Korjishan and Dingchang with it (QS, 310:4180). Korjishan himself served as an associate editor of *The General History*, and it is tempting to imagine that he had something to do with the presentation of the story. On Nurhaci's incorporation of these tribes, see Wakeman, *The Great Enterprise*, vol. 1: 52–53. I follow the practice of identifying Manchus by their Manchu names when those can be determined from *The General History*. For this purpose, I have used the index of names in "Ba qi tong zhi" *retsuden yinsoku*, ed. Kanda, Matsumura, and Okada, 12–98.

6. *Ba qi tong zhi*, 4:54–55. On companies in the early Manchu order, see Elliott, *The Manchu Way*, 58–61. The phenomenon of single companies being divided into two appears to have been quite common following the Wu Sangui Rebellion. On Hong Taiji's raid into China, see Wakeman, *The Great Enterprise*, 164–65. Keifu's name is written with different characters in the biographical section of *Ba qi tong zhi*.

7. *Ba qi manzhou shi zu pu*, 14:1b. There are no biographies of Kacilan's brothers. For vivid accounts of the Yunnan campaign from the Ming and Qing points of view, see Struve, *Voices from the Ming-Qing Cataclysm*, 234–60; and Wakeman, *The Great Enterprise*, vol. 2: 1030–36. The biographical section of *Ba qi tong zhi* (150:3833) refers to Kacilan as Keifu's son, but the record of Keifu's company (4:54) refers to him as Keifu's nephew.

8. *Ba qi tong zhi*, 150:3833–34; GCQXLZ, 277:3a–5b.

9. Norman, *Concise Manchu Chinese Lexicon*, 169–70.

10. *The General History of the Eight Banners, Authorized by the Emperor (Qin ding ba qi tong zhi)* refers to a separate biography for Kaimbu, but none appears in the text. The first pages of Korjishan's biography are, however, concerned with his father's life and achievements. See GCQXLZ, 171:32a; and *Qin ding ba qi tong zhi*, 153:1a–b.

11. Huang Pei, *Autocracy at Work*, 180–82.

12. *Ba qi tong zhi*, 4:54–55.

13. For the emperor's response, see the edict of Qianlong, 7 January 1737, in QLSL, 32:9b–10a (vol. 9: 633–34). See QLSL, 73:16a, 13 September 1738 (vol. 10: 168), which appoints Korjishan to manage the affairs of the commandant of the Beijing garrison.

14. For Korjishan's indictments, see GCQXLZ, 171:33a–b; for the emperor's response, see QLSL, 138:9b–14b (vol. 10: 988–91).

15. GCQXLZ, 171:40a–46a.

16. *Da yi jue mi lu*, 56–60, 116–99. The publication of this work was occasioned by the discovery in 1728 of an attempt by Zeng Jing to lure a Qing governor-general, Yue Zhongqi, into rebellion using the texts of an anti-Qing author of the seventeenth century, Lu Liu-

liang. On this case, see Spence, *Treason by the Book*; the Yongzheng emperor's discussion of Manchus is summarized on 166–68.

17. Crossley, *Translucent Mirror*, 260.

18. QLSL, 177:12a–b (vol. 11: 279).

19. Hang Shijun was almost correct about appointments. Manchus held the governor-ships of Anhui, Henan, Zhejiang, Shaanxi, Shanxi, and Sichuan in 1742. Chinese governors were appointed elsewhere, including in Yunnan, Guizhou, and Guangxi. All the governors-general were Manchus, except for the Yun-gui governor-general. Hang's anger may have been aroused by the appointment of Chang'an, the first Manchu to serve as governor of his native province of Zhejiang. QDZGNB, 3:1594–96.

20. QLSL, 184:46b–5b (vol. 12: 373).

21. Elliott, *The Manchu Way*, 186–87.

22. *Qianlong huangdi quan zhuan*, 91–103.

23. Waley, *Yuan Mei*, 29–30. The story originally appeared in Yuan Mei's biography of Ortai.

24. See "Sha Nuoqin," in Zhaolian, *Xiao ting za lu*, 1:7a–b. Nuoqin's grandfather was Ebilun, one of the four regents for the Kangxi emperor. Upon Nuoqin's death, his hereditary rank passed first to Cereng (governor of Guangdong, 1744–45, as well as governor-general of Guangdong, 1745–48, and Sichuan, 1748–53) and then to Aligun (governor of Shanxi, 1743–45, Shandong, 1745–48, and Shanxi, 1748–50, and governor-general of Huguang and Liangguang, 1750–53). See ECCP, 219–21.

25. See Kutcher, *Mourning in Late Imperial China*, 179–84.

26. *Qianlong zhupi*, vol. 1: 282. On Kaitai, see GCQXLZ, 172:1a–6b; and QS, 325:4293.

27. *Qianlong zhupi*, vol. 1: 197; on Zhongyin, see GCQXLZ, 83:38a–40a.

28. Twenty-three of those appointed were serving either in offices within the banner system or at military stations in central Asia at the time of their appointment. The majority of the direct transfers from the military into the civilian administration came during the last third of the eighteenth century, when a rebellion of White Lotus adherents raged through central and northwest China, and during the wars and rebellions of the nineteenth century. Another twenty-two appointees had been promoted to viceroy but returned to service as provincial governors to meet an immediate need. Some of those who were moved from positions as viceroys to governorships were in effect demoted, having reached their level of incompetence.

The emperor began to favor Manchus who held military postings at about the same time he appointed Fuheng chief of the Grand Council. It is tempting to imagine that Fuheng, whose experience was primarily military, influenced the emperor's choice of governors. But most sources, including Zhaolian, whose father may well have known Fuheng, assert that the guards captain was too young at the time of his appointment to do more than carry out the emperor's will. More likely, the appointment of Fuheng and the appointments of Manchus of military background came from the same source, Qianlong's emerging vision of the role of Manchus in the empire. See Zhaolian, *Xiao ting xa lu*, 1:11b.

29. Li and Kang, *Qianlong, He Shen yu Liu Yong*, 79–94.

30. Also included under the category of "court agencies" were mayors of the capital city (nine cases) whose appointments, though technically routine, were quite rare. There were also occasional appointments of men serving in the Hanlin Academy and in various ceremonial positions at court. In order to avoid clutter in the notes, I have not listed the

names of those appointed from various positions, with two exceptions: Table 5.1 lists the eighteenth-century governors who were reappointed after administrative discipline, and table 4.3 lists those who served as Grand Council clerks prior to their appointments.

31. Brunnert and Hagelstrom, *Present Day Political Organization of China*, 196–97. Eight of the nineteen appointments occurred during the eighteenth century, and eight were in the nineteenth century. Seven of the eight eighteenth-century appointees were Manchus; all of the nineteenth-century appointments were Chinese.

32. Other members of the Bordered Blue Banner who were appointed as governor include Ortai's sons and nephews, and Zhongyin, to whom the emperor addressed his remark that there was not a single good man among Manchu degree holders.

33. The emperor appointed Chen Hongmou to the post, although as Rowe has noted, the fabled governor was somewhat past his prime when he served in Guangdong.

34. QS, 325:4295.

35. GCQXLZ, 176:1a–6a. Other Manchus in the Plain Red Banner who served as governors were Shilin (Shanxi, 1727–37) and San Bao (Shanxi, 1771–73, and Zhejiang, 1773–77); San Bao was also governor-general of Huguang in 1777–80. See Qin ding ba qi tong zhi, juan 166.

36. On Huang Tinggui, see QS, 324:4264.

37. Mingde was demoted from his post in Gansu because two subordinates he had recommended while he was governor of Shanxi were found to be corrupt. See QLSL, 590:9a–b (vol. 16: 558). His mother died just as he was cashiered, and the emperor provided him with 1,000 *liang* to cover burial expenses and allowed him to go into mourning. After his mourning obligations were completed, he was assigned as lieutenant governor to Sichuan, under Huang Tinggui.

38. QLSL, 844:21b–22a (vol. 19: 281–82).

39. On the Jiang Zhou case more generally, see *Qianlong chao chengban tanwu dangan xuanbian*, vol. 1: 61–102; the reference to Mingde is on page 78.

40. On this case in general, see QLSL, juan 751–53 (vol. 18: 261–93) passim; and Li and Kang, *Qianlong, He Shen yu Liu Yong*, 96–103.

41. QLSL, 752:12b (vol. 18: 277).

42. Ibid., 755:12a–b (vol. 18: 313).

43. The thirty-one cases included nine governors who were cashiered, four who were demoted, four who were relieved, five who were summoned to the capital, and nine who were directly reappointed after illness.

44. For further development of this argument, see Guy, "The Administrative Punishment of Qing Provincial Governors," 92–94.

45. DQHDSL, 85:17a (vol. 2: 105).

46. See the case of Xu Rong, who was dismissed in 1736 and reappointed after he greeted the emperor in Henan, in QS, 292:4058. The regulations do not specify the significance of greeting the carriage, although in other instances, entertaining a visiting emperor could be a very expensive proposition.

47. Waley-Cohen, *Exile in Mid-Qing China*, 139–62 passim. Waley-Cohen identifies twelve governors who were sent into exile between 1758 and 182 (89 n. 47), of whom three were later reinstated to the position of governor.

48. Included here are the ten cases of direct reappointment after cashiering from table 5.1 plus another twelve cases in which officials were cashiered, reappointed shortly to lower-ranking posts in the government, and then promoted from those posts to governorships.

49. GCQXLZ, 177:1a–4; QS, 338:4366–67.

50. QLSL, 374:17b–19b (vol. 13: 1133–34).

51. QLSL, 532:18a–20a (vol. 15: 710–11). Tuerbing'a's case was not helped by the fact that the governors of Zhili and Shandong had distributed relief in counties across the border from the disputed areas of Henan.

52. QLSL, 537:13b–17b (vol. 15: 779–80), 538:10a–b (vol. 15: 798). See also the biography of Peng in QS, 339:4371–72, which is almost exclusively concerned with this case. Ultimately, Peng was executed, and his family's property was seized and distributed in order to relieve the flooding in his native district. In 1743, Peng edited a collection recording various unusual and unnatural occurrences in Henan during the end of the Ming and the Qing conquest; the Qing later banned the book. See Struve, *The Ming-Qing Conflict*, 219–20.

53. QLSL, 540:1a (vol. 15: 823). In fact, Tuerbing'a's duties may not have changed all that much as a result of this dismissal. One of his responsibilities as governor of Henan had been to manage the route of the southern army as it marched through his province. It is possible that he failed to provide relief in eastern Henan because this army drained the province's resources and his own time and energy. See Shun, *Qianlong zhongyao zhanzheng zhi junxu yanjiu*, 84.

54. See *Da Qing huidian*, juan 7 (59–68), for appointments procedures. Transfers, or *gai*, are treated in 7:13a–14b (62–63). Note that the index QDZGNB uses the term *gai* differently, to refer to officials who were moved to a different location but maintained the same position.

55. The most useful discussions of central government organization during the Qing are Li Pengnian, *Qingdai zhongyang guojia gaishu*; and Zhang Deze, *Qingdai guojia jiguan kaolue*. On the Board of Punishments specifically, see Li Pengnian, *Qingdai zhongyang guojia gaishu*, 383–97; and Zhang Deze, *Qingdai guojia jiguan kaolue*, 107–13. All the examples in this section are drawn from the Board of Punishments, in part because it contributed the most provincial governors and because the governors' correspondence with the board, known as *xingko tiben*, has been the subject of a number of recent studies on Qing administration.

56. On board fees in the early Qing, see Wang and Jin, "Cong qing chu di li zhi kan fengjian guanliao zhengzhi," 138–39. See also Lui, *Corruption in China*, 33. Examples from the Guizhou budget are in Zelin, *The Magistrate's Tael*, 144.

57. See Guo, *Shiba shiji di Zhongguo zheng zhi*, 248–65.

58. See QLSL, 154:15b–18a (vol. 10: 1203–4).

59. QS, 322:4254.

60. GCQXLZ, 174:6a–8a.

61. Ibid., 174:1a–3b.

62. DQHDSL, 20:1a–3a.

63. GCQXLZ, 188:5a–b.

64. See Guo, *Shiba shiji di Zhongguo zheng zhi*.

65. Rowe, *Saving the World*, 54.

66. The rules of avoidance for Manchu officials are in juan 35 (vol. 1: 441–46), and those for Chinese officials are in juan 47 (vol. 1: 590–602). Wei Hsiu-mei, *Qingdai zhi huipi zhidu*, provides a clear and useful discussion of the evolution and application.

67. Wei Hsiu-mei, *Qingdai zhi huipi zhidu*, 50.

68. GCQXLB, 20:8a.

69. QLSL, 555:22a (vol. 16: 24). These changes represented steps up for the Guizhou

and Fujian governors, though the transfer may have been a somewhat bitter development for Zhou Renji. Zhou was under a cloud, since he had been impeached and cashiered from his previous post in Zhejiang. He served in Guizhou for two years and then was recalled to the capital, where he died.

70. Wei Hsiu-mei, *Qingdai zhi huipi zhidu*, 149.

71. Perhaps to avoid the appearance of a demotion, Chen was made Protector of the Heir Apparent at the time of his appointment to Jiangsu. GCJXLB, 20:8b.

72. Wei Hsiu-mei, *Qingdai zhi huipi zhidu*, 149.

73. Kutcher, *Mourning in Late Imperial China*, 120–52 passim.

74. DQHDSL, 138:779–80. Quoted in Kutcher, *Mourning in Late Imperial China*, 137; see also the Oboi period regulations Kutchner discusses, which required that an official leave no unsolved legal cases and no tax arrears in the post he was departing (124).

75. JQSL, 318:13b–14a (vol. 32: 218).

76. QS, 360:4490. This was not the first time an impetuous act brought about delay in Zhang's career. During the late Qianlong reign, he served as a Grand Council clerk and was dismissed for disobeying Heshen. He had to wait for the ascension of the Jiaqing emperor before he was appointed to a senior posting. Zhang was particularly known for his governorship of Fujian.

Chapter 6. The Legacy of Military Occupation: The North and the Northwest

1. G. William Skinner, "Regional Urbanization," in *The City in Late Imperial China*, 213.

2. Ibid., 243–47.

3. Huang, *The Peasant Economy and Social Change*, 60; see also Lillian Li, "Grain Prices in Zhili: A Preliminary Study," in Rawski and Li, *Chinese History in Economic Perspective*, 72–73.

4. Joseph Esherick, "Introduction," in Esherick and Rankin, *Chinese Local Elites*, 21–22.

5. See Esherick, *The Origins of the Boxer Uprising*, 7–13; and Pomeranz, *The Making of a Hinterland*, 5–12.

6. SZSL, 44:10b (vol. 3: 354); quoted in Fu, *Qingdai dufu zhidu*, 12.

7. SZSL, 64:2a (vol. 3: 499); quoted in Fu, *Qingdai dufu zhidu*, 13.

8. Wakeman, *The Great Enterprise*, vol. 1: 424–36. For several accounts of north China holdouts against the Qing, see Struve, *The Ming-Qing Conflict*, 219–20.

9. SZSL 45:7a (vol. 3: 361); quoted in Fu, *Qingdai dufu zhidu*, 11.

10. On the dismissal of the governor-general, see SZSL, 117:1a (vol. 3: 909); on the elimination of the position, see SZSL, 117:16a (vol. 3: 916).

11. On the Green Standard Army forces in north China, see DQHDSL, 591:1a–16a (vol. 7: 638–46). On Shandong, see also *Shandong tongzhi* (1736), 16:1b–2a, 4ba–46b; for a map of the disposition of forces in west Shandong, see Naquin, *Shantung Rebellion*, 23. A third brigade was established at Caozhou in the nineteenth century; see *Shandong tongzhi* (1910), 114:3272–78. The Shandong governor's forces were in addition to the river troops commanded by the director-general of river conservancy and the garrison of Manchu troops in Qingzhou.

12. On Henan garrisons, see also *Henan tongzhi*, 16:1a–9b. A garrison of Manchu troops was stationed in Kaifeng in 1721. Henan was known as the "four battlefields," as it had been the scene of so much conflict in Chinese history. See Gu Zuyu, "Lun Henan," in HCJSWB, 78:38a–39b.

13. DQHDSL, 13:18a–b (vol. 1: 296–97). During the Oboi regency and again during the

Wu Sangui Rebellion, provincial commandants were assigned to Henan and Shandong, as they were to all provinces. See QDZGNB, 3:2437–51.

14. During the Yongzheng reign, a series of assistant directors-general of river conservancy was created to deal with specific regional problems. One assistant director-general for the Yellow River was appointed in 1724, a second assistant director-general for Jiangnan was created in 1728, and a third assistant director-general, responsible for the rivers around Beijing, was created in 1730. Subsequently, each river director was provided with a subordinate. In 1729, the post of director-general was eliminated, and its responsibilities were divided among the regional river coordinators for north and south. These new positions gave the Qing government the capacity to provide a more energetic response to local flooding, making possible a wider range of preventive and relief measures. But if the new positions enhanced the capacity of the dynasty to respond to natural disasters, they also increased the number of officials employed by the state and the range of local officials whose projects might require additional tax revenues. Possibly for this reason, the Yongzheng emperor's son and successor, who was more concerned with centralization and tradition than his father had been, gradually eliminated the new river positions, and by 1750, there were only two directors-general, one for the north and one for the south. For the documents creating and abolishing these positions, see QDZGNB, vol. 3: 388–1409.

15. Tian Wenjing, "Xün," in *Henan tongzhi*, 1b–12a. See also a collection of Tian's writings as governor of Henan, *Fu yu xuan hua lu*.

16. Yin Huiyi, *Yin shao zai zouyi*, 2:12a. In this memorial, Yin argues that the means of Henan peasants were so limited that the state could not afford to take any lands off the tax rolls. Specifically, he contends that Yongzheng era provisions for tax holidays on lands that had been reclaimed after war or neglect should be repealed for Henan.

17. The Henan governor was formally assigned responsibility for this task in 1677; see DQHDSL, 23:9b (vol. 1: 292). Regulations on dike maintenance are in DQHDSL, zhuan 904–14. The rules are divided into four subcategories: expenses (904–6), materials (907–10), construction specifications (910–12), and dredging (913–14). Surveys of the application of these regulations to Henan, are in *Henan tongzhi*, zhuan 16; and *Xu Henan tongzhi*, zhuan 21–23. *Yu he zhi*, which was compiled in the early twentieth century, provides a summary of work on the river during the Qing. For records of how two other governors dealt with Henan floods, see Yin Huiyi, *Yin xiao zai zouyi*, juan 7–8, and *Fu yu tiao jiao*, juan 4; and the biographies of the father-son team He Wei and He Yucheng, who served in Henan for much of the middle of the Qianlong reign, in GCQXLZ, juan 176.

18. Dunstan, *Conflicting Counsels to Confuse the Age*, 23–24, 44–47.

19. On Jiang Bing, see GCQXLZ, 78:23a–24a.

20. For Hu's 1745 assignment, see GCJXLX 83:37a; for his association with Fuheng, see Chen Hao, "Mu zhi ming," in GCQXLZ, 83:43a–4b.

21. On Henan's grain contributions to the western-route armies during the campaigns in Xinjiang, see Shun, *Qianlong zhongyao zhanzheng zhi junxu yanjiu*, 78–79, 83.

22. Cited in Esherick, *The Origins of the Boxer Uprising*, 32.

23. QSL, vol. 4: 267 (KXSL, 18:20b–22a); *Qing shilu Shandong shiliao xuanbian*, vol. 1: 36.

24. Gu Zuyu, "Lun Shandong," in HCJSWB, 78:35a–b.

25. *Qing shilu Shandong shiliao xuanbian*, vol. 1: 96.

26. Remittance rates are drawn from the chart in Zelin, *The Magistrate's Tael*, 28.

27. The longest-serving governors of Henan in the eighteenth century—Tian Wenjing (1725–35), Shuose (1743–48), and Asiha (1763–68)—were all special appointments. Shan-

dong tongzhi (1910), 75:9a–27a, has a list of Shandong governors with their major accomplishments. The list excludes, however, those governors who left office in Shandong because of administrative discipline.

28. Yunnan had the highest promotion rate in the empire, 37.3 percent. The figures for cashierings do not include cases in which governors were relieved of responsibility and subsequently indicted.

29. Documents on the Jiang Zhou case are reprinted in *Qianlong chao chengban tanwu dang'an*, vol. 1: 67–102.

30. KXSL, 85:2a–3a (vol. 4: 1076).

31. See David S. Nivison, "Ho-shen and His Accusers: Ideology and Political Behavior in the Eighteenth Century," in Nivison and Wright, *Confucianism in Action*, 233–34; *Qianlong chao chengban tanwu dang'an*, vol. 3: 2–3; and QS, 4261–62, 4378–79 (vol. 3: 2395–2492).

32. Wakeman, *The Great Enterprise*, vol. 1: 428–38; Spence. *The Death of Woman Wang*, 40–50.

33. See Esherick, *The Origins of the Boxer Rebellion*, 7–28; and Pomeranz, *The Making of a Hinterland*, 153–64.

34. Susan Mann, *Local Merchants and the Chinese Bureaucracy*, 58; Naquin, *Shantung Rebellion*, 3–25.

35. See Yang Zhengtai, "Ming qing Linqing di sheng shuai yu dili tiaojian di bianhua," 116–20. One indication of the pleasure of holding office in Shandong was that no less than eighteen officials wrote prefaces recalling their service in the province for the early Jiaqing reprint of the 1736 *Shandong tongzhi*.

36. On the complex political and social crisis precipitated by the death of the Xiaoxian empress, see Kutcher, *Mourning in Late Imperial China*, 157–89. The crisis led the Qianlong emperor to order the death of a provincial governor, Saileng'e, who seems to have been the first provincial governor executed during the reign.

37. QS, 333:4330–31. As I have argued in a review of Pamela Crossley's *Translucent Mirror*, such recognition of official family ties in the Qianlong reign was a part of the new "geneological thinking," which Crossley has suggested was characteristic of Qing thought about political orders in the eighteenth century. *Harvard Journal of Asiatic Studies* 61, no. 2: 470. Guotai offered once to go into exile in his father's place and, in the midst of his own extortion trial, offered to pay his father's fine so that Wenshou might return early from exile. See Waley-Cohen, *Exile in Mid-Ch'ing China*, 81.

38. Yu Yijian's sister was married to the head of the Kong clan in Shandong. See Rawski, *The Last Emperors*, 131. Most Shandong sources seem to regard Yu Yijian as an ineffectual, though not entirely benign, presence in the province.

39. *Qianlong chao chengban tanwu dang'an*, vol. 3: 1396. The emperor seemed particularly pleased that Chinese officials would regard a Manchu as brusque and businesslike.

40. The accusation is excerpted in ibid., vol. 3: 2396. See also Qian Feng's biography in QS, 323:4261.

41. QS, 333:4330–31. Wenshou was dismissed on 14 November 1781. Guotai was reprimanded in this case for his delay in memorializing to express the family's gratitude for the emperor's clemency in reducing Wenshou's sentence from execution to exile.

42. *Qianlong chao chengban tanwu dang'an*, vol. 3: 2474–76.

43. Ibid., vol. 3: 2418. Guolin's State Historiographical Commission biography refers to his serving as a "clerk" (*jiang jing*) during these years (National Palace Museum Archives, Taipei, *zhuanbao* 1756–6), but Liang Jiangzhu does not mention a Guolin serving as a Grand Council clerk. Liang does identify a Guo Lian serving as clerk in the council at

the time of Guotai's indictment. See Liang, *Shu yuan ji lue*, 16:10b. It has long been assumed that Guotai was Heshen's henchman and that Heshen was responsible for tipping off Guotai. However, Guolin's testimony is plausible, and scholars have recently suggested that there may not have been a special relationship between the two. See Li and Kang, *Qianlong, He Shen yu Liu Yong*.

44. *Qianlong chao chengban tanwu dang'an*, vol. 3: 2396, 2465–66.

45. For Lu Erchang's testimony, see ibid., vol. 3: 2455–56

46. *ECCP*, 944.

47. For the list of properties seized, see *Qianlong chao chengban tanwu dang'an*, vol. 3: 2491–92.

48. On Guolin, see National Palace Museum Archives, Taipei, *zhuanbao* 1756–6. Guolin's career in the banner service was only briefly interrupted by his brother's misfortune. Ironically, Guolin was appointed to a military position in Shandong in 1791 but dismissed from the post for incompetence a year later. On Wenshou, see QS, 4330–31 (333).

49. Huang, *The Peasant Economy and Social Change*, 87. See also Wakeman, *The Great Enterprise*, vol. 1: 469–76.

50. G. William Skinner, "Cities and the Hierarchy of Local Systems," in *The City in Late Imperial China*, 343.

51. The text of Yao's memorial is excerpted in the edict authorizing the creation of the Zhili governor-generalship, SZSL 45:7a–b (vol. 3: 361). His biography is found in QS, 264:3896; see also the characterization of him at the end of the *juan*, on 264:3901. Yao was a native of Tongcheng in southern Anhui and an important adviser to the Qing. Twenty-two of his essays, mostly on financial matters, were reprinted in *Essays on Statecraft in Our Times* (Huang chao jingshi wenbian).

52. *Jifu tongzhi* (1885 ed.), 952.

53. *ECCP*, 77–78; QS, 256:3743–45.

54. For the text of the edict, see KXSL, 262:10b (vol. 6: 583).

55. KXSL, 298:4a (vol. 6: 885). Zhao Hongxie's brother Zhao Hongcan had served as governor-general of Guangdong and Guangxi, and his son Zhao Zhihuan financed the printing of the illustrated records of the Kangxi emperor's sixtieth birthday. See *ECCP*, 78.

56. DQHDSL, 23:11a (vol. 1: 293); YZSL, 27:5a–b. (vol. 7: 414). It is interesting that the Yongzheng edict, which was expressly marked as a special edict, not to be taken as precedent, was included in *Collected Statutes and Precedents of the Qing*, whereas the Kangxi edict, which was not so marked but must have been regarded as special by the *Collected Statutes and Precedents* editors, was not included. Li Weijun was cashiered ten months after being appointed to office, but the title became permanent. The Yongzheng emperor went through nine governors-general in Zhili between 1724 and 1732 before settling on Li Wei, in whom he had great confidence.

57. The edicts collected in the first four *juan* of *Jifu tongzhi* (1735 ed.) provide a summary of the principal concerns of Zhili administration.

58. DQHDSL, 546:4a–547:19a (vol. 7: 55–75); Brunnert and Hagelstrom, *Present Day Political Organization of China*, 329.

59. DQHDSL, 543:2b–3b (vol. 7: 31).

60. This division of Zhili watercourses follows the account by Wu Bangqing in *Jifu hedao guan jian*. For a reprint, see *Jifu hedao shuili congshu*.

61. See *ECCP*, 923–24. Prince I's memorials to the throne on the situation are collected in *I xian xhinwang shu chao*. For a reprint, see *Jifu hedao shuili congshu*.

62. Will, Bureaucracy and Famine in Eighteenth-Century China, 14–16.

63. Gu Zuyu, "Lun Shanxi," in HCJSWB, 78:39b–40a.

64. DQHDSL, 545:5a–b (vol. 7: 45).

65. Ibid., 548:14a–30a (vol. 7: 82–90), 591:6b–11 (vol. 7: 641–44).

66. Ibid., 545:3b–4a (vol. 7: 44–45).

67. See Shanxi tongzhi (1736 ed.), 4:19b–42a. As a result of these changes, Qing Shanxi was larger than Ming or present-day Shanxi. These changes were made during the governorship of Fan Shijie and the broad regime of Nian Gengyao in the north and the west.

68. On grain prices and the difficulty of grain supply, see the memorial of Governor Liu Yuyi, translated in Dunstan, Conflicting Counsels to Confuse the Age, 48–52.

69. See Terada, Sansei Shonin no Kenkyu, 332–35; and Wei Qingyuan, "Qingdai zhuoming huang shang Fan shi di ying shuai." The account of Fan's property is cited by Wei from the Archives of the Imperial Household (Neiwufu Dang'an), 53. It appears that the Fans became sufficiently wealthy from all this such that they were able to underwrite logistical expenses for early Qing military campaigns in the northwest.

70. Da Qing huidian, 1690 Kangxi ed., 5:21a.

71. In 1723, the first year of his reign, the Yongzheng emperor formally ended the requirement, but this was one case in which practice prevailed over proclamation. To be sure, the edict, probably issued at the time Tian Wenjing was appointed lieutenant governor of Shanxi, ended Manchu monopolies on the lower levels of northwestern provincial administration. But at the governor's level, despite the Yongzheng edict, Manchus were appointed exclusively to the three northwestern provinces until the Qianlong reign, and even after the practice collapsed in Shaanxi and Gansu, it was maintained in Shanxi.

72. These reasons are for the most part inaccessible. Very few Manchu appointees to the province were the subjects of biographies. The first Shanxi Gazetteer (Shanxi tongzhi), compiled by Shilin in 1736, does not discuss officials after the Shunzhi reign, and the Shanxi Gazetteer compiled by Zeng Guoquan in 1877–80 is not terribly helpful either, identifying as distinguished (and hence worthy of biography) those governors whose biographies appear in other sources.

73. ECCP, 560–61.

74. Ibid., 268; Qing shi lie zhuan, 12.26a–29a.

75. GCQXLZ, 71:14a–b. See also the biography in Qin ding ba qi tong zhi, 166:5a–10b (vol. 27: 11071–82) Unfortunately, neither source provides enough information to determine Shilin's degree of closeness to the imperial house.

76. Will and Wong, Nourish the People, 20–24.

77. GCQXLZ, 171:33a–b.

78. QLSL, 138:10b (vol. 10: 988).

79. Yu Hongtu was indicted by Wang Shilun in October 1733 and executed in early January the next year. He had been implicated in the Cha Siting case. See YZSL, 135:1b–2a (vol. 8: 732–33).

80. QLSL, 138:13a–14b (vol. 10: 990).

81. QS, 325:4283; GCQXLZ, 187:11a–18a.

82. G. William Skinner, "Regional Urbanization," in The City in Late Imperial China, 234–35.

83. Wong, "Entre Monde et Nation," 21. His account is richly corroborated by two excellent full-length studies of northwest China in English: Jonathan N. Lipman, Familiar

Strangers: A History of Muslims in Northwest China, and James A. Millward, *Beyond the Pass: Economy, Ethnicity and Empire in Qing Central Asia, 1759–1864.*

84. Dai Yingcong, "The Rise of the Southern Frontier," 104.

85. The only other provincial governor outranked by both the garrison commander and the governor-general was the governor of Guangdong. But the Guangdong governor had many more resources at his command, as explained below.

86. See the map in *Shaanxi tongzhi*, reproduced in Elliott, *The Manchu Way*, 106.

87. See DQHD 23:5a (290); SZSL, 76:3b (vol. 3: 598); and KXSL, 93:3a–4b (vol. 4: 1174), 95:21a–b (vol. 4: 1194).

88. Rowe, *Saving the World*, 69.

89. QS, 308:4166. These imperial instructions do not appear in the QLSL edict reappointing Chen or in the State Historiographical Commission draft biography. They may have been preserved elsewhere, or been issued orally, or represent a comment by the editors of *History of the Qing* on the uniqueness of Chen's appointment in Shaanxi.

90. Rowe, *Saving the World*, 71.

91. GCQXLZ, 83:39b–40a; QLSL, 621:4a–b (vol. 17: 301); and QLSL, 660:16b–17b (vol. 17: 392–93). The Qianlong emperor's attitude toward the *jinshi*-degree holder Zhongyin is discussed in chapter 5.

92. ECCP, 622–24; QS, 4337–38 (333); and GCQXLZ, 185:18a–22a.

93. On Bi's relationship with Fuheng, see Qian Daxin, "Mu Zhi Ming," in GCQXLZ, 185:14a.

94. Mann, *Precious Records*, 103.

95. *Shaanxi tongzhi*, juan 19, outlines the requirements for provisioning the armies stationed in the province.

96. GCQXLZ, 185:8b.

97. Ibid., 73:37a–39b; QLSL, 64:8a–9a (vol. 10: 41).

98. Rowe, *Saving the World*, 224–26; HCJSWB, juan 214 (2875–98).

99. Wong, *China Transformed*, 19.

100. Bi, "Shaanxi nong tian shui li mu qu shu, in HCJSWB, 36:10a–13a (924–26).

101. A provincial judge was provided for the area in 1663.

102. *Gansu tongzhi, mulu*, 6a–b.

103. Gansu experienced the highest rate of interregional official transfers in the empire. Some 72 percent of Gansu governors were transferred to their posts from either the capital or the northwest.

104. DQHDSL, 23:14a–b (vol. 1: 294); QLSL, 329:21a–b (vol. 13: 451–52).

105. DQHDSL, 23:15a (vol. 1: 295); and QLSL, 597:5b–6b (vol. 16: 651–52), 637:3a–b (vol. 16: 1038). During this period, the governor-general's seat was moved from Lanzhou in the eastern part of the province to Suzhou in the west.

106. SZSL, 23:15a (vol. 1: 295); QLSL, 706:7a–b (vol. 17: 885). Quoted and punctuated in Fu, *Qingdai dufu zhidu*, 30.

107. Perdue, "Military Mobilization," esp. 777–81.

108. GCQXLZ, 172:28a–30b. During his term in Gansu, Changjun suggested a number of other changes in the province's administrative geography. See DQHDSL, juan 66. In between his various territorial postings, Changjun served a number of terms as a clerk in the Grand Council.

109. *Qing shi lie zhuan*, 22:22b.

110. An interesting case of imperial sensitivity to revealing administrative practice in the northwest occurred in 1779, when a grandson of Huang Tingjian's published Tingjian's memorial, with their vermilion endorsements. Huang Tingjian had served as governor of Gansu (1741–49) and as governor-general of both Sichuan (1751–53) and Shan-gan (1750–51, 1755–59). The grandson's motive seems to have been, not to reveal state secrets, but to call attention to himself and his family; the published text was distributed mostly to officials in the northwest. But the dissemination of the memorial made the Qianlong emperor very uncomfortable, and he ordered all copies of the book destroyed. See *Qingdai wen zi yu dang*, vol. 1: 395–418.

111. Millward, *Beyond the Pass*, 117. On Xu Rong, see QS, 4057 (292).

112. *Qianlong chao chengban tanwu dang'an*, vol. 2: 1192. On the rebellion of Su Forty Three, see Lipman, *Familiar Strangers*, 108–10, in particular, the ingenious translation of the "Ballad of Su Forty Three" discovered in the northwest by Gu Jiegang in 1837. The major documents for this case are reprinted with commentary in Yang Huaizhong, "Shiba shiji di Gansu chang mao an," in *Huizu shi lun gao*, 371–439.

113. "Jian-jue," in *Qianlong chao chengban tanwu dang'an*, vol. 2: 2.

114. On the investigation of Chen Huizu, see *Qianlong chao chengban tanwu dang'an*, vol. 3: 2499–2845. Chen Huizu's father was Chen Dashou, who had served as governor of Jiangsu from 1741 to 1746 and as governor-general of Liangguang from 1750 until his death in 1751. This extensive attack on Chinese families who had served in the Qianlong territorial service in the eighteenth century strongly suggests the hand of Heshen.

115. Dai Yingcong, "The Rise of the Southwestern Frontier," 4, 9. The chaos of early Qing administration in Sichuan is reflected in the preface to the 1735 edition of *The Sichuan Gazetteer*, which dismisses the previous compilation by Cao Yurong as inadequate because it had been prepared in a time of war.

116. DQHDSL, 23:5b–18a passim; QDZGNB, vol. 3: 1510–11.

117. These jurisdictional changes were spelled out especially vividly in the "Administrative Changes" (Yange) section of the 1816 *Sichuan Gazetteer*. *Sichuan tongzhi*, juan 2–5. In fact, the number of changes in local organization is offered as one of the rationales for recompiling a provincial gazetteer only eighty-one years after the first one.

118. "Yongqian shiqi defang guan que shiiao," 3–6. For a discussion of this case, see chapter 3 of this volume.

119. QS, 296:4081–86; *Qing shi lie zhuan*, 13:9b–17b; *Manzhou Ming Chen zhuan*, 32:4a–27b; ECCP, 587–90.

120. ECCP, 587–90. Dai Yincong, "The Rise of the Southwestern Frontier," 220–58. In 1724, Nian Gengyao published a work on military strategy deriving from his experience, *Zhi pin sheng xuan chuan shu*.

121. The character of the Yongzheng succession is one of the oldest issues in Qing history. Meng Sen was the first Chinese historian to address the question; see Meng Shen, "Qingchu san da yi an," 454–511. For a passionate defense of the Yongzheng emperor's legitimacy, see Silas H. L. Wu, *Passage to Power*.

122. YZSL, 3:10b–11a (vol. 7: 72). For the quotes from *The Book of Documents*, see Legge, *The Chinese Classics*, vol. 4, *The Shoo King*, 73–74.

123. The responses are reproduced in *Nian Gengyao zou zhe*, vol. 3: 877–1124.

124. For a summary of this indictment, see *Qing shi lieh zhuan*, 15a–17b.

125. ZPZZ, vol. 2: 794. On He Tianpei, see *Manzhou Ming Chen zhuan*, 35:5b–9b. A third

protégé of Nian Gengyao's involved in the case was Fan Shijie, who was governor of Shaanxi. Possibly because he was of more distinguished lineage, being a descendant of Fan Wencheng, he was spared execution.

126. See Meng Shen, "Qingchu san da yi an," i495–511. Meng's view is reflected in most of the secondary literature on the subject. See ECCP, 589; Silas H. L. Wu, *Communications and Control*, 80; and Silas H. L. Wu, *Passage to Power*, 175.

127. ECCP, 589.

128. Feng Ergang, *Yongzheng zhuan*, 104–20.

129. Nian Gengyao's memorials to the throne were published by the National Palace Museum in 1971; see *Nian Gengyao zou zhe zhuanji*. Most were written in Manchu. Nian's memorials were translated into Chinese and published in 1995; see Li, Li, and Xie, *Nian Gengyao man han zou zhe bian*.

130. QS, 297:4087–90; GCQXLZ, 280:4b–46a; ECCP, 957–59. See also Spence, *Treason by the Book*, 5–21; and Bartlett, *Monarchs and Ministers*, 56–64.

131. GCQXLZ, 280:1a–4b.

132. One reason for Yue's fall from grace may have been his rivalry with Ortai, who became the emperor's principal assistant in the war. See ECCP, 959.

133. Spence, *Treason by the Book*, 5–6.

134. Yue, "Yue xiang qing gong xing lue." This is a reprint of a reminiscence by one of Yue's great-grandsons, written in the early part of the nineteenth century. It is particularly interesting for the family details.

135. These two governors are credited with carrying out the first survey of the province since the Qing conquest, a necessary prerequisite to resettlement, although in this instance, both were ordered to cooperate with Yue Zhongqi in the task. See QS, 295:4076, 299:4107.

136. On this case, see Guy, "Zhang Tingyu and Reconciliation."

137. QSL, 321:655–713 (vol. 13:278); QLSL, 321. There is no extant biography of Jishan, who held a post in the Board of War before his appointment in 1743.

138. The best English-language account of the origins of this campaign is Herman, "National Integration and Cultural Hegemony," 215–85. See also Zhuang, *Qing Gaozong shi quan wugong yanjiu*, 109–82, which emphasizes the corruption of Sichuan armies.

139. QLSL, 329:19a–20b (vol. 13: 470).

140. Ibid.

141. Crossley, *A Translucent Mirror*, 29–30.

Chapter 7. Negotiated Orders: The Lower Yangzi Valley and the Southeastern Coast

1. See Meyer-Fong, *Building Culture in Yangzhou*, 14–20; and Struve, *Voices from the Ming-Qing Cataclysm*, 28–49.

2. See Struve, *Voices from the Ming-Qing Cataclysm*, 49–55.

3. See Dennerline, *The Chia-ting Loyalists*.

4. Struve, *The Southern Ming, 1644–1662*, 65.

5. On the conquest of Tongcheng, see Hilary Beattie, "The Alternative to Resistance: The Case of T'ung-ch'eng, Anhwei," in Spence and Wills, *From Ming to Ch'ing*, 241–75.

6. Faulkner, *The Town*, 386.

7. SZSL, 18:13b–14b (vol. 3: 164).

8. For these appointments, see DQSL, vol. 3: 167 (which contains the dynasty's charge to Hong Chengchou), 168, 173; and SZSL, 19:2a–4b. See also Wang Chenmain, *The Life and Career of Hong Ch'eng-ch'ou*, 146–70; and Struve, *Voices from the Ming-Ch'ing Cataclysm*, 141–55.

9. *Qing shi lie zhuan*, 5:28a.

10. SZSL, 30:17a (vol. 3: 253).

11. See James Polachek, "Gentry Hegemony: Soochow in the T'ung-chih Restoration," in Wakeman and Grant, *Conflict and Control*, 218. For a comparative view of Jiangnan tax assessments, see Bernhardt, *Rents, Taxes, and Peasant Resistance*, 43–46.

12. Zelin, *The Magistrate's Tael*, 253.

13. SZSL, 88:5b–6a (vol. 3: 692).

14. KXSL 1:16b–17a (vol. 4: 46). For a sample of regency attitudes, see the edict on indictments by censors, in ibid., 1:12b–13a. Incongruously, several days before this edict was issued, a censor asked for and received a reduction in the commutation rate of tribute taxes in the Susongtai region, because of the heavy burden of land taxes.

15. QS, 487:5288

16. Kessler, *Kang-hsi and Consolidation*, 30–39. Meng Sen, "Zouxiao An," in *Ming Qing shi lunzhuo jikan*, 434–52. Meng makes the point that few records of this episode survive in the official accounts of the history of the period. His essay takes the form of a collection of references to the case in contemporary literary collections.

17. QS, 487:5288. After his service at Jianging, Zhu was assigned to the southwest, where he was killed in the Wu Sangui Rebellion. Meng Sen suggests that it was a Jiangnan literatus, serving as adviser to Wu, who recommended the murder.

18. KXSL, 6:5a–b (vol. 4: 104).

19. Wakeman, *The Great Enterprise*, vol. 2: 1067–71. As Wakeman writes, the solution was achieved when "a new system of tax registers was established, land was properly recorded therein, and liability was attached to the individual household without relying on the old tax headman system" (1070).

20. KXSL, 5:5a (vol. 4: 92).

21. The appointments are noted in KXSL, 12:11b, 13:2a (vol. 4: 186, 195). See also *Chongxiu Anhui tongzhi*, 17:3a–b; QDZGNB, vol. 3: 1991; and *Jiangnan tongzhi*, 104:4b, 31a–b, 34b–35a. In view of the Qing's apparent concern with physical borders, it may be surprising that greater fanfare did not attend a new division of the empire. However, arrangements in Jiangsu appear to have been motivated more by a need to facilitate administration than by any desire to rethink the delta. Indeed, when the Yongzheng emperor ordered the preparation of provincial gazetteers, Jiangsu and Anhui shared a gazetteer. The first independent gazetteer for Anhui was not produced until 1830. The more commonly cited version of the Anhui gazetteer, the *Revised Anhui Gazetteer* (Chongxiu Anhui tongzhi), was complete in 1878 and, according to its prefaces, represented an effort to raise morale among the local elite after the destruction suffered during the Taiping Rebellion. No separate gazetteer was produced for Jiangsu.

22. KXSL, 5:12b (vol. 4: 96). The new commissioner, Sun Dai, was a somewhat mysterious figure. Prior to his assignment to Jiangnan, he held a post in the Grand Secretariat. He seems to have held no other high office in the Qing, and no biography of him is extant.

23. *Jiangnan tongzhi*, 20:4a–b; Xu, *The Chinese City*, 102.

24. See Spence, *Ts'ao Yin and the K'ang-hsi Emperor*, 65; and more generally on Suzhou, Clunas, *Fruitful Sites*.

25. The anomaly was compounded in the eighteenth century, when a second finance commissioner was established for Jiangsu and ordered to reside at Jiangning rather than at Suzhou.

26. Skinner, "Cites and the Hierarchies of Local Systems," in *The City in Late Imperial China*, 343.

27. The Qianlong figure is my own count, derived by checking all the governors in Qian Shifu, *Qingdai zhi guan nian biao*, against Hung's index and other biographical materials.

28. *Qing shi lie zhuan*, 12:21b–24b; *Jiangnan tongzhi*, 102:36a–b.

29. QS, 270:3932.

30. On Tian's appointment as education commissioner, see Zheng Fangkun, "Xiao zhuan," GCQXLZ, 52:39b; and Chen Kangqi "Jiwen," GCQXLZ, 52:42a. The practice of appointing *jinshi* holders as education commissioners was announced in an edict at the end of Tian's term. See KXSL, 118:9b–10a (vol. 5: 239–40). For official praise of Tian Wen, see *Meng Zhai nianpu*, 1:18a–19b.

31. For the appointment, see KXSL, 130:5b (vol. 5: 394). For the appointment letter and interview, see *Meng Zhai nianpu*, 23b–26a.

32. This was zhuan 173; *Qin ding "Si ku quan shu" zong mu ti yao*, vol. 4: 3701–27. On Tang Bin's collected writings, see ibid., 3705–6; on Song Luo's, see ibid., 3718; and on Song Luo's, see ibid., 3719–20. Because collected writings by Qing intellectuals were so numerous in the eighteenth century, the editors of the *Complete Library of the Four Treasuries* decided to include only a few in the collection.

33. QS, 266:3910. Song Luo's activity was parallel to Wang Shizhen's upriver at Yangzhou; the two were friends, and Song wrote an epitaph for Wang. See Meyer-Fong, *Building Culture in Early Qing Yangzhou*, 41, 46–74 passim.

34. For an account of the Zanglang Pavilion, where Song Luo held his gatherings, see ECCP, 689–90; and *Qin ding "Si ku quan shu,"* vol. 3: 1637. On the poetic anthology, see *Qin ding "Si ku quan shu,"* 4323–24 (192).

35. These two officials are named in GCQXLZ, 48:2a–b; and Peng Shaoshi, "Shizhuang," GCQXLZ, 48:38a. For Shi Lin's biography, see QS, 277.3961. The Hanlin official was Sun Zaifeng; see QS, 280:3985.

36. KXSL, 115:28b–29a (vol. 5: 202).

37. ECCP, 671–72.

38. For Mu Tianyan's memorials describing this work, see HCJSWB, 113:14a–16a, 113:56a–57b. On river work conducted along the lower Yangzi, see HCJSWB, juan 113. See also QS, 297:3975; and *Qing shi lie zhuan*, 12:22b.

39. This characterization appears in two sources: QS, 280:3988 (devoted to the lives of those who worked on the Yellow River), and the review of *He fang I lan*, in *Qin ding "Si ku quan shu,"* 68:1495. Implied in this characterization is the idea that Pan stressed scouring out the river channels rather than building dikes along the riverbank. In his recent book, Tani Mitsutaka disputes this characterization, arguing that while Pan did advocate allowing the three streams to flow together, he also built many dikes. Tani, *Mindai Kakoshi Kenkyu*, 371–85. See also Ray Huang's biography of Pan in Goodrich and Fang, *Dictionary of Ming Biography*, vol. 2: 1107–11. Some two hundred years later, North American and European civil engineers would debate the merits of dike building or scouring along the Mississippi and Rhine Rivers. See Barry, *The Great Mississippi Flood of 1927*, 32–45.

40. Hou Renzhi, "Jin Fu zhi he shimo," 47–49.

41. Jin was serving as secretary of the Wu Ying Dian throne hall at the time of his appointment to Anhui. All of his service prior to his appointment in Anhui was in Beijing.

42. Jin Fu's son published his father's memorials in Jin Wenxiang gong (Fu) zoushu, which was reprinted in 1967. A shortened version of Jin's edicts, together with other administrative documents from the river project, was published as He fan zou ji shu, in Si ku quan shu. For commentary, see Hou Renzhi, "Jin Fu zhi he shimo." Summaries of Jin's proposals are in ECCP, 161–63; and QS, 280:3982. Hou emphasizes that Jin was very much guided in his proposals by his muyu, Chen Huang. For a short account of Chen's conversations with Jin Fu, see He fan jou ji shu. See also Hou, "Chen Huang zhi he," 65–82.

43. Hou, "Jin Fu zhi he shimo," 83–84.

44. See DQHDSL, 903:1a–2b (vol. 10: 423); and Hou, "Chen Huang zhi he," 71–72. Confronted with significant flooding and a recalcitrant local elite, another Chinese bannerman, Tian Wenjing, would adopt the same expedient when he was governor of Henan.

45. Tang Bin, Qianan xiansheng shugao, 905–21.

46. After the conclusion of his term in Jiangsu in 1684, Mu had served briefly as governor of Huguang, then for two years as governor of Guizhou, after which he was promoted to governor-general for grain transport.

47. For Tian's history of his native district, Chang he zhi jie kao, see Tian Wen, Gu Huan Tang Ji, juan 40–48.

48. The elder Yu Chenglong is discussed in chapter 2, in the "Appointments Procedure" section.

49. For a description of the younger Yu Chenglong's role in the process, see Song and Li, Yu xiang qin gong (Chenglong) nianpu, 1:19a–48b. For an English-language summary, see Miller "Factional Conflict," 150–55.

50. See Miller, "Factional Conflict," 140–50.

51. This end was not accomplished, however, without a certain measure of bureaucratic turmoil. On the same day in 1688, Mu Tianyan and Jin Fu were dismissed from their appointments as directors-general, Mu of river conservancy and Jin of grain transport, as were five other court officials who had participated in the conflict. KXSL, 134:21–24a (vol. 5: 340). Six days later, Tian Wen was transferred to the governorship and to Guizhou. Meng zhai nianpu, 26b–27b. Tang Bin, who had used his access to the emperor, provided by his position of tutor to the heir apparent, to argue against Jin Fu's proposal, was demoted and died soon after. The best descriptions of Tang Bin's role in the controversy are in Yang Chun's biography of him, in GCQXLZ, 48:29a–31b; and Fang Bao's "I shi," in GCQXLZ, 48:43b–46a. A year later, when the Kangxi emperor made his second tour of the southeast, he was so impressed by what the people of northern Jiangsu told him about the advantages of the new Zhong He canal, that he reappointed Jin Fu to his post as director-general of river conservancy. The younger Yu Chenglong escaped the 1688 carnage because of his appointment to the governor-generalship of Zhili, where he devoted himself to conservancy work on the Yongding River, which provided water for Beijing. ECCP, 938.

52. Qin ding "Si ku quan shu," 68:1501.

53. Hang Shijun, "Zhang Boxing zhuan," in GCQXLZ, 61:10a.

54. There are eight biographical accounts of Zhang in GCQXLZ, juan 61:1a–42b. See also QS, 266:3910–11; and ECCP, 51–53.

55. He, "Kangxi yu Gali," 90.

56. Qing shi lie zhuan, 12:26b–30b; ECCP, 268.

57. See Zhang Boxing "Guo shi guan ben zhuan," in GCQXLZ, 61:2a.

58. This case is vividly described in Spence, *Ts'ao Yin and the K'ang-hsi Emperor*, 240–54; and Durand, *Lettres et Pouvoirs*, 229–42. Durand's focus is on the ongoing conflict between Manchus and Chinese literati in Qing government. My interest is more on what the case says about local rather than central politics. The information that military men sided with Gali and civilians sided with Zhang is found in Cao Yin's memorials on the Examination Hall case, in *Guanyu Jiangnan zhizao Cao jia dang'an shiliao*, 90.

59. See Zhang Boxing, "Li chen bei wu shi mo shu," in *Zheng yi tang wenji*, vol. 2: 17–27. The form of the references to Gali's indictment in Zhang's memorial suggest that the memorial was excerpted rather than merely paraphrased. The passages from the Gali memorial are fairly long and are set off from the rest of the text by the words *cheng* and *deng yu*, which were the verbal equivalent of quotation marks in Qing documents. Also, the language quoted in Zhang's edict matches that quoted in *Qing shi lie zhuan*, 12:28b–29a.

60. KXSL, 243:13a–b (vol. 6: 417). It is possible that Zheng Jinxin was a relative of Zheng Chenggong's, but the Manchu Brigade general identified him as a native of Ningbo.

61. Zhang Boxing, "Li chen bei wu shi mo shu," in *Zheng yi tang wenji*, vol. 2: 17–18.

62. KXSL, 244:15b–16a (vol. 6: 427).

63. See ibid. and *Qing shi lie zhuan*, 12:29a. This charge does not appear in Zhang Boxing's redaction of Gali's memorial.

64. Zhang Boxing, "Li chen bei wu shi mo shu," in *Zheng yi tang wenji*, vol. 2: 18–19. Zhang would spend much of his time as governor of Jiangsu pursuing Zhang Yuanlong.

65. On Mingzhu's attempted extortion during the Tang Bin's term, see Peng Shaosheng, "(Tang Bin) Shizhuang," in GCQXLZ, 48:39b; and QS, 270:3931. Fang Chao-ying describes Mingju, perhaps delicately, as a "skillful business executive" who "amassed a great fortune," which was ultimately confiscated in the late eighteenth century by another skillful Manchu "executive," Hoshen. ECCP, 577. On Mingju's influence in provincial government, see Kessler, *K'ang-hsi*, 129. Kessler observes that Mingju's was the first Manchu faction to include both Manchus and Chinese.

66. Zhang Boxing, "Li chen bei wu shi mo shu," in *Zheng yi tang wenji*, vol. 2: 20–21; *Qing shi lie zhuan*, 12:29b; *Guanyu Jiangnan zhizao cao jia dangan shiliao*, 90–92.

67. Zhang Boxing, "Li chen bei wu shi mo shu," in *Zheng yi tang wenji*, vol. 2: 20.

68. On Chen Pengnian, see ECCP, 95–96; QS 3972–73; and Durand, *Lettres et Pouvoirs*, 220–27. The editors of *The Annotated Catalog* took note of Chen's collected writings but did not copy them into the imperial library. See *Qin ding "Si ku quan shu,"* 37:4073. When Gali indicted Lieutenant Governor Yi Sigong shortly after his arrival in the delta, Chen Pengnian, then prefect at Suzhou, was ordered to serve as acting lieutenant governor. Gali in turn indicted Chen, who was sentenced to exile. However, a place was found for him on one of the imperial editing projects in Beijing. At the end of his career, Chen served as director-general of river conservancy from 1721 to 1723.

69. On Lü Lungqi, see ECCP, 547–48; and QS, 266.3909–10 (also the concluding note for *zhuan* 266, on p. 3911). Thirteen titles by Lü Lungqi were included in the *Complete Library of the Four Treasuries*. For the condemnation of Mu Tianyan, see 279.3975.

70. Zhang Boxing, "Li chen bei wu shi mo shu," in *Zheng yi tang wenji*, vol. 2: 22–23. Durand emphasizes that Zhang Boxing was not a good administrator. *Lettres et Pouvoirs*, 236–38.

71. On Fang Bao, see Durand, *Lettres et Pouvoirs*; and Guy, "Fang Bao and the Ch'in-ting *ssu-shu wen*," in Elman and Woodside, *Education and Society*, 150–83, particularly 153–54; and Goodrich, *The Literary Inquisition of Ch'ien-lung*, 77–80.

72. ECCP, 689, 565.

73. Zhang Boxing, "Li chen bei wu shi mo shu," in *Zheng yi tang wenji*, vol. 2: 24–25. It is not clear here whether Zhang Boxing refers to publications he commissioned in his official capacity or to his own collectanea, *Zheng yi tang wenji*, which included the works of Sung Neo-Confucian philosophers and was published in several editions between 1703 and 1707.

74. Zhang Boxing, "Xie fu ren shu," *Zheng yi tang wenji*, 29–30.

75. Spence, *Ts'ao Yin and the K'ang-hsi Emperor*, 215. Zhaolian relates that the Kangxi emperor was initially inclined to favor Gali in the dispute but changed his mind when Gali's mother told him how corrupt Gali was. It may be significant in this context that Gali was dismissed from office for plotting to kill his mother. Zhaolian, *Xiao ting za lu*, 10:24b. Zhang's victory was a personal one, however, not a victory for Chinese scholar-administrators. He was replaced in 1715 by a bannerman, and most Jiangsu governors during the Yongzheng reign were Chinese bannermen. Pierre-Henri Durand reads this case in the context of the succession crisis in Beijing and concludes that the emperor's actions represented a conscious choice of Chinese scholars over Manchu partisans of the heir apparent.

76. For an example of the use of this trope in the eighteenth century, see Kuhn, *Soulstealers*, 70–72.

77. See Elman, *Classicism, Politics, and Kinship*, 51–52, 70.

78. Wills, "Maritime China," 208.

79. For biographies of many of the Fujian officials, see *Guo chao ji xian lei zheng xuan bian*.

80. Struve, *The Southern Ming*, 75–94; and Wakeman, *The Great Enterprise*, 734–38.

81. ECCP, 415–16.

82. See Kessler, *K'ang-hsi*, 41–45. The edict banning trade is translated in Xie, "Removal of Coastal Population," 564.

83. Fu, *Qingdai dufu zhidu*, 14–15. The first governor-general was Zhang Cunren; for his pursuit of the Longwu emperor, see QS, 238.3727. Zhang first appears in the *Veritable Records* in 1645, remarking on the difficulty of forcing the Chinese to wear the queue and then resigning on account of illness. See SZSL, 19:10a (vol. 3: 171).

84. John Wills has hypothesized that Qing coastal officials had to have a combination of various skills often found singly in officials of other provinces. In the mainstream of Chinese officialdom, he suggests, there were places for the mediator, the merchant, and the military commander. But in the southeast, these skills could be combined powerfully in a single individual. See Wills, "Maritime China," 234.

85. Crossley, "The Tong in Two Worlds," 21; see also Crossley, *Translucent Mirror*, 57–88; and ECCP, 796–98. The Tongs have fascinated many historians of the early Qing. See Wakeman, *The Great Enterprise*, 737. On Tong Guoqi's writings, see Struve, *The Ming-Qing Conflict*, 277.

86. Twelve Tongs with names beginning with *guo*, all active in the late seventeenth century, are listed in Hung and Du, *Index*, 373.

87. ECCP, 792–93; GCJXLX, 151:23a–b.

88. See Mungelo, *The Forgotten Christians of Hangzhou*, 28–30.

89. See Wills, "Contingent Connections," 188–91.

90. On Tong's firing, see SZSL, 132:7b (vol. 2: 1020). On Zhu Changzo's allegiance to the regent Suksaha, see QS, 250.3805, where he is noted for pleading for relief on behalf of impoverished Manchu bannermen.

91. ECCP, 231–32. See also Crossley, *Translucent Mirror*, 123–25.

92. QS, 353.3823; for other memorials on land taxation by Fan, see Fan Chengmo, *Fan Zhongzhen gong quanji*, 129–31, 141–53.

93. "Qing dongnan da kun shu," in Fan Chengmo, *Fan Zhongzhen gong quanji*, 125.

94. Fan Chengmo, *Fan Zhongzheng gong quanji*, 201–13.

95. Ibid., 186; translation adapted from Xie, "Removal of Coastal Population," 185.

96. Not the least of the pressures Fan felt would have been family pressures. He had two brothers serving the Qing.

97. Peng Peng, "Min Zongdu Zhongzhen Fan Xiansheng zhuan," in *Fan Zhongzhen gong quanji*, 49–64. On Peng Peng, see ECCP, 613–14. In the nineteenth century, a popular novel celebrated Peng's status as a paragon.

98. Dai Zhen, "Fan Zhongzhen zhuan," in *Dai Zhen wenji*; and Qian Yiji, "Fan Zhongzhen gong quanji," in Fan Chengmo, *Fan Zhongzhen gong quanji*, 65–74. Dai Zhen's biography is printed with punctuation in Dai Zhen, *Dai Zhen wenji*, 185–87.

99. Fan Chengmo, *Fan Zhongzhen gong quanji*, 1–4.

100. For an outline of Wu's career and family history, see QS, 261.3879–80; for more details, see *Guo chao ji xian lei zheng xuan bian*, 519–22. See also Wills, "Maritime China," 231–32.

101. For Wan's appointment, see KXSL, 80:16b–17a (vol. 4: 1024). The edict makes clear that Wan's local expertise as a Fujian native was a decisive factor in his appointment. Wan was serving as naval commander in Hunan at the time and was authorized by the emperor to take with him to his new post those of his subordinates who knew something about Fujian.

102. On Wu's role, see particularly *Guo chao ji xian lei zheng xuanbian*, 522. See also Wan Zhengse's biography in QS, 262:3885. Shi Lang again held this post from 1681 until his death in 1696. In the mid-seventeenth century, the Qing experimented with posting a naval commandant in Zhejiang and Guangdong, but in neither case did the post become permanent.

103. On Yao Qixian, see *Guo chao ji xian lei zheng xuanbian*, 519–21; QS, 261.3877–79; and ECCP, 899–900. The information that Wu introduced Yao to the Qing is from Zhaolian, who, though well informed, lived in the early nineteenth century. Yao Qixian, Wu Xingzuo, and Wan Zhengse are grouped in QS, juan 262 .

104. Fan Chongzhen, "Tiao-chen Min sheng li-hai shu," in Fan Chengmo, *Fan Zhongzhen gong quanji*, 124–25; translation modified slightly from Xie, "Removal of Coastal Population," 573.

105. KXSL 121:19a–20a (vol. 5: 157); Kessler, *K'ang-hsi*, 97.

106. Wills, "Maritime China," 232. On Wu's collection of maps, see ECCP, 777.

107. *Guo chao ji xian lei zheng xuanbian*, 523; KXSL, 141:9b–10a (vol. 5: 549). Wu subsequently saw service in the Kangxi emperor's campaign against Galdan.

108. For a history of the borders of Zhejiang, see Gu Zuyu, *Du shi fang yu ji yao*, vol. 4: 3724.

109. *Guo chao ji xian lei zheng xuanbian*, 593–94; QS, 276:3958; and ECCP, 81.

110. ECCP, 51.

111. KXSL, 115:11b (vol. 5: 195).

112. DQHDSL, 65:2b–7b (vol. 1: 825–29).

113. Ibid., 65:18a–25b (vol. 1: 833–34); for the subsequent evolution of Taiwan's local government, see 834–37.

114. On the size of banner garrisons, see DQHD, 86:6a–7b (779–80). See also DQHDSL, 545:8b–11b (vol. 7: 47–48).

115. These numbers are drawn from QS, 133:1633. More complete information on the disposition of forces in Zhejiang is in *Zhejiang tongzhi*, juan 91–94.

116. Crossley, *Orphan Warriors*, 87.

117. On Fusong, see *Chengban tanwu*, vol. 4: 3290–3387.

118. QS, 295:4073–74; *Qing shi lie zhuan*, 13:37a–40a.

119. Li also defined the province for his capital superiors, supervising the production of both the *Zhejiang Gazetteer* (Zhejiang tongzhi), which was issued and reissued until the end of the nineteenth century, and *Gazetteer of Liangzhe Salt Regulations* (Liangzhe yan fa zhi).

120. Yang Qijiao, *Yongzheng di ji qi mizhe zhidu yanjiu*, 127–40.

121. Ho Ping-ti, *The Ladder of Success*, 228.

122. On the Zhejiang elite, see Brook, "Family, Continuity and Cultural Hegemony," 47.

123. QS, 292:4057; *Qing shi lie zhuan*, 13:30b–32b.

124. Goodrich, *The Literary Inquisition of Ch'ien Lung*, treats this legend as fact. Such a clumsy prosecution would have highlighted Cha's apparent point, that the Manchus were unfit to rule the Chinese literary elite.

125. The case is discussed in Goodrich, *The Literary Inquisition of Ch'ien Lung*, 80–82.

126. YZSL, 48:24a–26b (vol. 7: 730–32). Cha Siting was recommended as an examiner by Lungkodo.

127. Ibid., 48:26b–30b (vol. 7: 732–33). Although this edict clearly expressed the views of the Yongzheng emperor at the time he appointed Wang Guodong, it does not mention Cha Siting and perhaps was occasioned by another circumstance. Unlike most officials in Qing China, educational officials' were limited to terms of three years, and the commissioners for all provinces were appointed at the same time. In the autumn of 1726, a new set of commissioners was appointed, and this edict appears to have represented instructions for all of them.

128. Ibid., 49:6a–b, 7b (vol. 7: 737).

129. Ibid., 49:18b–21a (vol. 7: 743–44).

130. Ten memorials from Wang's term in Zhejiang are reprinted in ZPZZ, 1742–55. See also Yokohama, "Guanfeng zhengsu shi ko."

131. Undated memorial, ZPZZ, 1742–43.

132. ZPZZ, 1742–43.

133. Ibid., 1748–49.

134. See Guy, *The Emperor's Four Treasuries*, 124–29.

135. See Spence, *Treason by the Book*, 111–12, 136, 231.

136. Wills, "Maritime China," 232.

137. Rawski, *Agricultural Change and the Peasant Economy*, 57–101.

138. Naquin and Rawski, *Chinese Society in the Eighteenth Century*, 172.

139. *Guo chao ji xian lei zheng xuanbian*, 861.

140. Most scholars accept the fact of an economic decline in Fujian in the eighteenth century, and the proposition that it had something to do with the rise of Canton as a port and an economic engine, but the details of decline need further research. See Vermeer, "Introduction," esp. 11–13.

141. Macauley, *Social Power and Legal Culture*, 238.

142. Ownby, *Brotherhoods and Secret Societies*, 173.

143. Ibid., 175.

144. *Guo chao ji xian lei zheng xuanbian*, 858–59.

145. See Wu Shigong's essay in HCJSWB, 84:48a–49b.

146. QS, 310.4181:82.

147. *Guo chao ji xian lei zheng xuanbian*, 879–80.

148. These were Huang Jian, the son of Huang Tinggui, who was promoted from lieutenant governor to governor in 1778 and cashiered in 1779, and Wang Shiren, promoted in 1738 and cashiered in 1740.

149. *Guo chao ji xian lei zheng xuanbian*, 1052–60.

150. Macauley compares what she terms the "fruitless government exercises to construct customary law in Fujian to European attempts to construct customary law in sub-Saharan Africa." Fujian was not a colony of the Qing, although in some respects Taiwan was ruled like one, but government in the province clearly represented some imposition of central forms on complex local realities.

Chapter 8. Regions into Provinces: The Middle Yangzi and Lingnan

1. DQHDSL, 23:8a–b (vol. 1: 291).

2. The fullest English-language account of the Wu Sangui Rebellion is Kessler, *K'ang-hsi*, 75–90; see also Wakeman, *The Great Enterprise*, vol. 2: 1099–15. Its customary to refer to this episode as the "rebellion of the three feudatories," but since Wu Sangui was the driving force behind the rebellion, and the circumstances of the other two "feudatories" in Canton and Fujian were very different, I have adopted the practice recommended by Dai Yingcong and refer to this event as the Wu Sangui Rebellion.

3. G. William Skinner, "Regional Urbanization in Nineteenth-Century China," in *The City in Late Imperial China*, 211–53.

4. According to Gu Zuyu, the region that was to be the province of Hubei had multiple centers, with three potential strong points—Jingzhou, Wuchang, and Xiangyang. See Gu Zuyu, *Du shi fan yu ji yao*, vol. 4: 3171.

5. Yin Huiyi, "Zheng xue lu," 4:29a; quoted in Fu, *Qingdai dufu zhidu*, 15.

6. The Huguang governor-generalship was eliminated in the wake of a large corruption case in the area. For the elimination and reestablishment of the position, see KXSL, 134:14a–b (vol. 5: 455); and KXSL, 137:6b–7a (vol. 5: 489).

7. See KXSL, 61:2b (vol. 4: 789); and KXSL, 79:17a–b (vol. 4: 1013).

8. On Martino Martini's map of Chinese provinces (ca. 1654), all of the middle Yangzi is referred to as Huguang. There is no mention of Pianyuan or Yunyang. See Mungello, *Curious Land*, 118–19.

9. For descriptions of Hunan's river valleys, see Perdue, *Exhausting the Earth*, 31–33; on double-cropping in Hunan (which involved raising two different grains on the same land at the same time), see 131–35. On the degree of economic integration among the river valleys in Hunan, see R. Bin Wong and Peter C. Perdue, "Grain Markets and Food Supplies in Eighteenth-Century Hunan," in Rawski and Li, *Chinese History in Economic Perspective*, 126–44.

10. QS, 68:938.

11. For a translation of an account of fighting in Changsha in the 1650s, see Struve, *Voices from the Ming-Qing Cataclysm*, 155–61.

12. The name Hunan appears in official records before this date to designate a region, not a political apparatus.

13. *Hunan tongzhi* (1820), zhuan shou 1:11b.

14. Zhang Hong's preface to the 1820 gazetteer forcefully makes the case for a separate administrative identity for Hunan, and a separate gazetteer. See *Hunan tongzhi, shuzun,*

1a–20a. In their review of the *Huguang Gazetteer*, the editors of the *Annotated Catalog of the "Complete Library of the Four Treasuries"* fault the editors of the Huguang volume for ignoring materials from Hunan. SKQSZMTY, 68:1483.

15. QS, 240:3745.

16. Perdue, *Exhausting the Earth*, 80.

17. Ibid., 80–87. See also ECCP, 80; and QS, 269:3900. Zhao was recommended to the court by Li Guangdi and had close ties with many of the scholar-officials in the late Kangxi court. Thirteen biographies of Zhao are reprinted in GCQXLZ, 54:1a–44b; for the edict urging Zhao to reform corrupt officialdom, see 54:15a–b.

18. The governor involved was Wei Tingzhen, whose career and experience are discussed in R. Kent Guy, "Fang Pao and the Ch'in-ting ssu-shu wen," in Elman and Woodside, *Education and Society*, 155–56.

19. ZPZZ, vol. 3: 1752. The governor being appointed is Wang Guodong; the bannerman to whom the emperor refers is Bulantai.

20. This conflict is described in Akedun's biography, in QS, 304:4133–44.

21. Yang Xifu, "Chenming mi gui zhi you shu, " in HCJSWB, 39:21a–24b. The text is translated in full in Dunstan, *Conflicting Counsels to Confuse the Age*, 279–91. See also Perdue, *Exhausting the Earth*, 166–68, 168–234 passim.

22. Regulations on mourning are in DQHDSL, *juan* 138, 139. The mourning period often provided an official the chance to reassess his career.

23. QS, 309:4176–77; GCQXLZ, 173:6a–33a.

24. On Feng Qian, see GCQZLX, 178:37a–42a. On Kaitai, see QS, 327:4293; and GCQXLZ, 172:1a–6b.

25. For comments on this case from a slightly different point of view, see Guy "Rule of Man," 88–111. On official granaries in Hunan, see R. Bin Wong, "The Middle Yangzi," in Will and Wong, *Nourish the People*, 389–428.

26. ECCP, 501.

27. See Li Yuandu's assessment in GCQXLZ, 179:30b.

28. Tan Shangzhong and Fei Chun governed during the time when Heshen exercised tremendous power at the central court. Like Yang Xifu, both were degree-holding Chinese who had risen through the ranks of territorial administration to their posts. The collection possibly was published to make the point that Chinese-style administrators could be every bit as accomplished as the Manchu protégés of Heshen.

29. Will, "State Intervention," 295–348.

30. Rowe, *Hankow*, esp. 55–57.

31. On Nian Jialing, see *Qing shi lie zhuan*, 12:16a–17a; on Liu Dianheng, see GCQXLZ, 154:8a–9b. Liu Dianheng's father, Liu Chaoqi, had governed Hubei from 1661 to 1669.

32. The vigor of Hubei governors in the late seventeenth and early eighteenth centuries was manifested in, among other things, a "much more evident willingness to supervise the entire system of hydraulic installations" in the middle Yangzi basin than was apparent in earlier or later times. See Will, "State Intervention," 314–15.

33. On Yan and floods, see Will, *Bureaucracy and Famine*, 257 n.; and biographies in QS, 4183–84, and GCQXLZ, 169:23a–28a.

34. The increase in the number of short-term governors in Hubei broadly corresponded with the "Crisis" and "Phase B" periods of the Qing hydraulic cycle documented by Pierre-Etienne Will, times when the central government lost its capacity to effectively regulate hydraulic works in the middle Yangzi basin. These two developments were not coinciden-

tal, but neither were they related as cause and consequence. Most likely, both were related to the increasing power of local elites in the basin. See Will, "State Intervention," 320–40.

35. In its otherwise fairly complete account of Hubei officialdom, the 1825 edition of the *Hubei Gazetteer* (Hubei tongzhi) ignores these sojourning governors; see *Hubei tongzhi*, *zhuan* 121 passim.

36. Rowe, *Saving the World*, 211–14.

37. ZPZZ, vol. 2: 1199. The switch took place in 1727; see QDZGNB, vol. 2: 1582.

38. This account is drawn from Tang's biography, in GCQXLZ, 177:20a–23b.

39. For the charges against Asha, see QLSL, juan 632–33 passim (vol. 17: 1002–3, 1015, 1030, 1040). According to the edicts in *Veritable Records of the Qing*, the investigators were never able to determine the amounts involved, beyond the general sum of "several thousand *liang*."

40. QLSL, 642:24b–16a (vol. 17: 180–81).

41. In addition to Tang's biography, see the imperial edicts condemning Song Bangshou, in QLSL, 687:5b–11b passim (vol. 7: 692–95).

42. From his volunteer service in Hunan, Tang was promoted to Hunan provincial judge in 1764 and Shaanxi provincial judge in 1765.

43. Here, the issue was political and was far beyond Tang's control. The basic problem was the failure of the ill-fated Burma campaign; though Yang had recaptured areas along the border, he underestimated the strength of the resistance in his memorials to the court. Tang was blamed for not correcting Yang's report. See QLSL, 784:10a–11a. (vol. 18: 640–42).

44. Ho Ping-ti, *The Ladder of Success* , 228.

45. QS, 276:3960.

46. Gu Zuyu, *Du shi fang yu ji yao*, vol. 4: 3529–31.

47. On Haicheng and the Wang Xihou case, see Guy, *The Emperor's Four Treasuries*, 175–77. On Hao Shuo, see *Qianlong chao chengban tanwu dang'an*, vol. 4: 2847–81.

48. The governor was Ming Shan. See GCQXLZ, 173:36a.

49. On Haicheng's innovations, see Guy, *The Emperor's Four Treasuries*, 171. When I first wrote about the cases of Haicheng and Hao Shuo, I failed to note that they served in the same province and therefore to recognize how wonderfully a predecessor's execution can focus his successor's mind.

50. Gu Zuyu, *Du shi fan yu ji yao*, vol. 5: 4145.

51. Marks, *Tigers, Rice, Silk, and Silt*, 132.

52. Skinner, *The City in Late Imperial China*, 139–40.

53. SZSL, 32:4a–b (vol. 3: 263). A provincial finance commissioner, provincial judge, and circuit intendants were also appointed in this edict. Many appointees appear to have been Guangdong natives. On the appointment of Guangdong natives to posts in the province, see *Da Qing huidian*, Kangxi ed., 8:15a. Also see *Qing shi lie zhuan*, 4:27b–28a.

54. Struve, *The Southern Ming*, 128–29.

55. Descriptions from Dutch sources about the devastation this siege caused are in Marks, *Tigers, Rice, Silk, and Silt*, 149; and Struve, *The Southern Ming*, 142. In Guangdong at this time, there was also an epidemic, perhaps brought by the Manchu troops, and famine, owing to a series of cold winters known globally as the little ice age of the sixteenth century.

56. SZSL, 139:8b–9a (vol. 3: 1075).

57. KXSL, 21:2a (vol. 4: 279).

58. Ibid., 91:16b (vol. 4: 1158); see also the edict assessing the situation in Lingnan in ibid., 91:19a–21a (vol. 4: 1153–54).

59. *Guangdong tongzhi*, 17:1b–3a. This number includes multiple branch office of the provincial administration, granaries and schools, but it does not include prefectural or district officers.

60. See Zelin, *The Magistrate's Tael*, 218, for Guangdong reliance on commercial taxes. This reliance can only have increased as time went on. For an example of an official serving concurrently as governor and salt commissioner, see the case of Li Zhiying discussed in this chapter.

61. I include here the term of Li Zhiying, who, though ethnically Chinese, was a bond-servant attached to the Imperial Household Department.

62. A reader of this manuscript noted the eerie resemblance between early Qing and early Chinese Communist Party control of the southern city. See Ezra F. Vogel, *Canton under Communism*, 91–124. The Communists' ideological agenda was much more demanding than that of the Qing, but issues of distance, relations with the center, and garrison control proved to be somewhat similar.

63. The Yongzheng case is particularly vivid since both officials poured out their frustrations to the emperor via secret memorials.

64. On Yang Zongren and Yang Wenqian, see QS, 293:4061–62; and on Yang Yingju, see ibid., 328:4298–99.

65. On Akedun, see GCQXLZ, 17:1a–15a; and QS, 304:4133. For a brief but useful account of these lives, see ECCP, 5–8, 584–87.

66. QS, 293:4062.

67. On floods in 1725–27, see Marks, *Tigers, Rice, Silk, and Silt*, 210–12.

68. See ZPZZ, 367.

69. YZSL, 44:47a–48b.

70. For Yang's proposal, see ZPZZ, 381; for Akedun's response, see ibid., 5147.

71. For Yang's indictment, see ZPZZ, 398; for Akedun's, see ibid., 5157.

72. QS, 315:4218–19.

73. On Suchang, see QS, 310.3185; and GCQXLZ, 169:1a–7a. Zhaolian pronounced Suchang and his son Fugang among the most corrupt governors of the eighteenth century; see Zhaolian, *Xiao ting za lu*, juan 7.

74. On strongmen in Guangxi during the conquest, see Struve, *The Southern Ming*, 132–34. On Guangxi provincial officials during the Wu Sangui Rebellion, see KXSL, 46:14b, 60:14b–16a; and Xiao, *Qingdai tongshi*, vol. 1: 471–73.

75. On Chen, see QS, 290:4043–44. A legend exists that the future Qianlong emperor, who was born shortly before Chen was dispatched to Guangxi, was Chen's son, a baby switched at birth with a child of the Yongzheng emperor. Meng Shen finds this extremely unlikely. See "Haining Chen jia," in *Qingdai shi*, 511–31. Perhaps not surprisingly, Robert Marks finds Chen a rather inept administrator; see Marks, *Tigers, Rice, Silk, and Silt*, 241–51.

76. See Huang Chin-hsing, *Philosophy, Philology, and Politics*, 68.

77. See Marks, *Tigers, Rice, Silk, and Silt*, 131–32.

78. Hubei had almost as many newly promoted governors as did Guangxi, but it also had many more governors, since officials were transferred so rapidly in and out of a post that lay at the intersection of so many transport routes.

79. GSGBZ; and Yuan Mei, "Ji shi," in GCQXLZ, 78:11a–16b. Tuoyong was a member of the Fuca clan, then politically prominent at court, which is why his colleagues at Canton might have paid more attention to him and Yuan Mei might have been interested in him.

Despite being demoted in two provinces, he would eventually serve as president of the Board of War.

80. See Li Xiqin's biography in GCQXLZ, 172:17a–19a.

81. QSL, vol. 12: 809 (QLSL, 1191). Li Xiqin may not have known that in the mid-1740s the family of Ortai, of which Echang was a member, was in decline at the Qing court, whereas Tuoyong's family, which included the Qianlong emperor's favorite consort, was on the rise.

82. See Marks, *Tigers, Rice, Silk, and Silt*, 189.

83. Yang Jeou-yi, "The Muddle of Salt," esp. 593–608.

84. GCQXLZ, 178:32a–33b.

85. Guo, *Shiba shiji di Zhongguo zhengzhi*, 413–20; and Torbert, *The Ch'ing Imperial Household Department*, 117–20.

86. *Wen xian cong bian*, nos. 25 (1935), 26 (1936). These reports appear to be summaries of longer record books. Photographs of two of these volumes appear in Ju and Liu, "Qianlong Lesuo Panbo Guangshang Mi Shiliao," 68–80.

87. "Mi ji dang," *Wen xian cong bian*, no. 25 (1935): 4b–5a. GCQXLZ, 178:33b–34a.

88. QLSL, 1123:11a–18b, esp. 12b. For the memorials of investigation, see *Qianlong chao chengban tanwu dang'an*, vol. 3: 2099–2166.

89. Memorial of Kong Yuxun, in ZPZZ, vol. 1: 329.

90. Marks, *Tigers, Rice, Silk, and Silt*, 171.

91. "Mi ji dang," *Wen xian cong bian*, no. 25 (1935): 5a.

92. Ibid. For other cases of officials who sold personal property to pay Secret Accounts Bureau fines, see Torbert, *The Ch'ing Imperial Household Department*, 120.

93. "Mi ji dang," *Wen xian cong bao*, no. 26 (1936): 1b.

94. Marks, *Tigers, Rice, Salt, and Silk*, 131–32.

95. Gu Zuyu, *Du shi fang jiyao*, vol. 4: 4341.

Chapter 9. Communications and Provincial Government in Southwest China

1. Cited in Lombard-Salmon, *Un Example d'Acculturation Chinoise*, 93.

2. Ibid., 92–105. See also Jenks, *Insurgency and Social Disorder in Guizhou*.

3. For a vivid account of a French search for the sources of the Mekong, see Osborne, *River Road to China*.

4. G. William Skinner, "Regional Urbanization in Nineteenth-Century China," in *The City in Late Imperial China*, 241.

5. On the Mu family in Yunnan, see Goodrich and Fang, *Dictionary of Ming Biography*, vol. 2: 1079–83.

6. For the movements of the Yongli court between its expulsion from Canton in 1654 and its entry into the southwest, see Struve, *The Southern Ming*, 143–54. On the campaign against the Yongli court in the southwest, see ibid., 167–73.

7. On the establishment of provincial government in Guizhou, see SZSL, 118:2a (vol. 3: 918). On Yunnan, see SZSL, 123:3b (vol. 3: 950).

8. Wang Chenmain, *Life and Career*, 196, 171–208 passim.

9. *Da Qing huidian*, 1690 Kangxi ed., 8:15a.

10. *Qing shi lie zhuan*, 7:46a–b.

11. Li Dingguo was one of the warlords who supported the regime of the Ming pretender, the Yongli emperor.

12. Qing shi lie zhuan, 7:46b–47a.

13. KXSL, 24:8a (vol. 4: 331). One reason for the obliqueness of the language was that the emperor and Bian, following him, were determined to represent the resignation as a routine personnel transaction rather than as a challenge to the political order. This meant that neither could openly acknowledge the possibility that Wu Sangui was testing the system.

14. Qing shi lie zhuan, 7:47a–b.

15. QLSL, 1124:5a–6b (vol. 23: 24–25).

16. QDZGNB, vol. 2: 1543–46.

17. A brief memoir by Bian, covering the years 1679–81 and describing his reconquest of the southwest, titled "Ping nan ji lueh," has been published in Qing shi ziliao 3 (1983): 218–20. See also Xiao, Qingdai tongshi, vol. 1: 477–80.

18. The texts of these memorials are reproduced in Yunnan tongzhi, part 29, 4:11a–56a. For short summaries, see Qing shi lie zhuan, 7:6b–7a.

19. This memorial is anthologized in HCJSWB, juan 86.

20. This memorial is anthologized in ibid., juan 26.

21. This memorial is anthologized in ibid., juan 12.

22. Diamond, "Defining the Miao," 92–116; and Jenks, Insurgency and Social Disorder.

23. KXSL, 106:18a–b (vol. 5: 80). It is tempting to remark here that the Kangxi emperor's emphasis on the importance of the hunt for non-Chinese peoples may have been more strongly influenced by his own experience on the central Asian plains than by knowledge of the lives of peoples of the southwest.

24. This was another generic term for non-Chinese peoples.

25. KXSL, 124:46–5a (vol. 5:313).

26. "Xing lue," in GCQXLZ, 16:22b. Yuan Mei served in the Hanlin Academy from 1736 to 1739. He flunked the Hanlin final examination in Manchu but reported that Ortai told him this need not have a negative impact on his career and that the Qianlong emperor would appoint Yuan anyway. In fact, Yuan received an appointment as magistrate in Jiangnan. This brush with the Manchu elite seems to have fascinated Yuan and provided him with the raw material for many biographies of senior Manchu officials.

27. For Ortai's thanks to the emperor, see ZPZZ, 2569. See also Erong'an et al., "Xiang qin po," 62–68.

28. Erong'an et al., "Xiang qin po," 69–70. Ortai's fourth son, E'ning (governed Hubei, 1766–67, Guangdong, 1767–68, and Fujian, 1768–69), was born during Ortai's journey to Yunnan.

29. Smith, Ch'ing Policy, 16.

30. This seemed to be the practice of governors south of the Yangzi throughout the eighteenth century.

31. ZPZZ, 2578, 2600, 2616.

32. Most research using palace memorials has focused on specific issues, rather than the broader question of communication. Further careful analysis of monthly submissions for the south during the Yongzheng reign might indicate patterns here.

33. ZPZZ, 2587–88.

34. Ibid., 2599.

35. Eight of twenty-six memorials in the first period were concerned with military matters, as were nineteen of thirty-eight memorials in the second period. Because Ortai was a governor-general, his output was probably weighted more heavily toward warfare

than was that of the average provincial governor. He is worth considering here, however, since he was obviously the dominant figure in the south.

36. These three campaigns have been very capably treated in earlier studies that make possible the more modest methodological suggestions I offer here. The war against the Zhongjia is discussed in Smith, *Ch'ing Policy*, 44–101; the war in northeastern Yunnan is described in ibid., 101–79. Ortai's campaigns in Bawan-Guzhou are examined in Herman, "National Integration and Regional Hegemony."

37. ZPZZ, 2617; Smith, *Ch'ing Policy*, 133.

38. ZPZZ, 2901–5. The subject of governors' travels deserves further careful study. Reports of trips parallel in form to those submitted by Ortai in early 1731 appear fairly frequently in the eighteenth-century archives. It is possible, given that the intended purpose of *Memorials Endorsed in Vermilion* was to show how the memorial system should work, that early trip reports like the one cited here served as a model for later travel reports.

39. On the native chieftain system in the Qing, see Herman, "Empire in the Southwest"; and DQHDSL, 154, 589. See also the excellent discussion in Herman, "National Integration and Regional Hegemony," 15–73.

40. No source that I have found discusses the relationship of Shi Liha and Shi Wensheng. However, given Chinese naming practices, it seems very likely that Shi Wensheng was of the same family and generation as Shi Wenzhuo, Shi Liha's father. All were members of the Chinese Plain White Banner. See *Qin ding ba qi tong zhi*, 197:14a, 198:31a, 199:26a.

41. QS, 300:4107.

42. GCQXLZ, 70:25a.

43. On this enterprise and the mentality underlying it, see William T. Rowe, "Education and Empire in Southwest China: Ch'en Hung-mou in Yunnan, 1733–1738," in Elman and Woodside, *Education and Society*, 417–57.

44. Smith, *Ch'ing Policy*, 76.

45. Ibid., 84–91

46. See ibid., 36, 82–84.

47. ZPZZ, 2582. See also Smith, *Ch'ing Policy*, 81; and Feng Ergang, *Yongzheng zhuan*, 353–54.

48. Smith, *Ch'ing Policy*, 47.

49. Ibid., 194–219.

50. ZPZZ, 2603–4; anthologized in HCJSWB, 86.

51. Wang Yanfei, *Qingdai du fu Zhang Yunsui yū Yunnan shehui*, 12–13.

52. ZPZZ, 5, 2595–96.

53. Legge, *The Chinese Classics*, vol. 1, *The Great Learning*, 374.

54. YZSL, 43:5a–6a (vol. 7: 629); "He Shiqi guoshiguan benzhuan," in GCQXLZ, 70: 25a–26b.

55. ZPZZ, 2603.

56. Ibid., 2618.

57. GCQXLZ, 70:27a.

58. Pasquet, *L'Evolution du Système Postale,* esp. 107–10.

59. Wang Yanfei, *Qingdai di fu Zhang Yunsui*, 13–18.

60. Laura Hostetler, *Qing Colonial Enterpris*, 156–57.

61. Tian identifies twenty-eight categories of Miao. According to Hostetler, thirty-one categories were identified in 1692 and thirty-eight categories in 1741. Ibid., 238–39.

62. Qin ding "Si ku quan shu" zong mu ti yao, 68:1488.

63. QDZGNB, vol. 2: 1390–1410. Between 1736 and 1747, there were separate governor-generalships for Yunnan and Guizhou, which accounts for the overlap in the tenures of the two Zhangs.

64. The death rate among Guizhou governors was higher than that in other provinces and the rate of promotion lower, while Yunnan governors, working under the eye of the governor-general, were indicted and cashiered at a high rate.

Conclusion

1. QLSL 138:13a–b (vol. 10:990).

2. I have in mind here, among other instances, the debate over the past ten years over the meaning of gong, which took place in the course of efforts to determine whether China had a civil society.

3. Poggi, The Development of the Modern State, 62, 74.

4. Anderson, The Lineages of the Absolutist State, 18.

5. Marx and Engels, Selected Works, 13.

6. In the study of the Qing, Chinese historians have been inclined to see the eighteenth century as a period of muscular assertion of monarchical authority, whereas American scholarship has emphasized the growth of functions of an early modern state. In this respect, studies of the Qing have reproduced debates over the significance of absolutism long present in the European field.

7. See Anderson, Lineages of the Absolutist State, 69; and Lynch, Spain under the Hapsburgs, vol. 2: 19–20.

8. Stephen Saunders Webb has argued that the governors-general were principally military functionaries, but Richard R. Johnson disputes this. See Webb, The Governors-General; and Johnson, "The Imperial Webb."

9. The best study of the education and recruitment of the intendants is Gruder, The Royal Provincial Intendants.

10. Poggi, The Development of the Modern State, 71.

11. Ibid., 78.

12. Kuhn, Soulstealers, 230.

Appendix: Appointment Data for Qing Provincial Governors

1. Qian Shifu, Qingdai zhi guan nian biao.

Chinese Glossary

Ai Yuancheng 艾元徵
Aisin Gioro (Aixin Jueluo)
　愛新覺羅
Akedun 阿克敦
Aligun 阿里袞
an cha shi 按察使
An Lushan 安祿山
Anhui 安徽
Anqing 安慶
Aofeng Academy
　鼇峰書院
Asan (Ashan) 阿山
Asha (Asiha) 阿思哈

Bai Mao 白茅
Baoding 保定
bao-jia 保甲
Baqi Manzhou tongzhi
　八旗滿州通志
Ba qi tong zhi 八旗通志
Bawan 八萬
Bayansan 巴延三
Beijing 北京
Beiping 北平
ben zhuan 本傳
Bi Yuan 畢沅
Bian Sanyuan 卞三元
Bian Yongyu 卞永譽
Bishu Shanzhuang
　避暑山莊
bitieshi 筆帖式
Bolo 博落
Boxue Hongru 博學鴻儒
bu dang 不當
bu fei 部費
bu zheng shi 布政使

cai 才
cai (finance) 財
Cai Fangbing 蔡方炳
Cai Yurong 蔡毓榮
can zheng 參政
canzan junwu 參贊軍務
Cao Yin 曹寅
Cao Yishi 曹一士
caojiang xunfu 操江巡撫
Celeng 策稜
Chang'an 常安
Changjun 常鈞
Changlin 長麟
Changsha 長沙
Changshu 常熟
Chen Bangfu 陳邦傅
Chen Dashou 陳大受
Chen Hongmou 陳宏謀
Chen Huizu 陳輝祖
Chen Pengnian 陳鵬年
Chen Shiguan 陳世倌
Chen Xian 陳詵
Chen Yuanlong 陳元龍
Cheng Tao 程燾
cheng xuanbu zheng shi
　承宣布政使
Chenglin 成林
Chengtian 承天
che-qian 掣籤
chong 衝
Chongming 崇明
Chongqing 重慶
Chongxiu Anhui tongzhi
　重修安徽通志
Chongzhen 崇禎
Chuan-shaan 川陝
Chushan 出山

chushou 除授
chu-zhi you-ming
　黜陟幽明
cishi 刺史
congming 聰明
Cui Ji 崔紀

da 達
da ji 大計
Da Qing huidian shili
　大清會典事例
Da yi jue mi lu 大義覺迷錄
Dadu 大都
dai (lazy) 怠
Dai Mingshi 戴名世
Daming 大名
dan 石
dan wang 誕妄
dao 道
dao tai 道臺
Daoguang 道光
Daqing lüli 大清律例
Datong 大同
Daxing 大興
Deng Tingzhen 鄧廷楨
Denglai 登萊
Dengzhou 登州
Dezhou 德州
diao que 調缺
Ding Baozhen 丁寶楨
Ding Sikong 丁司孔
Ding Wensheng 丁文盛
Dingchang 定長
Dodo (Duoduo) 多鐸
Dong Qichang 董其昌
Dongping 東平
Dongting Lake 洞庭湖

419

Dorgon (Duo'ergun) 多爾袞

Duan Chenggong 段成功

Ebao 鄂寶
Ebi 鄂弼
Ebilun (Ebilong) 遏必隆
Echang 鄂昌
Ehai 鄂海
Eleshun 鄂樂舜
Ening 鄂寧
Erong'an 鄂容安

Famin 法敏
fan 煩
Fan Chengmo 范承謨
Fan Shichong 范時崇
Fan Shijie 范時捷
Fan Shishou 范時綬
Fan Shiyi 范時繹
Fan Wencheng 范文程
Fan Yuqi 范毓
Fan Zhongyan 范仲淹
Fang Bao 方苞
Fang Shijun 方世儁
fang zhi 方志
Fei Chun 費淳
fei yuan 廢員
Fen (river) 汾水
Feng Qian 馮鈐
Fengtian 奉天
Fengyang 鳳陽
fu 府
fu du tong 副督統
fu feng 腹封
Fu Zongmao 傅宗懋
Fuchang'an 福長安
Fude 輔德
Fuheng 傅恆
Fujian 福建
Fukang'an 福康安
Fulaihun (Fulehun) 富勒渾
Fuling'an 福靈安
Fulong'an 福隆安
Fushun 撫順

Fusong 福崧
fuyin 府尹
Fuzhou 福州

gai 改
Galdan (Ga'erdan) 噶爾丹
Gali 噶禮
Gan 灨
Gansu 甘肅
Ganzhou 甘州
Gao Bin 高斌
Gao Gong 高拱
Geng Jimao 耿繼茂
Geng Jingzhong 耿精忠
Giyesu (Jieshu) 傑書
Gu Yanwu 顧炎武
Gu Zuyu 顧祖禹
guan feng su zhi de shi 觀風俗之得失
guan feng zheng su shi 觀風正俗使
Guangdong 廣東
Guangdong Tongzhi 廣東通志
Guangxi 廣西
Guangxu 光緒
Guangzhaoluo 廣肇羅
Guangzhou 廣州
Guanxian 灌縣
Gubei kou 古北口
Guihuacheng 歸化城
Guilin 桂林
Guiyang 貴陽
Guizhou 貴州
guo 國
Guo shi guan 國史館
Guo Yiyu 郭一裕
Guolin 國霖
Guotai 國泰
Guzhou 古州

Haicheng 海成
Haihe 海河
Haining 海寧
Han 漢

Han Feizi 韓非子
Han Shiqi 韓世琦
Han Wudi 漢武帝
Hang Shijun 杭世駿
Hanlin 翰林
Hanzhong 漢中
Hao Shuo 郝碩
he bing 河兵
He Changling 賀長齡
He Shiqi 何世璂
He Tianpei 何天培
He Wei 何焴
He Yucheng 何裕城
Hecen 赫臣
Henan 河南
Hengwen 恆文
Henian 鶴年
Hening 和寧
Heqizhong 和其衷
Hesen (Heshen) 和珅
Hong Chengchou 洪承疇
Hong Taiji (Huang Taiji) 皇太極
Hong Zhijie 洪之傑
Hongguang 弘光
Hongze 洪澤
Hu Baoquan 胡寶瑔
Hu Zongxian 胡宗憲
Huai 淮
Huaiyang 淮陽
Huang Bing 黃炳
Huangchao jingshi wenbian 皇朝經世文編
Huang Tinggui 黃廷桂
Huangping 黃平
Huangpu 黃浦
Huan-Yun 黃運
Hubei 湖北
Huguang 湖廣
hui tui 會推
huidian 會典
Hunan 湖南
Hunhe 渾河
Huzhou 湖州

Ili 伊犁

Jia Yi 賈誼
Jiading 嘉定
jian (matured) 健
jiansheng 監生
jian xuan zai wai zhi que
　揀選在外職缺
Jiang Bing 蔣炳
jiang feng 疆封
jiang jun 將軍
Jiang Sheng 姜昇
Jiang Tingxi 蔣廷錫
Jiang Weiyuan 蔣爵遠
Jiang Youxian 蔣攸銛
Jiang Zhaokui 蔣兆奎
Jiang Zhou 蔣洲
Jiangbei 江北
Jiangnan 江南
Jiangnan Tongzhi
　江南通志
Jiangning 江寧
Jiangsu 江蘇
Jiangxi 江西
Jiangzhe 江浙
Jiaozhi 交阯
Jiaqing 嘉慶
Jiaxing 嘉興
jiedushi 節度使
jin (careful) 謹
Jin (dynasty) 晉
Jin 金
Jin Fu 靳輔
Jin Hong 金鉷
Jinan 濟南
Jinchuan 金川
Jing Daoqian 荊道乾
jingshen 精神
jing-shi 經世
Jining 濟寧
jinshi 進士
jinyao 緊要
Jinzhou 錦州
Jiqing 吉慶
Jishan 繼善
Jisule (Qisule) 齊蘇勒
juan 卷
jun 郡

juren 舉人

Kacilan 喀齊蘭
kai lie 開列
kai que 開缺
kai yan lu 開言路
Kaifeng 開封
Kaimbu 凱音布
Kaitai 開泰
Kangxi 康熙
Kangxi shilu 康熙實錄
kao gong qing li si
　考功清吏司
kaoman 考滿
ke jia mao bing 科甲毛病
Ke'erchin 喀爾欽
Keifu (Keyifu) 克宜福
Kong Yuxun 孔毓珣
Korjishan (Ka'erjishan)
　喀爾吉善
Kunming 昆明

Lanzhou 蘭州
laocheng 老成
laoshi 老實
Li 澧
Li Dingguo 李定國
Li Fu 李紱
Li Hu 李湖
Li Linfu 李林甫
Li Shijie 李世傑
Li Shiyao 李侍堯
Li Weijun 李維鈞
Li Xiqin 李錫秦
Li Yuandu 李元度
Li Zhiying 李質穎
liang 兩
Liang Guozhi 梁國治
Liangguang 兩廣
Lianghuai 兩淮
Liangjiang 兩江
liangxin 良心
Liaocheng 聊城
Liaodong 遼東
Licheng 歷城
liliang 力量

Lingnan 嶺南
Linqing 臨清
linxuan 遴選
Liu Dianheng 劉殿衡
Liu Kunyi 劉坤一
Liu Tongxun 劉統勳
Long Xiqing 龍錫慶
Longkodo (Longkeduo)
　隆科多
Longwu 隆武
lu 路
Lu Longqi 陸隴其
Lu Zhuo 盧焯
Lü Erchang 呂爾昌
Lü Liuliang 呂留良
lüli 履歷
Luocheng 羅城

Ma Guozhu 馬國柱
Ma Huibo 馬會伯
Ma Rulong 馬如龍
Maci (Maqi) 馬齊
Mengdu 孟瀆
Miao 苗
Min Eyuan 閔鶚元
Ming 明
Ming shi 明史
mingbai 明白
Mingde 明德
Mingshan 明山
Mingzhu 明珠
Minzhe, Min-zhe 閩浙
Miyun 密雲
Mozi 墨子
mu 牧
Mu Tianyan 慕天顏

nan 難
Nan Zhili 南直隸
Nanchang 南昌
Nanchong 南充
Nangan 南贛
Nanjing 南京
Nanshanji 南山記
neige xueshi 內閣學士
neng 能

Nian Gengyao 年羹堯
nian li 年力
Nian Xialing 年遐齡
Nianpu 年譜
Ningxia 寧夏
No Min 諾敏
Noqin 訥親
Nurhaci (Nu'erhachi) 努爾哈赤

Oboi (Aobai) 鰲拜
Ortai (E'ertai) 鄂爾泰

Pan Jixun 潘李馴
Peng Jiaping 彭家屏
Peng Peng 彭鵬
Pianyuan 偏沅
ping 平
Pingyue 平越
Pu 濮

Qian Feng 錢灃
Qian Mu 錢穆
Qian Yu 錢玨
Qiang 羌
Qianlong 乾隆
Qianlong huidian 乾隆會典
Qiao Guanglie 喬光烈
qin (diligent) 勤
Qin Cheng'en 秦承恩
Qin ding Li bu ze li 欽定吏部則例
Qin Huitien 秦蕙田
Qing 清
qing (incorrupt) 清
qing (young) 輕
Qing lüli tong kao 清律例通考
Qing shilu 清實錄
Qingdai zhi guan nian biao 清代職官年表
Qingfu 慶復
Qinghai 青海
Qinghe 清河
Qingshigao 清史稿

Qu Shisi 瞿式耜
quan cai 全才
quanxuan 銓選

Rehe 熱河
Ri zhi lu 日知錄
rong yuan 冗員
Ruan Yuan 阮元

Sahaliang 薩哈諒
Sailengga 塞楞額
Sanfan 三藩
Seleben (Shaluoben) 莎羅奔
Shaan-gan 陝甘
Shaanxi 陝西
Shandong 山東
shang 上
Shang Kexi 尚可喜
Shang Shu 尚書
Shang Yang 商鞅
Shanghai 上海
Shanxi 山西
Shen Buhai 申不害
sheng 省
shengbu 升補
Shenyang 瀋陽
shengyuan 生員
Shi Kefa 史可法
Shi Liha 石歷哈
Shi Weihan 施維翰
Shi Wenzhuo 石文焯
Shilin 石麟
shou 守
Shuntian 順天
Shunzhi 順治
shu shui gong sha 疏水攻沙
shui-shi ti-du 水師提督
Shuose 碩色
shu-sheng 書生
Sichuan 四川
Si ku quan shu 四庫全書
"Si ku quan shu" zong mu ti yao 四庫全書總目提要
Sima Zhao 司馬昭

Siming 四明
Si zhi tang wenji 四知堂文集
Song 宋
Song Bangsui 宋邦綏
Song Luo 宋犖
Song Quan 宋權
Songchun 嵩椿
Suchang 蘇昌
Suiyuan 綏遠
Sukeji 蘇克濟
Sun Qifeng 孫奇逢
Sun Shiyi 孫士毅
Sun Yuting 孫玉庭
Sun Zaifeng 孫在豐
Susongtai circuit 蘇松太道
Suzhou 蘇州

Taiji tu shuo 太極圖說
Taiping 太平
taishou 太守
Taiyuan 太原
Taizhou 台州
Tan Jixun 譚繼洵
Tan Shangzhong 譚尚忠
Tan Sitong 譚嗣同
Tang 唐
Tang Bin 湯斌
Tang Taizu 唐太祖
Ta-yong-ning 塔永寧
te 特
te jian 特揀
te shi 特使
te zhi 特支
te-can 特參
te-yu 特御
ti que 題缺
Tian Wen 田雯
Tian Wenjing 田文鏡
Tianjin 天津
tiao-li 條例
tong (vigorous) 通
Tong ban chiao 佟半朝
tong chuang 同窗
Tong Guoqi 佟國器

Tong Tulai 佟圖賴
Tong Yangjia 佟養甲
Tongcheng 桐城
Tongzheng Shisi
　通政使司
Tongzhi 同治
Tongzhou 通州
Tsereng (Celeng) 策棱
Tu Guobao 土國寶
Tumu 土木
Tuoyong 託庸

Ula 烏喇
Uliasutai 烏里雅蘇臺

wai guan 外官
Wan Zhengse 萬正色
Wang Danwang 王亶望
Wang Guodong 王國棟
Wang Mingyue 王命岳
Wang Shijun 王士俊
Wang Shu 王恕
Wang Yangming 王陽明
Wang Zhi 汪直
Wanli 萬曆
Wanxian 萬縣
Wei 渭
Wei Tingzhen 魏廷珍
Wei Yijie 魏裔介
Wei Yuan 魏源
wei zhi 維止
Wen Fu 溫福
wen xuan si 文選司
Wenshou 文綬
wu 物
Wu Dian 吳琠
Wu Sangui 吳三桂
Wu Shaoshi 吳紹詩
Wu Shigong 吳士功
Wu Tan 吳壇
Wu Xingzuo 吳興祚
Wu Yuan 吳垣
Wuhan 武漢
Wuhu 五湖
Wujin 武進
Wuyi 武夷

xia 下
Xiamen 廈門
Xi'an 西安
xian 縣
xian (worthy) 顯
Xiande 憲德
Xianfeng 咸豐
Xiang 湘
xiao chou 小醜
Xiaoxian 孝賢
Xie Cilü 謝賜履
xin yi ming bai 心意明白
xing zhong shu sheng
　行中書省
Xinjiang 新疆
Xiong Xuepeng 熊學鵬
Xu Chao 徐潮
Xu Hai 徐海
Xu Rong 許容
Xu Shizhen 許士貞
Xu Sizeng 徐嗣曾
Xuanfu 宣府
xuanweisi 宣慰司
Xun Xu 荀勖
xun-an 巡按
xunfu 巡撫
Xuzhou 敘州

Yan Sisheng 晏斯盛
yan zhang 煙瘴
Yang 楊
Yang Guozhong 楊國忠
Yang Suyun 楊素蘊
Yang Tingyao 楊廷耀
Yang Wenqian 楊文乾
Yang Xifu 楊錫紱
Yang Yingju 楊應琚
Yang Zongren 楊宗仁
Yangzhou 揚州
Yangzi 揚子
Yansui 延綏
Yanzhou 兗州
Yao 傜
Yao Chenglie 姚成烈
Yao Qisheng 姚啟聖
Yao Wenran 姚文然

Ye Cunren 葉存仁
Yehe 葉赫
Yende 音德
Yi Sigong 宜思恭
Yi sui suo ru bu zu heng yi
　sui suo chu
　一歲所入不足衡一歲
　所出
Yibin 宜賓
Yidu 益都
Yijing 易經
yin 蔭
Yin Huiyi 尹會一
Yinjiang'a 伊江阿
Yinjishan 尹繼善
Yinti 胤禵
Yinxing'a 伊星阿
Yixing 宜興
yong ren 用人
yong ren (servant) 傭人
Yongding 永定
Yongle 永樂
Yongli 永曆
Yongzheng 雍正
Yongzheng zhupi yuzhi
　雍正硃批諭旨
Yu Chenglong 于成龍
Yu Guozhu 余國柱
Yu Hongtu 俞鴻圖
Yu Minzhong 于敏中
Yu Wenyi 余文儀
Yu Yijian 于易簡
Yu Zhun 于準
Yuan (dynasty) 元
Yuan (river) 沅
Yuan shi 元史
Yuan Mei 袁枚
Yuan Zhancheng 元展成
Yuanzhou 沅州
Yude 玉德
Yue Jun 岳濬
Yue Zhongqi 岳鍾琪
Yun-gui 雲貴
Yunkai 雲開
Yunnan 雲南
Yunyang 雲陽

Zeng Jing 曾靜
Zeng Xian 曾銑
Zha Li 查禮
Zha Siting 查嗣庭
zhai 寨
zhang 長
Zhang Boxing 張伯行
Zhang Guangsi 張廣泗
Zhang Juzheng 張居正
Zhang Shicheng 張師誠
Zhang Shizai 張師載
Zhang Tingyu 張廷玉
Zhang Yuanlong 張元龍
Zhang Yunsui 張允隨
Zhangjiakou 張家口
Zhangqiu 章丘
Zhao Hongxie 趙弘燮
Zhaolian 昭槤
Zhao Liangdong 趙良棟
Zhao Shenqiao 趙申喬
Zhao Shilin 趙士麟
Zhao Xiangxing 趙祥星
Zhejiang 浙江

zhen meng-xiang zhi wai
　朕夢想之外
zhen zuo 振作
zheng 政
Zheng Chenggong 鄭成功
Zheng Jinxin 鄭盡心
Zheng Rui 鄭瑞
Zhengde 正德
Zhengding 正定
Zhengtong 正統
Zhengzhou 鄭州
Zhili 直隸
Zhili ting 直隸廳
Zhili zhou 直隸州
zhong 中
zhong (loyalty) 忠
Zhong He 中河
zhong ya 重雅
Zhong-jia 狆家
Zhongshan 鍾山
Zhongyin 鍾音
zhou 州
Zhou Dunyi 周敦頤
Zhou li 周禮

Zhou Renji 周人驥
Zhou Wan 周琬
Zhu Di 朱棣
Zhu Gui 朱珪
Zhu Guozhi 朱國治
Zhu Xi 朱熹
Zhu Xun 朱勳
Zhu Yihai 朱以海
Zhu Youjian 朱由檢
Zhu Yuanzhang 朱元璋
zhuang (middle-aged) 壯
zhuangyuan 狀元
Zhuang Yougong 莊有恭
Zhuang Gui 壯桂
zhuo 拙
zhuo-yi 卓異
Zhupi yuzhi 硃批御旨
Zi 淄
Ziya (river) 子牙河
zongbing 總兵
zongdu 總督
zui yao que 最要缺
zuofu duyushi 左副都
　御史

Bibliography

Anderson, Benedict. *Imagined Communities: Reflections on the Origin and Spread of Nationalism.* London: Verso, 1991.

Anderson, Perry. *The Lineages of the Absolutist State.* London: Verso, 1979.

Araki Toshikazu. "Yosei ninen no hikojiken to Ten Bunkei." *Toyoshi Kenkyu* 15, no. 4 (March 1957): 100–119.

Ba qi manzhou shi zu pu. Edited by Ortai. 1744.

Ba qi tong zhi. Edited by Ortai. 1737. Reprint, Changchun: Dongbei Chubanshe, 1986.

Ba qi tong zhi retsuden sakuin. Edited by Kanda Nobuo, Mitsamura Jun, and Okada Hidehiro. Tokyo: Tōyō Bunko Mambun Rōtō Kenkyūkai, 1965.

Backhouse, E., and J. O. P. Bland. *Annals and Memoirs of the Court of Peking (From the 16th to the 20th Century).* London: W. Heinemann, 1914.

Barfield, Thomas J. *The Perilous Frontier: Nomadic Empires and China.* Cambridge, Mass.: Basil Blackwell, 1989.

Barry, John M. *The Great Mississippi Flood and How It Changed America.* New York: Simon and Schuster, 1997.

Bartlett, Beatrice S. *Monarchs and Ministers: The Grand Council in Mid-Ch'ing China, 1723–1820.* Berkeley: University of California Press, 1991.

Beasley, William G., and Edwin G. Pulleybank, eds. *Historians of China and Japan.* London: Oxford University Press, 1962.

Beattie, Hilary J. *Land and Lineage in China: A Study of T'ung-Ch'eng County, Anhwei, in the Ming and Ch'ing Dynasties.* Cambridge: Cambridge University Press, 1979.

Beck, J. Mansvelt. "The Fall of the Han." In Twitchett and Loewe, *The Cambridge History of China*, vol. 1, *The Ch'in and Han Empires, 221 B.C.–A.D. 220.*

Bernhardt, Kathryn. *Rents, Taxes, and Peasant Resistance: The Lower Yangzi Region, 1840–1950.* Stanford, Calif.: Stanford University Press, 1992.

Bi Yuan. "Shaanxi nung tian shui li mu qu shu." In *Huangchao jingshi wenbian* 36:924–26.

Biot, Edouard. *Le Tcheou-li ou Rites de Tcheou.* Paris: Imprimerie Nationale, 1851.

Bourdieu, Pierre. *Outline of a Theory of Practice.* Translated by Richard Nice. Cambridge, Mass.: Harvard University Press, 1977.

Brook, Timothy. *The Confusions of Pleasure: Commerce and Culture in Ming China.* Berkeley: University of California Press, 1988.

———. "Guide for Vexed Travellers: A Supplement." *C'hing Shih Wen-t'i* 4, no. 6 (December 1981): 130–40.

———. " Family, Continuity and Cultural Hegemony: The Gentry of Ningbo, 1368–1911."

In *Chinese Local Elites and Patterns Dominance*, edited by Joseph Esherick and Mary Rankin, 27–50. Berkeley: University of California Press, 1990.

Brunnert, H. S., and V. V. Hagelstrom. *Present Day Political Organization of China*. Translated by A. Beltchenko and E. E. Moran. Shanghai: Kelly and Walsh, 1912.

Cai Fangbing. "Shu dian gu er jishi che qian shu hou." In *Huangchao jingshi wenbian*, 17:29a–b (vol. 1: 438).

———. "Shu jia Zhongcheng diao que fan jian shu hou." In *Huangchao jingshi wenbian*, 18:31b–32a (vol. 1: 468).

———, ed. *Yu Qingduan gong (Chenglong) zheng shu*. Reprint, Taipei: Wenhai, 1976.

Certeau, Michel de. *The Practice of Everyday Life*. Translated by Stevan Rendall. Berkeley: University of California Press, 1988.

Chan, Hok-lam. "The Chien-wen, Yung-lo, Hung-hsi and Hsuan-te Reigns, 1399–1435." In Mote and Twitchett, *The Cambridge History of China*, vol. 7, *The Ming Dynasty, 1368–1644, Part 1*.

Chang Yu-chuan. "Wang Yangming as Statesman." *Chinese Social and Political Science Review* 23 (1939–40): 30–99.

Chongxiu Anhui tongzhi. Edited by Shen Baozhen. 1878.

Chu, Raymond W., and William G. Saywell. *Career Patterns in the Ch'ing Dynasty: The Office of Governor-General*. Ann Arbor: Center for Chinese Studies, University of Michigan, 1984.

Clunas, Craig. *Fruitful Sites: Garden Culture in Ming Dynasty China*. Durham, N.C.: Duke University Press, 1996.

———. *Superfluous Things: Material Culture and Social Status in Early Modern China*. Cambridge: Polity, 1991.

Crawford, Robert Bruce. "The Life and Thought of Chang Chu-cheng, 1525–1582." Ph.D. diss., University of Washington, 1961.

Creel, Herrlee. "The Beginnings of Bureaucracy in China: The Origins of the Hsien." *Journal of Asian Studies* 23, no. 2 (February 1964): 155–84.

———. *Shen Buhai: A Chinese Political Philosopher of the Fourth Century B.C.* Chicago: University of Chicago Press, 1974.

Crossley, Pamela Kyle. *Orphan Warriors: Three Manchu Generations and the End of the Qing World*. Princeton, N.J.: Princeton University Press, 1990.

———. "The Tong in Two Worlds: Cultural Identities in Liaodong and Nurgan during the 13th–17th Centuries." *Ch'ing Shih Wen t'i* 4, no. 9 (June 1983): 21–46.

———. *A Translucent Mirror: History and Identity in Qing Imperial Ideology*. Berkeley: University of California Press, 1999.

Da yi jue mi lu. Edited and translated into the vernacular by Zhang Wenjun et al. Beijing: Zhongguo Chengshi Chubanshe, 1999.

Da Ming huidian. 1588. Reprint, Taipei: Dongnan Shubao She, 1963.

Da Qing huidian. 1899 Guangxu ed. Reprint, Beijing: Zhonghua, 1990.

Da Qing huidian. 1822 Jiaqing ed. Reprint, Taipei: Wenhai, 1992.

Da Qing huidian. 1690 Kangxi ed. Harvard Yenching Library, microfilm.

Da Qing huidian. 1733 Yongzheng ed. Harvard Yenching Library, microfilm.

Da Qing huidian shili. Guangxu ed. Shanghai: Commercial Press, 1908. Reprint, Beijing: Zhonghua, 1990.

Da Qing shilu. Tokyo: Okura Shuppan Kabushike Kaishu, 1937. Reprint, Beijing: Zhonghua, 1986.

Dai Yi. *Lu shuang ji*. Beijing: Renmin Chubanshe, 1986.

———. *Qianlong di ji qi shidai*. Beijing: Renmin Chubanshe, 1992.

Dai Yingcong. "The Rise of the Southwestern Frontier under the Qing, 1640–1800." Ph.D. diss., University of Washington, 1996.

Dai Zhen. *Dai Zhen wenji, Yuanshan, Mengzi Ziyi shuzheng*. Reprint, Taipei: He-le Chubanshe, 1975.

Dardess, John W. *Confucianism and Autocracy: Professional Elites in the Founding of the Ming Dynasty*. Berkeley: University of California Press, 1983.

———. *Conquerors and Confucians: Aspects of Political Change in Late Yuan China*. New York: Columbia University Press, 1973.

De Bary, William Theodore, Wing-tsit Chan, and Chester Tan, comps. *Sources of Chinese Tradition*. Vol. 1. New York: Columbia University Press, 1960.

Dennerline, Jerry. *The Chia-ting Loyalists: Confucian Leadership and Social Change in Seventeenth-Century China*. New Haven, Conn.: Yale University Press, 1981.

Des Rotours, Robert. *L'Histoire de Ngan Lou-chan*. Paris: Presses Universitaires de France, 1962.

Diamond, Norma. "Defining the Miao." In *Cultural Encounters on China's Ethnic Frontiers*, edited by Stevan Harrell. Seattle: University of Washington Press, 1995.

Duara, Prasenjit. *Rescuing History from the Nation: Questioning Narratives of Modern China*. Chicago: University of Chicago Press, 1995.

Dull, Jack. "The Evolution of Government in China." In *Heritage of China: Contemporary Perspectives on Chinese Civilization*, edited by Paul S. Ropp. Berkeley: University of California Press, 1990.

Dunstan, Helen. *Conflicting Counsels to Confuse the Age: A Documentary Study of Political Economy in Qing China*. Ann Arbor, Mich.: Center for Chinese Studies, 1996.

Durand, Pierre-Henri. *Lettres et Pouvoirs: Un Procès literaire dans la Chine Imperiale*. Paris: Ecole des Hautes Etudes en Science Sociales, 1992.

Ebrey, Patricia Buckley, ed. *Chinese Civilization: A Sourcebook*. 2nd ed. New York: Free Press, 1993.

Elliott, Mark C. *The Manchu Way: The Eight Banners and Ethnic Identity in Late Imperial China*. Stanford, Calif.: Stanford University Press, 2001.

Elman, Benjamin A. *Classicism, Politics, and Kinship: The Ch'ang-chou School of New Text Confucianism in Late Imperial China*. Berkeley: University of California Press, 1990.

Elman, Benjamin A., and Alexander Woodside. *Education and Society in Late Imperial China, 1600–1900*. Berkeley: University of California Press, 1994.

Endicott-West, Elizabeth. "Imperial Governance in Yuan Times." *Harvard Journal of Asiatic Studies* 46, no. 2 (December 1986): 523–49.

———. *Mongolian Rule in China: Local Administration in the Yuan Dynasty*. Cambridge, Mass.:

Council on East Asian Studies, Harvard-Yenching Institute, Harvard University Press, 1989.

Erong'an et al., eds. "Xiang qin po E wen duan gong nian pu." *Qing shi zi liao* 2 (1981): 555–152.

Esherick, Joseph W. *The Origins of the Boxer Uprising.* Berkeley: University of California Press, 1987.

Esherick, Joseph W., and Mary Rankin, eds. *Chinese Local Elites and Patterns of Dominance.* Berkeley: University of California Press, 1990.

Fairbank, John K. "Varieties of the Chinese Military Experience." In Fairbank and Kierman, *Chinese Ways in Warfare.*

Fairbank, John K., and Frank A. Kierman, Jr., eds. *Chinese Ways in Warfare.* Cambridge, Mass.: Harvard University Press, 1974.

Fan Chengmo. *Fan Zhongzhen gong quanji.* Compiled by Long Xiqin. Anhua, 1864. Reprint, Taipei: Wenhai, 1965.

Fang Bao. *Fang Bao ji.* 1746. 2 vols. Reprint, Shanghai: Gujie Chubanshe, 1981.

Farmer, Edward L. *Early Ming Government: The Evolution of Dual Capitals.* Cambridge, Mass.: East Asian Research Center, Harvard University Press, 1976.

———. *Zhu Yuanzhang and Early Ming Legislation: The Reordering of Chinese Society Following the Era of Mongol Rule.* Leiden and New York: E. J. Brill, 1995.

Faulkner, William. *The Town.* New York: Random House, 1957.

Farquhar, David M. "Structure and Function in the Yuan Imperial Government." In Langlois, *China under Mongol Rule.*

Feng Erkang. *Yongzheng zhuan.* Beijing: Renmin Chubanshe, 1985.

———. *Qingdai renwu chuanji shiliao yanjiu.* Beijing: Shangwu Yinshu Guan Chubanshe, 2000.

Feng Jianshi and Yang Yutang, eds. *Da Qing lüli tong kao jiao yu.* Beijing: Zhongguo Zhengfa Daxue Chubanshe, 1991.

Feng Zuozhe. *Tanke zhi wang He shen mi shi.* Changchun: Jilin Wenshi Chubanshe, 1989.

Fu Zongmou. *Qingdai dufu zhidu.* Taipei: Guoli Zhengzhi Daxue, 1962.

———. *Qing zhi lunwenji.* Taipei: Shangwu, 1977.

Gansu tongzhi. Edited by Qu Rong and Liu Didi. 1737. Reprinted in *Si ku quan shu,* vols. 557–58.

Gaozongshun (Qianlong) Huangdi shilu. Reprinted in *Da Qing shilu.* Tokyo: Okura Shuppan Kabushike Kaishu, 1937. Reprint, Beijing: Zhonghua, 1986. Vols. 9–27.

Gladwin, Irene. *The Sheriff: The Man and His Office.* London: Gollancz, 1974.

Gongzhongdang Qianlong chao zouzhe. 75 vols. Taipei: Guoli Gugong Bowuyuan, 1983.

Goodrich, Carrington L. *The Literary Inquisition of Ch'ien Lung.* Baltimore: Waverly Press, 1935.

Goodrich, Carrington L., and Chaoying Fang, eds. *Dictionary of Ming Biography, 1368–1644.* 2 vols. New York: Columbia University Press, 1976.

Graff, David A. *Medieval Chinese Warfare, 300–900.* New York: Routledge, 2002.

Gruder, Vivian R. *The Royal Provincial Intendants: A Governing Elite in Eighteenth-Century France.* Ithaca, N.Y.: Cornell University Press, 1968.

Gu Yanwu. *Gu Tinglin wenji*. Beijing: Zhonghua, 1959.

———. *Yuan chao ben Ri zhi lu*. Edited by Xu Wence. Reprint, Taipei: Minglun Chubanshe, 1958.

Gu Zhen. "Dui Yong Zheng gaige di pinglun zai pinglun." *Gugong Bowuyuan Yuankan* 1988.4: 61–66.

Gu Zuyu. *Du shi fan yu ji yao*. Ca. 1680. 6 vols. Reprint, Beijing: Zhonghua Shuju, 1955.

Guanyu Jiangnan zhizao Cao jia dangan shiliao. Taipei: Weiwen Chubanshe, 1977.

Guizhou tongzhi. Edited by Ortai and Jing Daomo. 1743. Reprint, 1841.

Guo cho qi xian lei zheng. Edited by Li Huan. Xiangyin, 1884–90.

Guo cho qi xian lei zheng xuan bian. Taipei: Wenhai Chubanshe, 1985.

Guo Chengkang. *Shiba shiji di Zhongguo zheng zhi*. Taipei: Zhaoming Chubanshe, 1991.

Guy, R. Kent. *The Emperor's Four Treasuries: Scholars and the State in the Ch'ien lung Period*. Cambridge, Mass.: Harvard University Press, 1987.

———. "Fang Pao and the Ch'in-ting Ssu-shu-wen." In *Education and Society in Late Imperial China*, edited by Benjamin Elman and Alexander Woodside, 150–82. Berkeley: University of California Press, 1994.

———. "Imperial Powers and the Appointment of Provincial Governors in Ch'ing China." In *Imperial Rulership and Cultural Change in Traditional China*, edited by Frederick P. Brandauer and Chun-Chieh Huang. Seattle: University of Washington Press, 1994.

———. "Li Hu and the Dusty Byways of Empire." Paper delivered at the International Conference on Qing History, Renmin Daxue, 1995.

———. Review of Huang Chin-hsing's *Philosophy, Philology, and Politics in Eighteenth Century China. Harvard Journal of Asiatic Studies* 57, no. 2 (December 1997): 615–23.

———. "Rule of Man and the Rule of Law in China: Punishing Provincial Governors during the Qing." In *The Limits of the Rule of Law in China*, edited by Karen G. Turner, James V. Feinerman, and R. Kent Guy. Seattle: University of Washington Press, 2000.

———. "Who Were the Manchus? A Review Essay." *Journal of Asian Studies* 61.1 (February 2002): 151–64.

———. "Zhang Tingyu and Reconciliation: The Scholar and the State in the Early Qianlong Reign." *Journal of Late Imperial China* 7, no. 1 (June 1986): 50–62.

Hartwell, Robert M. "Demographic, Political and Social Transformations of China." *Harvard Journal of Asiatic Studies* 42, no. 2 (December 1982): 365–442.

———. "Financial Expertise, Examinations and the Formation of Economic Policy in Northern Sung China." *Journal of Asian Studies* 30, no. 2 (February 1971): 281–314.

He Xiaorong. "Kangxi yu Gali." *Li shi dang an* 68 (1997.4): 88–92.

Henan tongzhi. Edited by Sun Hao and Tian Wenjing. 1735. Reprinted in *Si ku quan shu*, vols. 535–37.

Herman, John E. "Empire in the Southwest: Early Qing Reforms to the Native Chieftain System." *Journal of Asian Studies* 56, no. 1 (February 1997): 47–74.

———. "National Integration and Regional Hegemony: The Political and Cultural Dynamics of Qing State Expansion." Ph.D. diss., University of Washington, 1993.

Ho Ping-ti. "In Defense of Sinicization: A Rebuttal of Evelyn Rawski's 'Reenvisioning the Qing.'" *Journal of Asian Studies* 57, no. 1 (February 1998): 123–55.

———. The Ladder of Success in Imperial China: Aspects of Social Mobility, 1368–1911. New York: Columbia University Press, 1962.

———. "The Significance of the Ch'ing Period in Chinese History." Journal of Asian Studies 26, no. 2 (February 1967): 189–205.

Hoshi Ayao. Dai Unga. Tokyo: Kinfu Shuppanshe, 1971.

Hostetler, Laura. Qing Colonial Enterprise: Ethnography and Cartography in Early Modern China. Chicago: University of Chicago Press, 2001.

Hou Renzhi. "Jin Fu zhi he shimo." Shi xue nian bao 2.3 (November 1936): 43–88.

———. "Chen Huang zhi he." In Hou Renzhi yan yuan wen xue ji. Shanghai: Shanghai Jiaoyu Chubanshe, 1991.

Hu Chang-tu. "The Yellow River Administration in the Ch'ing Dynasty." Far Eastern Quarterly 14, no. 4 (August 1955): 505–13.

Huang Chin-shing. Philosophy, Philology, and Politics in Eighteenth Century China: Li Fu and Lu-Wang School under the Ch'ing. New York: Cambridge University Press, 1996.

Huangchao jingshi wenbian. Compiled by He Changling. Reprint, Taipei: Guofeng Chubanshe, 1965.

Huang He liu yu Ditu. Edited by Shui Li Bu. Beijing: Ditu Chubanshe, 1987.

Huang Pei. Autocracy at Work: A Study of the Yung-cheng Period. Bloomington: Indiana University Press, 1974.

Huang, Philip C. C. The Peasant Economy and Social Change in North China. Stanford, Calif.: Stanford University Press, 1985.

Huang, Ray. 1587: A Year of No Significance. New Haven, Conn.: Yale University Press, 1981.

———. "The Lung-Ch'ing and Wan-li Reigns." In Mote and Twitchett, The Cambridge History of China, vol. 7, The Ming Dynasty, 1368–1644, Part 1.

Hubei tongzhi. Compiled by Chen Shideng. Wuchang, 1804.

Hucker, Charles O. The Censorial System of Ming China. Stanford, Calif.: Stanford University Press, 1966.

———. A Dictionary of Official Titles in Imperial China. Stanford, Calif.: Stanford University Press, 1985.

Hunan tongzhi. Compiled by Wang Xudeng. Changsha, 1820.

Hung, William, and Du Lianzhe. Index to Thirty-three Collections of Ch'ing Dynasty Biographies. Reprint, Beijing: Zhonghua Shuju, 1959.

Hung, William, Fang Zhaoyin, and Du Lianzhe, comps. Chin Shih T'i Ming Pei Lu of the Ch'ing Dynasty. Beijing: Harvard Yenching Institute, 1941.

Jenks, Robert D. Insurgency and Social Disorder in Guizhou, the "Miao" Rebellion, 1854–1873. Honolulu: University of Hawaii Press, 1994.

Jiangnan tongzhi. Edited by Zhao Hong'en and Huang Zhijian. 1730. Reprinted in Si ku quan shu, vols. 507–12.

Jifu hedao shuili congshu. Compiled by Wu Bangqing. 1824.

Jifu tongzhi. Edited by Chen Yi and Tang Zhi. 1735. Reprinted in Si ku quan shu, vols. 504–6.

Jifu tongzhi. Edited by Li Hongzhang and Huang Pengnian. 1885. Reprint, Shanghai: Commercial Press, 1934.

Jin Wenxiang gong (Fu) zoushu. Compiled by Jin Zhiyu. Ca. 1725. Reprint, Taipei: Wenhai Chubanshe, 1967.

Johnson, David. *The Medieval Chinese Oligarchy.* Boulder, Colo.: Westview Press, 1977.

Johnson, Richard R. "The Imperial Webb: The Thesis of Garrison Government in Early America Considered." *The William and Mary Quarterly,* 3rd ser., 43 (July 1986): 408–30.

Jones, Susan Mann, and Philip A. Kuhn. "Dynastic Decline and the Roots of Rebellion." In *The Cambridge History of China.* Volume 10, part 1, edited by John K. Fairbank. New York: Cambridge University Press, 1978.

Ju Deyuan and Liu Yong. "Qianlong Lesuo Panbo Guangshang Mi Shiliao." *Gugong Bowuyuan Yuankan* 1 (1982): 68–88.

Kahn, Paul. *The Secret History of the Mongols: The Origin of Chinghis Khan; An Adaptation of the "Yuan Ch'ao Pi Shih," Based Primarily on the English Translation by Francis Woodman Cleaves.* San Francisco: North Point Press, 1984.

"Kangxi chunian yu guan guanyuan quanxuan zhi yushi zouzhang." *Lishi Dang'an* 2 (1992): 2–19.

Kessler, Lawrence D. "Chinese Scholars and the Early Manchu State." *Harvard Journal of Asiatic Studies* 31 (1971): 179–200.

———. "Ethnic Composition of Provincial Leadership during the Ch'ing." *Journal of Asian Studies* 27 (May 1969): 489–54.

———. *K'ang-hsi and the Consolidation of Ch'ing Rule, 1661–1684.* Chicago: University of Chicago Press, 1976.

Kocho Keisei Bunken So Mokuroku. Kindai Chūgoku Kenkyū Iinkai. 1957. Reprint, Taipei:Wenhai, n.d.

Kracke, E. A. *Civil Service in Early Sung China, 960–1067; With Particular Emphasis on the Development of Controlled Sponsorship to Foster Administrative Responsibility.* Cambridge, Mass.: Harvard University Press, 1953.

Kuhn, Philip A. *Reading Documents: The Rebellion of Chung Jen-chieh.* 2 vols. Cambridge, Mass.: John King Fairbank Center for East Asian Research, 1986.

———. *Rebellion and Its Enemies in Late Imperial China, Militarization and Social Structure, 1796–1864.* Cambridge, Mass.: Harvard University Press, 1970.

———. *Soulstealers: The Chinese Sorcery Scare of 1768.* Cambridge, Mass.: Harvard University Press, 1990.

Kutcher, Norman. "The Death of the Xiaoxian Empress: Bureaucratic Betrayals and the Crisis of Eighteenth Century Rule." *Journal of Asian Studies* 56, no. 3 (August 1997): 708–25.

———. *Mourning in Late Imperial China: Filial Piety and the State.* Cambridge: Cambridge University Press, 1999.

Langlois, John D., ed. *China under Mongol Rule.* Princeton, N.J.: Princeton University Press, 1981.

———. "The Hung-wu Reign." In Mote and Twitchett, *The Cambridge History of China,* vol. 7, *The Ming Dynasty, 1368–1644, Part 1.*

Lee, James, Cameron Campbell, and Wang Feng. "The Last Emperors: An Introduction to the Genealogy of the Qing (1644–1911) Royal Lineage." In *Old and New Methods in Historical Demography*, edited by Roger Schofield and David Reher. New York: Oxford University Press, 1993.

Legge, James, trans. *The Chinese Classics: With a Translation, Critical and Exegetical Notes, Prolegomena, and Copious Indexes*. 5 vols. Taipei: Wen Xing Shu Dian, 1966.

Lévi-Strauss, Claude. *The Savage Mind*. Chicago: University of Chicago Press, 1966.

Li Jingping and Kang Guochang. *Qianlong, Heshen yü Liu Yong*. Taipei: Zhishufang Chubanshe, 2000.

Li Pengnian et al. *Qingdai zhongyang guojia jiguan gaishu*. Beijing: Cijin Cheng Chubanshe, 1989.

Li Yuan, ed. *Guochao jixian leizheng*. Xiangyin: Li Family, 1884–90.

Li, Zhian. *Xingxheng zhidu yanyiu*. Tianjin: Nankai Daxue Chubanshe, 2000.

Liang Zhangju, comp. *Shu yuan ji lue*. 1875. Reprint, Taipei: Wenhai, 1967.

Library of Congress. Orientalia Division. *Eminent Chinese of the Ch'ing Period (1644–1912)*. Edited by Arthur W. Hummel. Taipei: Cheng Wen Publishing House, 1972.

Lin Yin, ed. *Zhouli jinzhu jinyi*. Taipei: Commercial Press, 1972.

Lipman, Jonathan N. *Familiar Strangers: A History of Muslims in Northwest China*. Seattle: University of Washington Press, 1997.

Liu Guilin. "Qing shizong xuan xian ren neng shu lun." *Li shi dang an*, no. 18 (1985.2): 88–97.

Liu Keyi. "Cong 'Zhu pi yin jian dan' kan Yongzheng di zhi ren." *Qing shi yanjiu Tongxun* (1988.4): 28–31.

Liu Ziyang. *Qingdai difang guanzhikao*. Beijing: Cijin Cheng Chubanshe, 1988.

Loewe, Michael. "The Former Han Dynasty." In Twitchett and Loewe, *The Cambridge History of China*, vol. 1, *The Ch'in and Han Empires*, 221 B.C.–A.D. 220.

Lombard-Salmon, Claudine. *Un Example d'Acculturation Chinoise: La Province de Guizhou au XVIIe Siècle*. Paris: Ecole Française d'Extrême-Orient, 1972.

Lui, Adam Y. C. *Corruption in China during the Early Ch'ing Period*. Hong Kong: Center for Asian Studies, 1979.

Lynch, John. *Spain under the Hapsburgs*. New York: New York University Press, 1981.

Ma Qihua. *Qing Gaozong chao zhi tanhe an*. Taipei: Huagang Chubanshe, 1974.

Macauley, Melissa. *Social Power and Legal Culture: Litigation Masters in Late Imperial China*. Stanford, Calif.: Stanford University Press, 1998.

Man-cheong, Iona. *The Class of 1761: Examination, State and Elite in Eighteenth-Century China*. Stanford, Calif.: Stanford University Press, 2004.

Mann, Susan. *Local Merchants and the Chinese Bureaucracy 1750–1950*. Stanford, Calif.: Stanford University Press, 1987.

———. *Precious Records: Women in China's Long Eighteenth Century*. Stanford, Calif.: Stanford University Press, 1997.

Manzhou ming chen zhuan. Jingdu: Rong Jin Shu Fang, n.d.

Marks, Robert. *Tigers, Rice, Silk, and Silt: Environment and Economy in Late Imperial South China*. Cambridge: Cambridge University Press, 1997.

Marx, Karl, and Friedrich Engels. *Selected Works*. Moscow: Progress Publishers, 1970.

Masui, Yasuki. "Qianlong chao 'Quan guo sheng fu xian guanqui biao' kao." *Lishi Dang'an* 3 (1992): 133–34.

Meng Sen. *Ming Qing shi lunzhuo jikan*. Taipei: Shijie, 1965.

———. "Qingchu san da yi an." In *Qingdai shi*. Taipei: Zhongchung Shuju, 1974.

———. *Qingdai shi*. Edited by Wu Xiangxiang. Taipei: Zhengzhong Shuju, 1971.

Meng Zhai nianpu. Compiled by Ni Fan. In *Tian shi cong shu*, edited by Tang Tongzhi. Dezhou, ca. 1740.

Meng Zhaoxin. *Kangxi dadi quanzhuan*. Changchun Shi: Jilin Wenshi Chubanshe, 1993.

———. *Kangxi pingzhuan*. Nanjing: Nangjing Daxue Chubanshe, Jiangsu sheng Xinhua Shudian faxing, 1998.

Metzger, Thomas A. *Escape from Predicament: Neo-Confucianism and China's Evolving Political Culture*. New York: Columbia University Press, 1977.

———. *The Internal Organization of Ch'ing Bureaucracy: Legal, Normative and Communicative Aspects*. Cambridge, Mass.: Harvard University Press, 1973.

Meyer-Fong, Tobie. *Building Culture in Early Qing Yangzhou*. Stanford, Calif.: Stanford University Press, 1993.

"Mi ji dang." In *Wen xian cong bian*, nos. 25 (1935), 26 (1936). Beijing: Guoli Gu Gong Bo Wu Yuan, 1935.

Miller, H. Lyman. "Factional Conflict and the Integration of Qing Politics, 1661–1690." Ph.D. diss., George Washington University, 1974.

Millward, James A. *Beyond the Pass: Economy, Ethnicity and Empire in Qing Central Asia, 1759–1864*. Stanford, Calif.: Stanford University Press, 1998.

Ming shi. Compiled by Zhang Tingyu et al. 1736. Reprint, Beijing: Zhunghua, 1974.

Mohorashi Tetsuji, comp. *Dai kanwa jiten*. 13 vols. Tokyo: Taishukan Shoten, 1955–60.

Mote, Frederick W., and Denis Twitchett, eds. *The Cambridge History of China*. Vol. 7, *The Ming Dynasty, 1368–1644, Part 1*. Cambridge: Cambridge University Press, 1988.

Mungello, David E. *Curious Land: Jesuit Accommodations and the Origins of Sinology*. Wiesbaden, Germany: F. Steiner Verlag, 1985.

———. *The Forgotten Christians of Hangzhou*. Honolulu: University of Hawaii Press, 1994.

Naquin, Susan. *Shantung Rebellion: The Wang Lun Uprising of 1774*. New Haven, Conn.: Yale University Press, 1981.

Naquin, Susan, and Evelyn S. Rawski. *Chinese Society in the Eighteenth Century*. New Haven, Conn.: Yale University Press, 1987.

Narakino Shimesu. *Shindai jūuyō shokkan no kenkyū*. Tokyo: Kazema Shobō, 1975.

Nian Gengyao zou zhe zhuanji. Taipei: National Palace Museum, 1971.

Nian Gengyao man han zou zhe bian. Translated and edited by Li Yonghai, Li Pansheng, and Xie Zhuang. Tianjin: Tianjin Guji Chubanshe, 1995.

Nivison, David. *The Life and Thought of Chang Hsüeh-ch'eng, 1738–1801*. Stanford, Calif.: Stanford University Press, 1966.

Nivison, David, and Arthur F. Wright, eds. *Confucianism in Action*. Stanford, Calif.: Stanford University Press, 1959.

Norman, Jerry. *Concise Manchu Chinese Lexicon*. Seattle: University of Washington Press, 1978.

Osborne, Milton. *River Road to China: The Mekong River Expedition, 1866–1873*. New York: Liveright, 1975.

Ownby, David. *Brotherhoods and Secret Societies in Late Imperial China: The Formation of a Tradition*. Stanford, Calif.: Stanford University Press, 1996.

Oxnam, Robert B. *Ruling from Horseback: Manchu Politics in the Oboi Regency, 1661–1669*. Chicago: University of Chicago Press, 1970.

Pan Xinghun. *Ming dai wen guan quan xuan zhidu yanjiu*. Beijing: Beijing Daxue Chubanshe, 2003.

Park, Nancy Elizabeth. "Corruption and Its Recompense: Bribes, Bureaucracy and the Law in Late Imperial China." Ph.D. diss., Harvard University, 1993.

Pasquet, Sylvie. *L'Evolution du Système Postal: La Province Chinoise du Yunnan à l'Epoque Qing, 1644–1911*. Paris: Institut des Hautes Etudes Chinoises, 1986.

Perdue, Peter C. *Exhausting the Earth: State and Peasant in Hunan, 1500–1850*. Cambridge, Mass.: Harvard University Press, 1980.

———. "Military Mobilization in Seventeenth- and Eighteenth-Century China, Russia, and Mongolia." *Modern Asian Sudies* 30, no. 4 (October 1996): 757–93.

Perry, Elizabeth. "Tax Revolt in Late Qing China: The Small Swords in Shanghai and Liu Depei in Shandong." *Late Imperial China* 6, no. 1 (June 1985): 83–112.

Peterson, Charles A. "Court and Province in the Mid- and Late Tang." In *The Cambridge History of China*, vol. 3, Sui and T'ang China, 589–906, Part 1, edited by Denis Twitchett. Cambridge: Cambridge University Press, 1979.

Poggi, Gianfranco. *The Development of the Modern State: A Sociological Introduction*. Stanford, Calif.: Stanford University Press, 1978.

Polachek, James M. *The Inner Opium War*. Cambridge, Mass.: Council on East Asian Studies, Harvard University Press, 1992.

Pomeranz, Kenneth. *The Making of a Hinterland: State, Society, and Economy in Inland North China, 1853–1937*. Berkeley: University of California Press, 1993.

Pulleyblank, Edwin. *The Background of the Rebellion of An Lu-Shan*. London: Oxford University Press, 1955.

Qian Mu. *Guoshi dagang*. 2 vols. Shanghai: Guo Li Bian Yi Guan, 1943.

———. *Zhongguo lidai zhengzhi de shi*. 1955. Reprint, Taipei: San Min Shuju, 1974.

Qian Shifu, ed. *Qingdai zhi guan nian biao*. 4 vols. Beijing: Zhonghua, 1980.

Qianlong chao chengban tanwu dang'an. Compiled by Zhongguo Di Yi Lishi Dang'an Guan. 4 vols. Beijing: Zhonghua Shufu, 1994.

Qianlong huangdi quan zhuan. Edited by Guo Chengkang and Zong Chengde. Beijing: Xueyuan Chubanshe, 1994.

Qianlong zhupi. Edited by Dong Jianzhong. 2 volumes. Hong Kong: Zhongguo Huaqiao Chubanshe, 2001.

Qin ding ba qi tong zhi. Edited by Tieh Bao. 1786. Reprint, Taipei: Xueshen Shuju, 1968.

Qin ding da qing huidian. 1818. Reprint, Taipei: Wenhai, 1991.

Qin ding Li bu ze li. 1848.

Qin ding "Si ku quan shu" zong mu ti yao. Edited by Ji Yun et al. 1782. Reprint, Taipei: Commercial Press, 1971.

Qin ding xin xuan liu bu chu fen ze li. 1828.

Qin ding "Si ku quan shu" zong mu ti yao. Edited by Ji Yun. 1782. Reprint, Taipei: Commercial Press, 1971.

Qing shi. Edited by Zhao Erxun. 1927. Reprint, Taipei: Guo Fang Yanjiuyuan, 1961.

Qing shi lie zhuan. Shanghai: Zhonghua, 1928.

Qing shilu Shandong shiliao xuanbian. 3 vols. Jinan: Jilu Shushe, 1984.

Qingchao wenxian tongkao. Reprint, Hangzhou: Zhejiang Guji, 2000.

Qingdai luli dang'an quan bian. 30 vols. Beijing: Shifan Daxue Chubanshe, 1997.

Qingdai wen zi yu dang. 1931. Reprint, Taipei: Wen-hai, 1975.

Qingdai wenxian zongmu. Taipei: Gugong Bowuyuan, 1982.

Que shi quanlan. 1904. Reprint, Taipei: Wenhai, 1967.

Rankin, Mary Backus. Elite Activism and Political Transformation in China: Zhejiang Province, 1865–1911. Stanford, Calif.: Stanford University Press, 1986.

Rawski, Evelyn S. Agricultural Change and the Peasant Economy of South China. Cambridge, Mass.: Harvard University Press, 1972.

———. The Last Emperors: A Social History of Qing Imperial Institutions. Berkeley: University of California Press, 1998.

———. "Presidential Address: Reenvisioning the Qing: The Significance of the Qing Period in Chinese History." Journal of Asian Studies 55.4 (November 1966): 829–50.

Rawski, Thomas G., and Lillian M. Li, eds. Chinese History in Economic Perspective. Berkeley: University of California Press, 1992.

Ricoeur, Paul. Time and Narrative. 3 vols. Translated by Kathleen McLaughlin and David Pellauer. Chicago: University of Chicago Press, 1984.

Ropp, Paul S., ed. Heritage of China: Contemporary Perspectives on Chinese Civilization. Berkeley: University of California Press, 1990.

Rossabi, Morris. Khubilai Khan: His Life and Times. Berkeley: University of California Press, 1988.

———. "Muslims in the Early Yuan Dynasty." In Langlois, China under Mongol Rule.

———. "The Reign of Khubilai Khan." In The Cambridge History of China, vol. 6, Alien Regimes and Border States, 907–1368, edited by Denis Twitchett and Herbert Franke. Cambridge: Cambridge University Press, 1994.

Rowe, William T. "Domestic Interregional Trade in Eighteenth-Century China." In On the Eighteenth Century as a Category of Asian History: Van Leur in Retrospect, edited by Leonard Blussé and Femme Gaastra, 173–92. Aldershot: Ashgate, 1998.

———. Hankow: Commerce and Society in a Chinese City, 1796–1889. Stanford, Calif.: Stanford University Press, 1984.

———. Saving the World: Chen Hongmou and Elite Consciousness in Eighteenth-Century China. Stanford, Calif.: Stanford University Press, 2001.

Rudolph, Jennifer. "Negotiating Power and Navigating Change in the Qing." Ph.D. diss., University of Washington, 1999.

Schwartz, Benjamin. The World of Thought in Ancient China. Cambridge, Mass.: Belknap Press of Harvard University Press, 1985.

Shaanxi tongzhi. Compiled by Liu Yuyi et al. 1733. Reprinted in Si ku quan shu, vols. 551–56.

Shandong tongzhi. Compiled by Yue Jun. 1736. Reprint, n.p., 1910.

Shandong tongzhi. Compiled by Yue Zhun and Du Zhao. 1736. Reprinted in Si ku quan shu, vols. 539–41.

Shang Hongkui. "Lun Kangxi." In Kang Yong Qian sandi pingyi, edited by Zuo Buqing. Beijing: Zi Jincheng Chubanshe, 1986.

Shanxi tongzhi. Compiled by Shilin. 1736. Reprinted in Si ku quan shu, vols. 542–49.

Shanxi tongzhi. Compiled by Zeng Guoquan et al. N.p., 1877–80.

Shengzong Ren (Kangxi) Huangdi shilu. Reprinted in Da Qing shilu. Tokyo: Okura Shuppan Kabushike Kaishu, 1937. Reprint, Beijing: Zhonghua, 1986. Vols. 3–6.

Shi liao xun kan. Gugong Bowuyuan. 1929–31. Reprint, Taipei: Guofang Chubanshe, 1963.

Shun Fulai. Qianlong zhongyao zhanzheng zhi junxu yanjiu. Taipei: Gugong Bowuyuan, 1984.

"Shunzhi chunian longluo yu kongzhi Hanzu guanshen shiliao." In Qingdai dang'an shiliao congbian, vol. 3, 1–110. Beijing: Zhonghua Shudian, 1994.

"Shunzhi qin zheng hou Han guan bei ke an." In Qingdai dang'an shiliao congbian 13 (1994): 111–260.

Sichuan tongzhi. Compiled by Yang Fangcan and Chang Ming. 1816.

Si ku quan shu. 1,501 vols. Beijing, 1787. Reprint, Shanghai: Shanghai Guji Chubanshe, 1987.

Si ku quan shu ji wei wei shou shu mu yinde. Edited by William Hung. Harvard Yenching Institute Sinological Index Series. 1932. Reprint, Taipei: Chinese Materials and Research Aids Service, 1966.

Si ku quan shu. Edited by Ji Yun. 15 vols. Reprint, Shanghai: Guji, 1987.

Skinner, G. William, ed. The City in Late Imperial China. Stanford, Calif.: Stanford University Press, 1977.

———. "The Structure of Chinese History." Journal of Asian Studies 44, no. 2 (February 1985): 271–92.

Smith, Kent C. Ch'ing Policy and the Development of Southwest China: Aspects of Ortai's Governor-Generalship, 1726–1731. Ann Arbor: University of Michigan Microforms, 1970.

Sommer, Mathew. "Wu Jianzhang and Xu Naizhao Dismissed from Office: Imperialism, Social Change and Political Transformation in Mid-Nineteenth-Century China." Paper delivered at "Qing Documents" seminar, University of Washington, 1988.

Song Luo and Li Shude, eds. Yu xiang qin gong (Chenglong) nianpu. In Qing chao Han zhen yuan lili bian nian Yu xiang qin gong (Chenglong) nianpu. Reprint, Taipei: Wenhai, 1968.

Spector, Stanley. Li Hung-chang and the Huai Army: A Study in Nineteenth-Century Chinese Regionalism. Taipei: Rainbow-Bridge Book Company, 1973.

Spence, Jonathan D. The Death of Woman Wang. New York: Viking, 1978.

———. Emperor of China: Self Portrait of K'ang Hsi. New York: Vintage, 1975.

———. Treason by the Book. New York: Viking, 2001.

———. Ts'ao Yin and the K'ang-hsi Emperor: Bondservant and Master. New Haven, Conn.: Yale University Press, 1966.

Spence, Jonathan D., and John E. Wills, eds. From Ming to Ch'ing: Conquest, Region, and Continuity in Seventeenth Century China. New Haven, Conn.: Yale University Press, 1979.

Struve, Lynn A. The Ming-Qing Conflict, 1619–1683: A Bibliography and Source Guide. Ann Arbor, Mich.: Association for Asian Studies, 1998.

———. *The Southern Ming, 1644–1662*. New Haven, Conn.: Yale University Press, 1984.

———. "The Uses of History in Traditional Chinese Society: The Southern Ming in Ch'ing Historiography," Ph.D. diss., University of Michigan, 1974.

———. *Voices from the Ming-Qing Cataclysm: China in Tigers' Jaws*. New Haven, Conn.: Yale University Press, 1993.

Sugimura Yuzo. *Kenryu Kotei*. Tokyo: Sangen Sha, 1961.

Sun, E-tu Zen, ed. and trans. *Ch'ing Administrative Terms: A Translation of the Terminology of the Six Boards with Explanatory Notes*. Cambridge, Mass.: Harvard University Press, 1961.

Tang Bin. *Qianan xiansheng shugao*. In *Tang Wenzheng gong (qianan) quanji*. 1871. Reprint, Taipei: Wenhai, 1965.

Tang Liangxiong. *Zhang jiangling xin zhuan*. Taipei: Zhonghua, 1968.

Tang Wenji and Luo Qingsi. *Qianlong Zhuan*. Beijing: Renmin Chubanshe, 1994.

Tani Mitsutaka. *Mindai Kakoshi Kenkyu*. Kyoto: Doshisha, 1991.

Terada Takenobu. *Sansei Shonin no Kenkyu*. Kyoto: Doshisha, 1972.

Tian Wen. *Gu Huan Tang Ji*. In *Si ku quan shu*, vol. 1324. N.p., n.d.

———. *Meng zhai nian pu*. In *De zhou Tian shi congshu*. N.p., n.d.

Tian Wenjing. *Fu yu xuan hua lu*. Kaifeng, 1726. Zhengzhou: Zhongzhou Guji Chubanshe, 1995.

Tong, James. *Disorder under Heaven: Collective Violence in the Ming Dynasty*. Stanford, Calif.: Stanford University Press, 1991.

Torbert, Preston. *The Ch'ing Imperial Household Department: A Study of Its Organization and Principal Functions, 1662–1796*. Cambridge, Mass.: Harvard University Press, 1978.

Turner, Karen G., James B. Feinerman, and R. Kent Guy, eds. *The Limits of the Rule of Law in China*. Seattle: University of Washington Press, 2000.

Twitchett, Denis. "Provincial Autonomy and Central Finance in the Late T'ang." *Asia Major*, n.s. 11, no. 2 (1965): 211–32.

Twitchett, Denis, and Herbert Franke, eds. *The Cambridge History of China*. Vol. 6, *Alien Regimes and Border States, 907–1368*. Cambridge: Cambridge University Press, 1994.

Twitchett, Denis, and Michael Loewe, eds. *The Cambridge History of China*. Vol. 1, *The Ch'in and Han Empires, 221 B.C.–A.D. 220*. Cambridge: Cambridge University Press, 1986.

Vermeer, Edward B. "Introduction: Historical Background and Major Issues." In *Development and Decline of Fujian Province in the Seventeenth and Eighteenth Centuries*. Leiden, Netherlands: E. J. Brill, 1990.

Vogel, Ezra. *Canton under Communism: Programs and Politics in a Provincial Capital, 1949–1968*. Reprint, New York: Harper Torchbook, 1971.

Wakeman, Frederic, Jr. *The Great Enterprise: The Manchu Reconstruction of the Imperial Order in Seventeenth-Century China*. 2 vols. Berkeley: University of California Press, 1985.

———. "High Ch'ing, 1683–1839." In *Modern East Asia: Essays in Interpretation*, edited by James B. Crowley, 1–28. New York: Harcourt, Brace & World, 1970.

Wakeman, Frederic, Jr., and Carolyn Grant, eds. *Conflict and Control in Late Imperial China*. Berkeley: University of California Press, 1975.

Waldron, Arthur. *The Great Wall of China: From History to Myth*. New York: Cambridge University Press, 1990.

Waley, Arthur. *Yuan Mei, Eighteenth Century Chinese Poet*. Stanford, Calif: Stanford University Press, 1956.

Waley-Cohen, Joanna. *Exile in Mid-Qing China: Banishment to Xinjiang, 1758–1820*. New Haven, Conn.: Yale University Press, 1991.

Wang Chenmain. *The Life and Career of Hong Ch'eng-ch'ou (1562–1655): Public Service in a Time of Dynastic Change*. Ann Arbor, Mich.: Association for Asian Studies, 1999.

Wang Mingyue. "Qi liu jiao zhi shu." In HCJSWB 18.466–67.

Wang Sizhi and Jin Chengdi. "Cong qing chu di li zhi kan fengjian guanliao zhengzhi." *Lishi yanjiu* 1 (1980).

Wang Yanfei. *Qingdai du fu Zhang Yunsui yü Yunnan shehui*. Kunming: Yunnan Daxue Chubanshe, 2005.

Watt, John R. *The District Magistrate in Late Imperial China*. New York: Columbia University Press, 1972.

Webb, Steven Saunders. *The Governors-General: The English Army and the Definition of Empire 1569–1681*. Chapel Hill: University of North Carolina Press, 1979.

Wei Xiumei. *Qingdai zhi huipi zhidu*.

Wei Qingyuan. "Qingdai zhuoming huang shang Fan shi di ying shuai." In *Dang fang lun shi wen bian*, 42–69. Fuzhou: Fujian Renmin Chubanshe, 1983.

Wei Xiangshu. "Qing fu ru qin kao cha shu." In HCJSWB 19.495–96.

Wei Xiumei. *Qingdai zhi hui bi zhidu*. Taipei: Zhongyang Yanjiu Yuan Jindai Shi Yanjiu So, 1992.

———. *Qing ji zhi guan biao*. Taipei: Zhong Yang Yanjjiu Yuan Jin Dai Shi Yanjiu So, 2002.

Wei Yijie. "Zhifu liu ren shu." In HCJSWB 18.467.

Whitney, J. B. R. *China: Area, Administration, and Nation Building*. Chicago: University of Chicago, Department of Geography, 1970.

Will, Pierre-Etienne. *Bureaucracy and Famine in Eighteenth-Century China*. Translated by Elborg Forster. Stanford, Calif.: Stanford University Press, 1990.

———. "State Intervention in the Administration of a Hydraulic Infrastructure: The Example of Hubei Province in Late Imperial Times." In *The Scope of State Power in China*, edited by Stuart Schram. Hong Kong: Chinese University of Hong Kong Press, 1985.

Will, Pierre-Etienne, and R. Bin Wong, eds. *Nourish the People: The State Civilian Granary System in China, 1650–1850*. Ann Arbor: University of Michigan Press, 1991.

Wills, John E., Jr. "Contingent Connections: Fujian and the Early Modern World." In *The Qing Formation in World Historical Time*, edited by Lynn A. Struve. Cambridge, Mass.: Harvard University Press, 2004.

———. "Maritime China from Wang Chih to Shih Lang: Themes in Peripheral History." In Spence and Wills, *From Ming to Ch'ing*, 201–38.

———. *Pepper, Guns, and Parleys: the Dutch East India Company and China, 1622–1681*. Cambridge, Mass.: Harvard University Press, 1974.

Wittfogel, Karl A. *Oriental Despotism: A Comparative Study of Total Power*. New Haven, Conn.: Yale University Press, 1957.

Wong, R. Bin. *China Transformed: Historical Change and the Limits of the European Experience*. Ithaca, N.Y.: Cornell University Press, 1997.

———. "Entre Monde et Nation: Les regions Braudelliennes en Asie." *Annales: Histoire et Science Sociale* 56.1 (January 2001): 5–42.

Woodside, Alexander B. "The Ch'ien-Lung Reign." In *The Cambridge History of China*, vol. 9, Part One, *The Ch'ing Dynasty to 1800*, edited by Willard J. Peterson. Cambridge: Cambridge University Press, 2002.

Wright, Mary C. *The Last Stand of Chinese Conservatism: The T'ung-chih Restoration.* Stanford, Calif.: Stanford University Press, 1957.

Wu Bangqing. *Jifu hedao guan jian.* In *Jifu he dao cong shu.* 1824.

Wu Chengming. "Lun Qingdai qianqi woguo guonei shichang." *Lishi yanjiu* 1 (1983): 96–106.

Wu, Silas H. L. *Communications and Imperial Control in China: Evolution of the Palace Memorial System, 1693–1735.* Cambridge, Mass.: Harvard University Press, 1970.

———. *Passage to Power: K'ang-hsi and His Heir Apparent, 1661–1722.* Cambridge, Mass.: Harvard University Press, 1979.

Xiao Yishan. *Qingdai tongshi.* 5 vols. Taipei: Commercial Press, 1966.

Xie Guozhen. "Removal of Coastal Population in the Early Tsing Period." Translated by Chen Tongxie. *Chinese Social and Political Science Review* 15 (1931): 539–56.

Xu Daolin. *Zhongguo fazhi shilunlue.* Taipei: Zhengzhong Shuju, 1959.

Xu "Henan tongzhi." Edited by Asha. 1767. Reprint, Kaifeng: Henan Jiaoyu Si Provincial Education Office, 1914.

Xu Yinong. *The Chinese City in Space and Time: The Development of Urban Form in Suzhou.* Honolulu: University of Hawaii Press, 2000.

Xue Fucheng. "Cha qiao He shen." In *Yong'an Biji.* Reprint, Nanjing: Jiangsu Renmin Chubanshe, 1983.

———. *Yong'an biji.* 1898. Reprint, Nanjing: Jiangsu Renmin Chubanshe, 1983.

Yang Huaizhong, ed. *Huizu shi lun gao.* Yinchuan: Ningxia Renmin Chubanshe, 1991.

Yang Jeou-yi. "The Muddle of Salt: State and Merchants in Late Imperial China." Ph.D. diss., Harvard University, 1996.

Yang Qijiao. *Yongzheng di ji qi mizhe zhidu yanjiu.* Guangzhou: Guangdong Renmin Chubanshe, 1983.

Yang Xifu. *Si zhi tang wenji.* Edited by Tan Shangzhong et al. N.p., 1803.

Yang Zhengtai. "Ming qing liu qing di sheng shuai tiaojian di bianhua." *Lishi Dili*, no. 3 (January 1983): 115–20.

Yeats, W. B. *The Collected Poems of W. B. Yeats.* New York: Macmillan, 1950.

Yeh, Wen-hsin, ed. *Landscape, Culture, and Power in Chinese Society.* Berkeley: Institute of East Asian Studies, University of California, Center for Chinese Studies, 1998.

Yin Huiyi. *Fu yu tiao jiao.* 1750. In Tian Wenjing, *Fu yu xuan hua lu.*

Yokohama Hirō. "Guanfeng zhengsu shi ko." *Toyoshi Kenkyū* 22, no. 3 (December 1963): 94–112.

"Yongqian shiqi difang gai zhi shiliao." Part 1, *Lishi dang'an* 3 (1992): 3–19; part 2, *Lishi dang'an* 4 (1992): 3–11.

Yongzheng zhupi yuzhi. Compiled by Ortai. 1738. 8 vols. Reprint, Taipei: Wenhai, 1965.

"Yongzheng chao zhupi yin jian dan." *Qingdai shi liao cong bian*, no. 9 (1983): 44–56.

Yu he zhi. Compiled by Wu Yongxiang. 1921. Reprint, Taipei: Guangwen, 1967.

Yu Qingduan gong (Chenglong) zheng shu. Compiled by Cai Fangbing. N.d. Reprint, Taipei: Wenhai, 1976.

Yuan shi. Compiled by Song Lian. 1370. Reprint, Beijing: Zhonghua Shuju, 1960.

Yue Jiong. "Yue xiang qing gong xing lue." *Qing shi zi liao* 4 (1983): 170–83.

Yunnan tongzhi. Edited by Ortai and Jing Daomo. 1736. Reprinted in *Si ku quan shu*, vols. 569–70.

Zelin, Madeleine. *The Magistrate's Tael: Rationalizing Fiscal Reform in Eighteenth-Century Ch'ing China.* Berkeley: University of California Press, 1985.

Zeng jiao Qing chao jinshi timing peilu fu yinde. Harvard Yenching Institute Sinological Index Series, No. 9, 1944. Taipei: Chinese Materials and Research Aids, 1966.

Zhang Boxing. *Zheng yi tang wenji.* Fuzhou, n.d. Reprint, Shanghai: Commercial Press, 1936.

Zhang Deze. *Qingdai guojia jiguan gaishu.* Beijing: Renmin Chubanshe, 1981.

Zhang Juzheng. *Zhang Wen gong quan ji.* Late Ming. Reprint, Shanghai: Shanghai Yin Wu Guan, 1935.

Zhang Pengge. *He fang zhi.* 1725. Reprint, Taipei: Wenhai, 1969.

Zhang Zhelang. *Mingdai xunfu yanjiu.* Taipei: Wen Shi Zhe Chubanshe, 1985.

Zhaolian. *Xiao ting za lu.* Reprint, Shanghai: Wenming Shuju, 1923.

Zhao Shenqiao. *Zhao Gongyi gong (Shenchao) sheng gao.* Edited by Zhao Tingxu. 1738. Reprint, Taipei: Wenhai Chubanshe, 1975.

Zhao Xiting. "Qingdai ge sheng di zhengzhi zhidu." *Lishi yanjiu* 3 (1980): 153–64.

———. "Qingdai zongdu yu xunfu." *Lishi jiaoxue* 10 (1963): 13–22.

Zheng Zao. "San dai kao ji, san sui da ji, he yi jie." In *Yuan xiang tong yi lu*, ed. Jiang Biao. 1897. Reprint, Shanghai: Ji Cheng Cong Shu, 1935.

Zhongguo lishi ditu ji. Beijing: Zhongguo Ditu Chubanshe, 1975.

Zhuang Jifa. *Qing Gaozong shi quan wugong yanjiu.* Taipei: Guoli Gugong Bowuyuan, 1982.

Zito, Angela. *Of Body and Brush: Grand Sacrifice as Text/Performance in 18th Century China.* Chicago: University of Chicago Press, 1997.

Zuo Buqing, ed. *Kang yong qian san di ping yi.* Beijing: Ci Jin Cheng, 1986.

Index

Note: page numbers followed by "t" and "n" refer to tables and endnotes, respectively.

www.ingramcontent.com/pod-product-compliance
Lightning Source LLC
Chambersburg PA
CBHW031820270326
41932CB00008B/477